Money and Banking

Richard H. Timberlake, Jr.

Edward B. Selby, Jr.
The University of Georgia

Wadsworth Publishing Company, Inc.
Belmont, California

To
Hildegard
and
Ashley and Courtenay

ISBN-0-534-00108-4

L. C. Cat. Card No. 73-178181

Printed in the United States of America

1 2 3 4 5 6 7 8 9 10 — 76 75 74 73 72

Preface

This volume is a money and banking textbook written primarily for college students who have successfully mastered elementary courses in economics. It presents orthodox principles of monetary theory and banking institutions, and it also offers some innovations that may make the subject more palatable and more easily assimilated than in traditional texts.

One major innovation of this volume is that appendices are included at the end of most chapters. These appendices consist of factual data, comprehensive problems, and selected readings that reinforce, freshen, or supplement the material presented in the text itself. The readings compose the bulk of the appendices; they should be easily understood by college students since they have been chosen with this constraint in mind. The few selections at an advanced level come near the end of the book and are aligned with subject matter near the frontiers of research.

The text is organized as its title indicates: monetary theory and its relationship to income and spending are presented first. Analysis and measurement of monetary value is followed by formal monetary theory and two national income models in which the role of money is examined.

Section two on commercial banking emphasizes fractional reserve bank credit creation and the institutional development of the banking industry. Both the history of banking in the United States and factual details of contemporary commercial banking practice are presented.

The third section on central banking makes explicit the differences between commercial banking and central banking, even though both of these institutions are involved in supplying money to the economy. Federal Reserve development is traced by means of serial combined balance sheets of the 12 Federal Reserve Banks. Many institutional details of Federal Reserve policy and structure since the end of World War II are also stressed.

Section Four is on international money flows — a subject that has gained new prominence in the 1960s. Its kinship to domestic monetary policy makes this subsidiary section almost necessary for a thorough treatment of the subject. However, only the fundamentals of international monetary flows are discussed here.

The last section is, of course, purely optional. It is meant for advanced students who are able to devote more than one semester or one quarter to the subject. It tries to show the direction of current interest and research in this branch of knowledge as well as to touch on issues that are somewhat peripheral to the main topics.

This order seems logical to us. However, we must make certain major disclaimers for the benefit of serious readers of the book who are necessarily its critics. First, other orderings of these topics are also logical. For example, a study of the institutions that supply money to the economy may seem to have priority over the analysis of monetary theory. If so, the reader should start with the second section and then come back to the first section. No author can determine the best arrangement of topics for every single student and instructor of this subject and for all time.

A second major disclaimer is that this text is not self-contained or encyclopedic. Every fundamental principle of the major topics has been exposed and analyzed, but these subjects are far from exhausted. Virtually every chapter has ramifications and extensions that require other books and other specialized studies. As Browning wrote, "On earth the broken arcs; in heaven the perfect round."

Several features of this book, however, are unique. One innovation is a Chapter 0, describing the operation of the market system and the establishment of relative price. It is intended to refresh the reader on the principles of value theory. An awareness of market behavior is valuable as a tool for interpreting general economic behavior, but it is also necessary for understanding the determination of monetary value. The reader should be aware that money fits into the market scheme of the economy in the same fashion as any economic good or service.

Another device of this text is the use of a "schematic sketch" chapter to introduce each major topic. These chapters divest their subjects of many confusing details that frequently obscure the principal behavior of institutions and individuals. Later chapters then attempt to bring in the practical qualifications and particulars of the real world.

Money, banking, and central banking is a beguiling and interesting field of study mainly because it deals with money, a subject that often has been plagued with priestcraft and mystique practiced by cranks and charlatans. The purpose of any text such as this one is to get the subject matter away from astrological methods and ideas and into a scientific environment. And, in fact, nowhere in economics can scientific method be put to better use than in the field of the demand for and supply of money.

The student then, should approach this subject with the same attitude with which he would begin the study of a physical science. Due to the large element of man-made institutions in banking and central banking and their rich history, the reader is also helped by some knowledge of political science, accounting, and social history. The basic goal of the book, however, is to present a systematic, coherent view of the factors determining the demand for and supply of money in the United States.

The student reading this book is advised to avoid thinking of the subject matter as isolated from other fields in the social sciences. Nor is it merely vocational: it gives little advice on how to run a bank. The truths it purports to teach cannot be injected into the reader's bloodstream as an inoculation against ignorance. The effort made to assimilate this material should be regarded also as a continuing and ramifying process. As the reader learns more about other related fields of study, more sense can be gleaned from this one.

In common with all textbooks, this one is a selection and distillation of traditional wisdom. Thus, it has ancestry and heritage, and to name all the human capital from which it has drawn interest would be an impossible task.

The readings directly reflect the work of the contributors. To all of these scholars and friends, our deepest appreciation. Special mention is also due to the economists who were our editorial critics — W. Philip Gramm, Texas A&M University, Thomas M. Humphrey and William Shropshire, Emory University — for trying to keep us rigorous. To Robert McTeer, Brenda George, and Jane Haws, an additional note of thanks for their thoughtful suggestions and comments.

We also are indebted to many of our colleagues at the University of Georgia, but especially to our Department Chairman, Robert R. Dince, for his many administrative felicities that gave us time to finish this work. Two errors in the earlier text were detected and pointed out for correction by Mr. Albert Caproni, Jr. Our thanks to him. Finally, our sorely missed colleague, the late David McCord Wright, made helpful suggestions on the chapters dealing with contemporary monetary policy. Mary Chambers and Julie Brooks typed a large part of the manuscript, and Grace Clifford Holloway rendered a final and valuable service by editing the text.

This text has been a joint effort. Nonetheless, primary responsibility for different parts has devolved upon one or the other of us. Selby wrote most of Chapters 11, 12, 13, 19, and the Appendices to Chapters 6 and 7. Chapters 8, 16, 22, and 27 were joint efforts. Timberlake wrote most of the remaining 22 chapters, and the Appendices to Chapters 2, 8, and 14.

Richard H. Timberlake, Jr.
Edward B. Selby, Jr.
Athens, Georgia

Contents

0
The Pricing Process in Competitive Markets and the Introduction of Money

The Private Enterprise Market Economy

The principal feature of a private enterprise economy is the existence of markets to effect the purchase and sale of goods and services. Free markets—markets that individuals may enter or leave without hindrance as either demanders or suppliers—may best be thought of as devices that transmit the wants of the consumer to the productive capacities of industry. They also are means by which industries channel new products to consumers for approval or rejection.

A typical market is an interesting phenomenon in the first place because it is not, as frequently thought, a specific geographical place. The New York Stock Exchange, a public auction, and a "farmers' market" are examples of markets at specific geographical points. Generally, however, a market is nothing more than a group of buyers in close communication with a group of sellers negotiating for the purchase and sale of a product that has definable and recognizable characteristics. The negotiation may be conducted between continents. This definition necessarily implies some formal principles, and it also permits some discretion by the observer in the scope of what may be included in "the" product. The observer may be interested in the automobile market but not in the vehicle market. Or he may be more narrowly interested in the market for Plymouths but not interested in the total market for automobiles. The problem the observer faces in dealing with a market may limit the extent of the market he examines to almost any degree he wishes. Thus,

1

a market is in part a concept in the mind of the person who faces some practical problem for which market investigation is required.

How many buyers and sellers make up a competitive market? When this question is faced by a person uninitiated in the wiles (or wilds) of economic analysis, he may try to frame an answer in terms of cardinal values, such as two, three, four, or ten. The economist simply says that the number of both buyers and sellers must be great enough that no individual or business firm can appreciably influence market sales volume or market price. Competition is then ensured. Here again, the judgment and discretion of the observer is required in estimating the necessary number of each.

Where are markets if they are not at specific places? The best answer is that they are everywhere—or, more accurately, anywhere that buyers and sellers can communicate to each other offers of goods for sale or bids to purchase goods in terms of some measure of value common to both. As communication and transportation facilities and techniques are improved, markets for goods and services may be extended indefinitely. Markets that once were only regional or local later may be world-wide.

The Economic Problem

Markets have become so pervasive in the last several hundred years that one might go to another extreme and ask what kind of economy could or did exist without markets. The answer is that only the primitive economy of a Robinson Crusoe or an isolated frontier household could exist without markets. In fact, these models of simple economic activity were simple because a market system was impractical if not impossible. They were, however, just as "economic" as today's interrelated market systems because they, too, had to face the problem of allocating relatively scarce factors of production among various competing demands for them. Crusoe's scarce factors, for example, were his island, the tools and equipment he salvaged from the ship he had been on, his time, and his own skills and abilities. The chronicle of his struggle to solve his economic problem is classic, both because it is a good yarn and because it exemplifies man's struggle against the odds of nature and misfortune.

The economic problem was central to the Crusoe struggle and is still *the* problem of contemporary economic activity. Isolation in the Crusoe epic focused attention on the economic problem by avoiding other important features of contemporary economic life. Since Crusoe was not in communication with anyone except his manservant, Friday, he was in no way involved in market behavior and he therefore had no use for money. When he salvaged a chest of coins from the foundering ship, he observed that a spool of thread would have been more useful for his purposes. Daniel Defoe, the author of the Crusoe model, thus demonstrated both the void of market activity in

Crusoe's world and the uselessness of money when no markets are present. Finally, on his island, Crusoe himself was the only government. If money is virtually a necessity for market activity and if its issue is in some realistic way a function of government, the utility of Defoe's simplifications can be appreciated.

A limited amount of primitive market behavior did take place without money. People swapped goods for goods, services for services, or goods for services. This kind of exchange is called *barter*. Perhaps the extension of economic activity beyond the walls of the medieval manor or frontier household required an intermediate stage of barter before money came into general use as a medium of exchange. In any case, if barter exchange preceded money exchange, barter today has declined outside the family household to an insignificant total of all economic activity primarily because the wants of the barterers for each other's offerings do not coincide.

The Introduction of Money

The use of a money as a *medium of exchange* generally divisible into small units solves the barter problem. As it becomes a generalized means for facilitating exchanges of goods and services, money also becomes a *standard of value:* The relative values of all goods and services are specified in monetary equivalents called *prices*. The substitution of money exchanging for goods in place of goods exchanging for goods does not alter these values. The relative (or real) economic value of a good or service is traditionally defined as the ability of that commodity or service to command other things in exchange. If one orange exchanges for two apples in a primitive pre-money market, one orange would exchange for enough money to buy the two apples after money became the customary exchange medium in this market.

The introduction of money into economic systems has yet other ramifications. For one thing, money offers universality of choice: It is a *bearer of options*. The seller of oranges does not have to take two apples for his orange; he may use the money he receives to buy two apples or anything he wants of equal market value. Likewise, the seller of apples may sell them to anyone who has the proper amount of money. He is not bound to swap them with someone who has oranges even though he intends to buy an orange with the proceeds from the sale of his apples.

If individual households and business firms realize greater utility from the implementation of a monetary system, the whole economy — the aggregation of households and firms — realizes a like increase in overall *efficiency* compared to what is possible in a barter economy. Exchange time is saved; exchange costs are lowered; and resources are conserved. The monetary system is thus an "industry" contributing a "product" that allows the economy to function much more efficiently. The system is similar in this regard to a highway or railroad system. Also, like these and other industries, the monetary system has a large capital structure, consisting of thousands of banks and the money itself, from which society realizes real returns. The total stock of money, then, must also be thought of as a *stock of capital*.

If all other economic values are expressed in units of the same kind of money at the same time that the money value of apples is given, the values of all goods and services relative to apples (and relative to all other goods and services as well) are immediately evident. Money thus has the function of being a *common denominator of value*, but it can perform this function properly only if it behaves itself—only on the condition that its own value does not change appreciably.[1] To simplify the analysis of markets, the value of money is assumed to be constant at some arbitrary "level." Otherwise, an unnecessary variable is added to the picture.

Description and Determination of Market Price

Everyone knows that "demand and supply" determine the market price of any specific good or service. This statement is virtually axiomatic or definitional, but the terms "demand" and "supply" require some elaboration. First, both concepts must be thought of as schedules, or better yet, as functional relationships. "Demand" expresses the *alternative quantities per unit of time that would be taken by demanders at various possible prices*. The various quantities demanded, therefore, are functions of the different possible prices. "Supply" expresses the *alternative quantities per unit of time that would be offered in the market by suppliers at various possible prices*. The quantities supplied are also functions of price.

People generally demand goods and services in order to obtain satisfaction or utility from them. Other people supply goods and services in order to obtain income by means of which they in turn will demand goods and services. In today's world every normal economic household is both a demander and a supplier. It demands heterogeneous goods and services, and supplies factors of production—usually the services of the head of the household—to some firm in the economy. What the head of the household supplies to the economy cannot be consumed or used by the household itself to any important extent. Thus, the modern household is in contrast to the Robinson Crusoe household. Crusoe demanded what he alone could supply, and he supplied within the limits of his environment only what he demanded. Nonetheless, the Crusoe economy is a microcosmic model of the sum of all households and firms in

---

[1]The scientific meaning of the value of money is discussed in the next chapter.

today's economy. Barring mistakes and accidents, the whole economy produces an annual volume of goods and services (a Gross National Product).
The multitudinous acts of production simultaneously generate the real income,
and thus the general demand, that is necessary for households and firms to be
able to buy all of the goods and services produced. Otherwise the goods and
services would not be produced in the first place or sold in the second place.

   This expression of total market behavior is known as *Say's Law of Markets*
after the famous French economist Jean Baptiste Say. In its least controversial
form, it simply defines truistically the roundabout but necessary linkage
between production and consumption.

   The signals for allocating factors of production into various income-
generating activities are furnished by market prices. In virtually all imaginable
cases alternative quantities demanded of any good diminish and the quantities
supplied increase as the money price becomes higher. These generalizations
are depicted in Figure 0.1.

Figure 0.1. The "Typical" Supply and Demand Concepts of Market Behavior

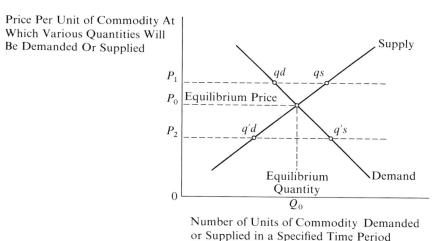

Price Per Unit of Commodity At
Which Various Quantities Will
Be Demanded Or Supplied

Number of Units of Commodity Demanded
or Supplied in a Specified Time Period

   The horizontal and vertical axes are labeled in detail to facilitate a proper
understanding of the diagram's meaning. Prices calibrated along the vertical
axis are expressed in terms of money units per unit of the commodity being
bought and sold in this market. The convenience of using money for this purpose is apparent if the observer imagines this diagram for a barter economy.
No price in terms of any other single commodity would be quotable. Instead,
many "prices" would be evident; the commodity would be valued in terms of
several other goods and services. Thus, a money unit, which acts as a common
denominator of value, greatly simplifies market behavior. To maintain the
efficiency of money in this role, however, the value of money must be under-

stood to remain constant throughout the pricing process. Since the value of money is expressed in terms of "all prices," all prices *on average* must be thought of as constant during the time in which a relative price is determined by supply and demand.

The horizontal axis lists the number of units of the commodity under consideration that would be demanded or supplied per unit of time. The use of a time period calibration on this axis allows the market scheme to become "fluid" and avoids the idea of a single unvarying stock to be bought and sold. "Quantity," then, is not a single quantity, but various possible quantities during some specified time period, such as a day, a week, or a year—whatever time period seems most practical or measurable to the observer. This method of calibrating the "quantity" axis allows a flow of the commodity to enter and leave the market. When the flow entering is equal to the flow leaving with no tendency to change, the market is in equilibrium with respect to both price and quantity.

Figure 0.1 depicts an equilibrium market condition in which the equilibrium price is P_o. Suppose, however, that people who quote prices make mistakes in estimating market conditions, and allow the market price to become "too high"—to, say, P_1 in the diagram. The flow of the commodity into the market from suppliers (q_s) at this price becomes greater than the flow out from demanders (q_d), who buy substitutes for this particular commodity. Furthermore, too many resources are being used by suppliers to produce this commodity and at too high a cost. Some of the overstocked suppliers reduce prices in order to avoid inventory losses and spoilage. In the process they attract new customers from competing commodities, and they force out of the supply picture some of the suppliers who can make supplies available in this market only at the higher than equilibrium price.

On the other hand, if the market price is "too low" (P_2), active measures to restore equilibrium can be expected to originate with demanders. At P_2 the quantities flowing into the market, q'_s, are less than the quantities demanded, q'_d, at that price. Demanders bid for the relatively scarce goods, encouraging additional quantities from firms that previously had not been supplying this market, as well as greater quantities from those suppliers already producing this commodity. At the same time, the higher price stimulates some demanders to seek substitute goods in other markets. Again, when the desired flow of goods into this market equals the desired flow out, an equilibrium price is obtained.

Simple Equilibrium between Money and Other Things

The method used to analyze equilibrium in all markets simultaneously is the same as the one that is used to determine equilibrium for one commodity in one market. When equilibrium is being sought in one market, demanders and suppliers can go into and out of this particular market, buying substitute or complementary goods. When all goods and services are considered as one homogeneous unit, only one choice is open: Demanders can either hold money that would purchase a unit of goods and services, or they can give up the money and get the things they want. Suppliers can either sell the goods and services they produce and get money, whereupon they become demanders and face the demanders' choices, or they can refuse to give up the goods and services under their control and keep possession of them until terms of sale are more favorable.[2] Since virtually all people are both demanders *and* suppliers, everyone faces the alternatives open on both sides of the markets that are compatible with his abilities and preferences.

The typical household's behavior in the light of these choices is to obtain money at the end of a pay period for services rendered or for goods sold and then bleed off the money gradually during the next pay period in order to satisfy ordinary household wants. Business firms, for their part, build up cash balances during the income period by selling their products and then pay out wages and other costs at the end of the period to the resource owners who work for them.

Given that people earn and spend their money income gradually in the normal course of events, they may still increase or decrease the *rate* at which they spend it for either consumption or investment purposes.[3] Just as the rate at which people buy apples depends on their taste for apples and the relative price or value of apples, so the rate at which they spend their money depends on their "taste" for money—their miserliness—and on the value of money as measured by the ability of each unit of money to command all other goods and services in exchange. The more each unit of money is worth in all markets, the less the number of money units the household needs to tide it over to the next payday. Or again, the less utility the household derives from money units relative to the utility it receives from goods and services, the smaller the average quantity of money units it will want to keep on hand. Once the utilities for money and all other things are given together with the incomes of all households and business firms, relative prices and the value of money are also determined through the market system.

A recapitulation may help at this point: Firms generate total product and households spend it when it is received as income. Supplies and demands in all specific markets establish the *relative* values of all goods and services to one another, including the values of the factors of production and the distribution of income (product) to the owners of the factors of production. Money may then be introduced as an intermediate device that allows an individual to adapt his total spending for goods and services to his income as expediently

---

[2]This discussion abstracts from the possibility of the purchase of financial assets that might have features of both money and commodities.

[3]They may also alter the rate at which their income is earned to some minor extent. The technological constraints of the production process limit this choice more than corresponding constraints on the spending side.

and efficiently as possible. When the various adjustments have been made such that the rate of spending for all individuals in the economy is constant, that is, such that the value of the money unit in terms of its purchasing power shows no tendency to change, money flows in the economy are in equilibrium.

The economic structures of the world are ever changing. Not only do the production patterns of goods and services change due to changing tastes on the demand side and to innovations and technological changes on the supply side, but the number of money units that is used to buy and sell these different galaxies of goods and services also changes.

The following chapters examine in more detail the institutions and conditions that influence or have influenced the quantity and value of money in the United States. To accomplish this project sensibly within the confines of one book, only monetary factors and institutions are surveyed. Industrial changes, the technology of producing goods and services, changing tastes of final consumers, and factors affecting economic growth are brought in only as peripheral influences.

Selected Bibliography

The student should refer to any standard principles of economics textbook for a review of the market mechanism. For example, see any of the following:

Alchian, Armen A., and William R. Allen. *University Economics,* 3rd ed. Belmont, Calif.: Wadsworth Publishing Co., 1972.

Bach, George Leland. *Economics: An Introduction to Analysis and Policy.* Englewood Cliffs, N.J.: Prentice-Hall, 1968.

Samuelson, Paul A. *Economics: An Introductory Analysis,* 8th ed. New York: McGraw-Hill Book Co., 1970.

Analysis of
Open-Market Pricing and Allocation

Armen A. Alchian and William R. Allen

The authors of this reading selection are widely known professional econo-mists whose text University Economics *has had considerable impact on the teaching and assimilation of Principles of Economics courses in colleges and universities. Professor Alchian is affiliated with the University of California, Los Angeles; Professor Allen with Texas A&M.*

This passage, from Chapter 8 of their text, explains in simple terms how a market operates in establishing an equilibrium price for a commodity and why a change in price may appear as the result of a change in costs. The two things—prices and costs—are related, but one does not "cause" the other. Rather, both are reflections of changes in demand and supply. The price system is seen as a rationing device that is more equitable than any other such device. Given an understanding of relative price determination, the reader now should be better prepared to understand the analysis of equilibrium for all prices taken together.

The Cost-Price Illusion

The avenue from increased demand to higher exchange-equilibrium prices often is concealed by inventories in the distribution chain from producer to consumer. As a result, prices appear to be set by costs of production instead of competition among consumers. The cause of this illusion is illustrated in the following example of an increased demand for meat.

To start, pretend that for some reason people's desire for meat increases. As you can guess, this implies a rise in meat prices. How does this happen and what does it accomplish?

Housewives express their increased desire for meat by increasing their market demand for meat. Market-demand schedules reflect what people do in the marketplace, not simply something they dream about doing at some later time. Housewives reveal an increased demand by buying more meat than formerly at the current prices in the meat markets. How can the prices remain unchanged? Retail butchers have inventories adequate for a day or two. As sales increase, that inventory is depleted more than expected. No single butcher knows that the demand has risen for the community as a whole. No single butcher knows that he could raise his price and make no fewer sales than earlier. All he knows is that *he* sells more meat at the existing price. But the increased demand takes its toll of inventories. Whether or not a butcher believes that the increased rate of sale is a temporary fluctuation, he will buy more meat than usual the next day in order to restore his inventory from its abnormally low level; and he will buy even more than that if he believes that the increase in sales will persist. If the demand for meat does increase so that one butcher's increase is not merely some other butcher's loss, the purchases by the aggregate of butchers from the packers will increase.

Just as butchers use inventories, so packers, on a larger scale, also rely on inventories to smooth out the effect of sales fluctuations on their pattern of purchases from cattlemen. We assume that the first day's change in demand was within that inventory limit and therefore was met without a price increase.

Packers restore inventories by instructing their cattle buyers (who travel around among the cattle raisers and fatteners and to the stockyards where cattlemen ship the steers for sale) to buy more cattle than usual. But with all the packers restoring their inventories in this manner, the numbers of cattle available for sale each day are inadequate to meet the increased total demand *at the old price*. There is not sufficient inventory in the stockyards to take care of this rise. Either some buyers for packers must report that they cannot get the number requested, or they must boost their offer prices in order to persuade cattlemen to sell the steers to them rather than to some other packers.

Rather than go without any increase in stock of meat, the buyers will begin to raise their offers in order to get more cattle. This rise in offer prices will occur nearly simultaneously, among the buyers, as if there was collusion among the cattlemen or buyers. The cattlemen simply let the buyers bid against each other until the price rises to a point where the packers will not want to buy more meat at the new higher price than they did at the old lower price; that is, the packers are induced by the higher price not to buy more than is available from the cattlemen.

In terms of our demand-and-supply apparatus, the supply curve of cattle is vertical. An increased demand by packers for cattle implies an intersection at a higher price. Each packer is therefore forced to slide or climb back up his new increased demand curve to a higher price, at which point he buys less than he had planned to at the old price. The total amount purchased is no greater than before, but the price of cattle is higher; at this high price, the amount wanted on the new demand curve equals the constant amount supplied. Each packer must pay a higher price for cattle in order to avoid getting less cattle and meat than he had before. Competition among the packers has raised the price of cattle during the immediate period when cattle production cannot be increased.[1]

---

[1]This "immediate" period in which cattle production cannot be increased is also called the "market" or the "very-short-run" period.

The cattle raisers bask in the glow of higher receipts. Business for them is more profitable. But the packers, faced with a higher price of cattle, experience *a rise in costs*. Why did their costs rise? The costs of raising cattle did not increase. Nor did the costs of getting cattle to market, nor of slaughtering, nor of distributing meat. The price paid by packers to cattlemen was pushed up in response fundamentally to the increased demand by consumers—the house-wives. Their demand, from butcher shops through packers, was met by de-pleting inventories. But the cattlemen did not have inventories that they could deplete and then restore quickly. Therefore, they simply let the buyers bid for the available amount brought to market (rather than allocating the cattle on some other principle).

Whether or not the packers are aware of the law of demand and supply, which says that a higher demand with the same old supply will permit higher prices, and whether or not they are aware that demand has increased, the higher price of cattle (higher costs to the packers) will mean that the packers must charge a higher price to butchers if they are to continue as profitable meat packers. In sum, a higher price occurs because the demand for meat has in-creased. The butchers, in turn, post higher prices to the housewives. When housewives complain about the higher price, the butcher in all innocence, honesty, and correctness says that it isn't his fault. The cost of meat has gone up. Cost, to him, is the cost of getting meat. The butcher can say, "I never raise prices until my costs go up." And the packers can honestly say the same thing. And if the housewife wants to know who is to blame for the higher costs and hence higher prices of meat, she can look in the mirror behind the butcher's counter and see her face and those of all her neighbors. She might then turn to each of them and say, "If you didn't want more meat, I could have more." But that observation and that tactless behavior are neither useful nor fostered by the competitive exchange system. The exchange system tends to conceal this fact of competition and make it appear as if the higher price of meat were caused by butchers' or packers' or farmers' greedy behavior—not that of ourselves or our neighbors.

The consumers' own increased demand for meat, then, brought about a rise in the price of meat to consumers. This rise in price *appeared* to be the result of a rise in costs because the first price effect of the increased demand occurred at the cattle raisers' end of the line. The demand increase pulled up the price paid in the first stages of the production and distribution channels. The first rise in price could have occurred in the butcher shops and then have been transmitted back step by step to the farmers. But butchers' inventories are usually adequate to cushion the changes in demand temporarily until the im-pact of increased sales goes all the way through the productive processes. This explains why the illusion is so common that increases in costs are responsible for higher prices.

Pricing and Prices

The foregoing analysis and examples show how the pricing process allocates the existing supply of a good among the competing claimants. Putting the matter emotionally, it is an analysis of discrimination among competing claimants, in which some obtain more favorable treatment — get more goods — while others get less. The discrimination or competitive criterion is heavily weighted by the amount of money offered in exchange for the particular good at issue. The pricing process is a distributive, discriminatory process; our interest in pricing is not in whether prices are high or low, but instead in how prices solve the problem of deciding who gets what amount of particular goods.

The analysis does not say that this system of competition or discrimination among claimants is either a good one or a bad one. Under this system, people bid for some goods by offering others in exchange (via the intermediary of money). Sometimes it is said that under this system of allocation the goods go where there are the most votes or dollars. Thus, a rich man's dog may receive milk that a poor child needs to avoid rickets — not because demand and supply are working ineffectively but because they "are working effectively, putting goods in the hands of those who can pay the most or who have the money votes." But surely this interpretation is faulty. First and fundamentally, suppose everyone had the *same* amount of wealth. Some people still would feed dogs while other people would be able to use more food for children. Some simply prefer to feed their dogs rather than feed more to children. A cruel statement? Yes, but it is honest and nonromantic and avoids blaming some "system" for people's preferences.

In the second place, it seems misleading to say that the private-property exchange (price) system puts goods where the most dollar votes are. Rather, it puts *more* goods where there are *more* dollar votes and less where there are less. It is not an all-or-none allocation like a political election in which the winner takes all while the loser gets nothing. It is more akin to proportional representation than to majority rule. The exchange system puts some goods *wherever* there are some dollar votes *per unit* of the good, rather than only where the most votes are. A poorer person, by concentrating more of his money on some goods, can express a higher value *per unit* of the goods for which he bids. In this way he can match the per unit *price* of a rich bidder, if he wishes, by bidding for a proportionally smaller amount: thereby he will get *some* of the goods. This may seem a small solace to a poorer person, and indeed it is; but compare it with the case in which the person who is outvoted or outcompeted gets nothing, as would occur if the goods went only where the most "votes" were.

We are not saying that the price-exchange system for allocating goods is desirable or undesirable — only that it is easy to misinterpret its operation.

This discussion, of course, suggests the desirability of investigating what determines how many dollar votes or how much wealth each person has... [But] for the present analysis, we are taking the distribution of wealth as simply given—not as something granted by heaven or "naturally proper."

Section One

Monetary Theory and National Income Analysis

1
A Schematic
Sketch of Money

Origins of Money

Money is, among other things, an abstract unit of account — a *numeraire* — as well as a tangible medium of exchange for consummating transactions and clearing debts. As a unit of account it is analogous to a yard length or a pound weight. A yard, a pound, and a dollar are all abstract, arbitrarily defined units of measurement. A yard-*stick,* a pound-*bob* and a dollar *bill* are all tangible media for representing the units of measurement.

A contemporary industrial economy is characterized by specialization of the factors of production. Almost every worker produces his specialty in a good or service many times the amount that he himself can use. He relies on exchanging the "excess" supply of his product for the "excess" supplies similarly produced by others. This kind of specialization enhances and enlarges the total product enormously. It also necessitates the use of a monetary system that can expedite exchanges of goods and services.

Barter, the exchange of goods for goods, preceded the exchange of goods for money. Even barter required methods for measuring values and keeping accounts. A primitive way of establishing values was to compare the sizes of things to be exchanged; but eventually standards of comparison in the form of some well-known commodity appeared. These standards differed from place to place. In Europe the cow or ox was commonly used as a standard of value;

in other places, the slave was used. Hoes and knives are said to have been used as money by the Chinese, and later miniature copies of these articles lacking any utility as commodities circulated as money. Ornaments, too, appeared early to serve as money. The American Indians' wampum, consisting of belts and necklaces of black and white polished shells, is an example of ornamental money.

Metals Assume Importance as Money

Any commodity could have evolved as money, but the precious and near-precious metals assumed this role because they possessed more characteristics required of a good money than other commodities. They were easily *identifiable* by the trading public; they were relatively *stable in quantity* and therefore in value; they were conveniently *divisible;* and their *durability* permitted the accumulation of a substantial stock over time, a stock so large that the production of more metal over a period of several years could not appreciably affect it. This last characteristic also made them *good stores of value*. By way of contrast, almost all other commodities suffer deterioration in storage, while their production can be altered relatively quickly to meet changing market demands.

Even the precious metals had their drawbacks. Their supply was subject to the hazards of accidental discovery and improvements in mining techniques, and they could be altered and adulterated and were not perfectly durable. Most importantly, their use tied up a lot of resources for producing, safe-keeping, storage, and transportation. These imperfections provoked methods for "economizing" monetary metals through the adoption of cheaper representations usually made of paper. Paper money has long since become conventional in contemporary societies, but its use has also included the major problem of how to manage its issue. Hence, much of the analysis and history that follow bears on two questions:

1. What economic effects are provoked by changes in the quantity of money?
2. How is the quantity of nominal money units controlled?

Legal Tender

Metallic coins, because of their utility as media of exchange, first were struck by private persons. Once established *ae facto* as money, the relationship between a weight of metal and some denomination of the unit of account was often formalized *de jure* by the fiat of a ruling government. A government that has a fiat (the power of "let there be") may specify this relationship. When it does, it stipulates by law that a debtor may clear his debt by proffering or tendering the proper amount of legal metal to his creditor. The government's role in this process is to formalize as the standard of value the commodity that has general public approval and to enforce the rule of legal tender. By the same token, a government that is overthrown and loses its power also loses its fiat. Then any laws it has made with respect to legal tender necessarily are null.

Throughout most of the nineteenth and the first part of the twentieth centuries in the United States, the legal tender value of an ounce of gold was $20.67. If a creditor refused to accept such legal tender as payment of debt, the debtor legally could clear his money debt by depositing the correct amount of gold (or other legal tender) with the courts. He was then absolved of any encumbrances for the debt, such as accruing interest.

The precious metals were usually chosen as ultimate legal tender because they were already in use, and because they lent themselves most conveniently to a self-regulating monetary system. Since precious metals as commodities were precious because of their relatively short supply, no wild inflation from a sudden over-abundance of these metals was likely to occur. This feature argued strongly for metallic monetary systems.

Acceptability of Money

Although a money metal such as gold has commodity value, the government action that declares it legal tender is as fiat as one that would make paper money legal tender. In each case the government is imposing its power to ensure that a debtor may clear his obligation to a creditor. The creditor is forced to accept the medium regardless of its intrinsic value.

Anything that has been declared legal tender by government for clearing money debts necessarily becomes accepted in transactions. A transaction may be thought of simply as a very short-term debt, undertaken at one moment and liquidated the next. When a buyer picks up a loaf of bread in a grocery store, he goes into debt to the grocer who automatically accepts the role of creditor. If legal tender is offered to clear the "debt" at the cash register, the grocer must accept. The only other money of any consequence that may be tendered is a check. A check is not legal tender but is usually acceptable if the recipient is reasonably certain that he can obtain legal tender for it. Banks are obliged to make this kind of redemption for their depositors.

Money may be accepted habitually, customarily, and thoughtlessly by many people, but its formal acceptance in the first place is neither routine nor mystical. Acceptance is based on the force of law behind legal tender money and the knowledge that other moneys, such as checks drawn on banks, can be converted readily into legal tender with negligible risk and cost. If cost of conversion becomes appreciable, money loses its moneyness and its corresponding ability to act as a medium of exchange. In a hyperinflation, for example, the cost of holding money for any length of time is the virtual certainty that its purchasing power will decline. When hyperinflation becomes extreme, money loses its utility. Sometimes under such conditions, the monetary system is forsaken entirely and barter is revived. The amount of hyperinflation people will endure, rather than abandon the monetary system completely, is a remarkable testimonial to money's social productivity. (See reading selections at the end of Chapter 3.)

The characteristics of legal tender and acceptability discussed above reduce to the fact that something becomes a money when it has the lowest relative cost in functioning as a medium of exchange. Different items, however, may enjoy the lowest cost attribute at different times. In stable political and economic environments, a legal tender paper money may be relatively riskless and therefore a less costly money to maintain than, say, gold. In circumstances of social upheaval, holders of paper money might have to assume the large risk that this kind of money would rapidly lose some or all of its value. Under such conditions, a money, such as gold, that previously had suffered a comparative cost disadvantage could well reassume monetary prominence.

The Value of Money

The *value* of money must be distinguished from its *acceptability* in the same manner that the quantity of a substance must be distinguished from its quality. The presence of acceptability does imply the existence of value, and vice versa. However, the two attributes may be usefully distinguished for purposes of analysis.

The economic value of a unit of money is its ability to command units of commodities and services in exchange. And this relationship is reciprocal: When 50 cents are exchanged for a dozen oranges, a dozen oranges are just as surely exchanged for 50 cents. Once barter is abandoned, money assumes a fundamental uniqueness; it becomes *the* standard of value—a general measure of the value of "other things." The value of money therefore must be expressed in terms of all the "other things" that it buys. This value is measured by the average of all "prices" paid for money in terms of the quantities of all the other things for which money is exchanged.[1]

---

[1]The technique of index number construction to determine an average of prices is presented in Chapter 2. Only the general concept is raised here.

Let a conventional and finite stock of money units be distributed among people in a free choice economy that includes a market system; and let "all other things" be thought of as a composite, homogenized "loaf" of goods and services. One unit of money (one dollar) will buy a thin slice of this loaf, and a slice of the loaf will buy a dollar. If the price or value of a slice of the loaf is P, then $P = \$1/1$ slice. Now, let the "price" or value of one dollar be p. Since one slice of the loaf also buys a dollar, $p = 1$ slice/$\$1$. The "price" of one dollar is one slice, and the relationship between P and p is $P = \dfrac{1}{p}$. That is, the price or value of goods in terms of money, P, equals the inverse of the value of money in terms of goods, $\dfrac{1}{p}$. Various hypothetical values for this equality are shown in Table 1.1, and are graphed in Figure 1.1.

Table 1.1

Time	Average of Prices	Value of Money
0	100	100
1	99	101
2	75	133
3	50	200
4	25	400
5	10	1,000
6	1	10,000
7	33	300
8	150	66
9	200	50
10	285	35
11	∞	0

Let P_o be the value of goods in terms of money at some time O, and P_1 be the value of goods in terms of money at time 1. Then the value of money at time O is p_o and the value of money at time 1 is p_1. Since $P_o = \dfrac{1}{p_o}$ and $P_1 = \dfrac{1}{p_1}$,

$$\frac{P_o}{P_1} = \frac{(1/p_o)}{(1/p_1)}$$

This expression may be reduced algebraically so that the relationship between the average of prices P and the value of money p at the two different times is

$$\frac{P_o}{P_1} = \frac{p_1}{p_o}$$

This equation relates changes in the value of money over time to changes in the average of prices. Notice that neither money nor "other things" have any *absolute* value. Therefore, adoption of a convenient number, such as "100," for both the value of money and the value of "other things" is possible at time *O*. Values at earlier or later times are relative to values at time *O*. In index number parlance, time *O* is called the "base year."

Figure 1.1

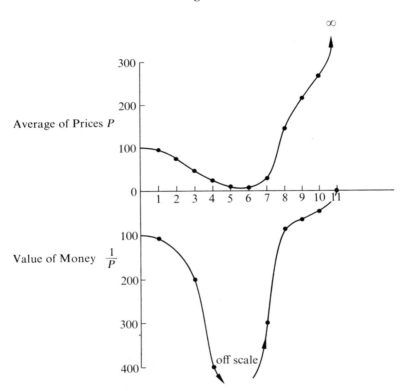

Given all money prices, one dollar is equal to some slice of goods and services generally offered for sale. If the average of all prices increased so that the price of a slice of the loaf was two dollars, *P* would equal two dollars per slice (*P* = $2/1 slice), and *p* would equal one slice per two dollars (*p* = 1 slice/ $2). Thus, a general change in prices is identical to an inverse change in the value of money.[2]

---

[2]Note that an "inverse change" is different from a "proportionally opposite change." If prices increase by 100 percent, the value of money *does not* fall by 100 percent, that is, to zero, but by 50 percent. In order for the value of money to approach zero, prices in general must become infinitely high.

The Price Level and Relative Prices

The average of prices *P* can be measured by an index of a representative sample of all money prices. While the framework of prices may increase, decrease, or remain constant, the relationship between an individual money price and all other money prices within the framework may behave completely independently. If the average of all money prices doubled, for example, and the money price of a loaf of bread increased from 15 cents to 20 cents, the relative or real price of the bread would have *fallen*. Here, relative price movements and their causes must be abstracted; the study of money and its value is the study of the framework of prices, not an investigation of value changes within the framework.[3]

Large-scale movements of prices can occur and have occurred in the past. Then again, price levels have remained almost constant for long periods. When they do, money prices become very meaningful to buyers and sellers because a money price approximates a real price. People do not need to make an implicit adjustment to any given money price because of changes in the general framework of prices. Such stability is a most desirable characteristic for any monetary system.

A Schematic Money Economy

An example of an economy using both gold and paper money may illustrate more concretely the principles discussed above. Consider a society that includes a government endowed with the usual policy-making powers. Assume that individuals in this society are free to choose among various goods and services offered for sale, and that they are also free to work at those trades or positions for which their abilities qualify them. Let this economy operate at relatively full employment and with no banking system.

Assume, next, that the government issues legal-tender paper dollars that are used in transactions and debt clearings. These units of paper money are noninterest-bearing, and could have been issued at a time when the government needed to finance large fiscal deficits.[4] Let the quantity of these money units be fixed at the moment, and assume that gold coin also circulates as the result of traditional private minting operations. The coins are of convenient sizes and denominations for purposes of exchange. They circulate even though

---

[3]However, both the study of relative prices and the study of absolute prices assume that money prices are flexible.

[4]For a historical example of this scheme, see Chapter 10.

the government has put no force of law behind them. Gold, then, is useful both as a commodity in the arts and as an exchange medium in the monetary system. The supply of gold is also virtually fixed in any short-run period.

The questions that now arise are these: (1) What gives each currency acceptability? and (2) What gives each currency value relative to the other currency and relative to all goods and services? Clearly, the paper money has acceptability because the government has invested it with legal tender privileges, while the gold coin is acceptable because it is recognized by everyone as a valuable commodity that may be used in various industrial activities. It is similar to other commodities in this respect, but superior to all others as a medium of exchange. The gold coins as such differ from, say, gold bullion only in their finished form. They are also different from the paper money in that they are not stamped with a unit of account denomination, such as "$10," but are marked by weight. For simplicity's sake, let them all be marked "1 ounce."

The value of an ounce of gold coin depends on the supply of and demand for gold relative to other things. The supply is almost fixed; the demand is a function of the utility of gold as an ornamental or industrial device, of its use as a store of value against contingencies and uncertainties, and of its transactive utility as a money. The value of paper money is also dependent on its demand and supply relative to other things, and has nothing to do with the trivial intrinsic value of the paper. The demand people have for it is a function of its efficacy as a transactive device and of its stability as a store of value.

The value of gold with respect to paper money is given once the demands for and supplies of each money with respect to all other commodities and services are established. Possibly this value would be one ounce of gold equals twenty paper dollars. People would then become accustomed to thinking of a gold coin in terms of twenty dollars of debt-clearing or transaction-effecting value, and they would perhaps call a gold coin a "twenty-dollar gold piece." Nevertheless, only the paper money would be legal tender unless the government formulated a gold standard on some terms. Gold would remain simply a commodity and a commodity money.

If the stock of paper money were doubled overnight, everyone would wake up some morning with twice as many units in his possession. Each person would have "too much money" relative to the other things he owns, and he would try to rid himself of the superfluous money units. But of course what one would spend another would receive; the aggregate supply could not be diminished. The attempt by people to do so, however, would force up paper money prices, including the paper money price of gold. The value of gold in terms of paper would become $40 = 1 ounce. The new monetary equilibrium would find all paper money prices twice as great as before, but no dollar price of any one good or service *relative* to other dollar prices necessarily would have changed. The prices of other commodities in terms of gold also would be the same.

Now, instead of a paper money expansion, assume that large quantities of new gold are discovered so that the stock of gold is doubled in just a very short time. People then would have "too much" gold. At first this surplus would be the property of gold miners; but in time it would spread through various spending channels to the whole economy. The price of gold in terms of other things, including the fixed amount of paper money, would fall. One ounce of gold would become equal to ten paper dollars. Again, all relative prices can be assumed to nave remained constant.

The hypothetical economy assumed in this example is uncomplicated and unchanging. In an economy that experiences changes in tastes, resources, and technology over time, demands for both money and commodities also change. The techniques of monetary analysis must then be used to gauge the supply that is necessary for fulfilling the objectives of monetary policy.

Summary

Money is a medium of exchange, a store of value, a standard of value, a unit of account, a bearer of options, and a stock of capital. When a money comes into general use as a medium of exchange in a market economy, the money prices of all the goods and services sold for money make up a general framework of prices sometimes referred to as a price level. The purchasing power or value of money is described by this general level of prices. This value declines as the price level rises and increases as the price level falls. Therefore, the value of the money unit (dollar, pound, or franc) may be defined as the inverse of the average of money prices.

The value of money and the acceptability of money are separate characteristics. The value of money is a function of its purchasing power; the acceptability of money depends upon its utility as a commodity if it is a metallic money (gold), or upon its investiture with legal tender power by government if it is a noncommodity money. Both kinds of money may exist side by side, in which case their respective values are established by the same principle that determines the economic value of any good or service — that is, the ability to command other goods and services in exchange.

Selected Bibliography

For interesting accounts of the development of forms of money, see:

Del Mar, Alexander. *A History of Money in Ancient Countries from the Earliest Times to the Present*. New York: Burt Franklin, originally published London 1885, reprinted 1968.

Einzig, Paul. *Primitive Money in Its Ethnological, Historical, and Economic Aspects*. Oxford: Pergamon Press, 1966.

For a discussion of monetary theory that would be hard to improve upon in terms of either lucidity or completeness, see:

Robertson, D. H. *Money*. New York: Pitman Publishing Co., 1948, Chs. 1-2. The interested student can easily read this book through.

Sixth Century Political Economy

Mark Twain

The Connecticut Yankee (Clarence) and King Arthur are traveling incognito in a kingdom adjacent to Arthur's when, by force of circumstance, they become guests of some hospitable villagers. After a hearty meal, the conversation becomes "shop talk"—more particularly, comparisons of wages and prices in the kingdom, where tariff protection is the rule with wages and prices in the kingdom that has reasonably free trade. The Connecticut Yankee, arguing in the present of the sixth century but with the helpful knowledge of the next 1,300 years, tries to explain to the villagers the difference between money wages and real wages, that is, the difference between wages expressed in terms of money and the same wages expressed in terms of the goods and services the money wages would purchase. The dubious success of his effort has been shared by many others over the centuries, and ignorant villagers are far from the only ones who have not profited from the verity of these simple illustrations.

The king got his cargo aboard, and then, the talk not turning upon battle, conquest, or iron-clad duel, he dulled down to drowsiness and went off to take a nap. Mrs. Marco cleared the table, placed the beer-keg handy, and went away to eat her dinner of leavings in humble privacy, and the rest of us soon drifted into matters near and dear to the hearts of our sort—business and wages, of course. At a first glance, things appeared to be exceeding prosperous in this little tributary kingdom—whose lord was King Bagdemagus—as compared with the state of things in my own region. They had the "protection" system in full force here, whereas we were working along down toward free trade, by easy stages, and were now about half-way. Before long, Dowley and I were doing all the talking, the others hungrily listening. Dowley warmed

---

From pp. 323-328 in *A Connecticut Yankee in King Arthur's Court* by Mark Twain, Harper & Row, Publishers, Inc.

to his work, snuffed an advantage in the air, and began to put questions which he considered pretty awkward ones for me, and they did have something of that look:

"In your country, brother, what is the wage of a master bailiff, master hind, carter, shepherd, swineherd?"

"Twenty-five milrays a day; that is to say, a quarter of a cent."

The smith's face beamed with joy. He said:

"With us they are allowed the double of it! And what may a mechanic get — carpenter, dauber, mason, painter, blacksmith, wheelwright, and the like?"

"On the average, fifty milrays; half a cent a day."

"Ho-ho! With us they are allowed a hundred! With us any good mechanic is allowed a cent a day! I count out the tailor, but not the others — they are all allowed a cent a day, and in driving times they get more — yes, up to a hundred and ten and even fifteen milrays a day. I've paid a hundred and fifteen myself, within the week. 'Rah for protection — to Sheol with free trade!"

And his face shone upon the company like a sunburst. But I didn't scare at all. I rigged up my pile-driver, and allowed myself fifteen minutes to drive him into the earth — drive him *all* in — drive him in till not even the curve of his skull should show above-ground. Here is the way I started in on him. I asked:

"What do you pay a pound for salt?"

"A hundred milrays."

"We pay forty. What do you pay for beef and mutton — when you buy it?" That was a neat hit; it made the color come.

"It varieth somewhat, but not much; one may say seventy-five milrays the pound."

"*We* pay thirty-three. What do you pay for eggs?"

"Fifty milrays the dozen."

"We pay twenty. What do you pay for beer?"

"It costeth us eight and one-half milrays the pint."

"We get it for four; twenty-five bottles for a cent. What do you pay for wheat?"

"At the rate of nine hundred milrays the bushel."

"We pay four hundred. What do you pay for a man's tow-linen suit?"

"Thirteen cents."

"We pay six. What do you pay for a stuff gown for the wife of the laborer or the mechanic?"

"We pay eight cents, four mills."

"Well, observe the difference: you pay eight cents and four mills, we pay only four cents." I prepared now to sock it to him. I said: "Look here, dear friend, *what's become of your high wages you were bragging so about a few minutes ago?*" — and I looked around on the company with placid satisfaction, for I had slipped up on him gradually and tied him hand and foot, you see, without his ever noticing that he was being tied at all. "What's become of those noble high wages of yours? — I seem to have knocked the stuffing all out of them, it appears to me."

But if you will believe me, he merely looked surprised, that is all! He didn't grasp the situation at all, didn't know he had walked into a trap, didn't discover that he was *in* a trap. I could have shot him, from sheer vexation. With cloudy eye and a struggling intellect he fetched this out:

"Marry, I seem not to understand. It is proved that our wages be double thine; how then may it be that thou'st knocked therefrom the stuffing?—an I miscall not the wonderly word, this being the first time under grace and providence of God it hath been granted me to hear it."

Well, I was stunned; partly with this unlooked-for stupidity on his part, and partly because his fellows so manifestly sided with him and were of his mind—if you might call it mind. My position was simple enough, plain enough; how could it ever be simplified more? However, I must try:

"Why, look here, brother Dowley, don't you see? Your wages are merely higher than ours in *name*, not in *fact*."

"Hear him! They are the *double*—ye have confessed it yourself."

"Yes-yes, I don't deny that at all. But that's got nothing to do with it; the *amount* of the wages in mere coins, with meaningless names attached to them to know them by, has got nothing to do with it. The thing is, how much can you *buy* with your wages?—that's the idea. While it is true that with you a good mechanic is allowed about three dollars and a half a year, and with us only about a dollar and seventy-five—"

"There—ye're confessing it again, ye're confessing it again!"

"Confound it, I've never denied it, I tell you! What I say is this. With us *half* a dollar buys more than a *dollar* buys with you—and *therefore* it stands to reason and the commonest kind of common sense, that our wages are higher than yours."

He looked dazed, and said, despairingly:

"Verily, I cannot make it out. Ye've just *said* ours are the higher, and with the same breath ye take it back."

"Oh, great Scott, isn't it possible to get such a simple thing through your head? Now look here—let me illustrate. We pay four cents for a woman's stuff gown, you pay eight cents four mills, which is four mills more than *double*. What do you allow a laboring-woman who works on a farm?"

"Two mills a day."

"Very good; we allow but half as much; we pay her only a tenth of a cent a day; and—"

"Again ye're conf—"

"Wait! Now, you see, the thing is very simple; this time you'll understand it. For instance, it takes your woman forty-two days to earn her gown, at two mills a day—seven weeks' work; but ours earns hers in forty days—two days *short* of seven weeks. Your woman has a gown, and her whole seven weeks' wages are gone; ours has a gown, and two days' wages left, to buy something else with. There—*now* you understand it!"

He looked—well, he merely looked dubious, it's the most I can say; so did the others. I waited—to let the thing work. Dowley spoke at last—and betrayed the fact that he actually hadn't gotten away from his rooted and grounded superstitions yet. He said, with a trifle of hesitancy:

"But—but—ye cannot fail to grant that two mills a day is better than one."

Shucks! Well, of course, I hated to give it up. So I chanced another flyer:

"Let us suppose a case. Suppose one of your journeymen goes out and buys the following articles:

> "1 pound of salt;
> 1 dozen eggs;
> 1 dozen pints of beer;
> 1 bushel of wheat;
> 1 tow-linen suit;
> 5 pounds of beef;
> 5 pounds of mutton.

"The lot will cost him thirty-two cents. It takes him thirty-two working days to earn the money—five weeks and two days. Let him come to us and work thirty-two days at *half* the wages; he can buy all those things for a shade under fourteen and a half cents; they will cost him a shade under twenty-nine days' work, and he will have about half a week's wages over. Carry it through the year; he would save nearly a week's wages every two months, *your* man nothing; thus saving five or six weeks' wages in a year, your man not a cent. *Now* I reckon you understand that 'high wages' and 'low wages' are phrases that don't mean anything in the world until you find out which of them will *buy* the most!"

It was a crusher.

But, alas! it didn't crush. No, I had to give it up. What those people valued was *high wages;* it didn't seem to be a matter of any consequence to them whether the high wages would buy anything or not. They stood for "protection," and swore by it, which was reasonable enough, because interested parties had gulled them into the notion that it was protection which had created their high wages. I proved to them that in a quarter of a century their wages had advanced but thirty percent, while the cost of living had gone up one hundred; and that with us, in a shorter time, wages had advanced forty percent, while the cost of living had gone steadily down. But it didn't do any good. Nothing could unseat their strange beliefs.

The Early History of Money

W. Stanley Jevons

In this selection from his book on money, the early British political econo-
mist W. Stanley Jevons (1835–1882) discusses the evolution of currency from
primitive objects, such as hides and skins, to the kind of metallic coin that is
easily identified as such. Jevon's economic interests were catholic; he wrote
books on principles of economics, labor economics, and money. He was both
a theorist and a scholar. The selection here is one of scholarship—that is,
of facts; and they are facts that the beginning student of the subject should
find enlightening.

Living in civilized communities, and accustomed to the use of coined metallic money, we learn to identify money with gold and silver; hence spring hurtful and insidious fallacies. It is always useful, therefore, to be reminded of the truth, so well stated by Turgot, that every kind of merchandise has the two properties of measuring value and transferring value. It is entirely a question of degree what commodities will in any given state of society form the most convenient currency, and this truth will be best impressed upon us by a brief consideration of the very numerous things which have at one time or other been employed as money. Though there are many numismatists and many political economists, the natural history of money is almost a virgin subject, upon which I should like to dilate; but the narrow limits of my space forbid me from attempting more than a brief sketch of the many interesting facts which may be collected.

Currency in the Hunting State

Perhaps the most rudimentary state of industry is that in which subsistence is gained by hunting wild animals. The proceeds of the chase would, in such a state, be the property of most generally recognized value. The meat of the animals captured would, indeed, be too perishable in nature to be hoarded or often exchanged; but it is otherwise with the skins, which, being preserved and valued for clothing, became one of the earliest materials of currency. Accordingly, there is abundant evidence that furs or skins were employed as money in many ancient nations. They serve this purpose to the present day in some parts of the world.

From *Money and the Mechanism of Exchange* by W. Stanley Jevons. New York: Appleton-Century-Crofts, 1902, pp. 19–28, 54, 55.

In the book of Job (ii, 4) we read, "Skin for skin, yea, all that a man hath will he give for his life"; a statement clearly implying that skins were taken as the representative of value among the ancient Oriental nations. Etymological research shows that the same may be said of the northern nations from the earliest times. In the Esthonian language the word *râha* generally signifies money, but its equivalent in the kindred Lappish tongue has not yet altogether lost the original meaning of skin or fur. Leather money is said to have circulated in Russia as late as the reign of Peter the Great, and it is worthy of notice, that classical writers have recorded traditions to the effect that the earliest currency used at Rome, Lacedaemon, and Carthage, was formed of leather.

We need not go back, however, to such early times to study the use of rude currencies. In the traffic of the Hudson's Bay Company with the North American Indians, furs, in spite of their differences of quality and size, long formed the medium of exchange. It is very instructive, and corroborative of the previous evidence to find that even after the use of coin had become common among the Indians the skin was still commonly used as the money of account. Thus Whymper says, "a gun, nominally worth about forty shillings, bought twenty 'skins.' This term is the old one employed by the company. One skin (beaver) is supposed to be worth two shillings, and it represents two marten, and so on. You heard a great deal about 'skins' at Fort Yukon, as the workmen were also charged for clothing, etc., in this way."

Currency in the Pastoral State

In the next higher stage of civilization, the pastoral state, sheep and cattle naturally form the most valuable and negotiable kind of property. They are easily transferable, convey themselves about, and can be kept for many years, so that they readily perform some of the functions of money.

We have abundance of evidence, traditional, written, and etymological, to show this. In the Homeric poems oxen are distinctly and repeatedly mentioned as the commodity in terms of which other objects are valued. The arms of Diomed are stated to be worth nine oxen, and are compared with those of Glaucos, worth one hundred. The tripod, the first prize for wrestlers in the 23rd Iliad, was valued at twelve oxen, and a woman captive, skilled in industry, at four. It is peculiarly interesting to find oxen thus used as the common measure of value, because from other passages it is probable, as already mentioned, that the precious metals, though as yet uncoined, were used as a store of value, and occasionally as a medium of exchange. The several functions of money were thus clearly performed by different commodities at this early period.

In several languages the name for money is identical with that of some kind of cattle or domesticated animal. It is generally allowed that *pecunia*, the

Latin word for money, is derived from *pecus*, cattle. From the Agamemnon of Æschylus we learn that the figure of an ox was the sign first impressed upon coins, and the same is said to have been the case with the earliest issues of the Roman *As*. Numismatic researches fail to bear out these traditions, which were probably invented to explain the connection between the name of the coin and the animal. A corresponding connection between these notions may be detected in much more modern languages. Our common expression for the payment of a sum of money is *fee*, which is nothing but the Anglo-Saxon *feoh*, meaning alike money and cattle, a word cognate with the German *vieh*, which still bears only the original meaning of cattle.

In the ancient German codes of law, fines and penalties are actually defined in terms of live-stock. In the Zend Avesta, as Professor Theodores . . . informs me, the scale of rewards to be paid to physicians is carefully stated, and in every case the fee consists in some sort of cattle. The fifth and sixth lectures in Sir H. S. Maine's most interesting work on *The Early History of Institutions*, which has just been published, are full of curious information showing the importance of live-stock in a primitive state of society. Being counted by the head, the kine was called capitale, whence the economical term capital, the law term chattel, and our common name cattle.

In countries where slaves form one of the most common and valuable possessions, it is quite natural that they should serve as the medium of exchange like cattle. Pausanias mentions their use in this way, and in Central Africa and some other places where slavery still flourishes, they are the medium of exchange along with cattle and ivory tusks. According to Earl's account of New Guinea, there is in that island a large traffic in slaves, and a slave forms the unit of value. Even in England slaves are believed to have been exchanged at one time in the manner of money.

Articles of Ornament as Currency

A passion for personal adornment is one of the most primitive and powerful instincts of the human race, and as articles used for such purposes would be durable, universally esteemed, and easily transferable, it is natural that they should be circulated as money. The *wampumpeag* of the North American Indians is a case in point, as it certainly served as jewelry. It consisted of beads made of the ends of black and white shells, rubbed down and polished, and then strung into belts or necklaces, which were valued according to their length, and also according to their color and luster, a foot of black *peag* being worth two feet of white *peag*. It was so well established as currency among the natives that the Court of Massachusetts ordered in 1649, that it should be received in the payment of debts among settlers to the amount of forty shillings. It is curious to learn, too, that just as European misers hoard up gold and silver coins, the richer Indian chiefs secrete piles of wampum beads, having no better means of investing their superfluous wealth.

Exactly analogous to this North American currency, is that of the cowry shells, which, under one name or another—*chamgos, zimbis, bouges, porcelanes,* etc.—have long been used in the East Indies as small money. In British India, Siam, the West Coast of Africa, and elsewhere on the tropical coasts, they are still used as small change, being collected on the shores of the Maldive and Laccadive Islands, and exported for the purpose. Their value varies somewhat, according to the abundance of the yield, but in India the current rate used to be about five thousand shells for one rupee, at which rate each shell is worth about the two-hundredth part of a penny. Among our interesting fellow-subjects, the Fijians, whale's teeth served in the place of cowries, and white teeth were exchanged for red teeth somewhat in the ratio of shillings to sovereigns.

Among other articles of ornament or of special value used as currency, may be mentioned yellow amber, engraved stones, such as the Egyptian scarabæi, and tusks of ivory.

Currency in the Agricultural State

Many vegetable productions are at least as well suited for circulation as some of the articles which have been mentioned. It is not surprising to find, then, that among a people supporting themselves by agriculture, the more durable products were thus used. Corn has been the medium of exchange in remote parts of Europe from the time of the ancient Greeks to the present day. In Norway corn is even deposited in banks, and lent and borrowed. What wheat, barley, and oats are to Europe, such is maize in parts of Central America, especially Mexico, where it formerly circulated. In many of the countries surrounding the Mediterranean, olive oil is one of the commonest articles of produce and consumption; being, moreover, pretty uniform in quality, durable, and easily divisible, it has long served as currency in the Ionian Islands, Mytilene, some towns of Asia Minor, and elsewhere in the Levant.

Just as cowries circulate in the East Indies, so cacao nuts, in Central America and Yucatan, form a perfectly recognized and probably an ancient fractional money. Travellers have published many distinct statements as to their value, but it is impossible to reconcile these statements without supposing great changes of value either in the nuts or in the coins with which they are compared. In 1521, at Caracas, about thirty cacao nuts were worth one penny English, whereas recently ten beans would go to a penny, according to Squier's statements. In the European countries, where almonds are commonly grown, they have circulated to some extent like the cacao nuts, but are variable in value, according to the success of the harvest.

It is not only, however, as a minor currency that vegetable products have been used in modern times. In the American settlements and the West India Islands, in former days, specie used to become inconveniently scarce, and the legislators fell back upon the device of obliging creditors to receive payment in produce at stated rates. In 1618, the Governor of the Plantations of Virginia ordered that tobacco should be received at the rate of three shillings for the pound weight, under the penalty of three years' hard labor. We are told that, when the Virginia Company imported young women as wives for the settlers, the price per head was one hundred pounds of tobacco, subsequently raised to one hundred and fifty. As late as 1732, the legislature of Maryland made tobacco and Indian corn legal tenders; and in 1641 there were similar laws concerning corn in Massachusetts. The governments of some of the West India Islands seem to have made attempts to imitate these peculiar currency laws, and it was provided that the successful plaintiff in a lawsuit should be obliged to accept various kinds of raw produce, such as sugar, rum, molasses, ginger, indigo, or tobacco....

The perishable nature of most kinds of animal food prevents them from being much used as money; but eggs are said to have circulated in the Alpine villages of Switzerland, and dried codfish have certainly acted as currency in the colony of Newfoundland.

Manufactured and Miscellaneous Articles as Currency

The enumeration of articles which have served as money may already seem long enough for the purposes in view. I will, therefore, only add briefly that a great number of manufactured commodities have been used as a medium of exchange in various times and places. Such are the pieces of cotton cloth, called *Guinea pieces,* used for traffic upon the banks of the Senegal, or the somewhat similar pieces circulated in Abyssinia, the Soulou Archipelago, Sumatra, Mexico, Peru, Siberia, and among the Veddahs. It is less easy to understand the origin of the curious straw money which circulated until 1694 in the Portuguese possessions in Angola, and which consisted of small mats, called *libongos,* woven out of rice straw, and worth about 1½d. each. These mats must have had, at least originally, some purpose apart from their use as currency, and were perhaps analogous to the fine woven mats so much valued by the Samoans, and also treated by them as a medium of exchange.

Salt has been circulated not only in Abyssinia, but in Sumatra, Mexico, and elsewhere. Cubes of benzoin gum or bees-wax in Sumatra, red feathers in the Islands of the Pacific Ocean, cubes of tea in Tartary, iron shovels or hoes among the Malagasy, are other peculiar forms of currency. The remarks of Adam Smith concerning the use of hand-made nails as money in some Scotch villages will be remembered by many readers, and need not be repeated. M. Chevalier has adduced an exactly corresponding case from one of the French coalfields.

Were space available it would be interesting to discuss the not improbable suggestion of Boucher de Perthes, that, perhaps, after all, the finely worked stone implements now so frequently discovered were among the earliest mediums of exchange. Some of them are certainly made of jade, nephrite, or other hard stones, only found in distant countries, so that an active traffic in such implements must have existed in times of which we have no records whatever.

There are some obscure allusions in classical authors to a wooden money circulating among the Byzantines, and to a wooden talent used at Antioch and Alexandria, but in the absence of fuller information as to their nature, it is impossible to do more than mention them....

The Invention of Coining

The date of the invention of coining can be assigned with some degree of probability. Coined money was clearly unknown in the Homeric times, and it was known in the time of Lycurgus. We might therefore assume, with various authorities, that it was invented in the mean time, or about 900 B.C. There is tradition, moreover, that Pheidon, King of Argos, first struck silver money in the island of Ægina about 895 B.C., and the tradition is supported by the existence of small stamped ingots of silver, which have been found in Ægina. Later inquiries, however, lead to the conclusion that Pheidon lived in the middle of the eighth century B.C., and Grote has shown good reasons for believing that what he did accomplish was done in Argos, and not in Ægina.

The mode in which the invention happened is sufficiently evident. Seals were familiarly employed in very early times, as we learn from the Egyptian paintings or the stamped bricks of Nineveh. Being employed to signify possession, or to ratify contracts, they came to indicate authority. When a ruler first undertook to certify the weights of pieces of metal, he naturally employed his seal to make the fact known, just as, at Goldsmiths' Hall, a small punch is used to certify the fineness of plate. In the earliest forms of coinage there were no attempts at so fashioning the metal that its weight could not be altered without destroying the stamp or design. The earliest coins struck, both in Lydia and in the Peloponnesus, were stamped on one side only....

2

Measuring the Value of Money

The Concept of Monetary Value

Economists, in common with most scientists, have been intensively concerned with values. The concept of economic value — the ability of a commodity or service to command other commodities or services in exchange — was fairly easy to come by in the development of classical economic thought. That is, it was easy until the value of money was at issue. Money was supposed to be a standard of value and a measure of value; and the question "How do you measure the standard?" was insoluble for several decades after economics itself had been identified as a distinct discipline.

The classical economists (Adam Smith through John Stuart Mill) approached the question of the value of the value measure by undertaking a minute intellectual search for something that had unvarying *absolute* economic value — a talisman of economic measurement. Adam Smith, for example, felt that silver served such a purpose in the short run, that "corn" (meaning, in England, grain generally) was a better measure in the long run, but that the best measure was the disutility (or unpleasantness) involved in "common labor" because it was always the same at all times and places to all men.[1] How could it be proven otherwise? Who can say that one man's labor is any more valuable or less onerous to him than another man's is to him? The labor cost theory of value thus became the hallmark of classical economic thought.

---

[1]Adam Smith, *Wealth of Nations*, ed. E. C. Cannan (New York: Modern Library, 1937), pp. 176–191.

In time, the presumption that each man's labor-time-given-up was equally costly, even if not equally disagreeable, was recognized as absurd; and the search for an absolute measure of value, against which even the value of money could be compared, was abandoned. From about the middle of the nineteenth century, concepts and practices for estimating the value of money focused on the inductive method of averaging money prices.

A unit of money buys a multitude of different goods and services, the prices or values of which are stated in monetary terms. The value of the money unit may be estimated by the amount it buys of any one of these many goods or services; but, clearly, the accuracy of the measure of monetary value is enhanced by including the prices of a larger and larger cross-section of the multitude of goods and services for which money is exchanged. Two problems then arise: (1) The number of prices included in the averaging may become statistically unwieldy, and (2) the method of averaging is subject to the discretion and judgment of the person computing the average.

Any average of prices is called a "price index." A price index must be distinguished from the price level. A price index is a statistical calculation of an average of money prices, while the price level is the abstract average of prices the statistician seeks to measure by means of a price index. The analogy of thermometer and temperature is applicable here. The temperature is a specific physical value that the thermometer measures with greater or lesser accuracy. The price index, likewise, is supposed to measure the general level of money prices. Clearly, any estimation of the price level is only as good as the quality of the device built to measure it. Just as a thermometer may be sensitive to pressure and not reflect the correct temperature, so a price index may record a higher or lower price average than it should. Unfortunately, biases in price indexes are not necessarily obvious or very likely measurable. Nonetheless, a user of indexes must be aware that biases exist, and he should try to have some general idea of their relative effects.

Biases or no biases, an economic analyst must use the tools he has, and a price index is a very useful tool. It is first of all an estimator of the price level. Therefore, it is also an estimator of the values of money and of all things measured in monetary terms by means of the inversion formula discussed in Chapter 1.

Only a representative sample of goods and services is necessary to give a reasonably accurate price index, and as a rule only a fraction of the economy need be surveyed in order to determine the general drift of the money prices paid for particular commodities and services. If people in different localities paid different prices for each commodity, no "average" of prices would have much validity because the dispersion of prices around the average would be too great. An average is a measure of central tendency. With too much dispersion of values, no central tendency is meaningful. Fortunately, in a free-choice, competitive economy the "law of one price" works fairly well. Prices of most goods and services are not only the same in local markets but are also reasonably uniform from city to city and from region to region.

The Construction of Index Numbers

An index may be a simple average of values, in which case each item has equal importance or "weight" in the index, or the items may be weighted differently according to their individual importance in the budgets of households and firms. To demonstrate construction of an index, first as a simple average, assume that the whole class of items exchanged for money in the economy is represented by the goods and services listed in Table 2.1.

Table 2.1. Hypothetical Money Prices of Six Commodities for Selected Years

Year	Bread (loaf)	Milk (quart)	Fuel Oil (gallon)	Tooth-picks (box)	Auto-mobile (per mile)	Housing (per room/day)
1950	0.15	0.24	0.16	0.10	0.07	1.00
1960	0.20	0.28	0.15	0.25	0.08	1.30

Notice that the beginning average of prices in 1950 has no relevance until it is compared with the average of prices in some other year. The sum of all six prices in 1950 is $1.72, and for 1960 it is $2.26. However, these sums of money prices are almost meaningless as they stand. First of all, housing dominates the average because of the size of the housing unit chosen. If toothpicks as a unit were cited in boxcar-load quantities, they might dominate the index. Second, using a sum of prices, such as $1.72, even though it expresses the cost of a specified bundle of goods and services, is awkward. If $1.72 is revalued as 100 percent of the cost of this bundle of goods, then subsequent changes in the cost of the bundle based on "100" indicate immediately the proportional change in the value of the monetary unit from this benchmark or "base year" value.[2] This kind of calibration is similar to that used in scaling centigrade thermometers, where, for example, 100 degrees is arbitrarily stated as the boiling point of pure water at a specified atmospheric pressure. If the average of prices is defined as "100" in 1950, the price average of the same commodities in 1960 is given by the ratio $\Sigma p\,1960/\Sigma p\,1950 = 131.4$. When prices are indexed in this way, the change in the measured level of prices

[2]When average prices over a span of years are used, the group of years is referred to as a "base period."

is immediately apparent: Prices are 31.4 percent higher in 1960 than they were in 1950.

The problem of what size unit should be selected for the index is still an issue. The usual way of handling this matter is to use units that are commonly exchanged in markets and then to weight the units chosen according to the proportion of the average consumer's budget devoted to the purchase of the particular item to be weighted. Assume that weights obtained by this means are those given in Table 2.2.

Table 2.2. Hypothetical Money Prices and Weights of Six Commodities for Selected Years

| | 1950 | | | 1960 | | |
Item	Price (dollars)	Weight 1950	$P \cdot W$	Price (dollars)	Weight 1950	$P \cdot W$
Bread (loaf)	0.15	25	3.75	0.20	25	5.00
Milk (quart)	0.24	19	4.56	0.28	19	5.32
Fuel oil (gallon)	0.16	20	3.20	0.15	20	3.00
Toothpicks (box)	0.10	1	0.10	0.25	1	0.25
Automobile (mile)	0.07	30	2.10	0.08	30	2.40
House (room/day)	1.00	5	5.00	1.30	5	6.50
Total		100	18.71		100	22.47

The prices are the same as those in Table 2.1; but the weights, instead of being implicitly the same for each commodity, now correspond to the proportional share each item absorbs of the average consumer's income for the base year (1950). Each price is multiplied by its corresponding weight, and the sum of these products is then compared to a similar sum for the values in another year. The sum of the weights is 100, implying that these items exhaust the average consumer's income.

The relationship between *weighted* prices in 1950 and *weighted* prices in 1960 is:

$$\frac{\sum p1960 \cdot W1950}{\sum p1950 \cdot W1950} = \frac{22.47}{18.71} = \frac{120.1}{100.0}$$

Since 1950 is the base year, the index value for that year again may be set at 100. The index value in 1960 then is 120.1. This value is significantly lower than the simple index value computed earlier because this index greatly deflates the implicit weight assigned to toothpicks in the simple index.

The weighting system used in this latter example is known as the *aggregative index method*. The weights in the base year are used for the computations in all other years. Clearly, the assumption of constant weights builds error or bias into the index. Weights change due to both independent changes in tastes and the influence of price changes on the proportions of commodities purchased. However, if weight changes as well as price changes are permitted, the index simply would measure the change in total money income. Price changes as such would be unidentifiable.

Various other weighting methods have been devised, but none is (or can be) completely exempt from criticism.[3] Fortunately, index values obtained by different weighting methods do not diverge markedly from each other, except that the values obtained from the simple aggregative index do differ significantly from all the weighted indexes. The consensus of statisticians is that weighting on some logical discriminating basis is better than weighting each item equally, as is done when "no weights" are imputed to the index.[4]

The two most commonly cited price indexes in the United States are the Consumer Price Index and the Wholesale Price Index. Both are prepared by the Bureau of Labor Statistics of the Department of Labor. They are, however, calculated from different data and are designed to cover different spending sectors of the economy.

The Consumer Price Index, or CPI, is the valuation of a "market basket" of goods and services purchased in the 3,000-odd cities and towns of 2,500 population and greater. The "market basket" includes all the items commonly purchased by urban wage earner and clerical worker families. It therefore eliminates purchases made by extremely large or extremely small incomes. The revised index of 1960 includes about 400 items. Its general composition is summarized in Table 2.3.

The CPI is calculated by the weighted aggregative method. It must, therefore, be rebased from time to time (at least every ten years) in order to account for changes in the "market basket" of goods and services that people buy. The most recent revision is based on the three-year period 1957–1959. As time passes, say over several decades, the index may come to contain hardly a fraction of things that had been in it originally. It must also be interpreted with other qualifications in mind. First of all, while it covers prices of items purchased by about 40 percent of the population in the United States, it excludes prices paid by nonurban, nonclerical workers anywhere, and of course it excludes prices on items purchased in towns of less than 2,500 population. These qualifications do not negate its general usefulness because price changes outside the index are fairly similar to those covered by the index. However, they must be kept in mind when the index is used to measure changes in the cost of living for any specific income class in the total population.

---

[3]For a clear and simple discussion of weighting methods, see Frederick E. Croxton and Dudley J. Cowden, *Applied General Statistics,* 5th ed. (Englewood Cliffs, N.J.: Prentice-Hall, 1967).

[4]One of the easiest ways for the student to remember the weighting process is to relate the computations for his course grade average at the end of each grading period to the method used for obtaining a price index. In such an analogy, course grades correspond to money prices and credit hours to weights.

Table 2.3. Groups of Items and Weights Used in Consumer Price Index

Item Group	Weight (%)
Food	30
Apparel	9
Housing	33
Transportation	11
Medical care	5
Personal care	2
Recreation	5
Other	5

Source: U.S. Department of Labor, Bureau of Labor Statistics, *The Consumer Price Index* (Washington, D.C.: U.S. Government Printing Office, 1960).

The Wholesale Price Index, or WPI, is not precisely an index of wholesale prices, but an index of prices quoted for about 2,000 commodities in primary markets. This large number is in response to the demands of users of the index. Table 2.4 summarizes its general composition.

Table 2.4. Groups of Items and Weights Used in Wholesale Price Index

Item Group	Weight (%)
Farm products	15
Processed foods	15
Textiles and apparel	10
Hides and leather products	2
Fuel, power, and light materials	9
Chemicals and chemical products	5
Lumber and wood products	3
Rubber and rubber products	2
Pulp, paper, and paper products	3
Metals and metal products	12
Machinery and motive products	14
Furniture and household durables	4
Nonmetal minerals	1
Tobacco manufacturers and bottled beverages	2
Miscellaneous (toys, jewelry, etc.)	3
Total	100

Source: U.S. Department of Labor, Bureau of Labor Statistics, *The Wholesale Price Index* (reprint of Ch. 10 from BLS *Bulletin No. 1168*), Washington, D.C.

"Wholesale," as used in the title of this index, refers to sales in large quantities. Price data used in constructing the index are those prices resulting from the *first important commercial transaction* each commodity experiences. For some commodities, such as agricultural products, prices quoted on commodity exchanges are used. For other commodities, such as ships and railroad rolling stock, custom-made machinery, and the like, direct measures of price movements are not possible. Instead, weights of the other commodities in the index used in the production of the above-mentioned goods are increased. In some cases, too, additional weight is assigned to commodities manufactured in a similar way. List prices quoted in trade journals and in manufacturers' brochures are also used in the index where appropriate. The index does not include prices of retail transactions, prices of services, prices for printing and publishing, and prices of real estate, transportation, and securities.

The WPI principally differs from the CPI in the characteristics of the commodities priced. The WPI includes more unprocessed commodities. For this reason it is of more concern to manufacturers who buy such things in their industrial operations. These commodities also have the characteristic of changing less in intrinsic content over time than commodities bought in retail markets. (An apple is always an apple, but applesauce may be processed in a number of ways.) Constancy of intrinsic content makes the WPI more useful and accurate for estimating changes in the value of money over long periods.

Limitations of Index Numbers

Even if the price indexes discussed above were computed with perfect arithmetical precision (i.e., perfect weights) and were used only to measure the value of money in the areas selected, they might still include either inflationary or deflationary biases. A *bias* may be defined as *a systematic tendency to err*. When it appears in an index, it makes the index read higher or lower than it would if it were reflecting *all* the data properly. Needless to say, such biases are inadvertent and largely unavoidable; statisticians do their best to get indexes that accurately register price level changes. Fortunately, factors that bias indexes have a relatively small influence on the overall accuracy of the index in its recording of general price level changes. Nonetheless, users of indexes must be prepared to compensate conceptually for these possible biases.

Biases may occur in at least three ways. First, intrinsic quality changes that do not provoke corresponding price changes are largely unaccountable in the index. Compilers of the indexes in fact try to prevent changes in the quality of the "market basket," but they cannot control manufacturers who build better mousetraps and consumers who buy them. Much of the competition in industry takes the form of improvements in quality either because the improvements themselves are technically costless or because quality improvements at constant prices are less costly administratively than constant quality products at lower prices. Technological indivisibilities also contribute to this phenomenon. Of course, when product quality improves and the money price increases at the same time, the price increase can be identified as roughly equal to the cost of the quality improvement. (The transition from gear-shift transmissions to automatic transmissions in automobiles is an example of this type of change.) The apparently unresolvable problem is the imputation of price changes to commodities and services that have shown quality changes only. Nor are these changes in the quality of items in the market basket likely to cancel out; improvements in the qualities of some goods are not usually offset by depreciation in the qualities of others. Improvements occur generally during periods of competitive business pressure ("buyers' markets"), while depreciation is most evident during periods of rapid inflation ("sellers' markets").

Another bias problem arises as new products enter the index computation. A new product may be thought of as an extreme case of quality change, but the problem of exit and entry in the index is different from the quality question discussed above. A new product is not necessarily a commercial success. It must first prove itself in its market before it can have a place in a price index. Nevertheless, while it is doing so, people are buying and using it, revenue is being generated by its sales, and resources are being allocated to its production.

If changes in production costs and in the corresponding price history of the typical new commodity coincided with changes in the money prices of established commodities, the time at which the new commodity entered the index would be inconsequential. But ordinarily a successful new commodity enjoys economies of scale. Its early history is marked by price declines as technical advantages in costs are realized and intensified competition is experienced. Then, as production techniques for the commodity mature and most of the economies of scale are capitalized, the price of the commodity tends to flatten out. Ultimately it follows, with more or less precision, money prices in general.[5]

The stage of its price history at which a commodity is brought into the index clearly influences the direction the index takes. Inclusion of every "new" commodity is uncalled for; many such commodities are commercial failures and never become a part of the economic fabric. If the index waits for commercial success, on the other hand, it fails to record the effect of some money price declines in the early history of the new commodity. *An index that does not register such a downward price influence must necessarily be biased upward.* For example, if an index with an inflationary bias registers a constant value over time, the general price level actually would be falling by the amount of the bias.

---

[5]A good example of this pattern in recent years is the price history of automatic dishwashers. When they were first marketed for households about 1954, their list price was $250, but they were immediately "on sale" for $230. Five or six years later, somewhat improved versions of the original sold for $115 to $130. More recently, the money price has shown little tendency to fall further.

A last source of bias is the possibility that the money prices used in the index are not the ones really paid across (or under) the counter. The actual money prices quoted may be altered by hidden discounts, sale prices, and rebates. Such hidden changes in quoted prices may have either an upward or a downward bias on the index, depending on circumstances. During periods of rapidly rising prices, the real price rise may be understated by the index as businesses use various means to apply hidden premiums to quoted prices. Under statutory money price and wage controls, this problem is most acute. Not only do "black market" prices become widespread but an official index cannot take account of them without admitting that the laws of the land are being broken! Government statisticians who compute indexes under such conditions must necessarily take as factual the "ceiling prices" statutorily given by the official government agency responsible for "stabilization."

Under conditions of business recession, pressures in the opposite direction develop. Stores have sales; automobile dealers give "exorbitant" trade-in values; rebates become common. These devices are used in place of quoted price reductions because they bring home the price reduction to the consumer without violating general "asking" or list prices.

Statisticians who compute the various indexes try to adjust to these three types of bias. However, these problems evade satisfactory statistical solution. They also tend to be cumulative, that is, not offsetting. During periods of rapidly rising prices, quality deteriorations and unquoted price premiums appear. When prices are under downward pressure due to a business recession, quality improves, hidden price declines are in evidence, and new products are more numerous.

While indexes may not adjust for these biases perfectly, the biases themselves are small. *They are of consequence only when small changes in the index occur from year to year.* To illustrate: Assume that under the relatively stable economic conditions of the ten-year period 1952–1962 the CPI had a 1 to 2 percent per year inflationary bias for some or all of the reasons considered above. Then if the price level actually had remained stable, the price index would have shown an increase of 1 to 2 percent per year. On the other hand, a fairly sizable price index increase of, say, 10 percent in one year really would be an 8 to 9 percent increase in the price level; so the index reading would be fairly accurate for this large a change. But an "increase" from a reading of 103.1 to 104.2 (the change cited by the CPI between 1960 and 1961) is clearly within the realm of the biases discussed above. With a built-in bias of 2 percent per year, this "increase" would actually indicate a 1 percent price level decline! The same thing is true for the measured increase in the index from 93.2 in 1953 to 100.7 in 1958. This change would be significant only if small inflationary biases in the index did not exist. Since much empirical study suggests that these biases do exist, the observer must implicitly recalibrate the index to take account of the biases. During years of product "shortages," such as the period 1942–1948, the biases work in the other direction. A deflationary bias is then said to exist in the index; prices actually increase by an amount greater than what the index registers.

Biases, of course, can only be judged in a discretionary sense; they cannot be pinpointed or given explicit quantitative values. If they could be quantified, price indexes would be adjusted for them and the foregoing qualifications would be uncalled for.

Table 2.5. Consumer Prices by Major Group, 1953 to 1970 (1957–1959 = 100)

Period	All Items	Food	Housing, Total	Apparel	Trans-portation	Medical Care
1953	93.2	95.6	92.3	97.8	92.1	83.9
1954	93.6	95.4	93.4	97.3	90.8	86.6
1955	93.3	94.0	94.1	96.7	89.7	88.6
1956	94.7	94.7	95.5	98.4	91.3	91.8
1957	98.0	97.8	98.5	99.7	96.5	95.5
1958	100.7	101.9	100.2	99.8	99.7	100.1
1959	101.5	100.3	101.3	100.7	103.8	104.4
1960	103.1	101.4	103.1	102.1	103.8	108.1
1961	104.2	102.6	103.9	102.8	105.0	111.3
1962	105.4	103.6	104.8	103.6	107.2	114.2
1963	106.7	105.1	106.0	104.8	107.8	116.7
1964	108.1	106.4	107.2	105.7	109.3	119.4
1965	110.0	108.8	108.5	106.8	111.1	122.3
1966	113.1	114.2	111.1	109.6	112.7	127.7
1967	116.3	115.2	114.3	114.0	115.9	136.7
1968	121.2	119.3	119.1	120.1	119.6	145.0
1969	127.7	125.5	126.7	127.1	124.2	155.0
1970*	135.2	132.7	135.6	132.2	130.6	164.7

Source: Federal Reserve Bulletins.
* June values.

Table 2.6. Wholesale Price Indexes, 1953 to 1970 (1957–1959 = 100)

Period	All Commodities	Farm Products	Processed Foods	Chemicals, etc.	Rubber, etc.	Lumber, etc.	Metals	Furniture, etc.
1953	92.7	105.9	97.0	96.1	86.8	99.4	83.6	92.9
1954	92.9	104.4	97.6	97.3	87.6	97.6	84.3	93.9
1955	93.2	97.9	94.3	96.9	99.2	102.3	90.0	94.3
1956	96.2	96.6	94.3	97.5	100.6	103.8	97.8	96.9
1957	99.0	99.2	97.9	99.6	100.2	98.5	99.7	99.4
1958	100.4	103.6	102.9	100.4	100.1	97.4	99.1	100.2
1959	100.6	97.2	99.2	100.0	99.7	104.1	101.2	100.4
1960	100.7	96.9	99.9	100.2	99.9	100.4	101.3	100.1
1961	100.3	96.0	100.6	99.1	96.1	95.9	100.7	99.5
1962	100.6	97.7	101.2	97.5	93.3	96.5	100.0	98.8
1963	100.3	95.7	100.4	96.2	93.8	99.1	101.3	98.0
1964	100.5	94.3	103.1	96.7	92.5	100.6	102.8	98.5
1965	102.5	98.4	106.7	97.4	92.9	101.1	105.7	98.0
1966	105.9	105.6	113.0	97.8	94.8	105.6	108.3	99.1
1967	106.1	99.7	111.7	98.4	97.0	105.4	109.5	101.0
1968	108.7	102.2	114.1	98.2	100.3	119.3	112.4	104.0
1969	113.0	108.5	119.8	98.3	102.1	132.0	118.9	106.1
1970*	117.0	111.3	124.8	100.5	104.1	120.2	129.1	108.6

Source: Federal Reserve Bulletins.
* June values.

Selected Bibliography

Almost any textbook on statistics can furnish the student with a reasonably good account of price index computation. For example, see the following:

Croxton, Frederick E., and Dudley J. Cowden. *Applied General Statistics,* 5th ed. Englewood Cliffs, N.J.: Prentice-Hall, 1967.

Huff, Darrell. *How to Lie with Statistics.* New York: W. W. Norton & Co., 1954. A light but fundamentally important caution on the use of statistics.

Morganstern, Oskar. *On the Accuracy of Economic Observations.* Princeton, N.J.: Princeton University Press, 1963. A recent book that discusses the tolerances possible in statistical computation and usage.

Wallace, William H. *Measuring Price Changes: A Study of the Price Indexes.* Richmond, Va.: Federal Reserve Bank of Richmond, 1970.

Measuring the Cost of Quality

Richard Ruggles

This selection is taken from the now defunct journal Challenge, *which published many articles on economics and business subjects aimed at intelligent and interested nonprofessional readers. In this article, Professor Richard Ruggles of the Department of Economics at Yale University, whose principal professional contributions are on the measurement and interpretation of national income data, discusses the problems and pitfalls of using price index figures "naively"—without allowing proper qualifications for biases. The cautions raised by Professor Ruggles have direct implications for too restrictive a monetary policy at certain times, but they should not be taken to mean that the standard price indexes are useless. They are only useless (or worse) if the intrinsic limitations on their accuracy are ignored.*

The bogy of inflation is with us again. This cry, which was chronic during the Fifties, has been a major factor in determining our monetary and fiscal policies. Since these policies are based on the movements in the price indexes, it is time to consider whether our confidence in these indexes is justified.

Since 1948 the Consumer Price Index has increased by approximately 25 percent. A large part of this increase—about one-third of it—occurred in the brief space of one year, at the beginning of the Korean war. The other two-thirds was spread more or less evenly over the other 12 years—an average increase of about one and a half percent a year.

In view of these statistics, policy makers might have concluded that we had relative price stability in the Fifties, except at the beginning of the Korean war when scare buying forced prices up. Instead, we hear much about a continual and insidious price creep. When price indexes continued to rise during periods of recession, such as in 1958, many policy makers concluded that rising prices stemmed from increasing costs due to excessive wage demands and administered prices of monopolies.

To understand what has *really* been happening to prices, we must first examine the factors responsible for the rises in the index. For this purpose let us take a look at the 12 percent increase in the Consumer Price Index that has occurred since the Korean war. There are major segments of consumer purchases for which prices have not risen at all since that time. The price index for consumer durables, for example, shows a decline of approximately three percent. On the other hand, the index for medical care rose by more than 30

From *Challenge: The Magazine of Economic Affairs,* Vol. 10, No. 2, November 1961, pp. 6–8. Reprinted by permission of the author.

percent. On the average, the prices of services rose a substantial 23 percent, while those of commodities rose only six percent.

This difference in behavior largely reflects the fact that the price of a service is generally the rate of compensation of those performing it. And these wages naturally rise as per capita income rises. In the last 50 years the prices of services relative to those of commodities have risen continually as a consequence of such general rises in living standards. Commodity prices, on the other hand, can sometimes reflect increased productivity. If the increase in output per man-hour is greater than the increase in the wage rate, the cost of production may actually fall, thus permitting lower commodity prices despite higher wages.

The identification of price indexes with rates of pay in the service industries involves the implicit assumption that the productivity of the service industries has remained unchanged. In some instances, this assumption may be correct, but in others quite wide of the mark.

In the case of medical care, for example, the apparent 30 percent price increase of the last eight years must be qualified by considering the increase in medical knowledge, better drugs and the new preventive medicines. Certainly the Salk vaccine was a tremendous medical advance which, in addition to sparing many lives, will save consumer dollars that would have gone for the treatment of polio.

Basically, then, the measurement of price changes comes down to a question of whether one gets more or less for his money. In the field of medical care it can be argued that most people would rather pay today's prices for today's medical care than yesterday's prices for yesterday's medical care. The fact that diseases were treated more cheaply in yesterday's world is more than offset by the increased knowledge and new drugs available for curing disease today. Although it is difficult to measure improvement in the *quality* of medicine in quantitative terms, there is no justification for ignoring it—which is what our present method of computing price indexes does.

The problem of measuring changes in quality also arises in the commodity components of the Consumer Price Index. In the Congressional hearings on government price statistics conducted early this year, Prof. Zvi Griliches of the University of Chicago reported on the effect that changes in specifications had upon automobile prices. Dr. Griliches computed the value of specifications such as size, automatic transmission, horsepower, etc., by taking the price differences for a given year among cars with these varying specifications. Automobile prices were then adjusted to take into account the different features included as standard equipment in each year.

On this basis, using the value of specifications given by the 1954 price schedule, the prices of the "low-priced three" dropped 27 percent from 1954 to 1960, although their unadjusted list price rose 34 percent, and the Consumer Price Index for these automobiles reported a rise of 11 percent. The significance of this study is not that the Consumer Price Index for automobiles needs some minor adjustment to reflect the true price situation, but rather that the overemphasis on price change is itself in question. Instead of an 11 percent price increase over this period, there may have been a price reduction of as much as 27 percent.

This same kind of analysis could, of course, be applied to other major kinds of consumer durables, such as home laundry equipment, refrigerators and freezers, portable radios, cameras and hi-fi equipment. Almost all of these have shown considerable change in recent years. If the change in *quality* were taken into account the price index for consumer durables would have fallen far more than the three percent now reported.

Besides the quality change in existing goods, we should also take into account the effect of the introduction of totally new commodities upon the consumer's purchasing power. The index of consumer prices is purposely designed so that the introduction of new goods or the dropping of old ones will have no effect. Thus the introduction of such things as television, synthetic fibers and plastic products has had no effect upon the index.

But the introduction of new products obviously *does* have an influence upon consumers' standards of living, just as do quality improvements in existing products. It is quite possible to imagine an economic system which obtains its higher standard of living through the introduction of new products which are superior to the old ones they replace. In such a system, the consumer might continuously get more value for his dollar, even though the prices of the old products rose steadily due to rising wage and material costs. Yet conventional price indexes would show this situation as one in which prices are rising and consumers are getting less for their dollars. Although, of course, in our economy not all of the improvement in the standard of living comes about through the substitution of new products for old, it does seem clear that much of it has been achieved in this way, despite the systematic exclusion of this factor from price indexes.

Make-Up of the Consumer's Market Basket*

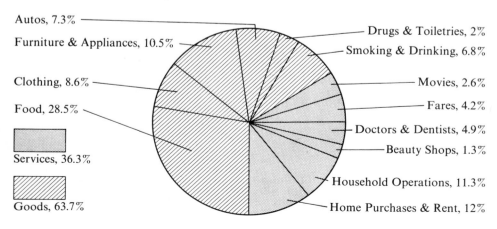

Autos, 7.3%

Furniture & Appliances, 10.5%

Clothing, 8.6%

Food, 28.5%

Services, 36.3%

Goods, 63.7%

Drugs & Toiletries, 2%

Smoking & Drinking, 6.8%

Movies, 2.6%

Fares, 4.2%

Doctors & Dentists, 4.9%

Beauty Shops, 1.3%

Household Operations, 11.3%

Home Purchases & Rent, 12%

Innovations and new products are not restricted to the durable goods field. They have, for instance, been highly significant in the food industry over the last decade. Meals are much easier to get and the choice available to the housewife is much greater. There will be those who claim that the additional packaging and processing now common is an undesirable element of cost, and that the personal contact between the individual proprietor and the customer has been lost. Conversely, it can be argued that increased attention to packaging not only standardizes the merchandise, but it raises the level of sanitation and grading. In addition, the freedom to examine goods allows the customer to make comparisons before buying in a way that would not have been possible before.

It is, of course, not possible to measure accurately the dimensions of quality and product change. Nevertheless, one can safely suggest that, given the size of the average yearly increase in the Consumer Price Index since Korea, quality and product improvements may well have been much greater, so that we may actually have had declining rather than rising prices.

This does not mean that price indexes are completely invalid. Price indexes are useful in that they can show the relative differences in price behavior over time or between countries. For example, the eight percent increase in the price index at the beginning of the Korean war indicates that prices were rising more rapidly in this period than at any other time in the decade of the Fifties.

In periods of hyperinflation, such as have been experienced by some Latin American countries in recent years, where the price index may rise by as much as 80 percent in a single year, the indexes give a good indication of what is happening since such large increases cannot be offset by quality change. It is only in periods when price changes are relatively small that it becomes a serious error to use the indexes as an exact measure of what is taking place in the economy. In such periods the systematic biases of the price index may well be greater than the reported price change.

The defects of the Consumer Price Index are also inherent in the other price indexes which are used to deflate the gross national product to measure the change in real output. Two major categories of goods are produced by the economy besides consumer goods. These are goods and services purchased by the government, ranging from school teaching to missiles, and plant and equipment purchased by producers for use in later production. To measure the quantity of output in these categories, we need price indexes to calculate it in noninflationary terms.

In measuring the output of government, it is assumed — as it is throughout the service sector — that the productivity of civil servants never changes. The price indexes for this area are merely based on the changes in pay of government employees. While one may be tempted to agree with this evaluation of civil servants, the fact is that the introduction of computers, office machines and other automatic equipment has greatly increased the effectiveness of the individual worker. For example, the 1960 census data were processed by microfilming the original schedules and automatically producing magnetic tape for the electronic computers. Automatic equipment performed jobs which took thousands of clerks in previous censuses. Not only was the payroll reduced, but far more information was made available in a much shorter space of time. Output per census employee thus rose very considerably.

Similar examples of the increased output of government employees can be cited at the local level. For example, policemen have been provided with radio-equipped patrol cars and, more recently, transistorized walkie-talkies. Street cleaners have been given mechanized equipment. In some areas — education, for instance — progress is more difficult to measure. Yet most of us would be unwilling to have our children given the same education as we received, especially in the areas of sciences and mathematics.

In producers' durable equipment, once again, the price indexes leave out quality change and new products. But there are probably very few industries in which producers in 1960 would have been willing to buy 1950 models of machines even if they could get them at the 1950 prices. According to the Wholesale Price Index the 1960 price of producers' durable equipment was 23 percent above the 1950 price; if producers' durable equipment showed as much quality change as was shown in the study referred to above for automobiles, it seems probable that in fact prices actually fell.

For construction, both industrial and residential, the index is computed on the basis of wage rates and material costs. Thus again it is assumed that productivity does not change. While the construction industry is notorious for its lack of progressiveness, if we consider the new methods of off-the-site fabrication of components it is obvious that this assumption is not entirely valid. Once again, it seems that price indexes have greatly exaggerated the actual price rise.

Thus, we see that for almost every category of goods, whether purchased by consumers for household consumption, by government for public services or by producers for plant and equipment, the conventional price indexes do not reflect the effects of the introduction of new products and the improvement of existing products, or the increased productivity of those performing services. These ommissions mean that the price indexes are higher than they should be. And since the indexes are used to deflate the value of current output and calculate its worth in noninflationary terms, our rate of growth is thus considerably understated.

The fact that our growth rate has probably been higher than we thought does not mean, however, that we should be any happier vis-á-vis the Russians. These elements would also have at least as much effect upon the Russian figures. As we well know, the Soviet rate of technological progress in some areas has exceeded ours, but even in the areas where they are still well behind us, the *rate* at which they introduce new technology might be faster than ours.

A half-century ago many more industries were producing the kind of output that could be measured quite satisfactorily in quantity terms. Today new major industries such as electronics, chemicals, machinery and household appliances account for an increasingly important share of our output. In all these industries the changes in prices and output are very difficult to measure, since the nature of the products is continually changing. It may mean, therefore, that the national concern over a sagging economic growth rate is really not warranted. The problem may be our inability to measure growth represented by product changes and increased productivity in the service industries. The inadequacy of the price indexes will become even more glaring in the years ahead.

It is interesting to speculate on what will happen to our measurement of output when further growth does not take the form of additional consumption of identical items, but rather of the consumption of goods of improved quality, the substitution of new products for old and the consumption of higher quality services. In such a world, our conventional price indexes would fail to catch the quality improvement; they would not recognize that the substitution of new products for old was any increase in the standard of living; and they would report the continued increase in the use of services solely in terms of the rates of remuneration. Thus they might show an economy with constant output and rising prices, even though the standard of living was increasing rapidly. What is perhaps more serious, the conventional price and output indexes would fail completely to distinguish between a dynamic economy and one that was truly stagnant.

Appendix: The Use and Misuse of Statistics and Common Sense

Richard H. Timberlake, Jr.

You are a research investigator for Associated Consumer Analysts. ACA assigns to you the task of exploring the possible changes that occurred in the standard of living in the United States just before, during, and right after World War II. What is your procedure?

You decide to attack the question by looking first at "secondary" source material in economic textbooks. The general consensus of the textbooks is that the United States economy was in a deep depression prior to World War II. While recovery was evident, it still was not complete by the time the United States entered the war at the end of 1941. Large-scale increases in government spending and the money supply, and the corresponding demands of the government for war production, generated labor and other resource "shortages" where a few years earlier the most obvious feature of the economy had been unemployment and "surpluses." (You determine *not* to be sidetracked into a polemic on the economic foolishness of "shortages" and "surpluses.") You find further that the real income of the general public increased during the war in spite of large diversions of resources into goods and services that were used up in the war effort. The explanation of this phenomenon seems reasonably plausible: All the previously unemployed factors of production became fully employed, so the total product of the economy increased by enough to support a 12 million man (and woman) armed force and still leave enough to increase consumer satisfactions in the domestic economy! Other factors that made such a phenomenon possible were (1) increases in the average work week and (2) supplementation of the labor force by people who ordinarily would not have been in it, that is, people past retirement age, housewives, and young people. After the end of the war, you find that the income per capita *and the income per worker* declined from their wartime highs, but not to the level of the prewar period. Not until the early 1950s did average income reach the value achieved in 1944.

If you have not been brainwashed by the authority and prestige of your sources, reflection on these conclusions generates some doubts. You grant the reemployment of idle factors of production and the other addenda to the labor force during the war. But how, you ask yourself, could a less skilled labor force in conjunction with the outworn and obsolete capital remaining from the depression decade of the thirties generate a product in 1944 that was greater than the product of 1948? By the latter year, practically all military forces had been demobilized. Furthermore, gross private domestic investment had expanded rapidly; for the three years 1946–1948 dollar volume for this item was greater than it had been for the previous ten years, 1936–1945. Thus, the economy generally was operating with a higher-productivity labor force and with a significantly increased stock of capital. On the other hand, the average work week for workers in manufacturing was greater in 1944 than in 1948. But could this factor have compensated for the greater productivity of labor and capital in the later years? If you think that it could not, where might be the statistical error that would allow what appears to be the anomaly of greater productivity per worker in 1944?

To pursue the matter rigorously, you gather together the relevant statistics and put them into a table. You obtain your data from *Historical Statistics in the United States,* published by the Department of Commerce. You select what seem to be relevant data and summarize them as shown in Table 1.

You notice that the deductions of your secondary sources are borne out by the figures in Column 5: Real Gross National Product per civilian worker reached a peak in 1944. The value for 1944 is not only much higher than the value for 1948, but is not surpassed until ten years later!

You now take a closer look at the possible reliability of the data. GNP in current prices, being the summed value of all goods and services produced and measured at their industrial origins, would be difficult to bias. Total employment as well is largely nose-counting after having solved the conceptual problem of what age and occupation groups to include. Average weekly hours

Table 1

Year	(1) GNP in Current Prices (billions of dollars)	(2) GNP in 1929 Prices (billions of dollars)	(3) Implicit Price Index (1929 = 100)	(4) Total No. Civilians Employed (millions)	(5) Real (1929) GNP/Civil- ian Worker (dollars per year)	(6) Average Weekly Hours Worked in Manufac- turing
1941	126	139	91	50.4	2,758	40.6
1944	211	184	115	54.0	3,407	45.2
1946	211	167	126	55.3	3,020	40.4
1948	259	174	149	59.4	2,929	40.1
1952	347	207	168	61.3	3,377	40.7
1954	363	213	171	61.2	3,480	39.7

Source: U.S. Bureau of the Census, *Historical Statistics of the United States, Colonial Times to 1957* (Washington, D.C.: Department of Commerce, 1960). Data in Columns 1, 2, and 3 were taken from Series F-1, F-3, and F-5, p. 139; data in Column 4 were taken from Series D-5, p. 70; values in Column 5 were computed by dividing deflated GNP data in Column 2 by employed civilian workers data in Column 4; and data in Column 6 were obtained from Series D-627, p. 92.

worked covers only manufacturing, but again no *a priori* biases can be established. The implicit price index, however, is another matter. Not only may biases be present in the form of quality changes (in 1944, quality deterioration), but also the construction of a price index at a time when money prices are controlled by law virtually invalidates the economic meaning of the index. Laws that institute general "price controls" are laws that make free market prices illegal. If the price ceilings are effective, the quantity of any good or service demanded exceeds its supply at the maximum money price that has been decreed. What happens then? People must keep more money than they wish to, not only because to do so is "patriotic" but also because to spend it at prices that are higher than the statutory maxima is against the law and punishable by fine and/or imprisonment. One can assume that for a while the ceiling prices are effective. Gradually, however, the "surplus" cash balances that people are forced to hold "burn holes in their pockets." Middlemen, not governed by too many scruples and willing to take risks in breaking the law, make available goods and services at prices necessarily much higher than those permitted by the legal ceilings. Under these auspices, "black markets" develop. The black market, you observe, is the free market; nonetheless, it is also an illegal market.

What would a statistician do about black market prices? First, they are illegal. Therefore, to incorporate the data of the black markets in a price index is to admit, even to emphasize, that the laws of the land are being broken. If this knowledge becomes general by its publication in an index, no one still following the letter of the price control laws would feel constrained to do so any longer. Furthermore, if the statistical bureau computing the index is also a government agency, admission of the law's ineffectiveness is tantamount to saying that the present administration's policy is a failure. This kind of conclusion is not politically acceptable, to put it mildly. Finally, black market data, by their very nature, are hard to measure accurately and completely. Thus, their inclusion is difficult, does not give an accurate picture, is politically inexpedient, and is unpatriotic(!).

The statistician faced with this dilemma really has no choice. He simply acts as though the ceiling prices were being adhered to and prices Gross National Product on these terms. In truth, however, GNP is being sold on some very different terms. Once the war is over and price ceilings are abandoned, total spending comes out into the open and can be counted accurately and legally. You thus conclude that the "real" values for GNP, when derived by using price index values of the war years, are spurious.

You feel satisfied that this conclusion is reasonably valid. However, it also leaves a vacuum: If the real product value for 1944 is not accurate, what was the real value?

You decide that the quoted income and price index figures for 1941 are probably legitimate. If the real GNP per civilian worker for that year ($2,758) is adjusted by the ratio of total civilian employees in 1944 to those in 1941 (54.0/50.4), the resulting value for real product per worker in 1944 becomes $2,958. This value is almost identical to the same kind of adjusted product per worker in 1948 ($2,929). You reason that these two values may very well be close together. The work week was 12.5 percent longer in 1944, but the labor force was 9.5 percent greater in 1948. Therefore, the longer work week in 1944 was almost equal to, and offset by, the increase in the labor force. This reasoning still leaves room for a real product in 1944 that was 3 percent greater than the corresponding product per worker in 1948. But, again, by 1948 some significant additions to capital had been made, quite probably enough to have made up this remaining 3 percent difference.

You rest on these deductions and submit your report to the directors of ACA.

3

The Theory of Money and Prices

The Interrelationship of Money and Prices

Market economies have found that money is a unique and functional device for standardizing economic values and for performing the awesome tasks of exchange in a world of heterogeneous goods and services. A monetary system performs these functions much more expediently than any other arrangement and with no necessity for detailed controls except regulation of the number of nominal money units.

The use of money as an exchange medium implies the existence of money prices. Political economists early recognized a relationship between the quantity of money units and the general level of prices. In fact, such recognition and the thought devoted to it identified a philosopher in general as a political economist in particular. As early as the middle of the eighteenth century one such person, the eminent David Hume, wrote:

> Though the high price of commodities be a necessary consequence of the encrease of gold and silver,... some time is required before the money circulates through the whole state, and makes its effect be felt on all ranks of people.... By degrees the price rises, first of one commodity, then of another; till the whole at last reaches a just proportion with the new quantity of specie which is in the kingdom.[1]

---

[1] David Hume, *Writings on Economics,* ed. and intro. by Eugene Rotwein (Madison: University of Wisconsin Press, 1955), pp. 37–38.

The word "money" to the classical economists meant only metallic money — gold, silver, and minor coin. Money as a medium of exchange had value imputed to it because of its value as a commodity. Since the money stocks of contemporary Western societies contain no more than trivial amounts of precious metals, modern monetary analysis must proceed along slightly different lines: Acceptability is given to intrinsically worthless paper money by governmental fiat, and value is obtained by governmental limitations on the number of debt-clearing units issued.

The Equation of Exchange

Money is channeled through an economy from two directions: First, firms pay the owners of the factors of production for their contributions to the total product, and second, households purchase the final products produced by the firms. Clearly, the money used for one purpose is the same money that is used for the other; and since the goods and services are produced in accordance with consumer demands, the total cost payments going to the factors of production comprise sufficient income to purchase the total final product.[2]

Since money units can be used again and again to purchase goods and services, the total stock of money can be of different quantitative magnitudes and still do the same "work." The same annual Gross National Product R in real goods and services may be valued at \$100 billion per year or \$500 billion per year in monetary terms, depending on the quantity of money used in purchasing the total flow of R and the corresponding money prices P of the goods and services.[3]

Money can also circulate at different velocities in purchasing R. The more rapidly money circulates, the fewer the units of money necessary to produce and to purchase R at any given level of money prices. The number of times the average dollar thus circulates in purchasing the total product R is defined as the velocity of money V_R with respect to the product purchased. It is a conceptual device. If PR is, say, \$500 billion per year and the stock of money M is \$250 billion, then each dollar on the average has "gone around the track" twice per year in consummating purchases of real R, and the velocity of money V_R has a value of "2/year." The total stock of money M multiplied by the average number of times V_R each dollar makes the income or product

---

[2]This generalized truism, known as Say's Law and referred to in Chapter 0, is only intended to be a device for systematizing thought. Clearly, the money income may be unspent after the goods are produced, or other events may promote disparity between the flow value of income and the flow value of spending. These exceptions do not invalidate the usefulness of the generalization as a methodological device.

[3]In this discussion R is always the *physical* flow of Gross National Product at yearly rates, while PR is the same flow priced so that it is in monetary terms.

circuit therefore describes the total money expenditures made on real product *PR*. This truism is stated symbolically as

$$MV_R = \sum_n pn \cdot qn$$

where *n* refers to any good or service. More simply, the expression can be summed to

$$MV_R \equiv PR$$

The average price of goods and services *P* can be thought of most easily as the money price of some cross-sectional "slice" of the Gross National Product *R*, and a price index, such as the Consumer Price Index, may be used to approximate it.

This identity is known as the Equation of Exchange. It reduces masses of data into a few workable forms. As an identity it is noncausative. It simply equates two flows that by definition must be equal; all money spent by all people to buy the total product must equal all money received by all people for producing and selling that product. Causative relationships can emerge only if the value of one term in the equation can be classified as logically dependent on the values of the other terms in the expression. A variable classified as "independent" is one whose value is determined by forces outside the equation. Deductive theorems that are logically rigorous are a first step, and empirical tests of these theorems a second step, in establishing any chain of cause and effect.

Another method of constructing the Equation of Exchange is to use the *total* exchanges of money for all goods and services *T* in place of the concept that sees money spent only on *final* products and services *R*. Exchanges involving purchases and sales of goods in process, secondhand articles, and financial assets would be included in *T* but not in *R*. The Equation of Exchange when constructed in this more inclusive form is expressed as

$$MV_T \equiv PT$$

The rationale for this form of the equation is just as logical as for the narrower concept that uses *R* instead of *T*. Money's work is certainly not limited to effecting the purchases and sales of finished goods and services; money spent on *R* is only a part of total money exchanges. Both equations, however, must use the same stock of money *M* even though the volume of exchanges in the *T* equation greatly surpasses the volume in the *R* equation. No means exist for distinguishing the quantity of dollars used for secondhand commodities from the quantity used for new commodities and services. The price average *P* for all goods and services may be thought of as approximately equal to the price average for finished goods and services; but here, too, no precise method of measuring divergences in the two price levels is possible. Since the dollar volume of *T* must be very much greater than the dollar volume of *R*, while the stock of money in both equations is identical, V_T must be much greater numerically than V_R.

Despite the greater inclusiveness of the T equation because it embraces the total exchange work that money effects, the R equation is a more useful device to the monetary analyst for one simple reason: The data to be fitted into the R equation are much more readily available and measurable. The form that includes R, therefore, is the one that must be used empirically in estimating monetary change in the real world. Furthermore, while it cannot be proven precisely, changes in the R equation are usually good approximations of changes in the T equation. Unless otherwise specified, the R equation is the one employed in the analyses that follow.

Several theorems that express contemporary views of monetary behavior are summarized below. Since the Equation of Exchange is a truism, each theorem must be some algebraically correct variant of it. Different theorems and alternative chains of causality are derived by assuming that different factors are held provisionally constant. The logic and relevance of the assumed conditions are in the final analysis measured by the degree of operational predictiveness contributed by the theorem posited.

Theorem I—The Quantity Theory of Money: *Changes in the price level P are directly proportional to changes in the quantity of money M.*

This theorem assumes: (1) a fixed number of resources (capital and labor), (2) full employment of these resources, (3) a constant flow of Gross National Product from these resources, (4) free markets and flexible money prices for resources and finished products, (5) constant consumer tastes for money as well as for all other things, and (6) a time period of adjustment that permits all money prices to change.[4] When in this form, the equation becomes

$$P = M \cdot \left[\frac{V_R}{R}\right]_o$$

The terms V_R and R are constants because consumer tastes and total output have been held constant. M is allowed to change because of the government's assumed discretionary control over the stock of money, while money prices P "have time" to be flexible and are obtained empirically as price index data from the market system. This theorem is the traditional quantity theory of money. It predicts a proportionate change in the price level given an independent change in the total stock of money. A rereading of the quote above by Hume shows that this particular way of looking at spending behavior was envisaged by the classical economists.

---

[4]All money prices do not, or cannot, change unless the time period of adjustment is extended over several years. Nevertheless, in, say, a six-month period the large majority of money prices can and do change, and the average change of prices is not necessarily inhibited by inflexibility of some prices. Those that are flexible can, and probably do, change more than they otherwise would if price rigidities for some other goods and services were completely absent.

Theorem II—The Velocity Theorem: *Changes in the stock of money are matched by corresponding inverse changes in the velocity of each money unit.*
This theorem has two methods through which the given conditions of Theorem I may be altered so as to produce the result posited. Either prices are presumed to be inflexible due to the political and social powers of organized groups, such as labor unions, the farm bloc, industrial combinations, and government regulatory agencies, or the time period of adjustment demanded by Theorem I is thought to be "too long" to be realistic. Even if prices are flexible in the long run, so that a new equilibrium of prices could ultimately be obtained, some economists argue that other presumed constants, such as R, may have changed appreciably long before the new equilibrium could be reached. The stock of money M may still be regarded as an independent variable under the control of the government. The variant of the Equation of Exchange that expresses this theorem is

$$V = \frac{1}{M} \cdot [PR]_o$$

Its conclusion is that any new money pumped into the economy is hoarded as additional cash balances. No effect on spending due to an increased stock of money is seen.
Quite obviously, the time period of adjustment could be narrowed down until this theorem had to be valid, just as time can be extended enough for Theorem I to be valid. Logic itself cannot prescribe any "correct" time period—one that is exclusively proper under all conditions. Choice in this matter rests entirely with the observer and what he regards as valid data for the particular problem he is trying to analyze.
The constants chosen also must be thought of as "constant" only within the particular framework defined by the case. Furthermore, they are constant at the beginning and end of the period under scrutiny but not necessarily for the whole time in which the other variables are acting and reacting. In the Quantity Theorem, for example, the increase in the quantity of money might at first be associated with a decline in velocity. Given more time, however, the effect of the new money on total spending would be accompanied by an increase in prices. Given further time, output would increase due to nominal year-to-year increases in the factors of production, and the price level would then resume its original value. The Quantity Theorem is valid only within the time period during which money prices have had a chance to establish new equilibrium values, and during which no significant increase in output has occurred.

Theorem III—The Political Theorem: *Changes in prices are functions of changes in the cost payments to the factors of production. The changes in the stock of money then necessary to maintain high-level employment are brought about by social-political pressures on the money-creating agency.*

This theorem is related to Theorem II and may be thought of as a possible second stage of that theorem. Higher wages or other costs are alleged to push up prices through the pressures of organized groups. Price level movements are regarded as social, and not strictly as economic, phenomena. The higher prices in one sector cannot be compensated by lower prices on other cost factors because the powers of competing groups are too great to permit overt price declines. Simple arithmetic is sufficient to show that, if some prices are pushed up and other prices are forced to stay constant, the general price average must also increase. The net result would be some unemployment in the cost-pushed industries. Salvation is possible, however, if the money-creating institution (the central bank) can be prevailed upon to increase the stock of money. Prices then rise (they are only inflexible downward); and the higher returns to the cost-pushing sector are vitiated in part by a more general reduction in the value of money. The principal feature of this theorem is that the stock of money M is an indirect political or social function of the price level P. To express this relationship, the equation of exchange takes the form

$$M = P\left[\frac{R}{V_R}\right]_o$$

Gross National Product R may be held at the full employment level as a part of a contrived policy, and V_R may be held constant in accord with the constraint of constant "tastes" for cash balances and other things. The time period of adjustment is the same as for Theorem I.

The role of money in this theorem is reversed completely from what it was under Theorem I. Changes in the quantity of money follow rather than lead changes in prices. While both theorems are algebraically correct, they are also contradictory. Clearly, only one can be a realistic illustrator of cause and effect at any given time.

Every theorem is vulnerable with respect to the variables held provisionally constant. Theorems I and II have particular time limitations, for example. Theorem III allows for no compensation effect; that is, the money prices allegedly pushed up are not offset by price declines of complementary commodities. Rigidities in money prices, rather than price flexibility, are assumed. A price increase on gasoline, according to this theorem, would not inhibit the sale of cars, batteries, tires, or other goods and services. Furthermore, the organized groups that push up prices must be able to gain more and more monopolistic power in order to continue their pushing effectively. This constraint is in opposition to the contention that monopolies are inherently unstable and costly to maintain and are only able to survive when sanctioned and encouraged by government.[5]

---

[5]This thesis is discussed more fully in Chapter 28. See also Milton Friedman, *Capitalism and Freedom* (Chicago: 1962), University of Chicago Press, Chap. 8.

Theorem IV—The Gold Standard Theorem: *Changes in the quantity of money are both cause and effect of changes in the Gross National Product.* This theorem is expressed as

$$M = R \cdot \left[\frac{P}{V_R}\right]_0$$

It assumes an institutional structure that includes a smoothly working commodity money such as gold. Given full employment equilibrium, a normal yearly increase in R tends to lower prices and costs, thus provoking an increase in the value of money. Gold mining and gold importation become more profitable. Assuming (heroically) that gold mining is carried on under cost conditions equal to the average of all other industries, the stock of money M would increase at the same rate as R. Prices under this scheme would suffer no more than minor deviations around some initial level. In an economy on the gold standard but without a gold mining industry, the tendency of prices to fall with increases in output would encourage the exportation of goods and services and the corresponding importation of gold. The result would be the same. Gold mining would be stimulated in countries endowed with gold lodes, but the gold would spread into all economies that dealt with the gold producing country.

This model is compatible with Theorem I because it also allows that the quantity of money acts on prices. The time period must be long enough, however, for the output of gold mines to be monetized. In practice, gold mining companies anticipate demand for their product; so the increase in Gross National Product and the increase in the quantity of money via the increase in monetary gold take place almost simultaneously. Since gold is generally procured only under conditions of increasing costs, except for occasional and spectacular discoveries, a rigorous gold-standard monetary system might well be marked by secular price level declines with occasional short periods of mild inflation.

Theorem V—The Unemployment Theorem: *Under conditions of less than full employment, increases in the stock of money increase effective demand, employment of resources, and Gross National Product.* This theorem may be stated symbolically as

$$R = M \cdot \left[\frac{V_R}{P}\right]_0$$

Money M is again the independent variable, but Gross National Product R is the dependent variable. Some defenders of this expression see velocity changes as inversely related to changes in the stock of money and amalgamate this theorem with Theorem II. Others contend that velocity V_R is relatively stable, so that changes in M have their full effect on R. Both groups agree that prices are relatively inflexible in the "modern industrial economy" until full employment is reached. Full employment of resources implies that R can no longer increase due to stimulation by M, and at this level the Quantity Theorem supposedly comes into its own. Otherwise, some cost-push model (Theorem III) must be adopted at the full employment point.

Since less than full employment is the assumed beginning condition, Gross National Product R can be a variable. In fact, any quantity theorist would agree that, in the event of unemployment, increases in the stock of money may have a primary effect on R. The deductions can be extended: Some specialized resources ("bottlenecks") become fully employed ahead of others. Their prices increase and a general price-level rise can be expected some time before all resources are fully employed. The quantity theorist would also allege that unemployment is a special case, and that under ordinary full employment conditions R could be regarded as a quasi-constant. In short, the provisional assumption of fixed real income (product) is useful, even though the Unemployment Theorem might have predictive value for special periods.

The dichotomies posed by Theorems I and II or by Theorems I and III demonstrate that theorizing can take the monetary analyst just so far. Any theorem, however, must fit into some variant of the Equation of Exchange. The "best" theorem, the one that predicts effects most accurately, can only be chosen by empirical evaluation. In this choice, as in most others, performance is what counts.

The Cambridge Equation
(The Cash Balance Approach)

The Equation of Exchange and its variants are useful for classifying aggregate phenomena into a few workable theorems. A similar approach with some distinct advantages is the "Cambridge Equation"—so-called because it was developed by a British school of economists centered at Cambridge University. It is another way of looking at the total monetary economy by starting with a definitional truism. Both it and the Equation of Exchange are equally valid, but each has some special advantages in clarifying the effects of money on the economy.

The Equation of Exchange uses an interval of time, say, one year, during which the flow value of money is presumed equal to the flow value of finished goods and services. The Cambridge Equation—also called "the cash balance theorem"—sees the process of exchange as imminent rather than accomplished. It freezes all monetary activity into an action that is about to take place. Its rationale is as follows. At any instant of time a stock of money M exists. This same stock could exist at some second of time, during some year, or forever. Assume for simplicity's sake that it is the same stock used during the year defined by the Equation of Exchange. At this same instant a mass of goods and services R is in the act of being produced, bought, and sold. These goods and services, and the market prices P for which they are bought and sold, are also to be thought of as identical to those described by the Equation of Exchange. The annual rate of production in monetary terms is again *PR* (or *PT* if *all transactions* are being considered). In this case, however, the rate at which the product is being generated, not the total yearly product, is under conceptual investigation.

The time interval considered in the cash balance equation is "too small" to allow exchanges to take place, and the stock of money does not turn over but must be held. It is held "against" goods and services about to be purchased. These goods and services are both product and income, so the money stock may be thought of as held "against" some part of total money income. In terms even less causative, the dollar value of the stock of money is some fraction *k* of the rate at which money income is being generated. That is,

$$M \equiv kPR$$

where *PR* is the money value of the total product and *k* is the appropriate fraction. This equation, similar to the Equation of Exchange, is true by definition. The fraction *k* adjusts to whatever value fulfills the conditions of equality.

Another way of approaching this equation is to conceive of an "average" man holding his "average share" of the money stock during a payment period. Since he holds an average stock, he may be thought of as holding it for the entire period or for any instant during the period. If the income recipient gets $600 per month and spends this amount at a constant rate ($/minute) during the month, the cash balance held at the beginning of the month is $600 and that held at the end of the month is zero. Therefore, the average amount held during the month is $300, and the fraction of his monthly income held in the form of a cash balance is ½. His yearly income is $7,200, so the fraction of his yearly income held in the form of a cash balance is 1/24.[6] Since the Cambridge Equation is constructed to show yearly values, numerical substitution of the above values would be expressed as

$$\$300 = \frac{1}{24} \cdot \$7,200$$

The example of the "average man" may be extended to the whole economy. At any instant the economy has a stock of money that people hold relative to their total money incomes. If the stock is $200 billion and the Gross National Product is $1,000 billion per year, then people altogether hold cash balances that are one fifth the monetary value of their collective product (income).

Since the Equation of Exchange and the Cambridge Equation use the same data except for one term in each expression, the two alternate terms can be related to each other. The Cambridge Equation states that $M \equiv kPR$; the

---

[6]The numerical value of 1/24 for *k* in this example is more logically a *k* for all transactions *T* than it is a *k* for total product generated *R*.

Equation of Exchange says $MV \equiv PR$. The k in the cash balance equation equals $\dfrac{M}{PR}$, while V in the Equation of Exchange equals $\dfrac{PR}{M}$. Therefore, $V_R = \dfrac{1}{k}$ or $k = \dfrac{1}{V_R}$. If k increases, people are holding a higher fraction of cash balances to income and, equivalently, the velocity of circulation of money is less. Both k and V_R, therefore, are determined by the same behavioral factor, that is, by peoples' tastes and dispositions for holding nominal money units.

Since each of the two terms is technically the inverse of the other, as one goes up the other goes down in the same proportion. For example, if people spend their money faster in anticipation of inflation, V_R (or V_T) increases. To say that people spend their money faster is equivalent to saying that their collective "taste" for holding cash balances has declined. They want to hold less money, so they spend it more rapidly. An individual could succeed in this venture only if other individuals were willing to hold more. However, the given condition of the example is that *everyone* wants to hold less money. In an economy where the supply of money is determined by the discretion of the government (central bank), the collective desires of individuals to rid themselves of money cannot succeed. All they can do is to force up prices, thus forcing down the value of each money unit, until the total real value of cash balances takes the value it would have taken if people could have destroyed the "excess" money they wanted to get rid of at the old price level.

Selected Bibliography

Fisher, Irving. *The Purchasing Power of Money*. New York: Macmillan Co., 1911. The principal work on the quantity theory of money.

Friedman, Milton. *Studies in the Quantity Theory of Money*. Chicago: University of Chicago Press, 1956.

Pigou, A. C. "The Value of Money." *Readings in Monetary Theory*. Ed. Friedrich A. Lutz and Lloyd W. Mints. Homewood, Ill.: Richard D. Irwin, 1951.

Robertson, D. H. *Money*. New York: Pitman Publishing Co., 1948. A comparison of the quantity theory and the cash balance theory.

Hyperinflation in Germany, 1923

The New York Times

Hyperinflation is a phenomenon that must be experienced to be believed. The news stories reprinted here from **The New York Times** *give some idea of the social upheaval that occurred in 1923 during the hyperinflation in Germany. As these items indicate, and as the tables following show in more detail, the stock of German marks approached "infinity" and their value dropped correspondingly. All fixed dollar claims, such as insurance policies, mortgages, and bonds, became virtually worthless. The wonder is that money was used at all! But used it was, because even at the rate at which it was depreciating (50 percent per week) it was still a cheaper medium for transacting ordinary items than barter would have been.*

Exchange rates for foreign currency (such as dollars) rose in approximately the same pattern as all other prices. The fact that these rates were fixed by law at too low a level meant that no traffic would occur in the exchange markets. The free market price would be a "bootleg" price. The nonsensical remark in the last item—"Berlin is suffering from an acute paper mark shortage"—reflects this situation.

Finally, these stories note the appearance of significant unemployment. When all money prices and the "price" of money are subjected to a high degree of uncertainty, many ordinary business operations are simply suspended to avoid the large losses that otherwise would occur. Ultimately, the whole monetary system was "washed out" and the mark revalued at 1 trillion hyperinflated marks to one new mark (rentenmark).

Berlin Prices Rise to Fantastic Figures

Loaf of Bread Costs 58,000,000
Marks, and a Ride on a Street
Car 10,000,000.

Berlin, Oct. 7. Nobody knows what Germany's paper circulation and floating debt are today, but a careful estimate places the floating debt at 40 quadrillions on Sept. 30 and possibly 80 quadrillions today, while 75 quadrillions is the estimated paper circulation.

A delayed Reichsbank statement for the week ending Sept. 22 shows the paper mark output nearly trebled in the week, 5 quadrillion, 500 trillion being issued, making a grand total of 8 quadrillions, 600 trillion. Twenty million gold marks were spent for foreign exchange. The Reichsbank's notes and bills discounted increased during the week by 10 quadrillions to 15 quadrillions. Treasury notes discounted totaled 12 quadrillion, 200 trillions. The paper mark today sank below 800 millions to the dollar.

Prices are rising with crazy speed. Butter is 180,000,000 marks, margarine 120,000,000, meat 120,000,000 to 200,000,000, beans 18,000,000, tomatoes 14,000,000, onions 8,000,000 by the pound. One herring is 10,000,000 marks and an egg is 18,000,000.

Berliners will pay on Monday 20,000,000 for milk, 30,000,000 for a cubic meter of gas, 68,000,000 per kilowatt-hour for electricity, 30,000,000 for a cubic meter of water, 58,000,000 for a standard loaf of bread, and 10,000,000 for street car fare.

Keep Mobs Moving as Mark Tumbles

*Berlin Security Policy Disperse Bands of
Would-Be Plunderers of Bread Shops.*

Women Attack Iron Works

*Ruhr Wives Infuriated by Failure to
Pay Husbands' Wages — 5 Dead
in Mannheim Riots.*

By Cyril Browns

Berlin, Oct. 18. The Security Police were kept busy today dispersing would-be plunderers of bread shops as the paper mark official rate was fixed at 8,000,000,000 to the dollar and later in the afternoon sank to 9,000,000,000. There were rumors even of quotations at 11,000,000,000.

Friedrichstrasse and Unter Den Linden this evening were patrolled by many individuals who cautiously approached anyone who looked like an American or other possessor of real money, eager to swap bales of paper marks therefor. Americans who must change dollars find it profitable to go shopping for bargains among these mark bootleggers.

Bales of new 50,000,000,000-mark notes were thrown into circulation today and the new 100,000,000,000-mark notes also made their debut. These are not confidence inspiring paper scraps, but they are more in demand than the new 1,000,000,000-mark notes, which likewise were put out today. In banking circles the paper mark has become the butt of ridicule. A bank clerk remarked to *The New York Times* correspondent today, as he handed out a big parcel of mark notes:

"Their real value is on the back." It was pointed out to him that there was nothing printed on the back. "That's what they are worth," the clerk replied.

The Boerse was strongly influenced today by the conditions throughout Germany, particularly Saxony. Various large failures are reported and a large section of the Boerse appears to be involved.

Depreciation has been so rapid that the German Chamber of Commerce and Industry urges the immediate adoption of the million-mark as the bookkeeping unit of calculation, and Hamburg is already using it.

The Reich's index figure for the minimum cost of living has leaped to nearly 700,000,000 times the pre-war figure and the cost of living has increased 534 percent over last week. Wholesale prices have jumped to over 1,000,000,000 times the pre-war level.

Living Costs Still Soaring

Fifty Percent above Last Week's
Standard Figure in Berlin.

Berlin, Nov. 29. Official index figures for the minimum standard cost of living for the week are 1,535,000,000,000 times the pre-war cost. This standard minimum living cost increased 50 percent over the preceding week.

Berlin is suffering from the most acute paper mark shortage. Many Americans are literally walking the streets of Berlin trying to part with real money dollars in return for worthless marks, but bootleggers have all taken to cover and there are no offerings.

Berlin, Nov. 29. Unemployment in unoccupied Germany showed a further increase for the first fortnight of November. About a quarter of a million persons were added to those already without work.

European Currency and Finance, 1914–1925

German Reichsbank, Principal Assets and Liabilities, 1914–1924

	Discounted Bills			
	Treasury Bills	Commercial Bills	Total Discounted Treasury and Commercial Bills	Advances
1914—January			828,657	70,699
July			2,081,075	202,190
1915—January			3,783,946	42,367
July			4,784,585	17,041
1916—January			5,273,184	21,658
July			6,542,001	12,735
1917—January			8,180,039	9,957
July			11,127,820	9,675
1918—January			13,105,525	8,721
July			15,988,653	8,397
1919—January			27,098,634	8,926
July			30,680,853	5,009
1920—January			39,322,418	11,340
July			46,093,364	10,109
1921—January	50,594,540	2,742,406	53,336,946	8,881
July	79,981,967	1,135,529	81,117,496	10,686
1922—January	126,160,402	1,592,416	127,752,818	20,548
July	207,858,232	8,122,066	215,980,298	141,276*
1923—January	1,609,081,121	697,216,424	2,306,297,545	95,316,552
February	2,947,363,994	1,829,341,080	4,776,705,074	27,422,282
March	4,552,011,661	2,372,101,737	6,924,113,418	2,132,906
April	6,224,899,348	2,986,116,724	9,211,016,072	20,466,948
May	8,021,904,840	4,014,693,720	12,036,598,560	61,030,322
June	18,338†	6,914,198,630	25,252,198,630	188,548,574
July	53,752†	18,314†	72,066†	2,553,177,597
August	987,219†	164,644†	1,151,863†	25,261†
September	45,216,224†	3,660,094†	48,876,318†	98,522†
October	6,578,650,939†	1,058,129,855†	7,636,780,794†	41,787,532†
15 November	189,801,468,187†	39,529,577,254†	229,331,045,441†	535,714,637†
30 November	96,874,330,250†	347,301,037,776†	144,175,368,026†	7,472,665,263†
December	‡	322,724,948,986†	322,724,948,986	268,325,819,530
1924—January§	...	...	755,866	336,520
February	...	...	1,165,649	306,618
March	...	...	1,767,443	143,102
April	...	...	1,916,969	156,362
May	...	...	1,954,930	128,597
June	...	...	1,897,959	108,789
July	...	...	1,798,097	62,489
August	...	...	1,860,843	59,983
September	...	...	2,169,684	54,424
15 October‖	...	...	2,153,943	15,947
31 October	...	...	2,339,616	33,443
November	...	...	2,290,166	18,628
December	...	...	2,064,094	16,960

		Demand Deposits			
Securities	Notes in Circulation (Paper Currency)	Public	Other	Total Demand Deposits	Due to the Rentenbank
298,201	2,052,782			690,579	
396,603	2,909,422			1,258,466	
15,759	4,658,588			1,452,612	
19,801	5,538,164			1,651,604	
49,745	6,502,402			1,785,921	
60,413	7,024,564			2,395,595	
104,546	7,858,489			3,452,429	
127,741	8,852,737			5,847,971	
98,891	11,138,934			6,676,327	
123,803	12,704,503			8,504,876	
148,150	23,647,640			12,522,737	
145,755	29,268,889			10,362,127	
181,547	37,443,385			14,121,542	
307,076	55,763,596			17,281,809	
147,126	66,620,804	4,055,904	11,778,060	15,833,964	...
283,381	77,390,853	4,810,026	11,014,130	15,824,156	...
198,725	115,375,766	5,286,950	18,125,502	23,412,452	...
313,488	189,794,722	9,197,727	30,778,489	39,976,216	...
483,318	1,984,496,369	157,058,537	605,205,692	763,264,229	...
1,209,935	3,512,787,777	253,915,266	1,329,065,770	1,582,981,036	...
1,690,011	5,517,919,561	368,550,293	1,903,533,291	2,272,083,584	...
1,207,105	6,545,984,355	454,403,079	3,399,871,714	3,854,274,793	...
697,611	8,563,749,470	652,575,366	4,410,494,865	5,063,070,231	...
344,819	17,291†	1,648,114,327	8,304,602,339	9,952,716,666	...
1,422,291	43,595†	3,779,235,298†	24,078†	27,857†	...
15,539,853	663,200†	206,168†	384,912†	591,080†	...
1,801,579,570	28,228,815†	8,185,467†	8,781,150†	16,966,617†	...
9,536,953	2,496,822,909†	606,660,673†	3,261,424,030†	3,868,085,703†	...
8,901,495	92,844,720,743†	72,457,230,513†	57,095,366,904†	129,552,597,417†	...
336,495,629†	400,267,640,302†	120,478,936,906†	253,497,803,653†	373,976,740,559†	...
65,791,385†	496,507,424,772†	303,114,560,004†	244,909,637,001†	548,024,197,005†	...
12	483,675	492,985	281,320	774,305	200,000
25	587,875	367,551	282,958	650,509	400,000
533	689,864	352,360	352,334	704,694	800,000
91,984	776,949	474,411	330,561	804,742	800,000
80,011	926,874	545,252	259,203	804,455	800,000
76,378	1,097,309	493,043	280,884	773,927	800,000
76,509	1,211,038	452,597	290,390	742,987	800,000
76,331	1,391,895	264,064	297,791	561,855	800,000
78,305	1,520,511	307,515	362,581	670,096	800,000
77,517	1,396,748	...	...	828,511	800,000
77,699	1,780,930	...	...	708,728	800,000
77,808	1,863,200	...	...	703,938	684,664
77,999	1,941,440	...	...	820,865	456,508

Source: John Parke Young, *European Currency and Finance, Foreign Currency, and Exchange Investigation,* Serial 9, Volume 1, Commission of Gold and Silver Inquiry, U.S. Senate, 67th Congress, 4th Session (Washington, D.C.: U.S. Government Printing Office, 1925), pp. 526-529.
  * A large increase of advances at the close of November 1922 was due to the fact that the Reichsbank had to take over temporarily the financing of food supplies from the loan bureaus (Darlehnskassen), as the latter were unable to extend the needed accommodation, their outstanding notes having reached the maximum amount permitted by law.
  † 000,000,000 omitted.
  ‡ According to a decree of November 15, 1923, further discounting of treasury bills by the Reichsbank was discontinued.
  § Since January 1924, figures are shown in thousands of rentenmarks or reichsmarks. One rentenmark is equivalent to one reichsmark or 1,000,000,000,000 former paper marks. The reichsmark is the equivalent of the gold mark worth 23.82 cents.
  ‖ Date of first statement of reorganized Reichsbank.

Wholesale Prices in Germany, 1914–1924 (1913 = 100)

Reichsamt index numbers, monthly averages, 38 commodities. The index numbers have been converted to a gold basis by applying to them the percentages which the corresponding average monthly exchange rates for dollars are of par. From April 1917 through June 1919, the exchange rates used were a combination of New York on Amsterdam and Amsterdam on Berlin.

	On Paper Currency Basis	Converted to Gold Basis
1914—January	96	96
July	99	99
1915—January	126	116
July	150	129
1916—January	150	118
July	161	123
1917—January	156	112
July	172	102
1918—January	204	166
July	208	151
1919—January	262	134
July	339	95
1920—January	1,260	89
July	1,370	146
1921—January	1,440	97
July	1,430	78
1922—January	3,670	80
July	10,160	85

	On Paper Currency Basis	Converted to Gold Basis
1923—January	278,500	82
February	558,500	94
March	488,800	103
April	521,200	88
May	817,000	69
June	1,938,500	81
July	7,478,700	94
August	94,404,100	134
September	2,391,889,300	189
October	709,480,000,000	2,025
November	72,570,000,000,000	131
December	126,160,000,000,000	120
1924—January	117,320,000,000,000	111
February	116,170,000,000,000	106
March	120,670,000,000,000	111
April	124,050,000,000,000	115
May	122,460,000,000,000	115
June	115,900,000,000,000	114
July	115*	115
August	120*	120
September	127*	127
October	131*	131
November	129*	129
December	131*	131

Source: John Parke Young, *European Currency and Finance, Foreign Currency, and Exchange Investigation,* Serial 9, Volume I, Commission of Gold and Silver Inquiry, U.S. Senate, 67th Congress, 4th Session (Washington, D.C.: U.S. Government Printing Office, 1925), p. 530.
* On basis of prices in terms of reichsmarks. (1 reichsmark = 1,000,000,000,000 former paper marks.)

Exchange Rates in Germany, 1914–1925

New York on Berlin. January 1914–March 1917, sight drafts: April 1917–June 1919, a combination of cable rates, New York on Amsterdam, and spot quotations in Amsterdam of German currency; July 1919–December 1919, cable transfers; January 1920–June 1921, sight drafts; July 1921–November 1924, cable transfers. Average rates 1914–October 1918 are midpoints between the monthly high and low rates; from November 1918 to date, the averages are simple arithmetic monthly averages of daily rates.

	Cents per Mark		
	High	Low	Average
1914—January	23.75	23.67	23.71
July	24.06	23.77	23.92
1915—January	22.10	21.66	21.88
July	20.56	20.28	20.42
1916—January	19.19	18.25	18.72
July	18.63	17.91	18.27
1917—January	17.86	16.28	17.07
July	14.48	13.82	14.15
1918—January	20.73	17.97	19.35
July	18.00	16.64	17.32
1919—January	12.71	11.82	12.21
July	8.00	6.25	6.64
1920—January	2.05	1.09	1.69
July	2.65	2.23	2.53
1921—January	1.81	1.33	1.60
July	1.35	1.22	1.30
1922—January	0.59	0.47	0.52
July	0.25	0.15	0.20
1923—January	0.013,9	0.002,1	0.007
February	0.005,2	0.002,4	0.004
March	0.004,8	0.004,4	0.005
April	0.004,8	0.003,1	0.004
May	0.003,3	0.001,4	0.002
June	0.001,5	0.000,6	0.001
July	0.000,6	0.000,088	0.000,3
August	0.000,095	0.000,008,9	0.000,033,9
September	0.000,009,95	0.000,000,403	0.000,001,88
October	0.000,000,32	0.000,000,007,5	0.000,000,068
November	0.000,000,000,29	0.000,000,000,014	0.000,000,000,043
December	0.000,000,000,024,9	0.000,000,000,015,3	0.000,000,000,022,7

		Cents per Mark		
	High	Low	Average	
1924—January*	23.6	21.9	22.6	
February	23.3	20.4	21.8	
March	22.3	21.3	22.0	
April	22.8	21.5	22.0	
May	23.3	22.4	22.3	
June	23.9	23.0	23.4	
July	24.0	23.8	23.9	
August	23.9	23.7	23.8	
September	23.8	23.8	23.8	
October	23.8	23.8	23.8	
November	23.8	23.8	23.8	
December	23.8	23.8	23.8	
1925—January*	23.8	23.8	23.8	

Source: John Parke Young, *European Currency and Finance, Foreign Currency, and Exchange Investigation*, Serial 9, Volume I, Commission of Gold and Silver Inquiry, U.S. Senate, 67th Congress, 4th Session (Washington, D.C.: U.S. Government Printing Office, 1925), pp. 531–532.

* Cents per rentenmark and (since October 1924) per reichsmark. One rentenmark is equivalent to one reichsmark or 1,000,000,000,000 former paper marks. The reichsmark is the equivalent of the gold mark worth 23.82 cents.

4

The Demand for Money

Utility and Marginal Utility of Money

Economists generally agree on the theoretical approach to the determination of relative value for any specific economic good or service. The traditional and customary way is to develop a supply and demand apparatus that, under given conditions, shows the determination of an equilibrium market price for a particular good or service and an equilibrium flow of the good or service in and out of the market (see Chapter 0). When it comes to money, particularly paper money having no commodity redemption value, economists have sometimes deserted the traditional principles of value determination and have contrived instead all sorts of awkward and mysterious schemes. One group argues that money has no utility of its own because it yields no specialized services. If this view is accepted, the same argument must be used for any endurable wealth item, and probably for everything else except outright services. One does not demand a house, but the services a house renders; and one does not demand money, but the services money renders.

Casual empirical investigation of the way people behave with respect to money is enough to verify the fact that people demand money in the same sense that they demand other wealth. If people had no "real" demand for money, they would not hold any of it for any length of time but would spend it all as quickly as they received it. The velocity of money would approach infinity. In reality, however, people receive income in the form of money and, after an initial bill-paying flurry, settle back and spend their money little by little until their next receipt of income. So some of the money people receive at the beginning of a payment period (say, one month) is held until the end of the month. If money had no utility—yielded no services of any sort—people would never demand it or hold it but would demand and hold other things in its place. The plain fact that they hold units of money for shorter or longer intervals confirms that money has utility of some sort; and therefore money, in the same fashion as other economic wealth, may be subjected to marginal analysis.

Money's utility may also be regarded as marginally diminishing. People do not ordinarily pile up greater and greater stocks of money indefinitely; that is, true miserliness is rare. Additional units of money, therefore, must give their owners successively smaller additional utilities. This reasoning suggests that the behavior of people with respect to money may be analyzed with the same tools that are used to estimate their behavior in purchasing and selling all other things.

Wherein lies money's utility if, as is certainly the case in today's world, it has no "intrinsic" utility and no commodity value? First, money is the best if not the only medium of exchange. It is also a store of value, and consequently the best medium of exchange that is also a store of value. These characteristics give money a unique utility: They permit an owner of money to transfer or exchange his wealth in the form of money to some other kind of wealth with minimum costs of transfer and with maximum discretion on his part as to the form in which he holds his wealth stock. If money were not a medium of exchange, converting it into other kinds of wealth would be more or less difficult and would require more or less time. (A system of barter demonstrates such awkwardness.) And if money were not a good store of value, people would have to exchange it immediately to avoid the risk of changes in its value. (The condition of hyperinflation exemplifies this behavior.) In sum, the use of money economizes resources and helps to maximize convenience, liquidity, and security for individuals.

Demand theory in economics derives from utility theory. Utility theory in turn has subjective origins: For a good or service to possess utility, it must satisfy a human want. Given that all goods, services, and money have characteristics of utility, some system must be devised to determine how people make logical choices in furthering their total satisfactions. Since choices would be unnecessary if people had unlimited incomes, the product of the whole economy and the income share of any individual must also be limited. Finally, in a "normal" world, diminishing marginal utilities of money and other things must be accepted as a matter of fact.

Diminishing marginal utility—the principle that additional units of like goods and services render additional but successively smaller amounts of utility to their owners within a given time period—is intuitive to anyone who thinks about the matter. Everyone knows that additional units of anything lead to satiety. A more compelling proof, however, is to imagine a society in which everyone by assumption had increasing marginal utilities for all goods and services. Every individual would then start by buying that item that gave him the most utility, and he would continue buying more units of that same item until he had exhausted his income. Society would be made up of individuals who specialized their purchases. Each individual might have a different specialty, but he would concentrate on just one thing. Casual observation denies this condition: People diversify their purchases of economic goods and services as much as possible. Diminishing and not increasing marginal utility would seem to be a datum of human behavior.

Cardinal Utility—An Example

The principle of diminishing marginal utility and its operational use for obtaining general equilibrium may be illustrated by means of a numerical example. Utility, of course, is an abstract and subjective reaction not given to precise numerical measurement. However, to simplify an understanding of its effects, assume that utilities for various goods and money are quantified in the mind of some "economic man" who is typical of a large group of economic men (see Table 4.1). His money income is fixed, and his tastes as described by the table are independent and constant. Finally, money prices for all commodities are determined in free markets and are constant during the period in which equilibrium is sought.

Table 4.1. Marginal Utilities of Successive Units of Various Commodities and Money to a Consumer

Units	MU Money*	MUa (apples)*	MUb (bread)*	MUc (coal)*
1	22	30	26	40
2	21	28 (3rd)	24 (6th)	34 (1st)
3	20	26 (4th)	20 (10th)	29 (2nd)
4	19 (12th)	24 (7th)	19 (12th)	26 (5th)
5	18 (11th)	22 (8th)	16	20 (11th)
6	17 (10th)	20 (9th)	15	15
7	16 (9th)	18	13	10
8	15 (8th)	16	12	5
9	14 (7th)	14	11	0
10	13 (6th)	12	10	0
11	12 (5th)	10	9	0
12	11 (4th)	8	8	0
13	10 (3rd)	6	7	0
14	9 (2nd)	4	6	0
15	8 (1st)	2	5	0

* The order in which exchanges are made is given in parentheses.

How, then, does this individual allocate his income between money and other things? If he is to maximize total utility at minimum cost, he will give up money and buy the various commodities until the utilities of the marginal units of commodities and money relative to their respective market prices are equal. This equilibrium for a maximizing consumer is described by the following expression:

$$\frac{mu \text{ apples}}{p \text{ apples}} = \frac{mu \text{ bread}}{p \text{ bread}} = \frac{mu \text{ coal}}{p \text{ coal}} = \cdots = \frac{mu \text{ money}}{p \text{ money}}$$

That is, the additional utility per dollar from a unit of apples must be equal to the additional utility per dollar from a unit of bread must be equal to the additional utility per dollar from a unit of coal must be equal to the additional utility per the "price" of money from a unit of money.[1]

Let a unit of money be one dollar, a unit of apples be ten pounds, a unit of bread be five loaves, a unit of coal be 100 pounds, and the market price of each unit of each commodity be one dollar. Finally, give the consumer fifteen dollars of new income and allow him a carryover or inventory of one unit each of apples, bread, and coal. Under these conditions, the consumer has "too much" money; that is, the marginal utility of his fifteenth dollar is 8, while the marginal utilities of the last units of other commodities in his possession are 30, 26, and 40, respectively. To begin with, his marginal utilities relative to prices are

$$\overset{\text{(money)}}{\underset{\text{"1"}}{\frac{8}{}}} \neq \overset{\text{(apples)}}{\frac{30}{\$1}} \neq \overset{\text{(bread)}}{\frac{26}{\$1}} \neq \overset{\text{(coal)}}{\frac{40}{\$1}}$$

so he logically wishes to give up money for the available alternatives. His first purchase, 'if he is to maximize utility, is for a unit of coal yielding 34 units of utility, for which he gives up a unit of money worth eight units of utility. Then, units of money are successively given up for the "best" units of the other goods until the consumer has three units of money, six units of apples, four units of bread, and five units of coal. With these acquisitions his marginal

---

[1]The "price" of a dollar is the inverse of the average money prices of all the commodities involved in purchase and sale. Units are devised here so that the price of one unit of any commodity is $1/1 unit. Therefore, the "average price" of the commodities is $1/1 composite unit, and the value of the dollar is 1 unit/$1 or "1." Computing an index which included various money prices (not all $1.00) would not change things, because some quantum of commodities could always be set equal to one dollar, and the "price" of money is then given.

utility for each unit relative to the price of each unit reaches equilibrium by approximating equality:

$$\underset{\text{(money)}}{\frac{20}{\text{``1''}}} = \underset{\text{(apples)}}{\frac{20}{\$1}} \simeq \underset{\text{(bread)}}{\frac{19}{\$1}} \simeq \underset{\text{(coal)}}{\frac{20}{\$1}}$$

Only the assumed indivisibility of the units prevents an exact equality.

Monetary Equilibrium under Inflation

The above analysis was carried out under conditions of constant prices for all things, including money, constant tastes, and constant real income. The next step is to analyze the process of a price level change, say an increase, when the stock of money is appreciably enlarged (or the available supply of goods is diminished), with other conditions remaining as before.

Assume in the example discussed above that no more goods are available after every consumer has obtained three units of apples, one unit of bread, and four units of coal.[2] Each consumer's marginal utilities relative to prices are then no better than 13/1, 26/1, 26/1, 26/1. The marginal utility of money relative to its "price" is only half as great as that for any commodity. People still have an incentive to get rid of money; but since full employment is in effect, their efforts can result only in raising prices. For simplicity's sake, assume all money prices go up together, so that all relative prices stay constant. Then the average of money prices must rise to "2," and the value of money—its "price"—must fall to "½" before equilibrium can be restored. At the same time that the value of money is falling (or the price level rising), the marginal utilities of the various units of money are also falling in the same proportion as the decline in the value of money. Each unit of money commands less in exchange, so the utility of each unit is correspondingly reduced. As the price level doubles and the "price" of money falls to "½," the marginal utilities of the successive money units are exactly half of the values noted in the first column of Table 4.1. Starting with the first unit of money, the utility values

---

[2] In the real world, this situation usually occurs because of a super-abundance of money rather than from a deficiency of goods. A deficiency in the available quantities of goods is assumed here only because it is simpler to handle numerically. Either change is the monetary equivalent of the other.

become 11, 10½, 10, etc. When final equilibrium occurs at a price level twice as high as the original, any one consumer's new equilibrium is then indicated as

$$\text{(money)} \quad \text{(apples)} \quad \text{(bread)} \quad \text{(coal)}$$
$$\frac{6\frac{1}{2}}{\text{``}\frac{1}{2}\text{''}} = \frac{26}{\$2} = \frac{26}{\$2} = \frac{26}{\$2}$$

In summary, an individual with higher money balances than he wishes gets rid of money in favor of other things—consumer goods, services, and investment goods. Individuals collectively do the same thing. However, when the economy is working with a maximum use of factors of production, additional goods and services are not available. Money prices then rise, and the "price" of money falls, until marginal utilities relative to prices are again in equilibrium.[3]

The Demand for Money in Terms of Purchasing Power: Traditional Demand

The preceding examples have demonstrated the principle of diminishing marginal utility of money with respect to the number of money units held by households and business firms. When the total stock of money units was doubled, the economic value and marginal utility of each money unit were halved before equilibrium in overall spending was reestablished.

A demand schedule is composed of the alternative quantities of a commodity that would be purchased per unit of time at various alternative prices. The two price-level equilibria associated with the two stocks of money in the above examples position two points on a demand curve for money. If further changes in the supply of money continue to provoke proportional price level increases and, therefore, proportional decreases in the "price" of money, the demand-for-money schedule generated assumes the form shown in Figure 4.1.

The vertical or *y*-axis in the diagram specifies alternative values of money units in terms of inverted price level values as such values would be estimated by a price index. As prices *P* become lower, the value of money $p = \frac{1}{P}$ becomes higher; so higher values on the vertical scale reflect lower price levels. The horizontal axis shows various possible quantities of dollars existing in the economy. The rectangular hyperbolic market demand for money *Dm*

---

[3]Full employment of resources does not obtain as abruptly as has been assumed here. When an economy approaches full employment, specialized factors become fully employed ahead of less specialized factors, and relative prices, therefore, change. Money prices of commodities that require the use of specialized resources rise sooner than other money prices, and the price level necessarily begins to rise before the last village laborer admits he has a job.

Figure 4.1. Value ("Price") of Money Unit as Measured by the Inversion of a Price Index

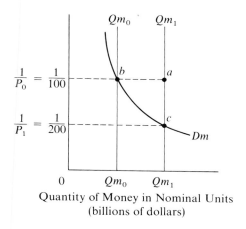

Quantity of Money in Nominal Units
(billions of dollars)

coordinates the alternative (average) quantities of money units that people desire to hold at different price levels, given (1) their tastes (utilities) for money and other things, (2) their real incomes, and (3) a time period of adjustment long enough for all prices to reach a new equilibrium when disturbed from an initial equilibrium. A rectangle under this curve formed by perpendiculars to the axes is equal to any other rectangle so described. These rectangles measure the "real" value of the total quantity of money units that the public desires to hold.

To demonstrate the operational utility of this particular market demand for money, assume that the money supply Qm_0 is given as an inelastic stock by governmental policies, and that the price level in the beginning is at $P_0 = 100$ in Figure 4.1. Then let the quantity of money be doubled to Qm_1. People now are holding a greater quantity of money than they wish to — they have an excess supply of money. At this price-level value they would rather hold b units than the a units supplied. An individual could get rid of his excess supply (a-b) by exchanging his units of money for goods and services. But since the money stock is fixed for all individuals, the whole community cannot rid itself of the excess units by spending them. What one person spends, another person must receive. The only adjustable variable for the community as a whole is the price level — a variable that also reflects the value of each money unit. Increased spending by individuals bids up prices of goods and services so that the price level rises to, say, P_1, and the value of each money unit declines to $\frac{1}{P_1}$. By spending money and forcing up prices, people force down the value of money to the level at which they are satisfied to hold the existing stock without further change in their spending. Such a situation describes static monetary equilibrium.

This particular construction of a demand for money is implicit in the quantity theory of money and in the Cambridge Equation. The Cambridge Equation, for example, states that:

$$PRk = M$$

or identically

$$\frac{kR}{p} = M$$

where $P = 1/p$.

The items k and R express constancy of tastes and real incomes for society. They are the same constants assumed in an analysis of the demand for any commodity. As long as their constancy is assured — that is, under normal, full employment, noninflationary circumstances — they may be replaced by a single constant term. For simplicity's sake, let that constant term be "1." The expression above then becomes

$$\frac{1}{p} = M \quad \text{or} \quad p = \frac{1}{M}$$

When the expression is written in this way, it shows again the proportional inverse relationship between the value of money p and the quantity of money M. These variables may be given explicit values and put into the form of a demand schedule. (If $M = 10$, $p = \frac{1}{10}$; if $M = 5$, $p = 1/5$; etc.) The graph of such a schedule is, again, the hyperbola of Figure 4.1.[4]

The Demand for Money in Terms of Interest Rates: Liquidity Preference

A demand for money that emphasizes interest rates on securities as the independent variable has been adopted by many economists as a generalized replacement for the quantity theory of money and the unitarily elastic demand for money just discussed. This later approach was initiated by John Maynard Keynes in *The General Theory of Employment, Interest, and Money*, published in 1936. The traditional view, including that of Keynes in his earlier

---

[4]This particular analysis has been supplemented by Don Patinkin to include the demand for money by individuals. While his method has some features that recommend it, it is also unnecessarily complicated and has logical inconsistencies that cannot be explored in an elementary text. In any case, his analysis ends with the same relationship emerging between prices and the quantity of money as the one presented here. See Don Patinkin, *Money, Interest, and Prices,* 2nd ed. (New York: Harper & Row, 1966), pp. 15–31.

writings, saw money's function as almost entirely a mechanical means for making transactions during the intervals between income payments. The newer Keynesian theory suggests that an appreciable part of the stock of money may be held as a store of value for reasons similar to those that make the holding of nonmoney assets attractive, that is, for so-called precautionary or speculative motives.

Keynesian theory not only adds a new dimension to money by bringing it into the asset fold, but also emasculates the effectiveness of money as a *determinant* of spending. Much money in the Keynesian model is still retained for transaction purposes (the transactions motive); but spending decisions are made *first* on the basis of anticipations, and then enough transaction money is set aside to handle them. Transaction balances are linked mechanically to total spending, which itself is decided upon prior to the receipt of money. This view reverses the process of cause and effect used in the traditional model.

The Keynesian concept of an "asset money," in conjunction with a "transactions money" concept that is functionless, makes necessary a different demand-for-money construction. While money is a store of value, some stores of value are not money. Almost any material commodity that is not immediately perishable may be held for this purpose. Since many of these possible forms of wealth are easily liquidated in markets, they are hypothesized by the Keynesian school as substitutes for money in money's store-of-value function. However, not all wealth qualifies; the effective substitutes are limited to certain classes of securities that fulfill a good marketability requirement. A wrist watch, for example, renders a stream of services to its owner and could be conjectured a money substitute in money's store-of-value function; but wrist watches are held primarily for the utility they render as commodities. They are seldom liquidated for money, and the market for used wrist watches is poor. Marketable securities, on the other hand, yield dollars of income — not a stream of specialized services — and markets for such items are very good. Such securities, therefore, cannot be dismissed *a priori* as inconsequential to the theory of money. Insofar as money is held as a store of value, and to the extent that high-grade securities are good stores of value, high-grade securities may substitute for money.

Given the possible validity of this argument, the following question can be posed: "Why do people hold *any* money with a zero yield rate when securities returning positive yields are available? Why does not everyone get rid of money, buy securities, then sell off the securities as cash for ordinary business or household transactions as needed?"

Two general answers are possible. (Clearly, people must have some reason, or reasons, for not following this pattern, because almost no one behaves this way under normal conditions.) One answer is that behavior of this sort would greatly increase total transaction costs. Going from cash received as income into securities and back into cash every few days would involve a great deal of extra time, trouble, and explicit cost payments to securities dealers. These costs would only be borne if the value of money was expected to depreciate substantially during the time intervals considered (hyperinflation) or if interest rates were high enough to compensate for such costs.

Another factor is interest rate uncertainty. People do not know from one moment to the next what the course of interest rates will be. If they go from cash into interest-bearing securities only to see the market value of the securities fall, they will realize net losses when they go back into money. Money, in a stable-price-level environment, offers insurance against such uncertainty. The "premium" paid for the insurance is the interest income that *might* have been realized if the securities had been purchased and not fallen in value. Interest rates in securities markets, in conjunction with the various money prices in commodity and service markets, present households and business firms with the data (prices and interest rates) that permit money and securities "to coexist peacefully" at a determinate price level and with a determinate interest rate structure.

A whole range of interest or yield rates for securities exists at any one time. Differences in rates are reflections of differences in risks and maturities of the securities considered. To simplify such a heterogeneous group, an index of interest rates may be assumed and a "typical" bond that promises to pay a given number of money dollars per year may be conceived. If people hold quantities of money in lieu of these bonds at various possible rates of interest that might be paid on the bonds, a demand schedule is defined such as is shown in Figure 4.2. This *Lm* curve is the so-called "liquidity preference" demand schedule for money. It describes the alternative quantities of money held as an asset at various possible interest rates for the low-risk bonds that seem to be good substitutes for money in money's store-of-value function. In this case the demand schedule has no particular shape, such as a rectangular hyperbola or the like. It is negatively sloped, however, reflecting the fact that people are more willing to hold money units when rates on fixed dollar claims are low than when these yields are high. To simplify, money may be thought of as an asset that normally has a zero yield rate; and the greater the difference between the yields on low-risk assets and the zero yield on money, the more incentive people have to economize on their holdings of money in favor of these assets.

Again assume a stock of money Qm_0 and an equilibrium rate of interest $r_0 = 4$ percent. Now let the stock of money be increased to Qm_1. The rate of return being realized on income-earning assets becomes too high, and people have an incentive to hold less money than before. The quantity of money they hold exceeds the amount they desire to hold by $c-d$, and they dispose of these excess money balances by buying securities. The prices of old securities are forced up, that is, the rate of return per dollar of money invested in them is forced down. In addition, new securities floated to finance new investments can be obtained only on less favorable terms. When the rate reaches $r_1 = 3$ percent, people have no further incentive for giving up money to get securities. The securities market is in equilibrium.

Figure 4.2. Rates of Anticipated Return on "Typical" Bond

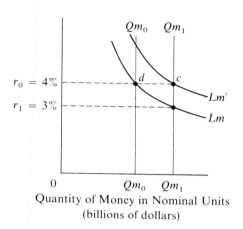

Quantity of Money in Nominal Units
(billions of dollars)

Equilibrium in Commodities, Securities, and Money

The two demand-for-money concepts presented above are the basic frameworks used by economists in analyzing monetary phenomena. As theories, both are logical; and in some regards the use of either theory in analyzing the impact of monetary changes on aggregate spending may result in identical conclusions. However, the two concepts involve fundamental differences. The Dm demand[5] is a traditional one that relates alternative quantities demanded to alternative possible prices under specified given conditions. Its vitality depends on an operational market system that specifies money prices. Changes in the stock of money make their effects felt through such a system. A monetary increase, for example, throws households and firms out of equilibrium. Their attempts to regain monetary equilibrium are expressed through the market structure by changes in prices. This process takes time; and many economists argue that the time it takes is too long and that money prices are too insensitive to allow the results posited by this theory.

The Lm demand is not a traditional concept. It has no counterpart in the theory of demand for specific goods and services. It relates alternative quantities of money to interest rates on some other asset, since money as such is usually presumed bare of interest returns.[6] It does not include the effect of

---

[5]From this point on, the quantity theory demand-for-money concept is referred to as "Dm," and the liquidity preference demand-for-money concept as "Lm."

[6]Treasury notes, a quasi-currency issued at various times during the nineteenth century, bore interest. Demand deposits did, too, until interest payments on them were prohibited by law. Service charges may be thought of as a "negative interest" rate for services rendered. These services may be paid for—an interest rate equivalent—by maintenance of minimal balances by depositors.

money on prices, either because its advocates do not believe money has a significant effect on the price level or because they believe such effects are too lengthy and roundabout to be relevant to the analysis.

In truth, one of the usual first effects of a policy that allows a sizable increase in the stock of money is a reduction of interest rates in securities markets. Not only are these markets excellent in a technical sense, they are also the markets through which increases in the money supply are channeled. To carry out such an operation, a central bank typically buys securities or commercial paper. Almost of necessity, the scale of these operations forces up prices of securities and thus reduces interest rates. And even if the increase in money were carried out, say, by a government lottery which distributed new money to private individuals at random, the first effect might well be the same. Windfalls of cash—what the new money would be to those people who won in the lottery—are first used to liquidate old debts or they are converted into fixed dollar claims, such as time deposits, government securities, savings and loan shares, and the like. Only after some deliberation by households and firms is new money used for the real goods, services, and investment capital that cannot be resold except at a substantial loss if an unwise or unprofitable decision is made.

All these factors—the machinery of money creation, the easy accessibility of certain "safe" securities, and the necessity of a longer time interval for making "real" decisions—suggest the high probability that the first impact of new money is a lowering of observable interest rates, say to r_i in Figure 4.2. Once enough time is allowed for households and firms to ponder their greater real wealth, however, they may well decide that fixed dollar returns do not yield the greatest utility. As consumers who maximize utility by diversifying wealth and income, they logically purchase other things as well: consumer durables, investment goods, services, "necessities," gifts to charities, and frivolities. Now the money is in channels where prices respond. Given the condition of full employment and a fixed output of goods and services, the new money would have to effect an increase in prices. In terms of the *Lm* demand concept, a greater amount of money would be needed to carry out total dollar transactions, so less would be left for security and speculative purposes. The arithmetic of this change forces the *Lm* demand in Figure 4.2 to shift to *Lm′*, implying that the additional quantity of money would be held only at the interest rate prevailing before the increase in the quantity of money. In effect, the new money is "used up" in supporting a higher cost-price framework, the conclusion predicted directly by the *Dm* construction.

Interest rates also can be introduced into the consumer equilibrium equation with similar results. Equilibrium was achieved there when marginal utilities of goods and services relative to their prices were equal to the marginal utility of money relative to its "price." If the typical household or business firm holding money and goods also wants to hold some sort of security-promising future income, equilibrium would be given when

$$\frac{mu_a}{p_a} = \frac{mu_s}{p_s} = \frac{mu_m}{p_m}$$

where a symbolizes any commodity, s refers to a security yielding an antici-pated return r_s, and m is again money. The security has a price p_s and yields an income y_s. The yield rate r_s of the security is equal to its anticipated income return y_s divided by its going price p_s.[7] That is,

$$r_s = \frac{y_s}{p_s}$$

The utility of such a security is due solely to the income it is expected to return. Thus, y_s is a proxy for mu_s and may be substituted in the equilibrium equation. The equation then becomes

$$\frac{mu_a}{p_a} = \frac{y_s}{p_s} = \frac{mu_m}{p_m}$$

However, since $\frac{y_s}{p_s} = r_s$, r_s may be substituted to make the equation read:

$$\frac{mu_a}{p_a} = r_s = \frac{mu_m}{p_m}$$

Given now an increase in the stock of money when the consumer is in equilibrium, the first effect again would be a reduction in the marginal utility of money mu_m. If the first reaction to "too much money" is the purchase of securities, or if the money-creating process itself involves the purchase of securities, the price of securities p_s rises and r_s falls. Ultimately, the prices of commodities p_a also rise and the "price" of money p_m falls until a new equilibrium is achieved. The money that at first prompted higher security prices would forsake that market for the commodity markets. If households and firms have a constant utility for anticipated future income from securities, r_s is a constant. This rate falls only so long as the money price of securities is bid up by bullish buyers ahead of increased general spending on everything else. Once the new money begins to be spent on commodities, and assuming

---

[7]Interest rate analysis is explored in detail in Chapter 5.

that y_s is fixed in dollar terms, the price of securities returns to its old level. The full effect of the monetary increase is reflected in the market prices of goods and services; the effect on interest rates is at most transitory.

If the special case of less than full employment is assumed—that is, the Keynesian framework—increases in the quantity of money may well provoke a "permanent" lowering of interest rates. At least, the reduction would be permanent until the resulting spate of business activity inspired renewed confidence in the future, leading to increased investment spending and finally to higher interest rates. This possibility is discussed more explicitly in later chapters. Only the static (nonexpectational) full employment case is treated here.

Selected Bibliography

Keynes, John Maynard. *The General Theory of Employment, Interest, and Money.* New York: Harcourt Brace Jovanovich, 1936. This is the "bible" of money and interest; see chs. 13, 14, and 21 for the essence of what Keynes says on money.

Contemporary work on monetary theory has revived the quantity theory in a somewhat new garb. See the following.

Friedman, Milton, ed. *Studies in the Quantity Theory of Money.* Chicago: University of Chicago Press, 1956. Best presentation of the counterattack by quantity theorists.

Patinkin, Don. "Price Flexibility and Full Employment." *Readings in Monetary Theory.* Ed. Friedrich H. Lutz and Lloyd W. Mints. Homewood, Ill.: Richard D. Irwin, 1951.

For an excellent review of both the neoclassical and the neo-Keynesian approaches, see:

Laidler, David E. W. *The Demand for Money: Theories and Evidence.* Scranton, Pa.: International Textbook Co., 1969. (Monetary Economic Series in paperback.)

Of the Value of Money,
as Dependent on Demand and Supply

John Stuart Mill

On the basis of his early intellectual accomplishments, John Stuart Mill (1806–1873) is seen as one of the greatest intellects in recorded history. His contributions to political economy reflect this endowment. If he had any fault, it was his classical felicity with word usage and grammar that made the substance of his exposition look too elementary!

In this selection from his Principles, *Mill presents the best discussion on the simple determination of the value of money that was ever written. The theory of value for money, he shows, is not a special case but fits into the general theory of value determination for all economic goods and services.*

The value or purchasing power of money depends, in the first instance, on demand and supply. But demand and supply, in relation to money, present themselves in a somewhat different shape from the demand and supply of other things.

The supply of a commodity means the quantity offered for sale. But it is not usual to speak of offering money for sale. People are not usually said to buy or sell money. This, however, is merely an accident of language. In point of fact, money is bought and sold like other things, whenever other things are bought and sold for money. Whoever sells corn, or tallow, or cotton, buys money. Whoever buys bread, or wine, or clothes, sells money to the dealer in those articles. The money with which people are offering to buy is money offered for sale. The supply of money, then, is the quantity of it which people are wanting to lay out; that is, all the money they have in their possession, except what they are hoarding, or at least keeping by them as a reserve for future contingencies. The supply of money, in short, is all the money in *circulation* at the time....

As the whole of the goods in the market compose the demand for money, so the whole of the money constitutes the demand for goods. The money and the goods are seeking each other for the purpose of being exchanged. They are reciprocally supply and demand to one another. It is indifferent whether, in characterizing the phenomena, we speak of the demand and supply of goods, or the supply and the demand of money. They are equivalent expressions.

We shall proceed to illustrate this proposition more fully. And in doing this, the reader will remark a great difference between the class of questions which

From *Principles of Political Economy* by John Stuart Mill, ed. W. J. Ashley. New York: Longmans, Green and Co., 1923, Book III, Ch. 8, pp. 490–495. Reprinted by permission of the publisher.

now occupy us, and those which we previously had under discussion respecting Values. In considering Value, we were only concerned with causes which acted upon particular commodities apart from the rest. Causes which affect all commodities alike do not act upon values. But in considering the relation between goods and money, it is with the causes that operate upon all goods whatever that we are specially concerned. We are comparing goods of all sorts on one side, with money on the other side, as things to be exchanged against each other.

Suppose, everything else being the same, that there is an increase in the quantity of money, say by the arrival of a foreigner in a place, with a treasure of gold and silver. When he commences expending it (for this question it matters not whether productively or unproductively), he adds to the supply of money, and, by the same act, to the demand for goods. Doubtless he adds, in the first instance, to the demand only for certain kinds of goods, namely, those which he selects for purchase; he will immediately raise the price of those, and so far as he is individually concerned, of those only. If he spends his funds in giving entertainments, he will raise the prices of food and wine. If he expends them in establishing a manufactory, he will raise the prices of labour and materials. But at the higher prices, more money will pass into the hands of the sellers of these different articles; and they, whether labourers or dealers, having more money to lay out, will create an increased demand for all the things which they are accustomed to purchase: these accordingly will rise in price, and so on until the rise has reached everything. I say everything, though it is of course possible that the influx of money might take place through the medium of some new class of consumers, or in such a manner as to alter the proportions of different classes of consumers to one another, so that a greater share of the national income than before would thenceforth be expended in some articles, and a smaller in others; exactly as if a change had taken place in the tastes and wants of the community. If this were the case, then until production has accommodated itself to this change in the comparative demand for different things, there would be a real alteration in values, and some things would rise in price more than others, while some perhaps would not rise at all. These effects, however, would evidently proceed, not from the mere increase of money, but from accessory circumstances attending it. We are now only called upon to consider what would be the effect of an increase of money, considered by itself. Supposing the money in the hands of individuals to be increased, the wants and inclinations of the community collectively in respect to consumption remaining exactly the same; the increase of demand would reach all things equally, and there would be a universal rise of prices. We might suppose, with Hume, that some morning, every person in the nation should wake and find a gold coin in his pocket: this example, however, would involve an alteration of the proportions in the demand for different commodities; the luxuries of the poor would, in the first instance, be raised in price in a much greater degree than other things. Let us rather suppose, therefore, that to every pound, or shilling, or penny, in the possession of any one, another pound, shilling, or penny, were suddenly added. There would be an increased money demand, and consequently an increased money value, or price, for things of all sorts. This increased value would do no good to any one; would make no difference, except that of having to reckon pounds, shillings, and pence, in higher numbers. It would be an increase of values only as estimated in money, a thing only wanted to buy other things with; and would not enable any one to buy more of them than before. Prices would have risen in a certain ratio, and the value of money would have fallen in the same ratio.

It is to be remarked that this ratio would be precisely that in which the quantity of money had been increased. If the whole money in circulation was doubled, prices would be doubled. If it was increased only one-fourth, prices would rise one-fourth. There would be one-fourth more money, all of which would be used to purchase goods of some description. When there had been time for the increased supply of money to reach all markets, or (according to the conventional metaphor) to permeate all the channels of circulation, all prices would have risen one-fourth. But the general rise of price is independent of this diffusing and equalizing process. Even if some prices were raised more, and others less, the average rise would be one-fourth. This is a necessary consequence of the fact that a fourth more money would have been given for only the same quantity of goods. *General* prices would in any case be a fourth higher.

The very same effect would be produced on prices if we suppose the goods diminished, instead of the money increased: and the contrary effect if the goods were increased or the money diminished. If there were less money in the hands of the community, and the same amount of goods to be sold, less money altogether would be given for them, and they would be sold at lower prices; lower, too, in the precise ratio in which the money was diminished. So that the value of money, other things being the same, varies inversely as its quantity; every increase of quantity lowering the value, and every diminution raising it, in a ratio exactly equivalent.

This, it must be observed, is a property peculiar to money. We did not find it to be true of commodities generally, that every diminution of supply raised the value exactly in proportion to the deficiency, or that every increase lowered it in the precise ratio of the excess. Some things are usually affected in a greater ratio than that of the excess or deficiency, others usually in a less: because, in ordinary cases of demand, the desire being for the thing itself, may be stronger or weaker: and the amount of what people are willing to expend on it, being in any case a limited quantity, may be affected in very unequal degrees by difficulty or facility of attainment. But in the case of money, which is desired as the means of universal purchase, the demand consists of everything which people have to sell; and the only limit to what they are willing to give is the limit set by their having nothing more to offer. The whole of the goods being in any case exchanged for the whole of the money which comes into the market to be laid out, they will sell for less or more of it, exactly according as less or more is brought.

From what precedes, it might for a moment be supposed that all the goods on sale in the country, at any one time, are exchanged for all the money existing and in circulation at that same time: or, in other words, that there is always in circulation in a country a quantity of money equal in value to the whole of the goods then and there on sale. But this would be a complete misapprehension. The money laid out is equal in value to the goods it purchases; but the quantity of money laid out is not the same thing with the quantity in circulation. As the money passes from hand to hand, the same piece of money is laid out many times, before all the things on sale at one time are purchased and finally removed from the market: and each pound or dollar must be counted for as many pounds or dollars, as the number of times it changes hands in order to effect this object. The greater part of the goods must also be counted more than once, not only because most things pass through the hands of several sets of manufacturers and dealers before they assume the form in which they are finally consumed, but because in times of speculation (and all times are so, more or less) the same goods are often bought repeatedly, to be resold for a profit, before they are bought for the purpose of consumption at all.

If we assume the quantity of goods on sale, and the number of times those goods are resold, to be fixed quantities, the value of money will depend upon its quantity, together with the average number of times that each piece changes hands in the process. The whole of the goods sold (counting each resale of the same goods as so much added to the goods) have been exchanged for the whole of the money, multiplied by the number of purchases made on the average by each piece. Consequently, the amount of goods and of transactions being the same, the value of money is inversely as its quantity multiplied by what is called the rapidity of circulation. And the quantity of money in circulation is equal to the money value of all the goods sold, divided by the number which expresses the rapidity of circulation.

The phrase, rapidity of circulation, requires some comment. It must not be understood to mean the number of purchases made by each piece of money in a given time. Time is not the thing to be considered. The state of society may be such that each piece of money hardly performs more than one purchase in a year: but if this arises from the small number of transactions—from the small amount of business done, the want of activity in traffic, or because what traffic there is, mostly takes place by barter—it constitutes no reason why prices should be lower, or the value of the money higher. The essential point is, not how often the same money changes hands in a given time, but how often it changes hands in order to perform a given amount of traffic. We must compare the number of purchases made by the money in a given time, not with the time itself, but with the goods sold in that same time. If each piece of money changes hands on an average ten times while goods are sold to the value of a million sterling, it is evident that the money required to circulate those goods is £ 100,000. And conversely, if the money in circulation is £ 100,000, and each piece changes hands by the purchase of goods ten times in a month, the sales of goods for money which take place every month must amount on the average to £ 1,000,000.

Rapidity of circulation, being a phrase, is still adapted to express the only thing which it is of any importance to express by it, and having a tendency to confuse the subject by suggesting a meaning extremely different from the one intended, it would be a good thing if the phrase could be got rid of, and another substituted, more directly significant of the idea meant to be conveyed. Some such expression as "the efficiency of money," though not unexceptionable, would do better; as it would point attention to the quantity of work done, without suggesting the idea of estimating it by time. Until an appropriate term can be devised, we must be content, when ambiguity is to be apprehended, to express the idea by the circumlocution which alone conveys it adequately, namely, the average number of purchases made by each piece in order to effect a given pecuniary amount of transactions.

5

Interest Rates and the Valuation of Capital

Definition of Interest Rates

No economic concept has been more subject to confusion, mysticism, and faulty inference than that of interest rate determination. The fundamental characteristic of an interest rate is that it is a rate, or ratio, that relates future income to a present value or price. The obvious contrast that should be made immediately is the one between an interest *rate* and a money *price*. A price expresses an equality of economic value between an amount of money and units of a good or service. It includes no time dimension. If an apple sells for 10 cents, it is a fact for here and now. If no apples are sold at this price, the 10 cent "price" is not a price because it does not express an existing operational relationship between the values of apples and money.

A rate of interest likewise is a fact, but it does not express "the price of money." If anything, it reflects the price or cost of borrowing someone else's income or wealth. It is a "price" expressed in a special way. Since it is a ratio, it does not need to involve units of money as a measuring device. In a rural economy, for example, a farmer may borrow 100 units of seed in the spring to plant his fields. If he signs a contract agreeing to pay back 103 units of seed six months later (in the autumn), he has subjected himself to an interest charge of three units of seed for the six-months loan of 100 units of seed. Since consistency of expression is needed to simplify meaning, rates of interest are given in annual terms. Therefore, this farmer pays a 6 percent *per annum* interest charge, even though the loan lasted only six months.

This example demonstrates that rates of interest are real and not just monetary. In a pecuniary economy, the farmer would borrow 100 units of money to buy seed; and he would pay back 103 units of money. The use of the money, however, would not change the fact that what the farmer borrows and pays back is someone else's real wealth. The three units of interest charge are properly thought of as interest *income* to the lender because they are a part of services rendered in the current time period.

This example also shows the necessity of a time interval in economic activity before an interest rate is either required or meaningful. Interest is occasioned by the fact that production and a large part of consumption are processes which involve significant lapses of time between inputs of resources and final utilization of goods and services.

The farmer in the above example borrowed someone else's wealth; but if he had used his own wealth—seed saved from last year's crop—to plant this year's crop, the accounting of interest charges would have been identical. He himself would have received the interest income in addition to possible income from his other functions as entrepreneur, laborer, or landowner. In this case, the interest charge would be implicit.

Interest rates, in fact, can be determined for anything that has a market price and requires some amount of time between its creation and utilization in the economy. Even services are not excluded, for while they are demanded and used immediately, they are supplied by an extensive buildup of resources over time. Commodities produced and consumed within short time periods (one year) are excluded definitionally, but need not be. A loaf of bread has an "annual yield *rate*" to whomever consumes it. However, the case of this type of commodity is too trivial to require definition in terms of interest rates, and would be too costly as well. Most notably, interest rates can be conceived of for human beings, who are "capital" in a very real sense. The institution of slavery confirms this example.

Determination of Interest Rates

An interest rate, from the viewpoint of a borrower, is a cost. The borrower is a demander. He borrows someone else's wealth to extend his own well-being. He may invest this wealth in some sort of enterprise, with the anticipation that the marginal product returned will equal or exceed the cost of the wealth borrowed; or he may simply throw a big party consuming all the borrowed wealth, in which case the pleasurable return or utility of the party is recompense for the cost of the borrowed wealth. In either case, the borrower is subject to marginal considerations. As an investor, he has a shelflist of particular projects from which he expects to gain specific amounts of revenue. Only when the expected gain is equal to or greater than the cost of the borrowed wealth would the borrowing take place. Obviously, the lower the interest rate on borrowed wealth, the more projects that were submarginal at higher rates become marginal or supermarginal. The process is similar for a borrower who wishes to consume more than his current income by giving a party, except that the return has to be measured in terms of hedonistic utility. In this case, the lower the rate of interest, the bigger and more elaborate the party.

These considerations of marginal decision-making by potential demanders of borrowed wealth suggest a typical negatively sloped demand schedule (Figure 5.1). The vertical axis is calibrated with a schedule of interest rates in the relevant range for the particular market under investigation, and the horizontal axis shows the amount of wealth or income per year that is borrowed. The demand for borrowed wealth, measured in dollars per year, is seen to be inversely related to the rate of interest; that is, as rates go down, the quantity of wealth demanded per year increases. This relationship traces out the demand function *D–B* (demand for borrowed wealth).

Figure 5.1. Demand Curve for Borrowed Wealth

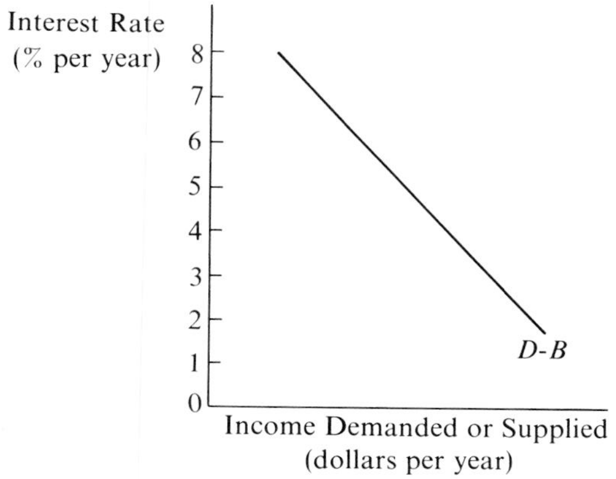

Lenders, by way of contrast, are suppliers. To lend their wealth, they must refrain from using it themselves. In short, they must have either so much income or so little disposition for consuming it that "surplus" income (saving) tends to appear.[1] This "surplus" is also dependent on marginal factors. If

---

[1]In fact, no actual "surpluses," except increased inventories, appear because the whole process is *continuous*. That is, markets are continually being supplied with unconsumed income in the form of money, and this income constantly is being absorbed by households and firms in their efforts to increase their total capital stock.

interest rates are low, suppliers of wealth are not as likely to forego consumption of their wealth as they might otherwise. This principle applies even though some wealth may be accumulated even at zero or negative interest rates; and some amount of saving at negative rates also implies that saving is a function of factors other than the explicit return promised in the market. However, it does not imply the impotency of market rates, only that they are not exclusive in determining the supply of income flowing into and out of capital markets.

A supply of wealth (or saving) function appears, then, in a positive relationship to rates of interest. Figure 5.2 combines this supply function *(S–W)* with the demand function depicted in Figure 5.1. The two functions respectively define the alternative amounts of income currently being generated that would be demanded or supplied at various rates of interest.

Figure 5.2. Demand and Supply Curves for Borrowed (Lent) Wealth

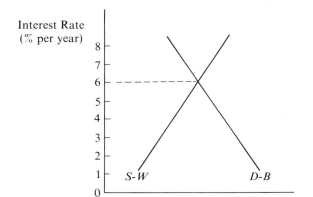

Income Demanded or Supplied
(dollars per year)

The equilibrium rate of interest in this market is 6 percent. At this rate, the supply flow of saving is just equal in quantitative terms to the demand for additional wealth by borrowers. The quantitative units used to express this equality are dollars, but they could be just as properly bushels of wheat or bottles of whiskey. Dollars, generalized units of purchasing power, are the most common units used.[2]

The determination of interest rates has been examined up to this point without an explanation of why interest rates exist in the first place. A money price is an expression of value right now and in this place (f.o.b.) for some identifiable commodity or service. A money price right now for the same object to be delivered one year from now is not the same price because the

---

[2]The modification that has to be made in interest rate determination when dollars suffer a change in value is discussed below.

object is not the same object, even if it has the same physical characteristics and even if the dollars paid for it have the same purchasing power. Nor does a dollar to be obtained one year hence have the value of a dollar today. In essence, economic goods and services and dollars are valued in the here and now. Any necessity for waiting—for allowing a time interval to elapse between contract and consummation—must include a discount on the thing waited for.

The reason for a premium on "waiting" should be immediately apparent. Income is derived from wealth, which is in turn owned by human beings who are mortal. If they are to forego certainty in the use of the income by consuming it, the wealth owners must be rewarded. This reasoning applies equally to the wealth owner who uses his own income to finance the increase in his own stock of wealth and to the wealth owner who lets his income be borrowed by others.

Borrowers of income, likewise, have an incentive for paying the wealth owners some amount of premium. They would not attempt to build up their own income-producing wealth stock unless they believed that the product they anticipate from their augmented wealth—the internal rate of return— would at least equal the external rate of interest they must pay to borrow it.

These decisions are, of course, variable and a part of a marginal process. The cost of getting more and more income for wealth-building purposes increases at the margin, and the productivity of additional units of wealth applied at the margin decreases. At some point the marginal productivity of capital, expressed as an internal rate of return, is reduced to equality with the marginal cost of getting new capital from the market—which is to say, to equality with the market rate of interest. In fact, this process, carried on hundreds of times a day by individual households and business firms, determines the market rate of interest.

The Capitalization Process

Any economically productive unit of wealth yields a stream of services to its owner for the period of time during which it exists. Real wealth consists of conventional capital, such as buildings and machinery; personal possessions, such as eyeglasses, dentures, and wrist watches; and intrinsically human assets, such as knowledge or technical skills. Nominal wealth includes all representations of real wealth—stock certificates, deeds to property, and fixed dollar claims of all kinds. Some real wealth is not customarily represented by tangible claim, title, or deed, These exceptions include most personal possessions, such as clothing, household equipment, and the corporate claim of an individual person to his own product. One important group of nominal wealth items in turn does not represent or is not offset by any real wealth. Included in this category are the outstanding obligations of the federal government to the public: government securities held by private investors, reserves of the banking system, and currency issued by the central bank or treasury. The last two items are specific liabilities of the central bank (or treasury) and constitute the basis for control over the monetary system.

Because of custom and the particular uses to which they are put, some wealth items, such as eyeglasses, enter the marketing process only once; others, such as houses, enter only infrequently. The values of some are commonly expressed as money *prices;* the values of others are given as *rates* of annual yield relative to present market values (or to the original costs) of the items.

To demonstrate as simply as possible the relationship between prices of assets and corresponding rates of return, assume that a politically stable government in an economic environment that includes free markets and a relatively stable price level issues consol bonds in order to make up a deficit between government expenditures and receipts. Let each consol declare that the government will pay, say, $40 per year forever to the holder of the consol. A consol has no maturity date on which the principal is paid. Its sole claim to value is that it pays an annual number of money dollars "forever." (If the government wishes to retire outstanding debt, it may buy back the consols from the open market in those years when its revenues exceed its expenditures.) Anyone may bid on the consols because they are "floated" in the securities market by investment banking houses or by individual dealers in securities. In making a bid, a potential buyer is motivated by various factors: how much money he wishes to hold relative to this type of bond asset; how much in common stocks he wishes to hold relative to this type of asset; how much food he wishes to consume relative to the total amount of income-earning assets he wishes to hold; what his anticipations are of the future states of the various markets; and many other factors, including the future course of prices. The potential buyer foresees, nevertheless, a stream of annual money income payments from the consols. But since he is standing in time present and must anticipate a future that is necessarily limited and uncertain, each anticipated year's income appears successively smaller from the vantage point of time present. An income-right-now is preferable to the same nominal income-a-year-from-now. Income-right-now is certain, certain to be received and certain to be used as one wishes, while income-a-year-from-now has some degree of uncertainty and inconvenience attached to it.

The premium that a person is willing to pay for present income relative to future income can easily be found by a simple experiment. Anyone can be asked to equate the number of dollars he would take right now at time zero as an exact equivalent to $40 one year from now. If this individual's future is rosy and he has no pressing need for the use of income now, he might allow that he would accept $39 now as equivalent to $40 a year from now. Another individual might have such an immediate preference for cash income that he would be willing to accept as little as $30 now rather than wait a whole year for $40. The difference in these demands for immediate income becomes quantifiable. The optimistic person has a rate of time discount of 2½ percent; that is, $40 ÷ 1.025 = $39. The rate for the second person is 33⅓ percent; that is, $40 ÷ 1.333 = $30.

Suppose, then, that the quantity of new consols supplied in the securities market by the Treasury Department is all taken by demanders of securities whose rates of time discount are 5 percent. Next year's $40 of income to anyone in this market is worth $40 ÷ 1.05, or $38.10 right now. Income-two-years-from-now would be worth income-one-year-from-now discounted by the same amount. That is, $38.10 ÷ 1.05 = $36.29, the value right now of the $40 income due *two* years hence. This result is the same as $40 divided twice by 1.05, and it is expressed as $40 ÷ (1.05)^2. In general, the value of income right now, Y', of any nominal income Y due in some future year, n years hence, at a rate of discount r is

$$Y' = \frac{Y}{(1 + r)^n}$$

As the future date of income receipt recedes in time, n becomes very large and Y' becomes correspondingly small for given values of Y and r. The anticipated income of $40 in 20 years and discounted at a rate of 5 percent is worth right now $40 ÷ (1.05)^{20}, or $15.08.[3]

The consol is expected to return an infinite number of future income payments of $40 per year. *Its present value is the sum of all the anticipated discounted future incomes the asset is expected to return.* This sum may be expressed as:

$$P = \sum_{n=0}^{n=\infty} \frac{40}{(1.05)^0} + \frac{40}{(1.05)^1} + \frac{40}{(1.05)^2} + \frac{40}{(1.05)^3} + \cdots + \frac{40}{(1.05)^n}$$

where n becomes as large as desired so that the final term in the expression becomes as small as desired. This sum of an "infinite" number of terms reduces to $P = $40 ÷ 0.05 = $800. That is,

$$P = \sum_{n=0}^{n=\infty} \frac{Y}{(1 + r)^n} \rightarrow \frac{y}{r}$$

It says truistically that if the bond market discounts this type of asset at a rate of 5 percent, the price that clears the market is $800. If the rate of return that investors seek and savers supply were only 4 percent, the consols would sell at $1,000. Generally, the present value P of an asset yielding an annual net income of Y dollars indefinitely, when a rate of return r prevails for this type of asset, is

$$P = \frac{Y}{r}$$

---

[3]This value is easily computed by means of logarithms. Required is the antilog of log 40 − 20 (log 1.05).

By definition, the value of a consol is entirely dependent on the sum of its future anticipated income yields. This example, therefore, demonstrates the limit that interest rate changes may have on capital or wealth values. Any change in the interest rate alters every future income value the consol is expected to return.

The analysis is somewhat different if the income-yielding article has an explicit maturity date. A three-year note with a maturity value of $800 and a 5 percent coupon rate ($40/year) would sell for $800 in the market if the market rate were also 5 percent. The buyer of the note pays $800. He then receives three payments of $40, each properly discounted, and a final payment of $800, similarly discounted. In this case, both annual incomes and principal must be discounted at the 5 percent rate. In general, the formula for obtaining present value P of an asset paying Y income per year for n years and having a maturity value W is

$$P = \frac{W}{(1 + r)^n} + \sum_{m=1}^{n} \frac{Y}{(1 + r)^n}$$

If the market rate of interest goes to 6 percent, the present value of the three-year note would be[4]:

$$P = \frac{800}{(1.06)^3} + \sum_{m=1}^{n=3} \frac{40}{(1.06)^3} = \$778.59$$

For a consol, a similar market change to a 6 percent interest rate would give a present value of

$$\frac{\$40}{0.06} = \$666.67$$

Thus, an identical change in interest rates affects the prices of long-term securities more than it affects those with short maturity dates. While economic forces in the various capital and securities markets do not necessarily move interest rates in parallel, they probably do tend to move them in the same direction. For this reason, yield rates on longer-term securities tend to change by smaller amounts than yields on shorter-term securities, but prices of short-term securities tend to change by smaller amounts than prices of long-term issues.

Money and Interest

The interest rate analysis presented above is appropriate either in a system that does not use money or in a system in which the unit of money has constant purchasing power. If either of these conditions prevails indefinitely in a real

---

[4]Such values are readily obtainable from bond tables.

economy, the effects of quantity-of-money changes on the interest rate structure can be ignored. Actual economies, however, are subject to the buffetings of monetary disturbances; so the next step is to trace out the short- and long-run effects of undue changes in the quantity of money and the price level on the structure of interest rates.

Assume an economy is thriving under conditions of full employment of resources, a stable general level of prices, and a stable interest rate structure. The government for fiscal or other reasons permits, encourages, or initiates an increase in the stock of money of more than nominal dimensions. Let this increase be on the order of, say, 10 percent over a short period of time, perhaps three months. The environment on which this change is imposed is stable — one in which people believe that the value of a unit of money will be the same tomorrow as it is today, one in which anticipations are "neutral."

To some extent, the results of this new money injection depend on the channels through which money makes its way into the economy. The usual channel in the United States is the central-commercial banking system, with an assist from the securities market. Without dwelling on the mechanics of this process here, assume that the central bank furnishes the commercial banking system with new reserves. Commercial banks then encourage borrowers to demand new credit by reducing rates of interest on business and other types of loans. The central bank, as well, has initiated a decline in rates of interest on government securities by its initial actions in creating new reserves.

As the process of bank credit creation increases the stock of money (bank demand deposits) in the economy, people realize larger disposable money incomes. The easiest channel for spending new income, which in the first instance takes the form of larger cash balances, is to pay off old debts or to buy highly secure, fixed dollar claims of some sort (time deposits, short-term government securities, savings and loan shares) until other kinds of new "real" wealth can be decided upon as permanent household or business capital. (See Chapter 4.)

When the new money is spent in the markets for consumer and capital goods and services, general spending increases and, by the same token, aggregate income also increases. The economy, already operating at full employment, cannot produce a greater volume of real goods and services. Greater spending must, therefore, result in a higher general price level. The real quantity of money, temporarily increased by the increase in the nominal stock, now depreciates as prices rise. Consequently, what had been regarded as "excess" money balances now become "necessary" for the higher dollar values of goods, services, and incomes. Interest rates then assume their former values, barring some further change in the monetary or real environment.[5]

---

[5]The existence of significant unemployment in the economy is a special case that requires a modified explanation. See Theorem V; the Unemployment Theorem, in Chapter 3.

The increase of 10 percent in the money stock, imagined in the above example, is assumed to be a once-and-for-all increase. Suppose now that the 10 percent increase is continued quarter by quarter indefinitely. Since all the people cannot be fooled all of the time, or even for very much of the time, the pattern of monetary increases and subsequent increases in the price level soon would provoke anticipations of the actual increases. Average cash balance holdings then would be economized *prior* to the actual increases in the stock of money. Interest rates would *rise,* rather than fall, as people sought to avoid holding fixed dollar claims (including money). Thus, pervasive increases of more than nominal proportions in the stock of money are seen to be associated with secularly rising nominal interest rates.

In order for increases in the stock of money to hold interest rates at a level lower than what they would be in their natural state, the increases would have to be larger and larger. Such action would generate hyperinflation and would be self-defeating: Eventually, no volume of monetary increases would be able to hold down interest rates, and ultimately people would refuse to use national money for making exchanges. Continuous increases of more than nominal amounts in the stock of money, therefore, are associated with increases in nominal interest rates, while continuous decreases in the stock of money provoke declining interest rates. The anticipated percentage rise of prices can be regarded as a premium the nominal rate of interest must include to equate it with the natural or real rate of interest.

The difference between this example of continuous increases in the stock of money, in an atmosphere made "dynamic" or expectational by these very increases, and the previous example of a once-and-for-all increase undertaken in an environment of stability demonstrates the limited role monetary policy can have on interest rate structures. The most that increases in the stock of money alone can accomplish is to maintain an environment of stability in the economy itself. Interest rates, similar to all other economic values, can then find their proper values in the capital and securities markets.[6]

Selected Bibliography

For a reconciliation of the liquidity preference and loanable funds theories of interest, see:

Fellner, William J., and Harold M. Somers. "Alternative Monetary Approaches to Interest Theory." *Review of Economic Statistics,* Vol. 23 (1941), pp. 43–48.

---

[6]For more discussion of this point, see the reading selection at the end of Chapter 22, Milton Friedman, "The Role of Monetary Policy."

For a more recent work at an advanced level, see:

Friedman, Milton. *The Optimum Quantity of Money and Other Essays.* Chicago: Aldine Publishing Co., 1969, Ch. 1.

Interest

William L. Miller

Interest theory rivals monetary theory in mystique and complexity. In this selection from A Dictionary of the Social Sciences, *Professor William Miller of the University of Georgia presents in short compass the essentials of the theory as they are currently understood. For the reader who wishes to explore the subject in more depth, Professor Miller has included all the major references. Especially recommended is the article by Professor Frank H. Knight in the 1932 edition of the* Encyclopedia of the Social Sciences.

A. In a money-using economy, interest denotes the price, or rent, paid in money in exchange for the use of a sum of money, the premium paid to get cash without which an attractive course of action must be temporarily or permanently forgone.

B. Economists have commonly not been much interested in this commonplace definition and have asked why interest must be paid and why the borrower is willing to pay it.

1. Economists first answered that interest must be paid, so that enough saving will be done to permit desirable progress from capital accumulation. While it is generally agreed that some saving would be done at zero interest, the amount would be undesirably small. Positive interest has been looked upon as a necessary bribe to get recipients of income to consume less than they might. N. W. Senior, one of the first to be clear-cut in his explanation, declared that interest compensated for the pains of abstinence (*An Outline of the Science of Political Economy* [1st edn., 1836], London: Charles Griffin, 6th edn., 1872, pp. 58–60; see also M. Bowley, *Nassau Senior and Classical Economics*, London: Allen & Unwin, 1937, pp. 137–66).

2. Socialists poured scorn upon the notion that interest is a reward for the pains of abstinence. If abstinence involves pain, they said, then the Rothschilds and other rich must have suffered monumentally. Senior, of course, could have admitted that saving by the rich involved no obvious or even hidden pain but

---

From William L. Miller, "Interest," in *A Dictionary of the Social Sciences*, ed. Julius Gould and William I. Kolb. New York: Free Press, 1964, pp. 341–343. Reprinted by permission of the publisher and author.

then have argued that without interest an insufficient amount of abstaining from consumption would be supplied. Marx himself argued that the capitalist wished to consume and at the same time to acquire power through accumulation of property. Of course marginal analysis clears up the difficulty by viewing interest merely as the opportunity cost of the marginal unit of saving. Where small savers represent marginal supply real 'pain' appears.

3. Socialist criticism, nevertheless, left economists uncomfortable. Help came through a shift in emphasis which converted abstinence into time preference. The time preference theory of interest had its early development in the work of W. S. Jevons and the Austrians, particularly E. von Böhm-Bawerk (*The Positive Theory of Capital*, trans. by W. Smart, London: Macmillan, 1891, pp. 285–424; W. S. Jevons, *The Theory of Political Economy* [1st edn., 1871], London: Macmillan, 4th edn., 1911, pp. 71–4). This theory has been criticized and refined by J. A. Schumpeter, I. Fisher, F. A. Fetter, F. A. Hayek, and others. Böhm-Bawerk imputed to man a "perspective undervaluation of future wants." For many people this undervaluation explains the preference for present goods over those available in the future, but the presence of this element is not a necessary ingredient of the time preference theory except in a stationary society. "All that is required in a progressive society for the existence of interest is that its members should feel some *reluctance to postpone* consumption of present income in order to increase future income beyond the present level at more than a limited rate" (F. A. Hayek, *The Pure Theory of Capital,* London: Routledge & Kegan Paul, 1941, p. 420). Some members cannot save because their incomes are at or near the minimum for biological subsistence, but since in rich countries this group is comparatively small, in them other factors account for the high rate of time preference of the great majority. Most people whose incomes are high enough to permit saving have high propensities to consume for the following reasons: (1) They try to approximate the consumption patterns of people in income brackets above theirs; (2) many, including the young, expect future to exceed present incomes; and (3) a large number, including some elderly people, have incomes too low to enable them to reach levels of living attained in the past. Few economists today deny the importance of time preference, but many of them do think that the schedule of saving, in which the quantity of saving is presented as a function of the rate of interest, has little elasticity through much of its length.

4. In 1936 J. M. Keynes emphasized liquidity preference as necessitating the payment of interest (*The General Theory of Employment, Interest, and Money,* London: Macmillan, 1936, pp. 136–7, 145–6, 166–74, 202). Interest must be paid because people and institutions have the alternative of hoarding their monetary savings. Lord Keynes thought that a decline in interest set up expectation of a return to a higher level. The lower the rate of interest, the stronger the incentive to accumulate hoards, for every fall in the interest rate "reduces the current earnings from illiquidity, which are available as a sort of insurance premium to offset the risk of loss on capital account, by an amount

equal to the difference between the squares of the old rate of interest and the new" (*ibid.*, p. 202). As Sir Dennis Robertson was prompt to point out, Lord Keynes came near to saying that interest exists because it is expected to differ in magnitude from what it is (D. H. Robertson, *Essays in Monetary Theory*, London: King, 1940, p. 25). An improved statement of the liquidity theory of interest is that interest cannot decline below a minimum because of the alternative of hoarding but that any rate above this minimum is adequate to induce dishoarding if higher future rates are not anticipated and if other circumstances are favourable. With justice Sir Dennis scolded Lord Keynes for failing to note that the rate of interest must in equilibrium satisfy both the "marginal convenience of holding money" and the "marginal inconvenience of refraining from consumption." Sir Roy Harrod noted that the borrower "will have to pay the price necessary to satisfy the lender in his capacity of waiter or the price necessary to satisfy him in his capacity of parter with liquidity, whichever is higher. There seems to be the assumption in Keynes that the second will be the higher" (*Towards a Dynamic Economics,* London: Macmillan, 1948, p. 70). Conversely, because of their assumption of flexible wages and prices, classical and Austrian economists saw no need for the liquidity preference theory of interest.

C. Regardless of the emphasis in their theory of interest, all economists recognize productivity or yield of capital as a determinant of interest. Much confusion, however, results from the intermingling of static and dynamic analysis. Both Schumpeter and Böhm-Bawerk pointed out that it was *value* productivity, not physical productivity, that mattered. Schumpeter, in his *Theory of Economic Development* (Cambridge, Mass.: Harvard University Press, 1934), pointed out that if there were no new technical changes or disturbance, and the process of capital accumulation continued uninterruptedly, the prospect of a marginal value product would disappear. He denied that there would be any reason for time preference in the resulting riskless equilibrium or "stationary state." F. H. Knight also maintained that without continual growth and change there would be no reason for Böhm-Bawerk's time preference; thus he said Böhm-Bawerk, despite his frantic denials, *had* a productivity theory. Knight, however, argued that Schumpeter's stationary state was an impossibility, in theory anyhow, as there are no "limits on the use of capital" (see F. H. Knight, "Interest," in E. R. A. Seligman [ed.], *Encyclopedia of the Social Sciences,* New York: The Macmillan Co., vol. VIII, 1932, p. 134). Any actual stationary society would be the result of "non-economic" or sociological forces (F. H. Knight, "Capital, Time and the Interest Rate," *Economica,* vol. I, new series, 1934, pp. 257–86; "The Quantity of Capital and the Rate of Interest," *The Journal of Political Economy,* vol. XLIV, 1936, pp. 433–53, 612–42). One can forget the controversy about zero interest and still concede that innovation can keep interest above the minimum which the time preferences of savers require. Interest is an alternative cost of consumption, and, when it is above the necessary minimum, savers can simply examine the existing rate and report it as their rate of time preference though a lower return would suffice. Shifts in the schedule of the marginal efficiency of investment also affect interest via induced changes in the demand for liquidity (D. McC. Wright, "The Future of Keynesian Economics," *American Economic Review*, vol. XXXV, 1945, pp. 292–3; also D. McC. Wright, *The Keynesian System*, New York: Fordham University Press, 1962).

Productivity theories of interest thus reflect the fact that in a free enterprise economy the motive for borrowing is in anticipation of return from investment. While a socialist state might figure costs differently and have different value scales, it also would need to consider returns for rational planning. But those who presented the cases for time preference and liquidity preference did great service for they showed that a simple productivity theory was never complete in itself.

Fewer and fewer economists now subscribe to any one of the extreme positions represented by Böhm-Bawerk, Keynes, or Schumpeter. On an empirical level one recognizes the influence of at least three dimensions: profit prospects from technical change, etc., liquidity preference, planned saving. To this may be added time preference. The majority conclusion is thus apt to be substantially that of D. Patinkin, "that interest exerts its influence in all markets and that, in particular, it operates simultaneously on the 'threefold margin' of time preference (consumption decisions), marginal productivity of capital (investment decisions), and liquidity preference..." (*Money, Interest, and Prices*, Evanston, Ill.: Row, Peterson, 1956, p. 267).

6

National Income
Accounting and Determination

The Generation of Income and Definitions of Concepts

The Equation of Exchange truism discussed earlier used four variables to show the identical relationship between money expenditures for goods and services and the money receipts obtained for those goods and services during some interval of time, say, one year. The "national income" view of the same process is also a truism. In place of the variables M, V, R, and P used in the Equation of Exchange, the income approach uses "spending" variables — consumption, investment, saving, and income. All of these concepts are two-dimensional; that is, they are *flows* of goods and services measured over some interval of time, ordinarily one year.

This approach to the spending process can be illustrated in the following manner. Assume an economy that includes a labor force of 1,000 people, all of whom are gainfully employed. In conjunction with 100 units of capital (including land), all of which is owned by the people in the labor force, a national product of 100,000 units of goods and services is generated. These goods and services are sold at constant prices of, say, one dollar per unit.[1] The value of the total product, or Gross National Product, is therefore $100,000 per year. If the economy also contains 50,000 units of money, each unit of which is a dollar, the income velocity of money is "2" per year.

---

[1] Each "unit" of goods and services is one "slice" of the composite "loaf" discussed in Chapter 1.

The community produces the total of goods and services and buys it back as well; otherwise, it would not have been produced in the first place. But in an interdependent economy that uses money, the product need not be purchased immediately with the money received as income. Money may be hoarded in the same way that goods and services may be stockpiled. However, the additional utility of stockpiling a particular good is offset eventually by the cost of storage and the increasing attractiveness of exchanging it for other things to satisfy household or business functions. The cost of storing money and the possibility of obtaining alternatives in the form of goods and services also eventually cause dishoarding of money.

Income analysis couches spending behavior in terms of "spending decisions." *Consumption spending results from individual decisions that lead to the disbursement of current annual income for those goods and services that render final utility in satisfying human wants.* It is a direct function of income. Assume that consumption absorbs $80,000 of the total product generated in the current year.[2]

Rather than spend all their incomes in fulfilling current needs, some people prefer to purchase goods that render services for periods longer than the current production year. Since these items are not used up currently, *they become additions to the stock of wealth or capital,* that is, to the stock of things that yields services or products in future years.[3] Expenditure on such goods is *investment.* Assume that the remaining $20,000 of total product is absorbed by investment spending.

People who divert current income to those products not immediately consumed must make provision for such expenditures. They can do so only by not consuming their own income or by borrowing the unconsumed income of other people. *This rather negative process of not consuming current income is called saving.* It is distinguished from investment because the two acts may be performed by different people for different reasons. However, if an individual does not consume his own income and at the same time uses this unconsumed income to build new equipment that will yield product in future years, he is saving his own income and investing this income concurrently. If he borrows the income from someone else who has not consumed, the investing and saving functions are specialized. Nonetheless, the total of investment spending must equal the total of saving because of the way each is defined: *Any addition to the existing stock of capital made from current income must be income that was not consumed; and any part of the total*

---

[2] Unless otherwise specified, the "current" production period will always be one year. All incomes or products, therefore, are calibrated in terms of annual rates.

[3] The common difference between "wealth" and "capital" is a loose distinction between those goods that are owned without necessarily contributing in direct fashion to the production of more goods or services and those goods that do so contribute. This distinction has no place in rigorous analysis. Even the most "frivolous" of wealth items, such as art objects, yield the "income" of utility to their owners and anyone else who looks at them.

product not consumed in the current year must, by some means or other, become an addition to the net stock of capital. A businessman may find that his inventory of unsold goods increases during the year. This change, unwitting as it may be, is an investment by him of the additional goods that are added to inventory. It is also saving because the additional inventory is product that is not consumed. In the example cited above, the $20,000 per year of investment spending must be matched by $20,000 worth of current income (product) not consumed, that is, saving. If Y is income, C is consumption, I is investment, and S is saving, equilibrium exists when total income (product) equals total spending (consumption plus investment). This relationship may be expressed as follows:

$$Y = C + I$$

Saving is defined as income or product not consumed:

$$S = Y - C$$

Therefore, saving must equal investment:

$$S \equiv I$$

The "typical" investor may be thought of as an ambitious entrepreneur who has the ability and imagination to make productive use of new capital. Unfortunately, his current income is insufficient for financing the volume of investment he would like to make. The "typical" saver is a retired widow with more income than her modest needs demand, and with no particular incentive or ability to augment society's stock of productive capital. On the advice of an intermediary, such as an investment counselor, or any of many kinds of bankers, she may make available to the entrepreneur the income she does not consume (her saving).[4] For this service she may ask for a fixed dollar income claim, in which case the entrepreneur would offer her a bond and a banker would give her a time or demand deposit; or she may prefer a claim on the residual income that the new capital will generate, in which case the entrepreneur would give her a common stock share in his enterprise. In any case the young entrepreneur's net investment in new capital must equal the saving which the widow has made available.

The flow of saving must equal the flow of investment at any particular instant or over any period because of the way the two flows are accounted as identities. However, the "ex-ante, ex-post" issue must be resolved before an equilibrium can exist. A discrepancy may exist between *planned* saving and *planned* investment. Saving anticipated before the fact of investment may be more or less than realized saving after planned investment spending has either stimulated or retarded total spending. Only when planned saving equals

---

[4]If she saves by taking out a deposit claim on a bank, the bank becomes the agent for channeling her saving to a would-be investor.

planned investment does an income flow become one that has no tendency to change and thus become an *equilibrium* flow.

The equilibrium flow of income was also seen in the Equation of Exchange when *MV* equaled *PR*. The income analyst argues that these products of single variables do not distinguish the motives that provoke spending on consumption goods and services from the motives that cause spending on investment goods, or from either of these types of spending motivation and the incentive to save. He also believes that the decisions made by people in determining the magnitude of these flows are more critical and more pertinent to the determination of total spending and the employment of resources (particularly labor) than are the variables in the Equation of Exchange. Investment he sees as the primary determinant of total spending and income, while consumption and saving in turn are largely determined by income. Investment spending is seen as "exogenous"; that is, it is generated or initiated by sociopsychological factors that may be rational or irrational, but they are factors that are "outside" the economic system. Expectations, confidence, apprehension, uncertainty, and the like are the keynotes to investment.

The Multiplier

In the simple example cited above, full employment of resources and equilibrium flows of income and spending have been assumed. Now, for whatever psychological reasons that might be appropriate, let investment spending decline to, say, $10,000 per year with no offsetting or compensating increase in consumption spending.[5] Investment is one part of expenditures, so total expenditures and total income decline to $90,000 per year. But this decline in income has ramifications for spending in the next short time period because consumption spending is assumed to depend on income. If consumption changes by, say, 0.6 and planned saving by 0.4 of the change in income, consumption expenditure then becomes $74,000 per year and planned saving declines to $16,000 per year. Total income, being the total of consumption plus investment, becomes $74,000 per year + $10,000 per year = $84,000 per year. This income value is yet another $6,000 per year less than that of the preceding period; and consumption spending must then fall to $80,400 per year, while planned saving becomes $14,400 per year. The essence of this process is that decisions to save exceed decisions to invest at every income level until the *n*th. At this income and expenditure level ($75,000 per year) planned saving again equals planned investment with no tendency for change. Figure 6.1 and accompanying Table 6.1 summarize this process.

[5]In terms of the quantity theory, this reduction in spending—or a reduction in any kind of spending—is a reduction in the velocity of money, or an increase in hoarding.

Table 6.1. Hypothetical Components of Income and Expenditure Given a Decrease in Investment (dollars per year)

Period	Expenditures (consumption plus investment)	Consumption	Investment (planned and actual)		Saving (planned)	Saving (actual)	Income
1st	100,000	80,000	20,000	=	20,000	20,000	100,000
2nd	90,000	30,000	10,000	$\neq$	20,000	10,000	90,000
3rd	84,000	74,000	10,000	$\neq$	16,000	10,000	84,000
4th	80,400	70,400	10,000	$\neq$	13,600	10,000	80,400
5th	78,240	68,240	10,000	$\neq$	12,160	10,000	78,240
...	...	...	...		...	...	...
...	...	...	...		...	...	...
nth	75,000	65,000	10,000	=	10,000	10,000	75,000

Figure 6.1. Determination of Equilibrium Income by Consumption, Saving, and Investment

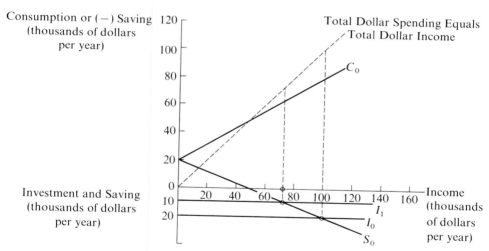

The decline in investment spending, brought about originally by any number of possible circumstances external to the other variables in the system, induces a multiple decrease in total income because every decrease in income causes a corresponding decline in consumption. Less consumption means that expenditures (and hence income) in the next period will be less. Each change in income is assumed to provoke a change in consumption spending that is 6/10 the change in income, the remaining 4/10 being a change in saving. In the language of the income analyst, the *marginal propensity to consume (MPC)* is 0.6 and the *marginal propensity to save (MPS)* is 0.4. The total change in spending is, first, the original decline in investment of $10,000 per year, plus 6/10 of this amount, or $6,000 per year, plus 6/10 of $6,000 per year, and so on. The total decline in income may be summarized thus:

$$\$10,000 + \left[\left(\frac{6}{10}\right) \cdot 10,000\right] + \left[\left(\frac{6}{10}\right)^{2} \cdot 10,000\right]$$

$$+ \left[\left(\frac{6}{10}\right)^{3} \cdot 10,000\right] + \cdots + \left[\left(\frac{6}{10}\right)^{n} \cdot 10,000\right]$$

where n becomes as large as desired, so that $(6/10)^{n}$ approaches zero. This expression is of the general form

$$\Delta Y = \sum_{n=0}^{n=\infty} (k^{n} \cdot \Delta I)$$

where k is the marginal propensity to consume and ΔI is the original change in investment. As n becomes very large, the expression approaches

$$\Delta Y = \frac{\Delta I}{(1 - k)}$$

In Figure 6.1, Y_{o} is the original equilibrium income. After the fall in investment, equilibrium income declines to Y_{1}, a level not compatible with full employment. Since $(1 - k)$ is $(1 - MPC)$, or simply MPS, the total change in income is equal to the change in investment divided by the marginal propensity to save:

$$\Delta Y = \frac{\Delta I}{MPS}$$

The expression $1/MPS$ is frequently referred to as the "multiplier." In the example here, ΔI is $10,000 and the MPS is 0.4. Thus, the multiplier is 2½ and ΔY is $25,000. Clearly, the smaller the marginal propensity to save, the larger the multiplier: The smaller the change in saving resulting from a change in income, the greater the ramifications a change in investment spending has on consumption spending.

No fault of logic can be found in this commonly held view of national income determination. If the explicit and implicit assumptions hold, a change in investment spending changes total income by some multiple. More important than the change in money income is the corresponding change in the employment of resources that accompanies a change in income. If full employment was obtained when income was generated at the rate of $100,000 per year, the income analyst sees employment falling significantly when income falls by 25 percent. In terms of the Equation of Exchange, this conclusion implies an independent change in V, the velocity of money, due to the assumed decline in investment spending. The change in velocity causes a decline in R, the Gross National Product, due to the effect on employment. A decline in one form of spending without compensation in some other form of spending necessarily implies a decline in the velocity of money. Income determinists see velocity fluctuating erratically, with all of the variations affecting money income and the level of employment.

The Accelerator

Income analysis also makes use of a concept known as "the accelerator." Where multiplier analysis is used to estimate the impact of investment spending on income, the accelerator analysis allows for an independent increase in consumption spending that *accelerates* the ordinary pace of investment.

Consider, for example, the hypothetical economy noted above in the multiplier analysis. When last observed, this economy was floating along at less-than-full-employment equilibrium with expenditure and income of $75,000 per year, consumption of $65,000 per year, and net investment and saving of $10,000 per year. Suppose that the total product of $75,000 per year requires a capital stock of 75 machines in addition to the labor force, and that five machines are replaced each year. This replacement rate implies that each machine lasts fifteen years. If labor and capital combine in fixed proportions to generate the total product, a machine is required for every $1,000 worth of product. Now, let a sudden surge in general demand, due basically to an independent increase in consumption, stimulate total product to a value of $100,000 per year. The economy needs 25 new machines in addition to the normal replacement of five machines. The investment demand, therefore, would be for a total of 30 machines rather than for the usual five. A 33 percent increase in general product demanded accelerates to a 500 percent increase in investment goods. In the following year, replacement demand would fall back again to five machines plus whatever part of the 25 new machines wear out during that year.

Accelerator theory is used most often as an explanation of cyclical swings in business activity. The surge in investment spending during the first year would result in successive damped surges in subsequent periods when the 25 extra machines came to be replaced.

When accelerator theory is used in analyzing spending for the economy in general, it is most often applied to the case in which total spending and income are extremely low with much unemployment, and in which net investment is virtually zero or even negative.[6] The U.S. economy during 1933–1934 is a possible example. From 1929–1933, national income fell from $88 billion to $40 billion per year. Gross private domestic investment declined from $16 billion to $1 billion per year, and net investment in 1933–1934 was estimated to be $–4 billion per year. These data imply that virtually all income was consumed and that investment spending was at a standstill or even negative.

If the same path were now traveled in reverse, the increase of consumption by, say, 120 percent ($40 billion to $88 billion) would stimulate investment spending to increase by 1,600 percent ($1 billion to $16 billion). Assuming that the investment goods industries had adjusted to a new low-level equilibrium position in 1933–1934, the ferment of recovery involving roughly a doubling of consumption would have accelerated to a sixteen-fold increase in investment. However, no great amount of theory or evidence supports either an accelerator or a multiplier concept when the economy is at full employment. Even if an accelerator could be assumed as the result of a large increase in the stock of money, economic processes in the economy do not gear up to sixteen times their normal rate in one year only to grind back down again the next year. This pattern would be too uneconomical for the industries involved. Business firms are not denuded of capital equipment by a recession. Far from it. As industrial activity improves, firms reemploy idle buildings and machinery just as they rehire unemployed workers. Furthermore, businessmen do not invest in a lot of new equipment if they have good grounds for believing that the surge in demand is temporary. They build output flexibility into their firms just to avoid this kind of problem.

Once something like an increase in the stock of money induces renewed spending in a depression, accelerators and multipliers may then have their impacts. New spending of any sort at a time of unemployed resources does not require an offsetting decrease in other spending. The new spending can generate demands to reemploy the unemployed factors of production and by this means generate increased real income. Both new investment and new consumption can then be "financed" by the new income.

An economy approaching full employment, however, is subject to a limitation of resources, which in turn means a limitation of real income. Further spending impulses of either a multiplier or an accelerator nature can only increase the price level component of national money income. These potential or realized price level increases inhibit spending (by means discussed earlier in Chapters 3 and 4). In addition, any kind of new spending in real terms at full employment must be compensated by a reduction in real spending in some other sector of the economy. Thus, analysis of aggregate spending and its ramifications may be very different for an economy at full employment than for one in a deep depression. A much later chapter (Chapter 26), makes some empirical examinations of spending for the U.S. economy at various time periods that include both full employment and depression.

---

[6]*Negative* investment implies that the community is using up its existing stock of capital by not maintaining and replacing it. By this means, capital can be consumed on net balance.

Selected Bibliography

Haberler, Gottfried. *Prosperity and Depression.* New York: Atheneum, 1963. Originally published by Harvard University Press as volume 105 of the Harvard Economic Studies.

Hansen, Alvin. *A Guide to Keynes.* New York: McGraw-Hill Book Co., 1953.

Knox, A. D. "The Acceleration Principle and the Theory of Investment: A Survey," *Economica,* New Series, Vol. 19 (August 1952), pp. 269–297, reprinted in M. G. Mueller, ed., *Readings in Macroeconomics.* New York: Holt, Rinehart and Winston, 1967, pp. 114–133.

Appendix:
Algebraic Formulation of Simple Keynesian Models

You may find the following exposition of simple national income models useful in understanding the attainment of equilibrium and factors causing changes in it. In simple Keynesian models equilibrium occurs when the aggregate demand for goods and services equals their aggregate supply. Aggregate demand comes from two sources: households and businesses. Household demand(consumption plans) depends upon many factors; $C = f$ (income, interest, wealth, prices, demographic factors, taste, etc.), but Keynes concluded that current real income Y was the most important one. Thus, $C = f(Y)$ with all of the other determinants of income held constant.[1] (See Figure 1.)

Figure 1

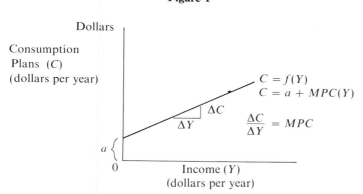

---

[1] In all of the following models prices are assumed to be constant unless otherwise noted. Also, these models are of a comparative static nature—they do not trace the continuous path of income changes through time.

If current income were to increase, consumption would also increase. The change in consumption divided by the change in income $\Delta C/\Delta Y$ is called the marginal propensity to consume (*MPC*); it is simply the slope of the consumption function. This is normally assumed to be less than 1 but greater than zero.[2] It should also be noted in the diagram that some consumption takes place when income is zero. This amount is designated a.[3]

. An algebraic notation of this line is $C = a + MPC\cdot Y$. Given the values for a and *MPC*, we can plug in any value for income and find the corresponding level of consumption. For example, if $a = 10$ and $MPC = \frac{4}{5}$, with income of 100, $C = 90$.

$$C = a + MPC\cdot Y$$

$$C = 10 + \left(\frac{4}{5}\right)(100)$$

$$C = 90$$

The other element of aggregate demand for goods and services is planned investment (*I*). Just as in the case of consumption, investment is a function of many variables—$I = f$ (marginal efficiency of investment, retained earnings, interest rates, business expectations, income, changes in income, etc.). We shall, however, assume that investment is constant. That is, $I = I_o$. If planned investment is 30, it will remain at that level regardless of changes in income (see Figure 2).

Figure 2

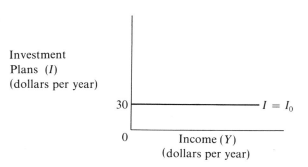

The other element of aggregate demand for goods and services is planned investment (*I*). Just as in the case of consumption, investment is a function of many

Adding together investment and consumption gives aggregate demand. In diagrammatic form it appears as shown in Figure 3,

---

[2] For simplicity's sake it is assumed that the function is linear.

[3] When income and output are zero, consumption can only take place through a reduction in the stock of capital—for example, a decline in inventories.

Figure 3

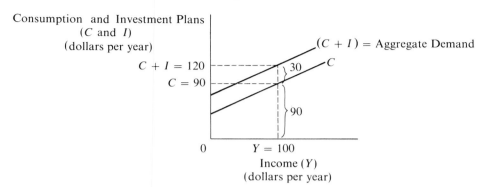

Consumption and Investment Plans
(*C* and *I*)
(dollars per year)

$(C + I)$ = Aggregate Demand

$C + I = 120$

$C = 90$

30

C

90

0

$Y = 100$
Income (*Y*)
(dollars per year)

and in tabular form as in Table 1.

Table 1

Y	C	I	C + I (aggregate demand)
0	10	30	40
100	90	30	120
200	170	30	200
300	250	30	280

The remaining element of our first simple model is aggregate supply. An easy way to derive it is to assume that businessmen respond to various expected levels of spending with equal amounts of output. Thus, if businessmen expect households and businesses to spend $100 for goods and services, businesses will produce $100 worth of goods and services. If total spending of $200 is expected, output of $200 will be forthcoming (see Figure 4). Aggregate supply becomes a line that intersects each axis at a 45° angle.

Now we are ready to combine aggregate demand with aggregate supply. It should be noted that through the act of production, output, income of an equal amount is generated—that is, income = output ($Y = O$). The horizontal axis of income in Figure 3 is the same as the horizontal axis in Figure 4. The vertical axes are also equivalent; total expected spending is equal to consumption and investment plans. Figure 5 combines the two.

Where aggregate supply and aggregate demand cross, at $200, equilibrium is found. At this point the demands of households and businesses are just being met by current output. If output were less, total demand would be greater than output supplied, inventories would be reduced, and signals would be sent to producers to increase output. Thus, income and output would rise to the equilibrium point. If

Figure 4

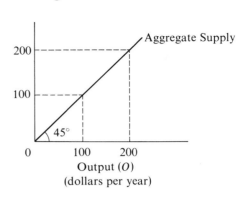

Total Expected
Spending
(dollars per year)

Output (O)
(dollars per year)

Figure 5

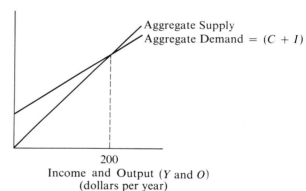

Total Expected Spending
(C and I)
(dollars per year)

Income and Output (Y and O)
(dollars per year)

income and output were greater than the equilibrium level, inventories would accumulate unintentionally and signals would be sent to trim production.

The elements discussed are sufficient to provide us with a simple algebraic model. Model IA:

(1) $Y = C + I$

(2) $C = a + MPCY$

(3) $I = I_o$

The first equation notes that in equilibrium aggregate supply, represented by Y, is equal to aggregate demand $(C + I)$. The second equation is the consumption function and the third the investment function. To solve these equations, the simultaneous method may be used. The variable we are seeking is the equilibrium level of income Y. The following steps may be used:

$$Y = C + I \qquad \text{(first rewrite the initial equation)}$$

$$Y = a + MPC \cdot Y + I_o \qquad \text{(second, substitute definitions as far as possible)}$$

$$Y - MPC \cdot Y = a + I_o \qquad \text{(third, move all } Y \text{ terms to the left-hand side of the equation)}$$

$$Y(1 - MPC) = a + I_o \qquad \text{(fourth, factor out } Y\text{)}$$

$$Y = \frac{a + I_o}{1 - MPC} \qquad \text{(fifth, isolate } Y\text{)}$$

This final equation is the equilibrium equation. By substituting in known factors, such as a, I_o, and MPC, we may derive the equilibrium level of income. For example, if $MPC = \frac{4}{5}$, $a = 10$, and $I_o = 30$,

$$Y = \frac{a + I_o}{1 - MPC}$$

$$Y = \frac{10 + 30}{1 - (\frac{4}{5})} = \frac{40}{\frac{1}{5}}$$

$$Y_e = 200$$

That is, the equilibrium level of income is 200.

Another simple model may be constructed by looking at the relationship between planned saving and investment. As discussed in Chapter 6, in equilibrium, savings plans and investment plans are equal ($S = I$). Saving is a function of the same determinants as consumption, but income is considered to be the most important one. Therefore, $Y - C = S$. A saving equation may be developed from this. (Also see Figure 6.)

$$S = Y - C$$

$$S = Y - (a + MPC \cdot Y) \qquad \text{(recalling that } C = a + MPC \cdot Y\text{)}$$

$$S = Y - MPC \cdot Y - a$$

$$S = (1 - MPC)Y - a$$

$$S = MPS \cdot Y - a \qquad \text{(recalling that } MPC + MPS = 1\text{)}$$

Model IB:

(1) $S = I$ (the equilibrium condition)

(2) $S = MPS \cdot Y - a$ (the saving schedule)

(3) $I = I_o$ (investment still constant)

Figure 6

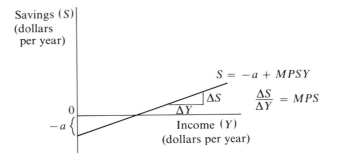

To solve the model, follow the same steps outlined for Model IA.

$$S = I$$
$$MPS{\cdot}Y - a = I_o$$
$$MPS{\cdot}Y = a + I_o$$
$$Y = \frac{a + I_o}{MPS}$$

or

$$Y = \frac{a + I_o}{1 - MPC}$$

which is the same equilibrium equation obtained from Model IA. Model IB is shown below in diagrammatic form.

Figure 7

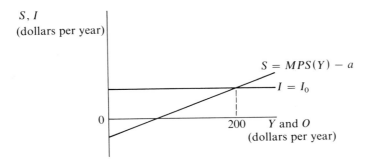

The impact of changes in investment, or a, may be readily seen in these models.[4] Assume that I_o increases from 30 to 40 (change of 10). There are two ways of finding

---

[4] A change in any of the determinants of C besides Y will cause the consumption function to shift— this is reflected in the model by a change in a.

the resulting change in the equilibrium level of income. First, the new level of investment may be placed in the equilibrium equation and the equation solved for the new equilibrium level: $(10 + 40) \div \frac{1}{5} = 250$. Then the old equilibrium level may be deducted from the new: $Y_e' - Y_e = \Delta Y_e$; $250 - 200 = 50$. A second method is as follows:

$$Y = \frac{a + I_o}{MPS}$$

$$\therefore \Delta Y = \frac{\Delta I_o}{MPS}$$

$$\Delta Y = \frac{10}{\frac{1}{5}}$$

$$\Delta Y_e = 50$$

The student should recognize that $1/MPS$ is the multiplier in this model (explained in Chapter 6).

Diagrammatically, in Model IA, aggregate demand would shift upward. In Model IB, investment would shift upward. (See Figure 8.)

Figure 8

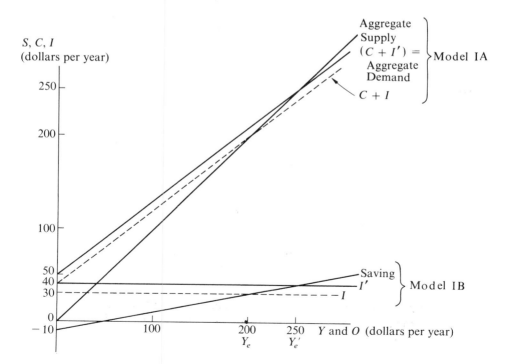

The introduction of government spending G and taxation Tx into the model allows the demonstration of the impact of fiscal policy. Model IIA:

(1) $Y = C + I + G$ (government spending is added to aggregate demand)

(2) $C = a + MPC{\cdot}Yd$ (consumption is now a function of disposable income)

(3) $Yd = Y - Tx$ (disposable income is income minus taxes)

(4) $G = G_o$ (government spending, taxes, and investment are all assumed to be constant)

(5) $Tx = Tx_o$

(6) $I = I_o$

Solving the model for the equilibrium equation:

$$Y = C + I + G$$
$$Y = a + MPC{\cdot}Yd + I_o + G_o$$
$$Y = a + MPC(Y - Tx_o) + I_o + G_o$$
$$Y = a + MPC{\cdot}Y - MPC{\cdot}Tx_o + I_o + G_o$$
$$Y - MPC{\cdot}Y = a + I_o + G_o + MPC{\cdot}Tx_o$$
$$Y(1 - MPC) = a + I_o + G_o - MPC{\cdot}Tx_o$$
$$Y = \frac{a + I_o + G_o - MPC{\cdot}Tx_o}{1 - MPC} \quad \text{or} \quad Y = \frac{a + I_o + G_o - MPC{\cdot}Tx_o}{MPS}$$

Given:

$$a = 10 \qquad I_o = 30$$
$$MPC = 0.8 \qquad Tx_o = 50$$
$$G_o = 60$$
$$Y = \frac{a + I_o + G_o - MPC{\cdot}Tx_o}{MPS}$$
$$Y = \frac{10 + 30 + 60 - (0.8)(50)}{0.2}$$
$$Y_e = 300 \quad \text{(the equilibrium level of income)}$$

The impact of changes in government spending or taxation may be found by substituting their new level into the equation or by examining the impact of their changes, as follows:

$$\Delta Y = \frac{\Delta G_o}{MPS} \quad \text{or} \quad \left(\frac{1}{MPS}\right)(\Delta G)$$

where $1/MPS$ is the government spending multiplier.

$$\Delta Y = \frac{-MPC(\Delta Tx_o)}{MPS} \quad \text{or} \quad \left(\frac{-MPC}{MPS}\right)(\Delta Tx_o)$$

where $-MPC/MPS$ is the taxation multiplier. Note that increases in taxation have a negative effect on income.

A similar model may be constructed around the savings-equal-investment relationship. Model IIB:

(1) $\quad S + Tx = I + G$

(2) $\qquad S = MPS{\cdot}Yd - a$

(3) $\qquad Yd = Y - Tx$

(4) $\qquad G = G_o$

(5) $\qquad Tx = Tx_o$

(6) $\qquad I = I_o$

$$S + Tx = I + G$$
$$MPS{\cdot}Yd - a + Tx_o = I_o + G_o$$
$$MPS(Y - Tx) - a + Tx_o = I_o + G_o$$
$$MPS{\cdot}Y - MPS{\cdot}Tx_o + Tx_o - a = I_o + G_o$$
$$MPS{\cdot}Y + (1 - MPS)Tx_o - a = I_o + G_o$$
$$MPS{\cdot}Y + MPC{\cdot}Tx_o - a = I_o + G_o$$
$$MPS{\cdot}Y = a + I_o + G_o - MPC{\cdot}Tx_o$$
$$Y = \frac{a + I_o + G_o - MPC{\cdot}Tx_o}{MPS}$$

In these models increases in government spending, reductions in taxation, or some combination of the two can be shown to have a positive impact on the equilibrium level of income, output, and employment. These are essentially "Keynesian" solutions to a depressionary period in which the economy has stabilized at less than full employment.

7

National Income Determination: The Money and Commodity Markets

Money in National Income Analysis

The simple version of national income analysis, as described in Chapter 6, neglects or denies the necessity for a stock of money as a prime mover in determining spending of any sort. Money is a necessary medium for carrying out spending decisions, but it is not necessary in determining those decisions.

The more sophisticated and complete model of income analysis, however, allows money to be a partial determinant of one type of spending—that of investment. The means by which money may have an effect on investment spending is by its prior effect on interest rates through the liquidity preference function. This relationship may be described as follows. Assume a liquidity preference schedule that shows the alternative quantities of money units held on average over time at various possible interest rates for high quality, fixed dollar securities. This schedule is a demand for money, but it applies only to "asset" money—that part of the money stock held for precautionary or speculative purposes. Furthermore, the various quantities of money held are functions of rates of return on something else—for example, "safe" securities such as short-term government bills.

Figure 7.1. Rates of Anticipated Return on "Typical" Security

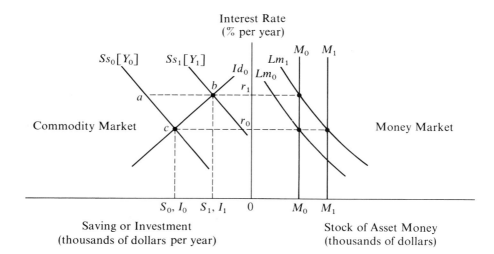

In Figure 7.1, Lm_0 and Lm_1 are liquidity preference functions; M_0 and M_1 are alternative stocks of money held for asset purposes; Ss_0 and Ss_1 are saving supply schedules shown as functions of rates of interest on high-grade bonds; and Id_0 is an investment demand schedule assumed here to be an inverse function of interest rates.

To say that an investment schedule, such as Id_0, is a negative function of some sort of "average" interest rate structure, and that a saving schedule, such as Ss_0 or Ss_1, is a positive function of an "average" interest rate structure, is not to deny the possible effects of other factors—most notably income. (To show the effects of income, the entire curve must be shifted—for example, from Ss_0 to Ss_1.) Nonetheless, both experience and reason suggest that interest rates have the kind of influence depicted here, other things being constant.

Figure 6.1 did not allow the saving and investment functions to depend on interest rates; investment was "exogenous," and saving was a linear function of income. In this more complete approach, the saving schedule Ss_0, while a positive function of interest rates, is also seen to be defined as it is only when income is at Y_0. If income shifts to Y_1 (a lower level of income), the alternative flows of saving at various interest rates must be correspondingly less. A similar condition holds true for the investment demand schedule Id_0. It is constructed here as a function of "exogenous" factors and of interest rates. If anticipations of profitable investments improve, the Id_0 schedule would shift out further from the origin. Income also could influence investment positively, as it does saving. However, to include this possibility would needlessly complicate the analysis.

Figure 7.1 is made to correspond with the simple model of a national income economy posed earlier by letting the intersection of S_0 and I_0 equal $20,000 per year. M_o, the stock of money available for asset purposes, might have a value of $5,000 when the total money stock is $50,000. This part of the money stock is seen as an asset; it is not spent on ordinary consumer goods and services but is held as a potential substitute for other financial assets.

The economy is at a full employment level of income. To get to a less than full employment equilibrium, the flows of investment and savings must be reduced, or in the language of the quantity theory the velocity of money must be less. In order for the velocity of money to decline, liquidity preference must shift to the right (increase). If the new liquidity preference schedule is Lm_1, people are more interested in holding the existing stock of money than they were and correspondingly less eager to hold securities. However, they cannot take money from their transactions balances because these balances are needed to consummate all ordinary exchanges. The interest rate on securities in the money market is forced up to r_1, a rate at which the existing flow of saving tends to be greater than the flow of planned investment.

The attempt to increase the flow of saving and the desire to increase cash balances, although complementary forms of behavior to the individual, are not the same thing and should not be confused. An increase in saving is a reduction of consumption spending; increased hoarding is diminished spending in general. Of course, the attempt to save more *must* result in increased cash balances if, but only if, investment spending is considered a datum as the income theorists assume it is. At the rate r_1 people wish to save at the point a on the Ss schedule, but the flow of investment spending is only b. Investment spending is reduced, triggering the multiplier. Income falls, causing a reduction in the alternative flows of saving at various interest rates. When the saving schedule falls to Ss_1 at income flow Y_1, a new equilibrium is obtained in the investment market at a saving investment flow of S_1, I_1. The vehicle for getting the saving schedule back to a position that ensures equilibrium is the reduction in income. If the old equilibrium level of income promoted full employment, the new income level necessarily allows less. It is seen as income Y_1 in Figure 6.1. (The saving investment value S_1, I_1 in Figure 7.1 corresponds to the intersection of S_o and I_1 in Figure 6.1.)

Sometimes the attempt by individuals to save more, which may end either in less saving due to the income decline or in the same amount of saving due to the constancy of investment, is known as "the paradox of thrift." A paradox is defined as "a statement seemingly self-contradictory, and yet explicable as expressing a truth." In this case, the mass attempt to be more thrifty results in less total saving. The crux of the matter is that the reduction in one kind of spending — consumption — reduces income and cannot be offset by increases in investment spending. Investment also would have declined either because it, too, was a function of income or simply because of the effect (shown in Figure 7.1) of higher interest rates.

The classical economists never recognized a "paradox of thrift." To them, a reduction in consumption spending — that is, an increase in saving — would lower interest rates, causing an increase in investment spending. In fact, the decline in interest rates would proceed until the increase in investment spending was just enough to make up for the decrease in consumption.

This conclusion is possible because the classical model allows investment spending to be determined "inside" the economic system. Both models, however, are perfectly logical. Furthermore, each may have some degree of explanatory power in assessing cause and effect in the real world. For example, one model may be more applicable in a severe depression and the other more realistic when business is prosperous.

The stock of money also has different effects in each system. If liquidity preference in the income model shifts to Lm_1 as described above, so that saving investment flows are reduced to S_1, I_1, and income is in turn reduced to Y_1, the overall stock of money may be increased by an amount sufficient to make M_1 the stock of asset money. Interest rates would then fall back to r_0, encouraging investment spending and increasing income via the multiplier. The saving schedule would shift back to Ss_0, and the S_0, I_0 position of saving and investment would again become equilibrium.

Full Employment or Less than Full Employment Equilibrium

The "revolutionary" aspect of the Keynesian system was its conclusion that full employment in a private enterprise market economy was capricious. It was no more probable than any of various states of unemployment and corresponding levels of business activity. Full employment especially was not an equilibrium condition. The particular equilibrium level of employment, flow of income, and state of business activity that would prevail would be determined by aggregate spending—consumption and investment spending, but particularly the latter. Such things as expectations of the future course of business activity and the future levels of interest rates were ultimate determinants of spending. Changes in the money stock could influence spending only to a limited extent. If business expectations were pessimistic enough, all increases in the stock of money simply would be hoarded by the public until some random event, or the belief that prices and interest rates could *not* go any lower, generated a resurgence of spending. Sometimes full employment might be achieved, but it would be accidental and short-lived.

The modern quantity theory brings in at this point of the argument the *real balance* effect.[1] This concept makes use of the movements of the level of prices, as determined by the system of private markets, on some existing stock of money. A price level by its inversion defines the value of each unit of money in a market economy. Therefore, households and firms would regard

---

[1] The classical theory has a necessary implication of the real balance effect in the quantity theory of money. Only in recent years, however, has the concept been made explicit.

an increase in their quantity of money as either an increase in real wealth or a quasi-capital–gains increase in income.[2] In either case the effect is the same: People would have too much money wealth and would wish to exchange some of it for other kinds of wealth. Or, if the new money is regarded as new income, it would be spent for consumption goods just as regular income is spent. These desired increases in consumption spending, given the flow of ordinary income currently being generated, necessarily reduce the amount of saving (so defined) out of given incomes. The saving schedule, therefore, can shift as far as necessary to promote a full employment flow of spending and income. If necessary, it can intersect the investment schedule at the point where net saving and net investment are *zero*! Under such circumstances, consumption spending would absorb total product. Since the stock of money can be increased by virtually infinite amounts at negligible costs, consumption spending can be made as large as required by monetary policy in order for full employment to be realized.

This situation can be described in the numerical example given in Chapter 6 as follows. If the full employment level of income is $100,000 per year and if investment drops to zero, increases in the stock of money can be used to induce consumption of the entire product of $100,000 per year. Net saving and net investment would then be zero, a position that has been described as "the classical stationary state." With no net investment the economy's net product and net income would be constant.

This same conclusion can also be obtained if, instead of allowing an increase in the stock of money at some given price level, a falling price level is imposed on a fixed nominal stock of money. Price levels that fall freely are less expedient to come by in practice than are increases in money stocks, the latter being a function of deliberate policy action by the central bank. Nevertheless, both means enable the real stock of money to be made as large as desired, and thus permit the consumption function to be shifted to the right as much as is necessary for a full employment level of income to be established.

In order for the real balance effect to be visualized completely, Figure 6.1 must be redrawn as Figure 7.2. Since consumption spending is now a function of the real value of cash balances, a multitude of consumption spendings are possible out of any given income. Two of these possibilities are shown. C_o is the consumption function of Figure 6.1. When investment shifted from I_o to I_1, income was reduced from the initial full employment flow, Y_o, to a less than full employment flow, Y_1. In Figure 7.2 the quantity of money and the price level are entered into the consumption and saving functions as the real stock of money M_o/P_o. Given the decline in investment to I_1, and income to Y_1 ($75,000), assume that the stock of money is increased to a value sufficient

---

[2] If the increase in the quantity of money is brought about by open-market purchases of the central bank, the total quantity of wealth may remain constant. Money would take the place of securities. In this case, the real balance effect is purely a liquidity effect. Because of money's unique transactive properties, such a substitution would be no less conducive to additional spending.

Figure 7.2. Determination of Equilibrium Income by Consumption, Saving, Investment, and the Real Stock of Money

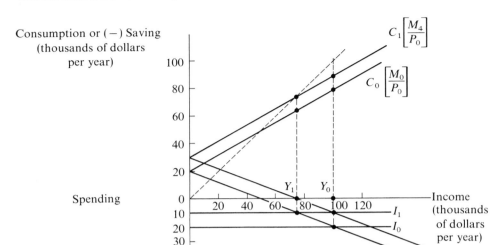

to provoke additional consumption spending to make up for the decline in investment. Let this value for the stock of money be M_4.[3] The new consumption function is C_1 and the corresponding saving function is S_1. The equilibrium intersection of S_1, I_1 is now at income Y_0, a full employment value.

The income theory cannot include the real balance effect because it eschews any real effects of price level changes on the economy. In fact, income theorists have never made the price level determinate, and many of them have scarcely acknowledged its existence. The implicit assumption is that the level of prices never makes any real difference. Declines in prices, according to this view, can exert no incentive toward increased spending because wage and salary incomes and consumption spending all decline together. Another, more rigid approach is the presumption that all money prices are completely flexible upward but are completely inflexible downward. The most casual sort of empirical observation disproves this opinion.

Since money prices are presumed either inflexible or indeterminate but generally of little consequence by income theorists, the influence of price level changes on the nominal quantity of money is not an issue with them. The quantity theorist grants the irrelevance of whether the price level is at "100" or "200." The important effect, he argues, is how a *change* in the price level

---

[3]The price level has been assumed constant at P_0. In fact, of course, it would fall, thus enhancing the real value of the money stock by more than the increase in the nominal stock to M_4. No matter whether the price level falls or the stock of money is increased, the desired level of consumption spending can be achieved.

reacts on the nominal stock of money units. When the prices of all goods and services change in one direction, the price or value of money as measured by a price index inversion changes proportionally in the opposite direction. The quantity theorist argues that this effect (of real balances) is a prime mover of people's spending behavior, particularly consumption, but possibly also investment.

The income theorists' rebuttal is that the time period required for changes in real balances to effect spending is too long, and that the economy may be in a deep depression before this effect is realized. Usually, the effect is seen only as a declining price level on a given stock of money. This tack brings into question the competence of the money-creating agency—the central bank—and its ability to get new money into the economy. If the central bank permits or encourages a *decline* in the stock of money (as the Federal Reserve System did in the early 1930s), a real balance effect is hardly possible. A price level, no matter how flexible, is hard put to catch up (down!) with a nominal stock of money declining at the rate of 6 to 10 percent per year. Even when central bank policy moves in the right direction, the constraints of a fractional reserve commercial banking system may further inhibit positive changes in the quantity of money. These issues, however, involve principles of monetary policy and the efficacy of control over the money supply, a subject that is discussed in later chapters.

The I-S, L-M Analysis

The most sophisticated model of what generally may be labeled "the income theory of spending"[4] makes use of a two-market model that distinguishes between a determination of equilibrium in the "money" market and a similar process in the "commodity" market. The common variables in each market for which equilibrium values must be determined are average rates of interest and corresponding levels of money income. The presumption is that various possible rates of interest are compatible with various possible levels of money income and money spending, depending upon the values of the determinants or "parameters" in each market. This result may be grasped more readily through diagrammatic analysis of each market.

The money market, described by Figure 7.3, contains the total stock of money divided into asset and transaction components by asset and transaction

---

[4]The "income theory of spending," in contrast to the "quantity of money theory of spending," may be thought of as initiated by Keynes, then developed and refined by subsequent thinkers who approved the general idea. The particular variant discussed in this section was developed by John R. Hicks in his well-known article "Mr. Keynes and the 'Classics': A Suggested Interpretation," *Econometrica*, Vol. 5, No. 2 (April 1937), pp. 147–169.

demands. The asset demand for money is the liquidity preference function discussed earlier. It shows the alternative quantities of money held as assets at various possible rates of interest on other securities that could be thought of as assets competing with money for the favor of the investor. If interest rates are "high," the investor gives up money, with its zero or slightly negative yield (due to service charges on demand deposits), to obtain the positive-yield securities. This logical possibility defines a demand curve such as Dm_a. (This demand curve is swiveled around 180° from its usual position and has its origin on the *right* extremity of the horizontal axis.) The total stock of money is represented by the length along the horizontal axis between O and M_0, although M_0 should be regarded as the zero point or origin of the money stock. Given some demand for money as an asset Dm_a, and some total stock of money M_0, the amount of money held for asset purposes at interest rate r_0 is $M_0 - Mt_0$, or Ma_0.[5]

Figure 7.3. The Money Market

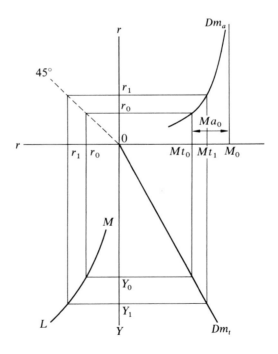

---

[5]This diagram is collapsed effectively from four quadrants to three quadrants by repeating interest rate values in the upper left-hand quadrant through the use of a 45° helping line.

The transactions demand is a passive function. It is similar in some respects to the unitarily elastic demand for money derived in Chapter 4, but it is fundamentally different in other respects. Its derivation is a sort of mechanical afterthought. At the beginning of an income period, the argument goes, the average income recipient has some plan of expenditures. To consummate this plan, he needs an average quantum of money during this period. The greater the anticipated volume of expenditure, the larger the transactions balances needed to carry out spending operations. For simplicity's sake, this relationship is assumed to be linear. That is, if a given amount of anticipated expenditure requires some quantity of money to effect transactions, twice as much anticipated expenditure would call for twice as much in transactions balances. This relationship is shown in the diagram by Dm_t, the transactions demand for money.

The fundamental difference between this function and the unitarily elastic demand for money lies in the implication of causality in each case. Here, spending is conceived *prior* to the determination of money holdings necessary to effect it. In the other case, money holdings largely determine the amount of spending that takes place.

The total money stock must be held by households and firms in the economy. Therefore, the two demands for money as conceived must exhaust the total stock of money and determine in the process the alternative money incomes compatible with various interest rates in financial or money markets. This last relationship is shown here as the *L-M* curve. It is constructed of coordinate points such as r_o, Y_o and r_1, Y_1. At these points the total stock of money M_o is divided between asset and transactions holdings as shown: At r_o, Y_o, asset money is $M_o - Mt_o$, and transaction money is Mt_o. At the higher interest rate r_1, less money is held for asset purposes ($M_o - Mt_1$) and necessarily more for transactions purposes (Mt_1). The greater amount held for transactions implies a higher anticipated level of spending in the first place. Thus, lower interest rates and lower levels of spending and higher interest rates and higher levels of spending are compatible with equilibria in this market.

The commodity market, sometimes called the saving investment market, makes use of a marginal efficiency of capital concept describing the alternative flows of investment spending that would occur at various interest rates. This curve is negatively sloped and is shown as *MEC* in Figure 7.4. At higher interest rates less investment spending would take place because of the necessarily greater internal rate of return that would need to be anticipated to cover the higher interest costs.

A saving schedule is another parameter. It is seen as a linear function of income beyond some minimal level. The saving function is shown as Ss_o in Figure 7.4.

From the definitions of consumption, saving, and investment, any determinate equilibrium requires that planned saving equal planned investment. Thus, at interest rate r_o, some amount of investment spending I_o takes place.

Figure 7.4. The Commodity Market

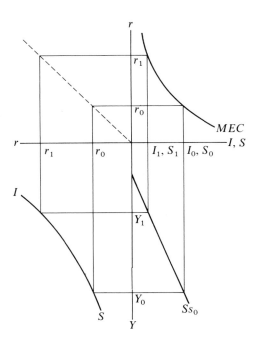

This amount of investment generates sufficient income, via the multiplier, to obtain a flow of saving S_o that equals it. The coordinates r_o and Y_o form a point of equilibrium in this market. Some other higher interest rate r_1 would discourage investment spending to the level I_1, income to Y_1, and savings to S_1. The combinations of points r_o, Y_o and r_1, Y_1 are possible equilibria in this market. These points form the *I-S* curve. By combining the *r-Y* axes of Figures 7.3 and 7.4, a complete equilibrium in both money and commodity markets can be seen at some such point as r_o, Y_o in Figure 7.5.

Figures 7.3, 7.4, and 7.5 include five determining parameters: (1) the marginal efficiency of capital *MEC*, (2) the saving-out-of-income function Ss_o, (3) the demand for money as an asset Dm_a, (4) the demand for money for transactions purposes Dm_t, and (5) a supply of money. Two common operations within this system might best show its efficacy as an engine of analysis. First, let the stock of money increase when the system is in its equilibrium state at r_o, Y_o. This change shifts the money supply point M_o to the right to some such value as M_2 (Figure 7.6) and necessarily restructures the *L-M* curve to L_2-M_2. Changes in interest rates and income now become pertinent. The magnitude and direction of possible changes depend on the time allowed for the change in the money supply to have its effects. Within a stable monetary environment, the first effect in the short run is probably a lowering of interest rates to r_2' while

Figure 7.5. Equilibrium in the Money and Commodity Markets

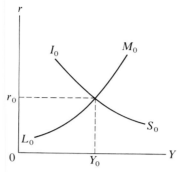

total spending and income stay constant at Y_0. The rationale of this conclusion is given in Chapter 4 in the original discussion of liquidity preference: The new money is more likely to be used to bid up security prices and to pay off debts, thereby lowering interest rates, than it is to extend overall spending. Assuming this extreme, the new interest rate–income position would be r_2',

Figure 7.6. The Money Market

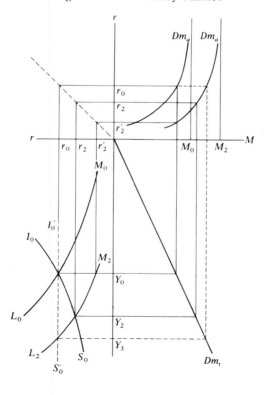

Y_0, a point that is not on the *I-S* curve as drawn.[6] The system is out of equilibrium. The lower interest rates in the money market, however, would encourage investment spending in the commodity market, the amount depending on the sensitivity of investment spending to interest rate changes. New investment spending would then increase total income through the agency of the multiplier, the multiplier's effect being a function of the slope of the saving parameter. The I_0-S_0 curve incorporates these two factors, and a final equilibrium of r_2, Y_2 is attained where the L_2-M_2 curve intersects the I_0-S_0 curve.

These new values indicate that the interest rate would decrease somewhat from its original value of r_0 and that total spending would increase. Whether any real factors change or not is unknown without further specifications because this model does not distinguish the price level and real output. Both are lumped together in Y. Neither does the model show the effect of new money on consumption. If the economy were operating at full employment and if the additional spending generated by the new money were in the old proportions of consumption and investment, real investment spending and real saving would not change. The I_0-S_0 curve would necessarily be vertical to the interest rate axis (I_0-S_0). All the new money would simply inflate the price level, and in this case would be reflected as an increase in money income to Y_3. This special case for this model is compatible with the way the quantity theorist would interpret matters. To argue otherwise is to postulate that an increase in the stock of money to some degree permanently lowers interest rates.

Another possibility is that the increase in money and spending encourages anticipations of further spending and higher prices. The parameter, Dm_a, would shift to the right (from its position in Figure 7.6), thus reducing money held as an asset and *increasing* the final value for the interest rate to something greater than r_0. Of course, income would also increase to some value greater than Y_3. This alternative is not within the realm of comparative statics. However, it is very possible in the real world after the economy has experienced several substantial and pervasive increases in the quantity of money.

Another common use made of the *L-M, I-S* model is to assess the effect of a shift of the marginal efficiency of capital in the commodity market. Assume again the stable equilibrium of Figure 7.5 with income Y_0 and interest rate r_0, and let this equilibrium be disturbed by a shift from MEC_0 to MEC_2, as seen in Figure 7.7. The new *MEC* curve calls as well for a shift of the I_0-S_0 curve to I_2-S_2. The points defining the I_2-S_2 curve, however, are equilibria for this market; they do not describe the process of adjustment from one set of equilibrium conditions to another.

Assume the shift from MEC_0 to MEC_2 is instantaneous due to some sort of "good news" in investment markets, such as government tax relief for corporations. The first reaction is likely to be a *desired* expansion of investment spending unmatched in the first instance by any corresponding flow of

---

[6]Of course, this point would be on *some* I-S curve, but not on the one constructed here.

Figure 7.7. The Commodity Market

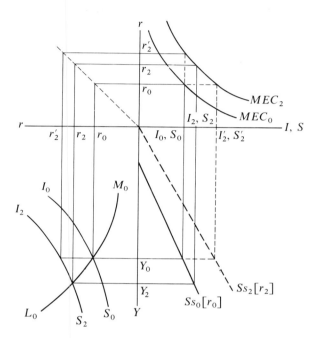

planned saving. The interest rate rises to r_2'. The necessary amount of planned saving is then generated by either or both of two possible reactions. First, if the flows of saving are sensitive to interest rates, the very increase in interest rates would itself induce increased saving flows out of given incomes. Such a reaction would require a shift in the saving function Ss_0 to some such value as Ss_2. If this shift in the saving function is large enough, which is to say that if the reduction in consumption spending is as large as the increase in investment because of a high sensitivity of saving to changes in interest rates, no further adjustments would be necessary. No increase in income would occur. Since the shift to MEC_2 would be matched exactly by the increase in the saving schedule to Ss_2, planned investment and planned saving would increase to I_2', S_2'. Interest rates would rise only infinitesimally, while consumption spending (not shown) would be reduced. This possibility is the one seen by the classical economists.[7]

Without any responsiveness of the saving function to interest rate changes, the immediate effect of the shift in the MEC curve would be an increase in

---

[7]This conclusion also would require that the change in the interest rate to r_2' have no effect on the demand for money in the money market. This aspect of the analysis also would be compatible with classical theory.

interest rates to r_2' while income would remain at Y_0. This value is not equilibrium. At this rate, asset money would leave its baliwick in the money market and seek securities in the investment market. The general increase in investment spending would trigger a multiplier, increasing income and, by this means, increasing the flow of saving along the Ss_0 curve until planned saving and desired investment again were equal at I_2, S_2. Income would stabilize at Y_2 and interest rates at r_2. These higher interest rates would have shifted just the right amount of asset money over to the transactions account to support spending and income at Y_2.[8]

How useful is the *I-S*, *L-M* analysis? The response depends on the criteria applied to what is "useful" in a theory. Generally, a theory is useful if it (1) can be given empirical content from the real world that in turn (2) endows it with the ability to predict the future reactions of present events, whether these events be planned policies or random happenings. The *I-S*, *L-M* analysis, while useful in some contexts, has some distinct shortcomings. First, it assumes money holdings are divided by the owners of this money into two compartments, one of which is dependent on a rate of return on *other* assets. It is similar to making some part of the total quantity of apples demanded depend upon the implicit rate of return obtained from other fruit. The other compartment contains transactions balances that have a functionless mechanical relation to total spending. Aside from the impossibility of getting information that would give an empirically satisfying measurement of the amounts in these two compartments, the question arises of whether such a concept is methodologically sound in the first place. All money is held for shorter or longer periods and for many mixed "reasons." The only universal reason for holding money is the purchasing power of a unit of it. Under this criterion all the "motives" can be collapsed. That is, when the purchasing power of a unit of money is cut in half by a doubling of the price level, it takes twice as much money to fulfill any of the motives—transaction, speculative, or precautionary. Furthermore, approaching the matter in this latter fashion immediately emphasizes the relationship between money and the price level, an issue that is completely neglected by the *L-M* scheme. Prices in this model are buried in income; and income, since it is a combination of both prices and real output, does not and cannot distinguish for the observer either prices or real output.

The commodity market section of the analysis also has its problems. Aside from the question of whether the saving function should have some interest elasticity is the question of how an *MEC* curve can be determined empirically. While some of these failings may be overcome by additional specifications in the model, it is still notably inadequate as useful theory.[9]

---

[8] In terms of the quantity theory, this change would be described as an increase in the overall velocity of money.

[9] For an extension of this system that includes a theoretical, albeit awkward, determination of prices and output, see Harry G. Johnson, "Monetary Theory and Keynesian Economics," in W. L. Smith and R. L. Teigen, eds., *Readings in Money, National Income, and Stabilization Policy* (Homewood, Ill.: Richard D. Irwin, 1965), pp. 32–43.

Selected Bibliography

Johnson, Harry G. *Money, Trade, and Economic Growth.* London: Allen and Unwin, 1962, pp. 107–126.

McKenna, Joseph P. *Aggregate Economic Analysis.* New York: Holt, Rinehart and Winston, 1966.

Pesek, B. P., and T. R. Saving. *Money, Wealth, and Economic Theory.* New York: Macmillan Co., 1967.

Appendix: Diagrammatic Treatment of I – S and L – M Curves and Algebraic Formulation

This section presents a different diagrammatic treatment of $I - S$ and $L - M$ curves as well as an algebraic formulation.

The Commodity Market

Continuing with Model IB as presented in the Appendix to Chapter 6, it is possible to relax the assumption that investment is constant and to make it a function of something. Part of Keynesian analysis is the response of investment, albeit an inelastic one, to changes in the rate of interest. If we assume a linear investment schedule, it may appear as in Figure 1. Our new investment equation

Figure 1

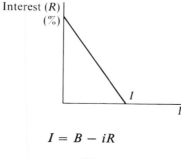

$$I = B - iR$$

or

$$R = \frac{B}{i} - \frac{1}{i}I$$

$$\frac{B}{i} = \text{vertical axis intercept}$$

$$-\frac{1}{i} = \text{slope of the line}$$

may be used in Model IB to form a new model. Model III, $I - S$ curve:

    (1) $S = I$
    (2) $S = MPS{\cdot}Y - a$
    (3) $I = B - iR$

Solution:

$$S = I$$
$$MPS{\cdot}Y - a = B - iR$$
$$MPS{\cdot}Y = a + B - iR$$
$$Y = \frac{a + B - iR}{MPS}$$

The equilibrium equation in this model is the $I - S$ curve. If we assume alternative rates of interest, we find corresponding levels of income that provide equilibrium in the commodity market. The equations that we have solved simultaneously above may also be solved in diagrammatic form (Figure 2).

Assuming an interest rate of R_1, we find that according to the investment schedule, investment of I_1 will take place. Tracing upward, we see that S must equal I, so

Figure 2

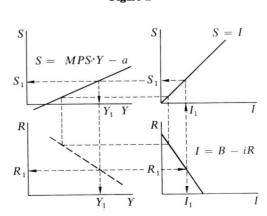

S_1 is found. Since $S = MPS\,Y - a$, income must be Y_1; finally, tracing to the diagram in the lower left-hand corner, we connect R_1 and Y_1. This provides us with a pair of values for interest and income that provide equilibrium in the commodity market. By repeating the process for alternative interest rates, a series of points is generated which, if connected, gives us the $I - S$ curve, shown in Table 1.

Table 1

R	I	S	Y
			$S = MPS \cdot Y - a$
			or, $Y = \dfrac{a + S}{MPS}$
	$I = B - iR$	$I = S$	or, $Y = \dfrac{a + B - iR}{MPS}$ (Model III)
0	20	20	150
2	16	16	130
4	12	12	110
6	8	8	90
8	4	4	70
10	0	0	50

Assuming:
$$MPS = \frac{1}{5}$$
$$a = 10$$
$$B = 20$$
$$i = 2$$

Relaxing a few assumptions, we may see the impact of changes in any of the parameters. For example, if business expectations improve, the investment schedule may shift to the right; that is, B may increase. If B increases to 30, we can see the result in Figure 3 and the equations below it.

Changes in the determinants of consumption—real balances, for example—can affect the $I - S$ curve, too. As discussed in Chapter 7, an increase in real balances will shift the consumption function up and the savings schedule down. A rightward shift in the $I - S$ curve results. In equation form a would be increased.

It is also possible to add government spending and taxation to this model. In the diagrams, government spending can be added to the investment function—this shifts the $I - S$ curve to the right, as does an increase in investment. Similarly, taxation can be added to the savings schedule. This shifts the $I - S$ curve to the left. Model IV, found in Figure 4 on p. 147 in algebraic and diagrammatic form, is but an expansion of Model III to include G and Tx (it is very similar to Model IIB).

Figure 3

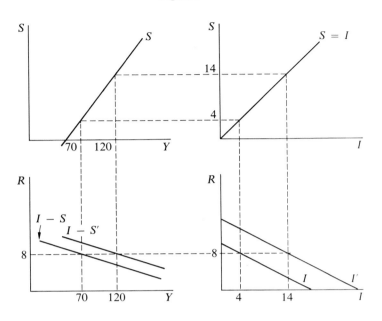

R	I	Y
0	30	200
4	22	160
8	14	120
10	10	100

$$Y = \frac{a + B - iR}{MPS}$$

$$\therefore \Delta Y = \frac{\Delta B}{MPS}$$

$$\Delta Y = \frac{10}{1/5}$$

$\Delta Y = 50$, at each rate of R

Assuming:

$$MPS = \frac{1}{5}$$

$$a = 10$$

$$B = 30$$

$$i = 2$$

(1) $\quad S + Tx = I + G$

(2) $\qquad S = MPS{\cdot}Yd - a$

(3) $\qquad Yd = Y - Tx$

(4) $\qquad Tx = Tx_o$

(5) $\qquad I = B - iR$

(6) $\qquad B = B_o$

(7) $\qquad G = G_o$

Solution:

$$S + Tx = I + G$$
$$MPS{\cdot}Yd - a + Tx_o = B_o - iR + G_o$$
$$MPS(Y - Tx) + Tx_o - a = B_o - iR + G_o$$
$$MPS{\cdot}Y - MPSTx_o + Tx_o - a = B_o - iR + G_o$$
$$MPS{\cdot}Y + MPCTx_o - a = B_o - iR + G_o$$
$$MPS{\cdot}Y = a - MPCTx + B_o - iR + G_o$$
$$Y = \frac{a - MPCTx_o + B_o - iR + G_o}{MPS}$$
$$\Delta Y = -\frac{MPC(\Delta Tx_o)}{MPS}$$
$$\Delta Y = \frac{\Delta G}{MPS}$$

Figure 4

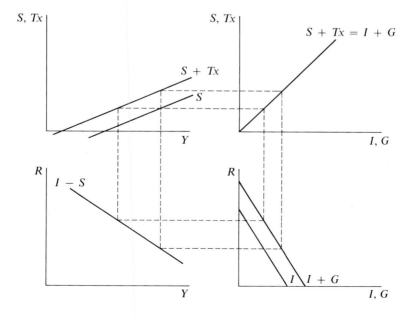

The Money Market

A money market model may be constructed around the demand for money L and the supply of money M. As discussed in Chapter 7, transactions demand L_t is assumed to be a function of income, $L_t = f(Y)$, and speculative demand L_s is assumed to be a function of interest R, $L_s = f(R)$. The combined demand for money can be represented as follows: $L = L_t + L_s$. The money stock is usually assumed to be constant, $M = M_o$. In equilibrium the demand for money and its supply are equal, $L = M$. This model is represented by Figure 5 and the equations following it.

Figure 5

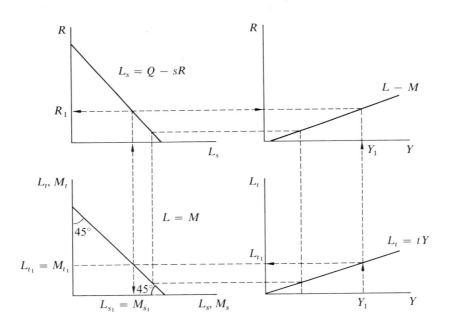

Model V, $L - M$ curve:

$$(1) \quad L = M$$
$$(2) \quad L = L_t + L_s$$
$$(3) \quad L_t = tY$$
$$(4) \quad L_s = Q - sR$$
$$(5) \quad M = M_o$$

Solution for income:

$$L = M$$
$$L_t + L_s = M_o$$
$$tY + Q - sR = M_o$$
$$tY = M_o - Q + sR$$
$$Y = \frac{M_o - Q + sR}{t}$$

Solution for interest:

$$L = M$$
$$L_t + L_s = M_o$$
$$tY + Q - sR = M_o$$
$$-sR = M_o - Q - tY$$
$$sR = Q - M_o + tY$$
$$R = \frac{Q - M_o + tY}{s}$$

Assuming an initial level of income Y_1, we can start in the lower right-hand diagram and locate the amount of transactions demand, L_{t_1}. Tracing to the left, we move into the diagram that represents both the money supply and the equality of the money supply and the demand for it. This line, at a 45° angle to each axis, shows that the money supply may be used to satisfy either speculative or transactions demand or some combination of the two. If M_{t_1} is being used to satisfy transactions demand, this leaves M_{s_1} for speculative demand. With speculative demand at L_{s_1} ($M_{s_1} = L_{s_1}$), interest must be at R_1. Projecting into the final diagram, we find a pair of values for interest and income that provide equilibrium in the money market. Continuing the process, we generate the $L - M$ curve. The $L - M$ curve is the money market equilibrium curve—the locus of all pairs of values of interest and income providing equilibrium in the money market.

Shifts in these functions may be shown in diagrammatic and algebraic form (see Figure 6). An increase in the money supply, perhaps caused by a desire on the part of monetary authorities to ease conditions, will shift the money supply curve to the right. This will, in turn, shift the $L - M$ curve to the right.

Figure 6

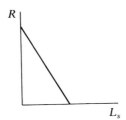

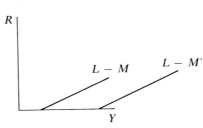

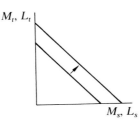

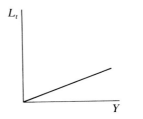

$$Y = \frac{M_o - Q + sR}{t}$$

$$\Delta Y = \frac{\Delta M_o}{t} \qquad \text{With } R \text{ constant an increase in } M_o \text{ will increase } Y.$$

or

$$R = \frac{Q - M_o + tY}{s}$$

$$\Delta R = \frac{-\Delta M_o}{s} \qquad \text{With } Y \text{ constant an increase in } M_o \text{ will decrease } R.$$

The last model in this appendix allows for a simultaneous solution of interest and income and provides a demonstration of the impact of monetary and fiscal policy. This is achieved by combining Model IV, the commodity market model, with Model V, the money market model. The algebraic solution is most easily obtained by first solving the money market equations for R, and then substituting that definition into the commodity market equations. Model VI, $I - S$ and $L - M$ curves is represented by the following equations:

$$
\begin{align}
(1) \quad & S + Tx = I + G \\
(2) \quad & S = MPS{\cdot}Yd - a \\
(3) \quad & Yd = Y - Tx \\
(4) \quad & Tx = Tx_o \\
(5) \quad & I = B - iR \\
(6) \quad & B = B_o \\
(7) \quad & G = G_o
\end{align}
$$

$$(8) \qquad L = M$$
$$(9) \qquad L = L_t + L_s$$
$$(10) \qquad Lt = tY$$
$$(11) \qquad Ls = Q - sR$$
$$(12) \qquad M = M_o$$

Solution:

$$R = \frac{Q - M_o + tY}{s} \quad \text{(see Model V)}$$

$$S + Tx = I + G$$

$$MPS{\cdot}Yd - a + Tx_o = G_o + B_o - iR$$

$$MPS(Y - Tx) + Tx_o - a = G_o + B_o - i\left(\frac{Q - M_o + tY}{s}\right) \qquad \text{(substitution)}$$

$$MPS{\cdot}Y - MPS Tx_o + Tx_o - a = G_o + B_o - \frac{iQ}{s} + \frac{iM_o}{s} - \frac{it\,Y}{s}$$

$$MPS{\cdot}Y + \frac{it\,Y}{s} + MPC Tx_o - a = G_o + B_o - \frac{iQ}{s} + \frac{iM_o}{s}$$

$$Y\left(MPS + \frac{it}{s}\right) = a + G_o + B_o - MPC Tx_o - \frac{iQ}{s} + \frac{iM_o}{s}$$

$$Y = \frac{a + G_o + B_o - MPC Tx_o - iQ/s + iM_o/s}{MPS + it/s}$$

By using this model, the impact of numerous changes can be traced. For example: fiscal policy changes:

$$\Delta Y = \frac{\Delta G}{MPS + it/s}$$

$$\Delta Y = \frac{-MPC(\Delta Tx_o)}{MPS + it/s}$$

monetary policy changes:

$$\Delta Y = \frac{i\Delta M_o/s}{MPS + it/s}$$

changes in the demand for money:

$$\Delta Y = \frac{-i\Delta Q/s}{MPS + it/s}$$

The important role of the slope of the investment schedule ($1/i$) and the speculative demand for money ($1/s$) may also be seen. In Keynesian models as the investment schedule becomes inelastic to interest rate changes (i approaches zero), monetary policy becomes ineffective. Adding a real balance effect to the savings schedule, however, would show that increases in M_o tend to increase a and allow monetary policy to work through shifts in the $I - S$ curve in addition to $L - M$ curve shifts. Similarly, the addition of a liquidity trap to the model where s approaches infinity would rob monetary policy of its effectiveness because interest rates would acquire a floor. Again, a real balance effect would overcome this.

Figure 7

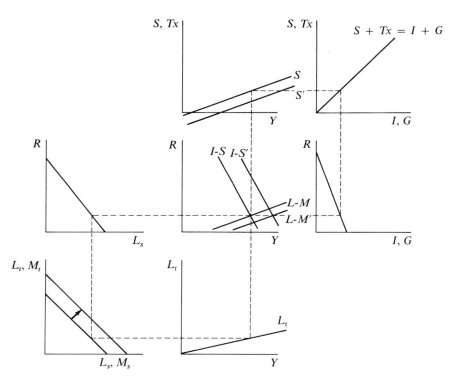

The student is encouraged to experiment with various changes in diagrammatic form. Also, if numerical values for the parameters are assumed, changes may be noted using equations.

Section Two

Commercial Banking

8

A Schematic Sketch of Fractional Reserve Banking

Development of Banking Corporations

Three institutions are responsible, directly or indirectly, for the creation of money in the United States. The Federal Reserve System and, to some extent, the United States Treasury Department determine what is called the "high-powered base" for the money stock, while commercial banks create most of the ordinary money used in day-to-day dealings as a result of their lending activities in pursuit of profits.

Society has accepted commercial banks as one way for borrowers to use the resources of lenders on mutually agreeable terms. Banks evolved in the Anglo-Saxon world primarily through the mediation of the goldsmiths in England during the sixteenth and seventeenth centuries. Successful merchants at times accumulated fairly large holdings of metallic coin; but unlike feudal barons, they lacked the means for keeping their treasure safely, so they delegated this function to goldsmiths, who had facilities for such purposes. Goldsmiths gave out receipts or notes that came to circulate as paper money equivalents to the gold itself. Eventually, some of the goldsmiths loaned out the gold or the notes at interest, keeping only a fraction of the gold as a reserve. When such an ancillary line of business became primary, the goldsmith had in fact become a banker.

Deposit Creation in a One-Bank Model

By the time the American economy was in its early stages, commercial banking was more than gold-smithing once removed. A bank was formed, typically, by a group of merchants who pooled their resources in order to incorporate a middleman institution that would act as a liaison between borrowers and lenders and that would earn a competitive return for its services. Ordinarily, the group applied at the appropriate governmental level for a charter. After they obtained it, the bank became a corporate body allowed to undertake banking operations.

To cast the scene in a present-day setting, imagine that ten businessmen each invest $10,000 cash (meaning legal tender currency) in this new enterprise and receive in return ten shares each of $1,000 par value stock. The balance sheet of the "Sound Money Bank Corporation" thus formed would be as shown in Table 8.1.

Table 8.1. Sound Money Bank Corporation*
(dollars)

Assets		Liabilities	
			0
		Net Worth	
Cash reserves	100,000	Capital	100,000
	Reserve ratio: ∞†		

* To keep this and subsequent balance sheets as simple as possible, furniture, fixtures, and other physical aspects of the bank are omitted.

† In this and all subsequent balance sheets, the stated reserve ratios are the actual reserve ratios, not the required ratios. The actual ratio is cash (and other) reserves/demand deposits. In this case the value for this expression is $100,000/0, or ∞.

At this point, the bank is nothing more than a legally proper organization. In an operational sense, it is not a bank; it has not yet created either loans for borrowers or deposits for depositors.

The directors of the bank, duly elected by the stockholders, are well aware that the only way for the corporation to earn income is for it to obtain interest-bearing assets by making loans to credit-worthy borrowers. Clearly, the bank does not "lend money"; it lends the control over resources (income) that the money represents. The stockholders are the (indirect) lenders; and since they exert no claims against the cash reserves—their claims being only against the residual income the bank earns—the bank can lend out all of its reserves without apprehension. In such an event the balance sheet of the bank would appear as in Table 8.2.

Table 8.2. Sound Money Bank Corporation
(dollars)

Assets		Liabilities	
			0
		Net Worth	
Cash reserves	0	Capital	100,000
Loans and discounts receivable in 30–60, 90 days	100,000		

$$\text{Reserve ratio:} \frac{0}{0}$$

This bank is still not a "typical" bank. It has loaned out at this point only the cash that was put into it. A typical bank would use the resources of other lenders and deposits that it creates itself in addition to the cash supplied by its stockholders. Indeed, the unique nature of commercial bank demand deposits distinguishes banks from all other corporations. Demand deposits are defined as fixed dollar claims payable in legal tender (or some other acceptable medium of exchange) on demand.

To demonstrate the process that gives rise to these deposits, assume that the Sound Money Bank receives another $100,000 in cash from households or business firms who accept in exchange demand deposit balances against which they can write checks. These deposits are called *primary* deposits. The balance sheet now appears as in Table 8.3.

Table 8.3. Sound Money Bank Corporation
(dollars)

Assets		Liabilities	
Cash reserves	100,000	Deposits	100,000
Loans and discounts	100,000		
		Net Worth	
		Capital	100,000

Reserve ratio: 100 percent

The bank may lend its new resources at interest in the same way it did the cash invested by stockholders, but it must take account of a new responsibility: Depositors, in contrast to stockholders, may demand cash at any time. The bank must therefore hold enough cash reserves to take care of such a contingency. The amount may be prescribed by law; but if banking is essentially a free enterprise, as it was in the United States between 1790 and 1860, the reserve proportion is left entirely to the discretion of the bank's directors.

When a person borrows money from a bank, bankers do not take cash from their vaults and hand it to the borrower. Instead, they open (or increase) a demand deposit (checking) account for the borrower in the amount desired. In turn, the borrower signs a promissory note, in which he promises to repay money to the bank after some interval of time and with some premium (interest) for the favor. In the absence of legal reserve requirements or an unusual demand for hand-to-hand currency, and if the Sound Money Bank Corporation is the only bank in existence (a single large bank), it would be able to create an infinite amount of asset loans and demand deposit money. Reserve requirements, however, are one constraint that limit potential monetary expansion. With, say, a reserve ratio of 20 percent, the bank must keep $0.20 in reserves for every $1.00 in deposit liabilities it faces. The total amount of deposits it could allow itself with this legal requirement and reserves of $100,000 would be $500,000. Its profit-seeking behavior would lead it to generate new loans; but in order to do so it must also create equal amounts of deposit liabilities. The bank's new balance sheet, after the maximum amount of loans and deposits had been created, would appear as in Table 8.4.

Table 8.4. Sound Money Bank Corporation
(dollars)

Assets		Liabilities	
Cash reserves	100,000	Demand deposits	500,000
Loans	500,000		
		Net Worth	
		Capital	100,000
	Reserve ratio: 20 percent		

Simple arithmetic shows that the bank's actual reserves (cash of $100,000) just match its required reserves ($0.20 \times \$500,000 = \$100,000$). The bank has created $400,000 of demand deposits that did not exist before, even though only $100,000 were originally deposited as *primary* reserves. Only with the entry of new cash reserves would the bank be able to create additional money. In its present state the bank is said to be "loaned up."

The bank's minimal reserve requirement is set by government decree through some agency such as a central bank or treasury department. The bank is "loaned up" with the reserve requirement now in force, but would not be if the requirement had a lower value. For example, if the minimal requirement were reduced to 10 percent, the bank would enjoy an "excess reserve" position; that is, its total reserves would be greater than the minimum amount of reserves necessary to satisfy the reserve requirement. In formula form,

$$E = R - rD$$

where E is excess reserves, R is total reserves, r is the reserve requirement expressed in decimal form, and D is the amount of demand deposits outstanding. With the reduced reserve requirement now in force,

$$E = \$100,000 - (0.10 \cdot \$500,000) \quad \text{or} \quad E = \$50,000$$

The bank could now expand its portfolio of earning assets and deposit obligations to the point described by Table 8.5. Given the constant value of this bank's reserves — a result of its being the only bank — the balance sheet could expand to any set of values desired by means of successive reductions in the minimal reserve requirement.

Table 8.5. Sound Money Bank Corporation
(dollars)

Assets		*Liabilities*	
Cash	100,000	Demand deposits	1,000,000
Loans	1,000,000		
		Net Worth	
		Capital	100,000
	Reserve ratio: 10 percent		

Deposit Creation in a Multi-Bank Model

The value of the isolated single-bank model is that it demonstrates, as will be seen shortly, the behavior of a complete banking *system*. However, a single bank operating in isolation is not realistic for a competitive, commercial economy. The commercial banking system in the United States, for example, includes over 13,000 banking corporations, not to mention branches. For all practical purposes, this number is "infinite." That is, it is large enough that no single bank is likely to hold a significant fraction of total reserves or deposits.

The multi-bank model presumes a commercial banking system that operates on such an infinite scale. To simplify the process of check clearing, assume that all the commercial banks are linked together by a central bank. The link is the reserve (or deposit) accounts they all keep with the central bank; so that when a check is drawn on one bank and deposited in another, the balance sheet changes are centrally accounted by the central bank. Obviously, what one bank loses another bank must gain; so net debits must always equal net credits.

Table 8.6. Accounting Chart of Multi-Bank Transactions

	Sound Money Bank Corporation				*Central Bank*	
	Assets	*Liabilities*			*Assets*	*Liabilities*
(1)	+ Cash 100,000	+ DD 100,000		(3)	+ Cash 100,000	+ MBR "Sound Money" 100,000
(2)	-- Cash 100,000 + Reserves with CB 100,000			(6)		− MBR "Sound Money" 80,000 + MBR "Second Bank" 80,000
(4)	+ Loan 80,000	+ DD 80,000				
(7)	− Reserves with CB 80,000	− DD 80,000		(10)		− MBR "Second Bank" 64,000 + MBR "Third Bank" 64,000

	Second Bank Corporation				*Third Bank Corporation*	
	Assets	*Liabilities*			*Assets*	*Liabilities*
(5)	+ Reserves with CB 80,000	+ DD 80,000		(9)	+ Reserves with CB 64,000	+ DD 64,000
(8)	+ Loan 64,000	+ DD 64,000		(12)	+ Loans 51,200	+ DD 51,200
(11)	− Reserves with CB 64,000	− DD 64,000				

DD = Demand deposits
MBR = Member bank reserves
CB = Central bank
r = 20 percent

In addition to its reserve account with the central bank, any one bank may keep currency reserves in its vault or "cash drawer" to take care of demands for cash from its demand depositors. Assume, now, that a depositor reverses this particular procedure and deposits cash in the Sound Money Bank for credit to his demand deposit balance (transaction 1 in Table 8.6). The Sound Money Bank may not want to hold more currency than it already has, so it sends the currency to the central bank and asks for credit to its reserve account (transactions 2 and 3). To further its income-earning position, the bank may now wish to make new loans and investments (transaction 4). The maximum it can lend legally is a multiple of its excess reserves. These excess reserves do not stay constant but decline as the bank starts to make new loans. People spend such new money by writing checks against the balances the bank has made available to them. These checks go to other people who deposit the checks in other banks. If the legal reserve requirement is 20 percent, and if the check clearings occur almost as fast as the new loans are made and the money spent, the Sound Money Bank will not be able to lend more than a dollar-for-dollar amount of its excess reserves. For simplicity's sake, assume that all the checks drawn against the Sound Money Bank go into the Second Bank Corporation, and are sent to the central bank for clearance (transaction 5). The central bank credits the reserve account of the Second Bank and debits the account of the Sound Money Bank (transaction 6). The Sound Money Bank is notified of this change and accordingly reduces its accounted reserves (asset) with the central bank and the demand deposit account (liability) of the person who wrote the check (transaction 7). In equilibrium with reserves at 20 percent of demand deposits, it would find itself in the position described by Table 8.7.

Table 8.7. Sound Money Bank Corporation*
(dollars)

Assets		Liabilities	
Loans and investments	80,000		
Reserves with central bank	20,000	Demand deposits	100,000
	Reserve ratio: 20 percent		

* This balance sheet is only partial. It shows just the values resulting from the last $100,000 deposit and the subsequent credit creation that takes place.

The Second Bank now has new deposits and reserves of $80,000 and *excess* reserves of $64,000. Assume that it follows the same procedure as the Sound Money Bank and lends dollar-for-dollar, so that $64,000 worth of loans are made. Again, the people who have borrowed money spend it, so that the accounting of other new deposits, reserve debiting and crediting, and new loan-making transactions must be carried out. This process is continued in numerical order in Table 8.6 through the "Third Bank Corporation." In the real world the process would include additional banks until the original reserves had generated the full amount of deposits allowed by law.

Every bank in the progression would have received additional primary reserves somewhat smaller in amount than the preceding bank due to the necessity of each bank's meeting the minimal reserve requirement on its total new deposits. When new loans and discounts then are generated by each bank in order to maximize income to the enterprise, reserves are lost to the next bank in the progression but demand deposits remain at their new level. Each bank has expanded deposits, therefore, not by expanding deposits directly, *but by reducing reserves held against these deposits to a fraction (20 percent) of their original value.*[1] The primary deposit of $100,000 has given rise to a succession of derivative deposits equal to $80,000 + $64,000 + $51,200 + ... As the nth term in this summation becomes insignificantly small, the total approaches $500,000. Each bank has experienced an enlargement of both assets and liabilities equal to $R(1 - r)^n$, where R is the value of primary reserves ($100,000 in this case), r is the reserve requirement expressed as a decimal (0.2 in this example), and n is the position of a particular bank in the progression (1st, 2nd, 3rd, ...). The sum of these individual cases may be expressed as:

$$\sum_{n=0}^{n=\infty} R(1 - r)^n \rightarrow \frac{R}{r}$$

Therefore, D, total demand deposits, equals or approaches as a limit R/r. This amount is also equal to the volume of demand deposits created by the single large bank. A bank that is the only bank in a community and has no contact with other banks does not lose reserves when it expands its loan and investment portfolio. A *system* of banks is in the same position; for while each individual bank may lose reserves, it loses the reserves to another bank in the *system*. Thus the balance sheet for either a single bank or for an "all banks" system would be the same (see Table 8.8).

---

[1]This unique and enlightening means for understanding how an *individual* bank creates money was first noted by Paul Samuelson. See any of the editions of his text, *Economics: An Introductory Analysis,* New York: McGraw-Hill.

Table 8.8. A Single Bank, or the "All Banks" System
(dollars)

Assets		Liabilities	
Loans and investments	400,000	Demand deposits	500,000
Reserves	100,000		

Reserve ratio: 20 percent

Limitations to the Expansion Process

A number of factors may limit the expansion process of fractional reserve banking. First, changes in the reserve requirement are important. If r were 100 percent, a multiple expansion of credit would be impossible; demand deposits would equal primary reserves. Second, the banking system may lose reserves because of the public's desire to convert bank obligations into hand-to-hand currency — a so-called cash drain. The commercial banking system furnishes the economy with all of its demand deposits, which constitute about 80 percent of the total stock of money. (The remaining 20 percent of the money stock is made up of currency and coin.) A cash drain is a decrease in bank reserves. Thus, the demand deposit expansion formula, $D = \dfrac{R}{r}$, in the presence of a cash drain C, would appear as:

$$D = \frac{R - C}{r}$$

A third exception to maximum credit expansion is seen when the banking system holds excess reserves, meaning that part of total reserves above the legal minimum. Excess reserves E have an effect similar to the cash drain. When they are present, the deposit expansion formula appears as:

$$D = \frac{R - C - E}{r}$$

Fourth, the public's preference for time deposits TD relative to demand deposits influences the expansion process because of the generally lower reserve requirements r^* on time deposits. If allowances must be made for time deposits, the expansion formula would be as follows:

$$D = \frac{R - C - E - (r^* \cdot TD)}{r}$$

Fifth, as far as the individual bank is concerned, the amount that it may lend safely depends upon the pattern of its clearing balances—adverse or favorable. If a bank has favorable clearing balances, then for every dollar it creates, it experiences a somewhat smaller loss of reserves than a dollar-for-dollar amount. This contingency, however, would not affect the total expansion process by the system. It would mean simply that reserves lost to other banks would be less than assumed, and the expansion process would take place with less than an "infinite" number of banks.

Sixth, several factors may influence the public's willingness to borrow and the banker's willingness to lend. These factors include the uncertainty and unpredictability of business conditions and the economic policies of the government. However, these intangibles would be mirrored by such things as cash drains and holdings of excess reserves, so they are not separate exceptions.

Monetary Contraction

Just as the commercial banking system when given new reserves can create a multiple expansion of money, so it may also trigger a multiple contraction when reserves are removed. Assume the banking system is loaned up, as in Table 8.9, and let the public withdraw $100,000 in cash.

Table 8.9. Combined Balance Sheet for "All Banks" in the Commercial Banking System (dollars)

Assets		*Liabilities*	
Cash	100,000	Demand deposits	1,000,000
Reserves with CB	100,000		
Government securities	100,000	*Net Worth*	
Loans	800,000	Common stock	100,000
	Reserve ratio: 20 percent		

With a reserve requirement of 20 percent, the system is just meeting its legal obligations. Cash (in vault) is counted as part of the bank's reserves. When depositors demand cash for their demand deposits, reserve ratios fall below the legal requirement. To restore the legal minimum, banks must call in loans and stop making new ones. For every dollar's worth of reserves that the system loses, demand deposits must be reduced by five dollars in order for the banks to regain a legal equilibrium.

Once the contraction process has been completed, the commercial banking system's balance sheet would appear as in Table 8.10.

Table 8.10. Commercial Banking System
(dollars)

Assets		Liabilities	
Cash			
Reserves with CB	100,000	Demand deposits	500,000
Government securities	100,000		
Loans	400,000	*Net Worth*	
		Common stock	100,000

One important difference should be noted between the multiple expansion and the multiple contraction processes. While banks *may* expand their loans when new reserves are placed in the system, they *must* contract them when reserves are withdrawn. The primary control that the central bank has is to add and subtract reserves and currency from the banking system. Thus it can cause such a contraction as that pictured here, or it can furnish enough new cash so that a contraction would not occur when depositors demanded more than the usual amount of hand-to-hand currency.

Selected Bibliography

Federal Reserve Bank of Chicago. *Modern Money Mechanics: A Workbook on Deposits, Currency, and Reserves.* Chicago: Federal Reserve Bank of Chicago, 1961. (No charge.)

Appendix: Comprehensive Problem and Solution
on Expansion of Bank Credit by a Commercial Banking System

Part A

Assume a commercial banking system is made up of 10,000 small banks, each of which has $1,820,000 in reserves. The minimal reserve requirement against demand deposits for all banks in the system is 13 percent. Compute the total dollar values of loans and demand deposits all banks can generate if credit is expanded to the limit. Assume the system does not use time deposits, and ignore incidental balance sheet items such as buildings and equipment.

Solution to Part A

In all such problems as this one, reserves in the banking system must be regarded as a datum—a given quantity—unless otherwise specified. These reserves are used to expand the deposit accounts of businessmen and householders who initiate loans. These people, in turn, spend their new deposits for the various purposes they had in mind when they asked for the loans. Assuming no desire by receivers of checks to convert demand deposits into currency, total reserves in banks remain constant. However, the effort made by each bank to increase loans and reduce reserves could result only in an increase of deposits in the whole system. Reserves could not be reduced under the constraints imposed here.

Originally, the system's combined balance sheet consists of equal amounts of reserves and primary deposits as in Table 1.

Table 1. All 10,000 Commercial Banks
(billions of dollars)

Assets		*Liabilities*	
Reserves	18.2	Deposits (primary)	18.2

The banking system then expands deposits, reserves remaining constant, in accordance with the formula $\frac{R}{r}$. Total deposits become $\frac{\$18.2 \text{ billion}}{0.13}$, or $140 billion. To effect this change, credit extension by commercial banks in the form of new loans, discounts, and investments are negotiated with borrowers. The newly acquired interest-earning assets in conjunction with reserves balance total demand deposits. The balance sheet for the system, when fully expanded, appears as in Table 2.

Table 2. All 10,000 Commercial Banks*
(billions of dollars)

Assets		*Liabilities*	
Loans, discounts, and investments	121.8	Deposits (derivative)	121.8
Reserves	18.2	Deposits (primary)	18.2
	140.0	Total deposits	140.0

* Only the monetary section of the system's balance sheet is shown. The nonmonetary items, such as buildings, equipment, and capital stock, would increase the total dollar values of both assets and liabilities by about 5 percent in an actual case.

Bankers, of course, do not distinguish between primary and derivative deposits. Both kinds are demand deposits and indistinguishable from each other in practice, even though they may be separated analytically.

Part B

Assume now that every banker in the system decides to hold excess reserves of $320,000. What will be credit expansion for the whole system in this case?

Solution to Part B

If excess reserves are $320,000 for each bank, required reserves must be $1.5 million. (Total reserves equal required reserves plus excess reserves.) Therefore, total deposits for all banks must be computed on the basis of the $15 billion in required reserves, even though total reserves are $18.2 billion.

Demand deposits become $\dfrac{\$15\ \text{billion}}{0.13} = \$115.4$ billion, and the combined balance sheet appears as in Table 3.

Table 3. All 10,000 Commercial Banks
(billions of dollars)

Assets		Liabilities	
Loans, discounts, and			
investments	97.2		
Reserves	18.2	Total deposits	115.4

Credit extension by the banking system is limited to $97.2 billion. Notice that the most important item to bankers is the portfolio value and earning power of their assets, while the most important item to society is the quantity of money (demand deposits) generated by the extension of credit via the expansion of the bank's portfolio of interest-earning assets.

Part C

Suppose reserve ratio requirements are decreased to 12 percent after the banking system has expanded to the maximum values shown in Part A. What volume of new credit would now be available to borrowers?

Solution to Part C

The answer to this part makes use of the methods employed in Parts A and B. Upon advertisement that reserve requirements were reduced, bankers immediately realize that they have excess reserves. Against outstanding demand obligations of $140 billion they now need to have only $16.8 billion ($140 billion $\times$ 0.12). But they have $18.2 billion; so excess legal reserves are $1.4 billion. Bankers then try to reduce reserves by making more loans and investments. Again, this attempt is unsuccessful, and deposits must increase to $\dfrac{\$18.2 \text{ billion}}{0.12} = \$151.7$ billion. Interest-earning assets become \$133.2 billion, and the combined balance sheet takes the form seen in Table 4.

Table 4. All 10,000 Commercial Banks
(billions of dollars)

Assets		Liabilities	
Loans, discounts, and investments	133.5		
Reserves	18.2	Total deposits	151.7

Reducing the percentage reserve requirement by one percentage point (more accurately, a reduction of 7.7 percent from what it was) "frees" reserves of \$1.4 billion, thus permitting a credit expansion of \$11.7 billion. This much additional credit potential would have required an open-market purchase by the central bank of \$1.52 billion if reserve requirements had remained constant. That is, to get an \$11.7 billion increase in demand deposits with a reserve requirement of 13 percent, the banking system would have had to obtain \$1.52 billion in new reserves. What appears to be a "small" change in reserve requirements constitutes a very large potential increase in bank credit and demand deposits.

Part D

To see how time deposits fit into a banking system, go back again to the conditions of Part A and assume that every bank in the system ends up with one-third of its total deposits outstanding in the form of time deposits and the remaining two-thirds as demand deposits. Let the reserve requirement for time deposits be 5 percent while the reserve requirement for demand deposits remains at 13 percent. What will be the balance sheet for the system when credit is fully expanded?

Solution to Part D

Solving this problem requires the use of simple algebra. Two unknown quantities are present — time deposits and demand deposits. Accordingly, let

X = time deposits, and let Y = demand deposits. Every bank expands credit in a way that generates twice as much demand deposits as time deposits. Therefore, the first equation is $\frac{Y}{X} = \frac{2}{1}$, or

$$Y = 2X$$

At the same time, all reserves are exhausted in the credit-creating process; that is, all reserves are used in sustaining the total of demand and time deposits. So,

$$0.05X + 0.13Y = \$18.2 \text{ billion}$$

Substituting $2X$ for Y in equation (2) gives

$$0.05X + 0.26X = \$18.2 \text{ billion}$$

Reducing this expression and solving for X shows that $X = \$58.7$ billion. Since $Y = 2X$, Y must be equal to $\$117.4$ billion. Thus, the final balance sheet for this system appears as in Table 5.

Table 5. All 10,000 Commercial Banks
(billions of dollars)

Assets		*Liabilities*	
Loans, discounts, and investments	157.9	Time deposits	58.7
		Demand deposits	117.4
Reserves	18.2	Total deposits	176.1

Notice that by using time deposits in the credit expansion process, banks can extend credit by many billions more than they were able to do by using demand deposits exclusively. This result, of course, is due to the much lower reserve requirement against time deposits. To the extent that demanders of credit insist on having demand deposits available for use, banks must conform by expanding along the demand deposit route.

9

Commercial Banking and the
Money Supply in the United States (I)

The Beginnings of Modern Banking

Contemporary commercial banking has at least two historical roots. It developed first as an accounting procedure by private entrepreneurs. In this respect bank credit was virtually money of account; that is, it had no necessary connection with monetary metal. Money of account, or the use of bookkeeping symbols to designate claims for and against others, was found frequently in societies where precious metals were scarce or nonexistent. Any private firm that engages itself as a middleman in the process of borrowing and lending these claims can rightfully call itself a bank. The presence of valuable money metal as a reserve is not necessary for the existence of banking institutions any more than it is necessary as a medium of exchange. Most commercial banks in contemporary economies, in fact, use very little tangible money for reserves; almost all bank transactions are handled by exchanges of ledger credits.

The precious metals, whether necessary or not, were important catalysts in the development of both monetary and banking institutions. The centuries preceding the evolution of the goldsmith bankers had witnessed the decline of self-sufficient fortress households, important increases in world trade, the extended use of metallic money, and an appreciable increase in the world's usable stock of money metal. As goldsmiths were called upon more and more to perform a warehousing function for precious metals, the possible utilization of the "dead" stocks in their custody became more and more obvious.

A competent goldsmith might have been satisfied with returns to his craft and the additional warehousing fee that involved little marginal effort on his part. A less successful craftsman, already committed to heavy fixed costs for his strongbox facilities and observing the "uselessness" of the latent treasure in his vaults, could have forsaken the role of craftsman and custodian for that of banker. His argument to depositors was simple: If they permitted him to oversee the lending of the precious metal entrusted to his care, the costs of storage could be foregone and a positive fee could be paid depositors for the use of their specie. When a goldsmith, turned banker, then made loans, he found out very soon that issues of paper representations of the gold were more expediently handled than the metal itself and just as acceptable. These paper representations commonly became currency, just as did the receipts of liability to the original (primary) depositors for their gold and silver.

The banker also discovered that he did not need to keep anywhere near the same value in metallic reserves that he had in notes outstanding against him. The paper representations circulated with little call for redemption so long as (1) the holder of the paper remained in the general vicinity of the bank, and (2) the bank's policies and actions gave no suggestion that redeemability was in question. If note holders either faced the necessity of making remittances to a foreign region or had reason to think that the reserves of the bank were insufficient, redemption of notes in metal would be called for.

The issue of paper currency and the generation of bank credit by banks were possible only because banks were inherently fractional reserve institutions. They could not *create* media of exchange and be otherwise. The question then became: How large must be the fraction that banks maintain? Clearly, it could be less than 1 percent or as much as 99 percent. In fact, bankers left to their own devices tended to keep reserve fractions of between 5 and 10 percent, while government statutes generally came to prescribe rates between 10 and 20 percent.

Bankers have wrestled for centuries with the conflict between the maintenance of reserves and the extension of earning assets. Either of these desiderata can be gained only at some expense to the other. To take advantage of profitable lending opportunities, bankers must risk a smaller fraction of reserves to outstanding demand obligations. To minimize this ratio safely, that is, to maximize the volume of safe earning assets, banking policy has perennially emphasized that commercial bank loans should be short-term, self-liquidating, and a means of facilitating the production and distribution of "real" goods. The goods in the process of being produced and marketed are regarded as proper collateral for the credit granted. This particular philosophy was most ably stated by Adam Smith in the following passage:

> When a bank discounts a real bill of exchange drawn by a real creditor upon a real debtor, and which, as soon as it becomes due, is really paid by that debtor; it only advances to him a part of the value which he would otherwise be obliged to keep by him unemployed and

in ready money for answering occasional demands. The payment of the bill, when it comes due, replaces to the bank the value of what it had advanced, together with the interest.[1]

Adherence to the "real bills" or commercial loan principle, it was believed, would promote "sound" banking and limit the expansion rate of bank notes and bank credit to the rate of real growth in the national product. Some spokesmen also argued that, under the operation of metallic standards and the use of coin or bullion as bank reserves, the "real bills" principle should be supplemented by the explicit requirement that every bank be able to convert any of its obligations into specie on demand. Competition among banks was supposed to provide an additional purifying influence on those banks that became too greedy.

Opponents of this rationale of commercial banking have pointed out that the real quality of a bank loan is never determinate. But even if loan quality can be verified, the same note can be rediscounted by another bank, and then by a third bank in favor of the second. The original loan could thus give rise to many times the original credit value imputed to it by the value of the goods in process. Convertibility of demand liabilities was necessary, the traditionalists agreed, but it was frequently jeopardized by the tendency of many banks to overextend credit during a period of business boom. The subsequent period of credit dearth and bank failures argued for quantitative controls in the form of reserve requirements. Bank notes and bank credit were not the sole province of banks themselves; their supply was a social concern and called for governmental rules to ensure the conditions for convertibility of notes and deposits into specie on demand.

Early Banking Development in the United States[2]

The push and pull of the banking doctrines summarized above were reflected first in the commercial banking system in England, and later by a similar system in the United States. Prior to 1800, banks in the United States were so few (four) that each one tended to act as if it were a complete banking system. Note clearing was limited by primitive transportation, and the few issues of bank notes required no special knowledge on the part of holders to determine the probability or price of note redemption in gold or silver.

---

[1]Adam Smith, *Wealth of Nations*, ed. E. C. Cannan (New York: Modern Library, 1937), p. 288. The general refutation of this doctrine as a sufficient condition for limiting the expansion of bank credit has been exhaustively treated by Lloyd W. Mints in *History of Banking Theory* (Chicago: University of Chicago Press, 1945).

[2]For a readable, stimulating, and competent account of nineteenth-century banking, see Bray Hammond, *Banks and Politics in America* (Princeton, N.J.: Princeton University Press, 1957).

The spate of bank growth after the War of 1812 resulted from the general suspension of the specie convertibility requirement and the issue of Treasury notes by the federal government. These note issues were inspired by fiscal necessities; but to the banks they were permissible reserves and greatly extended the possible generation of bank notes and credit over what had been feasible with just specie.[3] The economy boomed, banks flourished, and inflation ran. A *general suspension* of specie convertibility meant that *redemption* of notes was no longer a legal responsibility. It also showed the inadequacy of the "real bills" principle by itself as a factor that would limit bank credit.[4] Ultimately, the cold dawn of fiscal retrenchment in 1818 caused a general *contraction* of the money stock and made possible the *resumption* of specie payments.

During the more or less "normal" period between 1820 and 1860, the banking system showed a mixed growth. The convertibility requirement and competition among banks were not enough to keep all the banks solvent all of the time. Many banks started up on specie shoestrings with the bulk of their assets being notes receivable from stockholders who had simply given fixed interest claims to "their" banks in order to have residual income shares in enterprises that they thought would enjoy exorbitant gains. When such banks were unable to meet the specie claims of their note holders, they went bankrupt, with widespread effects on the business communities in which they operated. Some state governments, too, encouraged chancy bank ventures. The new states "needed" money, and banks were recognized as the institutions that provided it. Laws in some states were lax to the point of delinquency in their efforts to court the development of banking systems.

The hundreds of banks that came into existence issued both notes and checkbook claims against themselves. The notes circulated as currency in the economy; but while similar in general configuration they lacked uniformity of design and parity of value. One note, for example, stated that: "The Farmer's Bank of New Salem, Ohio, will pay the bearer ten dollars (in specie) on demand," and this bank might very well have paid such an amount on demand. But if the note turned up in a Cincinnati store, the storekeeper could not know its worth. He faced the costs of clearing the note through his local bank, and these costs included a transportation charge on the specie and the risk that any such bank existed. If it existed, it might have suspended specie payments sometime before. If it had suspended, however, the note might still be far from worthless although not worth its face (or par) value in gold. Notes of banks

---

[3]See Chapter 17 for an analysis of this process.

[4]To the extent that the "real bills" principle is valid, it is so for quantitative reasons. Ordinarily, the quantity of "good" loans available to banks is limited. Thus, the quality of loans may "limit" bank credit expansion if the *recognized quantity* of high quality paper is limited in the first place. This condition is ephemeral, however. As a business expansion gets under way, all credit possibilities look "good." Control through "quality" is thus a will-o'-the-wisp.

in the process of liquidation were still worth something because note holders had first lien on bank assets.[5]

The storekeeper thus had many possible variables to consider when such a note was presented as payment. He could reduce a great deal of this uncertainty by referring to a bank note "detector." This publication was similar to the stock market evaluation booklets now issued periodically by investment houses to interested investors. The "detector" gave a current evaluation of bank notes then in circulation. It was published monthly by dealers in bank notes who realized a return for the service, and it was useful to banks and merchants who handled any volume of nonlocal currency. With the establishment of a uniform and par value paper currency under the National Bank Act of 1863, the bank note detector became obsolete.

By 1830, bank deposits had also become an important fraction of the money supply, even though they were mistakenly regarded as less moneyish than bank notes. However, the distinction between demand and time deposits was not generally accounted by banks until after 1890. During the quarter century preceding the Civil War, total deposits were roughly 75 percent of bank notes, but had become about equal to bank notes in dollar volume by 1860..

First Controls over Commercial Banking

Two systems for improving the reliability of commercial bank notes were attempted during the first half of the nineteenth century. The first such system, known as the Suffolk System, was initiated by the Suffolk Bank of Boston in 1819 and continued in operation for the next 40 years. This scheme called for a minimum specie deposit from any bank that wished to keep the circulation of its notes in Boston in good standing. It was in a sense a permissive central banking arrangement for New England, but organized by a private interest. The deposits of specie by "country" banks in the Suffolk Bank were reserves against outstanding notes issued by these banks, and were to be replenished as they were used up in redemption of these notes. Banks that refused to join the arrangement would unexpectedly find large batches of their notes presented for redemption in specie, much to their chagrin. The Suffolk Bank, as the "central bank," benefited modestly from the deposits of out-of-city correspondents and from the service charges or fees for clearing the notes. Its influence was not sufficiently widespread to enable it to prevent general suspensions of specie payments, but it was able to impart a relatively high degree

---

[5]Banks operating under suspension were a problem. If they were forced into liquidation in order to pay off so many cents on each dollar of notes outstanding, the community faced a dearth of money. Forbearance was therefore common, at least for limited time periods.

of convertibility to note issues of New England banks. While it acted very much like a mixture of commercial and central banks, it was not a public depositor for government funds and was not in any way owned by either state or federal governments. Its utility ended with the advent of the national banking system.

The Suffolk Bank demonstrated most notably that one influential bank in a region could undertake reasonably effective quality control of the existing currency without governmental assistance and with little detriment to its own commercial interests. The explicit returns realized by the Suffolk Bank for its services suggested further that a questionable and uncertain bank note system had implicit costs that society would willingly pay a nominal premium to avoid.

Another attempt at control was the New York Safety Fund System, inaugurated in 1829. A tax as a percent of capital was levied on each bank in the state. The proceeds from the tax were put in a special fund and were to be used to pay off the "debts" of defunct banks. It was similar to federal deposit insurance, begun in the 1930s. It erred, however, in levying the tax (½ percent per year for six years) against capital in anticipation of a general payoff of all bad debts. The insured item itself should have borne the insurance premium. Since the principal concern at the time was the insurance of bank notes, the tax should have been levied against issues of bank notes, particularly because some of the most heavily capitalized institutions had relatively few note issues outstanding. Or, to put the matter more pointedly, some of the institutions with relatively little capital had large amounts of notes outstanding. Finally, the word "debts" as used in the law was ambigous. Depositors thought it was meant to cover deposits as well as notes. But when legal cases came up, the courts ruled otherwise.

This kind of scheme, more basically, cannot be thought of as insurance except in the sense of conflagration insurance. A banking system is not subject to random fatalities, the number of which is estimable on an actuarial basis. Banks generally fail in large numbers. When a typical bank crisis begins, one of its distinguishing features is a *general* scramble for limited liquid reserves and a *general* tightening or contraction of credit. Banks then fail in droves, while during years of plenteous reserves even the weak ones can survive.

The Safety Fund System was not equipped to cope with bank conflagrations. During the boom of the early 1830s, no calls were made on it, so of course it operated satisfactorily. With the worldwide decline in the level of the gold "table" in the early 1840s, a rash of bank liquidations exhausted the fund. The state of New York then had to fortify the fund by buying issues of bonds from it so that it could pay off the claims of note holders. (Depositors in many cases were bereft.) The fund thus differed from the Suffolk scheme by providing relief for sufferers rather than preventing the suffering in the first place. The premium it charged the banks, however, was insufficient for the situation it faced.

The Imposition of Reserve Requirements

The one other control over banking that made some headway before the National Bank Act was governmental imposition of reserve requirements. Before the corporate structure of banking was distinguished from that of other business firms, restrictions on banks were stipulated in terms of note issues to capital, or note issues to capital "actually paid in." The intentions of this type of law were good. However, banks were able to finance themselves by accepting deposits, a means not open to ordinary businesses, so a limitation on note issue in terms of capital value had little relevance. Furthermore, capital values were easily inflated by balance sheet manipulations.

The only control that means anything to a fractional reserve institution is one that specifies the fraction of reserves it must maintain to all note and deposit liabilities. The First and Second Banks of the United States sensed the necessity of keeping their own ratios large if they wished to be in a position to exert some degree of control over the commercial banking system. The better private banks, however, had no reason to assume any public responsibilities for one another. Their ratios of reserves to demand liabilities were only nominal — 5 to 10 percent. During prosperous times — that is, when the output of specie was high relative to the output of other goods and services — a 5 or 10 percent ratio was more than enough; but in times of bank panic, it was not half enough. Long experience thus demonstrated that statutory minimum reserve requirements were a necessity.

Congress almost imposed reserve requirements on the banks that held the federal government's funds in 1835–1836. The bill, in fact, was passed, but upon "reconsideration" was "laid on the table." The legislators of the day thought a provision of this sort would upset the delicate balance in the banking system and might trigger a typical bank credit "revulsion." It might well have. It specified reserve requirements of 20 percent against all note and deposit liabilities, a ratio much larger than that generally prevailing at the time.[6] After this movement finally stalled, the federal government did not try to prescribe reserve requirements again until the National Bank Act of 1863.

Several of the states, however, required minimal reserves against outstanding notes as early as 1837, and later against both notes and deposits. In 1842 Louisiana enacted a 33⅓ percent requirement of specie to notes and deposits. Many other states imposed similar restrictions during the 1850s. By January 1, 1859, actual ratios of specie to total deposits and circulation ranged from 53 percent in Louisiana to 4¼ percent in Illinois.[7]

---

[6]The interesting history of this bill can be found in *Register of Debates in Congress*, 23rd Congress, 2nd sess., and 24th Congress, 1st sess.

[7]Hammond, p. 716. As Hammond points out, the reliability of some of these statistics is questionable.

State reserve requirements were probably a necessary adjunct to the "free banking" laws that became prominent during the period. Prior to 1835, each bank was chartered individually by its appropriate state legislature. State legislatures in this way could maintain some control over the supply of credit generated, or so they presumed. When banking was permitted freedom of entry and exit, many organizations hardly recognizable as "banks" came into existence. In fact, the distinction between some types of "bankers" and ordinary counterfeiters was one of degree and not of kind. The centuries-old practice of transporting specie reserves from bank to bank just ahead of the state bank examiners was not unknown; and the basic principle of "plant location" was to place the "bank" as far from potential note holders as geography would permit.[8] Such banks were known as "wildcat" banks because they were in areas so remote that their only company would be wildcats.

Some states (Arkansas, California, Florida, and Texas) prohibited banking entirely prior to 1850, although corporations in those states that wished to act *as if* they were banks organized as "insurance" or "railway" companies and then went ahead and issued notes payable on demand. Some states also required deposits of state or other "approved" bonds as collateral for guaranteeing the convertibility of note issue. Since most of these bonds could be obtained on margin and since specie could be "stretched" by other sharp practices, state bank controls tended to be effective or ineffective depending on how careful or how liberal state governments were in encouraging local developments of credit. In some states, such as Indiana, a high quality state banking system flourished. In other states the temptation to establish going money and credit systems on terms that were too permissive ended in currency depreciation and bank disasters. By 1860, the banking and currency systems were of very mixed character; some were good and some were bad, but they were not *all* bad, as many observers have presumed.

Experience in banking and the gold boom of the 1850s resulted in fairly reliable banking institutions that issued reasonably good, that is, riskless, currency. Whether good or not, however, it circulated at varying rates of discount due to transportation and insurance costs. As in all industries, some marginal fringe of banking firms could stay in operation only by avoiding bank note holders who wanted redemption in specie, and by engaging in high risk banking practices, many of which failed in spite of general prosperity. The paper currency thus was not perfect. It lacked uniformity in design and parity of value. These deficiencies, however, were not much more than incidental to the productivity growth of the economy. Nonetheless, they were worth doing something about, and the National Bank Act was the measure that aimed at such a target. But it, too, would have been a scheme favored only by a minority had it not been seen as an expedient for helping to solve some of the financial problems raised by the Civil War.

---

[8]See, again, Hammond, especially Chs. 18, 19, and 21.

Selected Bibliography

Dewey, Davis R. *State Banking before the Civil War.* National Monetary Commission, Senate Document No. 581, 61st Congress, 2nd sess. Washington, D.C.: U.S. Government Printing Office, 1911. This volume explains the Suffolk System and the Safety Fund System.

Hammond, Bray. *Banks and Politics in America.* Princeton, N.J.: Princeton University Press, 1957. A most readable and thorough treatise on early banking. Also details the concept of central banking.

Hepburn, A. Barton. *A History of Currency in the United States.* New York: Macmillan Co., 1924.

Mints, Lloyd. *A History of Banking Theory.* Chicago: University of Chicago Press, 1945. For the advanced student who may wish to read a general critique of both the commodity theory of money and the commercial credit theory of banking.

Smith, Adam. *Wealth of Nations,* ed. E. C. Cannan. New York: Modern Library, 1937. Book II, Chapter 2, "Money," presents both the commodity theory of money and the commercial credit theory of banking.

Redemption

Bray Hammond

This view of redemption problems of early commercial banks in the United States is taken from the late Bray Hammond's Banks and Politics in America. *Dr. Hammond was a long-time research economist with and secretary to the Federal Reserve Board.* Banks and Politics *won him a Pulitzer Prize in 1957. It is a profound piece of research and most entertaining to read.*

In this section Dr. Hammond discusses the social and economic problems of communities that incorporated commercial banks at a time when conformity to specie redemption of paper bank note currency was the rule of the game. The conflict between the monetary needs of the community and restraints on banks is the principal issue examined here.

In June 1809, a matter of two or three months after the Dexter affair, the Massachusetts legislature imposed a penalty of two percent a month on notes that debtor banks failed or refused to redeem. The law was upheld by the courts, which in March 1812 found it "equitable and wise"; the failure of banks to be punctual in meeting demands "now that bank bills form almost exclusively the circulating medium of the country is a public inconvenience of great extent and introductive of much mischief." Mr. Gallatin considered the Massachusetts law one of the most efficient in restraining improvident issues. Daniel Webster, when a representative from Massachusetts, got a similar penalty included in 1816 in the charter of the new Bank of the United States, where it applied to payment of deposits as well as notes. The same month, April 1816, New York began, with the Bank of Niagara and the Bank of Jefferson County, to include in all charters a stipulation that the charters would be forfeited upon failure of the banks to redeem their notes. Pennsylvania and Maryland began enacting similar conditions early in 1819. But such stipulations were not effective.[1]

According to William Gouge, the Bank of Darien, Georgia, set up as a barrier to payment of its obligations the requirement that each person presenting its notes for redemption swear, at the bank, before a justice of the peace, in the presence of five directors and the cashier, that he was owner of the notes and not agent for another, besides which he had to pay a charge of $1.37½; and this had to be done separately as to each note presented.[2]

Individual creditors who sued to recover on unredeemed notes as on any unpaid debt seldom if ever gained anything. Stephen Girard's bank was sued in 1814 for refusing to redeem its notes during general suspension, but the plaintiffs seem to have sought to harass Mr. Girard rather than obtain payment —the amounts were small, one claimant, an umbrella-maker, suing for $25— and to have been discouraged by the firmness of his defense. Isaac Bronson, president of the Bank of Bridgeport, Connecticut, and a prominent capitalist in his day, sued in 1815, also during general suspension, for payment of notes of New York banks that he held. He seems to have got no satisfaction, but he got some prolix and extravagant abuse in the New York press for a course that was "unjust, impolitic, and odious." It was said in the New York *National Advocate*, 1 November 1815, that "any attempt at present or during the approaching winter to curtail discounts with a view to the payment of specie is fraught with misery and ruin to every class of society who depend upon their enterprise and industry for their prosperity in life."[3]

---

[1]Albert Gallatin. *Writings* (Henry Adams, editor) (Philadelphia, 1879), p. 318; *Brown v. Penobscot III Bank*, 8 Massachusetts Reports, 449; John Jay Knox, *A History of Banking in the United States* (New York, 1903), pp. 398, 448, 488; M. St. Clair Clarke and D. A. Hall. *Legislative and Documentary History of the Bank of the United States* (Washington, 1832), pp. 673–74.

[2]William M. Gouge. *A Short History of Paper Money and Banking in the United States*, Part II (Philadelphia, 1833), p. 141.

[3]John Bach McMaster. *Life and Times of Stephen Girard* Part II (Philadelphia, 1918), p. 281–84; "Aurelius," New York *National Advocate*, 26 October 1815; Abraham H. Venit. "Isaac Bronson," *Journal of Economic History*, V (1945), p. 202.

In Windsor County, Vermont, in 1808 an indictment was sought against a man who held notes of the Vermont State Bank and demanded specie for them. It alleged that Jireh Durkee, of Boston, "being an evil-disposed person and not minding to get his living by truth and honest labor but contriving how he might injuriously obtain...money to support his idle and profligate way of life and diminish and destroy the resources of the state of Vermont and rendering it difficult and impossible for the good citizens thereof to obtain money," had presented $9,000 of the bank's notes at the Woodstock office and obliged the bank to pay them. The effect of such action, which would enable Durkee "to realize a filthy gain," said the complaint, was to prevent the bank from making loans to "good citizens."[4]

Bank note redemption under pressure presented a dilemma that was long unsolved. The issue of notes was an exercise of the common law right to borrow and go into debt. It was the undisputed expectation, therefore, that bank notes, like other promissory notes, would be paid. That was the view in the courts and out. A bank note was not money but a promise to pay money; payment was redemption of the promise. It was also perceived that if the notes were not paid they depreciated in value as circulating media. So there were two important reasons why they should be paid.

But on the other hand a bank's payment of its notes involved a loss of specie reserves and an impairment of its power to lend. Local borrowers could readily see that—especially if the payment had to be made to strangers who came into town with valises full of notes, which had been acquired systematically at a discount, and who purposed carrying away a corresponding amount of gold and silver. That sort of thing was deflationary. It would frustrate local enterprise.

Public opinion wavered in confusion before the two evils, finding each in turn the worse. Should bank notes be kept at par or should bank credit be restricted? Few people could be consistent in all circumstances, for the two things seemed hopelessly incompatible. Sometimes it was dear money that troubled them and sometimes it was cheap money. The Maryland legislature, 15 February 1819, enacted a law against banks that refused to redeem their notes. Two days later, 17 February 1819, it enacted another against persons who demanded that they redeem them. The first was entitled an act "to compel ...banks to pay specie for their notes, or forfeit their charters"; the second, an act "to relieve the people of this state, as far as practicable, from the evil arising from the demands made on the banks of this state for gold and silver by brokers"—it forbade traffic in notes for less than their nominal value. Pennsylvania in a similar law, March 1819, made banks liable to forfeiture of their charters upon refusal to redeem their notes—except for brokers or dealers "habitually in the practice of receiving or buying notes at less than nominal values." The distinction the legislators had in mind is easy to recognize, but it was hard to define and establish.

---

[4]25th Congress, 2d Session, HR 79, 111.

The way out followed from the practical conclusion, enforced by usage, that the obligations of banks were not ordinary debts but money; and that a public interest was at stake in them which overrode that of any particular debtor and creditor. But that conclusion was reached slowly and with uncertainty.

Meanwhile banks themselves made the problem worse by their raids on one another. Loammi Baldwin, subsequently a well-known engineer, wrote in 1809 that a most important difficulty for banks arose from their imprudent jealousy in "running" upon each other for gold and silver in order to impair one another's credit and improve their own positions. If they would stop this, he said, and mutually aid and support each other "there would be little danger of failures." It was undoubtedly difficult or impossible to tell in many cases whether demands by some banks upon others were legitimate or greedy and malicious. John C. Calhoun in March 1816, doubting the wisdom of Daniel Webster's amendment penalizing the Bank of the United States two percent a month for any failure to redeem its obligations, said that too severe a penalty might produce combinations against it, and "be dangerous to the institution by inviting a run on it and thereby producing a suspension of payment." Actually, banks resorted to two extremes, both of them often. Sometimes they raided one another ruthlessly, which was strictly legal, though lethal. At other times they agreed to evade redemption and sustained one another's notes, which if not illegal was at least contrary to the law's intent and public interest though otherwise rather sensible. Proper practice, which combined the principle of both extremes, was maintained all the time by many banks, perhaps most, but not for a century was it generally achieved.[5]

In Massachusetts, conservative efforts to enforce payment of bank notes seem to have had better support than elsewhere. And it was bankers themselves, not legislators, who were responsible for them. In 1803 the Massachusetts Bank, the Union Bank, and the Boston office of the Bank of the United States united in systematically collecting out-of-town bank notes, and in 1804, as I have already said, the Boston Exchange Office was organized to specialize in such collections. It did so till Andrew Dexter got control and used it to delay rather than expedite note redemption. In 1809 sixty-four merchants and firms in Boston announced the following collective action against banks that evaded redemption of their notes:

> The subscribers, merchants and traders in the town of Boston, from a disposition to afford every facility and convenience to their country customers, have been in the habit, since the establishment of country banks, of receiving the bills issued by them in payment for goods or debts at par, — and which they were for a good while enabled again to circulate without loss.
>
> Within the last two years, however, many country banks have unwarrantably abused this confidence placed in their bills by refusing payment of them when presented or by opposing

---

[5]Loammi Baldwin. *Thoughts on the Study of Political Economy, etc.* (Cambridge, Massachusetts, 1809), pp. 46–47; Clarke and Hall, pp. 674, 809.

every obstacle which chicanery and artifice could invent to delay or evade it. The obvious consequences have followed, the public confidence has been shaken, their faith in written promises of institutions avowedly established as *patterns of punctuality* no longer exists. Country bank paper has depreciated and can not be negotiated without a discount which varies from two to four percent. We have, however, in hopes this unwarrantable conduct would be abandoned, continued to receive this paper at par and borne the loss of the discount till our patience is exhausted and our suffering interest calls loudly for a change of measures. We have therefore found ourselves compelled to send the bills home for payment and in case of refusal shall proceed to the collection by due course of law. We beg you will communicate this letter to the President and Directors of _____ Bank and hope that by a prompt payment of their bills they will save us from the disagreeable necessity of resorting to the legal alternative.[6]

In 1814 the New England Bank, Boston, incorporated the year before, arranged to receive the notes of out-of-town banks and charge the depositors only the actual cost of collection. Something promptly occurred which shows that resistance to note redemption was not merely a provincial affair. The bank had sent its agent to New York with about $140,000 of notes of New York banks. Silver coin in that amount had been collected in payment by the agent, had been loaded in three wagons, and had started on its way to Boston. The wagons had not gone far when they were halted by order of the federal Collector of Customs for New York; and the money was carried back by force and placed in the vaults of the Bank of the Manhattan Company, of which the Collector was a director. The action was protested by the New England Bank's agent, but the Collector declined to alter his purpose, alleging a suspicion that the coin was on its way to Canada, with which, since it was British, the States were then at war. In Boston, however, it was believed that his behavior "was chiefly actuated by dislike to the frequency with which the New England Bank dispatched large sums of the New York bills, which flooded Massachusetts, to be redeemed." The Massachusetts authorities laid the matter before the President of the United States, James Madison, "with the expression of their judgment that the collector had committed an outrage on one of their corporations, ought to relinquish the deposit, and be dismissed from his office." Their effort "so far succeeded as to have the money restored."[7]

The argument that redemption of notes was disadvantageous to borrowers, because it reduced the power of banks to lend, soon gave birth to the further argument that there were positive advantages in prolonged or even permanent suspension, because it augmented the power of banks to lend. To exclude or limit the use of bank credit was to confine the volume of money to small compass—gold and silver only—and deny the public the means adequate for an ever-expanding volume of monetary transactions. If banks were released from having to redeem their notes, they could lend more freely and every one would

[6]N. S. B. Gras. *Massachusetts First National Bank of Boston* (Cambridge, Massachusetts, 1937), p. 75; Massachusetts Historical Society, *Proceedings*, XI (1870), p. 307.
[7]J. B. Felt. *Historical Account of Massachusetts Currency* (Boston, 1839), p. 218.

be better off. In November 1814, Samuel D. Ingham of Pennsylvania, who fifteen years later was Secretary of the Treasury under President Jackson, expressed himself in Congress on the subject of suspension in this wise: "I do not apprehend any serious consequence will result from the temporary suspension of specie payments. The experiment was tried many years ago in England and has been continued up to this time, without injury to the commercial interests and with essential benefit to the nation at large." It had been demonstrated, he said, that but a small quantity of specie was sufficient when the public had faith in a bank; accordingly, since suspension made it impossible to get any specie at all, "necessity would become an auxiliary to faith and business would go on as usual." This happy conclusion was not unknown by any means in Britain, where, as Mr. Ingham said, the Bank of England's suspension of payments had been long continued. And the sarcastic comment upon it of Thomas Love Peacock, novelist and officer of the East India Company, was that "promises to pay ought not to be kept; the essence of a safe and economical currency being an interminable series of broken promises."[8]

In America too the conclusion that a circulating medium merely required faith, and no specie, seemed preposterous to the conservatives, both capitalist and agrarian. But the conservatives were becoming a minority. Though lawmaking and practice had now and then their nervous swings, the secular trend was toward easy money and expanding credit. Of the two evils, Americans in the long run stuck to the lesser: too much money was better than not enough.

It was in this period beginning around 1800 and on the complaint of chartered banks that the issue of notes by their unincorporated competitors began anew to be prohibited. The complaint was reasonable, for one of the purposes of incorporation was to establish limited and controllable privileges in the general interest; and if these privileges were of any use they should be protected. The earlier intent of these laws, however, had been to complete the ban on note issue, which they forbade for unincorporated banks and which was impossible for incorporated banks so long as the legislature incorporated none. But once some banks were incorporated and thereby authorized to issue notes, the prohibition became a means of protecting those banks.

It was an inadequate protection, however, for it bore on unincorporated banks and bankers only, but not on canal companies, academies, blacksmiths, etc., outside the field of banking, whether incorporated or not. These found that they could go into debt profitably by issuing notes which looked like money and circulated as money. The problem of the law-maker was to distinguish between notes which should be allowed to circulate as money and notes that should not. It was like the problem of distinguishing practically and equitably between creditors who should be allowed to demand payment of bank notes and those who should not. Restraining laws were tried in one version after another as the various state legislatures sought the verbal formula that would accomplish what they purposed. Massachusetts in June 1809 enacted a second

---

[8]Clarke and Hall, 501–02.

statute outlawing notes of banks not incorporated in Massachusetts. In March 1810, Pennsylvania forbade unincorporated banking companies either to receive deposits or to issue notes, but also declared that nothing in the act should interfere with others "in such manner and for such purpose as hath been hitherto usual and may be legally done." In the general act regulating banks, March 1814, sections XIII and XIV restated the prohibition against note issue by others than chartered banks "in the manner or nature of bank notes." Still another prohibition was enacted in Pennsylvania in March 1817, because "notes and tickets in the nature of bank notes" had been issued "as well by individuals as by corporations not established for the purpose of banking." Virginia again enacted a restraining act in February 1816 and New York in 1816 and 1818. Other states adopted like restraints.[9]

These restraints favored corporations at the expense of private individuals, and considering the prejudices both popular and official against the corporate form of business organization, it is remarkable that they were enacted at all. But they were supported by dissatisfaction with a monetary medium comprising the personal obligations of any Tom, Dick, and Harry. The restraints accordingly marked stages in the evolution of the business corporation and also in the evolution of the concept of money, which was expanding to include bank liabilities as well as coin. "Previous to the restraining acts," said the courts, "there was no power possessed by a bank not allowed to individuals and private associations. They could in common issue notes, discount notes, and receive deposits." Now it was different; the banking function, to the extent that it involved the *creation* of money (as distinct from the mere safe-keeping of it) was reserved to corporations authorized by the state for that purpose. The common law right to borrow was being distinguished from the right to borrow by the issue of obligations intended to circulate as money. The latter was being more and more positively reserved to chartered banks.[10]

This distinction between the legalistic and realistic concept of bank obligations had already been made years before in the courts of Great Britain, where the public had been making monetary use of such obligations for a much longer time than in America and where there had never been the abuse of them that Americans had experienced with their bills of credit. In *Miller* v. *Race,* January 1758, Lord Mansfield had rejected the fallacy, as he called it, of likening bank notes "to goods, or to securities, or documents for debts. Now, they are not goods," he said, "not securities, nor documents for debts, nor are so esteemed; but are treated as *money,* as *cash,* in the ordinary course and transaction of business, by the general consent of mankind; which gives them the credit and currency of money, to *all* intents and purposes. They are as much money as guineas themselves are, or any other current coin that is used in common payments, as money or cash."[11]

---

[9]Joseph Chitty. *A Practical Treatise on Bills of Exchange, Checks, etc.* (from the 5th London edition) (Philadelphia, 1821), 425 ff.

[10]*New York Firemen Ins. Co.* v. *Ely,* 2 Cowan 710.

[11]*Miller* v. *Race,* 1 Burrows 457.

10

Commercial Banking and the
Money Supply in theUnited States (II)

The National Bank Act of 1863–1865

Although the National Bank Act was passed originally in 1863, it was amended significantly in 1864 and 1865. It was primarily a "war measure" when passed, but it left a permanent impression on the banking system of the United States.

The Act had several notable features. First, it provided for national chartering of all banks that wished to become a part of the system. It was thus permissive, but it was also to some degree exclusive; banks were not forced to join, and some could not meet the requirements anyway. However, the system-wide regulation to which all would be subject promised a degree of insurance to reasonably sound banks that other national banks would also be sound. Second, reserve requirements were specified for all banks that joined— 25 percent for banks in "reserve" cities (the larger cities), and 15 percent for "country" banks. Third, all national bank notes were made similar in design and had to be accepted by all other national banks at par. Fourth, the notes were secured by government bonds held as collateral. Several hundred banks became participants in the first year of the Act, but the relatively rigorous standards caused a large majority to hold off.

The federal government was not completely motivated by considerations of monetary welfare in passing the Act. Like most governments faced with the problems of wartime financing, the two governments of that day lacked the revenues from taxes with which to maintain their war machines.[1] The federal

---

[1]Both Northern and Southern governments faced similar fiscal problems. For the sake of simplicity only Northern finances are discussed here.

government had passed acts that permitted the printing of legal tender paper money, but continuation of this practice would have promoted ever-increasing inflation. From the government's point of view, a means was needed to establish an effective demand for government bonds so that interest-bearing debt could be issued and its prestige maintained even if inflation was no less inhibited. The National Bank Act seemed to be the answer.[2] It called for all participating banks to buy and pledge government bonds to at least 33 percent of total capital value and to at least 110 percent of national bank notes issued. That is, notes could be issued up to 90 percent of the par or market value of the bonds, whichever was lower. Note-issuing national banks thus had three requirements to fulfill; two of them called for government bond holdings and the other for reserves that were by this time almost exclusively government issues of legal tender money (U.S. notes or "greenbacks").

To limit national bank notes, the law prescribed a maximum issue of $300 million to be apportioned, one half on the basis of population and the other half "with due regard to (existing) banking capital, resources, and business." Since the Southern states were outside the Union at this time, they were necessarily left out of the apportionment. Even an additional apportionment of $54 million in 1870 failed to improve upon the alleged intention of the law. The resulting antipathy in the South to national banking was thus understandable.

Many state banks found that they had little to gain by joining the new system. Weaker banks or those operating in risky or questionable paper could not or would not meet the more rigorous requirements of the Act. Congress thereupon passed an Act in 1865 that levied a 10 percent *per annum* tax on notes of banks that issued state bank notes. Clearly, a 10 percent tax could not be paid if the banks were to operate profitably. Many nonnational banks thereupon applied for national charters. The remainder, still a large majority of all banks, began using demand deposits exclusively. They were able, by this means, to avoid participation in the national scheme and to continue as state-chartered banks. From this time on, bank deposits dominated the total money stock. (See Table 10.1.)

Post–Civil War Monetary Problems

Between 1860 and 1866 the federal debt increased from almost nothing to approximately $2,700 million. U.S. notes, sometimes called "greenbacks" and sometimes "legal tenders," composed about $450 million of this amount; the remainder was interest-bearing debt having various maturities. The legal

---

[2]Bank purchases of securities, although they effectively monetized government debt, greatly simplified the marketing of the securities. National banks developed too late to further this process, but the intent of Congress and the executive branch was clearly in this direction.

tender issues had become a principal form of currency, as well as bank reserves and the basis of most bank credit. Much of the interest-bearing debt that had been issued by the government and purchased by the banks had been matched by increased deposit and note liabilities. The total money stock had approximately tripled and the price level had about doubled over the corresponding values for 1860.

Gold coin had become a commodity. Issues of legal tenders in the early years of the war, combined with the vast expansion in bank credit, had forced up the price level framework. Within this framework was the market price of gold, but outside of the market and fixed by law was the statutory mint price of gold. When the market price of gold tended to exceed the mint price, any accumulations of gold in the Treasury were thereupon demanded in redemption of, say, U.S. notes. The banks faced the same demands for their obligations. Since Treasury and bank-held gold was not unlimited, the Treasury and banks had no recourse ultimately but to admit inability to redeem notes and deposits for gold on demand. Suspension of specie payments in 1862 had the effect of giving some license for further expansion. Gold, no longer bridled by an effective mint price, went joyriding with other prices. In 1866, the premium on gold averaged 41 percent, meaning that a "mint dollar" exchanged for $1.41 worth of legal tender notes in the free gold market.

The general fiscal policy of the federal government in the postwar period was contraction of the money stock by means of budget surpluses in order to lower the price level and thus restore the convertibility of the dollar in terms of gold at the prewar parity.[3] Prices fell drastically until 1869, when they leveled off for several years and then fell again in 1876–1877. So far as the national banking system was concerned, a fiscal policy that retired outstanding federal debt meant that government bonds needed by the national banks as collateral against note issue and capital had become scarcer and therefore more expensive. Government bonds, far from being a glut on the market, almost reached their par value in gold in the early 1870s. At the same time United States notes were 87 percent of the prewar gold parity value.

National banking could not be extended as much as had been anticipated earlier, and national bank notes were always very limited in quantity. By the time resumption occurred in 1879, the total stock of currency consisted of U.S. notes, $346 million; national bank notes, $304 million; and a few odd millions of fractional currency. The U.S. notes served as both hand-to-hand currency and primary reserves for the banking system. National bank notes were an issued obligation of the national banks against which a reserve of either U.S. notes or specie had to be held; but national bank notes were also held as reserves by nonnational banks and used as hand-to-hand currency. The country banks, nonnational as well as national, deposited much of their

---

[3]This policy is reflected in Table 10.1 in the column "U.S. Notes and Treasury Notes" for the years 1865–1869.

Table 10.1. Monetary Statistics on Gold, Bank Deposits,
and Currency and Five-Year Average Values
for GNP: 1865–1913*
(millions of dollars)

| Year | Monetary Gold Stock | | Total Deposits | | Currency | | | GNP (averages for periods indicated) |
| | Gold Coin | Gold Certificates | National | Non-National | National Bank Notes | Government Issued | | |
						Silver and Fractional Currency	U.S. Notes and Treasury Notes	
1865	149		614	635	146	30	616	
1866	110	11	695	443	276	33	491	
1867	73	19	685	597	287	33	443	
1868	64	18	745	665	295	35	358	
1869	62	30	716	751	292	36	318	(1869–1873)
1870	81	32	706	868	289	43	327	6,710
1871	72	18	791	1,045	311	46	344	
1872	77	26	805	1,255	329	48	346	(1872–1876)
1873	63	34	836	1,276	339	52	349	7,530
1874	79	18	828	1,307	340	53	371	
1875	64	18	897	1,399	340	60	350	
1876	75	24	842	1,453	316	59	331	
1877	78	32	818	1,383	301	63	338	(1877–1881)
1878	85	25	814	1,275	311	76	321	9,180
1879	111	15	1,090	1,272	321	70	302	
1880	226	8	1,085	1,495	337	74	328	
1881	315	6	1,364	1,823	350	115	328	

Year								Period	
1882	358	5	1,365	1,844	353	133	325	(1882–1886)	
1883	345	60	1,337	2,016	348	133	323		11,300
1884	341	71	1,233	2,057	331	155	319		
1885	342	127	1,420	2,141	309	183	331		
1886	358	76	1,459	2,395	308	184	324		
1887	377	91	1,650	2,528	277	187	327	(1887–1891)	
1888	391	121	1,716	2,569	245	247	308		12,300
1889	376	117	1,920	2,694	207	307	316	(1889–1893)	
1890	374	131	1,979	2,971	182	363	335		13,500
1891	407	120	1,974	3,082	162	398	374		
1892	409	141	2,327	3,409	167	424	437	(1892–1896)	
1893	409	93	1,939	3,312	175	450	472		13,600
1894	496	66	2,228	3,311	200	438	461		
1895	480	48	2,279	3,604	207	432	435		
1896	455	42	2,141	3,545	215	443	351		
1897	518	37	2,386	3,884	226	469	390	(1897–1901)	
1898	658	36	2,799	4,245	223	513	408		17,300
1899	680	33	3,539	4,933	238	533	421		
1900	611	201	3,621	5,301	300	551	393		
1901	630	247	4,249	6,125	345	604	378		
1902	632	306	4,467	6,636	346	632	364	(1902–1906)	
1903	617	377	4,561	7,051	400	652	353		24,200
1904	646	466	4,834	7,507	433	662	347		
1905	651	485	5,406	8,366	480	666	342		
1906	669	517	5,691	9,012	548	699	343		
1907	562	600	6,188	9,571	589	715	348	(1907–1911)	
1908	613	783	6,328	9,112	632	736	344		31,600
1909	599	815	6,932	9,951	666	725	344		
1910	591	803	7,254	10,696	684	733	339		
1911	589	930	7,673	11,187	688	713	342		
1912	611	943	8,061	11,952	705	735	341	(1912–1916)	
1913	608	1,001	8,140	12,383	716	751	340		40,300

Source: Department of Commerce, *Historical Statistics of the United States, Colonial Times to 1957* (Washington, D.C., 1960), pp. 139, 646–649.

* Many of the statistics on the monetary stock involve double-counting. A large part of the gold stock, for example, was held by the Treasury as a reserve against other outstanding legal tender items (U.S. notes, etc.), and national bank notes were held frequently by non-national banks as reserves against demand deposits.

reserve balances with the reserve city national banks during seasons of slack business; so the demand obligations of the reserve city banks, particularly those in New York City, included a large share of the country banks' reserve assets. The assets of the nonbank public were largely deposit claims against the whole banking system. The banking and monetary system, therefore, was composed of three or four accounting "layers," the obligations of one layer being the cash assets of the next "inferior" layer. Of course, any layer could hold a "superior" asset such as specie or U.S. notes. Generally, however, the base of the system was specie and government currency, especially the portions of this stock in the reserve city national banks, and the monetary superstructure was the aggregate of demand obligations built on this base.

The fiscal-monetary policies of the Treasury and of the reserve city national banks largely determined the state of business. Treasury policy, and government policy generally, aimed at contracting the monetary base, but monetary amnesty was also granted from time to time at various points in the superstructure. Silver was remonetized to a limited extent in 1878, for example, and free national banking was permitted in the middle 1870s at the same time that U.S. notes were contracted. Something was given and something was taken away. On net balance the economy was pinched monetarily by governmental policies even though the rate of growth in real national product was high. Business never had the buoyancy it had enjoyed in the 1850s, although silver monetization made the 1880s easier to take than they otherwise might have been.

Black Banking

Shortly before the Civil War ended, the first black banks were organized in some Southern states. These banks were organized by the U.S. army and were opened in New Orleans, Louisiana; Norfolk, Virginia; and Beaufort, South Carolina. They were primarily for black soldiers and were called "military banks." They did not offer demand deposit services but acted primarily as savings institutions.[4]

To establish a permanent savings bank for blacks, President Lincoln signed a bill in 1865 authorizing the Freedmen's Savings and Trust Company. This bank was opened with headquarters in New York, and by 1872 it had established 34 branches, 32 of them in Southern states. In the words of a spokesman, the purpose of the bank "was to instill into the minds of the untutored Africans lessons of sobriety, wisdom and economy, and to show them how to rise in the world."[5] Unfortunately, the "lessons" were often trickery and deceit.

---

[4]Walter L. Fleming, *The Freedmen's Savings Bank* (Chapel Hill: University of North Carolina Press, 1927), pp. 20–21.

[5]Fleming, p. 88.

The bank tried to expand too rapidly, and also had the misfortune of trying to develop at a time of business recession and bank failures. In addition, the trustees of the institution, who were predominantly white, were not required to have a financial interest in the institution, and their legal obligations were practically nil. Discrepancies in accounts grew and questionable loans were made. According to Fleming, "Most of the inefficient officials, it seems, were Negroes; most of the dishonest ones were white."[6] The ill-trained black clerks and officers of the bank often became dupes for white schemes. The bank closed in 1874 with over $3 million in deposit liabilities on its books and practically nothing in reserve. During the next decade the bank's depositors were returned about $0.62 for every dollar they had deposited. In retrospect, one observer said that ten additional years of slavery could not have done more to discourage thrift among blacks.

Elasticity of the Money Supply

Most of the country banks found that their most profitable use of funds in the off-seasons of the year was as deposits in the principal financial centers, particularly in New York City. The New York banks frequently could loan these additional funds "on call," that is, callable within 24 hours. When the country banks demanded the return of their reserves, their New York "correspondent" banks would "call" the loans and send back the funds. At times, however, the call loans would be in use as tactical weapons in the stock market or for other speculative activities particularly reprehensible to "sound money" bankers. The "call" for the loan would thus get no answer. If the country banks insisted, call loan debtors would be forced to "sell off" security holdings and by so doing depress prices in the stock market. The ensuing stock market "crash" might then generate further apprehension and a general business depression.

The New York banks would frequently tighten credit and sometimes run their reserve positions dangerously low in their efforts to pay off the country banks. In September 1873, for example, reserves of New York City banks fell by more than 50 percent in four weeks. Reserve ratios that averaged 26 percent on September 6 averaged only 11 percent by October 4.

The seasonal demand for hand-to-hand currency and bank reserves that traditionally came in the fall seemed to be the trigger for the occasional money market panics and bank failures. Some observers thought that if additional demand for high-powered money could be met by additional supplies in season — if, in other words, the monetary system could be infused with a degree of seasonal elasticity — most of the current evils might be rendered innocuous.

[6]Fleming, p. 61.

Cyclical elasticity was another monetary problem. One of the features of a business recession is the increase in the demand for money due to an increase in uncertainty and apprehension of further trouble. A general increase in total product going to market would also increase the demand for money. If the money supply were inelastic or perversely elastic, the increased demands for money would not be met by increased supplies. Prices would then fall — that is, the value of money would increase — until the new value of money was high enough to satisfy the increased demand. This kind of bloodletting process was regarded with less and less complacency in the post-Civil War period, especially since prices tended to drag even when business was "good."

Any monetary system that uses more than one kind of money must make provision for the conversion of one form of money, say, bank deposits, into another form, say, currency, without allowing undue stress on the total quantity in existence. A system without such a characteristic lacks form elasticity. Under a system of fractional reserve banking, a demand for additional currency in place of deposits may well result in a decline in the total stock of money. Additional currency is obtained from bank reserves, and a loss of bank reserves forces the banks to contract their outstanding demand obligations by a multiple of the reserves lost if, as normally, they hold no "excess" reserves. "Elasticity of the money supply" thus implies: (1) *form elasticity,* or the ability of institutions in the system to convert one form of money into another without changing unduly the total quantity of money, and (2) *quantity elasticity,* or the ability of these institutions to alter the total quantity of money in order to prevent undue seasonal or cyclical changes in the value of money, which is to say, in the price level.

The elasticity problems can be solved in a variety of ways. First, the fractional reserve character of the system can be scrapped. This idea was given at least lip service by one of the more rigorous "sound money" schools of the past, but was too strong a medicine for later policy makers. A second method is governmental rules that prescribe various reserve requirements at different seasons of the year. But varying reserve requirements has never found much favor. To be operated properly, this policy requires a degree of sophistication not possessed by many policy makers, and it seems to be too cumbersome for seasonal adjustments. A third means is for some separate agency, governmental or otherwise, to supply extra reserves or currency when needed.

The national banking system was envisaged as an institution that might provide some of the elasticity required; and to some extent the national banks in the reserve cities did hold enough "excess" reserves relative to the rest of the system so that additional credit could be extended at critical periods. But national banks were essentially commercial enterprises. Their attempts to maximize returns from commercial lending were not conducive to maintenance of "excess" reserves. The Treasury, another possible candidate, was subject to the push and pull of politics and various ideologies, so it, too, could not be relied upon as an unqualified "lender of last resort." Furthermore, its "political" character made it subject to suspicion. The alleged inadequacies of these institutions gave rise to the "cheap money" palliatives of Greenbacks and Free Silver in the last quarter of the nineteenth century, and finally led to the formation of the Federal Reserve System in 1913.

Cheap Money Movements

A "cheap money" movement, first of all, should be corrected to read a "cheaper money" movement. One could in fact refer to it as a more buoyant price level movement. "Cheap money" has through the years been given an air of opprobrium that may be unwarranted; the word "cheap" has vulgar connotations. A cheaper money when prices are forever falling is a perfectly legitimate and monetarily valid principle. It may mean nothing more than a price level that does not fall as fast as what is currently being experienced, or it may imply the desire for a stable price level when prices are falling. Finally, if prices are relatively constant when unemployment is substantial, a policy that calls for slightly rising prices in order to stimulate real economic growth may have much merit. Thus, the advantages or defects of cheap money policies depend upon the degree of cheapness intended and upon the results that are actually obtained.

The Greenback and Free Silver movements were meant primarily as means for obtaining some elasticity in the money supply, but they also were reactions to the falling price level policies made mandatory by those who wished resumption of specie payments at the pre-Civil War parity. The Greenback movement came first. It developed in the late 1860s as the war-issued greenbacks began to be retired. Those who were most sensitive to falling prices (debtor groups generally) urged abatement of the contraction policy. They favored continuation of the greenbacks already in existence, and only a little more experience with paper money was necessary before suggestions were made for increasing the outstanding amount. Conversion of the interest-bearing debt into greenbacks was seen as one means for getting rid of the debt and for providing some sort of cyclical elasticity at the same time.

The advent of large quantities of silver obtained at lower and lower costs in the late 1870s made the Greenback movement obsolete. Silver had been demonetized formally by the Coinage Act of 1873. When its potential as a cheaper money became manifest a few years later due to discoveries of rich silver mines in the West, "cheap money" legislators, in efforts to cover up their failure to recognize and foster silver monetization, labeled this Act "The Crime of '73." The "crime," however, was adjudicated on the basis of *ex post facto* events.

Silver had many "advantages" over greenbacks once its original disadvantage — its dearness — had been safely overcome by ever-increasing supplies. It was a "precious" metal; it had been a legitimate money in the past; and it was recommended for use in lower denominations and as a fractional currency because of its relative cheapness with respect to gold. Finally, *it was sound:* Silver coins rang beautifully when tossed on counters.

Two Acts, the Bland-Allison Act of 1878 and the Sherman Silver Purchase Act of 1890, remonetized silver in limited amounts. The amounts had to be limited because the silver dollar was defined at a higher monetary value at the mint than what it could obtain in the free market. As a result of these two Acts, the Treasury put significant amounts of silver coin and silver certificates into circulation during the 1880s and early 1890s.

Total silver money in circulation was about $465 million by 1891. At the same time, U.S. notes outstanding were $343 million, and national bank notes were down to $162 million. Silver money thus composed almost half of the fiat currency outstanding. It had come to have the same position in the monetary system that U.S. notes had enjoyed twenty years earlier. In spite of the fact that it was "sound," the commodity value of the silver dollar was only 60 to 70 percent of its legal tender value. It was, therefore, a fiat money and a current demand obligation of the United States Treasury. The Treasury had to keep a portion of its gold stock as a reserve against this demand obligation in the same way that it kept gold reserves against U.S. notes. When the silver money outstanding became substantial, it would tend to raise domestic prices relative to prices in foreign countries and to stimulate an outflow of gold reserves from the Treasury and the banking system. U.S. notes and silver dollars were legal tender in the United States, but they were nothing more than commodities in foreign money markets. For international trading, gold was the only recognized balancer of payments.

During the heyday of the Greenback movement the gold standard system had been in suspension and thus inoperable. The infusion of silver started just as gold convertibility was resumed. The monetary effects of silver were not critical so long as enough gold also entered the system; and the silver augmentations to the money supply kept prices pleasingly buoyant in contrast to the depressed years of the previous decade. The early 1890s then witnessed a worldwide scramble for gold without enough in existence to keep price levels from falling competitively.

The United States fared reasonably well in the international struggle as evidenced by a favorable balance of trade, but it was the only major Western country that continued to monetize silver. Apprehension abroad over the ability of the banks and the Treasury to maintain gold convertibility for silver issues outstanding became acute in the middle 1890s. So in spite of the favorable balance of trade, gold did not flow in. Instead, outstanding government debt held abroad was returned in large part as "payment" for the trade balance. Suspension of gold payments was avoided only by the narrowest of margins in 1895 and 1896. Thereafter, fresh gold discoveries in the Yukon and South Africa furnished the commercial world with enough gold to make it, too, a money cheap enough for popular "consumption."

Greenbacks and silver had given some reasonable degree of secular increase (elasticity) to the money supply. However, bankers and legislators felt that elasticity was more critically a seasonal problem, and they most emphatically maintained that provision for elasticity was properly a job for the banking system. They held that all of the common forms of currency were necessarily inelastic in supply; and the constraint each bank faced in holding its own legal reserves prevented the system from expanding or contracting credit with regard to the "needs of business." They favored the formation of a "central reserve association" that would not only pool reserves of its members and thus make the strength of all available for the use of any one, but would also allow its members to obtain increases in reserves by discounting bona fide commercial paper with the central institution. On these principles the Federal Reserve System was originally formed. It provided for form-seasonal elasticity of the money supply at the initiative of the member banks, and it centralized reserves in the twelve regional Federal Reserve Banks. The System was not to act in contravention to the operations of the gold standard; it was seen simply as a more "economical" way of organizing gold reserves. It provided a reservoir of available funds for the discounting of high quality commercial paper, the only penalty for this privilege being the discount rate it charged.

Solution to the essential problem of inelasticity in the money supply required an arrangement within the monetary system for an "excess" reserve reservoir and some sort of rules for the disbursement of these reserves at the proper times. The Federal Reserve System was one such arrangement, but it was by no means the only one that had been used or the only one that could be used.

Growth in the Banking Industry to 1929

The banking industry in the nineteenth century grew at about the average rate for all industries. Between 1875 and 1896 the number of banks increased by a factor of 2.80, and the volume of bank deposits by a factor of 2.75. (See Table 10.1.) Prices fell somewhat during the same period and total money income about doubled. The number of banking firms and the "product" of the banking industry were thus expanding at rates comparable to the growth in the economy generally. Until just after World War I this trend continued; but the maximum number of banking firms (31,000) was reached in 1921. During the next eight years of prosperity and relatively full employment, the banking industry lost 7,000 firms — about 23 percent of the total number. At the same time total bank deposits increased from $34 billion to $61 billion, an increase of 80 percent. The volume of business of the average bank, therefore, increased considerably. This increase was also reflected in the value of total bank capital, which was $6.39 billion in 1921 and $9.75 billion in 1929. Since the value of the dollar was fairly constant during this interval, these dollar capital values are comparable. Taken with the decline in the number of banking firms, they show that the average size of the banking firm grew by about 50 percent.

Table 10.2. All Commercial Banks—Number of Banks by Federal Reserve Membership, Consolidations and Absorptions, Suspensions, Total Money Supply, and GNP: 1914–1969 (monetary statistics in billions of dollars; values near June 30)

Year	All U.S. Commercial Banks* Members of FRS	All U.S. Commercial Banks* Non-members	Mergers, Consolidations, and Absorptions	Suspensions	Demand Deposits Adjusted†	Currency outside Banks†	All Deposits in Commercial Banks plus Currency†‡	All Time and Savings Deposits	GNP for Calendar Year
1914	7,518	19,718		151	10.1	1.53	16.1	8.35	
1915	7,614	19,776		152	9.83	1.58	16.7	9.23	
1916	7,605	20,134		52	12.0	1.88	19.9	10.3	
1917	7,652	20,646		49	13.5	2.28	22.8	11.5	
1918	8,112	20,644		47	14.8	3.30	25.4	11.7	
1919	8,821	20,326		63	17.6	3.59	29.7	13.4	78.9
1920	9,398	20,893		168	19.6	4.11	34.2	15.8	88.9
1921	9,745	20,711	305§	505	17.1	3.68	31.7	16.6	74.0
1922	9,892	20,228	394	367	18.1	3.35	33.0	17.4	74.0
1923	9,850	19,973	329	646	19.0	3.74	36.1	19.7	86.1
1924	9,650	19,338	373	775	19.4	3.65	37.6	21.3	87.6
1925	9,538	18,904	363	618	21.4	3.57	40.9	23.2	91.3
1926	9,375	18,367	462	976	22.0	3.60	42.7	24.7	97.7
1927	9,099	17,551	567	669	22.0	3.56	43.9	26.5	96.3
1928	8,929	16,869	534	499	22.3	3.62	45.7	28.5	98.2
1929	8,707	16,263	636	659	22.5	3.64	45.7	28.6	104
1930	8,315	15,364	769	1,352	21.7	3.37	44.8	29.0	91.1
1931	7,782	13,872	798	2,294	19.8	3.65	42.2	29.0	76.3
1932	6,980	11,754	433	1,456	15.6	4.62	34.3	24.8	58.5
1933	5,606	8,601	322	4,001	14.4	4.76	30.0	21.7	56.0
1934	6,375	8,973	231	44§	16.7	4.66	33.3	22.9	65.0
1935	6,410	9,078	160	34	20.4	4.78	38.0	23.9	72.5
1936	6,400	8,929	176	43	23.8	5.22	42.7	24.9	82.7
1937	6,357	8,737	186	58	25.2	5.49	45.2	25.9	90.8
1938	6,338	8,529	100	52	24.3	5.42	44.5	26.2	85.2
1939	6,330	8,337	119	41	27.4	6.01	48.5	26.8	91.1

1940	6,398	8,136	96	22	32.0	6.70	54.2	27.5	101
1941	6,553	7,881	59	8	37.3	8.20	61.5	27.9	126
1942	6,644	7,709	89	9	41.9	10.9	68.4	27.3	159
1943	6,700	7,497	86	4	56.0	15.8	89.4	30.3	193
1944	6,770	7,368	72	1	60.1	20.9	102	35.7	211
1945	6,837	7,289	80	0	69.1	25.1	121	44.3	214
1946	6,884	7,268	94	0	79.5	26.5	138	51.8	211
1947	6,925	7,257	84	1	82.2	26.3	143	55.7	234
1948	6,922	7,267	75	0	82.7	25.6	144	57.4	259
1949	6,900	7,251	77	4	81.9	25.3	143	58.5	258
1950	6,882	7,264	91	1	85.0	25.2	147	59.7	285
1951	6,856	7,251	82	3	89.0	25.8	152	60.0	329
1952	6,812	7,257	100	3	94.8	26.5	161	63.7	347
1953	6,762	7,243	115	4	96.9	27.4	167	68.3	365
1954	6,717	7,219	206	3	98.1	27.1	171	73.3	363
1955	6,607	7,173	231	4	103	27.4	178	77.1	398
1956	6,495	7,183	189	3	105	28.3	183	80.6	419
1957	6,440	7,177	157	3	106	28.0	187	85.7	440
1958	6,312	7,192	151	8	107	28.0	197	95.5	445
1959	6,233	7,244	166	3	113	28.4	206	101	483
1960	6,174	7,300	131	2	110	28.1	205	104	503
1961	6,113	7,320			113	28.2	220	117	519
1962	6,047	7,380	322	18	114	29.3	235	132	554
1963	6,108	7,461			117.6	30.7	252.8	149.3	590.5
1964	6,225	7,536	288	13	120.8	32.7	270.1	165.9	632.4
1965	6,221	7,583			126.9	34.1	298.1	188.3	684.9
1966	6,150	7,620	286	25	131.3	36.3	322.4	208.7	749.6
1967	6,071	7,650			135.7	38.4	347.7	231.8	793.5
1968	5,978	7,701	266	19	145.9	40.8	375.8	251.9	865.7
1969	5,871	7,791	146	5	151.6	43.7	394.8	266.2	932.1
1970	5,768	7,920	n.a.	n.a.	162.2	47.7	418.2	277.3	976.5

Sources: Department of Commerce, *Historical Statistics of the United States, Colonial Times to 1957* (Washington, D.C., 1966), and *Banking and Monetary Statistics and Supplements* (Washington, D.C.: Board of Governors of the Federal Reserve System, 1943 and 1962).
* End of year.
† Averages of daily figures.
‡ This column includes time deposits in commercial banks plus the sum of the two preceding columns.
§ Data from this year on do not include private unincorporated banks.

The change in the average bank size with normal growth in commercial bank deposits was obtained in part by a net loss of banking firms in conjunction with a large number of consolidations and absorptions, and a sizable extension of branch banking. Consolidations and absorptions of banks numbered about 4,000 in the 1921–1929 period, while more than 5,500 banks suspended. At the same time about 2,500 new banks opened for business. To summarize, the total number of banking firms was fewer by 7,000 at the end of the period, but this loss was in part offset by the addition of over 2,000 branches to existing banks.

The decrease in the number of firms and the increase in the volume of business handled by each firm were possibly due to three factors: (1) internal technical changes within the banking firm, (2) technical changes external to the banking industry, and (3) legal changes in the rules of the game that prescribe the activity of each firm.[7] An example of technical change within the firm is the increase in the efficiency of accounting methods and practices due to the availability of machines that simplify the sorting and clearing processes. Use of such equipment allows a much larger volume of deposit business than is possible with hand methods. A change external to the industry that would cause the firms to centralize and to become larger and fewer is the general change in consumer buying and marketing habits brought about by the extended use of automobiles and other forms of transportation. With everyone able to get into the centers of business communities, many peripheral marginal businesses become unprofitable. The corner grocery store and the corner bank suffered the same fate. Finally, banking laws changed the maximum possible limits of bank size. Many of the states had long been suspicious of "moneyed monopolists." Banking firms had been regarded as pernicious, albeit necessary, institutions because they supplied the wheels of industry with financial "oil." During the 1920s public opinion softened somewhat and banking laws became less restrictive.

The Banking Industry in the Great Depression

The complexion of the industry changed radically in the four years of business decline (1929–1933) that marked the beginning of the Great Depression. Consolidations and absorptions gave way to suspensions as the dominant statistic for the industry. All told, the number of firms declined from 25,000 to 14,000, or by about 44 percent, and bank capital declined by 25 percent. Total deposits went from $61 billion to $36 billion, a decrease of 41 percent. (See Table 10.2.)

---

[7]The factors suggested here are only provisional. Much room for additional research on these issues is still evident.

Other industries also suffered, but not nearly so much as the banking industry. The number of firms in retail trade, for example, was reduced from 1,327,000 to 1,291,000, or by 3 percent, while the number of manufacturing firms declined from 257,000 to 166,000, or by 34 percent. (The Depression's effects on different industries varied greatly; the number of "second-hand" stores, for example, *increased* from 15,065 to 33,516.) Banking suffered the most, and, in addition, aggravated the decline by the destruction of the economy's money supply.

Since 1933, bank suspensions have been almost nonexistent. State and federal governments and the Federal Reserve System have generally conceded that society has a vested interest in the maintenance of an "adequate" number of banks. Banks have obtained a position similar to public utilities in official policies. In addition, the technical, legal, and organizational changes observed during the 1920s have continued. These factors, and the conspicuous absence of bank panics and bankruptcy during the last 35 years, have generated a contemporary bank image far different from that of the past.

Selected Bibliography

Friedman, Milton, and Anna Jacobson Schwartz. *A Monetary History of the United States, 1867–1960.* Princeton, N.J.: Princeton University Press, 1963. This work cannot be recommended too highly; its breadth, scholarship, and analytical rigor would be hard to surpass. Furthermore, it is written in a style that any layman or student of the subject can easily comprehend.

What Is the Average Recovery of Deposits?

Joseph Stagg Lawrence

The plight of the banker during the collapse of the thirties pervades this article by the late Princeton professor of economics and banker Joseph Lawrence. He tries to show that commercial business failures rather than bank failures were responsible for the economic debacle and that depositors' losses

From *Banking, Journal of the ABA,* February 1931, pp. 655, 656, 722, and 723. Reprinted by permission of the publisher.

from bank failures were not as severe, historically, as creditors' losses from corporate failures. The fact of the matter is that everyone was being injured by the failure of the government to pursue what we now understand to be appropriate monetary and fiscal policies (see especially the reading for Chapter 19 by Chandler). Also, it should be understood that the best type of "insurance" for bank depositors is a central bank that maintains a healthy banking and monetary system by means of intelligent and deliberate policies.

The banker seems fair prey for a host of facile thinkers seeking some scapegoat upon whom to unload that sense of personal inadequacy and fault which always accompanies misfortune. Shortly after the great debacle in the stock market, a speaker at the meeting of the American Academy of Political Science presented an involved, profound, obscure and atrociously erroneous analysis of the collapse which finally placed the American banker in the defendant's chair. The unfortunate part of the proceeding was the enthusiasm with which the diagnosis was greeted by an audience seeking intently for a salve with which to anoint its speculative wounds. The banker is compelled to say "no" so often that he becomes a popular candidate for this unpleasant role on the occasion of any national misfortune.

Business and Moral Risks

A year ago he was made responsible for the stock crash. Prior to that, he was the cause of speculation since he failed to heed the ineffable wisdom of Washington. During the past year his alleged penurious eccentricities have been the cause of commodity price declines. Now it appears that he is responsible for the extraordinary total of failures in the country. Bradstreet's, in its issue of Jan. 3, charges that the large total of commercial failures is to be accounted for by the extraordinary record of banking mortality. It is high time that a few rays of truth be focused upon this confused stage.

A banker is primarily a dealer in risks. Next to an insurance company no enterprise traffics so candidly with the fickle goddess of chance. A client comes in to borrow $10,000. He outlines his project to the banker and provides security, ample if the venture succeeds, inadequate if it fails. Often the collateral includes a generous allowance of moral risk, i.e., the confidence which the banker has in the capacity and integrity of the borrower. Perfect safety is impossible in ordinary banking. The best banker can never hope to eliminate losses entirely. His efforts are directed toward minimizing them. Over a period of years 1921–1928, net losses of national banks were equal to 10.3 percent of gross earnings. They amounted to more than half the payments for wages and salaries and exceeded the return to stockholders.

If a community or an industry is in distress, the banks cannot escape the consequences. The deflation of the land boom in Florida has left the landscape cluttered with the bleached bones of banks. Approximately three quarters of the banks in Florida have bitten the dust of insolvency during the past ten years, the grim reaper having done his most effective execution since real estate ceased selling by the ounce. If one examines the toll of banks which have passed on, one finds the majority of them throughout the South and West, particularly in regions where agriculture has suffered most. The banker's fortunes are tied to those of his community. If the sun of prosperity beams down upon it he may be able to benefit by the vital rays. Much has been said regarding the interdependence of business; not enough has been said about the interdependence of banking and business.

In another sense a banker's position is infinitely more precarious than that of his clients. Every business can present its statement of assets and liabilities which shows that the obligations due to the enterprise are matched by its own dues to its creditors. Insofar as the balance of the two sides of the statement is concerned the bank is no different from any other business.

The character of the obligations on the two sides reveals a startling difference. The bank has its debtors who must eventually repay their obligations to the bank but summary liquidation is impossible, except for a small fraction of the total. On the other hand, the greater part of the bank's liabilities are payable on demand. It normally relies on the operation of the law of averages, reinforced on occasion by its cash and secondary reserves. It knows from experience that demand will match deposits over a period of time. If there is an adverse movement it may resort to its liquid reserves and then secure additional assistance by the sale of marketable securities in its portfolios and by borrowing.

This falls far short of complete protection. If for any one of a number of reasons, sound or otherwise, the public decides to deny the bank its confidence there is nothing for it to do but close its doors, be its condition ever so good. If all the depositors of all our banks should demand payment at the same time, not one tenth of their claims could be met in cash and every bank in the country would be compelled to acknowledge insolvency. Recently several large banks have been forced to close their doors because of a collapse of public confidence, although subsequent examinations showed the institutions to be in excellent condition.

The organization of a bank or the acquisition of a proprietary interest in a bank is, like the state of matrimony, a condition which cannot be entered thoughtlessly. Our national banks and most of our state banks must first satisfy certain requirements of the law intended to recommend them to the confidence of the public. These relate to capital, the accumulation of surplus (to provide strength and a safety factor for the creditors), the maintenance of reserves (to be able to meet depositors' demands) and restraints upon lending and investing (to reduce risks). Furthermore the stockholders must pledge an amount equal to that which they have already invested as a hostage to the integrity, wisdom and efficiency of the bank's officers.

The banker is expected to stimulate the vital spark of enterprise with ample doses of credit. He must minimize risks and provoke no breath of suspicion regarding his prudence and honesty. Caesar's wife was a perfect wanton compared to the fleckless faultlessness of the banker's character. He must bow to the supervision of the state and bond his infallibility with double liability on his investment.

At the Public's Mercy

In these three respects then the position of the banker differs from that of the average entrepreneur. As the banker for community funds and its principal dealer in risks his business health is peculiarly and intimately bound with that of the community. The nature of the banker's liabilities leaves him at the mercy of the public's fickle apprehensions. An idle or malicious rumor starts a stampede of hysterical depositors. In every other line of business the debtor receives at least the same consideration as the creditor. Not so with the banker. His debts are, for the greater part, categorical and summary. His accounts receivable are conditional. In the third place the banker has submitted to an abridgment of his rights and the freedom of his judgment which leaves him in a class by himself.

Nevertheless as the elegiac notes of the funeral dirge swell, the voices of aspersion, suspicion and indictment are heard more distinctly. Six thousand bank failures in ten years! *Involving* $2,250,000,000 of deposits! We have borrowed the italicized word from the 1929 report of the Comptroller of the Currency. To those who know nothing of the liquidation of failed banks the sum conveys the impression of losses to depositors. The official mentioned did not establish the distinction between deposits involved and deposits lost in bank failures. The man in the street is not aware that such a distinction exists.

Actual Losses Small

Consider the record for 1930. About 1,100 banks have failed, with deposits amounting to (estimated partly) $800,000,000. This includes three large banks, two in New York City and one in Philadelphia, which account for almost one-half of that total. At the time of writing it seems reasonably certain that at least two of these institutions will be reorganized and that the third might be able to pay 100 cents on the dollar. This would immediately cut the horrendous aggregate in half. A study of national bank failures and subsequent liquidation since the Civil War reveals the fact that depositors on the average recover about ninety cents on the dollar!

The Depositor's Dollar in Average Bank Failure

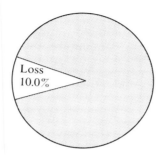

There is no intention here to mitigate the seriousness of bank suspension and failure even if the depositor does manage to salvage the greater part of his claim from the wreckage. To a client who has counted his deposit as so much liquid cash available to his draft, the announcement that the bank has deferred payment is calamitous. It immediately freezes his own business, not to mention any progressive commitments which he may have made and causes him grave embarrassment. Nevertheless it is an inconvenience rather than a loss. In many cases he can borrow against his certificate of deposit and eventually the bank thaws out its assets to pay back the greater part of his claim.

By Way of Contrast

What a contrast with the consequences of ordinary commercial failure! Sixty percent of these suspend without any assets whatsoever. The expenses of administration absorb the assets of a large part of the remainder. By the time the average creditor of the commercial bankrupt takes stock he finds that his dollar claim against the debtor has shrunk to 8¼ cents. (The figures quoted are taken from the statistical appendices of Colonel Donovan's report on Bankruptcy Reform.) So slim are the chances of recovery, so costly the process and so indulgent the law that 30 percent of the claims are abandoned by impatient or possibly wise creditors. During the five year period June 30, 1924, to June 30, 1929, commercial bankruptcies have resulted in $3,800,000,000 losses.

Creditor's Dollar in Average Commercial Failure

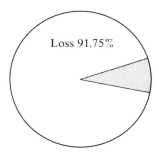

Loss 91.75%

In spite of the excellent comparative record of our banks, their detractors are dipping ardent brushes in ink and painting the picture black. The long sad list has been used as an indictment of the American system of banking and students more eager for reform than discerning in their examination of the facts have proposed the summary remedy of extinction for our unit banks. Branch banking has been brought forth as the all-embracing remedy.

What History Says

To indicate how far mistaken we may be in this matter it is necessary to go back to the decade following the panic of 1837. In the single year 1839, 403 out of a total of 850 banks failed, 47.6 percent. During the entire ten years 1921–1930 about 6,000 banks have failed out of an original total of 30,000, 20 percent. In the earlier period the failures were freely attributed to branch and chain banking and unentangled independent banking was urged as the remedy. Most northern states adopted it prior to the Civil War and in 1863 Congress excluded branch banking in the National Banking Act. At the present time the independent bank has been rather freely indicted and branch banking urged as a remedy.

In view of all the circumstances our bank failures are not so devastating as they have been painted. The extraordinary credit inflation of the war and post war period and the subsequent collapse; the prolonged depression in agriculture; the far reaching changes in the distribution of population, in transportation, in merchandising; and the benign guiding hand of Washington in many forms of private enterprise have been powerful contributing factors beyond the control of the individual banker.

11

The Regulation and Structure
of the Commercial Banking Industry[1]

Commercial banks act as both producers of money and middlemen between savers and investors. Some people have more current income than they wish to consume (savers), while others wish to construct new capital in some form or another but have insufficient current income for the purpose (investors). The economic justification for a banking firm is that it makes the income of the saver available to the investor. From this standpoint, the banking industry is not to be distinguished generally from any other financial industry. The short-term commercial loans and investments of various types which are held by banks do not differ essentially from many of the assets held by insurance companies, commercial credit houses, credit unions, and, to some degree, retailers, who themselves extend credit. It is the creation of some sort of *money* on the liabilities side of the balance sheet that makes a bank out of a firm that otherwise would be just another financial middleman.

Banking Regulation

Present-day banking regulations are a curious mixture of federal and state laws designed essentially to prevent bank failure. When a corporation fails, stockholders and bondholders are the ones who suffer the losses. When a bank

---

[1]For an excellent collection of articles on recent changes in the regulation and structure of banking, see *Law and Contemporary Problems*, Banking, Part I: Banking Regulation, Vol. 31, No. 4 (Autumn 1966), and Part II: Developments in Banking, Vol. 32, No. 1 (Winter 1967).

fails, the losses are borne not only by investors in the enterprise but also to some extent by depositors. A general loss of faith in the money and banking system, triggered by a few dramatic bankruptcies, can cause serious disruptions of production in the economy. To avoid such catastrophes, governmental regulations and supervision have been imposed on the banking system.

Fifty state agencies and three federal agencies are currently responsible for bank regulation. Federal supervision and regulation were initiated by the National Bank Act of 1863. Under this Act, the Comptroller of the Currency was given the power to charter banks provided certain requirements were met. The Federal Reserve Act of 1913 required all national banks to become members of the Federal Reserve System, and permitted all state banks which could meet the requirements to become members. The formation of the Federal Deposit Insurance Corporation (FDIC) in 1933 similarly afforded state banks the opportunity to obtain deposit insurance but also required national banks to do so. Banks that are state-chartered and not members of the Federal Reserve System or the FDIC are exclusively under state regulation. (On December 31, 1970, only 48 such commercial banks were left.) State banks that obtain FDIC insurance are subject to the regulation of two agencies, while state-chartered Federal Reserve members, all of whom must obtain FDIC insurance, are subject to the regulation of three agencies. National banks necessarily are under the regulation of the three federal agencies. This multiplicity of relationships has provoked a great deal of criticism and many suggestions for amendment and consolidation.

Dual Banking

The United States is said to have a *dual banking system* because banks may receive either a state or a federal charter and because they are free to shift from one type of charter to another. This shifting enables banks to substitute state regulation for federal or vice versa. Also, state banks may alter their degree of federal regulation by electing to become Federal Reserve members. Those who support dual banking say that it provides a safety valve against inequitable or discriminatory chartering or regulation procedures by either state or federal officials. Critics of dual banking say that it simply provides a means for banks to manipulate one regulatory authority against another, thus weakening banking regulation.

As mentioned above, banking laws were established essentially to prevent bank failure. An important part of these laws restricts bank competition in the interest of preventing such failures. Methods for limiting competition include: (1) restricting entry into the banking business; (2) erecting barriers to the branching of existing banks; (3) limiting the types and volume of earning assets which banks may hold; and (4) curbing the amount of interest which banks may pay on various types of deposits. Each of these techniques for restricting bank competition will be examined in turn.

Restriction of bank entry. Today a group of individuals seeking a bank charter must meet a host of requirements, whether the charter is state or federal. Applicants are expected to demonstrate not only that they have acquired the appropriate amount of capital subscriptions but also that there is a "need" for a new banking facility. This "need and convenience" criterion was established by the Banking Acts of 1933 and 1935 as a result of the belief that "overbanking" had caused the bank failures of the early 1930s. This new federal law charged the Comptroller of the Currency to certify to the Federal Deposit Insurance Corporation that he had examined not only the management and financial condition of the prospective bank but also the bank's "future earnings prospects... (and) the convenience and needs of the community to be served by the bank."[2] The Federal Reserve System was directed to follow the same guidelines in granting membership to newly organized state-chartered banks, and the FDIC was to consider the same factors in granting insurance to state-chartered banks that were not members of the Federal Reserve System. Since 98.6 percent of the commercial banks in the United States are insured and since many states have followed the same principle, virtually all new banks in the country have had to meet this criterion. One investigator has estimated that 50 to 100 percent more banks would have been chartered during the 1936–1962 period if such entry restrictions had been absent.[3] This estimate demonstrates the effectiveness of entry restrictions, although not necessarily the economic justification for them.

Branching barriers. A branch bank is a part of a single legal entity that operates more than one banking office. It is analogous to one firm with more than one plant. Branching provides existing banks with a means for expanding the supply of their services. Since the banking system generally is under dual jurisdiction, the laws for bank organization can be in conflict. In the case of branching, federal law has allowed state laws to be dominant. In 1865 the National Bank Act was amended to allow state banks with branches to become national banks while retaining their branches. The McFadden Act of 1927, and amendments in 1933 and 1962, allowed branch banking by national banks in states that permitted branching, subject to the same general rules imposed by the states.

For the most part, the states have been antipathetic to the idea of branch banking. Americans have traditionally opposed centralization of power, and have encouraged accordingly the development of unit banks (banks in which a single legal entity owns and operates one banking office). This procedure is in contrast to some other important industries and to the development of banking industries in many other countries. As seen in Table 11.1, only sixteen

---

[2]U.S.C. 1814, 1816.

[3]Sam Peltzman, "Bank Entry Regulation: Its Impact and Purpose," *Studies in Banking Competition and the Banking Structure,* articles reprinted from *The National Banking Review* (Washington, D.C.: United States Treasury, 1966), pp. 292–293.

states permit statewide branch banking. In sixteen others limited area branching is allowed, while unit banking is the mode in eighteen other states. In eleven states branching is prohibited altogether. Needless to say, banks may not branch across state lines, though some states allow foreign (international) branches. Branch banking has been most popular on the West Coast, although it is also prominent on the East Coast and around the Great Lakes. Its growth in these areas, in spite of restrictive law, suggests that it is an economical form of banking organization.

Table 11.1. Branch Banking, Limited Branch Banking, and Unit Banking States

States where Statewide Branch Banking Prevails	States where Limited Area Branch Banking Prevails	States where Unit Banking Prevails
Alaska	Alabama	Arkansas
Arizona	Georgia	Colorado
California	Indiana	Florida
Connecticut	Kentucky	Illinois
Delaware	Louisiana	Iowa
Hawaii	Maine	Kansas
Idaho	Massachusetts	Minnesota
Maryland	Michigan	Missouri
Nevada	Mississippi	Montana
North Carolina	New Jersey	Nebraska
Oregon	New Mexico	New Hampshire
Rhode Island	New York	North Dakota
South Carolina	Ohio	Oklahoma
Utah	Pennsylvania	South Dakota
Vermont	Tennessee	Texas
Washington	Virginia	West Virginia
		Wisconsin
		Wyoming

Source: *Annual Report of the Federal Deposit Insurance Corporation, 1964* (Washington, D.C.: Federal Deposit Insurance Corporation, 1965), p. 141

Earning asset limitations. Banks are subject to a bewildering array of limitations on the types of earning assets that they may acquire as well as on the sizes of the loans they may make in both total volume and the amount to any one borrower. Many of these limitations are a carry-over of the "real bills" doctrine.

The total amount that a commercial bank may lend is restricted by regulatory reserve requirements. In earlier times, reserves were a source of liquid assets that banks could call upon in case of financial need. In fact, only a system of 100 percent reserves would guarantee to depositors the liquidity of their deposits. Today, reserve requirements are recognized as a means for controlling bank credit by the central banking authorities. However, the application of reserve requirements is not uniform. Reserve requirements for all member banks of the Federal Reserve System are set by the System's Board of Governors; but reserve requirements within the System vary according to the classification of the bank—"country" or "reserve city," and according to the type of deposits being covered—"demand" or "time." State-chartered banks, not members of the System, are subject to the requirements set by their respective states.

The size of bank capital may limit the amount of bank lending in at least two ways. First, state, as well as federal, regulations usually specify that banks may not lend more than 10 percent of the value of their capital and surplus to any one borrower. This constraint is the familiar "don't-put-all-your-eggs-in-one-basket" theory. Second, banking authorities have traditionally believed that a certain portion of bank capital, relative to the total assets or liabilities of the bank, is needed to protect bank depositors against loss in the case of shrinkage in the value of bank assets. Banks that fall short in this respect are expected to obtain more capital or hold fewer risk assets. But not all students of banking agree with this approach. In the first place, bank capital, like the capital of other enterprises, has very little liquidation value. In addition, deposit protection for depositors stems from the banks' careful selection of an asset portfolio, FDIC insurance, and most critically on Federal Reserve policies. The size of the banks' capital stock and fractional reserve "backing" are popular but irrelevant misconceptions for measuring the security of bank credit. Nevertheless, reserve and capital requirements continue to limit the quantity of banks' earning assets.

Interest payment limitations. The amount of interest banks may pay on deposits directly influences the volume of deposits banks may attract. After the Banking Acts of 1933 and 1935, member banks of the Federal Reserve System or FDIC were prohibited from paying interest on demand deposits and were limited in the amount of interest they could pay on time deposits. These regulations are still in effect today. Competition among banks to attract demand deposits must exist on the basis of service. Some observers feel that these services are, in fact, *implicit* interest payments and that *explicit* payments should be allowed in order to broaden the channels of interbank competition.

Banks are not only in competition with each other for funds but also with other financial institutions. The rapid growth of nonbank financial institutions, such as savings and loan associations, credit unions, and others, has been attributed, at least in part, to the more attractive rates of interest these institutions have been able to pay. In 1960 a relaxation in the Federal Reserve's Regulation Q, governing the interest rates members may pay on time deposits, resulted in a partial reclamation of the commercial banks' former share of the financial markets. Some observers believe that an even more efficient allocation of funds among the various financial institutions would be forthcoming if additional freedom were allowed.

Conflicts in Federal Supervision

The large majority of banks in the country are subject to varying degrees of federal regulation, depending upon whether they are members of the Federal Reserve System and whether they possess a national charter. National banks have three masters to serve—the Comptroller of the Currency, the Federal Reserve System, and the FDIC. The complexities of bank supervision, especially national bank supervision, have rapidly multiplied as new laws have been passed, judicial decisions have been handed down, and new administrators have been appointed. Federal officials have spent much of their time coordinating the actions of their several agencies. Recent splits in the fabric of effective banking regulation have been due to both a complex organizational structure and an honest divergence of views by administrators.

A recent example of such conflicts is the question of bank absorption of certain "exchange charges" on the collection of checks for depositors. The Board of Governors maintains that such absorption is in fact a payment of interest on demand deposits—a violation of the statutes. The FDIC does not consider such absorptions to be interest payments and has argued with the Federal Reserve about the matter for years. A tripartite impasse occurred when the Comptroller of the Currency announced that national banks had the *right* and the *duty* to absorb exchange charges for their customers in the same fashion as their nonnational bank competition was doing.

Similar examples have occurred in the underwriting of revenue bonds by banks, bank purchases of corporate stocks, and bank mergers. While two sets of regulations, one federal and one state, are in accord with the principle of dual banking, two federal sets of rulings have been called poor government. Many proposals for the unification of federal supervision have been made. As early as 1919 several such bills were introduced in Congress. Since that time numerous reports have been made on the subject, including one by the Commission on Money and Credit in 1961. Opponents of the idea of a central authority, or Federal Banking Commission, fear the concentration of power in the hands of one federal agency. Some believe it would threaten the dual banking system, though supporters of a central commission claim the dual system would be strengthened. Clearly, the confusion in banking regulation that has been developed at the federal level is undesirable. One may argue that if other businesses should not and do not face this kind of bureaucratic regulation, neither should the banking industry.

The Changing View of Competition

Within the past decade a new view of banking regulation has arisen. While regulatory authority, at least for the past 40 years, has been concerned with safeguarding banks against failure, the new emphasis has been on fostering and preserving bank competition. An allied interest is the protection of borrowers, especially small borrowers, against monopoly situations in banking. James J. Saxon, Comptroller of the Currency in 1961–1966, encouraged the formation of national banks in areas that he felt were "underbanked." At least part of the conflicts that arose among federal agencies during this period must be attributed to the Comptroller's zeal for competition and the other agencies' inertia. During the Saxon era more national charter applications were received than in the previous 25 years. From 1936 to 1960 only 335 new national banking charters were granted, while from 1962 to 1965 a total of 513 new national charters were issued, a twelve-fold increase based on annual rates. Saxon's final report, the *103rd Annual Report of the Comptroller of the Currency,* states that new charters issued by his office during this period were needed in order to prevent stifling growth in particular communities. As often happens in a dual banking system, when one regulatory authority initiates changes others soon follow. This principle at least held true during the Saxon period as states stepped up their issues of charters. However, more recently the rate of chartering has slowed.

The Industrial Structure of Banking

The present structure of the commercial banking system in the United States is the product of institutions, laws, and circumstances. Prior to the National Bank Act of 1863, all banks except for the First and Second Banks of the United States were state-chartered. As noted in Chapter 10, state-chartered banks found little advantage in converting to national charters, so the percentage of national banks in the country initially was quite small. However, as Figure 11.1 shows, the number of national banks grew rapidly following the passage of a tax on state bank notes in 1865, though the growth of deposit banking kept state banks from being driven from the market. Starting in the early 1880s, a new spirit of free banking became pervasive, and a "charter race" appears to have occurred between state and federal officials. The number of national banks increased from approximately 2,100 in 1880 to about 8,000 by 1920. During the same period the number of state banks jumped from approximately 650 to over 22,000. Then in the early 1920s, federal chartering policy became somewhat restrictive. About half of the applications received during the 1926 to 1930 period were rejected. The Great Depression of the 1930s took its toll, with state-chartered banks disappearing more rapidly than national banks. During the past 30 years, with the exception of the Saxon era, the number of both state and federally chartered banks has gradually declined, but the ratio of national banks to all banks has remained at about 35 percent. During the past twenty years the growth of branch banking offices has been rapid enough to offset the decline in banks. In fact, the total number of banking offices (unit banks plus home offices and branches) has risen steadily. As of

June 30, 1970, the number of commercial banks in the United States was 13,671. Of this total, 4,640 were national banks, 1,167 were state-chartered members of the Federal Reserve System, 7,672 were state-chartered non-member insured banks, and 192 banks were not insured at all (see Table 11.2).

Table 11.2. Commercial Banking Offices in the United States
by Charter, Insurance, and Federal Reserve Membership, June 30, 1970

| Type of Office | Total | Insured | | | | Non-insured |
| | | Total | Federal Reserve Member | | Nonmember | |
			National	State		
All offices (number)	34,521	21,431	16,726	4,705	12,853	237
(percent of total)	100.00		48.45	13.63	37.23	0.69
Banks: Head office						
or unit (number)	13,671	5,807	4,640	1,167	7,672	192
(percent of total)	100.00		33.94	8.54	56.12	1.40
Branches, additional						
offices, and						
facilities (number)	20,850	15,624	12,086	3,538	5,181	45
(percent of total)	100.00		57.97	16.97	24,85	0.21

Source: Board of Governors of the Federal Reserve System, *Federal Reserve Bulletin*, Vol. 56, No. 8 (August 1970), p. A96.

State-chartered banks are more numerous than national banks, but the average national bank is larger. While comprising 33.94 percent of all the banks in the country, the national banking system has 58.89 percent of total commercial bank assets (see Table 11.3). However, the average state-chartered Federal Reserve System member bank is larger than the average national bank. The average state-chartered member bank has slightly over $102 million in assets compared to less than $68 million for the average national bank. Banks that are not members of the Federal Reserve System account for the least financial activity.

The recent proliferation of bank branches, as seen in Figure 11.1, has not been without mixed opinions and much comment. Branches now account for over 60 percent of all of the banking offices in the United States. The branch banking issue is but one part of a larger overall issue — competition and the growth of firms in banking. Extension of branches, consummation of new mergers, and formation of holding companies have been seen as possible limits to competition.

Table 11.3. Assets of Commercial Banks in the United States, December 31, 1969

	Total Assets (thousands of dollars)	Percent of Total Bank Deposits
Insured banks:		
Members of the Federal Reserve System:		
National	315,502,098	58.89
State	119,218,601	22.26
Nonmembers of the Federal Reserve System (state)	95,994,012	17.92
Noninsured banks (state)	4,965,029	0.93
Total	535,679,740	100.00

Source: *Annual Report of the Federal Deposit Insurance Corporation, 1969* (Washington, D.C.: Federal Deposit Insurance Corporation, 1970), p. 258.

Figure 11.1. Number of State-Chartered and Federally Chartered Banks

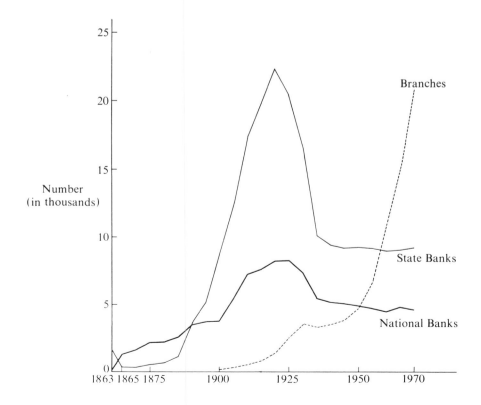

The Branch Banking Issue

The proponents of branch banking point to the many advantages that may stem from it. First, economists have discovered that the banking firm enjoys economies of scale: An expansion in the size of a bank frequently results in lower costs to the bank and either better service or lower rates on loans to the consumer of banking services. Since a unit bank can effectively serve only a small geographical area, significant economies in banking most likely can be attained only by permitting widespread branching—perhaps even across state lines.

Second, the mobility of bank funds is increased through branch banking. Some economic communities may have a higher loan demand than others. A unit bank usually can utilize only the savings of its own community in meeting loan demand, whereas a branch system can draw funds from areas with a high saving rate, and can shift those funds into the communities where they are needed most. The flexibility of branching thus provides more effective utilization of funds.

Third, the proponents of branch banking point out that a branch banking system is safer than a unit system. A unit bank survives or perishes with the community it serves. If the local mill or other sustaining industry closes, then the banks are likely to close with it. Branches, provided they are scattered throughout a wide area, are able to diversify their loans and escape some of the risks of the unit bank.

Fourth, customer service may be improved. Many unit banks still have not initiated a consumer loan department; many lack trust services; and others do not provide foreign exchange facilities. Advocates of branch banking point out that most branches provide a "department store" variety of services unavailable at small unit banks. (This advantage may be simply an extension of the "economies of scale" reasoning.)

Finally, there is the issue of competition. Branch banking does not necessarily lower competition but may increase it. Well-known business firms have access to both regional and national markets for loans, so the small borrower, consumer, or businessman at the local level stands to suffer if branch banking curtails sources of credit. However, in many cases the initiation of branch banking means that banking facilities are available where none existed before. So even if branching results in a net decrease in the number of banks in the country, competition does not necessarily decrease. In fact, it may intensify.

Opponents of branch banking take issue with most of these points. First, even though economies of scale are found in banking, recent studies show that unit banks of a certain size are more efficient, that is, have lower costs, than branch banks of the same size. Second, unit banks may achieve mobility of funds through the use of correspondent banks. Third, branch banks that are limited to a small geographical area of operation may not be able to achieve any greater diversity of loans (and thus safety) than unit banks. Fourth, branch banks are held to be guilty of "impersonal" service, and the making of loans on the basis of rigid guidelines which do not allow properly for the character of the borrower. The belief is that unit bank officers, who are often the owners, are better able to understand the needs of their community than branch managers who may be shifted from one area to another. Finally, opponents of branch banking fear that branching means the replacement of unit banks by branch banks, with a resulting increase in monopoly power and a decline in competition.

No clear-cut conclusion on branch banking is possible. The studies on the efficiency of branching are conflicting. It does appear, however, that branching systems are safer than unit systems. At least, the other nations of the world, where branching is widespread, have never experienced the widespread bank failures seen in this country. Also, recent studies indicate that branch managers have as much leeway in the size and type of loans they make as their unit counterparts. Thus far, branching has not resulted in a significant decline in unit banks; and the net increase in banking offices in the country has meant that consumers are receiving more convenient banking service than ever before.

Mergers

Bank mergers are necessarily attractive to the parties concerned; otherwise mergers would not take place. From the standpoint of the larger institution involved in the merger, the decision may be based on one or more of the following factors: (1) the desire to increase the size of bank operations; (2) a means of providing a branch bank in a growing community; (3) the opportunity to acquire a highly liquid institution (one with a low loan-to-deposit ratio); or (4) simply the opportunity to purchase another bank at a favorable price. Merger proposals often appeal to smaller banks for the following reasons: (1) The smaller bank may have failed to make adequate plans for managerial succession; (2) its earnings may be lagging; (3) it may wish to provide the larger stockholders of the bank with a means for increasing the value and liquidity of their stock; and (4) the officers of the smaller bank may be offered a higher salary package than they could have hoped for under the unit bank.

Bank mergers reached a peak of 231 in 1955 but have since declined to around 140 per year. Mergers are also seen as a threat to competition. This threat would be fulfilled if mergers both reduced the number of banks and increased the number of larger banks. A merger approved between two banks, say, in a two-bank town will decrease competition. In fact, though, mergers between two banks in the same town have occurred most often when there were five or more banks in the same town — not just two.[4] In other possible

---

[4]For example, almost two thirds of the intracity bank mergers that occurred in 1965 were in cities that initially had five or more banks. Derived from *Annual Report of the Federal Deposit Insurance Corporation, 1965* (Washington, D.C.: Federal Deposit Insurance Corporation, 1966); *Fifty-Second Annual Report of the Board of Governors of the Federal Reserve System* (Washington, D.C.; Board of Governors of the Federal Reserve System, 1966); and *Operating Banking Offices Insured by the Federal Deposit Insurance Corporation as of January 1, 1966* (Washington, D.C.: Federal Deposit Insurance Corporation, 1966).

cases of merger the situation closely resembles branch banking. On net balance, bank mergers have served more to increase the competitiveness and lower the costs of banking services.

Prior to 1960 bank mergers were largely a matter of state concern. The objective of merger laws was to protect the depositors and stockholders; little interest was paid to the competitive effects of mergers. The Bank Merger Act of 1960 changed this picture by making the merger of all insured commercial banks subject to the approval of federal agencies — the Comptroller of the Currency in the case of national banks, the Federal Reserve System in the case of state-chartered members, and the FDIC for insured state banks. The law specified, in addition to other criteria, that the agencies were to consider the effect of proposed mergers on competition, and on the convenience to and needs of the communities involved. Later decisions by the Supreme Court in 1963 and 1964 demonstrated that mergers were subject to the provisions of the Sherman Act and to section 7 of the Clayton Act. As a result of the Supreme Court decisions, Congress passed the Bank Merger Act of 1966. This act confirmed the applicability of antitrust laws to bank mergers, but recognized that the benefits from "need and convenience" may outweigh the anticompetitive effects of a merger. Under this new law, the Department of Justice has only 30 days in which to sue to enjoin a proposed merger; but it is the courts, not the regulatory agencies, that finally determine the legality of a merger. As most mergers do not involve substantially anticompetitive effects, the 1960 standards still apply in most cases.

Holding Companies

Another form of growth in the size of the banking firm has resulted from group banking. The ownership or control of two or more banks may take place through either chain banking or group banking. A banking chain includes two or more independently incorporated banks owned by the same individual(s). Chain banking is not subject to federal control, and there is little state regulation. Only one state, Mississippi, prohibits this kind of banking. Chain banking has not made much progress in the banking system due to the necessity of dispersing the stock upon the deaths of the original organizers and controllers. That is, the chain structure generally lacks an expedient means of perpetuating itself.

Group banking is an organizational means for providing the continuity lacking in chain banking. Group banks are independently incorporated but are brought under unified control by means of the holding company device. A holding company is a nonbank corporation that "holds" or "owns" the stock of the banks involved. The Bank Holding Company Act of 1956 gave the Federal Reserve System the authority to approve or disapprove all new bank holding company applications as well as the applications for extension of existing holding companies. This Act was amended in 1966 in order to make its wording consistent with the Bank Merger Act Amendment of 1966. This amendment emphasized that the anticompetitive effects of holding company formation or expansion were to be considered.

Bank holding companies exhibit their greatest popularity and growth in states that prohibit or limit branch banking. Many of the advantages of branch banking apply to holding companies. For example, the professional development of bank managers, mobility of resources, and a "department store" variety of services are all possible with a holding company system. However, the extent to which holding companies take advantage of these possibilities is not clear. Of course, group banking and branch banking are not mutually exclusive. Banks belonging to a group may have branches, and many do. However, holding companies provide a means for "branching" in those states which prohibit or limit branching, as well as a means for "branching" across state boundaries.

Since branch banking is a simpler and a more obvious means of extending the size of the banking firm, it preceded group banking. Group banking did not even begin until the late 1920s, but became a popular form of banking organization both in the latter part of that decade and again in the late 1950s. As of December 31, 1969, 97 bank holding companies existed in the United States and the District of Columbia. They controlled 10.1 percent of the banking offices in the United States and 14.3 percent of the nation's deposits.

Whether branch banking, group banking, or mergers have by themselves contributed to the size of the banking firm is problematical. The percentage of all deposits held by the 100 largest commercial banks has in fact declined. In 1934 the 100 largest banks in the country held 53.6 percent of the nation's deposits; in 1964, they held 46.3 percent. The average volume of deposits per bank for all commercial banks increased fourfold between 1940 and 1962, and the average capital value increased threefold. But if changes in the value of money are accounted, these dollar value increases are reduced by 50 percent. The rest of the growth, taking place as it does in larger firms, simply suggests that the most efficient size of the banking unit has become larger in real terms as well as in dollar terms. Thus, branch and group banking may not have had an appreciable effect on the degree of banking concentration in the United States; they may have been little more than the legal devices by means of which the economic size of the banking firm has been changed. As in most other industries, optimum size and maximum profitability of the firm have depended on the degree of entrepreneurial skill of the executive factor and the technical supply constants (such as the skills of accountants and the efficiency of computing machinery) that the executive must coordinate.

Correspondent Banking

Branch banking, mergers, and holding companies all provide a means for multiple office banking, but there is still another form — correspondent banking.

While stock ownership binds together group banks, interbank deposits forms the mutual bond in correspondent banking. The correspondent banking system provides a unifying force for thousands of unit banks, especially for banks that do not belong to the Federal Reserve System.

The need of small country banks for a means of collecting out-of-town checks and other items originally gave rise to correspondent banks in adjoining towns and cities. The city banks would collect out-of-town items for the country banks in return for the deposits the small banks placed in them. These correspondent deposit balances are very important accounts to many small city banks as well as to the leading New York and Chicago banks. Today, the large correspondent bank provides a host of services for its small depositing correspondents. The most frequently used of these services in descending order of use are as follows: (1) collection of checks and other out-of-town items; (2) storage of securities; (3) purchase and sale of securities; (4) participation in loans; (5) analysis of portfolios; (6) dispensation of credit information; (7) provision for foreign exchange service; and (8) access to bank wire service.[5] In addition, correspondents may provide information to the small banks through seminars, conferences, and publications. These correspondent relationships have provided benefits to the banks involved and have undoubtedly enhanced the vitality of the unit banking system. A matrix bank for many small correspondents is, in effect, a sort of microcosmic central bank.

The Federal Deposit Insurance Corporation

The Federal Deposit Insurance Corporation was formed in 1933 to help restore public confidence in the banking system following the wholesale bank failures during the first years of the Great Depression. The concept of deposit insurance was not new; several states had experimented with it prior to that time. The original capital for the FDIC was obtained from both the United States Treasury ($150 million) and the Federal Reserve System ($139 million). According to later congressional direction this capital was repaid by 1948, and the interest on it by 1951.

The moneys received by the FDIC through bank assessment are invested in government securities to form the deposit insurance fund.[6] Total government

---

[5]"The Corner of Main Street and Everywhere: A Special Report on the Correspondent Banking System," *Banking*, Vol. 52, No. 3 (September 1959), pp. 44–50.

[6]"As provided by statutes, the assessments are levied at an annual rate of $1/12$ of one percent of assessable deposits. However, a portion of the difference between assessments and the Corporation's administrative and operating expenses and insurance losses each year is returned to banks in the form of a credit against future assessments. This share was established at 60 percent under the Act of 1950, and raised to 66⅔ percent in 1961. The total credit in 1967 ... had the effect of reducing the net assessment rate to about one thirty-second of one percent of assessable deposits." *Annual Report of the Federal Deposit Insurance Corporation, 1967* (Washington, D.C.: Federal Deposit Insurance Corporation, 1968).

security holdings were $4,261 million as of December 31, 1969. Income from these securities ($192 million in 1969) now exceeds net assessment income ($144 million). On December 31, 1968, the fund had a net capital value of $4,051 million.

The FDIC has assumed that its responsibility is to prevent bank failures as well as to redeem deposits after a failure has taken place. To this end the FDIC sets minimal standards for participation in the program, and it regularly examines banks. Generally, the Comptroller of the Currency examines national banks, the Federal Reserve examines state-chartered members, and the FDIC examines state nonmember insured banks. However, the FDIC has access to the examination records of the Comptroller and the Federal Reserve, and it may conduct its own examinations of the other two categories of banks if it wishes. If insurance is withdrawn from banks that the FDIC considers too risky, depositors have two years in which to remove their money from the bank before the insurance lapses.

Banks in weak financial condition may receive direct loans from the FDIC, a succession of their ownership may be arranged, or they may be encouraged to merge with stronger banks. In these ways the FDIC has accumulated a spectacular "record" of avoiding large numbers of outright failures. Since deposit insurance has been in force, the rate of failure for insured banks has been less than three banks per year. For all banks, it has been five banks per year. But the FDIC is not necessarily responsible for this achievement. To argue otherwise is to commit the *post hoc ergo propter hoc* fallacy.

Many of the weaker banks in the system failed during the Great Depression, prior to the formation of the FDIC, when the Federal Reserve System allowed the stock of money to decline at an unprecedented rate. The better record of the central bank in recent years has been a major force in preventing bank failure. A prosperous economy aided by enlightened monetary and fiscal authorities is a far more substantial guarantee of the safety of bank deposits than "insurance" provided by the FDIC.

The original amount of maximum insurance coverage for a depositor was $2,500. This amount has been raised on several occasions, the most recent change being to $20,000 as of December 1969. Although over 98 percent of the banking offices in the country are covered by deposit insurance, only 58 percent of the value of bank deposits is insured. While full protection of all bank deposits is possible, the FDIC claims that such protection was not the intention of the original program. According to K. A. Randall, present chairman of the Board of Directors of the FDIC, the insurance program was designed to protect the small depositors who presumably had less information concerning security of banks than did large depositors. Contrary to Randall's argument, accumulated evidence suggests that the larger, more knowledgeable depositors, who would not have been covered by the FDIC, started the disastrous runs on banks in the 1930s.

Randall has also stated that complete coverage might give banks an "unfair" advantage over their nonbanking financial competitors, and that total insurance might weaken scrutiny of banks by the public and lead to less cautious policies by bank management. On the other hand, less cautious policies need not be followed if the insurance premium is based on a formula taking into account the size of the bank's capital and the risk involved in the bank's earning assets. Some students of money and banking feel that 100 percent insurance should be part of a logical program for streamlining banking regulation and increasing the competitiveness of the banking system. Cumbersome entry and operating restrictions could be relaxed, and smaller banks would be on more equal footing with larger ones in the attraction of deposits. Other observers believe the whole structure should be scrapped. They contend that the program is not and cannot be true insurance; that it inhibits bank competition; and that the central bank can provide all the deposit "insurance" needed by means of proper monetary policies.

Monopoly and Competition in Banking: A Summary View

A great deal of speculation and opinion has been put forth on the degree of competition within the banking industry. Competition in industry generally requires a number of given conditions in the business environment. First, entry and exit of firms must be reasonably easy. Second, the product of each firm in the industry must have good substitutes easily available from many other firms. Finally, the rules provided by law must be neutral with respect to the industry; that is, laws should neither discourage nor encourage entry of firms if an intrinsic measure of competitiveness is what is wanted.

The banking industry produces a most homogeneous product—bank deposits. Furthermore, the number of firms is sufficient to ensure that the competitive model of industry will provide the best prediction of behavior. A town of, say, 50,000 people usually has about three or four banks. This number might seem small, but it is larger than the number of Chrysler dealers and comparable to the number of milk distributors and five-and-dime stores. The firms in a circle competitive with banks must include as well two or three savings and loan institutions, several financial offices of the larger insurance companies, commercial credit companies, and, last but not least, the local pawnshops. In terms of supply alternatives, conditions would seem to be excellent for a competitive banking industry.

Several minor factors and one major factor, however, have clouded what might otherwise have been a neat competitive picture. In small town communities banks are notably high cost, low volume businesses, and given to discriminating their loan rates on the basis of personal relationships with their customers. Frequently, this behavior leads to a conclusion of monopolism; but it is more likely to be a result of small town economic practices generally, where economies of scale are markedly absent for most firms. The antiquated grocery store survives in the same milieu and does business in much the same personalized way. That large banks and supermarkets might be more profitable and lend at lower rates in these communities than the small "mamma and papa" banks and grocery stores is not pertinent. The larger firms gravitate to those markets that offer less restricted opportunities for the executive factor and where economies of scale can be realized. The law of comparative advantage works here as well as in international trade.

Efficacy in the entry and exit of banking firms is another necessary condition for competition. "Efficacy" is chosen as the modifier rather than "free" because entry is never free even under optimal conditions. The risk of failure, the necessity of making irrevocable decisions, the commitment of resources: All these actions involve costs that cannot be recovered in case of failure.

Laws may be a further impediment. In fact, restrictive law, far more than all other factors, seems to have been responsible for any lessening of competition in banking. Ever since the bank debacle of the 1930s, both state and federal governments and the Federal Reserve System have taken the position that a "need" must exist before a bank charter can be granted. As Alhadeff has said critically: "Need can be a highly ambiguous concept, particularly if it is interpreted to mean that the status quo in an area must not be disturbed in a competitive sense."[7] Many public officials and public laws have stated explicitly and officially that competition is neither necessary nor desirable in the banking industry, and public opinion has given sanction to such prescriptions. The image of banking as a healthily competing industry furnishing capital to small businesses and households has been overshadowed by the knowledge that the banking system is the major supplier of the money stock. While the apprehension that the banks would fail in their money-supplying role might well have been prevented by appropriate public policies at the right times, the impression of bank-stimulated disaster has been strong. General ignorance of the complexities of fractional reserve banking and monetary policy has resulted in focusing responsibility on the institution that suffers the immediate impact of failure—the local bank.

In view of this general social attitude, competition within the banking industry probably never will be as free as it once was. However, as high level employment conditions extend over time, the fears of the public about its money supply may lessen. Federal agencies, such as the Federal Deposit Insurance Corporation and the Federal Reserve System, as well as state supervisory agencies, contribute to a pattern of confidence by upholding standards of safety in banking. And even though these regulatory agencies do not permit cutthroat competition, or a banking business that is conducted by extremely high risk institutions, competitive rejection of the inefficient is still both possible and desirable.

---

[7]David Alhadeff, *Monopoly and Competition in Banking* (Berkeley: University of California Press, 1952), p. 205.

Safe banks are not necessarily efficient banks; that is, banks whose depositors are certain of being able to withdraw deposits on demand at any and all times are not necessarily those banks that earn high returns on invested capital. Nor are efficient banks necessarily unsafe banks. Supervisory agencies that enforce minimal standards of safety restrain mediocre and inefficient banks from "improving" their profit positions by recourse to high risk loan and investment procedures. The banks that chronically return low yields to their investors may be gradually liquidated without harming their depositors, and the capital invested in these institutions may then seek more profitable returns elsewhere. Limited competition of this kind is not "ideal" in a free economy; it is not intense enough to provide as efficient a service from the banking industry as might otherwise be expected. On the other hand, it may inhibit dramatic bankruptcies and resulting general financial ruin. It is perhaps as good as can be expected from a banking system that bears the burdens of multiple governmental supervision and legal inhibitions on the scope of enterprise open to the banking firm.

Selected Bibliography

Alhadeff, David. *Monopoly and Competition in Banking.* Berkeley: University of California Press, 1952.

Brown, William J. *The Dual Banking System in the United States.* New York: American Bankers Association, 1968.

Gramley, Lyle E. *Scale Economies in Banking.* Kansas City, Mo.: Federal Reserve Bank of Kansas City, 1965.

Lamb, W. R. *Group Banking.* New Brunswick, N.J.: Rutgers University Press, 1961.

Law and Contemporary Problems. Banking, Part I: Banking Regulation, Vol. 31, No. 4 (Autumn 1966), and Part II: Developments in Banking, Vol. 32, No. 1 (Winter 1967).

Studies in Banking Competition and the Banking Structure. Washington, D.C.: United States Treasury, 1966.

The One-Bank Holding Company—
History, Issues, and Pending Legislation

Larry Mote

A few years ago one-bank holding companies were practically unheard of. Today they control the largest banks in the nation. Bankers' natural propensity to increase profits had led them to seek new and varied ways of offering services to the public. A loophole in a federal holding company regulation overlooked one-bank holding companies and allowed bankers to venture into lucrative financial and nonfinancial areas heretofore unaccessible to them. This loophole was plugged on December 31, 1970, by the "Bank Holding Company Act Amendments of 1970." Major provisions of the Amendment include placing the responsibility for administration in the hands of the Board of Governors of the Federal Reserve System, defining holding companies as including any company that "has power to vote 25 per centum or more of any class of voting securities of the bank or company," making the grandfather clause date as of June 30, 1968, and limiting the activities of holding companies to those "closely related to banking or managing or controlling banks," as determined by the Board of Governors.

The following article, by Larry Mote, economist with the Federal Reserve Bank of Chicago since 1966, is condensed from the July 1970 issue of Business Conditions, *published by the Federal Reserve Bank of Chicago. It lucidly summarizes the issues.*

The one-bank holding company is a form of organization that is at least 50 years old. Yet as recently as five years ago one-bank holding companies were mentioned only in learned treatises on banking. Today, they are a prominent issue of public economic policy.

Briefly defined, a one-bank holding company is a company owning or controlling 25 percent or more of the stock of a single bank. On the surface, these companies would not appear to deserve the attention, and controversy, they have inspired. Yet, one-bank holding companies have generated support in some quarters, fear in others, and outright hostility in still others. Legislation is now being considered by Congress that would circumscribe their growth and activities.

The controversy over one-bank holding companies is attributable partly to their rapid increase in numbers from about a hundred to more than a thousand in the past 15 years. Also at issue is the enormous size of the banks owned by

From a review by the Federal Reserve Bank of Chicago, *Business Conditions*, 1970.

the most recently established one-bank holding companies. As of December 31, 1969, nine of the ten largest banks in the country were owned by one-bank holding companies.

But the fundamental reason for concern has been the tendency of one-bank holding companies to acquire non-banking businesses. To some, this development poses a serious threat to the traditional separation of banking from commerce. It raises the spectre of an American economy dominated by multi-industry combines similar to the Japanese *Zaibatsu* or German *Kartellen*. To others, the same development holds promise of greatly improved efficiency in meeting modern demands for financial services.

It may be that the potential of the one-bank holding company for either good or ill has been exaggerated. But it is undeniable that the questions raised by this once obscure form of banking organization are immediate and important.

Definitions

Affiliate — A legal term fully defined in the Banking Act of 1933. Generally, the term pertains to any organization which a bank owns or controls through stock holdings, or which the bank's shareholders own, or whose executive officers are also directors of the bank.

Bank holding company — In general usage, any company which owns or controls one or more banks. However, a bank holding company as defined in the Bank Holding Company Act of 1956 is one which controls two or more banks. Such companies must register with the Board of Governors of the Federal Reserve System and are commonly referred to as "registered bank holding companies."

Commingled investment fund — A bank-operated trust fund in which accounts of individual customers are commingled and lose their identity. Each customer, in effect, owns a share of the entire fund. Such a fund differs only in detail from a mutual fund.

Congeneric — Meaning "of the same kind," this term has been used to designate one-bank holding companies that have diversified into areas beyond the traditional bounds of banking, but within the financial field.

Conglomerate — In the field of banking, the term is used to designate one-bank holding companies whose subsidiaries engage in activities totally unrelated to the banking or financial areas.

Grandfather clause — A clause inserted in legislation which exempts those who, before a specified cutoff date, were engaged in the activities made illegal by the legislation.

Group banking — The common ownership or control of two or more separately incorporated banking institutions.

Holding company — Any company that holds the stock of another company for the purpose of exercising control over it.

Holding company affiliate — A legal term fully defined in the Banking Act of 1933. Generally, it pertains to any organization which owns or controls any one bank either through stock ownership or through any means that allow it to elect a majority of the bank's directors.

Multiple-bank holding company — A bank holding company, however defined, that owns or controls two or more banks.

One-bank holding company — At present there is no legal definition of a one-bank holding company. A very broad definition would be any company that owns or controls a single bank. Several alternative legal definitions have been proposed in the bills now pending before Congress. One would simply replace the words "each of two or more banks" with the words "any bank" in the present legal definition of a "bank holding company." Others would define a "single-bank holding company" as a company that owns or controls 51 percent or more of the stock of a single bank.

One-bank — The bank that is owned or controlled by a one-bank holding company.

Subsidiary — A legal term fully defined in the Bank Holding Company Act of 1956. Generally, any company owned and controlled by another.

Some Reasons Why

Virtually all commercial banks in the United States are confined to a fairly narrow range of activities within the broader area of financial activities. The basic statute regulating the activities of national banks is the National Bank Act of 1864. Section 8 of that act authorized national banks to exercise "all such incidental powers as shall be necessary to carry on the business of banking..." This "incidental powers" clause, as it is commonly known, could be construed either broadly or narrowly. Until recently, both the Comptroller of the Currency and the courts have tended to interpret it narrowly. Since 1962, however, the Comptroller has issued a number of rulings reflecting a much more liberal view of the permitted scope of bank activities. When some national banks rushed to take advantage of this new attitude, they found themselves face to face with lawsuits from non-banking firms and trade associations firmly opposed to bank encroachment on their industries.

In some states, to be sure, state banks are permitted to carry on activities, primarily of an insurance nature, that are prohibited to national banks. Nevertheless, many state banking codes are just as, or more, restrictive than the laws applying to national banks. But, because most of the largest banks in the United States are national banks, it is the restrictions on national bank activities that have had the greatest influence on the development of the bank-originated one-bank holding company. As of April 1, 1970, 30 of the 40 largest banks associated with one-bank holding companies were national banks.

Unlike one-bank holding companies, registered multi-bank holding companies offer no escape from the restrictions on bank activities. Under the Bank Holding Company Act of 1956, the activities of non-banking subsidiaries of multi-bank holding companies must be, with a few exceptions explicitly stated in the act, "of a financial, fiduciary, or insurance nature and which the Board... by order has determined to be so closely related to the business of banking or of managing or controlling banks as to be a proper incident thereto..."

As matters stand, the one-bank holding company represents one of the few loopholes left to banks seeking to expand their activities beyond the boundaries set by state and federal banking laws. Once the opportunity presented by one-bank holding companies became evident, and until restrictive legislation appeared on the horizon, banks moved quickly to diversify their operations. Most, though not all, of the new one-bank holding companies have restricted themselves to activities of a financial nature or at least bearing some resemblance to services already performed by banks. Hence, they are properly classified as congenerics, rather than conglomerates. But a few have announced their intentions to diversify as far as the law allows.

First, it may be concluded that restrictions on banking activities are no longer necessary. If so, the law should be amended to permit banks to engage in the prohibited activities directly.

Second, the current separation of banking from other activities may be deemed vital to the health of the banking system. In this case, one-bank holding companies should be subject to the same restrictions that now apply to registered bank holding companies.

Third, it may be found that certain activities dangerous for banks to engage in directly can be safely performed by related but separately incorporated holding company subsidiaries. This, provided that the bank bears no liability for losses of the non-banking subsidiaries. If this conclusion is the correct one, the major threat to bank safety posed by one-bank holding companies can be eliminated by restricting dealings between the bank and its subsidiaries to prevent the shifting of risky assets to the bank.

An example of the type of restriction that might be required is the provision of the original Bank Holding Company Act of 1956 which limited the loans by a subsidiary bank of a registered bank holding company to other subsidiaries of the holding company. (For a summary of proposed changes, see Table 1).

In principle, at least, diversification of activities could reduce the overall risks of earnings fluctuations to the parent holding company, just as industrial and geographic diversification of the loan portfolio of an individual bank lessens the risk of a large loss through default. For one-bank holding companies to achieve appreciable reduction in risk through diversification, however, would require that they assume the conglomerate, rather than the congeneric form.

The earnings of closely related activities tend to move up and down in unison. On the other hand, when several lines of activity are truly unrelated, as would be the case in a pure conglomerate one-bank holding company, unusually high (or low) earnings in one line of activity will often be offset by unusually low (or high) earnings in another.

This does not mean that even the limited diversification achievable by a congeneric would necessarily lead to any greater variability in earnings than that experienced by the bank alone. But it does suggest that the congeneric form has little to contribute to the year-to-year stability of a holding company's overall earnings. In any case, keeping the bank's earnings separate from those of other holding company subsidiaries would make the variability of holding company earnings less important from the standpoint of bank safety. The risks associated with any increased variability in earnings that did result from affiliation with a one-bank holding company would be borne—as they should be—by the shareholders of the holding company rather than the depositors of the bank.

The real danger to bank safety from combining banking and non-banking businesses in a one-bank holding company is the possible effect on business confidence. Poor earnings by a non-banking subsidiary may give rise to psychological unrest disproportionate to any objective assessment of the bank's prospects.

Efficiency

To be worth the risks, the combination of banking and non-banking activities must result in some improvements in the efficiency with which services are provided. Improved efficiency, in turn, could be expected to lead to a number of benefits to the public, including the introduction of new services, reduced prices for new or existing services, improved quality of services, and increased convenience.

Proponents of the congeneric form of organization consistently stress the convenience argument. They contend that the typical customer prefers to obtain most or all of his financial services from a single, familiar source. Indeed, this emphasis is no more than an extension of a line of reasoning pursued by commercial banks for years in their promotions for "full-service banking." The success of the department store and the shopping center demonstrates that consumers do value the convenience of one-stop shopping.

When it comes to productive efficiency in the narrow sense—the expenditure of real resources in the form of land, labor, and capital to produce any specified output of financial services—the congeneric form of organization would also seem to have the upper hand. For it is expansion into closely related product lines that is most likely to lead to production economies. Most such economies result from the more complete utilization of skills or resources that are readily transferable from one activity to another. A rather obvious example is the simultaneous provision of a trust department and investment counseling services. The same expertise in portfolio management is required by each.

Table 1. Major Features of Proposed One-Bank Holding Company Legislation

Bill	Sponsor	Definition of One-Bank Holding Company	Administering Agency	Date of Grandfather Clause, Other Exemptions	Limitations on Activities of One-Bank Holding Companies	Other Major Provisions
H.R. 6778	Rep. Wright Patman, Texas	Any company that "... has control over any bank ..."	Board of Governors	None in original bill. May 9, 1956 is the cutoff date in amended version passed by House. Exemption would not apply to one-bank holding companies with bank assets of more than $30 million and non-bank assets of more than $10 million.	Original bill retained provisions of Bank Holding Company Act of 1956 allowing entry into financial, fiduciary, and insurance businesses "so closely related to the business of banking as to be a proper incident thereto." The version passed by House permits activities found by Board to be "functionally related to banking" and that "produce benefits to the public...that outweigh possible adverse effects...." The House-passed bill also lists as not related to banking and "not in the public interest to be carried on by bank holding companies or subsidiaries thereof" the following activities: dealing in securities, providing insurance other than in connection with granting credit, acting as a travel agency, providing accounting services or data processing services, and leasing property.	Original bill prohibited tying arrangements and interlocking personnel relationships among banks, savings and loan associations, mutual savings banks, and insurance companies.
H.R. 9385	Administration (introduced by Rep. William B. Widnall, New Jersey)	Any company that "... owns, controls, or holds with power to vote 25 per centum or more of the voting shares of any bank ..."	Board of Governors, Comptroller, or FDIC depending on status of subsidiary banks.	March 1, 1969	Activities must "have been determined by unanimous agreement of the Comptroller of the Currency, the Federal Deposit Insurance	Permits "[a]ny party aggrieved by an order under this Act" to obtain review of order in U.S. Circuit Court of Appeals.

Bill	Sponsor	Definition	Administering agency	Effective date	Permitted activities / acquisitions	National Commission
S. 1052	Sen. William Proxmire, Wisconsin	Replaces words "each of two" in Bank Holding Company Act of 1956 with "one."	Board of Governors	January 1, 1969	Corporation, and the Board (1) to be financial or related to finance in nature or of a fiduciary or insurance nature and (2) to be in the public interest when offered by a bank holding company or its subsidiaries." Acquisitions of non-banking businesses not exempted under grandfather clause would be subject to same restrictions applicable to acquisitions by registered bank holding companies.	Establishes National Commission on Banking to "appraise the role of banking in the national economy" and report findings by June 30, 1971.
S. 1211	Sen. John Sparkman, Alabama	Any company that "...owns, controls, or holds with power to vote 51 per centum or more of the voting shares of a single bank..."	Board of Governors, Comptroller, or FDIC depending on status of bank for whose shares tender offer is made.	Exempts tender offers by persons controlling 50 per centum or more of bank's stock on February 28, 1969.	Bill requires prior approval by responsible agency of "tender offers and exchange offers for, and certain acquisitions of, the equity securities of certain regulated bank holding companies, and banks insured by the Federal Deposit Insurance Corporation."	None
S. 1664	Administration (Introduced by Sen. Wallace F. Bennett, Utah)	(same as H.R. 9385)				
S. 3823	Sen. Edward W. Brooke, Massachusetts	Any company that "...owns, controls, or holds with power to vote 25 per centum or more of the voting shares of any bank..."	Board of Governors	None	Activities must be determined by Board to be "functionally related to banking." Nonrelated activities permitted providing banking services not provided to customers of subsidiary engaged in such activities.	Establishes National Commission on Banking to study "role of banking in the national economy" and report findings by June 30, 1972.

Moreover, once the market research necessary for one of these activities has been done, there is little additional cost involved in applying the knowledge acquired to other investment purposes.

There is no comparable transferability of skills and resources among the disparate activities of a conglomerate. Only if economies of size in management and finance — economies found at the level of the entire firm, as opposed to those of the individual "plant" — turn out to be much more important than they have so far been shown to be could the conglomerate one-bank holding company be justified in terms of efficiency.

Fairness

Public policy makers cannot be indifferent to matters of equity. Equity is at the heart of questions regarding the treatment that a nonaffiliated customer can expect to receive from the subsidiary bank of a one-bank holding company. It is feared that such a bank may favor subsidiaries of the holding company in granting credit. Should this become common practice, competitors of holding company subsidiaries, and a broad range of other nonaffiliated companies, would be at a distinct disadvantage.

It is argued that this is a groundless fear, that it is not in the holding company's interest for its bank to favor holding company subsidiaries when higher yields are available elsewhere. The gains to the subsidiary from favoritism would be cancelled by the foregone interest income to the bank. Consequently, the holding company can have no incentive to induce its bank to favor other subsidiaries. Moreover, an upper bound to such favoritism, if it did occur, could be imposed in the form of a legal restriction on loans to subsidiaries of the holding company.

On the other hand, it has been pointed out by some writers that the existence of legal and institutional barriers to the use of interest rates to ration credit during periods of tight money may make such favoritism profitable.[1] Suppose, for example, that the market rate of return on a loan to a non-affiliated company is 10 percent, while the rate of return earned by a holding company subsidiary is only 8 percent. It would clearly be unprofitable to accept the lower rate of return by favoring the subsidiary. But if there is a usury ceiling of 7 percent, then the total return that can be earned on money invested in the subsidiary — including, besides interest, dividends and retained earnings — is greater than the maximum that can be realized on loans to outsiders. Although such situations can readily be imagined, their importance has not been ascertained.

---

[1]George R. Hall, "Some Impacts of One-Bank Holding Companies," *Proceedings of a Conference on Bank Structure and Competition* (Chicago: Federal Reserve Bank of Chicago, 1969), pp. 84–86.

Competition

The competitive questions stemming from the affiliation of one-bank holding companies with non-banking activities are more difficult to assess than those already considered. The most frequently mentioned danger to competition from the combination of banking with non-banking activities is the possibility of what are known in the antitrust literature as "tie-ins." Tie-ins occur when, in exchange for the privilege of purchasing one item, the customer is required to purchase his requirements of a second item from the same seller. A common hypothetical example is that of the loan customer who is forced, as a condition of obtaining a loan, to purchase his insurance from another subsidiary of the bank's parent holding company. Thus, the purchase of insurance is tied to the loan.

Several recent articles have discounted the importance of this danger.[2] They stress a point that few students of economics would dispute: for a tie-in to be effective, there must be some degree of monopoly power in the sale of the "tying" product. Otherwise the buyer would be under no compulsion to agree to the tie-in. Given that monopoly power results when one or a few sellers control a large proportion of sales in a specific product and geographic market, the contention is that the number of unrelated product lines offered by a one-bank holding company has little or nothing to do with the degree of competition within any one of these lines.

There is a possibility, however, that the degree of competition in any given product line may depend on the extent to which banking and non-banking activities are combined under common ownership. For example, if all existing commercial finance companies became affiliated with banks — on which they are at times heavily dependent for temporary credit pending the placement of large blocks of commercial paper — a prospective new entrant might find it excessively risky to enter the industry unless it, too, could first become affiliated with a bank. But this would raise the capital requirements for entry, perhaps to the point of excluding all but the largest and best-financed potential entrants.[3]

Another important factor determining the effect of one-bank holding companies on competition is the degree of substitutability between the services of the bank and those of other holding company subsidiaries. Although much of the criticism of one-bank holding companies has been directed at their proposals to enter fields totally unrelated to banking, the effects on competition are probably greater when a bank holding company acquires a firm in a closely

---

[2]See, *e.g.*, Franklin R. Edwards, "Tie-In Sales in Banking and One-Bank Holding Companies," *Antitrust Bulletin*, XIV (Fall, 1969), pp. 587–605.

[3]George R. Hall, p. 86.

related industry. The reason is that the actual or potential competition subject to elimination is much greater.

Much of the monopoly power that exists in banking derives from entry requirements designed to protect bank solvency. These requirements have little or nothing to do with the one-bank holding company form of organization. However, a one-bank holding company may enable a bank to exercise such power as it already possesses more effectively than would otherwise be possible. For example, a usury ceiling may prevent a bank from taking full advantage of its monopoly position by limiting the interest rate that can be charged on loans. However, if the bank can tie the purchase of services from other holding company subsidiaries at inflated prices to the availability of a loan, it can circumvent the constraint imposed by the ceiling.

It has been argued that coercive tie-ins could be dealt with adequately through vigorous enforcement of Section 1 of the Sherman Act.[4] However, it may happen that tie-ins occurring in connection with the granting of a bank loan are of a "voluntary" nature. That is to say, the lender may make no overt attempt to persuade the borrower to purchase the tied product. Rather, the borrower may do so of his own volition, in order to improve his chances of obtaining a loan at a future date. Tie-ins of this sort are extremely difficult to detect and, because no illegal behavior is involved, impossible to prosecute.[5] They can be prevented only by eliminating the particular organizational arrangement that brings them about—in this case, the combination of banking and non-banking activities under common control.

So far, only the negative impacts of one-bank holding companies on competition have been considered. It is far from clear, however, that the net effect of bank expansion into unrelated fields via the one-bank holding company is anticompetitive. On the contrary, bank expansion into unrelated fields may give a powerful impetus to competition. The evidence for this has been the reaction of existing firms when banks have attempted to invade their fields directly. Individual firms or trade associations have brought suit to prevent national banks from offering electronic data processing services, underwriting revenue bonds, selling insurance other than that "related in any direct way to protection of the security for loans made," and operating travel agencies and commingled investment funds. The plaintiffs have relied primarily on a narrow interpretation of the "incidental powers" clause of the National Bank Act and the dangers to bank solvency in expansion into unfamiliar lines of activity.

These lawsuits demonstrate the potential effects on competition of bank entry into new fields. Bank-sponsored credit cards offer a prime example of banks actually entering an established line of business. Entering the field years

---

[4]Edwards, pp. 602–605.

[5]See Donald I. Baker, "An Antitrust Look at the One-Bank Holding Company Problem," *Proceedings of a Conference on Bank Structure and Competition* (Chicago: Federal Reserve Bank of Chicago, 1969), pp. 126–127.

after the oil companies, major retailers, and independent credit card organizations, banks unveiled a whole new array of tactical weapons designed to facilitate penetration of the market. Mass mailings of cards, intensive advertising, and sharp reductions in merchant discounts characterized the banks' plunge into credit cards. Many mistakes were made and initial losses exceeded projections. But the major lesson of this experience is that commercial banks are a competitive force to be reckoned with in any field that they choose, and are permitted by law, to enter. This fact was not lost on the potential competitors of commercial banks. They have rallied to the support of those in Congress who advocate stricter controls over one-bank holding companies.

12

Instruments of the
Money Market and Government Bonds

The term "money market" refers not to one specific market but to a conglomeration of markets where certain short-term negotiable instruments may be issued or traded.[1] Usually included in such markets are negotiable certificates of deposit, commercial paper, federal funds, bankers' acceptances, dealer loans and repurchase agreements, call loans, and United States Treasury bills. Need for such instruments arises because of the occasional imbalance between the current receipts and expenditures of both business and government. While the maintenance of some amount of cash balances is necessary in the conduct of business, excessive balances pose a cost to the holder either in the form of interest charges on borrowed money or in lost opportunities for financial return. The money market provides a means through which economic units (business or government) with cash surpluses may place their funds and where other units in deficit may seek funds.

Negotiable Certificates of Deposit

A relative newcomer to the money market field, negotiable certificates of deposit, or CD's as they are called, have in the last decade grown in volume

---

[1]Excellent supplementary sources include *Instruments of the Money Market*, available from the Federal Reserve Bank of Richmond, and *Money Market Instruments*, available from the Federal Reserve Bank of Cleveland.

to the point where they are the leading privately issued money market instrument (see Table 12.1). During the 1940s and 1950s, New York City banks' share of the nation's bank deposits declined due to the less rapid population growth of the Northeast, the decentralization of business there, and the growing sophistication of corporate managers who were reluctant to leave surplus funds in demand deposit balances where they would draw no interest. Common practice was for these banks not to accept time deposits from corporations. The banks believed that the corporations would simply transfer balances back and forth between their demand deposit and time deposit accounts, increasing banks' operating expenses and interest payments without a corresponding increase in total deposit business. The outflow of corporate funds into Treasury bills and other money market instruments, however, caused a reassessment of this view.

Table 12.1. Dollar Volume of Selected Money
Market Instruments in Selected Years, 1950–1969
(millions of dollars)

Date*	Treasury Bills	Negotiable Certificates of Deposit†	Commercial and Finance Company Paper	Bankers' Acceptances
1950				642
1955	22,300			2,027
1960	39,400	796	4,497	3,392
1965	60,200	16,251	9,058	
1966	64,700	15,642	13,279	3,603
1967	69,900	20,330	16,535	4,317
1968	75,000	23,474	20,497	4,428
1969	80,600	10,919	31,624	5,451

Source: Board of Governors of the Federal Reserve System, *Federal Reserve Bulletin*, selected issues.
* As of year-end.
† Issued by large banks in excess of $100,000.

In February 1961, the expanded use of negotiable certificates of deposit began with an announcement by the First National City Bank of New York that it would issue such certificates in large denominations and that a secondary market for these instruments would be provided by a large U.S. government securities dealer. These certificates are fixed denomination, marketable receipts for money deposited in a bank for a specified period of time at a contractually set rate of interest. Their large minimal values (normally $1 million for New York banks) and the fact that they may be redeemed only after a specified period of time help to ensure that the funds attracted are not those which would have been left in demand deposit accounts. In addition, CD's allow corporate purchasers to maintain goodwill relationships with their banks while at the same time gaining a return on their idle balances. The negotiable nature of CD's and the substantial secondary market in them means that the liquidity of corporations is not significantly reduced by the addition of CD's to their portfolios.

While the basic forces of supply and demand determine the yield of CD's, this yield is constrained by the existence of the Federal Reserve's Regulation Q. This regulation sets the maximum rate of interest which member banks and FDIC members may pay on time deposits. If market rates of interest rise above the minimal level prescribed by Regulation Q, CD's are placed at a competitive disadvantage and commercial banks experience difficulty selling new ones as existing ones mature. Such a situation occurred in 1966 and to a much greater degree in 1969, when CD volume was reduced by more than one half (see Table 12.1). Bankers showed much imagination at this time in seeking deposits from other sources, including the Euro-dollar market, the commercial paper market (via finance companies related to banks by the holding company device), and the federal funds market. Correspondents were also called upon to participate in loans.

Commercial Paper

Commercial paper is short-term, unsecured, discounted promissory notes sold by a relatively small group of large businesses, directly or through dealers, in order to raise cash. The unsecured nature of such notes means that only large firms with impeccable credit ratings are able to use this means of financing. Developed in earlier times to finance the purchase of resalable goods, commercial paper was purchased by manufacturing firms and then sold to banks or commercial paper dealers. In 1920 the General Motors Acceptance Corporation pioneered the direct placement of commercial paper by selling directly to investors rather than going through the traditional dealer channel. Directly placed paper now accounts for about two thirds of the market.

Manufacturers, wholesalers, and retailers were once the volume borrowers in the commercial paper market, but their place has been taken by large-sales finance companies. The former group tends to rely on bank credit as a main source of short-term funds and to use commercial paper as a supplement. Large sales finance organizations behave in the opposite way. The main advantage of borrowing through the commercial paper market rather than through commercial banks is its lower cost. Even after allowing for dealer commissions or for the cost of direct placement, the total cost of borrowing is usually less than the prime rate charged by banks.

Since World War II the volume of commercial paper has burgeoned. From a low of about $100 million during the war, the outstanding volume grew to

$1.75 billion by the end of 1952, and to about $9 billion by 1965. Since then, it leaped to over $31.6 billion by the end of 1969! As seen in Table 12.1, commercial paper now exceeds CD's as the leading privately issued money market instrument.

Several explanations have been offered for this sharp growth: First, the need for funds during this period has been greater than internal sources would supply; second, the higher cost of borrowing in the long-term market has encouraged borrowing in the short-term market; and third, the tight money period of 1966 and credit rationing by banks caused firms to substitute commercial paper for bank indebtedness in unprecedented amounts and for an extended period.

Since the 1920s the major buyers of commercial paper have been non-financial corporations. Firms directly placing commercial paper tailor it to meet corporate demands as to amount and maturity, and usually stand ready to repurchase the paper should the corporate purchaser experience unanticipated cash needs. Many corporate treasurers feel that the interest income from this source more than compensates for its added risk.

Federal Funds

Commercial banks, as well as nonfinancial corporations, attempt to minimize their idle balances. On any given day some banks may experience a temporary excess of reserves while other banks have a temporary shortage. The federal funds market provides a means for these surplus and deficit units to make a deal.

Member banks of the Federal Reserve System must maintain a reserve that is a certain proportion of their deposit liabilities. These reserves may be in the form of either vault cash or deposits with the Federal Reserve Bank of their district. Since bank reserves draw no return, commercial banks are eager to minimize their reserves in excess of the legal requirement. Similarly, banks are anxious to avoid a reserve deficit because they may be penalized at the discount rate plus 2 percent. Member banks of the Federal Reserve System have the privilege of writing checks that are *immediately* debited against their excess reserves held by the Federal Reserve System. Trading in these reserve balances constitutes the federal funds market. Such trading is normally on an overnight basis and at a rate of interest determined by market conditions.

The federal funds market has been in existence since 1921, when the first such exchange was made in New York City. During the Great Depression the market died out almost completely because there were large excess reserves, few buyers, and depressed interest rates. During World War II, Federal Reserve pegging of bond prices encouraged banks to make their reserve adjustments through buying and selling government securities, because the risk of loss in that market had been effectively eliminated. With the return to flexible monetary policy signaled by the Treasury–Federal Reserve Accord of March 1951, the federal funds market revived and expanded.

The main participants in the federal funds market have been large money market banks. Typical trading units are for $1 million, an amount that effectively eliminates smaller banks. However, rising interest rates have encouraged small banks to enter the market through larger correspondent banks willing to negotiate for small amounts.

The federal funds market is national; amounts in even multiples of $1,000 may be transferred instantaneously and without charge to any part of the country through the Federal Reserve's wire service. But even with the more widespread participation in federal funds by smaller banks, New York remains the market center. Many smaller banks are correspondents of the New York banks; special federal funds brokers are located in New York; and the New York banks are generally net buyers of federal funds.

Bankers' Acceptances

Everyone is accustomed to writing bank drafts or checks that order a bank to pay a third party. Under certain conditions a person may direct a bank to pay him money at some future date even though he does not have balances on deposit with the bank. When a commercial bank "accepts" such a draft or bill, it becomes known as a bankers' acceptance. It is a money market instrument much like a certified check payable to the bearer at some future date.[2] It is an instrument that was used primarily in international trade to provide a means for importers, whose credit reputations may have been unknown to foreign exporters, to substitute a commercial bank's credit standing for their own.

Consider a jeweler in the United States who wishes to import a line of fine silver products from Great Britain and decides to finance it on an acceptance basis. After completing the terms of the agreement with the seller, the U.S. jeweler arranges for his commercial bank to issue an irrevocable letter of credit in favor of the British exporter. That is, the jeweler negotiates with his bank to accept a bill or bills drawn on it by the seller. The time period specified in the letter is based upon how long the transaction will take, including the shipment of the goods. The maximum time allowed is 180 days. The jeweler must sign a contract with his commercial bank promising to pay the bank in time for the bank to redeem the acceptance.

---

[2]According to the Federal Reserve System, "A banker's acceptance...is a draft or bill of exchange, whether payable in the United States or abroad and whether payable in dollars or some other money, accepted by a bank or trust company or a firm, person, company, or corporation engaged generally in the business of granting bankers' acceptance credits." *Advances and Discounts by Federal Reserve Banks, Regulation A* (Washington, D.C.: Board of Governors of the Federal Reserve System, 1955), p. 5.

Once the British exporter receives the letter of credit, he presents it to his bank, along with a bill of lading that allows the holder to receive the shipment of goods, and with a draft that he has drawn on the American bank. He may simply ask his bank to collect the payment for him; or more likely, he will ask his bank to give him the present value of the draft in British money. The British bank then forwards the draft, bill of lading, and letter of credit to the United States (normally through a correspondent bank) for collection. Providing the terms of the agreement have been fulfilled, the U.S. bank issuing the letter writes its acceptance on the face of the draft. Thus, the draft becomes a bankers' acceptance, maturing in an agreed-upon time. The jeweler may then be given the bill of lading under trust agreement so that he may claim the goods when they arrive. He then markets the goods in order to repay his commercial bank before the maturity date.

The British bank may elect to retain title to the acceptance, in which case it would, effectively, be lending money to the jeweler until the maturity date; or it may decide to sell the acceptance in the U.S. money market. In that way the acceptance might end up in the portfolio of any bank in the country, or even the issuing bank may elect to buy it. The transaction is completed when the acceptance is presented by its holder at maturity for collection.

Bankers' acceptances have been in use in Europe for hundreds of years. They also enjoyed some popularity in this country before the Civil War and after the establishment of the Federal Reserve System. Since 1955 the Federal Reserve System has been trading in bankers' acceptances in an effort to strengthen and broaden the market. Recent dollar volume of bankers' acceptances, as seen in Table 12.1, is in excess of $5.4 billion.

In addition to their uses in importing and exporting, bankers' acceptances may be used for transactions involving the shipment of goods within the United States or between foreign countries, in the storage of goods in the United States or foreign countries, and in the creation of dollar exchange between U.S. and foreign banks. There are six dealers in the United States who "make a market" in bankers' acceptances, and most of these dealers trade primarily in government securities. The predominant holders of bankers' acceptances are foreign banking and nonbanking institutions. The accepting banks themselves constitute the next most important group. They hold chiefly their own acceptances; only a small number of their acceptances have been issued by others. Because of their liquidity, acceptances offer commercial banks a greater degree of portfolio flexibility than do conventional loans.

Dealer Loans and Repurchase Agreements

The rapid growth of the national debt since the 1930s has been accompanied by an increase in the number of dealers specializing in trading government securities. These private parties purchase substantial quantities of new offerings of government securities from the Treasury and then sell them to the public in hopes of making a profit from the transaction. At the initiative of the Federal Reserve, these dealers also purchase from and sell to the System's Open Market Account. Similarly, they stand ready to purchase existing government securities from financial institutions, general corporations, and private investors in order to resell them for profit. Since they must maintain large inventories, they are in constant need of financing. This need gives rise to dealer loans and also to repurchase agreements as a means of financing.

Loans to dealers, primarily by commercial banks, account for less than half of the dealers' short-term financing needs. Such loans may be of a demand or call nature, or they may have specific maturities. The pledging of securities as collateral is a normal feature of such transactions. The remaining short-term financial needs of dealers are met through repurchase agreements. These agreements closely resemble collateral loans; only the title to the government securities is actually transferred from borrower to lender. The borrowing dealer contracts to "repurchase" the securities the next day, at some fixed future date, or whenever one of the parties wishes to terminate the contract.

Nonfinancial corporations are a main source of repurchase agreement funds. Such agreements afford corporations a relatively riskless means of minimizing their holdings of cash balances while gaining some return. To commercial banks, especially New York banks, both repurchase agreements and collateral loans are important in the adjustment of reserve balances. The Federal Reserve participates in repurchase agreements (or reverse repurchase agreements) as a means of temporarily supplying (or absorbing) funds.

Call Loans

Call loans at one time were the most important money market instrument and the most important source of commercial banks' secondary reserves, but they have slipped into relative obscurity since 1932. Commercial banks make these loans to securities brokers and dealers so that they can finance their customers' common stock purchases. The customers' stock purchases become the main collateral of the loan. The call feature provides for the termination of the loan at the initiative of either the borrower or the lender on one day's notice.

Call loans developed in New York City about 1830 and functioned as secondary reserves for large banks. Their existence was due in part to the lack of suitable alternatives, such as commercial bills used in London or present-day Treasury bills. Most of the correspondent bank deposits which flowed into New York during the 1800s found their way into call loans because of the alleged liquidity of these loans. At times, 50 percent of New York City bank loan portfolios consisted of call loans. (The seasonal and cyclical elasticity problems which resulted from these policies were discussed in Chapter 10.)

The volume of call loans outstanding diminished after the formation of the Federal Reserve because System policies on "eligibility" proscribed the rediscounting of call loans. After World War I, the growth of equity financing returned the use of call loans to favor. Just before the stock market collapse of 1929, brokers' loans again accounted for 50 percent of New York City bank loans, and in retrospect were alleged to have encouraged speculative excesses. The Banking Act of 1933 and the Securities Exchange Act of 1934 contained passages that respectively limited the percentage of bank capital that could be used for security loans and set margin requirements (discussed in Chapter 14). Call loans remain important in New York, the center of stock market activity, but their volume is much below the 1929 level.

Government Securities

In order for a government to obtain command over the factors of production it needs for maintaining itself, it can resort to four alternatives. First, it can simply confiscate. Such a practice must be rejected for government "financing" on a continuing basis because of its disruptive influences on the normal channels of trade and individual incentives. A second, and perhaps more common means, is through the printing of money. While money itself cannot be turned into highways, ships, or cannon, it can command the resources that have this ability. Unbridled printing of money usually results in successive rounds of inflation. Prices of resources are bid up in order to wrest them from the private sector. The redistribution effects of this method are well known. Individuals with fixed dollar claims suffer declines in the real value of their dollars. In addition, price level increases may cause a loss of faith in the value of the circulating medium and a tendency to "economize" on holdings of dollars. By this means, the velocity of money spending generally rises.

The third and most conventional method of financing is through taxation. Economic literature abounds with discussions of various types of taxes and their impacts, be they progressive, regressive, or proportional. Suffice it to say that at times tax receipts may be insufficient to cover the current expenditures of government. Then the fourth means of commanding resources is brought into practice—that of government borrowing. The government persuades the private sector, by means of interest rate inducements, to part with current purchasing power in the form of money. The present national debt is but the summation of that part of federal borrowing over time that has not been repaid. Rising most dramatically during periods of war, the national debt today is in excess of $396 billion (see Table 12.2); but as seen in Table 12.3, federal agencies themselves hold over 40 percent of the debt. They purchase these securities for various trust funds, while the Federal Reserve System purchases securities to provide collateral for increases in high-powered money (currency and member bank reserves).

Treasury Bills

The United States Treasury issues an array of securities designed to attract money from almost every type of portfolio investor. One of the securities issued by the Treasury, the Treasury bill, has gained considerable importance in the money market—see Table 12.1. It serves as a flexible means of federal financing and is a highly liquid, virtually riskless asset to the holder. These bills are very different from the Series E savings bond, with which the general public is most familiar. Savings bonds are on sale continuously at a fixed price and with a stipulated rate of interest; Treasury bills are periodically auctioned. Bills for 91 days and 182 days are auctioned weekly, while 270-day and 365-day bills are auctioned monthly. The price—and therefore yield—of these securities is determined by the forces of supply and demand. Issued at discount and in several denominations from $10,000 to $1 million, bills may be redeemed at par value when mature. The dollar amount of interest earned by the bearer is the difference between his purchase price and the par value at maturity.

Statistics of marketable government securities maturing in one year or less include securities of longer than one-year maturity when issued, but which are currently approaching their redemption date. The following sections include discussions of each of the marketable securities issued by the Treasury and a brief summary of the nonmarketable ones. All securities directly issued by the Treasury are obligations of the U.S. government.

Ordinary savings bonds can be redeemed at any time but are not transferable through markets. Marketable securities, such as Treasury bills, can be sold by one holder to another but cannot be redeemed until maturity. As mentioned above, a well-organized dealer market handles the tremendous volume of marketable government securities that change hands each business day. Government securities dealers, commercial banks, and others who wish to obtain newly issued three- and six-month Treasury bills submit their bids (tenders) in writing to the Federal Reserve System each Monday before 1:30 PM New York time. The Federal Reserve promptly closes the subscription books at 1:30 PM, then opens and tallies the bids, and finally submits the bids to the Treasury for allocation.

Bids are either competitive or noncompetitive. Competitive bids state the price which the bidder is willing to pay and the quantity which he desires. Competitive bidders are normally large investors who are familiar with the money market and who have up-to-the-minute knowledge of market rates of interest. Smaller investors, who may not have such intimate knowledge of the market but wish to be assured of getting newly issued securities, submit a noncom-

Table 12.2. Gross Public Debt, by Type of Security
(billions of dollars)

End of Period	Total Public Debt*	Public Issues									Special Issues§
		Total	Marketable					Nonmarketable			
			Total	Bills	Certificates	Notes	Bonds†	Convertible Bonds	Total‡	Savings Bonds and Notes	
1941—December	57.9	50.5	41.6	2.0	...	6.0	33.6	...	8.9	6.1	7.0
1946—December	259.1	233.1	176.6	17.0	30.0	10.1	119.5	...	56.5	49.8	24.6
1962—December	303.5	255.8	203.0	48.3	22.7	53.7	78.4	4.0	48.8	47.5	43.4
1963—December	309.3	261.6	207.6	51.5	10.9	58.7	86.4	3.2	50.7	48.8	43.7
1964—December	317.9	267.5	212.5	56.5	...	59.0	97.0	3.0	52.0	49.7	46.1
1965—December	320.9	270.3	214.6	60.2	...	50.2	104.2	2.8	52.9	50.3	46.3
1966—December	329.3	273.0	218.0	64.7	5.9	48.3	99.2	2.7	52.3	50.8	52.0
1967—December	344.7	284.0	226.5	69.9	...	61.4	95.2	2.6	54.9	51.7	57.2
1968—December	358.0	296.0	236.8	75.0	...	76.5	85.3	2.5	56.7	52.3	59.1
1969—December	368.2	295.2	235.9	80.6	...	85.4	69.9	2.4	56.9	52.2	71.0
1970—May	371.1	295.8	236.6	80.1	...	93.5	63.0	2.4	56.9	52.0	73.3
June	370.9	292.7	232.6	76.2	...	93.5	63.0	2.4	57.7	52.0	76.3
July	376.6	298.5	237.8	81.4	...	93.5	62.9	2.4	58.3	52.0	76.1
August	380.9	301.4	240.5	81.9	...	99.9	58.7	2.4	58.5	52.1	77.5
September	378.7	300.1	239.3	80.7	...	99.9	58.7	2.4	58.4	52.1	76.7
October	380.2	302.9	242.2	83.7	...	99.8	58.7	2.4	58.3	52.2	75.4
November	383.6	306.0	244.4	84.6	...	101.2	58.6	2.4	59.2	52.4	75.6
December	389.2	309.1	247.7	87.9	...	101.2	58.6	2.4	59.1	52.5	78.1
1971—January	388.3	308.8	247.7	87.9	...	101.2	58.5	2.4	58.7	52.6	77.7
February	390.7	309.8	248.1	89.3	...	104.1	54.5	2.4	59.3	52.8	78.9
March	391.7	309.7	247.5	89.0	...	104.3	54.2	2.4	59.9	53.0	80.0
April	391.9	310.4	245.9	87.5	...	104.3	54.1	2.4	62.1	53.2	79.7
May	396.8	313.2	245.6	89.1	...	102.5	54.0	2.3	65.2	53.4	81.7

Source: Board of Governors of the Federal Reserve System, *Federal Reserve Bulletin*, Vol. 57, No. 6 (June 1971), p. A42.
* Includes non-interest-bearing debt (of which $627 million on May 31, 1971, was not subject to statutory debt limitation).
† Includes Treasury bonds and minor amounts of Panama Canal and postal saving bonds.
‡ Includes (not shown separately): depositary bonds, retirement plan bonds, foreign currency series, foreign series, and Rural Electrification Administration bonds; before 1954, Armed Forces leave bonds; before 1956, tax and savings notes; and before October 1965, Series A investment bonds.
§ Held only by U.S. Government agencies and trust funds and the federal home loan banks.

Table 12.3. Ownership of Public Debt
(par value, billions of dollars)

End of Period	Total Public Debt	Held by— U.S. Government Agencies and Trust Funds	Federal Reserve Banks	Held by Private Investors Total	Commercial Banks	Mutual Savings Banks	Insurance Companies	Other Corporations	State and Local Governments	Individuals Savings Bonds	Individuals Other Securities	Foreign and International*	Other Miscellaneous Investors†
1939—December	41.9	6.1	2.5	33.4	12.7	2.7	5.7	2.0	.4	1.9	7.5	.2	.3
1946—December	259.1	27.4	23.4	208.3	74.5	11.8	24.9	15.3	6.3	44.2	20.0	2.1	9.3
1962—December	303.5	53.2	30.8	219.5	67.1	6.0	11.5	18.6	20.1	47.0	19.1	15.3	14.8
1963—December	309.3	55.3	33.6	220.5	64.2	5.6	11.2	18.7	21.1	48.2	20.0	15.9	15.6
1964—December	317.9	58.4	37.0	222.5	63.9	5.5	11.0	18.2	21.1	49.1	20.7	16.7	16.3
1965—December	320.9	59.7	40.8	220.5	60.7	5.3	10.3	15.8	22.9	49.7	22.4	16.7	16.7
1966—December	329.3	65.9	44.3	219.2	57.4	4.6	9.5	14.9	24.3	50.3	24.3	14.5	19.4
1967—December	344.7	73.1	49.1	222.4	63.8	4.1	8.6	12.2	24.1	51.2	22.8	15.8	19.9
1968—December	358.0	76.6	52.9	228.5	66.0	3.6	8.0	14.2	24.4	51.9	23.9	14.3	22.4
1969—December	368.2	89.0	57.2	222.0	56.8	2.9	7.1	13.3	25.4	51.8	29.1	11.4	24.1
1970—April	367.2	90.2	56.5	220.5	54.5	2.8	7.1	11.9	24.7	51.6	31.1	13.2	23.6
May	371.1	92.3	57.3	221.4	53.9	2.9	6.9	12.5	25.2	51.6	31.4	13.8	23.3
June	370.9	95.2	57.7	218.0	53.3	2.9	6.8	11.1	24.6	51.6	30.9	14.8	22.0
July	376.6	94.8	58.6	223.2	55.1	2.8	7.1	12.0	24.2	51.6	31.2	15.9	23.4
August	380.9	96.4	59.9	224.6	58.0	2.9	7.2	11.7	24.2	51.7	30.6	16.5	21.8
September	378.7	95.5	60.0	223.2	56.9	2.9	7.1	10.3	24.0	51.7	31.0	17.4	23.1
October	380.2	94.4	60.0	225.8	58.9	2.8	7.0	11.1	24.2	51.9	30.5	18.2	21.4
November	383.6	94.6	61.2	227.9	59.8	2.7	6.9	10.8	23.2	51.9	30.4	20.0	22.1
December	389.2	97.1	62.1	229.9	63.2	2.8	7.0	10.6	22.9	52.1	29.8	20.6	21.1
1971—January	388.3	96.7	61.8	229.9	62.1	2.7	7.3	11.1	23.0	52.1	29.5	20.9	21.1
February	390.7	98.0	62.5	230.2	62.1	2.8	7.2	10.2	23.8	52.3	28.8	22.9	20.1
March	391.7	98.8	64.2	228.7	61.2	2.8	6.8	11.0	22.6	52.5	27.5	25.4	18.9
April	391.9	99.1	63.7	229.1	60.2	2.8	6.8	10.0	22.0	52.8	26.5	29.2	19.0

Source: **Board of Governors of the Federal Reserve System**, *Federal Reserve Bulletin*, Vol. 57, No. 6 (June 1971), p. A42.

* Consists of investments of foreign and international accounts in the United States.

† Consists of savings and loan associations, nonprofit institutions, corporate pension trust funds, and dealers and brokers. Also included are certain government deposit accounts and government-sponsored agencies.

Note: **Reported** data for Federal Reserve Banks and U.S. government agencies and trust funds; Treasury estimates for other groups.

The debt and ownership concepts were altered beginning with the March 1969 *Bulletin*. The new concepts (1) exclude guaranteed securities and (2) remove from U.S. government agencies and trust funds and add to other miscellaneous investors the holdings of certain government-sponsored but privately-owned agencies and certain government deposit accounts.

petitive bid. Upon receiving the bids the Treasury first makes the noncompetitive awards, usually in full up to $200,000, and then allocates the rest to the competitive bidders, starting from the highest offer and continuing downward until the amount being issued, an amount often in excess of $2 billion, is exhausted. The average accepted price is then calculated and the noncompetitive bidders are charged that price.

From the standpoint of the Treasury, the flexibility of the size of offerings and the market-determined rate of interest are the most attractive features of Treasury bills. Treasury cash needs vary on a seasonal and cyclical basis, and additional bills can quickly and easily be offered to meet such needs. Because the rate of interest is market determined, the Treasury can be assured that the interest charge on an issue is "fair" and that the interest rate is not so low as to make the issue unattractive. These characteristics are not present with Federal securities that carry a predetermined rate of interest when issued.

Outside of the Federal Reserve System and other government investment accounts, commercial banks are the most important holders of Treasury bills. Commercial banks maintain them as an important part of their secondary reserves. Corporations and state and local governments are the next most important users. Treasury bills offer the holder a highly liquid alternative to the possession of excessive cash balances. The short-term nature of Treasury bills and the highly developed market in them assures the holder of relatively stable prices and of smooth transitions to new prices.

Tax Anticipation Bills

A variation of the Treasury bill is the tax anticipation bill. These bills are designed to provide corporations with attractive means of accumulating funds for tax purposes while smoothing the flow of tax receipts to the Treasury. They mature in nine months or less, are issued in the same manner as regular Treasury bills, and are designed to mature about a week after tax payment dates. They may be submitted in payment of taxes at par or they may be cashed at maturity.

Coupon Issues

Coupon issues—certificates of indebtedness, Treasury notes, and bonds—unlike Treasury bills, which are auctioned, are normally issued at par and with a set coupon rate of interest. Once in circulation they are subject to price fluctuations, and, therefore, market yield and yield to maturity fluctuates, just as in the case of Treasury bills. Treasury offerings of these securities are preceded by an announcement some ten to twenty days in advance notifying the public of the amount and terms of the offering as well as the subscription period.

The primary difference between certificates, notes, and bonds lies in their initial maturity. When issued, certificates mature in one year or less, and notes mature in not less than one year but not more than seven. Bonds may have *any* original maturity, though it is usually in excess of five years. Certificates of indebtedness have not been offered in recent years. As of May 1971, none was outstanding. Treasury notes are generally offered four times a year. The maturity range of notes makes them attractive to commercial banks — the most important private holders. Notes maturing within about eighteen months seem especially attractive to nonfinancial corporations. As seen in Table 12.2, $102.5 billion of notes were outstanding as of May 1971. In recent years, new Treasury bonds have been offered less frequently than notes but more frequently than certificates. Treasury bonds are available in either coupon or registered form. However, the total value of bonds outstanding has decreased markedly in recent years. The interest ceiling imposed by Congress on newly authorized issues has made sales almost impossible. Other securities not subject to interest rate ceilings have replaced bonds.

Nonmarketable Securities

Over 90 percent of the nonmarketable federal securities outstanding are savings bonds and notes. They were originally issued in 1935 to provide the small saver with a safe place for his funds and to promote a wider distribution of the ownership of the public debt. During World War II, U.S. savings bonds became an important means of absorbing increases in consumer purchasing power. Sales are actively promoted today through payroll savings plans. The only savings bonds currently offered by the Treasury are Series E and H.

Series E bonds are on sale continuously through commercial banks, Federal Reserve Banks, the U.S. Treasury, U.S. Post Offices, and other qualified agencies. They are sold on a discount basis, that is, at 75 percent of maturity value. They mature in five years, ten months and, if held to maturity, presently yield 5.0 percent plus a ½ percent bonus. They may be redeemed by the owner at a lesser rate of interest two months after the date of issue, but they may not be sold or transferred. Designed for the small saver, their fixed price and redemption schedule protect the holder against adverse market fluctuations and encourage their holding until maturity. They range in denomination from $25 to $1,000, but no one person can purchase more than $5,000 issue value of these bonds annually.

Series H current income bonds are sold continuously by Federal Reserve Banks and the Treasury. While carrying about the same rate of interest as Series E bonds, current income bonds are sold at par, mature in ten years, and interest (closely following the Series E graduated scale) is paid semiannually by check. Investors are limited to purchasing $5,000 of these bonds per year.

Other nonmarketable bonds currently issued by the Treasury include U.S. Retirement Plan bonds, available to self-employed individuals under certain pension and profit-sharing plans, and special issues, sold directly to various government agencies and trust funds. Other issues outstanding include depositary bonds, R.E.A. Series, Foreign Series certificates and notes, and Foreign Currency Series certificates and bonds.

Other Federal Agency Securities

Within the past few years, the amount of outstanding securities issued by federal agencies other than the Treasury has increased significantly. Although these securities are not United States obligations or guaranteed, they are obligations of the issuing agency and are considered to be of good quality. Table 12.4 shows that the total value of the publicly held securities of major government agencies was $38.3 billion as of the end of 1970. The Tennessee Valley Authority and other government agencies also issue limited amounts of securities.

Table 12.4. Publicly Held Securities of Selected Federally
Sponsored Credit Agencies, 1961–1970
(millions of dollars)

End of Year	Federal Home Loan Banks	Federal National Mortgage Association	Banks for Cooperatives	Federal Intermediate Credit Banks	Federal Land Banks	Total
1961	1,571	2,453	435	1,585	2,431	8,475
1962	2,707	2,422	505	1,727	2,628	9,989
1963	4,363	1,788	589	1,952	2,834	11,526
1964	4,369	1,601	686	2,112	3,169	11,931
1965	5,221	1,884	797	2,335	3,710	13,947
1966	6,859	3,800	1,074	2,786	4,385	14,519
1967	4,060	4,919	1,253	3,214	4,904	18,350
1968	4,701	6,376	1,334	3,570	5,399	21,380
1969	8,422	10,511	1,473	4,116	5,949	30,471
1970	10,183	15,206	1,755	4,799	6,395	38,338

Source: Board of Governors of the Federal Reserve System, *Federal Reserve Bulletin*, selected issues.

State and Local Government Financing

The first public bonds of a modern nature offered by the states were issued in the 1820s. New York state's highly successful Erie Canal project encouraged borrowing by other states and helped to attract Eastern and European capital. Present-day offerings of state and municipal bonds are primarily absorbed by commercial banks. As shown in Table 12.5, commercial banks purchased 82.5 percent of such newly issued securities in 1967. At the same time, commercial banks also held 42.2 percent of the total state and local issues outstanding. While state and municipal issues are not strictly instruments of the money market, but mainly instruments of the capital market, several features make them attractive to commercial banks: Their safety record is surpassed only by federal government securities; their interest income is exempt from federal income tax; and many bonds are now issued with the short and intermediate maturities desired by commercial banks.

Table 12.5. The Volume of State and Local Government Securities Outstanding and Commercial Banks' Participation in Them in Selected Years, 1950–1967

Year	Total Volume Outstanding	Amount of Holdings by Commercial Banks		Change in Holdings by Commercial Banks	
		In Billions of Dollars	As Percentage of Total Issues Outstanding	In Billions of Dollars	As Percentage of Net New Issues
1950	24.7	8.1	32.8	1.6	59.2
1955	44.9	12.7	28.3	0.1	3.1
1960	68.8	17.6	25.6	0.6	16.7
1961	75.5	20.3	26.9	2.8	57.1
1962	82.7	24.8	30.0	4.4	88.0
1963	88.0	30.0	34.1	5.2	77.6
1964	93.8	33.5	35.7	3.6	59.3
1965	100.3	38.6	38.5	5.1	67.3
1966	104.6	41.0	39.2	2.4	40.0
1967	117.3	49.5	42.2	8.5	82.5

Source: Board of Governors of the Federal Reserve System, *Federal Reserve Bulletin*, Vol. 54, No. 7 (July 1968), p. 617.

The exemption of state and local issues from federal taxation arises from the famous case of *M'Culloch* v. *the State of Maryland,* which was heard before the Supreme Court in 1819. James William M'Culloch, a bank cashier managing the Baltimore branch of the Bank of the United States, refused to pay a newly levied Maryland stamp tax on the notes issued by his branch. Daniel Webster, in summarizing his case on behalf of M'Culloch, made this often quoted statement: "An unlimited power to tax involves, necessarily, a power to destroy...."[3] Justice Marshall, delivering the Court's unanimous opinion against the Maryland statute, said, "...This is a tax on the operations of the bank, and is, consequently, a tax on the operation of an instrument employed by the government of the Union to carry its powers into execution. Such a tax must be unconstitutional."[4] The opinion still stands today and is also applied in reverse.[5] The federal government cannot levy taxes that interrupt the operations of the states or their political subdivisions.

The tax exempt feature of these securities substantially increases their effective yield—especially to individuals and corporations in the upper income tax brackets. To an individual in the 50 percent tax bracket, a Treasury security paying 7 percent has no greater after-tax yield than a municipal bond yielding 3½ percent. State and local securities are thus able to offer low nominal interest rates and still compete with other types of issues in the marketplace. This feature both provides a tax loophole for the wealthy and in effect allows a subsidy to the states. Some students of the matter think that a more effective and equitable subsidy could be devised.[6]

Public bonds can be separated into two major categories—full faith and credit bonds, and revenue bonds. Full faith and credit bonds are secured by the full credit and property-taxing power of the issuer. They are commonly known as general obligations, or "G.O.'s." Revenue bonds are secured by and payable from the earnings of the project or agency which issues them or, in some cases, by state excise taxes. An example of the use made of revenue bonds is the financing of toll roads and bridges.

The number of bonds issued by state and local governments has been increasing rapidly in recent years (see Table 12.5). Only the adverse impact of high interest rates has dampened this trend.[7] Most of the increase has been in the form of revenue bonds. These bonds allow state and local governments to escape debt limitation ceilings. The escape is possible because the interest and principle of revenue bonds are payable from the earnings of the enterprise being financed, not from the general revenues of the state or local government. State and local governments are also coming to rely almost exclusively on serial bonds. When issued in serial form, some bonds mature each year. This

---

[3] 4 Wheaton 327.

[4] 4 Wheaton 436–437.

[5] For a brief summary of subsequent legal developments on tax exemption, see Roland I. Robinson, *Postwar Market for State and Local Government Securities,* a study by the National Bureau of Economic Research (Princeton, N.J.: Princeton University Press, 1960), pp. 22–26. For a more complete treatment of the legalities, see Cushman McGee, "Exemption of Interest on State and Municipal Bonds," in House Committee on Ways and Means, *Tax Revision Compendium,* Vol. 1 (1959), pp. 737–741.

[6] An excellent summary of the arguments, pro and con, is included in David J. Ott and Allan H. Meltzer, *Federal Tax Treatment of State and Local Securities* (Washington, D.C.: The Brookings Institution, 1963), Ch. 2.

[7] Two studies on the topic by Paul F. McGouldrick and John E. Petersen are "Monetary Restraint and Borrowing and Capital Spending by Large State and Local Governments in 1966," *Federal Reserve Bulletin,* Vol. 54, No. 7 (July 1968), pp. 552–581, and "Monetary Restraint, Borrowings, and Capital Spending by Small Local Governments and State Colleges in 1966," *Federal Reserve Bulletin,* Vol. 54, No. 12 (December 1968), pp. 953–982.

arrangement gives potential purchasers a better selection and requires the issuing government to redeem a certain portion of the principle each year, thus eliminating the "spending" temptation which sinking funds used to pose for financially burdened legislatures.

Interest Rate Calculation, Variation, and Yield Curves

Marketable bonds simultaneously have four rates of interest or yields: the coupon yield, the current market yield, the yield to maturity, and the after tax yield to maturity. The nominal yield which is stated on the face of the bond, is the coupon yield. For example, a Treasury bond maturing in 1985 and having a par value of $1,000 may carry a coupon yield of 3½ percent, meaning that the holder of the bond can expect to receive $35 in interest payments from the Treasury each year until the bond is retired at maturity.

Since the price of marketable bonds is free to fluctuate in the marketplace, the bond currently may not be selling at par value. If it is presently selling for $700, its current market yield is in excess of 3½ percent and can be found by dividing the current market price of the bond into the dollar amount of the annual coupon yield. In this case, the actual yield would be 5 percent ($35/$700 = 0.05).

For investment purposes, the market yield more accurately reflects the return on the security than the coupon yield, but both fail to consider the annual appreciation in value which the owner would gain by holding the security to maturity. While a complex formula is needed to determine the precise yield to maturity (see Chapter 5), a simpler one can approximate this return. It is:

$$\frac{\text{Annual dollar interest} + \text{average annual appreciation}}{\text{Average price from present until maturity}}$$

The annual dollar interest, or the coupon yield in dollar terms, is $35. The bond's price of $700 is discounted, so the total dollar appreciation to be gained on the bond is $300 — the difference between its purchase price and its maturity value. Assuming that the time of evaluation is in the year 1970, and knowing that the bond matures in 1985, the average annual appreciation in value is $20 — ($300/15 years = $20/year). The average price from present until maturity is $850. This value is derived by summing the present price and the maturity value and then averaging: ($700 + $1,000)/2 = $850. Placing these values in the yield-to-maturity formula, the yield to maturity becomes 6.47 percent — $($35 + $20)/$850 = 0.0647.

If the bond were selling at a premium, that is, at a price above its maturity value, the yield to maturity could be calculated by subtracting the average annual depreciation *from* the annual dollar interest and dividing by the average price from present until maturity. Today's investor does not have to perform these calculations; tables are readily available to provide him with all the necessary information on yields to maturity and prices. Similarly, after-tax-yield-to-maturity tables are available, which take into consideration the capital gains tax on the appreciation of investment principal and the effect of the federal income tax on interest income.

Economists are given to speaking of "the" interest rate as if it were unique. In fact, there is a whole range of interest or yield rates, and each of the money market instruments has a determinate rate of interest (see Figure 12.1). While interest rates in general may rise or fall, a spread is usually maintained between each of the interest rates for the various securities. Each instrument has a different risk of loss by default. United States Treasury bills are secured by the taxing power of the government, while commercial paper is secured only by the income-earning ability of the issuing corporation. Other things being equal, instruments of higher risk have to carry correspondingly higher interest rates to compensate for their risk. Second, the liquidity of each security differs. A large active market in Treasury securities means an easy conversion into cash; other instruments may be more difficult to sell. Third, the preferential tax treatment of some securities, such as that given to state and local government bonds, makes them competitive with securities of comparable quality paying higher rates of interest. Fourth, the cost of making a loan or of placing a security on the market may influence its yield. Last, similar securities differing only in maturity may offer different yields. Several theories have been offered in explanation of this phenomenon.[8] The segmented markets hypothesis states that the difference in yields of short- and long-term securities arises from the differences in the supply and demand of securities in each of these markets. According to this hypothesis, institutional buyers and sellers are active only in those maturity ranges which fit their particular needs. An extra supply of securities placed in the long-term market, for example, would depress market prices in that market and raise yields. This effect would not be transmitted readily to the short end of the market because of the imperfect substitutability of instruments with different maturities. Thus, long-term rates would remain above short-term ones.

Other market analysts see high interest rates on long-term securities relative to those on short-term ones as normal, since holders of long-term securities face a greater risk of price fluctuation. When market rates of interest change, the prices of various securities adjust to bring their yields into line.

---

[8]For a summary of these theories, see Frederick M. Struble, "Current Debate on the Term Structure of Interest Rates," *Monthly Review,* Federal Reserve Bank of Kansas City (January-February 1966), pp. 10–16.

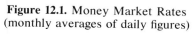

Figure 12.1. Money Market Rates
(monthly averages of daily figures)

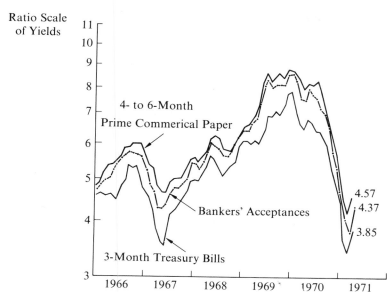

Using the yield-to-maturity formula, a given change in the market rate of interest results in a greater change in the price of long-term securities than in the price of short-term ones. Consider the 3½s85 bond currently selling at $700 and with a yield to maturity of 6.4 percent. If the rate of interest in the market were to increase to 7 percent, the price of that bond would have to fall by $44 in order to adjust. The same 3½s bond maturing in one year instead of fifteen years would suffer a price drop of only $6.

Finally, the pure expectations theory of market yields states that current differences in yields exist because the investors expect market prices and yields to change in ways that provide the same yield over any given period to holders of any maturity security. The yield of similar securities with different maturities can be graphically demonstrated by means of a yield curve. In Figure 12.2, the yield curve is formed so that long-term securities have lower yields than short-term securities. Expectationists would say that this curve demonstrates that investors expect interest rates to fall in the future, with short-term interest rates falling more than long-term ones. Thus, over the same period of time, if interest rates do fall, holders of short-term securities will obtain the same yield as the holders of long-term ones.

Figure 12.2. Yields of Treasury Securities, February 27, 1970
(based on closing bid quotations)

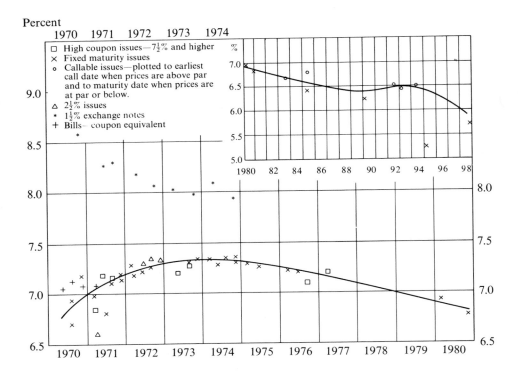

Selected Bibliography

Federal Reserve Bank of Chicago. "A Larger Role for Commercial Paper." *Business Conditions* (December 1968), pp. 2–12.

Federal Reserve Bank of Cleveland. *Money Market Instruments*. Cleveland: Federal Reserve Bank of Cleveland, 1967.

Maxwell, James A. *Financing State and Local Governments*. Washington, D.C.: The Brookings Institution, 1965.

Monhollon, Jimmie R., ed. *Instruments of the Money Market*. Richmond, Va.: Federal Reserve Bank of Richmond, 1968.

Scott, Ira O., Jr. *Government Securities Market*. New York: McGraw-Hill Book Co., 1965.

Selden, Richard T. *Trends and Cycles in the Commercial Paper Market*, Occasional Paper 85. New York: National Bureau of Economic Research, 1963.

13

Banking as a Business

A commercial bank is a profit-seeking business firm. It is similar in this respect to other businesses. It is also an institution that creates demand deposits. In this respect it is dissimilar to any other business firm and, indeed, to any other type of bank or financial institution.

A typical commercial bank may begin its business life by obtaining capital funds through conventional channels. It may be a single proprietorship, a closed or family corporation, or a corporation owned by a multitude of investors.

As a profit-seeking operation, it needs a proper geographical setting and an adequate physical plant. The "proper" place is near the center of the financial community it serves. The physical plant has traditionally been a stone or marble temple suitably appointed with iron bars, heavy vaulted doors, and other paraphernalia that imply solidarity and security. The contemporary trend, however, is toward a less rigorous atmosphere of aluminum and glass exteriors, and interiors featuring plush carpets and canned music.

The part of the institution that meets the eye of the public is only a small fraction of the total bank plant. Much capital in present-day banking is required for computing machines, special card-processing machines, and other time-saving and labor-saving equipment. An average-sized contemporary bank can be capitalized at about $1.5 million, an amount not too different from the value of capital in the average department store. Once a bank is physically settled, it, too, becomes a kind of "store." Its fundamental input after it is capitalized is primary deposits; its principal output is loans.

Commercial Bank Assets

Commercial bank assets fall into three major categories: cash on hand and due from banks, investments (primarily in government securities), and loans and discounts. Each of these categories serves a different function. Most of the cash on hand and due from banks can be considered to be banks' primary reserves. That is, portions of these funds are used to meet legal reserve requirements and daily liquidity needs. Investments may fulfill a secondary reserve function if they are readily convertible into cash. Finally, loans and discounts generate the bulk of the income that banks earn. Each of these categories and functions is discussed below.

As of December 30, 1969, all commercial banks in the United States had the following cash assets.

	(millions of dollars)
Currency and coin	7,347
Reserve with Federal Reserve Banks	21,453
Balances with other banks	19,941
Cash items in process of collection	40,594
	89,335

(Note that this total appears in Table 13.1.)

Commercial banks normally hold some currency and coin in their vaults for day-to-day transactions. Under current Federal Reserve regulations, member banks may count vault cash as part of their *legal reserves.* The other component of legal reserves for members is deposit accounts with Federal Reserve Banks. State-chartered banks, which are not members of the Federal Reserve System, are usually allowed to count balances with other banks as part of their legal reserves.

The discussions of check clearing (Chapter 8) and correspondent banking (Chapter 11) have shown that banks may deposit a larger amount of funds with Federal Reserve Banks or other commercial banks than is needed to meet legal reserve requirements.[1] The sum of these first three assets—currency and coin, reserves with Federal Reserve Banks, and balances with other banks—is regarded by banks as *primary reserves,* the amount that banks have available to meet claims presented for payment.

Another balance sheet item, "cash items in the process of collection," consists of checks that have been received by a given bank and drawn against other banks. These checks have been presented by customers (individuals or correspondents) for cash or deposit, and they are in the process of being cleared

---

[1] Of course, required reserves may not be used to satisfy ordinary withdrawal demands, so a bank must keep *some* small amount of excess reserves on hand.

against the debtor banks. This item is not included as part of primary reserves because a given bank not only has claims on other banks, but simultaneously other banks have claims on it. If all bank depositors were to stop writing checks at any given moment and allow all checks already in existence to clear, the balance in this account would quickly approach zero.

The investment account for all banks as of December 30, 1969, was composed of the subitems shown below.

	(millions of dollars)
Obligations of the U.S. government, direct and guaranteed	53,263
Obligations of states and subdivisions	57,572
Securities of federal agencies and corporations	9,239
Other securities	2,129
	122,203

Part of a bank's investments can be classified as *secondary reserves*. Secondary reserves do not make up an actual item but are a concept that usually includes short-term, highly liquid securities that may be converted into cash quickly, easily, and without loss. The need to do so may be either anticipated or unpredictable. Banks in agricultural communities regularly experience a seasonal demand for loans. Secondary reserves can be liquidated to meet this need. Large unanticipated withdrawals also may be met by secondary reserves. If the seasonal lending situation is not reversed, the bank may adjust its ordinary lending in order to restore secondary reserves.

The instrument most commonly held by banks as part of secondary reserves is the Treasury bill.[2] Treasury securities maturing in one year or less ideally fit the requirements for secondary reserves—they have little risk of default and their short maturity minimizes the risk of price fluctuation through changing market yields. These securities account for about one third of insured commercial banks' investment holdings. Treasury bonds and Treasury notes maturing within one to five years are the next-most-popular federal security, followed by bonds maturing within five to ten years. Commercial banks hold very few federal issues maturing in more than ten years.[3]

Commercial bank holdings of federal securities expanded sharply during World War II but have been declining since then. In contrast, holdings of state and local government securities have risen markedly in the past decade (see Table 12.5). Their attraction is their safety record, the exemption of their interest from federal income taxes, and the fact that many of them are now

---

[2]For a review of Treasury bills and other U.S. government securities, see Chapter 12.

[3]During periods of "high" interest rates, however, banks are willing to undergo reductions in liquidity in order to expand the number of loans made at favorable rates of interest. Unless offset by monetary authorities, an expansion of the money supply may follow. For further discussion, see the "Management of Bank Assets and Liabilities" section later in this chapter.

offered with short- and intermediate-range maturities. Other securities that banks hold include issues by federal agencies and corporations, Federal Reserve Bank stock (which must be held by members), and small amounts of other bonds, notes, debentures, and corporate stocks.

Both loans and investments earn income for the bank, while primary reserve items do not. Thus, the typical bank faces a minimax situation: It wishes to maximize interest-earning assets and the interest returns on these assets, and to minimize the risk and illiquidity of these assets. Of course, higher interest returns accrue on the higher risk paper that is less easily convertible into cash, while less risky, more liquid loans and investments return lower yields. The achievement of the proper minimax position is a function of the individual banker's skill as an entrepreneur.

All of the typical bank's assets have some degree of liquidity, cash and reserves being completely liquid. The bank can take any of its interest-earning assets—from a business loan to a 30-year government security—into the financial markets and either sell them outright or obtain a loan itself by using the assets as collateral. All of the bank's portfolio then has some potential degree of reserve power. In fact, if a bank is a member of the Federal Reserve System, the reserve potential of its interest-earning paper is further enhanced because of the discounting facilities available. Most monetary authorities argue, however, that only short-term government securities provide secondary reserve possibilities. But the difference between them and other paper is one of degree and not of kind as far as supplementing existing reserves is concerned.

The major asset in commercial bank balance sheets is loans and discounts. As seen in Table 13.1, they account for slightly over one half of the value of commercial bank assets. Loans and discounts have been disaggregated in Table 13.2 for closer analysis. The major types of loans and discounts—commercial and industrial, real estate, bank and other financial institution, security, farmer, and individual—are discussed in turn.

Commercial and industrial loans have been and continue to be the mainstay of commercial banking. In earlier days only the largest of businesses could attract capital from abroad; the rest had to secure funds locally. Commercial banks in the United States eschewed long-term financing and instead made short-term commercial loans because they appeared to be both safe and lucrative. The imagined safety of these inventory-type loans lay in their "self-liquidating" nature. That is, the loans allegedly were made for production, not consumption, purposes. According to the commercial loan theory of banking, when the goods so produced were sold they would afford income to repay the loan, plus interest and profit for the borrower. This theory collapsed during periods of business recession, when goods could not be sold and loans could not be repaid. Loans that seemed of high quality during a business boom lost much of their luster under the strictures of a depression.

Today commercial and industrial loans fall into one of two categories, short-term or term. Short-term loans, or the working capital variety discussed above,

Table 13.1. Assets and Liabilities of Insured Commercial Banks
in the United States, December 31, 1969

Asset or Liability Item	Amount in Millions of Dollars	Percent
Assets		
Cash and due from banks	89,335	16.8
Investments	122,203	23.0
Loans and discounts	296,464	55.9
Bank premises and furniture	8,070	1.5
Miscellaneous assets	14,643	2.8
Total assets	530,715	100.0
Liabilities		
Demand deposits	240,131	45.2
Time deposits	196,859	37.1
Other liabilities and bad debt reserves	54,149	10.2
	491,139	92.5
Capital accounts		
Capital stock, notes, and debentures	12,631	2.4
Surplus	17,461	3.3
Undivided profits	8,427	1.6
Reserves	1,057	0.2
Total capital accounts	39,576	7.5
Total liabilities and capital accounts	530,715	100.0

Source: *Annual Report of the Federal Deposit Insurance Corporation, 1969* (Washington, D.C.: Federal
Deposit Insurance Corporation, 1970), pp. 264–266.
* Includes states and other areas in this and following tables using the same source.

account for about 60 percent of the total commercial and industrial loans made
by commercial banks. Since they are regarded as aids to businesses in meeting
seasonal and unexpected demands, most banks insist on an annual cleanup of
these loans. Borrowing businesses are expected, sometime during the year,
to balance their accounts to demonstrate that the funds were needed only on a
temporary basis. If a business is unable to fulfill this requirement, the commercial banker may monitor the account more closely for signs of financial
weakness.

Term loans are defined as business loans with an original maturity of more
than one year. They are usually granted for the purchase of the tools of whatever trade is being financed — a freezer, cutting boards, and scales for the

Table 13.2. Loans and Discounts of Insured Commercial Banks
in the United States, December 30, 1969

Loans and Discounts		Amount in Millions of Dollars	Percent
Commercial and industrial loans (including open market paper)		108,394	36.6
Real estate loans		70,326	23.7
Loans to domestic commercial and foreign banks		2,425	0.8
Loans to other financial institutions		14,939	5.0
Federal funds sold (loaned)		9,712	3.3
Loans to brokers and dealers in securities		5,647	1.9
Other loans for purchasing securities		3,995	1.3
Loans to farmers (excluding loans for real estate)		10,324	3.5
Other loans to individuals—total		63,356	21.4
Passenger automobile installment loans	22,706		
Retail (charge account) credit card plans	2,639		
Check credit and revolving credit plans	1,083		
Other retail consumer installment loans	6,270		
Residential repair and modernization installment loans	3,655		
Other installment loans for personal expenditures	9,937		
Single-payment loans for personal expenditures	17,066		
All other loans (including overdrafts)	7,346		2.5
Total loans and discounts		296,464	100.0

Source: *Annual Report of the Federal Deposit Insurance Corporation, 1969* (Washington, D.C.: Federal Deposit Insurance Corporation, 1970), p. 264.

butcher, ovens, pots, and pans for the baker, and office furnishings for the dentist. The funds for the repayment of these loans must come out of the future earnings of the business. They are often repaid on an installment basis rather than in one single payment, although the interest charged may be only on the balance outstanding. They are therefore, more like short-term business mortgages than installment loans.[4]

---

[4]The calculation of real rates of interest charged on installment loans is discussed later in this chapter.

Real estate loans account for almost one fourth of the value of commercial bank loans and discounts (see Table 13.2). At one time, commercial banks were prohibited from making (as well as being reluctant to make) real estate loans. Short-term liabilities of commercial banks (primarily demand deposits) were supposed to be matched by short-term assets (commercial loans). With the expansion of longer-term liabilities by banks (time deposits), regulations have been relaxed and commercial banks have actively entered the mortgage market.

Commercial banks also make loans to one another and to other types of financial institutions. A correspondent bank may lend to its principal simply by crediting the borrowing bank's deposit account. Similarly, one bank may lend to another through the federal funds market (discussed in Chapter 12). In such a case the borrowing bank's reserves with the Federal Reserve System are immediately increased and the lending bank's reserves immediately reduced. Other financial institutions, especially sales finance companies and small loan companies, borrow from banks. Such institutions in turn make loans to their customers.

Banks also make loans for the purchase of securities. These loans may be to brokers or dealers (see Chapter 12), or directly to individuals. Dealers may borrow to finance the purchases of their customers. Some individuals borrow directly from banks in order to finance the purchase of securities.

Farmers also have uses for long-term, intermediate, and short-term credit. Long-term credit is needed for financing land purchases, intermediate credit for machinery and equipment, and short-term credit for fertilizer, seed, pesticides, and other items associated with annual crop production. Banks have traditionally met these short-term credit needs. In so doing, they strive to obtain an annual cleanup from farmers just as from other small businesses. The special problems of farming—weather, price fluctuations, and so on—plus farmers' lack of adequate financial records, preclude rigid financial guidelines for farm loans. Instead, the country banker must draw heavily on his personal experience in deciding what loans to make and in what amount.

Commercial banks located in an agricultural region may face the problem of not being able to diversify their loan portfolio adequately. When one farmer experiences crop failure and thus financial difficulties, all of the farmers in the region are likely to suffer the same troubles. The country bank may be severely pressed for funds if loan renewals are sought while the region is suffering a net outflow of funds. Though commercial banks make intermediate-term farm loans for equipment purchases, federal agencies are the predominant lender of long-term funds.

Following commercial and industrial and real estate loans, other loans to individuals is the third-largest category of loans made by commercial banks. (See Table 13.2.) Adherents of the commercial loan theory of banking thought loans for consumption unsound. The lagging demand for business loans during the 1930s caused banks to reevaluate this philosophy. Studies showed that consumer loans produced far fewer losses than expected, in some cases less than industrial loans; and they also showed that consumer lending was highly profitable. Today's banks actively compete for consumer loans. They finance purchases of automobiles, household durables, and home repair and modernization.

While accounting for only a small percentage of loans extended to consumers, the growth of bank credit card and check credit plans has attracted considerable attention. About 100 small commercial banks began to offer credit card and check credit services in 1952 and 1953. An upsurge of these programs occurred in 1958 and 1959, when the largest banks in the country entered the field. Since 1966, with the introduction of "interbank" cards, these plans have taken another jump. By September 30, 1967, 197 credit card plans were in existence, with 129 entering the field during the preceding 21 months, and the estimated number of participating banks (counting both principals and agents) was in excess of 1,000.[5] Principal banks start the credit card programs, issue the cards, maintain the accounting records, and extend credit. Agent banks play a more limited role. They sign up local merchants and forward merchants' sales slips to the principal bank. In some areas the agent banks share in the issuing of credit cards and in the revolving credit.

When the merchants using the plan present their sales slips to the bank, they are given credit for them, less a discount (the average being 3½ percent), and the bank assumes the responsibility for collection. Individuals using bank credit cards are billed at the end of each month for the total amount of their purchases. They have the option of paying the entire bill within 30 days without a service charge or of making a minimal payment, thus converting the account into a revolving credit plan. The service charge on the unpaid balance usually ranges from ¾ to 1½ percent per month.

Prior to the introduction and enforcement of the Truth in Lending Act, consumer borrowing on an installment basis, regardless of whether the lender was a commercial bank or a small loan company, usually resulted in the borrower paying about twice the stated rate of interest.[6] When repaying on an installment basis, the borrower paid interest on the full amount of the loan while having use on the average of only one half of the funds borrowed. For example, if one borrows $120 and agrees to repay it in twelve equal monthly installments, the average balance that he has is approximately $60. The full $120 is borrowed only during the first month. During the second month, he is borrowing $110, during the third, $100; and so forth. By the twelfth month, only $10 of the original amount of the loan is left. If the lender said that he was charging 5 percent interest and calculated it as (5% × $120 = $6.00), the true rate of

---

[5]For an excellent review of the development and impact of credit card and check credit plans, see *Bank Credit Card and Check Credit Plans* (Washington, D.C.: Board of Governors of the Federal Reserve System, 1968).

[6]An important exception to this is mortgage lending. There the stated rate of interest on the loan is in fact the true annual rate.

interest is closer to 10 percent than 5 percent. That is,

$$\frac{\$6 \text{ (the dollar amount of interest paid per year)}}{\$60 \text{ (average balance outstanding during the year)}} = 10\%$$

A formula that permits calculation of the real rate of interest on installment loans a bit more precisely is:

$$R = \frac{2mI}{P(n + 1)}$$

where m = the number of payment periods per year, I = the dollar amount of interest paid, P = principal — the amount of money actually advanced to the borrower — and n = the number of payments to be made.

Using the previous example:

$$R = \frac{(2)(12)\$6}{\$120(12 + 1)} = \frac{144}{1,560} = 0.092 = 9.2\%$$

Another way in which lenders effectively increase the rate of interest charged is to discount a loan; that is, the dollar amount of interest is deducted from the amount advanced to the borrower. Using the same example but discounting, the lender would receive only $114 ($120 − $6 = $114). When these figures are substituted in the interest rate formula, the real rate of interest is 9.7 percent, a full ½ percent increase:

$$R = \frac{(2)(12)\$6}{\$114(12 + 1)} = \frac{144}{1,482} = 0.097 = 9.7\%$$

Another means for increasing the effective rate of interest is to require the borrower to maintain a "compensating balance" of a certain minimum amount. Since money held in demand deposits draws no return, the bank has free use of this money, while the borrower gets no return from it. Service charges, investigation fees, and the like also serve to increase the true rate of interest.

Because of the widespread public ignorance of how to calculate true rates of interest, Congress passed the Truth in Lending Act in 1968. The provisions of this Act require lenders to spell out clearly the dollar finance charge and the true rate of interest borrowers are paying. The purpose of the law is to make customers aware of the cost of credit so they can shop more effectively for credit at desirable rates. The Federal Reserve System, through Regulation Z, in effect since July 1, 1969, provides for administration of this law. Regulation Z applies not only to banks, consumer finance companies, and savings and loan associations, but to department stores, credit card issuers, doctors, dentists, automobile dealers, and any other individual or group which extends or arranges for consumer credit.[7]

Commercial Bank Liabilities

After an initial injection of capital, commercial banks secure most of their funds by attracting deposits. Only primary deposits (as opposed to loan-created deposits) serve to increase reserves. Demand deposits are used by the public for paying, receiving, and transacting business. Today demand deposits account for almost 80 percent of the money supply in the United States.

Most commercial banks offer customers their choice of two checking plans. Special accounts are designed for the individual who does not write many checks per month. The customer is charged a certain fee for each check written, plus a small monthly charge. No minimum balance is required. Regular accounts are used by individuals and businesses with moderate to substantial balances. Provided a minimum monthly balance is maintained, no service charge is levied on these accounts.

All commercial banks with federal insurance have been prohibited from paying interest on demand deposits since 1935, and Federal Reserve members have been prohibited since 1933. Many observers felt that the "high" rates of interest banks were paying on demand deposits encouraged higher-yielding speculative loans and that such practices were partially responsible for the banking collapse of the period. Thus, restrictive regulations were passed. The present banking practice of absorbing service charges for large deposits is considered by most economists to be an implicit payment of interest. Many economists have urged that regulations limiting the payment of interest on time deposits be dropped, and that restrictions of interest payments on demand deposits be loosened.

The most important depositors in commercial banks are individuals, partnerships, and corporations (see Table 13.3). They account for three fourths of both the demand deposit and the time deposit liabilities of commercial banks. While businesses account for but a small number of the total bank accounts in the United States, they own a majority of the demand deposit balances. Interbank

---

[7]Board of Governors of the Federal Reserve System, "Truth in Lending," and "Regulation Z: Truth in Lending," *Federal Reserve Bulletin,* Vol. 55, No. 2 (February 1969), pp. 98–103 and 126–145.

deposits, forming the bond of correspondent banking, account for over 9 percent of commercial bank demand deposit liabilities.

Table 13.3. Liabilities of Insured Commercial Banks in the United States, December 30, 1969

Liability Item	Amount in Millions of Dollars	Percent
Demand deposits		
Individuals, partnerships, and corporations	178,186	36.3
Domestic interbank	24,412	5.0
U.S. government	5,051	1.0
States and subdivisions	17,560	3.6
Foreign governments and banks	3,415	0.7
Certified and officers' checks, letters of credit, travelers' checks, etc.	11,507	2.3
	240,131	48.9
Time deposits		
Individuals, partnerships, and corporations	176,241	35.9
Domestic interbank	446	0.1
U.S. government	223	0.0*
States and subdivisions	13,260	2.7
Foreign governments and banks	6,689	1.4
	196,859	40.1
Other liabilities		
Federal funds purchased (borrowed)†	14,685	3.0
Other liabilities for borrowed money	3,367	0.7
Acceptances outstanding	3,387	0.7
Other liabilities and bad debt reserves	32,710	6.6
	54,149	11.0
Total liabilities (excluding capital accounts)	491,139	100.0

Source: *Annual Report of the Federal Deposit Insurance Corporation, 1969* (Washington, D.C.: Federal Deposit Insurance Corporation, 1970), p. 265.
* Less than ½ of 1 percent.
† Includes securities sold under repurchase agreements.

The United States Treasury maintains what are known as tax and loan accounts at commercial banks. These accounts help to smooth the withdrawal of reserves from commercial banks when tax payments are due. The Treasury also has checking accounts with the Federal Reserve Banks; so when the Treasury receives a check from a corporation in payment of taxes, the Federal

Reserve Bank, in order to collect the check, has only to reduce the reserve account of the commercial bank on which it is drawn. If this procedure were followed at the end of each tax payment date, it would result in a massive reduction of commercial bank reserves. With the operation of tax and loan accounts, the Treasury simply returns the corporate tax payment check to the commercial bank on which it is drawn and asks that the tax and loan account be credited. In this way bank reserves are not immediately reduced. The Treasury then periodically checks against these balances as government appropriations are spent. State and local governments also maintain sizable demand deposit and time deposit balances in commercial banks. Other minor accounts with commercial banks include those of foreign governments, banks, and individuals.

Several types of savings and time deposit accounts are available to bank customers. The one most familiar to the general public is the passbook-type savings account. Other accounts include certificates of deposit and time deposit open accounts.

The general savings account is characterized by a passbook that the owner presents for deposit or withdrawal of funds. These accounts are owned primarily by individuals. Nonprofit corporations may open them, but profit-seeking corporations may not. Banks may require 30 days notice of intention to withdraw from these accounts, but in practice this regulation is rarely exercised. While accounting for over 50 percent of the total of savings and time deposit accounts by individuals, partnerships, and corporations (see Table 13.4), savings accounts have not been growing as rapidly in recent years as other types of time accounts. The growing sophistication of savers has resulted in a shift of deposits to higher-interest-yielding items such as certificates of deposit and open account plans.

Under current federal regulations commercial banks may pay a higher rate of interest on time accounts than on savings accounts (see Table 13.5). Purchasers of nonnegotiable certificates of deposit are required by law to give up a certain degree of liquidity in order to obtain this return (Table 13.5). Commercial banks normally require CD holders to give 90 days notice of their intention to return the certificate; or, in lieu of the 90 days notice, they may allow the holder to redeem the certificate only at certain intervals — for example, the 10 days immediately following each calendar quarter provided the money has been on deposit for the full quarter. (The characteristics and rapid growth of negotiable CD's were discussed in Chapter 12.)

While certificates of deposit are "sold" to the depositor for a fixed sum (some minimum amount), open account time deposits allow the depositor to increase his account by any amount. Withdrawal regulations closely parallel those for CD's: The depositor is required to give notice of his intention to withdraw some minimum amount of time prior to the actual withdrawal. (For recent trends and the composition of time and savings deposits of individuals, partnerships, and corporations in insured commercial banks, see Table 13.4.) Other liabilities of commercial banks include federal funds borrowed and bankers' acceptances outstanding, both of which were discussed in Chapter 12.

Table 13.4. Time and Savings Deposits of Individuals, Partnerships, and Corporations in Insured Commercial Banks on January 31 in 1968 and 1970

| | Amount in Millions of Dollars | |
Type of Deposit	January 31, 1968	January 31, 1970
Time deposits in denominations of less than $100,000 issued mainly to		
Consumers		
Certificates of deposit	37,754	45,863
Open account	2,955	16,039
Businesses		
Certificates of deposit	4,987	3,161
Open account	1,334	1,609
	47,031*	66,672
Time deposits in denominations of $100,000 or more (issued mainly to businesses):		
Negotiable CD's	15,202	6,445
Nonnegotiable CD's	4,437	3,986
Open account	1,651	1,404
	21,278	11,835
Christmas savings and other special funds	4,278	4,999
Savings accounts (passbook)	99,994	89,898
Total time and savings deposits	165,592	173,404

Source: Board of Governors of the Federal Reserve System, *Federal Reserve Bulletin*, Vol. 55, No. 3 (March 1969), p. 190, and Vol. 56, No. 5 (May 1970), p. 409.
* Certain numbers may not total precisely because of rounding.

Capital Accounts

A commercial bank raises its initial funds by sale of stock. Thereafter, the value of the capital account is held to "insure" depositors by the ability of this account to offset a certain shrinkage in the value of bank assets. Of course, other forms of "insurance" are equally if not more important in protecting bank depositors. Primary among these are the competence of the bank's managers and their ability to make sound loans; deposit insurance coverage by the FDIC; and perhaps most important, a healthy economy promoted by sound fiscal and monetary policies of the government. The value of the bank's capital also limits the amount that the bank may lend to any one borrower. Finally, for

Table 13.5. Maximum Interest Rates Payable on Time and Savings Deposits
(effective January 21, 1970)

Type of Deposit	Maximum Interest Rate*- Payable (percent *per annum*)
Savings deposits	$4\frac{1}{2}$
Other time deposits:	
Multiple maturity:†	
30–89 days	$4\frac{1}{2}$
90 days to 1 year	5
1 year to 2 years	$5\frac{1}{2}$
2 years and over	$5\frac{3}{4}$
Single maturity:	
Less than $100,000:	
30 days to 1 year	5
1 year to 2 years	$5\frac{1}{2}$
2 years and over	$5\frac{3}{4}$
$100,000 or more:	
30–59 days	rate suspended
60–89 days	rate suspended
90–179 days	$6\frac{3}{4}$
180 days to 1 year	7
1 year or more	$7\frac{1}{2}$

Source: Board of Governors of the Federal Reserve System, *Federal Reserve Bulletin*, Vol. 57, No. 6 (June 1971), p. A11.

* Maximum rate banks that are members of the Federal Reserve System may pay as established by Regulation Q of the Board of Governors. Since February 1, 1936, the same rates set by the Board of Governors have been used by the FDIC for non-member insured banks.

† "Multiple-maturity time deposits include deposits that are automatically renewable at maturity without action by the depositor and deposits that are payable after written notice of withdrawal." *Ibid.*

Federal Reserve System members, the value of the bank's capital and surplus is used in determining how much stock a member must purchase in the Federal Reserve Bank of its district.

Traditionally, commercial banks have increased the value of their capital accounts through the sale of *common stock* and through the accumulation of retained earnings. The massive number of banks failing during the 1930s changed this practice. The Reconstruction Finance Corporation was authorized in 1933 to make loans to commercial banks in difficulty by accepting their preferred stock and subordinated debentures as security.[8] Through the sale

---

[8]Debentures, or debenture bonds, are unsecured obligations to repay borrowed money. Normally, they carry a certain coupon rate of interest. When subordinated, the holders of these debentures have to wait until the claims of all depositors have been paid before their own can be presented.

of such senior securities to the RFC and others, commercial banks quickly raised over $1 billion. With the return to more normal banking conditions, commercial bankers were quick to retire these debentures and preferred stock, for they viewed them as a sign of weakness.

Some bankers, however, noted that the issuance of senior securities provided them with greater financial flexibility and wished to continue using them. But federal and state officials, with the exception of those in New York and New Jersey, were wary of the use of these securities as a source of bank capital and either discouraged or prohibited them. The Board of Governors has maintained that these debentures are not capital, that they increase financial risks to the issuer in periods of poor earnings, and that they may hurt the sale of common stock by the bank. While previously concurring in such views, the Comptroller of the Currency, after a study of bank practices and problems in 1962, authorized national banks to issue preferred stock and debentures. Today most of the states have amended their regulations to allow the same thing. The recent rapid growth of these securities, particularly debentures because of their tax deductible nature, can be seen in Table 13.6.

Table 13.6. Capital Accounts of Insured Commercial Banks, December 30, 1961, and December 31, 1969

| Capital Accounts | Amount in Millions of Dollars | |
	December 30, 1961	December 31, 1969
Common stock	6,585	10,529
Preferred stock	15	103
Capital notes and debentures	22	1,998
Surplus	10,798	17,461
Undivided profits	4,157	8,427
Reserves	546	1,058
Total	22,123	39,576

Source: *Annual Report of the Federal Deposit Insurance Corporation, 1969* (Washington, D.C.: Federal Deposit Insurance Corporation, 1970), p. 266.

Other capital accounts include surplus, undivided profits, and reserves. An increase in the surplus account may occur in one of two ways. First, if bank stock is sold for more than its par value, the difference is placed in the surplus account. Second, undivided profits may be transferred to the surplus account. The undivided profits account reflects current and accumulated net income of the bank which has not yet been added to surplus (part of the stockholders' investment) or distributed to the stockholders in the form of dividends. A declaration of dividends, of course, reduces the undivided profits account. The reserve account, which may also acquire value from undivided profits, is maintained to meet contingencies and absorb extraordinary losses.

Capital Ratios

Capital ratios serve as a measure of the "insurance" of deposit liabilities by capital accounts. A traditional favorite of bankers and regulatory authorities has been the total capital to total asset ratio. For years, a 10 percent ratio was thought to be the minimum desirable. During the early 1940s, as the federal government launched its wartime finance program, commercial bank holdings of government securities and deposits increased rapidly without a corresponding increase in capital accounts. Even though the capital ratio weakened, both the bankers and the regulatory authorities agreed that the security of depositors had not been compromised because of the soundness of the new assets (government securities) held by the banks.

With this development a new measure of capital adequacy was stressed — the risk asset ratio: total capital to total assets minus primary reserves and investments in federal securities. Bankers came to question the relevance of this ratio because certain types of secured loans and obligations issued by state and local governments may be as riskless as federal securities. Thus, "secondary risk asset ratios" have been devised which omit various "riskless" assets in their calculation. While the meaning and value of these ratios obviously change with time and events, they are nevertheless useful to regulatory authorities, who can at a glance identify banks with ratios that drastically deviate from the national norm.

Management of Bank Assets and Liabilities

Bankers are continually faced with the dilemma of balancing the need for safety with desire for profit. The variation of deposits over time, therefore, is of considerable interest to them. Lending adds to the profits of the bank but reduces the volume of reserves available to meet withdrawal demands. If bankers can anticipate the ebb and flow of deposits, they can make better lending and investing decisions. A recent study has shown that interbank deposits are the most variable, with an average fluctuation of 64 percent per year around their mean; U.S. government deposits are next, with 45 percent; and other types of demand deposits follow, with an average fluctuation of 6 percent. The variability of time deposits is only 1½ percent.[9]

---

[9]Hugh Chairnoff, "Deposit Variability: A Banker's Headache," *Business Review,* Federal Reserve Bank of Philadelphia (September 1967), pp. 9–15.

The traditional theory of bank management holds that banks first meet their liquidity, primary and secondary reserve needs and then make loans to their customers. Liquidity needs are determined by deposit stability and management preferences. If loan demand is slack, investments are treated somewhat as residuals after the satisfaction of liquidity needs. The newer theory of bank management combines the microeconomic theory of the firm with the theory of portfolio management and treats banks as profit-maximizing economic units.[10] Bank loans and investments are no longer seen as residuals but as integral parts of portfolio management. The inducement for banks to reduce their liquidity by making loans is the interest return expected on loans. That is, higher rates of interest are seen as necessary in order to induce banks to increase their ratio of loans to deposits because (1) the higher the ratio, the greater the chance that loans would have to be liquidated on unfavorable terms through deposit withdrawals; and (2) with a higher ratio large depositors, who are not covered by deposit insurance, are more likely to move their deposits to a bank that they feel is safer (more liquid). A higher rate of interest must be earned on loans in order to induce banks to face these risks.

Recent years have witnessed greater flexibility in both asset management and liability management. Banks have discovered that in order to compensate for deposit withdrawals they can attract new deposits by varying CD rates to supplement the older options of borrowing from the Federal Reserve System, liquidating secondary reserves, or purchasing in the federal funds market.[11] The selection of a source of funds depends upon the relative cost of each. The relaxation of regulations on the issuance of capital notes, debentures, and preferred stock has added another note of flexibility — the expansion of capital accounts. Now the total size as well as the composition of bank portfolios can be easily changed. The profit-maximizing bank can issue new CD's or debentures until the marginal cost of the issuance approaches the marginal return on new loans.

Commercial Bank Income

An income statement for all insured commercial banks in the United States is found in Table 13.7. The statement should hold few surprises for the student reading this far. The largest source of income for commercial banks is the interest received on loans — approximately 67.3 percent of all bank income. When interest and dividends received on securities are added, these sources account for about 86 percent of commercial bank income. The largest single expense for commercial banks is the interest paid on time and savings deposit

---

[10]For a good survey of this approach, see James L. Pierce, "Commercial Bank Liquidity," *Federal Reserve Bulletin*, Vol. 52, No. 8 (August 1966), pp. 1,093–1,101.

[11]The latest borrowing techniques by banks include tapping the Euro-dollar market and selling commercial paper through finance companies controlled by bank holding companies.

accounts—40.6 percent of total expenses. Salaries, wages, and employee benefits follow, accounting for 28.2 percent of bank operating expenses.

While net income after taxes was only 0.84 percent of the value of total bank assets, it was 11.34 percent of total capital accounts. Because capital accounts are equal to only about 8 percent of the value of total assets, a small percentage return on total assets provides a much larger percentage return to the banks' owners.

Table 13.7. Income of Insured Commercial Banks in the United States in 1969

Income Item	Amount in Millions of Dollars	Percent
Current operating revenue		
Interest on U.S. government obligations	3,396	11.0
Interest and dividends on state and other securities	2,351	7.6
Interest and fees on loans	20,726	67.3
Income on federal funds sold and repurchase agreements	812	2.6
Service charges on deposit accounts	1,120	3.6
Other charges, commissions, fees, etc.	694	2.3
Trust department	1,022	3.3
Other current operating revenue	686	2.3
Total revenue	30,807	100.0
Current operating expenses		
Salaries and wages of officers and employees	5,879	24.4
Officer and employee benefits	904	3.8
Interest on time and savings deposits	9,790	40.6
Expense of federal funds purchased and repurchase agreements	1,206	5.0
Interest on other borrowed money	433	1.8
Occupancy expense of bank premises, net	1,073	4.5
Furniture and equipment	773	3.2
Other current operating expenses	4,019	16.7
Total expenses	24,077	100.0
Income before income taxes and securities gains or losses	6,730	
Less: Applicable income taxes	2,164	
Securities gains or losses, net	238	
Net income before extraordinary items	4,328	
Net extraordinary charges or credit	7	
Net income	4,335	

Source: *Annual Report of the Federal Deposit Insurance Corporation, 1969* (Washington, D.C.: Federal Deposit Insurance Corporation, 1970), p. 276.

Selected Bibliography

American Bankers Association, Commission on Money and Credit. *The Commercial Banking Industry*. Englewood Cliffs, N.J.: Prentice-Hall, 1962.

Bank Credit Card and Check Credit Plans. Washington, D.C.: Board of Governors of the Federal Reserve System, 1968.

Cawthorne, D. R., Sam B. Chase, Jr., and Lyle E. Gramley. *Essays on Commercial Banking*. Kansas City: Federal Reserve Bank of Kansas City, 1962.

Chairnoff, Hugh. "Deposit Variability: A Banker's Headache." *Business Review*, Federal Reserve Bank of Philadelphia (September 1967), pp. 9–15.

McKinney, George W., Jr. "New Sources of Bank Funds: Certificates of Deposit and Debt Securities." *Law and Contemporary Problems*. Banking, Part II: Developments in Banking, Vol. 32, No. 1 (Winter 1967), pp. 71–99.

Robinson, Roland I. *The Management of Bank Funds*, 2nd ed. New York: McGraw-Hill Book Co., 1962.

Guide to Reserve Computation

Federal Reserve Bank of Richmond

Everyone knows that commercial banks must keep dollar reserves as fractions of outstanding demand and time deposits. Almost no one besides bankers and central bankers ever bothers to learn the details of reserve computation. Yet an awareness of this process is valuable to both the practical banker and the academician interested in the creation of money.

The selection included below is a slightly abridged version of a Guide to Reserve Computation *compiled by the Federal Reserve Bank of Richmond. (Further details on allowances and deductions are given in the complete explanation of reserve computation. This supplement would be important to member banks but is of too limited value to students to be included here.) The reader should note that required reserves are computed for a one-week period. Data for making this computation include deposits accounted during the week two weeks prior to the week in question, vault cash also held two weeks earlier (as a part of legal reserves), and member bank reserve balances at the Federal Reserve Bank* for the current week. *In formula form, the computation is as follows:*

$$\frac{\text{Required reserves}}{\text{for current week}} = \frac{\text{Legal reserve}}{\text{requirement}} \cdot \frac{\text{Deposits for week}}{\text{two weeks earlier}}$$

Allowable reserves for fulfilling this requirement are:

$$\text{Allowable reserves} = \begin{array}{c}\text{Vault cash held}\\ \text{during week two}\\ \text{weeks earlier}\end{array} + \begin{array}{c}\text{Member bank reserves}\\ \text{with FRB during cur-}\\ \text{rent week}\end{array}$$

Regulation D of the Board of Governors of the Federal Reserve System was amended effective September 12, 1968, resulting in several changes in the method of computing member banks' required reserves. The principal changes are:

1. Establishing a one-week reserve period for all member banks, regardless of reserve classification.
2. Using deposits held two weeks earlier in calculating the required reserves for the present period.
3. Using vault cash held two weeks earlier, together with reserve balances at the Federal Reserve Bank for the current week, in the computation of reserves held in satisfaction of the requirements.
4. Providing that either excesses or deficiencies of up to 2 percent of required reserves will be carried forward to the next reserve week.

The amended regulation does not represent any change in Federal Reserve monetary policy, but is merely an alteration in a technical regulation designed to facilitate the efficient functioning of the reserve mechanism. The changes are expected to reduce uncertainties, for both member banks and the Federal Reserve, about the amount of reserves required during the course of any reserve period. They should also moderate some of the pressures for reserve adjustments within the banking system that produce sharp fluctuations in the availability of day-to-day funds.

Report of Deposits, Currency and Coin, Loans, and Securities — BK 1 (Table 1)

All figures should be entered on this report *as of the close of business.* Since it is prepared by member banks from their own books, the report provides the necessary data for computing required reserves. The need for accuracy of preparation and timely dispatch cannot be overemphasized.

From time to time the figures on this report may be compared with like figures contained in other reports and statements. This is done in an effort to correct any inconsistencies in reporting procedures which materially affect the computation of reserves and/or affect monetary studies.

Columns 1 through 9 contain figures necessary for computing the amount of reserves required to be maintained on the books of the Federal Reserve Bank *two weeks later*. Table 1 has been supplied with sample figures for the week of August 7 through August 13 that would determine the amount of reserves required at the Reserve Bank in the week of August 21 through August 27.

Cash Items in Process of Collection, Column 4, should include amounts of cash letters forwarded to the Reserve Bank while awaiting credit on the Federal Reserve daily statement. For example, checks forwarded to a Federal Reserve Bank on August 7, with credit deferred until August 12, should be reported in Column 4 for five days, August 7 through August 11. Banks which customarily charge the Reserve Bank immediately upon mailing a cash letter may utilize a memorandum or subsidiary account to facilitate reporting proper amounts in Column 4. Otherwise, net demand deposits upon which required reserves are figured may be overstated.

Columns 10 and 11, Federal Funds Sold and Federal Funds Purchased, along with the Loans and Securities section at the bottom of the form, are memorandum items which do not affect the reserve computation. These data are needed for monetary studies, but are collected on this report in lieu of burdening member banks with separate reporting forms. Figures in Column 10 should agree with item 7 under *Assets* in the Call Report of Condition; Column 11 should agree with item 23 under *Liabilities* in the Call Report of Condition. Banks which submit a weekly condition statement (Form FR 416) need not complete the Loans and Securities section of the Report of Deposits.

Statement of Required Reserves (Table 2)

Each Wednesday night the Federal Reserve Bank dispatches to each member bank a Statement of Required Reserves for the following week. This statement should be received on the first day of the week in which such reserves are to be maintained. Table 2 furnishes a computation of reserves required in the week of August 21 through August 27, and it would be received by the member bank on August 21. This statement was prepared from the Report of Deposits, Currency and Coin, Loans, and Securities for the week of August 7 through August 13 (Table 1).

Table 1. Report of Deposits, Currency and Coin, Loans, and Securities

Please mail to the

FEDERAL RESERVE BANK OF RICHMOND
RICHMOND, VIRGINIA 23261

XYZ BANK
ANYWHERE, U. S. A.

0555–0555–2
ACC 515

on Thursday after the close of the weekly period
Base period ending Wednesday ___ August 13 ___ 19 69

Official Signature

PLEASE REPORT IN NEAREST THOUSANDS AS OF CLOSE OF BUSINESS EACH DAY

DAY	DATE		1 DEMAND DEPOSITS OF BANKS (Schedule E, items 1,7, & 8) Mil.	Thous.	2 U.S. GOV'T. DEMAND DEPOSITS (Schedule E, item 4) Mil.	Thous.	3 OTHER DEMAND DEPOSITS (Schedule E, items 2,5,6 & 9) Mil.	Thous.	4 CASH ITEMS IN PROCESS OF COLLECTION (Schedule D, item 1) Mil.	Thous.	5 DEMAND BALANCES DUE FROM BANKS (Schedule D, item 2) Mil.	Thous.	6 NET DEMAND DEPOSITS Columns 1,2,3,4 Minus 5 & 6 Mil.	Thous.	7 SAVINGS AND CLUB DEPOSITS (Schedule F, item 1 plus club deposits) Mil.	Thous.	8 OTHER TIME DEPOSITS (Schedule F, items 3,4,6,7,8,9 & 10 minus club deposits) Mil.	Thous.	9 CURRENCY AND COIN (including currency and coin in transit with F. R. Bank) (Schedule D, item 5) Mil.	Thous.	10 FEDERAL FUNDS SOLD (including securities purchased under resale agreements) (Assets, item 7) Mil.	Thous.	11 FEDERAL FUNDS PURCHASED (including securities sold under repurchase agreements) (Liabilities, item 23) Mil.	Thous.
Thurs.	8/7	1	2	265		348	21	409	1	458	8	386	14	178	11	762	4	943		859				
Fri.	8/8	2	2	373		346	28	615		972	16	280	14	082	11	874	4	948		859				
Sat.	8/9	3	1	405		305	23	205	1	973	9	936	13	006	11	880	4	951		645				
Sun.	8/10	4	1	405		305	23	205	1	973	9	936	13	006	11	880	4	951		645				
Mon.	8/11	5	1	449		313	26	118	1	062	10	270	16	548	11	878	4	950		651		100		–
Tues.	8/12	6	1	650		269	23	152	1	662	4	488	18	921	11	912	4	955		672				–
Wed.	8/13	7	1	472		268	22	319	1	969	3	907	18	183	11	910	4	921	1	224				–
Total		8	12	019	2	154	168	023	11	069	63	203	107	924	83	096	34	619	5	555		100		–

LOANS AND SECURITIES

Complete the form below if your bank does not submit Weekly Report of Condition (Form F. R. 416)

CLOSE OF BUSINESS ON ___ August 13 ___ 19 69
Wednesday

			Mil.	Thous.
1	LOANS AND DISCOUNTS INCLUDING FEDERAL FUNDS SOLD AND SECURITIES PURCHASED UNDER RESALE AGREEMENTS (Assets, items 7 & 8)		20	333
2	UNITED STATES TREASURY SECURITIES – (Include securities sold under repurchase agreements.) (Assets, item 2)		6	988
3	OTHER SECURITIES – (Obligations of States and political subdivisions, securities of Federal agencies and corporations, and other securities and corporate stocks, including Federal Reserve Bank stock. Include securities sold under repurchase agreements) (Assets, items 3, 4, 5, & 6)		4	441
4	TOTAL LOANS AND SECURITIES (Total of items 1, 2 and 3 above)		31	762
5	TOTAL ASSETS (Item 4 above plus total of all other assets) (Assets, item 14)		37	854

Budget Bureau No. 55 – R171.7

Table 2. Specimen Form—Statement of Required Reserves

FEDERAL RESERVE BANK OF RICHMOND
STATEMENT OF REQUIRED RESERVES – IN THOUSANDS OF DOLLARS

0555–0555–2 ACC 515
XYZ BANK
ANYWHERE, U. S. A.

RESERVE PERIOD ENDING 8/27/69

	WEEK ENDING 8/13/69	REQUIRED RESERVES %	REQUIRED RESERVES
1. REQUIRED RESERVES			
AGGREGATE DEPOSITS			
A. NET DEMAND			
1. FIRST $35 MIL.	35,000	12.5	4,375
2. REMAINDER	72,924	13.0	9,480
B. SAVINGS	83,096	3	2,493
C. TIME & COMMERCIAL PAPER			
1. FIRST $35 MIL.	34,619	3	1,039
2. REMAINDER	0	5	0
D. TOTAL REQUIRED RESERVES			17,387
2. RESERVES CARRIED OVER FROM PREVIOUS WEEK			−302
3. CURRENCY AND COIN			5,555
4. AGGREGATE RESERVE BALANCES NEEDED WEEK ENDING 8/27/69			12,134

The first vertical column of figures shows the amount of deposits subject to reserve requirements. The second vertical column shows the required reserve percentages.[1] The third vertical column shows the amount of reserves required against each classification of deposits, with total required reserves shown on line 1D. This figure is adjusted by allowable reserve carry-over from the previous week (line 2), and currency and coin held two weeks earlier (line 3), to arrive at aggregate reserve balances needed for the week (line 4).

Cumulative Reserve Status Computation (Tables 3, 4, and 5)

Each day, along with the Statement of Reserve Account, each bank is sent a cumulative reserve status computation. This statement is received on the next business day and reflects: (1) the aggregate amount of funds needed for the remainder of the week; and (2) the daily average balance needed for the remainder of the week. The figures shown in the Statement of Required Reserve (Table 2) have been used to prepare specimen copies of the Cumulative Reserve Status Computation.

The statement for Thursday, August 21 (Table 3) reflects the bank's position after the first day of the reserve week. Line 7 indicates that *aggregate* balances of $10,143 thousand are needed for the remainder of the week. Line 8 indicates that this amount calls for an *average* balance of $1,691 thousand per day for the remaining six days. The statement for Friday, August 22 (Table 4), bears a multiple date (Friday, August 22–Sunday, August 24), and reflects the bank's position through Sunday. Line 7 shows *aggregate* balances of $4,275 thousand needed for the remainder of the week; line 8 indicates that this amount requires an *average* balance of $1,425 thousand per day for the remaining three days.

To complete the picture, refer to the statement for Wednesday, August 27, the last day of the week (Table 5). The XYZ Bank ends the week with excess reserves of $53 thousand. Immediately after preparation of this statement, the Statement of Required Reserves (Table 2) is prepared for the week August 28 through September 3. The amount of reserves to be carried over to the week ending September 3 is determined at this time. Since excess reserves are less than 2 percent of required reserves in the example, all of the excess reserves ($53 thousand) may be carried forward. The carry-over provision of the revised regulation is covered more fully in the section "Illustration of Carry-Over Provision."

---

[1]Reserve city bank requirements against net demand deposits will exceed the percentages shown in Table 2. All banks' requirements are subject to change and current requirements are always contained in the latest supplement to Regulation D.

Table 3. Specimen Form – Cumulative Reserve Status Computation

FEDERAL RESERVE BANK OF RICHMOND

CUMULATIVE RESERVE STATUS COMPUTATION – IN THOUSANDS OF DOLLARS

0555–0555–2   ACC 515   8/21/69
XYZ BANK
ANYWHERE, U. S. A.

1.	REQUIRED RESERVES – CURRENT WEEK		17,387
2.	CURRENCY AND COIN HELD DURING BASE WEEK	5,555	
3.	RESERVE BALANCES HELD SO FAR DURING CURRENT WEEK	1,991	
4.	NET ALLOWANCES AND DEDUCTIONS	0	
5.	CARRYOVER OF EXCESS OR DEFICIENCY FROM PREVIOUS WEEK	–302	
6.	CUMULATIVE RESERVES TO MEET REQUIREMENTS – CURRENT WEEK		7,244
7.	AGGREGATE RESERVE BALANCES NEEDED FOR REST OF WEEK		10,143
8.	DAILY AVERAGE RESERVE BALANCE NEEDED FOR REST OF WEEK	1,691	*******

Table 4. Specimen Form—Cumulative Reserve Status Computation

FEDERAL RESERVE BANK OF RICHMOND
CUMULATIVE RESERVE STATUS COMPUTATION – IN THOUSANDS OF DOLLARS

0555–0555–2 ACC 5l5
XYZ BANK
ANYWHERE, U. S. A.

8/22 – 24/69

1.	REQUIRED RESERVES – CURRENT WEEK		17,387
2.	CURRENCY AND COIN HELD DURING BASE WEEK	5,555	
3.	RESERVE BALANCES HELD SO FAR DURING CURRENT WEEK	7,859	
4.	NET ALLOWANCES AND DEDUCTIONS	0	
5.	CARRYOVER OF EXCESS OR DEFICIENCY FROM PREVIOUS WEEK	–302	
6.	CUMULATIVE RESERVES TO MEET REQUIREMENTS – CURRENT WEEK		13,112
7.	AGGREGATE RESERVE BALANCES NEEDED FOR REST OF WEEK		4,275
8.	DAILY AVERAGE RESERVE BALANCE NEEDED FOR REST OF WEEK		1,425 ******

Table 5. Specimen Form—Cumulative Reserve Status Computation

FEDERAL RESERVE BANK OF RICHMOND
CUMULATIVE RESERVE STATUS COMPUTATION -- IN THOUSANDS OF DOLLARS

0555–0555–2 ACC 515
XYZ BANK
ANYWHERE, U. S. A.   8/27/69

1.	REQUIRED RESERVES – CURRENT WEEK	17,387
2.	CURRENCY AND COIN HELD DURING BASE WEEK	5,555
3.	RESERVE BALANCES HELD SO FAR DURING CURRENT WEEK	12,137
4.	NET ALLOWANCES AND DEDUCTIONS	+ 50
5.	CARRYOVER OF EXCESS OR DEFICIENCY FROM PREVIOUS WEEK	–302
6.	CUMULATIVE RESERVES TO MEET REQUIREMENTS – CURRENT WEEK	17,440
7.	EXCESS RESERVES HELD FOR CURRENT WEEK	+ 53

****

Final Reserve Computation

Several days after the end of the reserve week, a final computation is prepared reflecting the final reserve position as well as certain reserve management ratios. The final position, in most instances, is identical to the position shown on the Cumulative Reserve Status Computation for the last day of the week (Table 5). Any differences between the two result from analysis adjustments (allowances and/or deductions) that come to light between the last day of the week and the day the final computation is prepared.

Section Three

Central Banking

14

A Schematic Sketch of Central Banking

Definition of Central Banking

A fitting, though perhaps corny, conundrum with which to introduce this subject is by posing the question "When is a bank not a bank?" The straight answer: "When it's a central bank." Both commercial banks and central banks use the label "bank," but a commercial bank operates as a private business that attempts to return a net return (profit) to its owners. A central bank, on the other hand, is an institution that creates and destroys the community's stock of money through consciously contrived policies in order to further well-understood economic goals, such as price level stability and high levels of employment. Its most positive impact is primarily through its influence on the reserves of the banking system. The particular institutional framework used, its implicit or explicit objectives, and its techniques of control are all subject to some variation; but a central bank that has powers enabling it to effect national monetary objectives must have some formal relationship to the government.

The most prolific development of central banks occurred during the nineteenth century, but under the pressures of different social stimuli, and sometimes within different political frameworks. Since central bank development in the United States has been extensive and discontinuous, the factual history of central banking thought and institutions in this country is left to subsequent chapters. This chapter presents only skeletal details of contemporary central bank techniques.

Formation of the Central Bank

A twentieth century central bank, as an institution distinct from a commercial bank, can be understood and analyzed most easily by means of progressive balance sheet development. Since the central bank's influence is channeled through the commercial banking system, the analysis may begin at the point where balance sheet interpretation of commercial banking left off.

Assume that the Sound Money Bank, developed in Chapter 8, has the balance sheet shown below. This bank multiplied "infinitely," say 10,000 times, constitutes a commercial banking system. The total amount of deposits furnished by this system is a function of the reserve ratio maintained by the banks in the system and the total amount of reserves they hold. Since bankers obtain income from interest paid in on loans and discounts, they maximize returns for their enterprises by judicious manipulation of their asset portfolios. As private profit seekers, they neither attempt to operate consciously in the public interest nor have any responsibility for doing so. Yet their normal portfolio operations of lending and investing notably affect the money supply—which is vital to the health of the economy.

Table 14.0. Sound Money Bank
(thousands of dollars)

Assets		Liabilities	
Loans and discounts	280,000	Deposits	200,000
Specie	20,000		
		Net Worth	
		Capital	100,000

Actual reserve ratio: 10 percent

The supply of money in the economy must adjust, or be adjusted, to various economic changes that change the demand for money. Economic variations with monetary side effects may occur (1) from time to time during the year (seasonal), (2) at other times when the demand for money undergoes sudden random shifts (cyclical), and (3) more or less continuously and predictably to provide for increases in the economy's rate of real output (secular). The private banking system cannot very well adjust to all such shifts in demand while operating under profit-seeking motives. Consequently, some policy-making governmental agency or institution must be given powers of some sort to administer changes in the monetary base. One such institution is a self-regulating metallic standard.[1] In the twentieth century, however, the controlling institution is a central bank.

---

[1]While a gold standard clearly is not a bank, neither is a central "bank" a bank. For purposes of analysis a self-regulating monetary institution, such as a gold standard system, may be thought of *as if* it were a central bank automatically functioning through the self-interest of gold miners.

Assume that a democratic government sets up a central bank called the "National Central Bank" (NCB). Let it have the exclusive legal right to issue paper currency and the exclusive responsibility for holding the specie reserves of the commercial banking system. The commercial banks transfer their specie reserves to the NCB and receive in return "reserve bank credit." This item is a liability of the NCB against which the NCB holds the specie as a reserve asset. Excluding furniture, fixtures, and other such items, the balance sheet for the NCB would be as shown in Table 14.1, while all 10,000 commercial banks would have assets and liabilities described by Table 14.2.

Table 14.1. National Central Bank
(thousands of dollars)

Specie	200,000	Reserves of, credits to, or deposits by commercial banks	200,000

Actual reserve ratio: 100 percent

Table 14.2. All Commercial Banks
(thousands of dollars)

Assets		*Liabilities*	
Loans and discounts	2,800,000	Deposits	2,000,000
Reserves (credit with central bank)	200,000		
		Net Worth	
		Capital	1,000,000

Actual reserve ratio: 10 percent

Central Bank Control by Discount Rates

The central bank's three principal techniques for controlling the stock of money can now come into play. It can, first of all, raise or lower the interest (discount) rate it charges the commercial banks for granting them reserve credit. If the commercial banks are hard pressed for liquid reserves to redeem demand obligations, they can take some of their interest-earning paper to the central bank for discount at a lower rate of interest than what they have charged their customers.[2] Assume that they discount $100 million. If, for simplicity's sake, the interest charge that would ordinarily be deducted ahead of time is not counted, the commercial banking system's balance sheet would be as shown in Table 14.3, and the NCB balance sheet would appear as in Table 14.4.

Table 14.3. All Commercial Banks
(thousands of dollars)

Assets		Liabilities	
Loans and discounts	2,800,000	Notes and discounts	
Reserves	300,000	payable	100,000
		Deposits	2,000,000
		Net Worth	
		Capital	1,000,000

Actual reserve ratio: 15 percent

Table 14.4. National Central Bank
(thousands of dollars)

Assets		Liabilities	
Discounts for		Reserves of	
commercial banks	100,000	commercial banks	300,000
Specie	200,000		

Actual reserve ratio: 66⅔ percent

The reserve ratio of the commercial banks has been increased by this operation from 10 percent to 15 percent. At the same time the reserve ratio of the central bank, its specie to demand obligations, has been diminished from 100 percent to 66⅔ percent. Commercial banks sense "relief" in their enhanced reserve position. While the central bank may face a limiting reserve requirement of, say, 25 percent of specie to demand obligations,[3] such a limitation causes the central bank no discomfort and might be little more than window dressing to assure the unsophisticated that *something* is "backed" by gold.

---

[2]Ordinarily, the rate charged by a central bank to a commercial bank is lower because the paper discounted is usually the less risky in the commercial bank's portfolio, and the bank as well adds its own responsibility for the ultimate payoff of the note. At present, most of the collateral pledged by commercial banks is government securities.

[3]This legal requirement is the one the Federal Reserve Banks faced from 1944 to 1966.

The central bank operating in the realm of public policy is not interested in earning income from its discounting operations. Its sole function as a central bank is to maintain stability in the monetary system. Its reserve ratio can indeed limit it as well, but if it does the central bank can no longer act as a central bank. Its role as the ultimate source of liquidity is lost.

If no central bank had existed in the above example, the commercial banks could have discounted their loans in private money markets with private investors who deal in such paper. When *all* commercial banks face a liquidity pinch and *all* try to discount at once, however, the cash reserves available from the money market are never enough. Private investors simply do not keep sufficient cash balances for such a purpose. Interest rates at these times go very high on short-term securities and loans, reflecting a demand that cannot be satisfied. Primary depositors, as they sense a deficiency of bank reserves, "panic"; and the fractional reserve feature of commercial banking ensures that much of the deposits or notes, previously expanded on a given reserve base, will be contracted. This kind of action and reaction has given the fractional reserve banking system a reputation for provoking a "perverse elasticity" in the supply of money: The supply declines when both the quantity demanded and the "price" paid increase.

The central bank differs in its technique of discounting paper from that of a private money market. When private dealers in the money market buy bank paper or lend directly to the banks, they give up their cash balances for the loan paper, and are paid for their trouble and risk by the interest income they obtain. The central bank may also have to pay out specie when it discounts commercial paper; but if it operates in the mode of central banks today, the central bank simply *creates* the liability—reserve bank credit[4]—with which to "pay for" the commercial paper or other securities it purchases from banks.

Discount rates set by the central bank are supposed to influence commercial bank borrowing and discounting at the central bank. If rates are lowered, the banking system is encouraged to lend and invest; if rates are raised, banks are discouraged from lending and investing. Nevertheless, in the presence of other powerful and independent variables, nominal rate changes may be ineffective. For example, raising rates when the banking system has a large volume of "excess" reserves may have little effect: The banks are able to create new loans and deposits anyway. Conversely, if a severe depression develops, lowering the rate even to zero may have little effect on bank reserves. Banks may be so apprehensive over the risks of the loans and the uncertainties of the future state of the economy that they may not supply additional credit to potential borrowers on any terms. Fortunately, other weapons of the central bank are more positive than discount rate changes.

---

[4]The credit that commercial banks obtain from the central bank is referred to here as a liability (of the central bank). Current Federal Reserve System practice is to call "reserve bank credit" an asset, since it is extended on the basis of the interest-earning assets (mostly government securities) the Reserve Banks obtain from the member banks.

Central Bank Control by Reserve Requirements

Another controlling device of central banks is specification of minimum reserve ratio requirements for commercial banks. In Table 14.3 the banking system had reserves equal to 15 percent of its demand obligations, where the banks voluntarily had maintained 10 percent previously. If the central bank statutory reserve requirement for member banks is 10 percent, banks in the system have a total of $100 million in "excess" reserves and are free to expand loans and discounts until their reserves are "used up."[5] If the NCB instead should raise the requirement to 20 percent without allowing the banking system "relief" in other ways, the system would have to contract to a position described by Table 14.5. Since the bank deposits people hold, while liabilities of the banks, also constitute an important component of the total money stock, a decline of $100 million in this stock could not help but affect prices, incomes, and employment.

Table 14.5. All Commercial Banks
(thousands of dollars)

Assets		Liabilities	
Loans and discounts	2,300,000	Notes and discounts	
Reserves	300,000	payable	100,000
		Deposits	1,500,000
		Net Worth	
		Capital	1,000,000

Actual reserve ratio: 20 percent

While minimal reserve requirements were thought of initially as a means for ensuring that banks would be able to meet demand obligations, they are now regarded only as a control device. However, they are not used as frequently as other forms of control by central banks. They are too cumbersome for expedient administration, and open market operations are more effective.

---

[5]The student should verify for himself the value of "excess" reserves. He should understand the simple arithmetic involved in computing both required reserves and the total deposits the system could develop given the volume of reserves and the reserve ratio requirement.

Open Market Operations

Open market operations in government securities are probably the most effective device used by central banks because the results of these operations immediately and directly affect the supplies of currency and bank reserves. Open market procedure is extremely simple; its only prerequisite is the existence of something the central bank can monetize. Government securities are an ideal asset for acquisition and monetization because central bank ownership of these securities implies nothing more than retirement. Central bank possession of private assets, such as corporate bonds or stocks, would bring the central bank — that is, the government — into the arena of private enterprise as an unwarranted and unwelcome participant.

Assume that government expenditures exceed tax revenues in some year by $200 million and that the government sells interest-bearing perpetual bonds (consols) in the money market to make up the deficit. The bonds pay $40 per year and are all sold to the nonbank public for a price of $1,000 each.[6] The Treasury Department pays out the money it has collected from the sale of the bonds to the government's creditors. The economy then has the same quantity of money that it had but $200 million more "wealth" in the form of interest-bearing assets.

A government fiscal deficit of $200 million for the year supplies the economy with public debt of the same amount. A useful characteristic of interest-bearing public debt is that it can be converted into noninterest-bearing legal tender and thus furnish the economy with money. The existence of a Treasury Department in a government that has power and authority is enough to effect such monetization; that is, the Treasury if authorized could issue noninterest-bearing legal tender notes with which it could buy back the interest-bearing debt.[7] However, this medicine has usually been too strong for societies to swallow, and when swallowed has frequently produced disastrous internal convulsions. Public officials prefer to vest money-making institutions with mystique and priestcraft, so that the unseemly realities of money creation are becomingly concealed.

In accordance with contemporary practices, then, let the executives of the NCB decide that the economy needs an injection of money. They contact dealers who specialize in government securities, and buy enough, say, $100 million worth, at going prices to effect the particular policy they have decided upon. If the volume they wish to buy is very large, their demand may sensibly

---

[6]The price of $1,000 for each bond means that people equate income of $40 per year "forever" with $1,000 of potential consumption that must be given up "right now." (See Chapter 5.)

[7]In fact, procedures of this general nature were followed in the Civil War, when about 20 percent of new (federal) government debt took the form of currency (U.S. notes). (See Chapter 10.)

increase the market price. Of course, the price paid for the securities has nothing to do with any anticipation of profit by the NCB on the possible future sale of the securities. Since prices of government securities move within a fairly narrow range, the amount of premium (or discount in the case of a sale) that the central bank must pay is small compared to price movements in other securities or in commodities. In the case of the consols a par value would not exist; central bank action would be reflected only by changes in the market prices of the consols.

If the securities are all purchased from people who wish currency payments for the securities given up, the central bank pays for the securities by writing checks payable to the security dealers, who in turn have written similar checks to the sellers of the securities. (For simplicity's sake, assume that the NCB checks go directly to the sellers of the securities.) The sellers of the securities take the checks to the local banks and demand currency for them, and the banks remit the checks to the NCB, relaying, in effect, the demand for the currency. The NCB prints National Central Bank notes, using the securities it has just purchased as collateral for the new notes, and its balance sheet then appears as in Table 14.6.

Table 14.6. National Central Bank
(thousands of dollars)

Assets		Liabilities	
Discounts for		NCB notes	
commercial banks	100,000	outstanding	100,000
Government securities	100,000	Reserves of	
Specie	200,000	commercial banks	300,000

Actual reserve ratio: 50 percent

Both sides of the balance sheet have expanded by $100 million. Again, the NCB has "paid for" what it purchased by creating the means; for every dollar's worth of government securities obtained, the NCB has produced a dollar's worth of currency. This kind of alchemy encourages spending because currency can be used to purchase goods and services currently produced, as well as to purchase previously produced wealth, while government securities may be held only to earn income or to anticipate a price level decline.

If the sellers of the securities prefer demand deposits instead of currency, they deposit their checks from the NCB in commercial banks. The commercial banks send the checks back to the NCB for "clearance," and the NCB "clears" the checks it has previously written by crediting the accounts of the commercial banks and destroying the checks. Commercial banks now realize an increase in their reserves. Their combined balance sheets appear as in Table 14.7, and the central bank's balance sheet is described by Table 14.8. Both the banks' reserves and their deposits have increased by $100 million.

Assuming that the reserve requirement remains at 20 percent, the banks could now expand until their combined balance sheet is as shown in Table 14.9. Central bank action in this case has resulted in *multiple* alchemy: Government security holdings by the public have been converted into money (demand deposits) worth five times the dollar value of the securities.

Table 14.7. All Commercial Banks
(thousands of dollars)

Assets		Liabilities	
Loans and discounts	2,300,000	Notes and discounts	
Reserves	400,000	payable	100,000
		Deposits	1,600,000
		Net Worth	
		Capital	1,000,000

Actual reserve ratio: 25 percent

Table 14.8. National Central Bank
(thousands of dollars)

Assets		Liabilities	
Discounts for		Reserves of	
commercial banks	100,000	commercial banks	400,000
Government securities	100,000		
Specie	200,000		

Actual reserve ratio: 50 percent

Table 14.9. All Commercial Banks
(thousands of dollars)

Assets		Liabilities	
Loans and discounts	2,700,000	Notes and discounts	
Reserves	400,000	payable	100,000
		Deposits	2,000,000
		Net Worth	
		Capital	1,000,000

Actual reserve ratio: 20 percent

The Central Bank and Its Reserves

The National Central Bank, when in the position described by Table 14.8, has specie reserves of $200 million and outstanding demand liabilities of $400 million. Its reserve ratio is, therefore, 50 percent. As long as the NCB is operating within the framework of a specie standard, it must keep a "free" reserve position; that is, it must keep specie reserves greater than the statutory minimum so that it can lend to commercial banks when monetary conditions become "stringent." People ordinarily are satisfied with the central bank notes as currency, and banks ordinarily are satisfied with central bank credit. However, in both the nineteenth and the twentieth century, central banks at times have faced acute demands for specie to redeem notes or checks, particularly when balances of trade were unfavorable. A deficit in the trade balance meant that foreign dollar claims exceeded domestic claims on foreign currencies. The balance could be made up either with specie or by sales of interest-bearing securities at long or short term. Specie, the only internationally acceptable means of payment, was almost always demanded in part payment of net debts to foreigners, particularly during times of international uncertainty.

Banks that deal primarily in foreign exchange would experience the impact of this demand. To protect their reserve positions, they would transmit the demand for specie to the central bank by discounting some of their commercial paper. If the central bank accommodated them, its "discounts for commercial banks" would increase and its holdings of specie decrease. The specie would become the property of the banks who shipped it as bullion or coin to foreign creditors (in the twentieth century, to foreign central banks).

Assume that the amount of specie called for under some such circumstances is $100 million. The National Central Bank balance sheet then takes the position shown by Table 14.10. The balance sheet for the commercial banking system shows a loss of deposits and an increase of indebtedness to the central bank, as in Table 14.11. The decline in deposits is from the accounts of importers who have converted their deposits into gold. Reserves, of course, would remain at $400 million because of central bank accommodation.[8] The whole system on net balance has lost $100 million of specie, but has gained $100 million in promises to pay, so total balance sheet values show no net change.

The internal price level has little reason to change appreciably, so the favorable balance of payments may continue. At the same time, prices in exporting countries need not rise if central banks in those countries "neutralize" the

---

[8]The commercial banks would have a small amount of excess reserves in this example, but their greater indebtedness to the central bank, their awareness of credit "stringency," and higher interest rates probably would inhibit any credit expansion.

Table 14.10. National Central Bank
(thousands of dollars)

Discounts for		Reserves of	
commercial banks	200,000	commercial banks	400,000
Government securities	100,000		
Specie	100,000		

Actual reserve ratio: 25 percent

Table 14.11. All Commercial Banks
(thousands of dollars)

Assets		*Liabilities*	
Loans and discounts	2,700,000	Notes and discounts	
Reserves	400,000	payable	200,000
		Deposits	1,900,000
		Net Worth	
		Capital	1,000,000

Actual reserve ratio: 21 percent (approximate)

inflow of specie. The whole price-specie-flow mechanism can thus be offset temporarily.[9] But this mechanism is a corrective device. If it is not allowed to function, the correction must come from some other source. In this example the National Central Bank has expanded its holdings of government securities and discounts for commercial banks to the point where its minimum reserve requirement (25 percent) has been reached. The central bank is now "just another bank," since it too must obey the law. If gold continues to flow out of the country, the central bank not only loses gold but must contract (sell) its holdings of government securities and reduce its accommodations to commercial banks. Such a reaction could very well trigger a commercial bank credit contraction. The classic price-specie-flow mechanism would then operate according to the blueprint. As the money supply shrank, money incomes and prices would fall until the deficit in the balance of payments disappeared.

One way of avoiding the stress a central bank might sustain from a threat to its statutory specie reserve requirement is to abolish its reserve requirement

---

[9]For a more extensive discussion of international monetary adjustment, see Chapter 23.

altogether. The United States Congress took such steps in 1966 and 1968, so the Federal Reserve System no longer faces any internal or external legal gold convertibility requirement.[10] The System now may expand or contract currency and bank reserves so that the total stock of dollars in people's hands may expand or contract in accordance with some preconceived policy goals.

Selected Bibliography

As supplementary reading for this chapter and for most of the remaining chapters in this section the student should read *The Federal Reserve System — Its Purposes and Functions,* published by the Board of Governors of the Federal Reserve System. Current statistics for the monetary system and the banks are carried monthly in *The Federal Reserve Bulletin,* also published by the Federal Reserve System. Both these publications can be obtained free or for a nominal cost from any Federal Reserve Bank or directly from the Board of Governors in Washington, D.C.

Appendix: Comprehensive Problem on the Relation of the Central Bank to the Money Supply

The combined balance sheet for "The 12 Federal Reserve Banks" for June 30, 1968, includes the following items and their values in billions of dollars:

Consolidated Statement of Condition*

Assets		Liabilities	
Gold certificate account	10.0	Federal Reserve notes	41.9
(Total) U.S. government		Member bank reserves	21.5
security holdings	52.2		

* This statement contains only the major items. Therefore, it is incomplete and does not balance exactly.

1. Assume the member banking system faces an overall reserve requirement against demand deposits of 14 percent, that it holds $4 billion of Federal Reserve notes as part of its total reserves, that it holds no excess reserves, that $7 billion of total reserves are held against time deposits, and that all

---

[10]The general obligations of the Treasury Department and the federal government to meet gold "commitments" are another story. See Chapter 23.

commercial banks are members of the system. Estimate the "narrow" stock of money in the economy.

Answer: Total reserves available for demand deposits are $21.5 billion (member bank reserves), plus $4 billion cash (Federal Reserve notes), less $7 billion held against time deposits, equals $18.5 billion. This amount is expanded through the banking system by a multiple equal to the inverse of the average reserve requirement; that is, $\dfrac{\$18.5 \text{ billion}}{0.14} = \$132.1$ billion demand deposits. Hand-to-hand currency outside banks is equal to F.R. notes outstanding ($41.9 billion), less F.R. notes held by the banking system ($4 billion), for a net total of $37.9 billion. Thus, the total money stock is:

(a) $132.1 billion demand deposits, plus
(b) $ 37.9 billion hand-to-hand currency, for a total of
(c) $170.0 billion

2. The total money-to-currency ratio in this example is 4.49 to 1. Assume that people change their "taste" for money in a way that requires this ratio to become 5.00 to 1. The Federal Reserve System supplies the changes required by open market operations in government securities, at the same time keeping the total stock of money constant at $170 billion.[1] Assuming no changes in bank-held currency or reserve requirements, what would be the values in the combined balance sheet at the new ratio?

Answer: With a total money stock of $170 billion, the component of hand-to-hand currency outside banks would have to equal $34 billion ($170 billion × 1/5), a reduction of $3.9 billion from the existing amount. Thus, the F.R. note *item* in the combined balance sheet would have to become $37.0 billion ($41.9 billion − $3.9 billion), and demand deposits would have to increase to $136 billion. To obtain this value with no changes in bank-held currency or reserve ratios, banks would have to have reserves of $19.04 billion ($136 billion × 0.14), an increase of $0.54 billion in their reserve accounts over the $18.5 billion they already have available. After these changes are incorporated, the liabilities side of the combined balance sheet would be:

(a) Federal Reserve notes 38.0 (41.9–3.9)
(b) Member bank reserves 22.04 (21.5+ 0.54)

The net change in total demand obligations would have been −3.90 + 0.54, or −3.36 net. The asset side of the balance sheet would reflect this change by an equal change in government security holdings. Securities would be sold until their total value was $48.84 billion ($52.20 billion − $3.36 billion). The asset side of the balance would then appear as:

---

[1]This constraint satisfies the condition for form elasticity of the money supply.

(a) Gold certificate account 10.0
(b) U.S. government securities 48.84

What this solution says is that the change in tastes for the two forms of money necessitates a net contraction of the monetary base supplied by the central bank if the total money stock is to remain constant. As the demands of the public become known, the central bank sells the appropriate amount of government securities to effect the necessary changes.

3. During the coming year, suppose the Federal Reserve System purchases $3 billion of government securities in the open market, and that this purchase is reflected on the liabilities side of the consolidated balance sheet as a $2 billion increase in F.R. notes and a $1 billion increase in member bank reserves. If time deposits in the economy stay constant and commercial banks demand an additional $1 billion in F.R. notes as "till money," what will be the new stock of money in the economy after the commercial banking system has reduced its new excess reserves to zero?

Answer: The new consolidated balance sheet would appear as shown below.

Consolidated Statement of Condition

Assets		Liabilities	
Gold certificate account	10.0	Federal Reserve notes	40.0
U.S. government security holdings	51.8*	Member bank reserves	23.0*

* Rounded to nearest $100 million.

Total reserves now available for private demand deposits are $23.0 billion (member bank reserves), plus $5 billion cash (Federal Reserve notes), less $7 billion held against time deposits, equals $21 billion. Expanding this reserve base by the inverse of the reserve requirement, $\frac{\$21 \text{ billion}}{0.14}$, gives $150 billion demand deposits. Federal Reserve notes held as hand-to-hand currency by the nonbank public are total notes outstanding ($40.0 billion), less the amount held as till money by the banking system ($5 billion). The total stock of money becomes $185 billion; and the increase in the stock of money brought about by the $3 billion purchase of government securities is $15 billion.

15

The Central Bank and the Treasury

Fiscal-Monetary Functions of the Treasury

Treasury departments in the executive branch of the government traditionally have maintained intimate relationships with securities markets, the banking system, and central banks. Their interest results from the fiscal functions they must perform for the central governments of which they are a part.

A secretary of the treasury, or a chancellor of the exchequer, or a minister of finance, is the head of an executive department and a member of the cabinet.[1] His opinions and decisions on fiscal policy are influential, and he is made responsible for his policies by the electorate's control over the President. He, along with the President and the other members of the cabinet, is in a politically competitive market: His policies must "deliver the goods" within the framework of law or he is out of a job. By way of contrast, the directors of the central bank are appointed for long terms, and the organization is structured to minimize political influences. In practice, however, central banks have had to operate in the presence of administrations that have faced immediate and formidable political pressures. When conflicts of financial policies have appeared between the central bank and the current executive branch, the

---

[1]The Treasury Department of the United States includes the Treasurer, the Comptroller of the Currency, the Director of the Mint, the Register, auditors, and others, over whom the Secretary presides as the executive head.

executive branch (usually with the treasury department as its spokesman) has had its way. The compulsions and behavior of the typical treasury department, therefore, are important data to central bank directors in their formulations of monetary policies.

The treasury department is usually spoken of as the "fiscal agency" of the government.[2] Its operations are to a large extent dependent on the volume of appropriations the legislature provides for government services and the amount of tax revenue received to pay for what has been appropriated. Even when the budget is balanced — the traditional norm for a governmental budget — the treasury must administer the expenditures and act as a custodian of the public moneys. When a budget deficit occurs, that is, when annual governmental expenditures tend to exceed annual receipts from taxes, the treasury becomes instrumental in getting before the legislature the necessary information on how much additional revenue is needed, how it should be obtained, and what economic effects proposed legislation may have. Given the certainty of, say, a $5 billion deficit, the only alternative to the possibility of higher taxes is legislative authorization for the treasury to float new issues of public debt. The volume of new debt authorized and the prices at which it may be sold usually are limited by the authorization act itself, although an acceptable price is more likely to be left to the discretion of the treasury than any other feature. The treasury then has the job of marketing the securities to banks, corporations, institutions, and individuals. To perform this task, at times a Herculean one, the treasury enlists the aid of investment houses, securities dealers, and the central bank.

The new securities floated to make up a deficit may be long-term, short-term, or some combination of both.[3] The monetary effects of the security sales depend almost entirely upon the volume of new money created in the process of getting the securities into the hands of their new owners. If the securities all go to nonbank investors, no new money is created. The treasury, in effect, receives checks from the buyers of securities. As is shown in Table 15.1, its accounts in commercial banks or central banks are increased while the accounts of securities purchasers in commercial banks are debited.

This partial balance sheet is meant to be explanatory rather than realistic. In floating new debt the treasury in effect substitutes a longer-term debt (government securities outstanding) for debts due immediately to creditors. After the creditors of the government are paid, the "demand deposit account" is credited and "due creditors" is debited. Recipients of treasury checks deposit their checks in banks, and the economy has the same amount of money it had prior to treasury debt flotation, although new assets to the public of $5 billion in government securities remain outstanding.

---

[2]The word "fiscal" comes from the Latin word *fiscus,* which means "basket."

[3]The longest long-term debt possible is a consol with no maturity date (or one that matures in "infinite" time). The shortest short-term treasury obligation is for 91 days, although any debt maturing in less than a year is usually called "short-term."

Table 15.1. Treasury Department (Partial Balance Sheet)
(billions of dollars)

Assets		Liabilities	
Demand deposit accounts with commercial or central banks	(+5)	Due creditors on current account	(+5)
		Government securities outstanding	(+5)

The treasury conceivably could build up cash balances by either selling securities in the presence of a balanced budget or raising taxes, thus effecting a decline in the quantity of money used by the private economy. But treasury action of this kind would be highly unorthodox. The legislature would not usually authorize the treasury to sell debt in the first place if such discretionary policy were either likely or possible. The treasury obtains money only to pay off its creditors. The money then goes right back into the economy in payments to these creditors, and the economy has the same quantity of money as before. Its net gain is additional fixed dollar claims in the form of government securities.[4]

A second possibility is for the new securities to be sold to commercial banks who use only excess reserves to make the purchases. New bank credit and corresponding amounts of new demand (or time) deposits are then created. Furthermore, the banking system can purchase securities equal to a multiple of the excess reserves it maintains. Again, the treasury does not pile up a cash balance but pays off its creditors with the new bank deposits. In this case the mode of financing the debt is by means of commercial bank monetization of government securities. The stock of money is increased by the amount of new securities bought by the banks.

If commercial banks have no excess reserves, they can buy government securities only if they give up an equal amount of their normal accommodation to private businesses and individuals. To effect such a redistribution of bank credit in a free system, yield rates on government securities must rise (prices of securities fall) while interest charges on commercial paper also must rise to meet the sales competition. Bank credit then seems stringent, especially to treasury officials who wish to borrow at "low" interest rates. As interest rates rise and prices of most fixed dollar claims including treasury security issues turn "soft" in the open market, the treasury may pressure the central bank to buy enough of the securities to keep up the price. Since security prices tend to fall as fresh supplies of securities are made available, "supporting" the market price almost necessarily means buying some amount of the securities

---

[4] The balance sheet of the treasury need not balance. On net balance, that is, the government is a net debtor to the private economy to the extent of the net public debt outstanding plus any issues of fiat paper money it might have made in the past.

in the open market, although it may also mean refraining from selling securities that otherwise would have been sold in order to counter inflation.

The central bank ordinarily is proscribed by law from buying the securities directly from the treasury. However, the effect is the same if the central bank buys securities in the open market at the same time the treasury is selling them. The central bank has more securities in its portfolio, and the checks the treasury gets from its security sales may be deposited with the central bank in the "treasury account," as shown in Table 15.2.

Table 15.2. National Central Bank
(billions of dollars)

Assets		*Liabilities*	
Government securities	(+5)	Treasury account	(+5)

The treasury then may write checks to pay its creditors, who either deposit the checks in commercial banks or cash them in for currency. If currency is desired, commercial banks transmit the demand to the central bank, and the balance sheet given in Table 15.2 is changed to the form shown in Table 15.3. The new government securities previously purchased serve as legal collateral for the issue of new NCB notes.

Table 15.3. National Central Bank
(billions of dollars)

Government securities	(+5)	NCB notes	(+5)
		Treasury account	(+5)(−5)

If recipients of treasury checks are satisfied to hold demand deposits, they redeposit the checks in commercial banks who in turn send the checks to the central bank for clearance. The central bank then credits the reserves of commercial banks and debits the treasury's account. The balance sheet in this case changes from Table 15.2 to Table 15.4.

Table 15.4. National Central Bank
(billions of dollars)

Government securities	(+5)	Reserves for com- mercial banks	(+5)
		Treasury account	(+5)(−5)

The commercial banks now may expand loans and investments with their new reserves. The investments they make might well be purchases of government securities. The central bank's original purchase then would have furnished additional bank reserves for the additional multiples of demand deposits that would be created to purchase the remaining government securities offered by the treasury. This procedure, as can be surmised, allows a given purchase of government securities by the central bank to serve as a fractional base for a multiple purchase of securities by commercial banks *and* a multiple expansion of their demand deposits.

Metallic Monetization Functions of the Treasury

Authorization to issue inconvertible legal tender paper money without any kind of "backing" or collateral is another channel through which the treasury may alter the monetary structure. Ordinarily, this procedure is unconstitutional; but strong-willed and strong-armed executives have employed or usurped this mechanism, and pliant legislatures have been known to grant such powers to meet fiscal "emergencies." Under such conditions, the paper money becomes both currency and bank reserves, while the monetary metals simply become market commodities.

Monetization of metal is a more routine and usual function of treasuries. Under a gold standard the treasury is charged by law with the duty of buying and selling gold at a fixed money price. (Other gold traffic may be carried on with or without the agency of the treasury, but only the amount monetized is of concern here.) Under the current institutional setup, a seller of gold to the amount of, say, $5 billion receives a treasury check. The treasury also issues a gold certificate liability that gives the certificate holder legal title to the gold just purchased. This certificate is equal in monetary value to the check that paid for the gold, and it is also equal to the monetary value of the gold. The treasury deposits the certificate in the central bank in the same way that an individual deposits currency in an ordinary commercial bank. The central bank's partial balance sheet then changes to the position shown in Table 15.5.

Meanwhile, the seller of the gold, who now has a treasury check payable at any bank or at the National Central Bank, either deposits the check in a commercial bank or demands currency. As in the previous example, if currency

Table 15.5. National Central Bank
(billions of dollars)

Assets		Liabilities	
Gold certificates	(+5)	Treasury account	(+5)

is demanded, the central bank clears the check by debiting the treasury's account and issuing National Central Bank notes as in Table 15.6. If the seller of the gold is satisfied to maintain a deposit in a commercial bank, the commercial bank's reserve account is credited and the treasury account is debited when the check is cleared. This change is shown by Table 15.7.

Table 15.6. National Central Bank
(billions of dollars)

Gold certificates	(+5)	NCB notes	(+5)
		Treasury account	(+5)(−5)

The treasury is involved in the process only fleetingly no matter how its check is converted. The central bank's balance sheet reflects the change "permanently," and the central bank retains title to the gold.[5]

Gold that comes into a domestic economy from foreign countries in order to clear international balances is handled by a similar procedure. If the central bank wishes to prevent the new gold from having any influence on the monetary system, it may sell some other asset as the gold certificate account increases. The usual candidate for this policy action is central bank holdings of government securities that are duly sold in the open market to banks and individuals. These sales may be distributed and timed to offset completely the buoyant effects that the gold inflows might otherwise have provoked. Table 15.5 then changes to Table 15.8. Monetization of the gold is offset by an equal demonetization of government securities.

Table 15.7. National Central Bank
(billions of dollars)

Assets		*Liabilities*	
Gold certificates	(+5)	Reserves of commercial banks	(+5)
		Treasury account	(+5)(−5)

Table 15.8. National Central Bank
(billions of dollars)

Gold certificates	(+5)	NCB notes	(no change)
Government securities	(−5)	Reserves for commercial banks	(no change)

---

[5]While the central bank has *title* to the gold, control of the actual movement of the gold is vested in the treasury by means of licensing powers and other restrictions.

The treasury similarly can neutralize gold inflows by conducting open market sales of its own in the presence of a balanced budget. The proceeds from security sales would need to be impounded in a treasury account, and the treasury would have to achieve and maintain a cash balance position to keep the new money out of the economy. It could do the same thing with silver. In sum, treasury purchases of either gold or silver do not necessarily mean that the stock of money must be increased. If the government agency doing the buying has government securities at its disposal, sales of securities "pay for" the monetary metal purchased.[6] Contrarily, gold or silver outflows can be prevented from diminishing the stock of money in the private economy if the public and banks hold government securities that can be purchased by the treasury or central bank, and that are then purchased and paid for either through dishoarding of treasury cash balances or through the money-creating machinery of the central bank.

The possible similarities of monetary policy techniques by treasury and central bank become manifest. Granted legislative authorization, either agency can conduct open market operations; either agency can create or destroy money.[7] The questions might then be asked: Why maintain both agencies when either could do the job? And, assuming both exist, by what means are their respective areas of influence defined? Answers to these questions are not necessarily very rational or very brief. The chapters that follow, however, attempt to trace the institutional development and influence of the two agencies in the United States as well as their relationships to each other.

Selected Bibliography

Gaines, Tilford. *Techniques of Treasury Debt Management.* New York: Columbia University Press, 1962.

Smith, Warren. *Debt Management in the United States.* Study Paper No. 19 for the Joint Economic Committee. Washington, D.C.: U.S. Government Printing Office, 1960.

Tobin, James. "An Essay on the Principles of Debt Management," in Commission on Money and Credit, *Fiscal and Debt Management Policies.* Englewood Cliffs, N.J.: Prentice-Hall, 1963, pp. 143–218.

---

[6]Federal Reserve and United States Treasury policies that worked along these lines are examined in Chapters 18 and 19.

[7]In fact, both agencies in the United States have issued currency. The Treasury issues included silver certificates, U.S. notes, Treasury notes, and fractional coins. All of these items except coins were paper bills identical in design to Federal Reserve notes and for denominations of $1, $2, and $5. Federal Reserve notes outstanding replaced most treasury currency, except fractional coin, in 1962.

The Supply of Money in the
United States: The Monetary Framework[1]

Richard H. Timberlake, Jr.

The following selection, which appeared in the February 1971 issue of the
Monthly Review *of the Federal Reserve Bank of Richmond, presents a systematic explanation of the money supply in the United States at the present time. A supplement of money supply equations is also included.*

High-Powered Money

The units of money in common use are the final products of a refined technical operation. Two different industries combine and coordinate resources and raw materials to generate the dollars that compose this product. The primary industry is the central bank. It produces what is sometimes known as high-powered money (HPM), which consists of (1) currency and (2) commercial bank reserve accounts in the central bank. These components make up the base on which the actual money supply of hand-to-hand currency and demand deposits is formed. Most currency is a part of the actual money supply, but it also may be held by banks as reserves on which demand deposits are expanded.[2]

Two institutions, other than the gold and silver industries, have furnished the monetary system with HPM in the past. First, the Treasury Department at various times printed paper currency (e.g., U.S. notes, Treasury notes, and silver certificates) when authorized to do so by Congress. During the late nineteenth and early twentieth centuries it also manipulated its deposit balances in national banks as a part of deliberate policy to increase and decrease bank reserves at different seasons of the year.

Since 1914, the Federal Reserve System has been the more prominent institution for furnishing HPM. It issues Federal Reserve notes and maintains the reserve (or deposit) accounts of member banks. The Treasury still has some outstanding currency in the form of silver certificates and fractional coin, and

---

From *Monthly Review*, February 1971, Federal Reserve Bank of Richmond.

[1]Much of the following discussion on high-powered money and the two determining ratios are presented in greater depth in Philip Cagan, *Determinants and Effects of Changes in the Stock of Money, 1875–1960*, NBER, Columbia University Press, 1965.

[2]The total stock of HPM as of June 30, 1970 was $80.0 billion. This total consisted of (1) member bank reserve accounts with Federal Reserve Banks—$22.2 billion; (2) Federal Reserve notes outstanding—$50.6 billion; and (3) Treasury currency outstanding—$7.2 billion. The defined narrow stock of money was $222 billion, consisting of $172 billion private demand deposits adjusted for interbank holdings and $50 billion of currency held outside commercial banks and the Federal government.

it still has substantial balances (tax and loan accounts) with commercial banks. However, the Federal Reserve System has taken over most of the currency-issuing job, and member bank deposits in Federal Reserve Banks have been substituted for the specie reserves that used to be held by the banks themselves.

Both the central bank and the Treasury may carry out seasonal policies with HPM but only the central bank can provide year-to-year (secular) increases in this basic stock. Where the Treasury must rely on bank reserves already in existence to change its balances at commercial banks, the Federal Reserve System creates HPM from scratch by buying government securities or acquiring other assets. The final payment for the securities takes the form either of an issue of Federal Reserve notes or of a new credit to the reserve accounts of member banks. Both of these items are counted as liabilities of Federal Reserve Banks, and both of them are HPM.

Once HPM has been created by the central bank, its final monetary effect depends on its route through the second of the two money-generating industries — the commercial banking system. Most Federal Reserve notes are channeled through commercial banks to become a part of hand-to-hand currency. However, commercial banks keep about 10 percent of these notes as reserves in addition to their deposit reserve accounts in the central bank.

The Currency-Deposit Ratio

In addition to the quantity of HPM, two ratios have an important influence in determining the ultimate quantity of money. One is the ratio of currency to demand deposits, expressed as

$$r_C = \frac{C}{D_d},$$

that households and business firms wish to maintain. This ratio is a function of technical factors, such as checking facilities available to the nonbank public. It also depends on such behavioral factors as trust or mistrust of banks, desire to avoid inflation or evade taxes, black market activities, and the extent of personal travel. Given the total amount of the HPM base, the narrow money supply (defined in footnote 2) is larger when the currency-deposit ratio is smaller, and vice versa. For example, let this ratio be one-to-five at some point in time. Then assume that households and business firms experience some change in preferences that prompts them to maintain a ratio of only one dollar in currency to six dollars in checkbook balances, and let them deposit some of their currency in commercial banks in order to achieve this new ratio. The net effect of currency deposited in the banks is to give the banks excess reserves. If the central bank holds constant the stock of HPM, that is, if it does nothing to offset the additional currency in the commercial banks, these banks now have the means to expand credit on the asset side and deposits on the liability side. The volume of deposits then increases by the amount of excess reserves times the inverse of the average ratio of reserves to demand deposits maintained by the commercial banking system. Thus, a unit of HPM held as hand-to-hand currency by the nonbank public has much less monetary influence than the same dollar held as a reserve unit in a commercial bank.

The Reserve-Deposit Ratio

The second of the two determining ratios is largely a function of central bank policy. It is the ratio of all banks' reserves to their total demand deposits. It may be expressed as

$$r_R = \frac{R}{D_d},$$

where R is the dollar volume of commercial bank reserves held against demand deposits and D_d is the dollar value of demand deposits. Generally, the banks make loans and investments until the actual ratio is reduced to the legal minimum ratio required by law. By increasing earning assets and thereby reducing this ratio, banks maximize the earnings potential of their portfolios.

The minimum required ratio varies from one bank classification to another and between state banks and member banks of the Federal Reserve System. Reserve requirements for state chartered banks are subject to state laws. While these laws may be very different one from another, they generally specify reserve requirements in terms of vault cash (currency), deposits in "other" banks—usually member banks of the Federal Reserve System—and "approved" government securities. The "approved" securities are limited issues of state or Federal government securities bearing relatively low rates of interest. Most of the reserves maintained by these banks, however, are interbank deposits with member banks; so the reserve requirement limitations imposed by the Federal Reserve System on member banks indirectly restrict creation of state bank deposits as well.

For the commercial banking system as a whole, some ratio of total reserves to total deposits exists at any given moment. If the quantity of HPM and the value of the currency-deposit ratio mentioned above are already determined, the volume of demand deposits (and also the total stock of money) is greater when the reserve-deposit ratio is lower and smaller when this ratio is higher.

These three basic parameters define an unadjusted money stock. However, several factors involving monetary accounting and classification must be disposed of before the narrow stock of money is obtained.

Accounting Issues in Classifying the Stock of Money

One item to be considered is interbank demand deposits — deposits to the credit of one bank and accounted as a liability by another bank. According to current Federal Reserve regulation, a commercial member bank that makes such a deposit in another member bank may deduct this amount from the total of its own demand deposits subject to reserve requirements. Even though the *recipient* bank must keep reserves against these deposits, the net effect is to exempt the member banking system as a whole from maintaining reserves against interbank deposits. If this allowance were not made — if reserve requirements were in full force against interbank deposits — an increase in this item would diminish the *measured* narrow money supply even though gross demand deposits remained constant. As it is, the reserve allowance permits an increase in interbank deposits with no corresponding decrease required in deposits held by the nonbank public, foreigners, or the government. Member interbank deposits, therefore, neither absorb reserves nor are a part of a classified money stock.

Another difficulty, one which cannot be handled so readily, is the fact that both time and demand deposits require reserves. Therefore, reserves held against time deposits in commercial banks must be deducted from total reserves in order to count the amount of reserves that can be used to expand demand deposits.

Time deposits raise yet another problem. Since interest is paid on them, they are in competition with a whole complex of interest-earning assets in financial markets. Therefore, their creation by commercial banks is subject to interest rate effects and interactions of demands and supplies of other financial assets. These feedbacks may alter the reserves available for demand deposit creation, so that interest rates on financial assets may have some indirect bearing on the volume of demand deposits. This influence is so roundabout that it is difficult to measure. The opinion here is that it is visible but of low significance.

Dollar demand deposits held by foreigners in U.S. commercial banks also require an accounting pigeonhole. These deposits absorb reserves just as any other deposits do. Since they may be used to buy goods and services produced in the United States and are largely behavioral, they are included in the narrowly defined money supply.

The Federal government also has demand deposit balances in commercial banks, as well as vault cash (currency) in government offices, and deposit accounts with Federal Reserve Banks. The latter two of these three items remain relatively constant, but the tax and loan accounts at commercial banks are another matter. While subject to reserve requirements, they are not usually counted as a part of the narrowly defined stock of money. The government is assumed to carry out policies and make decisions that require spending without regard to its cash balance holdings. Only money held by private households and business firms can influence (or be influenced by) individual behavior. However, classifying *the* money supply to include or exclude government balances is purely arbitrary. It can be done either way. The way it is done should depend on the function of the money supply so classified.

Short-Run Effects of Treasury Balances

The ability of the Treasury to create HPM has become negligible. Its fiscal powers of taxing and spending, however, cause the balances it keeps in com-

Genesis of the Money Supply

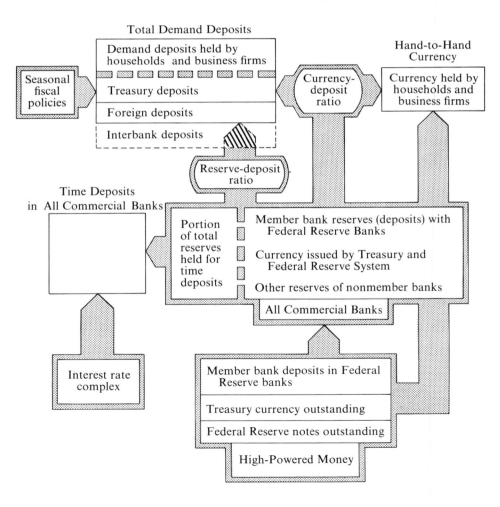

mercial banks to fluctuate widely. These balances average about $6 billion, but their month-to-month variation is often $2 billion and is sometimes more than $4 billion due to a lack of synchronization between federal tax receipts and disbursements. Since none of the government's cash holdings is created by the Treasury, increases and decreases in government balances must be reciprocated by corresponding decreases and increases in the money holdings of households and business firms in the private economy. Sometimes, the change of the month-to-month money supply in the private economy from this source is larger than the annual secular change due to Federal Reserve policy effects either on HPM or on the reserve-deposit ratio. This datum emphasizes that the Treasury's short-run influence on the private money stock is frequently massive.

Figure 1, in which some nonmonetary details are condensed, gives a schematic view of the whole money-generating process. HPM originating in the Federal Reserve System (and to some extent in the Treasury) is channeled through commercial banks to become either hand-to-hand currency or bank reserves. The currency-deposit and reserve-deposit ratios establish the ultimate amounts of deposits and currency that will be generated as well as the total of both. Offstage, a complex of interest rates in the money market has some possible effects on total time deposits created, and thus on the total of demand deposits. Seasonal fiscal policies, finally, are seen defining the short-run volume of Treasury deposits held in the aggregate of total demand deposits.

A Symbolic View of the Money Supply

Items

1. Reserve accounts of member banks with Federal Reserve Banks R
2. Treasury currency outstanding C_T
   a. Treasury currency held by public C_{TP}
   b. Treasury currency held by banks C_{TB}
3. Federal Reserve notes outstanding C_N
   a. Federal Reserve notes held by public C_{NP}
   b. Federal Reserve notes held by banks C_{NB}
4. Total demand deposits D
   a. Private demand deposits D_P
   b. Interbank demand deposits D_B
   c. Government demand deposits D_G
   d. Foreign-owned demand deposits D_F
5. Time deposits in commercial banks T_B
6. Reserves held against demand deposits R_D
7. Reserves held against time deposits R_T

Identities

1. $C_N = C_{NP} + C_{NB}$
2. $C_T = C_{TP} + C_{TB}$
3. $D = D_P + D_B + D_G + D_F$

Exogenous Determinants

1. Stock of high-powered money

$$\text{HPM} = R + C_N + C_T$$

2. Reserve-deposit ratio

$$r_R = \frac{(R + C_{NB} + C_{TB} - R_T)}{(D_P +. D_B + D_G + D_F)}$$

3. Currency-deposit ratio

$$r_C = \frac{C_{NP} + C_{TP}}{\dfrac{(R + C_{NB} + C_{TB} - R_T) - (D_B + D_G)}{r_R}} = \frac{C_{NP} + C_{TP}}{D_P + D_F}$$

Equations

1. Currency holdings of nonbank public

$$C = C_{NP} + C_{TP}$$

2. Total reserves of commercial banks

$$R_R = R + C_{NB} + C_{TB}$$

3. Total demand deposits

$$D = \frac{R_D - R_T}{r_R} = \frac{R + C_{NB} + C_{TB} - R_T}{r_R}$$

4. Private demand deposits

$$D_P = D - (D_B + D_G)$$

5. Currency held by nonbank public

$$C = C_{NP} + C_{TP}$$

6. Narrow stock of money

$$M = C + D_P$$

16

Goals, Targets, Indicators, and Lags of Monetary Policy

Goals, Targets, and Indicators

The goals of any one policy-making agency of the government are limited by both the philosophy of the group in power and the technical resources of the particular agency. Some of the time, the stated goals of policy degenerate into meaningless platitudes, such as the classic "greatest good for the greatest number."[1] Usually, however, some sort of emphasis can be gleaned from the pronouncements of the political majority that is getting its will into action. For example, a group that pledges "a maximum of price level stability consistent with full employment and economic growth" is, by implication, giving priority to full employment or to economic growth or to some combination; but it is ranking price level stability behind both of the other two. If the statement pledged "maximum levels of employment within a framework of stable prices," the reverse interpretation could be made.

All of these characteristics—full employment, price level stability, a high rate of growth in real output, and various economic freedoms as well—are recognized as "good." They are as invulnerable as mother, home, and apple

---

[1]This familiar slogan of the classical hedonist Jeremy Bentham is also self-contradictory: If the number of people is "greatest," the greatest good is impossible to achieve. Another classical writer, Thomas Malthus, pointed out this unpleasant correction to the rosy view of Bentham. Contemporary ecology takes the matter further.

pie. No policy makers promise their contraries. Therefore, the ordering or ranking of the possible goals and the degree to which the goals are achieved become the benchmarks for an evaluation of policy. In any policy-making agency, results are what count. But the results that are counted also must be weighed in the value systems of the people doing the accounting. To some people rigorous price level stability might weigh more heavily than a very high level of employment. Others might reverse the priorities; and still others might trade off one of these desirable features for the other at different possible levels of achievement.

A central bank, then, as a policy-making agency, has goals to aspire to. Technically, Congress is supposed to specify such goals for the central bank in the United States; but during the early years of the Federal Reserve System, the issue was almost neglected. Since World War II, the Employment Act of 1946 has come to be the understood statement of principles for the System to follow. This Act simply states (in many words) that it is "the continuing policy of the Federal Government to use all practicable means ... to promote maximum employment, production, and purchasing power."[2] Of course, such a statement is too general to serve as a blueprint for policy. It has more utility in preventing, say, a central bank from doing foolish things that might be foisted on it by, say, a Treasury Department.

Given the generalities in an Employment Act, the policy-making agency must select targets within the technical scope of its competence that offer the best probabilities for achieving the more general goals. Whether a target is within the technical scope of the agency is sometimes debatable. For example, a central bank may or may not be able to keep stable a price index or an interest rate complex. By itself, and in the face of other government policies to the contrary (such as effective minimum wage laws), it probably could not maintain both full employment of the measured labor force and a stable price level as measured by a price index.

Another characteristic close to achievability that the target should embody is verifiability. Observers from outside the agency should be able to match the agency's performance against the desired target. If adequate results are not forthcoming, the electorate should be able to recognize inadequacy or failure.

An identifiable target is a necessary condition for fixing responsibility on the policy makers. In addition, the political machinery for effecting a change must be available and utilizable. Only then can democratic procedures bear fruit. A policy-making agency usually cannot be counted on to admit failure; it cannot be considered self-critical and self-regulatory. Everything it does will be "right" according to its rationale. Nor is there an economic market in which it can be tested, as is the case with private business. Its efforts can be measured only in the political market, where its concepts of policy and its target achievements are weighed, judged, and approved or condemned by the electorate.

---

[2] *U.S.C.*, title 15, sec. 1021.

An economy using a central bank to regulate its monetary system necessarily gives some degree of discretion to the central bankers who administer the institution. If the monetary system is thought of as self-regulatory, as is the case with an operational metallic standard, the monetary managers cannot have much discretion in the first place, and therefore need not be bound tightly by explicit rules for target selection and policy procedure. When a central bank has virtually complete control of the money supply, however, the rights of administrative discretion must be matched by clear-cut responsibilities for policies undertaken.

In the absence of policy rules prescribed by Congress, or even in conjunction with many possible rules, central bank managers, as well as many academic economists, undertake continuous studies on the current state of the economy. They have at their disposal for this task some 88 business and economic indicators, many of which customarily lead the turning points in general business activity.[3] Economists and other officials of the Federal Reserve System study these economic indicators and report their opinions to decision-making centers of the System, especially to the Federal Open Market Committee. Members of the FOMC then try to reach a consensus on existing conditions in the real and monetary sectors of the economy and to take whatever action seems appropriate. If the committee concludes, for example, that an economic peak has been reached and that a downturn is underway, they may ease monetary policy by changing the directive to the account manager. Due to the indirect impact of the actions of monetary policy on the economy and to the time lag between the taking of action and the response of the economy, monetary managers logically select target variables that respond fairly quickly and directly to policy actions. Similarly, intermediate indicators affected by policy action may be used to determine whether other policies are on the right track.

Selection of targets and policy indicators is, of course, predicated by the monetary managers' views of how monetary policy affects the economy. If the selection of targets and indicators results in economic crises and general instability despite the good intentions of the individuals involved, the political structure should encourage the incumbents to resign and allow a new group of managers, who have different concepts of policy, to succeed them. Unfortunately, the machinery for such a succession has not yet been incorporated into the political framework. A shorter term in office for governors might be an improvement.

A number of targets and indicators of policy action have been used by the Federal Reserve System, and still others have been suggested by economists. The most important of these targets and indicators are or have been price indexes; prices of government securities; "orderliness" in the market for government securities; interest rates; free reserves; "tone, color, and feel" of the

---

[3]See Geoffrey H. Moore and Julius Shiskin, *Indicators of Business Expansions and Contractions* (New York: National Bureau of Economic Research, 1967), pp. 1–7. For current statistics see the U.S. Department of Commerce's monthly, *Business Conditions Digest.*

market; the monetary base; and the money supply. These targets are reviewed briefly below, and the more significant ones are discussed in greater detail in the later sections that deal with policy history.

During most of the Fed's existence, some target or other has been prominent either because the System has adopted one on its own, or because many academic economists and influential congressmen have argued for one. Significantly, none was written into the original Federal Reserve Act. Before long, however, some sort of target was bound to develop; something as specific as monetary policy begs for a guideline.

Whether a target is a target or a goal is a goal is a definitional or taxonomic question. Goals are more general than targets. A target implies a specific and technically realizable objective for the institution involved. Thus, maintenance of the price of government securities by the operations of the central bank correctly may be thought of as a target, even if it is a poor one. Maintenance of a stable price level for the economy is more logically a goal. A parallel situation applies to interest rates. A central bank may keep the interest rates on government securities low or high, but it cannot do the same thing to an interest rate complex (except in the short run), much less to the real rate of interest.[4] The latter two ideals can only be thought of as goals.

During the history of the Federal Reserve, this distinction between goals and targets has not always been observed by people interested and involved in policy making. For example, the first "target" of consequence proposed for the Fed was one calling for maintenance of a stable price index by means of central bank manipulation of the money stock. This proposal was suggested by prominent economists in the twenties and had some serious congressional consideration and support. Federal Reserve officials resisted it vigorously both on the grounds that the central bank should not try to manipulate the price level, and on the grounds that it could not be expected to do so because its power to control the money supply was limited. In fact, this objective was a goal and not a target, and the Fed's objections were better taken if this distinction had been made. Price level stability, in short, may be a good goal but a bad target. Willy-nilly, the principle was never adopted for policy in spite of the cooperative efforts of many congressmen and academic economists.

From the late twenties through the early thirties, a hazy amalgam of interest rates and the U.S. balance of payments became a target of sorts. In the later thirties and early forties, the growing volume of government securities outstanding brought the securities market into greater prominence. At that time, monetary policy was well down on the list of things that mattered, so the job given to monetary policy was correspondingly trivial: Keep an "orderly market" in government securities — clearly a target and clearly a very poor one. During World War II, an "orderly market" came to mean pegging the market prices of these securities. Pegging the prices also pegged the yield rates. Prices

---

[4]See Chapter 5 and the reading selection at the end of Chapter 22.

and yields were not set for countercyclical purposes; they were pegged in order to facilitate the massive issuance of Treasury securities being made to finance the war.

The Treasury–Federal Reserve Accord of March 1951 freed the Federal Reserve of this constraint, principally because the goals written into the Full Employment Act of 1946 were seen to be incompatible with this target. During the early sixties, some return to an interest rate target was undertaken. Yield rates of short-term securities were maintained in order to achieve balance in international payments.

The economic rationale of an interest rate target is that lower interest rates during a recession stimulate spending, particularly investment, and that higher rates during inflationary periods dampen spending. The records of the Federal Open Market Committee, however, do not confirm that the System managers have specifically followed this reasoning. The minutes of the committee do reveal that it has often been preoccupied with interest rates as an indicator of the ease or tightness of the economy, and has used them to gauge the effectiveness of monetary policy. "High" interest rates are considered to be depressing, while "low" ones indicate ease. Aside from the questions of how high is "high" and how low is "low," this interpretation has also led critics to point out the misleading nature of interest rate levels and movements. For example, rising interest rates may be the result of an expanding demand for investment rather than a restrictive supply of money or credit. Similarly, low interest rates may be the result of lagging demand rather than an indication of easy money. Pursuit of a fixed interest rate may even cause *procyclical* monetary policy, as measured by changes in the money supply. For example, suppose that the Fed attempts to maintain what it feels is a "low" interest rate target (r_1 in Figure 16.1). If investment demand independently drops (I-S shift from I-S_1 to I-S_2 in Figure 16.1), then interest rates will tend to fall (r_1 to r_2). With an interest rate target of, say, r_1, the Fed will try to send interest rates back up by restricting the growth of the money supply (L-M_1 to L-M_2), thus accelerating the business contraction (total drop in income from Y_1 to Y_3). Because of this type of possible reaction, some critics have argued that the Open Market Committee needs an indicator of the responsiveness of monetary policy that is not affected by anything except what the committee does.

Beginning in the early fifties, the concept of the free reserve target developed considerable importance in Federal Reserve policy discussions.[5] The very definition of this quantum would seem to combine both positive and negative elements of bank liquidity in one neat package. The alleged role of free reserves

---

[5]Free reserves is defined as excess reserves of member banks minus member bank borrowing. If member bank borrowing from the System exceeds excess reserves, the resulting figure is termed net borrowed reserves. The concept of free reserves seems to have had some roots in the early use of System open market operations. For a succinct survey of the history of the free reserve concept, see Karl Brunner and Allan H. Meltzer, *The Federal Reserve's Attachment to the Free Reserve Concept,* Subcommittee on Domestic Finance, House Committee on Banking and Currency, 88th Congress, 2nd sess., May 1964, pp. 2–10.

Figure 16.1. The Use of *I-S* and *L-M* Curves to Show the Pursuit of an Interest Rate Target under Conditions of Falling Investment Demand

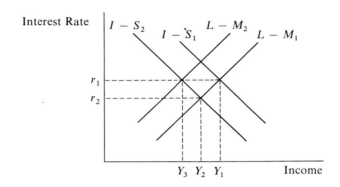

in the causal process of monetary policy is illustrated in the following statements made by System spokesmen:

> The Federal Reserve exerts its influence upon the availability of bank credit, upon the money supply, and upon the interest rates, almost wholly by influencing bank liquidity....
>
> Measurement of the primary liquidity position of banks requires consideration of both positive and negative elements. Positive primary liquidity assets consist of balances held by banks with Federal Reserve Banks. For liquidity purposes, i.e., for meeting drains on deposits and reserves, reserve balances held in excess of requirements are generally a more significant and useful measure than total reserves.
>
> The negative element of primary liquidity for banks arises from member bank borrowings from the Federal Reserve....
>
> The Federal Reserve restrains (or encourages) bank credit expansion by reducing (or increasing) the banks' primary liquidity. This is ordinarily accomplished through open market operations....The effect of these actions, after allowance for the various other factors that influence the availability and use of reserves, may be reflected either in excess reserves or in member bank borrowing at the Reserve Banks. The over-all result for bank liquidity is commonly measured by the figure of "free reserves" or "net borrowed reserves...."[6]

After the 1951 Accord, the Open Market Committee began using free reserves as a target. Positive levels of free reserves or a positive range of free reserves were often cited by committee members during meetings and were

---

[6]Commission on Money and Credit, *The Federal Reserve and the Treasury: Answers to Questions from the Commission on Money and Credit* (Englewood Cliffs, N.J.: Prentice-Hall, 1963), pp. 6–8.

used in the consensus statement to direct the open market account manager. During the middle and late 1950s, enchantment with free reserves waned as economists both inside and outside the System attacked its validity and as some of the members of the committee questioned its reliability. Even with a constant free reserve level it is possible for total bank reserves and the money supply to expand or contract. Those economists who emphasize the importance of total bank reserves or the money supply, therefore, find the use of a free reserve target unnecessarily crude and uncertain.

The committee's recognition of the limitations of free reserves led to what has been called a "modified free reserve doctrine." That is, the use of the free reserve concept continued but was tempered by an awareness that total bank liquidity, the demand for bank credit, some interest rates, the discount rate, and various other factors alter the significance of a particular level of free reserves. The extent to which the committee still relies on free reserves as an indicator or as a target is not clear. However, it has not abandoned the concept altogether.

A somewhat unique target frequently used by the Federal Open Market Committee is the "feel" of the market. The "feel" of the market and its importance in the Open Market Committee's policies are difficult to specify accurately. During the later 1950s "feel" bridged the gap between the modified free reserve target and the degree of ease or tightness indicated by the committee during its discussion. Though the committee would often mention a desired free reserve level in its discussion, it would really be indicating a feeling about the desired degree of ease or tightness. Since market conditions may change, the numerical target that the committee had set might be revised between meetings. The account manager, however, would attempt to adhere to the "spirit" of the free reserve target while not following it to the "letter." The committee frequently set a range of free reserves as a target. The account manager would then vary the free reserve level within that range according to his "feel" of the market in adhering to the spirit of the committee's wishes.

The apparent looseness of such directions and yet the committee's faith in them are seen in the following statement made by Alfred Hayes, President of the Federal Reserve Bank of New York, in the March 1, 1960, Federal Open Market Committee meeting:

. . . I believe that our usual instructions couched in terms of "the same degree of restraint" or "more" or "less" are sufficiently precise to make it possible for the Manager to react to changing developments flexibly and in such a way as to carry out fully the spirit of the Committee's instructions. As we have often noted, our system of reports, including the daily conference call, is so extensive that each member has ample opportunity to inform the Manager if he sees any deviation from the Committee's instruction. I think we would be giving up a highly advantageous technique, developed over many years, if we were to attempt to couch the instructions in some very exact mathematical terms. Of all the tested statistical guides we have available, net borrowed reserves are still probably the best, but this guide is certainly a long way from being sufficient by itself.[7]

Many economists believe that interest rates, free reserves, and "feel" of the market are misleading targets and unreliable indicators. Targets, they argue, should be single-valued, clear-cut, recognizable, and technically achievable. They urge the use of a monetary base or a money supply or some combination of the two. Table 16.1 shows how the monetary base is calculated from a combined United States Treasury–Federal Reserve System balance sheet. The base may be found either by summing the factors that supply it from the central bank's point of view (Federal Reserve credit, gold stock, Treasury currency outstanding, Treasury deposits at Federal Reserve Banks, Treasury cash holdings and other deposits, and Federal Reserve accounts), or by summing monetary liability items generated by the Federal Reserve Banks (member bank reserves at Federal Reserve Banks, and currency held by banks and by the public).[8]

Table 16.1. Calculation of the Monetary Base, June 1969, Average of Daily Figures*
(in millions of dollars)

Federal Reserve credit			
Holdings of securities	+ 56,695†	Member bank deposits	
Discounts and advances	+ 1,408	at Federal Reserve	+ 22,741
Float	+ 2,435	Currency held by banks	+ 5,903
Gold stock	+ 10,367	Currency held by the	
Treasury currency outstanding	+ 6,746	public	+ 44,800
Treasury deposits at Federal Reserve	− 970		
Treasury cash holdings	− 672		
Other deposits and other Federal			
Reserve accounts	− 2,575		
Monetary base	73,444		73,444

Source: Board of Governors of the Federal Reserve System, *Federal Reserve Bulletin*, Vol. 55, No. 7 (July 1969), p. A4.
* Data not seasonally adjusted.
† Includes acceptances of $53 million and other assets of $2,614 not shown separately.

The monetary base is felt to be highly useful as a target for three reasons. First, it is directly controllable by the Federal Reserve System. Federal

---

[7]*Minutes of the Federal Open Market Committee, 1936–1960, and of Its Executive Committee, 1936–1955.* Roll No. 15, Microcopy No. 591, Record Group 82 (Washington, D.C.: The National Archives, 1965).

[8]For an excellent explanation of the monetary base, see Leonall C. Anderson and Jerry L. Jordan, "The Monetary Base — Explanation and Analytical Use," *Review*, Federal Reserve Bank of St. Louis (August 1968), pp. 7–11. Available as Reprint No. 31 from the Federal Reserve Bank of St. Louis.

Reserve credit accounts for three fourths of the size of the base, and adjustments in Federal Reserve credit, for example, by open market operations, can easily offset movements in other items of the base. Second, monetary managers can change the base in a predictable manner. And, third, changes in the base are believed to affect significantly levels of employment, flows of real product, and prices. Changes in the supply of the base cause adjustments in the real and monetary holdings of the public in order to align the quantity of money demanded with the amount supplied. During such an adjustment, the prices of real and financial assets and the pace of economic activity are all changed.

Since shifts in the demand for monetary items making up the base cannot easily affect the size or supply of the base without central bank policy adjustments, changes in the base also reflect the direction of monetary policy. Rapid growth in the base indicates monetary ease; a slow rate of growth indicates tightness.

The target of a monetary base is very close to the target of a specific money supply. Several studies have found a close and predictable relationship between changes in the money stock and changes in economic activity.[9] Further, the money supply appears to be the independent variable. While not denying the importance of the money supply, contemporary Federal Reserve System officials have been reluctant to adopt it as a short-run target because of the difficulty of bringing the money supply under daily or even weekly control, because of the adverse impact they thought a rigidly controlled money supply might have on interest rates and other variables in the short run, and because they associated a money supply target with rules that might reduce their discretionary powers. More recently, system officials have modified their objections to the money supply as a target and are using it much of the time as a desirable guideline for policy. They continue to exercise discretion over the annual rate of increase. Proponents of a nominal and constant rate of increase (3 to 5 percent per year) in the money supply as a rule for policy feel that various lags in the monetary system make discretionary policy procyclical rather than countercyclical. A rule implies constraints on discretion, but the degree of constraint is infinitely variable. A money supply rule, for example, might specify 4 percent per year, but leave the week-to-week variation to the discretion of the monetary managers.

Lags

Contemporary theory recognizes two general types of monetary lags. The need for a change in economic policy and the initiation of a new course of

---

[9]See Chapter 26, "The Velocity of Money and the Investment Multiplier in the United States."

action by policy makers give rise to one type labeled the "inside lag." Then, the interval between the time monetary managers take action and the time such action exerts an influence on the economy is termed the "outside lag." Each of these lags can be further subdivided. The inside lag is composed of (1) a recognition lag—the time between a need for a change in policy and the recognition of that need; (2) a decision lag—the time it takes to decide on a course of action; and (3) an action lag—the time necessary to put the decision into operation. Once action has been taken by monetary authorities, some time may elapse before the monetary system shows any quantitative change. This interval is one aspect of the outside lag. The remainder of the outside lag is the period from the time the banking and monetary system realizes changes in reserves and currency to the time the economy begins to respond. For the sake of clarity, these definitions are presented in Table 16.2.

Table 16.2. Monetary Lags

Lags	Description of the Dating Point	Lag Designation	
	——— An economic change occurs———————————————————		
1	Recognition of the need for a	The recognition lag	The
	——— change in policy———————————————————————		Inside
2		The administrative or decision lag	Lag
	——— A policy decision is made———————————————————		
3		The action lag	
	——— The authorities commence action		
4		Part 1 of the outside lag	The
	——— The banking system is affected———————————————		Outside
5		Part 2 of the outside lag	Lag
	——— The economy begins to respond———————————————		

In monetary policy decision making, the first task is to recognize the existence of a turning point in economic activity. Various indicators may be scanned to get such information. If the coming of an economic downturn is discernible, corrective action can be taken in time to offset most of the decline. A study of the forecasting record shows, however, that turning points become evident only about three months *after* they have occurred. Thus, for monetary as well as fiscal policy purposes, the recognition lag is about three months in length.

The major economic policy-making body of the Federal Reserve System, the Federal Open Market Committee, meets about every four weeks. It can meet oftener and frequently does so via telephone conferences. A study of the minutes of the committee shows that the decision lag for this committee is practically zero. Similarly, once a decision has been made by the committee it may be implemented immediately. Thus, the total inside lag of monetary policy is about the same as the recognition lag, that is, three months.[10]

The outside lag is more difficult to specify. Each economist tackling the problem seems to use his own set of criteria. After the commencement of policy action by central banking authorities, monetary variables are affected within two to five weeks. The measured money supply also changes at about this speed. Once the money supply does change, however, agreement is not unanimous on how or when the economy reacts. The lag interval depends upon the defined stock of money, the identified peaks and troughs in economic activity, and the monetary impulse thought to be geared to a particular change in activity. Outside lags of three to eighteen months have been identified by various economists doing empirical research on the subject. In any case, "the" lag seems to be highly variable. The probability that the outside lag is variable and often longer than a year has given much substance to the policy ideal of a rule specifying a nominal growth rate in the money stock. A monetary growth rate kept constant by the central bank on a month-to-month basis is seen as a means of keeping business fluctuations dampened and thus reducing monetary uncertainty. Other economists remain skeptical, so no thoroughgoing consensus can be said to have developed.

Selected Bibliography

Andersen, Leonall C., and Jerry L. Jordan. "The Monetary Base — Explanation and Analytical Use." *Review,* Federal Reserve Bank of St. Louis, Vol. 50, No. 8 (August 1968), pp. 7–11.

Brunner, Karl, and Allan H. Meltzer. *The Federal Reserve's Attachment to the Free Reserve Concept.* Subcommittee on Domestic Finance, House Committee on Banking and Currency, 88th Congress, 2nd sess., May 1964.

Fels, Rendigs, and C. Elton Hinshaw. *Forecasting and Recognizing Business Cycle Turning Points.* New York: National Bureau of Economic Research, 1968.

Saving, Thomas R. "Monetary-Policy Targets and Indicators." *The Journal of Political Economy,* Vol. 75, No. 4, Part 2, Supplement (August 1967), pp. 446–456.

---

[10]The absence of decision and implementation lags does not mean that decisions are correct in either magnitude or direction, or that other inside lags of a nonmonetary nature might not exist. Political factors, for example, may inhibit some action that the central bank might otherwise take.

Selby, Edward B., Jr. "The Inside Lag of Monetary Policy, 1953–1958." *The Quarterly Review of Economics and Business,* Vol. 5, No. 2 (Spring 1968), pp. 39–52.

Willes, Mark H. "Lags in Monetary and Fiscal Policy." *Business Review,* Federal Reserve Bank of Philadelphia (March 1968), pp. 3–10.

Federal Open Market Committee Decisions in 1968—A Year of Watchful Waiting

Jerry L. Jordan and Charlotte E. Ruebling

While the FOMC issues several types of directives, the Current Economic Policy Directive is the one most concerned with the domestic economic situation. Although the phrases excerpted from these directives for 1968 and reprinted on the following pages appear somewhat imprecise and unclear, to the open market account manager and to the trained observer they provide a clear map of FOMC thinking. Not only can the shifts in FOMC policy be seen—from tightness in early 1968 to ease in December—but the target of money market conditions is evident. Not until early 1970 did the FOMC shift officially to a monetary aggregates target. Jordan and Ruebling capture the divergence between signals given by market conditions and monetary aggregates. Also, they review the reason for the shift to ease during 1968 while inflation was continuing.

Summary

In the first half of 1968 the operating instructions sent to the Federal Reserve Bank of New York, and implemented by the Desk Manager, indicated that operations should be conducted with a view to maintaining firm conditions or attaining firmer conditions. High and rising short-term market interest rates in early 1968 indicated monetary restraint to some observers, but were probably only the result of rapidly rising demands for loan funds. The growth rates of the money stock and the monetary base on balance were very rapid throughout the first half of last year, indicating stimulative monetary actions. The growth of total bank deposits and bank credit slowed substantially in the spring of 1968 as market interest rates rose sharply relative to the ceiling rates banks were permitted to pay on time deposits, and banks were unable to compete effectively for time deposits. The majority of the FOMC interpreted the slowing of bank credit growth, coupled with rising market interest rates, as a sign

From *Review,* May 1969, Federal Reserve Bank of St. Louis.

of significant monetary restraint. Therefore, direct actions to slow the growth of Federal Reserve credit, the monetary base and the money stock were not taken.

Beginning with the first meeting after the passage of the fiscal package at midyear, the FOMC instructed the Desk manager to accommodate less firm conditions or to maintain prevailing conditions in the money markets. Until the final meeting of the year in mid-December, the majority of the Committee remained convinced that substantial restraining influence was forthcoming from the fiscal package, and concluded that monetary restraint was inappropriate.

There was considerable support for the majority opinion of the FOMC throughout the economics profession. Business and financial periodicals in the summer and early fall cited the majority of economic analysts as concluding that the fiscal package would soon have a substantial restraining impact on the economy. The Wharton School forecasting model indicated that the immediate impact of the fiscal package would slow the growth of GNP to $8.7 billion in the third quarter of 1968, less than half the actual result for that quarter. Similarly, most other forecasting models indicated there would be immediate slowing of economic activity and that by the first quarter of 1969 there was a strong possibility of a recession or "fiscal overkill."

The easing of market rates of interest from June into August last year may be attributed to the widely held expectation that substantial slowing of the economy, smaller price increases, and lower interest rates were soon to be forthcoming. However, as the second half of 1968 progressed it became increasingly evident that the immediate restraining impact of the fiscal action had been considerably overestimated and that rapid price increases and high market rates of interest would continue into 1969.[1]

Analysis based on the growth of money, on balance, does not indicate monetary restraint in early 1968. Furthermore, monetary growth during the period from June to November was about as stimulative as during the first part of the year. According to the monetary view, these actions were so expansive as to offset any restraint which might have developed from the more restrictive Federal budget.

If a tighter monetary policy was warranted in December, as it surely was, then it would also have been appropriate during the summer when total spending and expectations of price rises were also increasing rapidly. The decision to slow monetary growth probably would have been made if the FOMC and other analysts had not overestimated the restraining effects of the fiscal action and ignored the probable expansionary impact of the rapid growth of the money supply.

---

[1]The Council of Economic Advisers held firmly to the view that the economy would slow as a result of the fiscal action. In early November, Arthur Okun, the Chairman of the CEA, announced that the nation had "turned the corner toward price stability." He observed that "it should be emphasized that our over-all price performance is still far from satisfactory. But improvement is a fact—and no longer just a forecast."

Federal Open Market Committee Economic Policy Directives

Date of FOMC Meeting	Policy Consensus	Operating Instructions	Proviso Clause of Directive
1968 **January 9**	. . . to foster financial conditions conducive to resistance of inflationary pressures and progress toward reasonable equilibrium in the country's balance of payments. Dissents: None	To implement this policy, System open market operations until the next meeting of the Committee shall be conducted with a view to maintaining the somewhat firmer conditions that have developed in the money market in recent weeks . . .	provided, however, that operations shall be modified as needed to moderate any apparently significant deviations of bank credit from current expectations.
February 6	No change Dissents: None	. . . while taking account of Treasury financing activity, System open market operations until the next meeting of the Committee shall be conducted with a view to maintaining firm conditions in the money market,	and operations shall be modified to the extent permitted by Treasury financing if bank credit appears to be expanding as rapidly as is currently projected.
March 5	No change Dissents: None	. . . System open market operations until the next meeting of the Committee shall be conducted with a view to attaining somewhat firmer conditions in the money market;	provided, however, that operations shall be further modified if bank credit appears to be expanding more rapidly than is currently projected.
March 14	. . . current policy directive should be modified to permit adaptation of open market operations to the changed circumstances brought about by recent events including the discount rate action. Dissents: None	In light of recent international developments, System open market operations until the next meeting of the Committee shall be conducted with a view to maintaining firm but orderly conditions in the money market, taking into account the effects of increases in Federal Reserve discount rates.	
April 2	. . . to foster financial conditions conducive to resistance of inflationary pressures and attainment of reasonable equilibrium in the country's balance of payments. Dissents: None	. . . System open market operations until the next meeting of the Committee shall be conducted with a view to attaining slightly firmer conditions in the money market;	provided, however, that operations shall be modified if bank credit appears to be deviating significantly from current predictions or if unusual liquidity pressures should develop.

April 19	. . . achieving firmer money market conditions in keeping with the higher discount rate while facilitating orderly market adjustments to the increase in that rate. Dissents: None	System open market operations until the next meeting of the Committee shall be conducted with a view to achieving firmer but maintaining orderly conditions in the money market, while facilitating market adjustments to the increase in the **Federal Reserve discount** rates.	
April 30	. . . to foster financial conditions conducive to resistance of inflationary pressures and attainment of reasonable equilibrium in the country's balance of payments. Dissents: Mr. Hickman	. . . while taking account of Treasury financing activity, System open market operations until the next meeting of the Committee shall be conducted with a view to maintaining the firmer conditions prevailing in the money market;	provided, however, that operations shall be modified to the extent permitted by Treasury financing, if bank credit appears to be deviating significantly from current projections.
May 28	. . . to foster financial conditions conducive to resistance of inflationary pressures and attainment of reasonable equilibrium in the country's balance of payments, while taking account of the potential for severe pressures in financial markets if fiscal restraint is not forthcoming. Dissents: None	. . . System open market operations until the next meeting of the Committee shall be conducted with a view to maintaining firm conditions in the money market;	provided, however, that operations shall be modified if bank credit appears to be deviating significantly from current projection or if unusual pressures should develop in financial markets.
June 18	. . . to foster financial conditions conducive to resistance of inflationary pressures and attainments of reasonable equilibrium in the country's balance of payments, while taking account of the potential impact of developments with respect to fiscal legislation. Dissents: None	. . . System open market operations until the next meeting of the Committee shall be conducted with a view to maintaining generally firm but orderly conditions in the money market;	provided, however, that if the proposed fiscal legislation is enacted, operations shall accommodate tendencies for short-term interest rates to decline in connection with such affirmative congressional action on the pending fiscal legislation so long as bank credit expansion does not exceed current projections.

Federal Open Market Committee Economic Policy Directives

Date of FOMC Meeting	Policy Consensus	Operating Instructions	Proviso Clause of Directive
July 16	. . . to foster financial conditions conducive to sustainable economic growth, continued resistance to inflationary pressures, and attainment of reasonable equilibrium in the country's balance of payments. Dissents: None	. . . while taking account of forthcoming Treasury financing activity, System open market operations until the next meeting of the Committee shall be conducted with a view to accommodating the tendency toward somewhat less firm conditions in the money market that has developed since the preceding meeting of the Committee;	provided, however, that operations shall be modified to the extent permitted by Treasury financing, if bank credit appears to be deviating significantly from current projections.
August 13	No change Dissents: None	. . . System open market operations until the next meeting of the Committee shall be conducted with a view to maintaining, on balance, about the prevailing conditions in money and short-term credit markets;	provided, however, that operations shall be modified if bank credit appears to be significantly exceeding current projections.
August 19	No change Dissents: None	System open market operations until the next meeting of the Committee shall be conducted with a view to facilitating orderly adjustments in money market conditions to reductions in Federal Reserve discount rates;	provided, however, that operations shall be modified if bank credit appears to be deviating significantly from current projections.
September 10	No Change Dissents: None	System open market operations until the next meeting of the Committee shall be conducted with a view to maintaining about the prevailing conditions in money and short-term credit markets;	provided, however, that operations shall be modified if bank credit appears to be deviating significantly from current projections.

1968		
October 8	No change Dissents: Messrs. Hayes Hickman Kimbrel	System open market operations until the next meeting of the Committee shall be conducted with a view to maintaining about the prevailing conditions in money and short-term credit markets;	provided, however, that operations shall be modified to the extent permitted by the forthcoming Treasury refunding operation, if bank credit expansion appears to be significantly exceeding current projections.
October 29	No change Dissents: Mr. Hayes	... while taking account of the current Treasury financing, System open market operations until the next meeting of the Committee shall be conducted with a view to maintaining about the prevailing conditions in money and short-term credit markets;	provided, however, that operations shall be modified, to the extent permitted by Treasury financing, if bank credit expansion appears to be exceeding current projections.
November 26	No change Dissents: Messrs. Hayes Hickman Kimbrel Morris	... System open market operations until the next meeting of the Committee shall be conducted with a view to maintaining about the prevailing conditions in money and short-term credit markets;	provided, however, that operations shall be modified, if bank credit expansion appears to be exceeding current projections.
December 17	... to foster financial conditions conducive to the reduction of inflationary pressures, with a view to encouraging a more sustainable rate of economic growth and attaining reasonable equilibrium in the country's balance of payments. Dissents: None	... System open market purchases until the next meeting of the Committee shall be conducted with a view to attaining firmer conditions in money and short-term credit markets, taking account of the effects of other possible monetary policy action;	provided, however, that operations shall be modified if bank credit expansion appears to be deviating significantly from current projections.

Source: Federal Open Market Committee Policy Record Entries, Current Economic Policy Directive.

17

Early Development of
Central Banking in the United States

Commercial Banks and Central Banks

Commercial banks are privately owned, profit-seeking institutions. Inadvertently, and because of the particular type of demand liabilities they issue, they have been responsible for the great bulk of the circulating media commonly used as money in contemporary societies. Such an important function is not consciously undertaken by banking systems; it is simply an ancillary result of the demand obligations they generate in the process of creating interest-bearing loans and investments. Their purpose is to maximize returns; but the net social effect is that the community is supplied with money. Ordinary competitive processes in banking cannot protect society from bank credit fluctuations because a fractional reserve banking system can create variable amounts of deposits against a given amount of reserves. Only when some disinterested controlling agency is formed to regulate variation in the volume of bank credit can large fluctuations in the money supply be tempered and unforeseeable changes in the demand for money be counteracted.

An agency that causes increases or reductions of the circulating media or in any way exercises positive control over the nominal money supply is a central banking institution. Such an institution may be a quasi-bank; or it may be the treasury department of the central government, or a clearing-house association organized by a group of commercial banks. When a central banking institution is a central bank proper, it may look and sometimes act as if it is a commercial bank as well. But such a facade is usually out of place, since the central bank is an institution that effects public policy, while a commercial bank is an institution that aspires to private profit.

Central banking, probably as much as any other institution, has been subject to what philosophers would call "emergence"; that is, central banks have obtained functions in their maturities not given to them in their infancies. This evolution can best be understood and appreciated by an examination of their origins.

What came to be *central* banks usually took form first as *public* banks, although they were referred to frequently as *national* banks. These first "central" banks were hybrid organizations. They were fiscal agents for the government, and thus had preferential access to specie deposits. They absorbed a sizable fraction of outstanding government debt as one of their principal earning assets, and, from the government's point of view, they provided lodging for that much of the government's interest-bearing obligations. Finally, they issued uniform currencies as balancing liabilities for either the government debt they purchased or the limited amounts of commercial loans they made. Again, from the government's point of view, they allowed the retirement of any fiat currency the government may have issued without undue disturbance to business. Commercial banks could issue paper currency, but governments could not do so without embarrassment and loss of prestige.

Governments usually retained fractional control over the direction of the public banks by holding stock in such institutions. At the same time, the public bank was a competitor of private commercial banks in the commercial loan market. A public bank, therefore, had both public and private interests, and was regarded invidiously by its commercial bank competitors.

The First Bank of the United States

Proponents of banking in the United States have usually been of a conservative school and strongly oriented toward the "need" for banking. They have argued that banking systems could not overissue demand obligations as long as individual banks were in competition with one another and were obliged by law to pay specie on demand. The "needs of legitimate business" would functionally determine the correct volume of bank credit.[1] Such independence by the banking system, together with the assumed "natural" control of the money supply base through political adherence to metallic standards, allowed little reason for central banks that would necessarily interfere with or

---

[1]See Jacob Viner, *Studies in the Theory of International Trade* (New York: Harper & Row, 1937), and Lloyd W. Mints, *History of Banking Theory* (Chicago: University of Chicago Press, 1945), for the history and analysis of these theories.

supplant these other institutions. The "central bank" that first developed, therefore, was nothing much more than a federally chartered commercial bank and an administrative aid to the Treasury.

Alexander Hamilton, first Secretary of the Treasury, suggested such a bank in 1790. He saw this national bank "vitalizing as well as economizing the dead stock of gold and silver" by means of high-quality paper money issues. It would also absorb a fair amount of outstanding government debt in the process and yield fiscal service to the government. These points were discussed extensively in Congress.[2]

Even though it faced some strenuous opposition in the process, the First Bank of the United States was incorporated by the federal government in 1791. At this time the United States was what today would be labeled an "underdeveloped" country. Its economy was correspondingly primitive. The First Bank, upon incorporation, became the sixth bank in existence. Each bank tended to be a model of a single large bank: Derivative deposits created by commercial lending were not immediately accompanied by losses of primary reserves to other banks. Transportation and communication were slow. Each bank ultimately could lose reserves through an increase in the demand for hand-to-hand coin or by clearings to other banks and to banks in foreign countries through payment of international balances.

The federal government was to take up one fifth of the capital stock of the First Bank, and the bank was to hold about $7.5 million of government securities. The national debt at this time was $75.5 million, so the First Bank would hold 10 percent of the total debt. As the bank developed its commercial business by granting loans and discounts, it also issued notes that were used extensively as hand-to-hand currency. Its total liabilities, including capital, were limited to $15 million on the original specie deposit. Presumably it would get private and public deposits of primary reserves (specie) on which it could expand commercial loans and notes outstanding still further. No specific reserve requirement was mentioned. Table 17.1 shows the principal items in the closing statement of the bank in 1811.

The difference between the First Bank and the commercial banks was the First Bank's relation to the federal government. All government revenues were deposited in it, and its currency was vested with limited legal tender powers; that is, its notes were legal tender for all government disbursements and receipts. The commercial banks were not favored with government deposits, and their notes were not legal tender in any respect.

As long as the First Bank provided service to the government by "accommodation," its advantageous competitive position relative to other banks was permitted in spite of some severe criticisms. But similar to the Bank of England, the U.S. bank had so much private business as early as 1800 that its "public

---

[2]The very interesting history of the course of the Bank Bill through Congress can be read in the *Annals of Congress,* 1st Congress, 3rd sess.

Table 17.1. Balance Sheet of First Bank, December 31, 1811
(millions of dollars)

Assets		Liabilities	
Commercial loans and		Notes in circulation	5.0
discounts	14.6	Deposits	
U.S. government		Individual 5.9	
securities, etc.	2.8	Government 1.9	
			7.8
Notes and debts against			
other banks	1.3	Due to banks	0.6
Real estate	0.5	Unpaid drafts	0.2
Specie	5.0	Capital and surplus	10.5
		Total liabilities	
Total assets	24.2*	and capital	24.1*

Source: Andrew M. Davis, *The First Bank of the United States*, National Monetary Commission, Senate Document No. 571, 61st Congress, 2nd sess., Washington, D.C., 1910, p. 112.
* Totals do not equal because of rounding and exclusion of minor items.

function was to many persons quite unapparent except as usurpation and privilege."[3]

By the time recharter was a question in 1809–1811, the national debt had declined from $75.5 million (1791) to $41.0 million, and the First Bank held only $2.75 million of the latter amount. No one felt that its agency was needed any longer in financing deficits. Furthermore, the freshly sprung banking system was not regarded as a subordinate complement of the First Bank but as a competitor for the government's funds and the government's business. The First Bank's position was typical of the institutional dichotomy public banks were to face in the nineteenth and twentieth centuries: If they were too commercial, they faced the criticism of being government-favored monopolies; if they acted simply as public depositories and overseers of a uniform currency, they were duplicating a job that the central treasuries might do better; if they were too influential as central banks, they were assuming powers implicitly attached to metallic standards. Public banks walked a thin line. When a conflict of interests developed, their very existence was threatened. Sometimes they survived, and sometimes they were abolished.

Neither those who were for nor those who were against the bank's reincorporation in 1809–1811 generally understood its emergence as a regulator of commercial bank credit. The influential Democrats in favor of recharter saw the bank only in an ancillary and subordinate fiscal role to the Treasury, while those opposed to it stressed nonmonetary factors—that is, constitutionality, the "dominance" of British stockholders, and the desire that local banks "profit" from the deposits of the public money.

[3]Bray Hammond, *Banks and Politics in America* (Princeton, N.J.: Princeton University Press, 1957), pp. 115–116, 198–200.

The Second Bank of the United States

The Second Bank of the United States was chartered in 1816. The provisions of its incorporation were almost identical to those of the First Bank. Its capital was $35 million instead of $10 million, and again the government held 20 percent of the stock.

In the period 1818–1821 the Treasury Department effected a 30 percent decline in the price level by retiring through fiscal surpluses the large volume of limited legal tender Treasury notes it had issued during the War of 1812. Specie payments were resumed. The Second Bank, acting as a fiscal agent for the Treasury, took no central bank action. However, its specie reserve position was greatly strengthened by deposits of government receipts and by its curtailment of outstanding notes and deposits. As can be seen from Table 17.2, its reserve ratio increased from 12 percent to 61 percent during this period.

The Second Bank's central banking activities evolved from its relationship to the government, a relationship not enjoyed by any of its commercial peers. First, the bank received all the government's deposits interest free. Second, its notes outstanding were legal tender for all debts owed by and payable to the government. Third, the size of its capital and its specie resources made it an appreciable fraction of the total banking structure. The government, for its part, could appoint or remove five of the 25 directors, remove its own deposits, exact weekly statements, and inspect the accounts generally. In spite of this intimate relationship between bank and government, nothing in the debates over its incorporation, the provisions of its charter, or its activities for the first eight years of its existence suggested or indicated any central banking overtones.

Nicholas Biddle became the third, last, and most famous president of the Second Bank in 1823. Under his aegis the bank began its career of central banking, although it continued to operate as both a commercial bank and a public bank. Its principal means of regulating the commercial banks was by varying its holdings of their notes outstanding. If it wished to restrain the banks, it promptly presented these notes to them for redemption in specie. State bank credit was then inhibited because the banks would keep at least a minimal reserve ratio (5 to 10 percent) on their own volition. If the bank wished bank credit to expand, it would hold notes of other banks or pay them out in the normal course of business. At the same time, it would expand its own accommodations to both business and other banks.

The Second Bank's sheer size and its fiscal relationship to the government guaranteed that a substantial volume of money would pass through its offices. By keeping a relatively high ratio of reserves to demand liabilities, it allowed itself "room" to effect policy. It was, nevertheless, operating within the framework of the international specie standard. If the balance of payments ran against the United States, the Second Bank could borrow from foreign sources. It could also bleed off its own stock of specie; but ultimately the adjustments

Table 17.2. Selected Assets and Liabilities, and Reserve Ratios
of the Second Bank of the United States, 1817 to 1840
(millions of dollars)

Year	Loans and Dis- counts	Notes of State Banks Held by Second Bank	Specie	Circula- tion*	Deposits†	Total Circula- tion and Deposits	Reserve Ratios Specie ÷ Circulation + Deposits‡ (%)
1817	3.49	.59	1.72	1.91	11.23	13.14	13.1
1818	41.18	1.84	2.52	8.34	12.28	20.62	12.2
1819	35.77	1.88	2.67	6.56	5.79	12.35	21.5
1820	31.40	1.44	3.39	3.59	6.57	10.16	33.4
1821	30.91	.68	7.64	4.57	7.89	12.46	61.3
1822	28.06	.92	4.76	5.58	8.08	13.66	34.9
1823	30.74	.77	4.43	4.36	7.62	11.98	37.0
1824	33.43	.71	5.81	4.65	13.70	18.35	31.7
1825	31.81	1.06	6.75	6.07	12.03	18.10	37.3
1826	33.42	1.11	3.96	9.48	11.21	20.69	19.1
1827	30.94	1.07	6.46	8.55	14.32	22.87	31.1
1828	33.68	1.45	6.17	9.86	14.50	24.36	25.3
1829	39.22	1.29	6.10	11.90	17.06	28.96	21.0
1830	40.66	1.47	7.61	12.92	16.05	28.97	26.3
1831	44.03	1.50	10.81	16.25	17.30	33.55	32.2
1832	66.29	2.17	7.04	21.36	22.76	44.12	15.9
1833	61.70	2.29	8.95	17.52	20.35	37.87	23.6
1834	54.91	1.98	10.04	19.21	10.84	30.05	32.9
1835	51.81	1.51	15.71	17.34	11.76	29.10	54.0
1836	59.23	1.74	8.42	23.08	5.06	28.14	29.9
1837	57.39	1.21	2.64	11.45	2.33	13.78	19.1
1838	45.26	.87	3.77	6.77	2.62	9.39	40.2
1839	41.62	1.79	4.15	5.98	6.78	12.76	32.5
1840	36.84	1.38	1.47	6.70	3.34	10.04	14.6

Source: *Historical Statistics of the United States, Colonial Times to 1957*, U.S. Department of Commerce, Bureau of Census, Washington, D.C., 1949, Series N, p. 261.
* Circulation is the sum of the bank's own notes in circulation.
† Deposits is the sum of both private and government deposits.
‡ The reserve ratios given are computed by dividing the sum of circulation and deposits into specie.

required by the international specie standard would dominate. The stock of money had to be compatible with external economic conditions; that is, in the case of a worldwide "shortage" of specie, internal prices had to fall. In the event of a specie plethora, the Second Bank was able to control the nominal money supply by accumulating and impounding specie. For short periods it could and did use many of the tricks that comprise the "art" of central banking. In 1831–1832, for example, it conducted policies that were instrumental in checking a developing recession.

By 1830 the central banking activities of the Second Bank were well recognized. Recognition meant acceptance by some but condemnation by others; and these differences were at issue as the question of recharter became prominent. Congress discussed the matter exhaustively, the Whigs generally being in favor of recharter and the Jacksonian Democrats opposed. Those in favor of rechartering the bank viewed it as an instrument of monetary policy, as an auxiliary to the fiscal operations of the government, and as the only possible source of a sound currency.

The minority view was much more concerned about the power position the bank was assuming, or the position they thought it was assuming. This group objected to a bank that "would regulate commerce, which, if left to individual enterprise, will regulate itself without any such agency, under the rules which have been prescribed by law."[4]

The conflict that ensued from 1832 to 1836 over the existence or nonexistence of the Second Bank was also a jurisdictional dispute involving the Second Bank, the Treasury, and Congress. The question at issue was: Which agency, if any, is responsible for monetary policy? The Whig position was that such powers constitutionally belonged to Congress, but that by chartering the Second Bank Congress had made the bank its agent. The Whigs abhorred power in the Treasury Department; they thought that Andrew Jackson had already assumed too much power for his administration.

The Jacksonians were ambivalent. One wing was irrevocably committed to "hard money" (specie) in all commercial and financial dealings. Paper money of both the Second Bank and other banks was anathema to them. The other wing wanted only the destruction of the Second Bank for one or a number of reasons. They regarded commercial banks as innocuous institutions that could act as fiscal agents for the government, but that were at a competitive disadvantage with the Second Bank.

The Whigs had a majority in Congress during much of the time in which the "bank war" raged; but Andrew Jackson was too tough and too wily. The Second Bank's charter was not renewed in 1836. It subsequently became a state bank in Pennsylvania and failed during the international economic decline of 1839–1843. The Whigs then brought out several other "national bank" bills in 1841-1842 and again would have had a quasi-central bank similar to the Second Bank had not President Tyler unexpectedly vetoed each bill in turn.

The concept of monetary control was clearly envisaged in these proposals. In debates over the bills, one senator said that the central board in Washington would have "the sovereign power to make prices high or low at pleasure." Another observed: "The object of this bank is to regulate the currency—that is, to make it *more or less*—and as a consequence, to make prices *more or less*." Another saw a central bank as necessary to offset the presumably unfavorable

---

[4]*Register of Debates in Congress,* 22nd Congress, 1st sess., Appendix, pp. 132–145.

actions of European central banks.[5] One of the proposals outlined by the Secretary of the Treasury in 1842 charged that a government-sponsored bank had the *duty* of furnishing a paper money with a countercyclical bias. The credit it would generate, he wrote, "would be a fructifying and vivifying germe, amid general blight and barrenness."[6]

None of the Whig plans succeeded. Shifting political tides and party defections obstructed acceptance in each case. Monetary policy had to continue, however, and from 1836 to 1913 the principal agency for both monetary and fiscal policy was the Treasury Department of the federal government.

The Independent Treasury

The Independent Treasury was thought of as early as 1834. The original plan proposed that the Treasury be completely divorced from the banks, Banks of the United States or otherwise, and that all Treasury dealings be conducted only on a specie–Treasury note basis. The law formally establishing this system was passed in 1846. While the Treasury thereupon was freed from the influences and risks incurred in depositing its funds in commercial banks, force of circumstances almost immediately placed the banks in a position of dependence on it.

The Treasury was in a position of appreciable strategic importance. Given (1) international specie standards, (2) a relatively fixed volume of government expenditures, (3) tariff revenues that were elastic with respect to domestic money income, and (4) government transactions that were an appreciable fraction of the national total, any untoward deviation from general economic equilibrium brought in the Treasury Department as an "automatic" stabilizer. Assume, for example, a decline in internal spending. A favorable balance of trade would arise, contributing to an inflow of specie. In addition, the decline in tariff revenues from reduced imports would leave the government with a deficit that had to be financed. The government could finance its deficit by either selling interest-bearing debt in the open market or issuing Treasury notes. If it sold interest-bearing debt to the banks, the new bank credit and corresponding deposits would stimulate the economy. Or if (as frequently occurred between 1837 and 1860) Treasury note issues were authorized to provide for the deficit, the stock of high-powered money (currency and bank reserves) would be increased *ipso facto*. The Treasury Department, the administrator for these notes, necessarily would assume certain central banking characteristics.

---

[5]The authors of these expressions were respectively Senators Robert J. Walker, John C. Calhoun, and Henry Clay. See *Congressional Globe*, 27th Congress, 1st sess., pp. 81, 169–170.

[6]U.S. Congress, *Report to Congress on a Board of Exchequer*, 27th Congress, 2nd sess., Senate Document No. 18, p. 8.

Treasury notes were always authorized as "temporary debt." Most often they were issued for one year and usually they bore interest, although the rate ordinarily was low (often one-tenth of 1 percent per year). Their most important feature was their limited legal tender status for all debts of and due the government. They thus were regarded more as money than as "investments," and were used mostly as hand-to-hand currency and bank reserves. While the issues were supposedly only occasional and nominal, their volume from time to time was as much as 40 percent of the total amount of bank-held specie, and some volume of notes was outstanding for thirteen of the 22 years between 1837 and 1859.

Until 1850 the Treasury was almost constantly impoverished. Its incursions into monetary policy were largely idealistic expressions by the Secretaries over the Treasury note authorizations discussed above. In 1850 government revenues began to increase rapidly, along with general buoyancy in trade, as a result of the gold discoveries in the West. Since government expenditures tended to rise more slowly than receipts, a substantial specie balance accumulated in the Treasury. Secretary of the Treasury James Guthrie, during 1853–1856, conducted extensive open market purchases in government securities, not only to retire the national debt, but also to relieve "disorder in money matters...[from] the failure of many...banks, and the curtailment of the circulation and discounts of others."[7] During his four years as Secretary, $38 million of the $63 million of outstanding interest-bearing federal debt was repurchased.

At the end of his Treasury career, Guthrie gave an unequivocal statement of Treasury policy with respect to business fluctuations. Uncertainties in economic life due to wars, political strife, and other phenomena, he said,

> destroy confidence and with it credit, inducing the hoarding of the precious metals, the withdrawal of deposits, the return of bank notes for redemption, the consequent stagnation of commerce in all its channels and operations, the reduction of prices and wages, with inability to purchase and pay, bank suspensions and general insolvency....The independent treasury, when overtrading takes place, gradually fills its vaults, withdraws the deposits, and pressing the banks, the merchants and the dealers, exercises that temperate and timely control which serves to secure the fortunes of individuals, and preserve the general prosperity....
>
> The independent treasury, however, may exercise a fatal control over the currency, the banks and the trade of the country...whenever the revenue shall greatly exceed the expenditure. [Without the repurchases of debt since March 4, 1853], the accumulated sum would have acted fatally on the banks and on trade.[8]

---

[7]*Report of the Secretary on the State of the Finances* (Washington, D.C.: U.S. Government Printing Office, 1854), p. 6.

[8]*Report of the Secretary on the State of the Finances* (Washington, D.C.: U.S. Government Printing Office, 1856), p. 31.

Guthrie is quoted at length to show the extent to which the Treasury had evolved as a central banking institution even at this early date. The Treasury's required fiscal functions made it a timely and sensitive policy agent. It too, however, operated within the framework of the international specie standard. It could obtain significant specie balances only during a boom. When these balances were bled off, although it might still be able to resort to authorized note issues, it lost much of its leverage for carrying out policy. Such was its plight in the crisis of 1857, when notes again were issued. Shortly thereafter, the extraordinary financial maneuvers of the Civil War provoked entirely new problems for monetary policy.

Selected Bibliography

Hammond, Bray. *Banks and Politics in America.* Princeton, N.J.: Princeton University Press, 1957.

Kinley, David. *The Independent Treasury of the United States.* New York: Thomas Y. Crowell Co., 1893. An account of the monetary operations of the Independent Treasury.

Mints, Lloyd W. *A History of Banking Theory.* Chicago: University of Chicago Press, 1945. For more advanced reading.

Timberlake, Richard H., Jr. "The Independent Treasury and Monetary Policy before the Civil War." *Southern Economic Journal,* Vol. 27, No. 2 (October 1960), pp. 92–103. Another account of the Independent Treasury, somewhat different from Kinley's.

Timberlake, Richard H., Jr. "The Specie Standard and Central Banking in the United States before 1860." *Journal of Economic History,* Vol. 20, No. 3 (September 1961), pp. 318–341. A point of view on early central banking different from Hammond's.

Viner, Jacob. *Studies in the Theory of International Trade.* New York: Harper & Row, 1937. For more advanced reading.

Two Congressional Speeches on Banking

John C. Calhoun

John C. Calhoun (1782–1850) of South Carolina has historical notoriety for a number of well-understood reasons. He was a great secessionist and a proponent of states' rights, Vice President under John Quincy Adams and Andrew Jackson (only to resign), Secretary of State under John Tyler, a long-time United States senator, a political genius—but never President.

The passages reproduced here from the Register of Debates in Congress *are parts of speeches Senator Calhoun made early in 1834 over the issue of where government cash deposits should be made. The three possibilities were (1) the Second Bank of the United States, (2) the state ("pet") banks, and (3) no banks at all. In suggesting this last alternative, he was foreseeing the Independent Treasury System, which ultimately was incorporated twelve years later. However, at this stage of events in 1834, when the Bank of the United States still hoped for the possibility of recharter, he favored the bank. His arguments on banks, the executive, and the state of the monetary system show that he was just as able a monetary policy theorist as he was a statesman and jurist.*

January 13, 1834

What, then, is the real question which now agitates the country? I answer, it is a struggle between the executive and legislative departments of the Government; a struggle, not in relation to the existence of the bank, but which, Congress or the President, should have the power to create a bank, and the consequent control over the currency of the country. This is the real question. Let us not deceive ourselves. This league, this association of banks, created by the Executive, bound together by its influence, united in common articles of association, vivified and sustained by receiving the deposites of the public money, and having their notes converted, by being received everywhere by the treasury, into the common currency of the country, is, to all intents and purposes, a Bank of the United States, the Executive Bank of the United States, as distinguished from that of Congress.

However it might fail to perform satisfactorily the useful functions of the Bank of the United States as incorporated by law, it would outstrip it, far outstrip it, in all its dangerous qualities, in extending the power, the influence, and the corruption of the Government. It was impossible to conceive any institution more admirably calculated to advance these objects. Not only the selected banks, but the whole banking institutions of the country, and with them the entire money power, for the purpose of speculation, peculation, and corruption, would be placed under the control of the Executive. A system of menaces and promises will be established; of menace to the banks in possession of the deposites, but which might not be entirely subservient to executive views; and of promise of future favors to those who may not as yet enjoy its favors. Between the two, the banks would be left without influence, honor, or honesty; and a system of speculation and stock-jobbing would commence, unequalled in the annals of our country....

So long as the question is one between a Bank of the United States incorporated by Congress, and that system of banks which has been created by the will of the Executive, it is an insult to the understanding to discourse on the pernicious tendency and unconstitutionality of the Bank of the United States. To bring up that question fairly and legitimately, you must go one step farther — you must divorce the Government and the banking system. You must refuse all connexion with banks; you must neither receive nor pay away bank notes; you must go back to the old system of the strong box, and of gold and silver. If you have a right to receive bank notes at all, to treat them as money, by receiving them in your dues, or paying them away to creditors, you have a right to create a bank. Whatever the Government receives and treats as money, is money; and, if it be money, then they have the right, under the constitution, to regulate it. Nay, they are bound, by a high obligation, to adopt the most efficient means, according to the nature of that which they have recognized as money, to give to it the utmost stability and uniformity of value; and, if it be in the shape of bank notes, the most efficient means of giving those qualities is a Bank of the United States, incorporated by Congress. Unless you give the highest practical uniformity to the value of bank notes, so long as you receive them in your dues, and treat them as money, you violate that provision of the constitution which provides that taxation shall be uniform throughout the United States. There is no other alternative. I repeat, you must divorce the Government entirely from the banking system, or, if not, you are bound to incorporate a bank, as the only safe and efficient means of giving stability and uniformity to the currency. And, should the deposits not be restored, and the present illegal and unconstitutional connexion between the Executive and the league of banks continue, I shall feel it my duty, if no one else moves, to introduce a measure to prohibit Government from receiving or touching bank notes in any shape whatever, as the only means left of giving safety and stability to the currency, and saving the country from corruption and ruin.

March 21, 1834

All feel that the currency is a delicate subject, requiring to be touched with the utmost caution; but in order that it may be seen, as well as felt, why it is so delicate, why slight touches, either in depressing or elevating it, agitate and convulse the whole community, I will pause to explain the cause. If we take the aggregate property of a community, that which forms the currency, constitutes, in value, a very small proportion of the whole. What this proportion is in our country and other commercial and trading communities, is somewhat uncertain. I speak conjecturally in fixing it as one to twenty-five or thirty, though I presume that is not far from the truth; and yet this small proportion of the property of the community regulates the value of all the rest, and forms the medium of circulation by which all its exchanges are effected; bearing, in this respect, a striking similarity, considering the diversity of the subjects, to the blood in the human or animal system.

If we turn our attention to the laws which govern the circulation, we shall find one of the most important to be, that, as the circulation is decreased or increased, the rest of the property will, all other circumstances remaining the same, be decreased or increased in value exactly in the same proportion.

What, then, is the currency of the United States? What its present state and condition? These are the questions which I propose now to consider, with a view of ascertaining what is the disease, what the remedy, and what the means of applying it, that may be necessary to restore our currency to a sound condition?

The legal currency of this country—that in which alone debts can be discharged according to law, are certain gold, silver, and copper coins, coined at the mint of the United States, and issued by their authority, under an express provision of the constitution. Such is the law. What now are the facts? That the currency consists almost exclusively of bank notes; gold having entirely disappeared, and silver in a great measure, expelled by banks constituted by twenty-five distinct and independent powers, and notes issued under the authority of the direction of those institutions. They are, in point of fact, the mint of the United States. They coin the actual money (for such we must call bank notes), and regulate its issue and consequently its value. If we inquire as to their number, the amount of their issue, and other circumstances calculated to show their actual condition, we shall find that, so rapid has been their increase, and so various their changes, that no accurate information can be had. According to the latest and best that I have been able to ascertain, they number at least four hundred and fifty, with a capital of not less than one hundred and forty-five millions of dollars, with an issue exceeding seventy millions; and the whole of this immense fabric standing upon a metallic currency of less than fifteen millions of dollars, of which the greater part is held by the Bank of the United States. If we compare the notes in circulation with the metallic currency in their vaults, we shall find the proportion about six to one; and if we compare the latter with the demands that may be made upon the banks, we shall find that the proportion is about one to eleven. If we examine the tendency of the system at this moment, we shall find that it is on the increase—rapidly on the increase.

This increase is not accidental. It may be laid down as a law, that where two currencies are permitted to circulate in any country, one of a cheap and the other of a dear material, the former necessarily intends to grow upon the latter, and will ultimately expel it from circulation, unless its tendency to increase be restrained by a powerful and efficient check. Experience tests the truth of this remark, as the history of the banking system clearly illustrates. The Senator from Massachusetts truly said that the Bank of England was derived from that of Amsterdam, as ours in turn are from that of England. Throughout its progress, the truth of what I have stated to be a law of the system is strongly evinced. The Bank of Amsterdam was merely a bank of deposit—a storehouse for the safe keeping of the bullion and precious metals brought into that commercial metropolis, through all the channels of its widely-extended trade. It was placed under the custody of the city authorities: and, on the deposit, a certificate was issued as evidence of the fact, which was transferable, so as to entitle the holder to demand the return. An important fact was soon disclosed; that a large portion of the deposits might be withdrawn, and that the residue would be sufficient to meet the returning certificates; or, what is the same in effect, that certificates might be issued without making a deposit. This suggested the idea of a bank of discount as well as deposit. The fact thus disclosed fell too much in with the genius of the system to be lost, and accordingly, when transplanted to England, it suggested the idea of a bank of discount and of deposit; the very essence of which form of banking, that on which their profit depends, consists in issuing a greater amount of notes than it has of specie in its vaults. But the system is regularly progressing under the impulse of the laws that govern it, from its present form to a mere paper machine—a machine for fabricating and issuing notes, not convertible into specie. Already has it once reached this condition, both in England and the United States, and from which it has been forced back, in both to a redemption of its notes, with great difficulty.

After a full survey of the whole subject, I see none—I can conjecture no means of extricating the country from its present danger, and to arrest its farther increase, but a bank—the agency of which, in some form, or under some authority, is indispensable. The country has been brought into the present diseased state of the currency by banks, and must be extricated by their agency. We must, in a word, use a bank to unbank the banks, to the extent that may be necessary to restore a safe and stable currency—just as we apply snow to a frozen limb, in order to restore vitality and circulation, or hold up a burn to the flame to extract the inflammation. All must see that it is impossible to suppress the banking system at once. It must continue for a time. Its greatest enemies and the advocates of an exclusive specie circulation, must make it a part of their system to tolerate the banks for a longer or a shorter period. To suppress them at once, would, if it were possible, work a greater revolution, a greater change in the relative condition of the various classes of the community, than would the conquest of the country by a savage enemy. What, then, must be done? I answer, a new and safe system must gradually grow up under, and replace, the old; imitating, in this respect, the beautiful process which we sometimes see, of a wounded or diseased part, in a living organic body, gradually superseded by the healing process of nature.

How is this to be effected? How is a bank to be used as the means of correcting the excess of the banking system? And what bank is to be selected as the agent to effect this salutary change? I know, said Mr. C., that a diversity of opinion will be found to exist, as to the agent to be selected, among those who agree on every other point, and who, in particular, agree on the necessity of using some bank as the means of effecting the object intended; one preferring a simple recharter of the existing bank — another, the charter of a new Bank of the United States — a third, a new bank ingrafted upon the old — and a fourth, the use of the State banks, as the agent. I wish, said Mr. C., to leave all these as open questions, to be carefully surveyed and compared with each other, calmly and dispassionately, without prejudice or party feeling; and that to be selected which, on the whole, shall appear to be best — the most safe; the most efficient; the most prompt in application, and the least liable to constitutional objection. It would, however, be wanting in candor on my part, not to declare that my impression is, that a new Bank of the United States, ingrafted upon the old, will be found, under all the circumstances of the case, to combine the greatest advantages, and to be liable to the fewest objections; but this impression is not so firmly fixed as to be inconsistent with a calm review of the whole ground, or to prevent my yielding to the conviction of reason, should the results of such review prove that any other is preferable. Among its peculiar recommendations, may be ranked the consideration, that while it would afford the means of a prompt and effectual application for mitigating and finally removing the existing distress, it would, at the same time, open to the whole community a fair opportunity of participation in the advantages of the institution, be they what they may.

18

Central Banking from 1860 to 1914

The Monetary Effects of Civil War Finance

During the Civil War both opposing governments resorted to issues of legal tender notes in order to finance parts of their fiscal deficits. The volume of outstanding Treasury currencies soon became a significant multiple of the gold and silver in their vaults. These currency measures were not without precedent. What distinguished the Civil War issues from previous issues by the federal government was the sheer volume, and the fact that the war-issued currencies were *full* legal tender.

The monetary effects of these issues followed a pattern as old as fiat money itself. When the paper money went into circulation as payment for government purchases of goods and services, prices in general, including the market prices of silver and gold, tended to rise. But anyone desiring to purchase specie could get it from the Treasury or the banks at the mint price until these sources effectively were exhausted. Since the prices of foreign goods in terms of specie could rise only slightly, the principal demand for specie came from importers who exported the specie to the countries from which they bought goods and services.[1]

The banking system was in a position similar to, but also dependent on, the Treasury. Treasury issues of legal tender notes (called "greenbacks," "United States notes," or "legal tenders") were also legal as bank reserves. As people

---

[1]For a detailed discussion of this process, see Chapter 23.

deposited these notes in banks, the banking system effected a multiple expansion of bank credit. Government supplies of interest-bearing securities to the banks aggravated the process. Once the supplies of specie in banks and the Treasury were exhausted in paying for relatively cheaper foreign goods, paper money could no longer be redeemed for gold and "suspension" of specie payments resulted. The mint price of gold then became nothing more than a legal fiction, while the market value of gold went up more or less with the general price level.

The National Bank Act of 1863–1865 was intended to keep the bank credit expansion within manageable bounds. It required banks obtaining national bank charters to hold government securities against both capital and note issues, and it also imposed reserve requirements on them of 15 and 25 percent. Finally, it included a 10 percent annual tax on state bank note issues with the intention of forcing state banks into the scheme. The state banks, however, avoided both national bank membership and the necessity of note issue by using deposit creation as their means of extending credit.

National bank notes became the only bank-created currency. These notes were liabilities of the national banks but could be held as bank reserves by state banks, while U.S. notes were used as reserves by either national or non-national banks. The $350–$400 million of U.S. notes became the base on which rested the next "layer" of national bank notes and deposits, which in turn supported nonnational bank credit. Government policy with respect to the volume of its own notes outstanding, and with respect to its influence on national bank notes and credit, regulated the monetary environment.

The Policy of Contraction (1865–1868)

The first policy of the post–Civil War government was to contract what had been expanded during the war. Tax receipts greatly exceeded government expenditures; since a large part of total receipts was in the form of U.S. notes, the notes were simply destroyed, thus diminishing the total money supply. Between 1865 and 1868, government currency outstanding was reduced from $646 million to $394 million, and the price level fell approximately 8 percent per year.[2] Although this policy was formally approved by Congress, it was initiated and carried out by the Treasury Department.

---

[2]Increases in bank notes and deposits offset the government's policy to some extent. (See Table 10.1.)

Growing Up to the Money Stock
(1868–1874)

The price level decline proved to be more than the body politic would take, and Congress prohibited further contraction in 1868. Policy for the next six to eight years was a more moderate "growing up" to the money stock; the money stock was held relatively constant, while the output of real goods and services in the economy increased.

A monetary system not controlled by the restriction of specie convertibility had to be subject to the executive influence of the Treasury Department. The revenues to the government did not coincide with disbursements; so for extensive periods of the year the Treasury had a cash balance available with which it could influence the condition of the New York money market and the state of business generally. The Secretary did not *need* to keep a balance, and many strict constructionists in Congress thought he ought not to. He could spend the accruing balance by buying government securities in the open market as soon as more than a nominal amount accumulated. Most Secretaries, however, took the position of Secretary McCulloch, who said in 1866 that one of his duties was to "keep the business of the country as steady as possible while [it was] conducted on the uncertain basis of an irredeemable currency. To accomplish this," he concluded, "... it [is] necessary to hold a handsome reserve of coin in the treasury."[3]

George Boutwell, Secretary of the Treasury during Grant's first administration, initiated a policy of purchasing bonds in the open market during the early fall. The purchases were technically for the so-called "sinking fund" of the Treasury, but were made particularly in the fall to facilitate crop movements and to provide for other seasonal demands for money. In 1872 Boutwell also reissued some of the U.S. notes previously "retired," for the same seasonal purposes.[4] His action simulated contemporary central bank note issue. At that time congressional sentiment was divided over Boutwell's discretion. No resolutions or statutes were passed against this policy, but Boutwell's successor, William Richardson, assumed that he should not undertake such action without congressional sanction. As panic developed in the fall of 1873, Richardson did not use any of the "reserve" of U.S. notes to relieve the stress on the banking system. The issue of the reserve "for the sole purpose of affecting the money market," he said, "ought not to be the business of the Treasury Department."[5] The panic therefore ran its course. Fractional reserve bank credit contracted, and the economy experienced severe financial hardship.

---

[3]*Finance Report* (Washington, D.C.: U.S. Government Printing Office, 1866), p. 9.

[4]Congress in two different acts had prescribed a *maximum* of $400 million of U.S. notes and a *minimum* of $356 million. Thus, a $44 million range existed between maximum and minimum. Boutwell argued that the volume of currency issued *within this range* was a function of Treasury discretion.

[5]*Finance Report* (Washington, D.C.: U.S. Government Printing Office, 1873), p. xx.

The Path to Resumption
(1874–1879)

After the panic of 1873, the principal issue of monetary policy before Congress was again the resumption of specie payments. To obtain resumption at the pre–Civil War parity of gold to the dollar, the domestic price level had to fall to the point where the gold and paper dollars were at parity (i.e., one paper dollar would exchange for one minted gold dollar). By 1874 the paper dollar still was worth only $0.87 of the gold dollar. Various acts of Congress in 1874–1875 inhibited the growth in the money supply and brought about the necessary decline in the price level by 1878. At the same time silver gained prominence because its value declined as a result of increased supplies from the West. Those who were against a falling price level, and hence against resumption, embraced the remonetization of silver as a cheaper, more expedient, and more respectable standard than greenbacks. Various silver acts, starting with the Bland-Allison Act in 1878, were passed with the intention of tempering the harshness of what seemed to be the never-ending decline in prices necessary to reach parity of the gold dollar.

Resumption was, nevertheless, accomplished as scheduled in 1879. The Secretary of the Treasury, John Sherman, accumulated over $200 million in gold in the Treasury as a reserve against the $346 million in U.S. notes outstanding. This huge gold balance was obtained through fiscal surpluses and through bond issues floated in New York and London. When "Resumption Day" occurred on January 1, 1879, very little of the gold was called for to redeem the outstanding greenbacks. Such disinterest in the redemption of U.S. notes simply indicated that the price level in the United States relative to price levels abroad was low enough to ensure an external balance without further depreciation of the dollar in terms of gold.

The Silver Issue
(1879–1898)

The difference between the pre–Civil War Treasury and the post-1879 Treasury was that the latter had substantial *demand* obligations outstanding. It stood ready, however, to redeem these obligations in specie. The prewar Treasury had also issued some note obligations but sporadically and incidentally. Similar to most central banks of issue, the U.S. Treasury Department maintained only a fractional reserve of specie against outstanding legal tender notes. It also kept part of this cash balance in national bank depositories.

Silver had regained legal tender status in limited quantities by the Act of 1878; but its legal acceptability did not prevent it from losing market value.

By 1880 the Treasury had coined $73 million worth of silver, but had put only $47 million of this amount into circulation. Holding back the silver coin was necessary to prevent an external gold drain and was made possible by domestic fiscal surpluses in the federal government budgets. Silver was thus in the same monetary position in the 1880s as U.S. notes had been in the 1860s. That is, it was a fiat currency and an outstanding demand obligation of the Treasury against which the Treasury had to keep a gold reserve. If the silver currency in circulation had substantially increased the total stock of money, prices would have risen and provoked an outflow of gold. If prolonged, such an outflow would have depleted the banks and the Treasury of their gold reserves and resulted in a *de facto* silver standard.

Silver accumulation in the Treasury was a conscious and deliberate monetary policy. The quantity of silver allowed to go into circulation was at the discretion of the Secretary of the Treasury. He also had to decide what percentage of gold reserves to keep against total outstanding note obligations. The extent to which he could follow his judgment with respect to the outstanding amount of silver depended on whether the Treasury could afford to keep the silver that it was by law (Bland-Allison Act) required to purchase and coin. The Treasury could buy and retain the silver in its vaults by means of either a fiscal surplus or an issue of its own securities in the open market.

Various Secretaries were faced with different degrees of difficulty in their attempts to maintain adequate reserve ratios. Some had "too much" of a reserve and called for reductions of taxes to hold down the Treasury's balance. Others realized that disbursement of accumulated balances could have detrimental or beneficial effects on business conditions depending on when the money was spent. The means used to disburse surplus Treasury balances included (1) prepayment of interest on the public debt, (2) purchases of government securities in the open market, and (3) deposit of Treasury balances in national bank depositories. During the year 1890–1891 particularly, $104 million in bonds were purchased in the open market, and prepayments of interest were made. These actions added about $1 million per day to the economy during the summer of 1890, an increase that amounted to 6 percent *per month* of the outstanding currency stock.[6]

The Treasury Note Act was also passed in 1890. It called for silver purchases by the Treasury and corresponding issues of Treasury notes with the silver bullion to be held at its market value as collateral for the notes. The issues of these notes helped to alleviate the threatening panic of 1890, but they also tended to strain the Treasury's gold reserve in the years following.[7]

---

[6]*Finance Report* (Washington, D.C.: U.S. Government Printing Office, 1890), pp. xxvii–xxxii.

[7]From the time that U.S. notes were first issued, the Treasury kept a reserve of gold against both these notes and the various silver issues (silver certificates, treasury notes of 1890, and silver currency). Ordinarily, the gold reserve in the latter quarter of the nineteenth century was $100-$300 million, and outstanding currency obligations were $350-$700 million. The Treasury was thus a currency-issuing agency ("central bank") maintaining a reserve ratio of about 33–50 percent.

The United States was not alone in facing financial difficulties in the early 1890s; the lack of gold was worldwide. Silver policy in the United States tended for a while to prevent the decline in money, wages, prices, and incomes called for by the gold scarcity, but ultimately the "cheaper" silver money "drove out" the gold. The U.S. balance of payments was favorable in the middle 1890s, but the ability of the government to maintain gold convertibility was so much in question and raised so much corresponding uncertainty that foreigners on net balance returned outstanding debt of individuals, corporations, and government to pay for their trade deficits. Gold was a "hot money." In anticipation of loss of convertibility, $90 million in gold left the United States in 1894 in spite of a favorable balance of trade of $392 million.[8]

The Golden Era
(1898–1914)

The worldwide declines in prices and incomes that reached a trough in 1896 encouraged gold production by lowering the real costs of acquiring it while mint prices remained fixed. Such circumstances also provoked fresh gold discoveries in the Klondike and South Africa, thereby making the world safe for gold standards.

Gold accumulated in the United States Treasury as it did after the California and Australia strikes in 1849. The plethora again ended a period of worldwide declines in prices. Some of the gold accumulated as an independent balance in the Treasury's offices, and some was deposited with national banks as routine fiscal receipts. Of the gold held in Treasury offices, $150 million was required as a statutory reserve against outstanding Treasury obligations.[9] The remainder was uncommitted, and, in the absence of prescriptive legislation by Congress, its use was under the discretion of the Treasury Department.

By 1902 this gold balance had become appreciable. Secretary of the Treasury Leslie Shaw felt that it should be used to meet seasonal variations in the demand for money. Under his direction between 1902 and 1906, policies that had been used in the past were greatly enlarged and some new ones were introduced. Open market operations were not used to any great extent, except in 1902, because the volume of the national debt outstanding had become relatively small. Government securities, therefore, were at a substantial premium in the open market. In addition, they were needed by the national banks as collateral against outstanding issues of national bank notes and Treasury deposits.

---

[8]*Finance Report* (Washington, D.C.: U.S. Government Printing Office, 1894), p. LXXII.

[9]This requirement was set in the Gold Coin Act of 1900, in which the gold dollar was declared the "standard unit of value." The gold certificate requirement faced until recently by the Federal Reserve Banks was very similar.

Shaw's principal monetary policy was to deposit the Treasury's independent balances with the national banks, and to accept high-grade securities as collateral at 75 percent of their face value. Accepting nongovernment securities as collateral for Treasury deposits in national banks "freed" the government securities for use as collateral against national bank notes. Since these notes were held in great part as primary reserves of country banks, maintenance of their outstanding volume was most important.

Shaw's policy was analogous to the method the Federal Reserve System later used of increasing member bank reserves by advancing them credit on the discount of short-term commercial paper. Instead of commercial paper, the national banks operating under Shaw's plan pledged state, municipal, and other high-grade bonds; and in place of being granted Reserve Bank credit, the national banks received tangible gold and note reserves from the Treasury.

Shaw used two indexes for policy initiation: (1) short-term rates of interest in the money market and (2) the volume of reserves held by the New York national banks. When reserves in the New York banks were unusually low during the summer, credit might well be insufficient during the fall. Country correspondent banks needed their balances from New York and other reserve centers in order to meet seasonal "crop-moving" demands. Short-term rates of interest in the money market tended to become very high as banks called loans and scrambled for funds in order to fulfill their commitments in the hinterlands.

Shaw counteracted this variation in demand by letting gold accumulate in Treasury offices during the summer. These balances were then dumped into the New York banks in the fall, and subsequently were bled off in the winter. This method was followed in 1903 and again in 1906.

Ordinarily Treasury action could provide $25-75 million as additional national bank reserves. In 1906, for example, Treasury deposits in national banks increased by $72 million, or by 10 percent of existing reserves. National banks held about two thirds of total bank reserves, but also furnished reserves to nonnational banks. On net balance, total monetary variation through seasonal Treasury policies was on the order of 10 percent.

Shaw's policies were almost universally criticized by economists and business journalists of his day. Most economists felt that he had strained the law and exercised unwarranted discretion.[10] In his own defense Shaw correctly pointed out that the policy of the Treasury Department for more than half a century had been to anticipate monetary stringencies and, so far as possible, to prevent financial panics. Panics, he thought, were to be put into the same category as pestilences, the difference being that the former caused more hardship. He was moved to an official statement in 1906 that reflected a high

---

[10]For a more detailed discussion of Shaw's policies and the position of his critics, see Richard H. Timberlake, Jr., "Secretary Shaw and His Critics: Monetary Policy in the Golden Era Reviewed," *Quarterly Journal of Economics*, Vol. 77, No. 1 (February 1963), pp. 40–54.

degree of sophistication in the conduct of monetary policy. If the Secretary of the Treasury, he said,

> were given $100 million [in gold] to be deposited with the banks or withdrawn as he might deem expedient, and if in addition he were clothed with authority over the reserves of the several banks, with power to contract the national bank circulation at pleasure, in my judgement no panic as distinguished from industrial stagnation could threaten either the United States or Europe that he could not avert.[11]

In spite of his confidence in the monetary policies he had furthered, Shaw was a conservative Middle Western banker who believed wholeheartedly in the gold standard. He never presumed that he could counter a persistent drain of gold; he was only confident of results for the short run, that is, in the efficacy of monetary policy to offset seasonal variations in the demand for money.

His critics not only favored the gold standard in the same light as did Shaw, they also felt that the money market, similar to any other market in a relatively laissez faire economy, could better regulate itself. They did not distinguish money from other things; they did not allow for the aggravating effects of fractional reserve banking on the credit structure; and, worst of all, they complained of the disturbing monetary effects that the fiscal actions of the Treasury might provoke, while in the same breath they disallowed it to use limited discretion in order to prevent such trouble. If some agency had to be given power over monetary affairs, asked one critic, to whom should this power be given?

> To an irresponsible treasury official, or to the banking institutions of the country, which are in close touch with business conditions? Is not the Treasury *ex natura* in a position where it cannot possibly know the banking needs of the country, since it is not in contact with the world of trade?[12]

Conservative opinion of the time thus had a common focal point: opposition to the active monetary policies sponsored by the Treasury. On the other hand, this same conservative element had long recognized the inelasticity of currency and credit in responding to the needs of business. The organization the conservatives would form that could satisfy these two constraints had to be a privately owned institution with a centralized and mobilized reserve available to commercial banks at times of duress. Such an agency was the original Federal Reserve System of twelve banks.

---

[11]*Finance Report* (Washington, D.C.: U.S. Government Printing Office, 1906), p. 49.

[12]Eugene B. Patton, "Secretary Shaw and Precedents as to Treasury Control over the Money Market," *Journal of Political Economy,* Vol. 15 (February 1907), p. 86. Another academic critic, David Kinley, made almost exactly the same criticism.

Selected Bibliography

Bagehot, Walter. *Lombard Street: A Description of the Money Market.* London: Kegan Paul, 1906 (originally published in 1873). Bank of England policies and problems are analyzed very vividly.

Friedman, Milton, and Anna Jacobson Schwartz. *A Monetary History of the United States, 1867–1960.* Princeton, N.J.: Princeton University Press, 1963.

The Gold Panic. 41st Congress, 2nd sess., House Report No. 31, James A. Garfield, Chairman, Washington, D.C., 1870. The congressional investigation of the "Black Friday" gold price break of September 24, 1869.

Hepburn, A. Barton. *A History of Currency in the United States.* New York: Macmillan Co., 1924.

Sharkey, Robert P. *Money, Class, and Party.* Baltimore, Md.: Johns Hopkins Press, 1959. An excellent treatise on Civil War and post–Civil War monetary developments.

Timberlake, Richard H., Jr. "Mr. Shaw and His Critics: Monetary Policy in the Golden Era Reviewed." *Quarterly Journal of Economics,* Vol. 77, No. 2 (February 1963), pp. 40–54.

Lombard Street

Walter Bagehot

This selection from Lombard Street, *was written by the great English man of letters Walter Bagehot (1826–1877) and published in 1873. In this passage from Chapter 7, "The Bank's Administration of the Reserve," Bagehot critically assays Bank of England policies. He further argues for the particular policy that came to be known as "Bagehot's Rule": During a bank panic or crisis, the central bank should lend freely but at high rates of interest.*

Nothing, therefore, can be more certain than that the Bank of England has in this respect no peculiar privilege; that it is simply in the position of a Bank keeping the banking reserve of the country; that it must in time of panic do what all other similar banks must do; that in time of panic it must advance freely and vigorously to the public out of the reserve.

From *Lombard Street* by Walter Bagehot, 1873.

And with the Bank of England, as with other banks in the same case, these advances, if they are to be made at all, should be made so as, if possible, to obtain the object for which they are made. The end is to stay the panic; and the advances should, if possible, stay the panic. And for this purpose there are two rules.

First. That these loans should only be made at a very high rate of interest. This will operate as a heavy fine on unreasonable timidity, and will prevent the greatest number of applications by persons who do not require it. The rate should be raised early in the panic, so that the fine may be paid early; that no one may borrow out of idle precaution without paying well for it; that the banking reserve may be protected as far as possible.

Secondly. That at this rate these advances should be made on all good banking securities, and as largely as the public ask for them. The reason is plain. The object is to stay alarm, and nothing, therefore, should be done to cause alarm. But the way to cause alarm is to refuse some one who has good security to offer. The news of this will spread in an instant through all the Money Market at a moment of terror; no one can say exactly who carries it, but in half an hour it will be carried on all sides, and will intensify the terror everywhere. No advances indeed need be made by which the Bank will ultimately lose. The amount of bad business in commercial countries is an infinitesimally small fraction of the whole business. That in a panic the bank, or banks, holding the ultimate reserve should refuse bad bills or bad securities will not make the panic really worse; the 'unsound' people are a feeble minority, and they are afraid even to look frightened for fear their unsoundness may be detected. The great majority, the majority to be protected, are the 'sound' people, the people who have good security to offer. If it is known that the Bank of England is freely advancing on what in ordinary times is reckoned a good security—on what is then commonly pledged and easily convertible—the alarm of the solvent merchants and bankers will be stayed. But if securities, really good and usually convertible, are refused by the Bank, the alarm will not abate, the other loans made will fail in obtaining their end, and the panic will become worse and worse.

It may be said that the reserve in the Banking Department will not be enough for all such loans. If that be so, the Banking Department must fail. But lending is, nevertheless, its best expedient. This is the method of making its money go the farthest, and of enabling it to get through the panic if anything will so enable it. Making no loans, as we have seen, will ruin it; making large loans and stopping, as we have also seen, will ruin it. The only safe plan for the Bank is the brave plan, to lend in a panic on every kind of current security, or every sort on which money is ordinarily and usually lent. This policy may not save the Bank; but if it do not, nothing will save it....

As we have seen, principle requires that such advances, if made at all for the purpose of curing panic, should be made in the manner most likely to cure that panic. And for this purpose, they should be made on everything which in common times is good 'banking security'. The evil is that, owing to terror, what is commonly good security has ceased to be so; and the true policy is so to use the banking reserve that if possible the temporary evil may be stayed, and the common course of business be restored. And this can only be effected by advancing on all good banking securities.

Unfortunately, the Bank of England does not take this course. The Discount Office is open for the discount of good bills, and makes immense advances accordingly. The Bank also advances on Consols and India securities, though there was, in the crisis of 1866, believed to be for a moment a hesitation in so doing. But these are only a small part of the securities on which money in ordinary times can be readily obtained, and by which its repayment is fully secured. Railway debenture stock is as good a security as a commercial bill, and many people, of whom I own I am one, think it safer than India stock; on the whole, a great railway is, I think, less liable to unforeseen accidents than the strange Empire of India. But I doubt if the Bank of England in a panic would advance on the railway debenture stock; at any rate no one has any authorised reason for saying that it would. And there are many other such securities.

The *amount* of the advance is the main consideration for the Bank of England, and not the nature of the security on which the advance is made, always assuming the security to be good. An idea prevails (as I believe) at the Bank of England that they ought not to advance during a panic on any kind of security on which they do not commonly advance. But if bankers for the most part do advance on such security in common times, and if that security is indisputably good, the ordinary practice of the Bank of England is immaterial. In ordinary times the Bank is only one of many lenders, whereas in a panic it is the sole lender; and we want, as far as we can, to bring back the unusual state of a time of panic to the common state of ordinary times.

In common opinion there is always great uncertainty as to the conduct of the Bank: the Bank has never laid down any clear and sound policy on the subject. As we have seen, some of its directors (like Mr. Hankey) advocate an erroneous policy. The public is never sure what policy will be adopted at the most important moment; it is not sure what amount of advance will be made, or on what security it will be made. The best palliative to a panic is a confidence in the adequate amount of the Bank reserve and in the efficient use of that reserve. And until we have on this point a clear understanding with the Bank of England, both our liability to crises and our terror at crises will always be greater than they would otherwise be.

19

Structure of the
Federal Reserve System

Original Concept of the Federal Reserve System

The contemporary Federal Reserve System is a central banking institution that can provide all the elasticity to the money supply needed to fulfill various policy objectives. Its original purpose, however, was to furnish only form-seasonal elasticity; an expanding gold base supposedly took care of secular needs.

The lack of form elasticity, that is, the inability of the monetary system to provide a ready conversion of demand deposits into currency without undue change in the total quantity of money, was held largely responsible for the monetary panics of 1857, 1873, 1884, and 1893. The crisis of 1907 was supposedly the last straw and led to an acute demand for a centralized, reserve-holding institution that would adjust the supply of currency and credit to the "needs" of business. The institution finally agreed upon was a central banking system that would absorb reserve moneys during ordinary times and supply these reserves to banks during seasons of excessive demand for money and credit.

Just as important as the positive sentiment of the times pointing toward a central bank was the negative attitude toward the Treasury. The "interferences" of the Treasury in the money market were repudiated. Accordingly, the central bank was supposed to be "independent" of politics, to be operated largely by bankers with overall governmental supervision, to follow the principles of the commercial credit theory of banking, but to function largely automatically and with very little discretion. Its chief weapon of control was to be the discount rate. Generally, this rate would be raised when business was booming in order to prevent the boom from becoming an inflation, and lowered during a recession to stimulate bank credit and recovery.

One other discretionary control given to the System, and often overlooked, was the application of the "eligibility" principle. Commercial paper, to be eligible for discount by a Federal Reserve Bank, was supposed to have the "real bills" qualities long since sanctified as proper and respectable for commercial banks. In the words of the Federal Reserve Act, it was paper presumed to have arisen "out of actual commercial transactions . . . [and] issued or drawn for agricultural, industrial, or commercial purposes. [Moreover], the Board of Governors of the Federal Reserve System . . . have the right *to determine or define* the character of the paper thus eligible for discount."[1] Notes "secured by staple agricultural products" were eligible, but paper issued for "trading in stocks, bonds, or other investment securities" was not eligible. Finally, maturity of the paper had to be "not more than 90 days, exclusive of grace." The power of the Board to define eligibility of commercial paper and the power of each regional Reserve Bank to pass judgment on given requests by member banks for discount meant that the discount rate would not exclusively ration central bank credit.

Nevertheless, the System was supposed to be passive. Though it had discretion to set discount rates and to say what paper was eligible for discount, it was thought of as a standby agency, one that would act only when called upon to do so. It was a servant of the banks, a banker's bank. It was also a debtor of the banks because their reserves were deposited (centralized) in the twelve Reserve Banks. It was, as well, out of politics, a quasi-scientific organization that would respond to the short-term ebb and flow of business the way the gold standard responded in a long-run sense. In the eyes of its sponsors it required very little in the way of political checks and balances. This image of the Federal Reserve System was given more substance by the superficial fact that it was a privately owned institution, that is, "owned" by the "member" banks.

The conceptual limitations on the original Federal Reserve blueprint were not oversights; the institution was created within a monetary framework ruled by a gold standard. To have ordered the newly created central bank to undertake the functions it has assumed or been granted during the last 35 years would have been regarded as sacrilege.

The original concept of the Federal Reserve System as a loosely federated group of twelve banks, with each regional bank largely autonomous in its

---

[1]Legal Division of the Board of Governors of the Federal Reserve System, *The Federal Reserve Act* (approved December 23, 1913), as amended through November 5, 1966 (Washington, D.C.: Board of Governors of the Federal Reserve System), Section 13, pp. 43–44. (Italics supplied.)

powers to make executive and policy decisions, has never been realized. The System is most usefully regarded as a unified institution. Only administrative details are left to the individual Reserve Banks. Such unification is, of course, logical because the U.S. economy is more of an economic entity than it is a group of heterogeneous regions. Just the fact that the economy uses a single monetary unit of account, the dollar, argues for a unified central bank.

Evolution of the Central Bank's Administrative Power Structure

The power structure of the Federal Reserve System is complex because the administrative role of the Reserve Banks has never been rigorously segregated from the policy-making function. Each Reserve Bank has a board of nine directors who are chosen according to a statutory formula prescribed in the Federal Reserve Act. The Board of Governors is a superboard of directors consisting of seven men appointed by the President of the United States. Each member has a term of fourteen years, but the terms are staggered so that a vacancy occurs every two years. The Board of Governors chooses the chairman of the Board of Directors for each Reserve Bank, but each Reserve Bank's Board of Directors chooses its own president and vice president subject to the approval of the Board of Governors. (See Figure 19.1.)

Figure 19.1. Organization of the Federal Reserve System

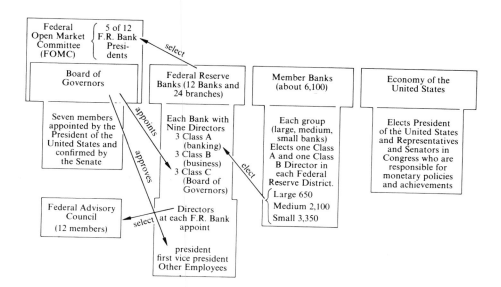

The individual Reserve Banks handle most of the administrative details for the member banks in their respective districts, such as check-clearing operations and currency movements, while the Board of Governors generally controls all important policy matters. In the early years of the System, the only policy at the discretion of the Board was the discount rate at the Reserve Banks; and even this power was originally held by the Reserve Banks themselves, the Board having only the power of "review and determination." In fact, the discount rate almost always has been consistent throughout the System, whether the Board directly controlled the rate or not.

The President appoints the Governors, but he does not have direct control over them as he does, say, over members of his Cabinet. The Board reports to Congress. Furthermore, a Governor's term in office and the staggering of appointments means that a President would have to be in office almost eight years before he could appoint a majority of members to the Board. Even the Chairman's term of four years is not coterminous with that of the President, and no tradition has grown of a Chairman offering his resignation when a new President takes office.

But Congress, too, finds that it has little effective control over the policy decisions of the System. This situation has prompted one congressman to claim that the Federal Reserve System has seceded from the federal government. According to him, the United States now has four branches of government — executive, legislative, judicial, and Federal Reserve System.

These incongruencies emphasize the lag between growth in the functions of the central bank and the original jurisdictional structure within which it was conceived. In the beginning, the central bank was private; it did not make policy that was all-important; its decisions were much less controversial than they are today. In fact, in many ways the Federal Reserve System has evolved into the kind of power structure that it was supposed to supplant (i.e., the Treasury). It is not, however, as independent of presidential, congressional, and public pressures and control as the above discussion might indicate. The Chairman of the Board of Governors frequently meets with presidential aides, principally the Secretary of the Treasury and the Council of Economic Advisers. Exchanges of information and views can lead to coordination and cooperation, but they may also lead to improper pressures of a political nature on the central bank. Congressional committees also call the members of the Board of Governors and Federal Reserve Bank presidents to testify as expert witnesses on the monetary state of the economy. In these hearings exchanges of information and suggestions take place, and some pressure may be applied when the System has made what seem to be impolitic or unpopular decisions.

Prior to 1935, members of the Board of Governors were perhaps too well schooled in the needs of the banking system and not so much aware of their responsibilities to the economy as a whole. As recently as the early 1950s one "mossback," as some of the older political appointees were known, was overheard asking a staff economist what that "GNP thing" was that people kept mentioning. The contemporary Board has more professional economists on it, although bankers and lawyers are also represented.

The Federal Open Market Committee (FOMC) is composed of the Board of Governors and five of the twelve Federal Reserve Bank presidents. It is responsible for managing the System's portfolio of government securities, bankers' acceptances, and foreign currencies in order to stabilize the monetary sector of the economy. The original Federal Reserve Act made no provision for the FOMC. Federal Reserve Banks were authorized to purchase and sell limited quantities of government securities, but they were not aware of the implications of such activities for economic stabilization. In fact, the first sizable open market purchases were made in 1922 in order to increase the earnings of the Federal Reserve Banks. The obvious impact of this action on member bank reserves prompted formation of an *ad hoc* committee composed of five presidents of the eastern Reserve Banks to coordinate such operations. Changes in the composition of the committee were made during the following years. The Banking Act of 1935 placed the seven Governors on the committee and officially vested the power of open market operations in the committee's hands. The president of the Federal Reserve Bank of New York is permanently on the committee because open market operations are conducted through that bank. The remaining Federal Reserve Bank presidents serve on a yearly rotating basis.

Federal Open Market Committee meetings take place in Washington about every four weeks. In addition to the Governors, all of the Federal Reserve Bank presidents usually attend. Others in attendance include the open market account manager, a special manager for foreign currency operations, legal counsel, secretaries, staff economists, and vice presidents or economists from each Federal Reserve Bank. In the days immediately prior to the meeting, the presidents and Governors receive publications from the Board's staff. The "Blue Book," the "Green Book," and supplements update them on current economic trends and events. Similarly, they receive a series of reports on the activities of the account manager and the minutes of the most recent FOMC meeting.

When the meeting itself is opened, various reports are presented. The open market account manager reviews domestic trading in government securities, the special account manager reports on foreign currency operations, and senior staff economists report on the real, financial, and international aspects of the economy. Then the discussion begins. Starting with the president of the Federal Reserve Bank of New York, each president and Governor has the opportunity to question staff economists, make a statement on the condition of the economy, and advance his own recommendations. In this way the FOMC serves as a forum where the appropriate policies for all of the System's tools of control can be discussed. The chairman of the committee, who is also the Chairman of the Board of Governors, is usually the last to speak. He presents his own views and then composes a consensus statement encompassing the views of the whole committee.

After the consensus statement, the official directive to the Federal Reserve Bank of New York for domestic open market operations—the Current Economic Policy Directive—is either reaffirmed or changed. This directive reflects the current thinking and wishes of the FOMC and is supposed to convey to the New York Bank and the account manager just what action the committee wants taken. Voting is recorded on this action. The Continuing Authority Directive, which limits the types and maturities of securities that may be traded by the manager, is changed much less frequently. Further discussions on foreign currency operations may follow.

Committee decisions are carried out by the open market account manager. FOMC policy is translated into the actual purchase and sale of government securities through the "trading desk" located in the New York Bank. Contact is maintained with major government securities dealers, numbering perhaps eighteen to 24, in the New York money market. When the manager wishes to sell securities, he sells to those dealers currently bidding the highest prices; similarly, he purchases from those dealers offering securities at the lowest prices. The reserve balances of New York commercial banks are immediately affected when the checks written in payment for the securities are deposited. Then the effects quickly spread as the securities dealers trade with other regions.

Each Federal Reserve Bank shares in purchases or sales depending on its proportional share of gold certificate holdings, which are in turn apportioned on the basis of the average amount of Federal Reserve notes it has outstanding on the last five business days of the month. Indirectly, therefore, security purchases or sales are allocated among the Reserve Banks on the basis of their Federal Reserve notes outstanding.

Many, if not most, of the activities of the open market account are designed to offset what might be disruptive short-run movements in member bank reserves. Bank reserves are affected by such factors as Treasury tax collections and disbursements, the public's demand for currency—especially during holidays—and changes in "float."[2] Defensive operations are designed to counter such fluctuations. For example, if a rise in float is anticipated, the account manager may sell securities in order to keep bank reserves from rising more than a nominal amount.

---

[2]The Federal Reserve System does not give immediate credit for all checks deposited with it for collection. If, however, after a certain period of time (maximum of two days) a check has not cleared, the Federal Reserve debits the depositing bank's reserve account even though the reserves of the bank on which the check was drawn have not been reduced. This item is termed "deferred availability cash items." Its counterpart on the asset side of the balance sheet is "cash items in the process of collection"—checks deposited but not yet "mature" enough to obtain "deferred availability" status. The difference between these two items is known as "float."

Another aspect of System activity, "dynamic operations," is aimed at countering long-run cyclical forces in order to achieve relatively stable prices, a high level of output and income, and a reasonable balance in international payments. These goals are taken from the Full Employment Act of 1946. Net buying of securities by the account manager in order to increase the level of member bank reserves is an example of such operations. In practice the two operations or responsibilities are difficult to separate because defensive and dynamic needs may at times coincide and at other times conflict.

Open market operations are considered to be the most important tool of control used by the System. It is both flexible and powerful; it carries no announcement effect; and it is undertaken at the initiative of the Federal Reserve System. The FOMC, however, has been subject to much criticism. It is said to be too large for effective decision making, and its composition is open to question. Perhaps the most challenging criticisms are that the FOMC at times may use the wrong targets and indicators, and that at other times it may be swayed more by what is fiscally expedient for the administration than by what is good for the economy. A fuller discussion of this problem is reserved for Chapter 29.

The Federal Advisory Council is another group within the Federal Reserve System. It consists of twelve members, one from each Federal Reserve District, who are selected by the directors of the banks in their districts. They serve a one-year term and have only advisory power. The council meets in Washington at least four times a year and confers with the Board of Governors on general business conditions. It can make written or oral recommendations on the activities of the System.

Although the council adds to the decentralized image of the Federal Reserve System, it has only the power of suggestion. Perhaps the most condemning criticism of the council is that it is useless. The minutes of the FOMC from 1951 to 1960 give no indication that the council's recommendations were brought into the FOMC discussion or used in any way. Even if the council had any value or power, its composition could also be criticized on the ground that only bankers seem to serve on it. Since general business conditions are within its province for discussion, representatives of other groups should be included in its deliberations. In any case, the intent of the original Federal Reserve Act was to give the council the role of special adviser to the Board of Governors. In large measure, the FOMC has absorbed this function, leaving the council without any function.

The Administration of Federal Reserve Banks

Perhaps in no other part of the System is decentralization so much a reality as in the actual administration of the Federal Reserve Banks. Each Bank has nine directors, six of whom are selected by the member banks of that district. The directors are grouped into three categories: Class A directors, who may be from banking; Class B directors, who must be engaged in agriculture, commerce, or some industrial activity in the district, and who may not be associated with a commercial bank; and Class C directors, who also may not be associated with a commercial bank, and who are appointed by the Board of Governors. The small member banks in the district select one Class A and one Class B director, and the medium-sized and the large banks of the district do likewise. The Board of Governors also designates one of the Class C directors as chairman and another as deputy chairman. The directors in turn appoint the Federal Reserve Bank president and the first vice president, subject to the approval of the Board of Governors.

Decentralization was supposed to avoid the aggregation of power in the hands of one "central bank" or central banker, but this principle has not worked. Nor is there any evidence that it could work. At the outset there was a struggle for power between the Federal Reserve Bank of New York and the Board of Governors.[3] In the 1930s, the focus of power shifted decidedly to the Board of Governors, and today the Federal Reserve Banks and their directors perform little more than administrative and service operations—as opposed to policy-making functions. The power of open market operations, most notably, was centralized in the 1930s by placing the Board of Governors on the FOMC, leaving the Reserve Bank presidents in the minority, and by making FOMC decisions binding on all of the Banks. Though the directors of each Bank still meet dutifully to vote on the discount rate, their decision is subject to the "review and determination" (with emphasis on the "determination") by the Board of Governors. The real discussion of the rate takes place in FOMC meetings, and the final decision on its level is in fact in the hands of the Board of Governors.

Federally chartered (national) banks are required to become members of the Federal Reserve System, while state-chartered banks have the option of joining or not. All members are subject to certain obligations. They must meet the operating regulations of the System, such as redeeming their checks at par, conform to System reserve requirements, and follow certain administrative practices. Also, they must purchase stock in the Federal Reserve Bank of their district equal to 3 percent of their own capital and surplus with another 3

---

[3]The Board of Governors was originally conceived of as nothing much more than a liaison body between the several Banks and the federal government. It had almost no policy-making powers.

percent subject to call. In return, member banks are extended certain privileges. They may borrow from their District Reserve Bank, use System check-clearing facilities, obtain currency for reserve accounts when needed, use the wire service and other informational facilities of the System, elect Reserve Bank directors, and receive 6 percent cumulative statutory dividends on their paid-in Federal Reserve stock. Even though slightly less than one half of the nation's commercial banks are members of the Federal Reserve System, member banks account for over 82 percent of the total value of commercial bank deposits. Thus, policy actions directly affect the bulk of the means of payment in the economy. In addition, nonmember correspondent banks indirectly feel the effects through their normal borrowing, loan sharing, and correspondent relationships with members.

Functions of the Federal Reserve System

Three broad categories or functions of the Federal Reserve System can be observed — public service, bank supervision, and economic stabilization. The System serves member banks, the United States Treasury Department, foreign central banks and governments, and the general public. It acts as a fiscal agent for the federal government; that is, it, along with a large segment of the commercial banking system, maintains the Treasury's deposit accounts. Tax receipts, when called from the tax and loan accounts deposited in commercial banks, flow into the Treasury's account with the Fed and are then used by the Treasury to pay government debts. The Fed also assists the Treasury in floating certain securities — for example, the Treasury bill (see Chapter 12, "Instruments of the Money Market"). Postal money orders are cleared through Federal Reserve Banks, and foreign central banks also maintain checking accounts with the Fed.

Federal Reserve Banks are sometimes called bankers' banks. Just as the public may keep deposits with and borrow from commercial banks, so bankers may do the same thing with Reserve Banks. Other administrative services to commercial bankers were mentioned earlier in this chapter.

Research is another important service of the System. Each Federal Reserve Bank has a staff of economists who analyze economic conditions in their district. Monthly publications on district business conditions are available to the public from each of the Banks.

The Board of Governors also maintains a staff of research economists. Operational types of research are performed, for example, to find ways that would permit checks to be cleared faster, to investigate the implications of the growth and use of credit cards, and to review the possible development of electronic payments mechanisms. Other economists analyze current economic

Figure 19.2. Boundaries of the Federal Reserve Districts and Their Branch Territories

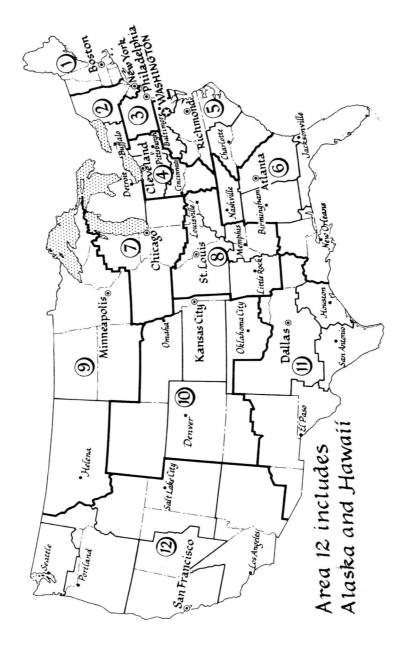

Area 12 includes Alaska and Hawaii

Source: Board of Governors of the Federal Reserve System, *Federal Reserve Bulletins.*

trends for the Board of Governors and the FOMC. More recently, System economists have been doing basic research on how monetary policy works. The recent Federal Reserve–MIT model is an example of this research.[4] Some of the research, most notably that of the Federal Reserve Bank of St. Louis, has answered controversial questions that did not conform to the current doctrine of the FOMC and the Board's staff.

Supervision of member banks is another important function. Members wishing to merge, branch, or otherwise change their structure must obtain approval of the Board of Governors. Examinations of state-chartered member banks are regularly conducted.[5] In addition, the System supervises the administration of certain regulations, such as "truth in lending" and margin loans for the purchase of common stocks.

Table 19.1. Tools of Control of the Federal Reserve System

Tool of Control	Component of the Federal Reserve System Responsible for the Tool
Quantitative or general controls	
Open market operations	Federal Open Market Committee
Reserve requirements	Board of Governors (within the range specified by Congress)
Discount rate	Directors of each of the Federal Reserve Banks (subject to review and determination by the Board of Governors)
Quantitative or selective controls	
Margin requirements	Board of Governors
Mortgage credit controls	the Board of Governors when granted by Congress—not presently in use
Consumer credit controls	the Board of Governors when granted by Congress—not presently in use
Other	
Moral suasion	any part of the System
Regulation Q	Board of Governors

---

[4] See Frank de Leeuw and Edward Gramlich, "The Federal Reserve–MIT Econometric Model," *Federal Reserve Bulletin,* Vol. 54, No. 1 (January 1968), pp. 11–40.

[5] A division of labor is strived for in bank examination. The Office of the Comptroller of the Currency examines national banks, the Federal Reserve System and the state examiners examine state-chartered member banks, and the FDIC and state examiners examine state-chartered nonmember banks. The results of the examinations are available to any agency with a legitimate interest.

From the standpoint of the economy as a whole, economic (or monetary) stabilization is probably the most important function. Through the use of all its tools, the Federal Reserve System is supposed to promote a healthy expanding economy, reasonable price stability, a low level of unemployment, and a reasonable balance in international payments. Although the implementation of policy is delegated to various parts of the System (see Table 19.1), the FOMC and the Board serve as focal points for generating and coordinating policy decisions. Not only is the System charged with domestic stabilization, but its decisions must also reflect an awareness of international trade and payments problems.

Selected Bibliography

Carson, Deane. "Is the Federal Reserve System Really Necessary?" *Journal of Finance,* Vol. 19 (August 1955), pp. 321–342.

Clifford, A. Jerome. *The Independence of the Federal Reserve System.* Philadelphia: University of Pennsylvania Press, 1965.

Hastings, Delbert C., and Ross M. Robertson. "The Mysterious World of the Fed." *Business Horizons,* Vol. 5 (Spring 1962), pp. 97–104.

Keir, Peter M. "The Open Market Policy Process." *Federal Reserve Bulletin,* Vol. 49 (October 1963), pp. 1,359–1,370.

Meek, Paul. *Open Market Operations.* New York: Federal Reserve Bank of New York, 1964.

Reagan, Michael D. "The Political Structure of the Federal Reserve System." *American Political Science Review,* Vol. 55 (March 1961), pp. 64–76.

Wayne, Edward A. *Come with Me to the F.O.M.C.!* Richmond, Va.: Federal Reserve Bank of Richmond, 1967.

Impacts of Theory on Policy:
The Early Years of the Federal Reserve

Lester V. Chandler

Students of money and banking often question the need for studying theory. The following article, by Professor Lester Chandler of Princeton University, portrays the tremendous importance of ideas and theories as guides for policy. But Professor Chandler's message is the negative counterpart of this principle: how adherence to the commercial bank theory of lending prevented positive and effective monetary policies from being applied by the central bank to retard and reverse the course of the Great Depression.

Professor Chandler is well known in the profession as the author of several excellent studies on monetary policy. He originally wrote this article for the book Men, Money, and Policy: Essays in Honor of Karl R. Bopp, *edited by David P. Eastburn and published by the Federal Reserve Bank of Philadelphia (1970). It very accurately conveys the characteristics of central bank philosophy and policy during the period 1919–1932.*

...the ideas of economists and political philosophers, both when they are right and when they are wrong, are more powerful than is commonly understood. Indeed the world is ruled by little else. Practical men, who believe themselves to be quite exempt from any intellectual influences, are usually the slave of some defunct economist.[1]

J. M. Keynes

The Federal Reserve Act was clearly not designed to create a monetary agency with ample powers for controlling the stock of money in accordance with any rational objective, although some of the provisions of the Act are not wholly unsuited to such a purpose.[2]

Lloyd W. Mints

How different the original Federal Reserve Act would have been if it had been based on some sort of quantity theory of money, and how different might have been the speed, if not the direction, of evolution of Federal Reserve policies! The Act would undoubtedly have referred repeatedly to the supply of money and to regulation of its quantity in line with the needs of the economy for money balances. And a natural line of evolution would have been to use Federal Reserve powers ever more positively to stabilize price levels, or perhaps to regulate some specific flow of expenditures, such as MV. However,

From *Men, Money, and Policy: Essays in Honor of Karl L. Bopp,* David P. Eastburn, ed., Federal Reserve Bank of Philadelphia (1970), pp. 41–53.

[1]*The General Theory of Employment, Interest and Money* (New York: Harcourt, Brace and Company, 1936), p. 383.

[2]*A History of Banking Theory* (Chicago: University of Chicago Press, 1945), p. 281.

the Act was based not on a type of quantity theory but on a commercial loan theory of banking, and its prime concern was not with money but with credit. A major purpose was to adjust credit to "the needs of trade" as evidenced by demands for commercial loans, not to adjust the supply of money to the economy's demand for money balances; its infrequent references to quantities were to the quantity of credit, not that of money; and it emphasized the "quality" of credit.

Though, as many of them claimed, other Congressional leaders influenced the new legislation; the original Federal Reserve Act bore the unmistakable imprint of Carter Glass and of his closest advisor on banking affairs, H. Parker Willis, the most unbending and best-known commercial loan theorist of the period. Nor did their adherence to the commercial loan theory or their influence end with the passage of the Act. For example, Senator Glass declared in 1931 that the Federal Reserve Act would never have permitted the Reserve Banks to lend on Government security collateral if its proponents had not believed that the Federal debt would continue to decline.[3] During the next year he agreed only reluctantly and under strong pressure to permit Government securities to serve as collateral for Federal Reserve notes, and he tolerated an amendment broadening the Federal Reserve's lending power only on condition that the ineligible paper not be used as collateral for Federal Reserve notes. Even at that late date Willis was still inveighing against "artificial" easing through Federal Reserve purchases of Government securities and was advocating passive adjustment of credit to the "needs of trade."

Many provisions of the Federal Reserve Act betray its origin in commercial loan ideas. The two enumerated purposes of the new System, other than to provide a more effective supervision of banking, were to furnish an elastic currency and to afford means of rediscounting commercial paper. Even the provision of an elastic currency was basically a credit rather than a monetary reform; its basic purpose was to prevent currency flows into and out of the banking system from having adverse effects on credit conditions. Only types of paper conforming to the commercial loan theory were eligible for discount at the Federal Reserve—"notes, drafts, and bills of exchange arising out of actual commercial transactions; that is, notes, drafts, and bills of exchange issued or drawn for agricultural, industrial, or commercial purposes, or the proceeds of which have been used, or are to be used, for such purposes...." Only such paper and Federal securities were eligible as collateral for Federal Reserve advances. Specifically excluded were "notes, drafts, or bills covering merely investments or issued or drawn for the purpose of carrying or trading in stocks, bonds, or other investment securities, except bonds and notes of the Government of the United States." As examples *par excellence* of commercial loans, acceptances were given favored treatment; member banks were permitted to create them on the basis of "real transactions," and they were

---

[3]*Hearings on S. Res.* 71, 71st Congress, 3rd Session (Jan. 20, 1931), p. 53.

made eligible for purchase by the Reserve Banks. This, it was believed, would both adapt credit to the legitimate needs of trade and divert loan funds away from the stock market. To provide an appropriate elasticity of Federal Reserve notes to the needs of trade, they should be collateraled only by gold and eligible paper.

Thus the Federal Reserve Act clearly favored types of paper conforming to the commercial loan theory, intended that the Federal Reserve should issue and withdraw funds primarily by dealing in such paper, and implied rather vaguely that the System could control the use of funds created by it by regulating the types of assets acquired. However, the Act provided but little guidance concerning the amounts of funds to be provided or withdrawn, or the general principles which should guide discounting. Such guidance as was implied suggested a policy of more or less passive accommodation of "the needs of trade." For example, it stressed "elasticity" of Federal Reserve notes and provided that discount rates should "be fixed with a view of accommodating commerce and business." The following statement by Governor Norris, of the Federal Reserve Bank of Philadelphia, in September 1930, was not an unreasonable interpretation of the intent of the Act.

> We have always believed that the proper function of the System was well expressed in the Tenth Annual Report of the Federal Reserve Board—"The Federal Reserve supplies the needed additions to credit in times of business expansion and takes up the slack in times of business recession." We have therefore necessarily found ourselves out of harmony with the policy recently followed of supplying unneeded additions to credit in a time of business recession, which is the exact antithesis of the rule above stated.[4]

In view of the basic theory of the Act, it is ironic that the first large-scale provision of funds—that during the World War I period, 1917–1920—did not conform to the commercial loan theory at all. The Reserve Banks supplied funds not on the basis of commercial paper but on the basis of Government securities, and their prime purpose was not to "accommodate commerce and business" but to accommodate the borrowing needs of the Treasury. However, at the end of this episode commercial loan ideas again came to the fore and for the next decade and a half vied with new ideas for supremacy.

Commercial loan ideas, with their emphasis on the "quality" of credit, were one reason, though not the only one, for the deflationary policies of 1920–1921. Both Federal Reserve and commercial bank credit based on Government securities, which did not reflect "the needs of trade," should be eliminated in order to restore "normal" conditions. Many Federal Reserve officials accepted the definition of "normal" offered by Governor Seay, of the Federal Reserve Bank of Richmond, in October, 1920.

---

[4]Except where indicated otherwise, quotations are from records and memoranda in Federal Reserve archives.

...It would probably be fair to say that a normal credit condition exists when bank loans are made very largely, and loans from Reserve banks entirely, for the purpose of producing, purchasing, carrying, or marketing goods in one or more steps in the process of production, manufacture, and distribution.

The rise of open market operations in Government securities as a major policy instrument after 1922, sponsored primarily by Governor Benjamin Strong and his colleagues at the Federal Reserve Bank of New York, challenged the basic tenets of the commercial loans policy prescriptions in at least two ways. For one thing, such operations supplied Federal Reserve funds not on the basis of paper arising out of "real transactions" but on the basis of Government debt. Also, they supplied funds not in response to "the needs of trade" as reflected in applications for discounts but on the initiative of the Federal Reserve itself. They were "forcible insertions" or "forcible withdrawals," which were likely to lead to "artificial credit conditions," especially if purchases were made when "the needs of trade" were declining or if sales occurred when "the needs of trade" were rising. The fact that large Federal Reserve operations in Government securities did occur during the remainder of the 1920s might be viewed as an unqualified victory of the new concept of positive control on the initiative of the Federal Reserve over the older concept of accommodation of "the needs of trade." However, commercial loan ideas were by no means dead, and they continued to influence thinking, attitudes, and policies.

Neither open market operations in Government securities nor the positive use of Federal Reserve powers to promote stability of prices and business conditions enjoyed full support within the System. How numerous and strong were the dissents did not become fully apparent before the 1930s, though objections were voiced earlier. For example, Governor Roy A. Young, Governor of the Federal Reserve Board, stated in 1928 that the primary concern of the System should be to maintain "a healthy banking situation" and that "it would be unfortunate if the Federal Reserve System were to be charged with still further responsibilities which are not directly related to banking, such as responsibility for the stability of the general price level or for moderation of ups and downs in business conditions."[5] In the early 1930s, as Governor of the Federal Reserve Bank of Boston, he consistently opposed purchases of Government securities and favored allowing credit to adjust to the declining "needs of trade." Adolph C. Miller, another member of the Board, was generally unfavorable to open market operations until the depression had been under way for more than a year. He stated in early 1931: "I believe that our troubles will be enormously minimized—in fact I think we will pretty nearly get rid of most of them—if the Federal Reserve banks are operated as institutions of rediscount."[6]

---

[5]*Journal of the American Bankers Association*, October 1928, Vol. XXI, p. 281.
[6]*Hearings on S. Res.* 71 (January 23, 1931), p. 150.

The commercial loan theory, or at least ideas consistent with that theory, continued to appear in various other ways during the remainder of the 1920s.

1. In evaluations of the behavior of bank credit. Many writers referred to the "excessive" expansion or inflation of bank credit during the 1920s, usually inferring that a sound basis for recovery could be established only when the "excess" was eliminated. Empirically, it would be difficult, if not impossible, to establish that there was, in the 1920s, an "excessive" rate of growth in the quantity of either total bank loans and investments or of the money supply, whether narrowly or broadly defined. Those who found "excessive" growth appear to have based their judgments on "quality" rather than quantity. Commercial loans grew only slowly during this period; a far larger part of the increase of bank credit was in the form of loans on security collateral, real-estate loans, and bonds. To commercial loan theorists, this was clearly an "excessive" expansion; it was an expansion in excess of "the needs of trade" as evidenced by demands for commercial loans. Also, some credit, including some bank credit, was used for speculation in securities and real estate. This, in itself, was convincing evidence of overexpansion for those who believed that only credit in excess of the legitimate needs of trade would flow into speculative uses.

2. In contentions that the form of assets acquired by the banking system controlled the use to which the resulting money would be put—e.g., that money issued for commercial loans would remain in commercial uses and that issued on the basis of collateral loans or bonds would remain in the securities markets. Some believed this true of both the Reserve Banks and the commercial banks. Strong and others had shown the errors of such ideas in the early 1920s, yet they lingered on. For example, Adolph Miller testified as late as 1931:

> ...when the Federal Reserve banks operate as investment banks, by buying investments, they force the member banks of the country also to operate as investment banks by buying investments or loaning against investments or by making loans of the kind here described as loans on real estate.[7]

Apparently such effects would not follow when the Federal Reserve supplied funds by discounting commercial paper or by purchasing acceptances or gold.

3. In the Federal Reserve's concern, in 1928 and 1929, with the alleged "absorption of credit in the stock market." It is still not wholly clear why the Federal Reserve became so deeply concerned about the use of credit in stock speculation that it virtually abandoned its other objectives and adopted a policy of severe and prolonged restriction, with deleterious effects on the domestic and international economy. However, the idea stressed most at the time was that loans on security collateral led to "absorption of credit in the stock

---

[7]*Hearings on S. Res.* 71 (January 1931), p. 139.

market" and to a decrease in the supply and increase of the cost of funds for legitimate business. They concentrated on the form of the loan and ignored subsequent uses of the money. It was, of course, clear that a lender, whether a bank or nonbank, on security collateral could not lend the same money to another borrower. But the money was not "absorbed" by the borrower; he passed it on to the seller of securities, who was free to use it as he wished to finance his own consumption or productive activities, to lend to someone else, and so on. We do not know the net effects of the rise of bank loans on security collateral on the total supply of funds, both equity and debt, to "legitimate" business or on the cost of capital to business. But two things are clear. First, the fact that loans were collateraled by securities did not necessarily mean less money or higher interest rates for business. And second, the highly restrictive policies adopted to remedy the situation contributed far more to higher interest rates for "legitimate" business than did any "absorption of credit in the stock market."

The first years of the great depression brought a sharp conflict between those who believed that the Federal Reserve should use its powers actively and on its own initiative in an expansionary way and those who favored a more passive policy of "accommodation" or of allowing credit to adjust to "the needs of trade." Commercial loan theorists were highly prominent in the second group, though some others shared their policy views. This group was especially antagonistic to Federal Reserve purchases of Government securities, but it also opposed "excessively easy" policies of purchasing acceptances and lowering discount and bill-buying rates.

The failures of Federal Reserve policies, which allowed the money supply to decline by a quarter during the first three years of the depression, are well known. The rate of liquidation was especially rapid in the months following the international financial crisis which hit the United States in September 1931. However, the money supply had already fallen more than 10 percent before the crisis impinged upon the United States and while the freedom of Federal Reserve action was not in any way limited by considerations relating to its gold reserve or free gold position or to the nation's balance of payments.

Why were Federal Reserve policies so inadequate and inappropriate in the early years of the great depression? One fundamental reason was the unsatisfactory, confused, and conflicting state of business-cycle and monetary theory, both within and outside the Federal Reserve System, and among professional economists as well as laymen. There was simply no valid, comprehensive, and generally accepted theory that could command a consensus and provide solid theoretical support for an appropriate and ambitious expansionary monetary program. The Keynesian Revolution was still years in the future. There was one type of monetary theory that suggested a positive policy of monetary expansion—the quantity theory. It is no coincidence that the principal proponents of large purchases of Government securities by the Federal Reserve were such well-known quantity theorists as Irving Fisher, John R. Commons, Wilford I. King, James Harvey Rogers, and Harry Gunnison Brown. However, both their theory and their policy prescriptions were rejected by large numbers of other professional economists, including some of the most prestigious names of the time. Among them were H. Parker Willis of Columbia and most other commercial loan theorists; Benjamin M. Anderson, Jr., influential economist of the Chase National Bank; O. M. W. Sprague of Harvard, Economic Advisor to the Bank of England and frequent consultant to the Federal Reserve and the Treasury; most members of the Yale Economics Department except Fisher and Rogers; Edwin W. Kemmerer of Princeton, famed "money doctor" and author of the most widely read book on the Federal Reserve; and George W. Dowrie of Stanford.

Though members of this group were united in their opposition to positive and ambitious measures for monetary expansion, they offered a wide variety of reasons for their opposition.[8]

1. Such a policy would be harmful and would prolong the depression by inhibiting the "natural process of liquidation." The depression was caused, it was claimed, by maladjustments created in the preceding period of prosperity, and a sound basis for recovery could be created only by liquidating these maladjustments. The preceding "inflation" and "excessive expansion of credit" had to be purged from the system. Expansionary monetary and credit policies would only prolong both the necessary process of liquidation and the depression.

2. The appropriate policy was to allow the volume of credit to adjust to the needs of trade at "normal" interest rates, and it was healthful for the volume of credit to fall in response to a decline in the needs of trade reflecting a decline of business activity or price levels. Central bank attempts to manipulate interest rates "artificially" to induce recovery would generate troubles and lead later to excessively high interest rates.

3. The Federal Reserve, as custodian of liquidity for the entire financial system, should conserve its own liquidity, and this could be assured only by limiting its earning assets to short-term, self-liquidating paper conforming to the commercial loan theory. Even short-term Government securities were not self-liquidating, and longer-term Government securities were still less liquid. Even as late as 1935 a group of 69 economists sent a memorandum to Congress urging that:

> ...The supply of non-commercial paper eligible for discount should be further restricted, not enlarged.... It is the function of a central banking system to maintain at all times a liquid portfolio, since the system holds the ultimate reserves of the nation's banks.
>
> All measures designed to correct weaknesses in the Federal Reserve System should seek...to increase, not reduce, its commercial nature. They should assure, not impair, its liquidity.[9]

---

[8]The state of economic theory at this time is discussed more fully in a forthcoming study of American monetary policies, 1928–1941.

[9]*Hearings before the House Banking and Currency Committee on H. R.* 5357, 74th Congress, 1st Session (March 1935), pp. 760–761.

4. Even if an expansionary monetary policy did no harm, it had little chance of inducing recovery. For example, Kemmerer believed that the large Federal Reserve purchases in 1932 lowered "confidence," made business unwilling to invest and banks unwilling to lend, and lowered the velocity of money.[10]

Under the conditions of early 1931, Sprague stated, "... I am disposed to think that monetary agencies are almost helpless of themselves to stay the downward course of the price level, to say nothing of being able to induce an upward movement."[11]

Such wide differences in theory and in policy prescriptions were by no means confined to professional economists; they were also evident in Government, in the financial community, among businessmen, and in the community at large. In this confusion of theory and policy advice, Federal Reserve officials must have wondered: which advice should we take? Should we take positive measures to expand money and credit? Should we encourage "natural liquidation"? Should we simply respond passively to demands for credit at "normal" interest rates reflecting "the needs of trade"? Should our primary concern be to conserve the liquidity of the Reserve Banks themselves? Or should we relax because what we do or don't do isn't very important anyway?

Theories and policy attitudes within the Federal Reserve System during the early 1930s were almost as diverse as those outside. A few officials were strong and consistent advocates of active expansionary policies, including both large purchases of Government securities and sharp reductions of discount and bill-buying rates. But these were few indeed. Of the members of the Federal Reserve Board, only one consistently took this position—Governor Meyer after his appointment in September 1930. Harrison of New York and Black of Atlanta were the only Reserve Bank Governors to advocate and support consistently active expansionary policies. Even these officials tended to think in terms of credit conditions rather than the money supply, and they sometimes, but not always, judged credit conditions by the behavior of interest rates. Thus they sometimes made the mistake of assuming that a decline of interest rates signified in some sense an "easier monetary policy" even if the fall of rates resulted largely from declines in demands for credit. Such a mistake would have been less likely if their guide had been the quantity of money or of total bank credit.

The ideas and policy positions of the other members of the Federal Reserve Board and of the other Governors of the Reserve Banks differed considerably. Some did on occasion support active expansionary policies. However, a large majority of them displayed a strong affinity for commercial loan ideas, including the desirability of "natural liquidation," passive adaptation of credit to the needs of trade, and avoidance of "artificial" easing measures. Their general

---

[10]*American Economic Review Supplement,* March 1933, p. 134. See also same publication, March 1934, p. 99.

[11]*Minutes of Evidence Taken Before the Committee on Finance and Industry,* Vol. II, February 19, 1931, p. 312.

approach was indicated in a recommendation made in January 1930 by Governor Norris of the Philadelphia Reserve Bank for the majority of the members of the Open Market Investment Committee.

...the recommendation is made that we see no necessity for operations in Government securities at this time either to halt or to expedite the present trend of credit. The majority of the Committee is not in favor of any radical reduction in the bill rate or radical buying of bills which would create an artificial ease or necessitate reduction in the discount rate. If that reduction comes about naturally from further liquidation or reduced demand, all well and good, but we do not feel that there should be any active effort to bring that about.... We distinctly feel that no operation in bills should be undertaken for the purpose of either forcing or facilitating a reduction of discount rates by any bank.

These and other similar attitudes were expressed repeatedly by Reserve Bank Governors. For example, Governor McDougal of Chicago consistently opposed purchases of Government securities, complained that credit conditions had become so easy as to be "sloppy," and sometimes advocated sales of securities or reductions of bill holdings in order to firm money market conditions. Chairman Austin of the Philadelphia Reserve Bank objected to purchases of securities and bills in March 1930, noting that:

...it lays us open to the apparent undesirable charge that the action is not justified by the demand for credit but for some other purpose, it may be for boosting business, making a market for securities, or for some other equally criticizable cause that will certainly come back to plague us.

In refusing to participate in purchases of Government securities in June 1930, Governor Calkins of San Francisco explained:

With credit cheap and redundant we do not believe that business recovery will be accelerated by making credit cheaper and more redundant.

We find no reason to believe that excessively cheap money will promote or create a bond market, seeing evidence in the recent past to the contrary, and, further, do not consider the promotion or creation of a bond market one of the functions of the Federal Reserve System.

In early 1930, officials of the Boston Bank preferred "to see things go along as they were for a time" because "there is more cleansing to be done." As late as August 1931 Governor Young voted against further purchases of Government securities, commenting that he "...would rather see the portfolios of the Federal Reserve System composed of bills and discounts, and regretted to see two important functions nullified by operations in government securities."

Governor Talley of the Dallas Reserve Bank complained in March 1930: "Everyone wants to keep business jazzed up all the time, and have it run along at boom figures. It seems to me the sounder course to pursue, after having done this for some time, is to catch up and let the public pay some of its debts." He added later, "Satisfaction of a demand for further capital supplies would tend to increase overproduction."

Governors Seay of Richmond and Fancher of Cleveland sometimes supported positive expansionary actions, but on several occasions they objected that interest rates had been pushed too low. Deputy Governor Atteberry of St. Louis expressed the view in mid-1930 that "fictitiously easy money" might have adverse effects.

> The discussion here develops the idea that excessive efforts in the interest of fictitious easy money may have just the opposite effect from that intended. It has been suggested that such efforts have the psychological effect of increasing the feeling of uncertainty and thus discouraging buying other than necessity demands.

Officials of both the Minneapolis and Kansas City Reserve Banks usually opposed positive expansionary actions.

As noted earlier, Governor Meyer was the only member of the Board who strongly and consistently supported positive expansionary policies. The others were generally no more than reluctant supporters of security purchases before September 1930; some became more favorably inclined after that time. They were usually more favorable to reductions of discount and bill-buying rates, though they often favored less rapid and smaller reductions than those proposed by New York.

The examples cited above suggest the wide variety of implicit theories and policy attitudes which permeated the System during the early 1930s, influenced policy decisions, and made it impossible for the System to formulate and carry out strong active expansionary policies.

In concentrating on the influence of theory on monetary and credit policies, I do not imply that policies can be explained wholly in terms of theory, either of current theory or that of "some defunct economist." A full explanation would require an investigation of the entire intellectual, social, political, and economic environment. For one thing it would have to explain why, when alternative theories are available, one theory is chosen over another. Why, for example, did so many adhere to the commercial loan theory, with its implications of relatively passive accommodation to private demands for commercial credit, rather than to the quantity theory, which suggests more positive control? Yet the commercial loan theory did have profound effects on the Federal Reserve. It influenced the very structure of the System; no quantity theorist setting up an agency to control the nation's money supply would have created 12 central banks, each originally expected to be largely autonomous. It influenced the powers granted to the System, and especially its emphasis on commercial credit. It influenced the thinking of professional economists and others outside, and thus the environment in which the System operated. And it had a profound effect on large numbers of Federal Reserve officials.

Nor can we be certain that this theory, with its remarkable ability to survive repeated refutations, is finally dead.

20

Federal Reserve
Policies from 1914 to 1941

World War I and the Postwar Inflation

A central bank is created to further monetary stability and to reduce the level of uncertainty in monetary affairs. It also may promote *indirectly* real growth and high levels of employment in the economy. These objectives may be specified precisely or only vaguely. The central bank may have limited powers to carry out such functions—its position under a true gold standard—or it may have virtually complete control of the monetary system. Whatever its institutional setting, a central bank's performance is no better summarized and preserved than in a serial view of its balance sheets.

The balance sheet of the twelve Federal Reserve Banks, which is titled "Consolidated Statement of Condition," is a record of Federal Reserve performance. With some qualifications, it can be used to analyze and evaluate the policy actions of the Federal Reserve System over the past 50-odd years.

This balance sheet has always contained two principal assets and two principal liabilities. These four items usually have been so large relative to the other minor items that they have dominated the balance sheet; and because of their relative importance in the balance sheet, the two major assets are always approximately equal to the two major liabilities.

In the formative years of the System the two principal assets were gold certificates and discounts and advances for member banks; the two principal liabilities were Federal Reserve notes outstanding and member bank reserve accounts. In 1917, just before the outbreak of World War I, values for these items were as shown in Table 20.1.

Table 20.1. All Reserve Banks as of January 1917*
(billions of dollars)

Assets		Liabilities	
Gold certificates	0.79	Federal Reserve notes	0.26
Discounts and advances	0.11	Member reserves	0.69
Government securities	0.05		

Reserve ratio: 83 percent

Source: *Banking and Monetary Statistics* (Washington, D.C., Board of Governors of the Federal Reserve System, 1943). Monthly averages of daily figures.
* In this balance sheet and in all subsequent ones of the Federal Reserve Banks, only principal items are shown. Therefore, the statement does not balance exactly, and reserve ratios are not precisely calculable from the data given here. The reserve ratio shown is the one that was calculated from the total balance sheet. It is the ratio of gold certificates and other reserves to the sum of Federal Reserve notes outstanding and member bank reserve accounts.

During World War I the principal policy of the System was to "assist" the Treasury in financing the war. (See Table 20.2.) The Reserve Banks faced statutory reserve requirements of 40 percent gold to Federal Reserve notes outstanding, and 35 percent gold to member bank reserves. Gold flows from Europe were appreciable, and the System had plenty of "room" to expand credit. Discounts and advances to member banks were extended. Although government security holdings by Reserve Banks were legally limited at this time, the System encouraged member banks to obtain these securities by favoring them as collateral security for the credit it granted on the basis of commercial paper. Long after the end of hostilities, Reserve Bank credit continued to expand under pressure from the Treasury Department.[1]

Two years later, when the economy was at the peak of its postwar boom, the combined balance sheet was as shown in Table 20.3.

Table 20.2. All Reserve Banks as of December 1918
(billions of dollars)

Assets		Liabilities	
Gold certificates*	2.13	Federal Reserve notes	2.63
Discounts and advances	2.11	Member reserves	1.59
Government securities	0.21		

Reserve ratio: 48 percent

* Besides gold certificates, Reserve Banks originally held small amounts of other "lawful money" reserves.

---

[1]For a summary analysis of Federal Reserve policy development, see E. A. Goldenweiser, *American Monetary Policy* (New York: McGraw-Hill Book Co., 1951).

Table 20.3. All Reserve Banks as of December 1920
(billions of dollars)

Assets		Liabilities	
Gold certificates	2.22	Federal Reserve notes	3.26
Discounts and advances	2.96	Member reserves	1.76
Government securities	0.34		

Reserve ratio: 44 percent

If the function of a central bank is to provide fresh supplies of credit as requested by a treasury department, then the Federal Reserve System's record during and after World War I was an unqualified success. Its actions in expanding its own notes and credit were part, parcel, and proximate cause of the general inflation that took place. In acceding to Treasury pressures, the Federal Reserve provided for inflation in the same manner that the Treasury and the National Banking System had followed during the Civil War. Supplying the economy with credit presupposed a lack of restrictive actions against inflation and extended the Reserve Banks so far that they could do nothing to assist the economy in the postwar recession of 1921. Gold certificates and other reserves exceeded minimum requirements by less than $0.3 billion. The System, in fact, felt obliged to raise discount rates to very high values in 1920 to protect its own reserves. Many observers felt that this policy triggered the recession of 1921. By the middle of 1922, when the upturn came, the combined balance sheet was as shown in Table 20.4.

Table 20.4. All Reserve Banks as of June 1922
(billions of dollars)

Assets		Liabilities	
Gold certificates	3.14	Federal Reserve notes	2.14
Discounts and advances	0.57	Member reserves	1.82
Government securities	0.59		

Reserve ratio: 78 percent

Analysis of Federal Reserve policy for the war and postwar period, 1917–1922, indicates that the primary purpose of the System at that time was to serve as a public bank: to "assist" the Treasury by making credit available on easy terms. It did not counter inflationary pressures during the war nor deflationary pressures after 1920. In fact, it did as much to generate the inflation as any other institution. This experience does not very much condemn the System's policies; it serves only to emphasize that World War I financing with a Federal Reserve System was not significantly different in the end from War of 1812 financing under a Treasury Department alone, or Civil War financing under a Treasury Department in conjunction with a National Banking System. The more that things are different, the more they are the same.

Federal Reserve Policy during the 1920s

Open market operations were *not* a discovery of the Federal Reserve System. During the period 1853–1857, and many times thereafter, the Treasury had undertaken extensive open market operations in government securities with the residual gold balances that had accrued from fiscal surpluses. Its purposes had been to reduce the national debt and interest charges on it, and to give stimulus to business. In 1922 the Federal Reserve began open market operations in government securities. In contrast to the Treasury's motives in 1853–1856, the Federal Reserve System was at first induced to buy securities in order to earn a little income. Its interest-earning advances and discounts to member banks had almost all been liquidated in the recession of 1921–1922, so the Reserve Banks had little in the way of earning assets to meet their business costs, including the "dividends" to member banks.

The open market purchases in 1922 had little monetary effect. They did lead, however, to the formation of the Open Market Committee and to the principle of using open market operations as an instrument of monetary policy. In 1924, the System again engaged in open market purchases, so that the Reserve Banks held $477 million by July 1924. This amount made up 60 percent of Reserve Banks' earning assets.

Two conditions that occupied the attention of Federal Reserve policy makers during the 1920s were international gold flows and the stock market boom. The Fed undertook easy money policies in the mid-1920s to aid the British policy of reestablishing gold convertibility at the prewar parity. Nevertheless, gold gradually but steadily came into the United States from 1921 until late in 1927 with the exception of 1925, when Great Britain made its big effort to restore convertibility. By the middle of 1929 the combined balance sheet of the Reserve Banks was as shown in Table 20.5.

Table 20.5. All Reserve Banks as of June 1929
(billions of dollars)

Assets		Liabilities	
Gold certificates	3.01	Federal Reserve notes	1.67
Discounts and advances	1.08	Member reserves	2.31
Government securities	0.18		

Reserve ratio: 75 percent

Official attention had been directed for some time to "speculation," particularly the unusual activity in the stock market. In order to curb the credit that permitted "speculative" stock market dealings, the Board raised Reserve Bank discount rates from 3½ percent in 1927 to 6 percent in 1929. This action had little effect. A speculator buying stocks in hopes of, say, 50 percent in capital gains over a short period is not likely to be inhibited very much by a 3 percent per year increase in the terms on which he can borrow. Furthermore, a normative question can be raised about such an interest on the part of a central bank. The stock and commodity markets are just a small part of the total market structure. A central bank can hardly support or suppress any *particular* market without having possibly undesirable effects in other markets, and without the dangerous claim being made that it intervene in other private markets in similar fashion. Nor does intervention in specific market areas guarantee stability in the economy generally. *General* economic stability was the problem that had to be faced as the 1920s became the 1930s.

Federal Reserve Policy in the Early Years of the Depression

The stock market collapse of 1929 was an apparent realization that the prices of securities were too high with respect to both annual yields and future growth rates. The influence of declining security values on monetary behavior was certainly depressive. Not only did price declines of such large magnitude breed general uncertainty, they also destroyed any suppositions investors might have had about the utility of securities as stores of value. Both the effects of uncertainty and the need for money as wealth to offset the large-scale depreciation of securities caused a general increase in the demand for real cash balances and a consequent decline in the velocity of money. Added to these factors was some apprehension in 1932 that gold convertibility of the dollar might not be maintained.

The Federal Reserve Banks lowered discount rates from 6 percent in 1929 to about 3 percent by late 1931, and open market purchases increased the System's portfolio of government securities from $200 million to over $700 million in the same period. Total earning assets of the Reserve Banks were $1.28 billion; but this amount was 8 percent *less* than the amount outstanding two years earlier, and the Reserve Bank's reserve ratio was higher. (See Table 20.6.)

Table 20.6. All Reserve Banks as of September 1931
(billions of dollars)

Assets		*Liabilities*	
Gold certificates	3.56	Federal Reserve notes	2.03
Discounts and advances	0.54	Member reserves	2.33
Government securities	0.74		

Reserve ratio: 82 percent

This phase of Federal Reserve policy making demonstrated very well the folly of using interest rates as an index or signal for monetary policy. The apparently "high" discount rates of the late twenties did not retard speculation or other economic activity, and the "low" rates that prevailed after 1931 did not restore the vigor of the economy. The paradox is that the "high" rates were not high relative to the anticipations of the investing public, and the "low" rates of around 3 percent were by 1931–1932 too *high* relative to the depressed state of business and household spending behavior to encourage new borrowing for consumption and investment spending.

This case also shows the fallibility of the real bills principle. As the Depression developed and banks and businesses failed, loans and discounts that would have been of good quality in a period of prosperity became more and more dubious and therefore less and less "eligible" for discount by banks or rediscount by Federal Reserve Banks. Thus, the very mechanism that was supposed to be used deliberately by the central bank to prevent monetary crises proved to be no better than the same device when under the push and pull of the free market. In fact, it was worse when under the auspices of the central bank. Under a free money market, the excess gold stocks built up by the central bank between 1929 and 1932 would have been used as a means of credit extension — at least to some extent, judging by the experience of the past. The Federal Reserve Board, however, simply allowed the money supply to dwindle as the gold reserves in the Reserve Banks accumulated.

Another weakness in the Federal Reserve System at this time was its inability to function without decisive leadership. No outstanding executive had appeared to assume the leadership vacuum that developed upon the death of Benjamin Strong in 1928. Strong had been president of the Federal Reserve Bank of New York, and a competent central banker. The System had no rules for selecting a leader, as well as no rules (except the "eligibility" principle) for its technical procedures. It therefore drifted purposeless and rudderless as the Depression deepened.

Domestic monetary problems were further complicated by the worldwide gold "crisis" of 1931. During the year the United States lost $600 million in gold, and the central bank desideratum of maintaining domestic stability found itself in apparent conflict with the workings of the international gold standard.

The Federal Reserve System then raised the discount rate to prevent gold drains and in so doing put additional pressure on the hard-pressed commercial banking system. At that time world central banking operated along "traditional" lines; that is, central bankers felt obliged to pay some heed to gold movements. Even though central banking policy might frequently attempt to counteract short-run gold flows, long-run movements could not be avoided if the international gold standard was to be preserved. Central bankers were at least intuitively aware of the rules of the game.

Another impediment to Federal Reserve operations at this time was the law that prescribed Reserve Bank collateral for the issue of Federal Reserve notes. This collateral had to be either gold or eligible short-term paper. Government securities could be held as collateral only against member bank reserves. With bank liquidations taking place and the corresponding decline of commercial bank earning assets, less and less commercial paper was being created, and the amount that was extant looked less and less "eligible" to Reserve Bank authorities as suitable collateral for Reserve Bank issues of currency. The demand for currency that became acute in 1931 resulted in large part from the popular uncertainty that was rapidly becoming popular hysteria. The System felt that its ability to increase the currency supply was limited until the law was changed to permit government securities to serve as collateral against Federal Reserve notes. Nonetheless, securities were eligible as collateral for member bank reserves, and purchases of securities, if carried out earlier, might well have mitigated the demand for currency by improving business confidence and spending through commercial bank credit expansion.

Table 20.7 shows how the total supply of money continuously declined through 1933. The data also show that the stock of currency *increased* simultaneously with the *decline* in bank deposits, especially after 1931. The increase in the currency supply was made possible by both the Federal Reserve and the Treasury. It was a response to a demand for conversion of bank deposits into currency by the nonbank public, but it was achieved only at a formidable cost in bank credit destruction. Between 1929 and 1931, the price level fell faster than the nominal stock of money, indicating that the real value of money was increasing. After 1931, both the nominal *and real values* of the money stock declined, indicating that an increased demand for money was being met by an even shorter supply. Such a disequilibrium situation is also unstable.

Congress passed an amendment to the Federal Reserve Act early in 1932 that permitted government securities to be held as collateral against Federal Reserve notes. The Federal Reserve System then began its belated policy of buying government securities in the open market. Reserve bank credit reached a high plateau in July 1932 and stayed more or less constant through 1933.

On net balance the security buying by the Reserve Banks in 1932 did little more than neutralize the outflow of gold. (Compare with Table 20.6.) Gold certificates and other reserves reached a high point of $3.62 billion in August 1931, declined to $2.79 billion in July 1932, then increased and remained constant at about $4 billion during 1933. (See Table 20.8.)

Table 20.7. Real and Nominal Values for Selected
Components of the Money Supply and the Price Level, 1929–1933

Year (near June 30)	Total Deposits in Comm. Banks and Currency		Total Deposits in Comm. Banks		Currency outside Banks		Price Index (1947–1949 = 100)
	Billions of dollars	Real (billions of dollars, 1947–1949)	Billions of dollars	Real (billions of dollars, 1947–1949)	Billions of dollars	Real (billions of dollars, 1947–1949)	
1929	46.1	62.8	42.5	58.0	3.64	4.97	73.3
1930	45.1	63.2	41.7	58.4	3.37	4.72	71.4
1931	42.6	65.6	39.0	60.0	3.65	5.62	65.0
1932	34.7	59.5	30.1	51.6	4.62	7.92	58.4
1933	30.9	55.9	26.1	47.2	4.76	8.60	55.3

Sources: Dollar values for the stock of money and its components were taken from *Banking and Monetary Statistics* (Washington, D.C.: Board of Governors of the Federal Reserve System, 1943). The price index is the BLS Consumers' Price Index (1947–1949 = 100) and is used to compute the "real" values from the given money values.

Even in July 1932, the Reserve Banks still had almost $1 billion in excess gold certificate reserves on which credit could have been extended to member banks, or on which Federal Reserve notes could have been issued. Neither of these actions took place. By November 1933, the balance sheet for all Reserve banks reached the level shown in Table 20.9. Excess reserves fell as low as $800 million only once (March 1933) and were generally between $1,500 million and $2,000 million during the entire period.

Table 20.8. All Reserve Banks as of July 1932
(billions of dollars)

Assets		*Liabilities*	
Gold certificates	2.79	Federal Reserve notes	2.86
Discounts and advances	0.58	Member reserves	2.00
Government securities	1.82		

Reserve ratio: 56 percent

Note: From this time on "discounts and advances" were never more than a trivial amount in the Reserve Banks' balance sheet (except during early 1933). Future extensions of credit were due almost entirely to gold inflows or purchases of government securities.

Table 20.9. All Reserve Banks as of November 1933
(billions of dollars)

Assets		*Liabilities*	
Gold certificates	3.79	Federal Reserve notes	2.99
Government securities	2.44	Member reserves	2.63

Reserve ratio: 65 percent

The ineffectual behavior of the System has been described by E. A. Goldenweiser, a long-time central banker, as follows:

Federal Reserve authorities were still thinking of themselves as lenders of last resort rather than as regulators of the money supply....That the Federal Reserve Banks could not fail the way commercial banks could as the result of deposit withdrawals, because the Reserve Banks could always issue notes to meet their deposit liabilities, was not part of the System's thinking at that time. As a matter of fact, so long as currency was redeemable in gold a Federal Reserve Bank could be forced to suspend by an excessive gold drain, but no such drain was in prospect and the possibility of suspension for such a reason was not contemplated. Commercial bank concepts were simply being applied to a central bank, to which they are not relevant.[2]

---

[2]Goldenweiser, p. 161.

In summary, Federal Reserve monetary policy in the crisis period of 1929–1933 failed primarily because of anachronistic theories on the scope and methods of central banking. The real bills concept on rediscounting, the collateral restrictions on currency issue, the failure of Congress and officials in the System to realize the fundamental and unique position of a central banking institution for regulating the money supply, and the inability of the System to provide itself with leadership all gave rise to a neutralization of policy that was the equivalent of no policy at all. One cannot say from this experience, however, that monetary policy had failed. Positive monetary policy had not even been tried.

Banking and Monetary Legislation of the Thirties

Most of the so-called banking legislation passed in the period between 1932 and 1935 in fact dealt with both the central bank and the commercial banking system. The Glass-Steagall Act of 1932 was an attempt to relieve collateral restrictions on the issue of Federal Reserve notes. Up to this time, note issues required a minimal gold reserve of 40 percent; the remaining 60 percent could be eligible commercial paper. The public's abnormal demand for currency thus might have been satisfied by central bank discount of the $2.5 billion in commercial paper held by member banks. However, the Reserve Banks would not discount this paper on the grounds that it was not "eligible" enough. Note issues, therefore, tied up much more gold reserves than the 40 percent minimum prescribed by the Federal Reserve Act. The Glass-Steagall Act, by specifying the eligibility of government securities as collateral for note issues, legally freed $750 million in gold reserves held by the Reserve Banks for a further credit expansion that also could have been matched by concurrent issues of Federal Reserve notes.

For a few months during 1932 after the passage of the Glass-Steagall Act, the Federal Reserve System made substantial open market purchases. However, its actions were too late; or if not too late, too little. The monetary and banking structure still had some bloodletting to endure. The new spate of purchases ended in August 1932.

The next bit of major legislation passed was the Emergency Banking Act of March 1933. Its principal provisions were to shore up the crumbling commercial banking system by means of various palliatives. It also provided for an emergency issue of $2 billion in Federal Reserve *bank* notes backed by government securities or commercial paper and without gold. Only about one tenth of the authorized issue was ever made.

Another piece of legislation that resulted from the popular demand for currency was the so-called "Inflation bill," the Thomas Amendment to the Agricultural Relief Act of May 1933. This Amendment authorized the President at his discretion to allow additional purchases of $3 billion in government securities by the Federal Reserve Banks, or to have the Treasury issue $3 billion in U.S. notes (greenbacks). These notes were to be a simple issue of fiat legal tender currency just as they had been during the Civil War. This provision was clearly an "or else" directive to the Federal Reserve System. It implied that the executive branch would take over money-creating powers if the Fed did not do something. However, the executive never issued any of the authorized currency, partly because the Federal Reserve took some positive monetary actions thereafter, and partly because the New Deal administration had little faith in the ability of monetary policy to alleviate the Depression.

The Thomas Amendment also authorized the President to reduce the gold content of the dollar (devalue) by as much as 50 percent. This power was used until the price of gold in dollars reached approximately $35 per ounce. Congress then passed the Gold Reserve Act of 1934. This Act allowed the President to proclaim the price of $35 per ounce as "permanent."

The Banking Act of 1933 was aimed primarily at commercial banks. Its major effect was to institute deposit insurance under a government corporation—the well-known Federal Deposit Insurance Corporation. All Federal Reserve member banks were required to join, and nonmember banks had the option of doing so if they could qualify. Other provisions of this Act regulated the branch-banking activities of national banks, separated commercial from investment banking, and inhibited "speculative" activity of banks.

The Banking Act of 1935 was the most important single piece of legislation during the 1930s with respect to control over the monetary system. Though titled a "Banking" Act, it was primarily a central banking act. It vested complete control of open market operations in the FOMC, and enlarged the powers of the Board of Governors to alter reserve requirements of member banks between the minimum percentages specified in the original Federal Reserve Act and a maximum that was double the minimum (13–26 percent for central reserve city banks, 10–20 percent for reserve city banks, and 7–14 percent for country banks). These two provisions effectively changed the focus of decision making and power within the System from the presidents of the separate Reserve Banks to the Board of Governors, and it extended greatly the money-creating and money-destroying powers of the Board as well.

This Act also broadened the lending powers of the Reserve Banks, empowered the Board to set a maximum limit to interest rates paid by member banks on time deposits, granted the Board power to set margin requirements for loans made by member and nonmember banks on stocks and bonds, and made other technical changes in organization and procedure. From this point on, the Federal Reserve System was the dominant monetary institution; the gold standard was reduced to a virtually functionless façade. This switcharound essentially distinguishes what may be defined as a "nineteenth century central bank" from a "twentieth century central bank." Unfortunately, the tremendous increase in powers given the central bank was not complemented by corresponding responsibilities and accountabilities of the Federal Reserve System to Congress.

The Depression Years:
Excess Reserves and the
Reserve Requirement Experiment

Increased gold flows from Europe, and the "capital gain" in the dollar value of gold holdings due to devaluation in 1934, gave the Reserve Banks and the commercial banking system an excess of legal reserves. The disinclination of commercial banks to use these reserves indicated to contemporary Reserve Bank officials — and to some economists — that supplying reserves and money to the economy through the banking system was pointless unless some positive spending apparatus was erected to provide a demand for the available supply of money and credit. What Federal Reserve officials and many economists failed to realize was that these reserves were not "excess" so far as the commercial banks themselves were concerned. The bloodletting experience of recent years had left the banks skeptical about self-styled lenders of last resort, and the general climate of business in the near future appeared unpromising. The reserves the banks kept, therefore, were only excess in a legal sense, that is, greater than what were required by law.

By late 1935 excess legal reserves were almost $3 billion out of total reserves of approximately $6 billion. As Table 20.10 shows, the total money supply at this time was $41.1 billion. If all of the excess *legal* reserves had been used in the way that reserves were being used at that time, the volume of member bank deposits would have increased by $29.8 billion. If the money supply and labor force of 1929 are accepted as benchmarks of full employment, and if the money supply is presumed to increase in proportion to the growth in the labor force as a proxy for growth in real output, the stock of money would have had to increase to $48.4 billion in late 1935 before full employment could have been reached. Or if the price level of 1929 is taken as the full employment benchmark, the money supply could have been increased to $50.7 billion on a strict quantity theory basis before the price level of 1929 was recovered. To obtain *both* the price level of 1929 *and* the full employment level for the labor force in late 1935, the money stock would need to have increased to $58.0 billion, or to about 84 percent of the total potential money stock value of $70.9 billion.

The Federal Reserve Board did not like the loose rein enjoyed by the member banks. The Board felt that such freedom put the Reserve authorities out of contact with the banks. To regain liaison, the Board raised reserve requirements by 50 percent in August 1936, that is, from 13, 10, and 7 percent — the requirements that had been in effect for the three classes of member banks since 1917 — to 19½, 15, and 10½ percent. This action reduced legal excess reserves from $2.71 billion on June 30, 1936, to $1.99 billion by December 31. Not only were the reserves available for expansion reduced, but the multiple of expansion — the inverse of the average reserve ratio faced by all the banks — was also lower, and the remaining potential increase in total deposits at this

Table 20.10. Selected Data from the Combined Balance Sheet of All Member Banks and of the Twelve Federal Reserve Banks, Together with the Total Money Supply, the Potential Money Supply, and a Computed "Full Employment" Money Supply
(billions of dollars)

Year (near date)	Total Member Bank Reserves	Excess Legal Reserves	Total Member Bank Deposits Adj.	Potential Increase in Deposits*	Actual Total Money Supply†	Potential Total Money Supply‡	Computed "Full Employment" Money Supply§
1935—Dec. 31	5.59	2.84	28.8	29.8	41.1	70.9	58.0
1936—June 30	5.63	2.71	30.5	28.3	43.9	72.2	60.3
—Dec. 31	6.61	1.99	32.4	13.9	46.0	59.9	62.1
1937—June 30	6.90	0.87	32.5	4.7	45.9	50.6	59.8
—Dec. 31	7.03	1.21	31.7	6.6	45.2	51.8	60.4
1938—June 30	8.02	2.88	32.2	18.0	45.1	63.1	62.5

Source: *Banking and Monetary Statistics* (Washington, D.C.: Board of Governors of the Federal Reserve System, 1943).
* The figures in this column are obtained by assuming that the excess reserves would generate a proportionate increase in total deposits. If the banks changed the demand deposit–time deposit relationship, this assumption would not hold. This value is computed only for member banks of the Federal Reserve System.
† The values in this column include all deposits in all commercial banks, adjusted for interbank deposits, plus currency outside banks and government agencies.
‡ The figures in this column are the sums of the values in the two preceding columns. They do not include possible growth in deposits of non-member commercial banks or allowance for possible changes in currency holdings.
§ The economy's "full employment" stocks of money for the various dates listed here are computed on a strict and simplistic quantity theory basis in the following manner. The money stock, labor force, and price level for June 1929 are assumed to be bench marks. To get the full employment money stock M_f for any subsequent date, the actual money stock M_t for that date is multiplied (1) by the ratio of the full employment labor force to the number of workers actually employed, N_f/N_t, and (2) by the ratio of the price level of 1929 to the price level for the date being investigated, P_0/P_t. By subtracting the actual money stock from each of these computed values, the increases in money necessary for financing increases in total product (assumed to be proportional to growth in the labor force) and for restoring prices to their 1929 level are obtained. Summing the actual money stock and both increases gives the "full employment" values in this column. In formula terms,

$$M_f = M_t + \left(\frac{N_f}{N_t} \cdot M_t - M_t\right) + \left(\frac{P_o}{P_t} \cdot M_t - M_t\right) \tag{1}$$

This expression reduces to

$$M_f = M_t\left[1 + \left(\frac{N_f}{N_t} - 1\right) + \left(\frac{P_o}{P_t} - 1\right)\right] \tag{2}$$

point was about $14 billion. This amount, if fully extended by commercial bank action, would have been just about sufficient to restore the price level of 1929 and achieve the full employment level of 1936. In the climate of spending prevalent in 1936, it would have been *no more* than enough, especially because of the reticence displayed by the commercial banks in using their "excess" reserves.

But the Federal Reserve Board still was not satisfied. Gold imports continued and bank reserves increased slightly. In January 1937, the Board again raised requirements, this time to the legal maxima of 14, 20, and 26 percent, and 6 percent on time deposits. Half of this last increase took effect in March and the remainder in May. By May 1937 the member banks had only $0.87 billion in excess reserves. (See Table 20.11.) Their potential expansion was reduced to $4.7 billion, an amount that would have permitted a total money supply of only $50.6 billion, or $9 billion less than the quantity necessary to achieve full employment.

The commercial banking system did not share the Federal Reserve Board's opinion on the excessiveness of reserves. Adjusted demand deposits of all banks declined by $1.50 billion (6 percent) during 1937, and the economy, not yet out of the previous depression, found itself in another one. The most incredible part of the story is that, once the business decline was underway, the Board took almost no remedial action to counteract the new depression regardless of what had caused it. One explanation of the Board's reticence, given by Goldenweiser, was that the Board felt open market purchases were inconsistent with the higher reserve requirements, and would be an admission of official error for having raised requirements in the first place! In any case, this experiment demonstrated only too clearly both the massive impact resulting from changes in reserve requirements and the incompetence and irresponsibility of the Federal Reserve Board in using them.

During the period from 1938 to 1941, the economy continued to function at only three-quarter speed. Gold inflows again became heavy after 1938 because of the political situation in Europe, but the business and banking sectors of the U.S. economy had been burned too often to attempt any large expansion of industry and credit. Not until the inordinate fiscal and monetary excesses during World War II was full employment again achieved. Then the turnaround came. The problem for policy consideration changed from one of

Table 20.11. All Reserve Banks as of January 1937
(billions of dollars)

Assets		*Liabilities*	
Gold certificates	11.30	Federal Reserve notes	4.19
Government securities	2.43	Member reserves	6.72

Reserve ratio: 80 percent

depression and unemployed factors of production to one of inflation with "shortages" of labor and capital.

Selected Bibliography

Burgess, W. R. *The Reserve Banks and the Money Market,* rev. ed. New York: Harper & Row, 1946. A well-known work.

Chandler, Lester V. *Inflation in the United States.* New York: Harper & Row, 1951. An account of Federal Reserve policy in the 1940s.

Friedman, Milton, and Anna Jacobson Schwartz. *A Monetary History of the United States, 1867–1960.* Princeton, N.J.: Princeton University Press, 1963. Critique of Federal Reserve policy in the 1930s.

Goldenweiser, E. A. *American Monetary Policy.* New York: McGraw-Hill Book Co., 1951.

Other works on the early development of the Federal Reserve System are easily obtainable.

Monetary Control under the Federal Reserve Act

Clark Warburton

A notable exception to the theoretical Keynesian economists of the 1935–1955 era is Dr. Clark Warburton, who did incisive empirical and theoretical work in monetary economics during this period. Possibly his adherence to the quantity theory school of thought, which was widely regarded as obsolete, was due to the fact that he was a research economist with the Federal Deposit Insurance Corporation and not subject to the Keynesian persuasions that conquered academia.

The reading that follows is excerpted from a much longer article originally published in The Political Science Quarterly *in 1946 and republished in his collection of essays,* Depression, Inflation, and Monetary Policy *(Baltimore: Johns Hopkins Press, 1966). Dr. Warburton's exposition gives an idea of the transition problems encountered in the 1930s when the central bank that had*

Reprinted with permission from the *Political Science Quarterly,* 61 (December 1946), pp. 527–534.

functioned in the limiting monetary environment of an earlier era was given comprehensive monetary powers without direction from Congress or accountability to any department of the government.

Attempts to Modify the Theory of
Monetary Control Underlying the Federal Reserve Act

The theory of monetary control underlying the Federal Reserve Act — that monetary responsibility need not be given a federal government agency, if monetary convertibility is maintained — was challenged in the middle 1920s. In 1926, and at various times since that date, efforts have been made to place the operations of the system on an entirely different theoretical basis by instructing the Federal Reserve Board to use its powers to stabilize the price level.[1] These efforts are obviously based on the belief that the central bank should be given definite responsibility for the prevention of price inflation on the one hand and of price deflation on the other, and on the assumption that the powers of the Federal Reserve Board are adequate to achieve this purpose. The Federal Reserve Board has repeatedly opposed the price-level-stabilization proposal, and no other proposal to give Federal Reserve authorities precise or definite responsibility for monetary control has been seriously considered by Congress.

The basic character of monetary law embodied in the original Federal Reserve Act has, nevertheless, been decisively modified. Gold coinage and its circulation, and redemption of circulating notes in gold, were suspended in 1933 under emergency legislation and were permanently prohibited by the Gold Reserve Act of 1934. These changes, together with numerous modifications of the loan powers of Federal Reserve banks and of member banks, constitute a complete abandonment, in law, of the convertibility theory of monetary control. Of the three principles on which the convertibility theory

---

[1]*Stabilization.* Hearings before the Committee on Banking and Currency, House of Representatives, 69th Cong., 1st Sess., on H.R. 7895 (1926 and 1927). The difference between the monetary theory which underlay this price stabilization proposal and that which was dominant in the original Federal Reserve Act was not clearly stated by its supporters or by its opponents. The Federal Reserve Board, for example, opposed the price stabilization proposal on the grounds (*a*) that the price situation and the credit situation are interrelated but only in a complex manner, (*b*) that decisions of "credit administration" must be made in advance of the dates when effects of the use of credit might show up in prices, (*c*) that no credit system could perform satisfactorily the function of regulating credit by reference to prices without failing in the endeavor, and (*d*) that the powers of the Federal Reserve System were inadequate to exercise the degree of price control implicit in the proposed legislative instructions. (Testimony of Adolph C. Miller, member Federal Reserve Board, *ibid.*, Part 2, pp. 623 *et seq.*, and *Tenth Annual Report of the Federal Reserve Board*, 1923, pp. 29–39.) These criticisms are valid if the word "credit" and the phrase "credit administration" are understood to refer to the loans made by member banks, Federal Reserve banks, or other loan institutions, and the context of the Board statement makes it clear that the words are so used. The Board's statement ignores the problem of the relation of bank obligations — whether deposits in commercial banks or circulating notes of Federal Reserve banks — to the quantity of money (circulating media) and the relation of the quantity of money to prices.

of monetary control was based — (1) assurance of convertibility of each kind of money with another kind, (2) direct convertibility of the standard form of money, and therefore indirect convertibility of all other forms of money, into some highly prized durable commodity, and (3) the predominance, in the assets of banks with obligations serving as money, of loans based on commodities in process of production or storage — only the first remains.

The place in monetary legislation vacated by abandonment of the convertibility theory of monetary control has not been filled. Feeble gestures in the direction of the responsibility theory of monetary control have been made by insertion of references to "injurious credit expansion or contraction," and "maintainance of sound credit conditions," for these ambiguous phrases can be interpreted to refer to the injuries to the country resulting from price changes and the presumed connection of price changes with expansion or contraction of bank obligations used as money. But in view of the loan powers and duties of the Federal Reserve System and the changes which have been made in those powers, the word "credit" in the ambiguous phrases is, with one exception, more reasonably assumed to refer to loan control than to monetary control. The exception is a clause relative to the prevention of undue credit expansion in Title III of the Act of May 12, 1933, which deals in part with the exercise of the constitutional power to coin money and to regulate the value thereof.[2] In this Act responsibility for action to prevent undue credit expansion is divided between the Federal Reserve Board and the Secretary of the Treasury.

In no legislation has the Board of Governors of the Federal Reserve System been given responsibility for monetary control. The Federal Reserve System has never been given the duty, either directly or by reasonably clear inference, of adjusting the quantity of money to the needs of the economy.

Monetary Theory of the
Board of Governors of the Federal Reserve System

In view of the ambiguous character of the criterion for central bank action embodied in the Federal Reserve Act, it is natural that Federal Reserve authorities should attempt to develop a reasonable and consistent theoretical basis for their operations.

As early as 1923 the Federal Reserve Board implicitly recognized the inadequacy of the convertibility theory of monetary control in its comments on the "anomalous situation" confronting the central banking administration when gold movements are not in accord with gold-standard theory, and in its

---

[2]U.S.C.A. Title 31, Chapter 13, section 821.

discussion of quantitative and qualitative guides to Federal Reserve credit policy.[3] As has been mentioned above, however, the Board failed to clarify the nature of the monetary problem to which quantitative guides are relevant.

Another Federal Reserve document which implicitly assumed the validity of the responsibility theory of monetary control was the report in 1931 by the Committee on Bank Reserves and the proposed amendment to the Federal Reserve Act which was drafted by that Committee. Unfortunately the Committee's statement of the theory underlying its proposals was couched in an ambiguous use of the word "credit" and of phrases such as "credit control" and "credit policy." Their report was not sufficiently clarified to make economists or the general public aware of the difference between the convertibility theory of monetary control which underlay the original Federal Reserve Act and the responsibility theory of monetary control which was involved in the rejected proposal to require the Federal Reserve Board to adjust its policies to the purpose of price-level stabilization and in the Committee's own proposal.[4]

In the annual reports of the Board of Governors of the Federal Reserve System in recent years much more recognition is given to the responsibility theory of monetary control. The report for 1935 opens with a paragraph referring to the Banking Act of 1935, stating that this Act "places responsibility for national monetary and credit policies on the Board of Governors and the Federal Open Market Committee"—notwithstanding the fact that the Banking Act of 1935 contains no reference to monetary policy, nor mentions any "monetary powers," nor contains any provisions indicating an alteration of the monetary theory underlying the original Federal Reserve Act. More recent annual reports and official statements of policy make frequent use of such terms as "monetary system," "monetary policy," "monetary contribution to economic stability," "monetary authorities," "monetary measures and objectives," and customarily use the word "monetary" along with the word "credit" when speaking about Federal Reserve policy.

---

[3] *Tenth Annual Report of the Federal Reserve Board,* 1923, pp. 30–31.

[4] In a section of the report entitled, "Control of Credit," the Committee notes that overexpansion of bank credit (referring to bank assets), whatever the character of bank loans, has the effect of temporarily inflating the general purchasing power of the community, and states that the function of reserve requirements is to restrain such overexpansion and that for adequate performance of this function reserve requirements must reflect both the volume and activity of credit outstanding. (*Nineteenth Annual Report of the Federal Reserve Board,* 1932, pp. 264–65.) It is difficult to find any meaning in this passage, unless "volume and activity of credit" refer to bank deposits as a part of the circulating medium, or money, of the nation. If the passage is thus interpreted it must mean that changes in reserve requirements should be made with primary reference to monetary control, and presumably other phases of Federal Reserve policy impinging on the amount of bank reserves—such as open-market operations and the rediscount rate—should also be focused primarily on monetary control. But nowhere in the report of the Committee is any further consideration given to the effect which changes in the quantity or rate of use of bank deposits may have upon the total money supply of the country or the operations of the entire monetary system. Neither is there any recognition of the fact that such an approach to reserve policy involves subordination of the duty imposed upon the Board of establishing discount rates for the *accommodation*— obviously through loans—of commerce, industry and agriculture.

The most detailed discussion of monetary theory and monetary policy by the Board of Governors of the Federal Reserve System is contained in a pamphlet, *Monetary Measures and Objectives,* consisting of three policy statements, two of which were transmitted by the Board of Governors to Congressional Committees.[5] The principal conclusions of these statements were reaffirmed in the *Annual Report of the Board of Governors* for 1943.[6]

Regarding the major problem of monetary theory, namely, the value of money or relation of the quantity of money to prices, the Board states, "The facts show clearly that the volume of money does not control the price level," and "Usually other things have a greater influence on prices than has the amount of money."[7] The Board of Governors supports this conclusion by statistical data relating to the quantity of money and to prices in 1929 and 1938 compared with 1926. The assumptions and methodology of this comparison are subject to criticism for several reasons:

1. No allowance is made for the increased need for money in 1929 and 1938, relative to 1926, resulting from growth in population or in the nation's productive capacity.

2. No allowance is made for the tendency of the population to hold, as time goes by, larger cash balances relative to its expenditures—a trend which was manifested during the 1920s when the price level was approximately stable.

3. Use of demand deposits adjusted plus currency outside banks as the measure of the quantity of money ignores the change which took place between 1926 and 1938 in the conditions attached to the use of time and demand deposits and the consequent fact that in the latter year a significant proportion of demand deposits was serving a monetary function —that of a store of value or money held in readiness for use—which was served to a much greater extent in 1926 by time deposits.

4. Price changes are judged solely by wholesale prices, with no attention to prices at which the products of the economy are sold to their final purchasers.

An examination of the annual changes, during the period since 1918, in the supply of money relative to the need for money, and comparison of those changes with an index of prices of final products, lead to conclusions different from those stated by the Board of Governors. These statistical data give unqualified support to a conclusion closely approximating that of orthodox monetary theory prior to World War I, namely, that changes in the general level of prices depend principally upon changes in the quantity of money relative to the need for money, taking into account the productive capacity of the country and the established monetary habits of the population.

---

[5]"Objectives of Monetary Policy," statement to Chairman of the Senate Committee on Agriculture and Forestry, July 30, 1937, reprinted from *Federal Reserve Bulletin,* September, 1937, pp. 827–28; "Proposals to Maintain Prices at Fixed Levels Through Monetary Action," statement released to the press March 13, 1939, reprinted from *ibid.,* April, 1939, pp. 255–59; and "Statement on Monetary Measures and Objectives," to the Chairmen of the Committees on Banking and Currency of the Senate and House, April 8, 1939, reprinted from *ibid.,* May 1939, pp. 363–64.

[6]*Thirtieth Annual Report of the Board of Governors of the Federal Reserve System,* 1943, p. 10.

[7]*Federal Reserve Bulletin,* April 1939, p. 256.

Regarding the central problem of monetary policy, the relation of such policy to economic stability, the Board of Governors concludes that monetary policy has little influence on economic stability, and that the major cause of inadequate use of the country's economic resources and price fluctuations is variation in the rate of use of money. The Board states:

> It has been the Board's view that, since the money supply, however measured, is larger now than at any previous time, the difficulty must lie not in the scarcity but in the inadequate use of the existing supply.
>
> In the past quarter century it has been demonstrated that policies regulating the quantity and cost of money cannot by themselves produce economic stability, or even exert a powerful influence in that direction.[8]

These views, like those on price theory, are not confirmed by the available factual data. When the appropriate statistical data are examined, the conclusions appear to be inescapable (1) that the reduction in the rate of use of money associated with the production and sale of goods and services during the great depression of the 1930s followed rather than preceded monetary contraction; (2) that the worldwide severity of that depression was primarily due to monetary contraction in the United States; (3) that monetary deficiency is the chief factor originating business depressions or amplifying minor recessions into severe depressions; and (4) that the monetary deficiency preceding each business depression since establishment of the Federal Reserve System — 1921, 1924, 1927, 1930–33, and 1937–38 — has been produced by Federal Reserve action impinging on the quantity of bank reserves.[9]

These conclusions of the Board of Governors regarding the relations of the quantity of money to the price level and to business fluctuations, based on inadequate examination of the factual data, are an effective barrier to the development of the kind of monetary policy needed for full production without price inflation. The attempt of Federal Reserve authorities to develop a theoretical basis for exercise of their monetary powers has been unsuccessful.[10]

---

[8]*Federal Reserve Bulletin*, May 1939, p. 363, and *Thirtieth Annual Report of the Board of Governors of the Federal Reserve System*, 1943, p. 10.

[9]See the following publications: "The Tripartite Problem of Scarce Currencies," *Political Science Quarterly*, LXIV, No. 3 (September 1949), 388–404; "Bank Reserves and Business Fluctuations (*Journal of the American Statistical Association*, Vol. 43 [December 1948], pp. 547–58); and "The Theory of Turning Points in Business Fluctuations" (*Quarterly Journal of Economics*, LXIV [November 1950], pp. 529–49).

[10]For the author's views regarding monetary policy, see, in addition to the references in note 15, the following: "Normal Production, Income, and Employment, 1945 to 1965," *The Southern Economic Journal*, XI, No. 3 (January 1945), 219–45; "Business Stability and Regulation of the Cost of Money" (*The American Journal of Economics and Sociology*, Vol. 4 [January 1945], pp. 175–84); "Monetary Policy in the United States in World War II," *The American Journal of Economics and Sociology*, Vol. 4, No. 3 (April 1945), pp. 375–83; and "The Monetary Theory of Deficit Spending" and reply to comments by H. W. Arndt (*The Review of Economic Statistics*, XXVII, No. 2 [May 1945], 74–84, and XXVIII, No. 2 [May 1946], 92–94).

The views expressed in these articles are summarized in the following statement from one of them: "A suitable volume of money in the economy is a *necessary* condition for maintenance of normal production, and this volume of money, it has been indicated, is a volume which increases as time goes by at a rate approximating the sum of the average annual rate of growth in population, trend of production per capita, and the trend of increased use of money as a store of value" (*Southern Economic Journal*, XI, 234).

Conclusions

The conclusions which emerge from the foregoing discussion may be stated in summary fashion, as follows:

1. The convertibility theory of monetary control embodied in the original Federal Reserve Act was not adequate to meet the monetary problems of modern society, and in fact was abandoned by monetary legislation in the early 1930s.

2. The United States government now has no agency responsible for regulating the value of money, that is, it has no agency which is responsible for preventing, on the one hand, monetary expansion leading to price inflation and, on the other hand, monetary contraction leading to price deflation and business depression.

3. The Board of Governors of the Federal Reserve System, which is generally considered to be the chief monetary agency of the federal government and has stupendous monetary power, has never been given responsibility for monetary control.

4. Monetary law in the United States is ambiguous and chaotic, does not contain a suitable principle for the exercise of the monetary power held by the Federal Reserve System, and has caused confusion in the development of Federal Reserve policy.

5. Extreme monetary maladjustments have occurred since the establishment of the Federal Reserve System, and those maladjustments are primarily responsible for the violence of economic fluctuations during the past three decades.

6. The monetary theory which is held by the Board of Governors of the Federal Reserve System is based on inadequate examination of factual data and is a barrier to development and adoption of the kind of monetary policy needed for full production without inflation.

21

Federal Reserve
Policy from 1941 to 1960

The Creation of Money during World War II

By the beginning of the 1940s, the Federal Reserve System was loaded with monetary dynamite. In December 1940 the balance sheet for all Reserve Banks was as shown in Table 21.1.

Table 21.1. All Reserve Banks as of December 1940
(billions of dollars)

Assets		Liabilities	
Gold certificates	19.92	Federal Reserve notes	5.87
Government securities	2.19	Member reserves	14.05

Reserve ratio: 90 percent

When the values in this balance sheet are compared with those in Table 20.8, the changes between 1932 and 1940 are seen to be almost entirely in gold certificate holdings on the asset side and member bank reserves on the liability side. The member banks held a tremendous amount of excess reserves ($6.62 billion out of a total of $14.05 billion). The total money stock was, however, only $54.2 billion—almost the entire increase since 1929 having been dollar-for-dollar increases with gold.

World War II required the government to spend a great deal of money in the exercise of its military functions. That is, the government had to have control of a much larger share of currently produced goods and services than it had had previously, and it had to have money to effect this control. It could get already existing money by either taxing or borrowing from the nonbank public; it could generate new money by selling securities to the commercial banking system or to the Federal Reserve Banks. With their excess reserves of almost $7 billion, just the member banks alone could generate at least $35 billion in new credit.[1] This amount, however, was small relative to what the Reserve Banks could supply with $18 billion in "excess" gold certificates. Once the Reserve Banks bought government securities, whether firsthand from the Treasury or secondhand in the open market from individuals and commercial banks, their purchases necessarily increased either the outstanding stock of currency or the reserves of the banking system. To see what actually transpired during the war years, compare the Reserve Banks' balance sheet for December 1945 (Table 21.2) with the one for December 1940.

Table 21.2. All Reserve Banks as of December 1945
(billions of dollars)

Assets		*Liabilities*	
Gold certificates	17.9	Federal Reserve notes	24.7
Government securities	24.3	Member reserves	15.9

Reserve ratio: 42 percent

Note: This statement and all subsequent balance sheets were derived from the *Federal Reserve Bulletin*. From this time on, the minimal reserve requirement was 25 percent gold against both Federal Reserve notes and member bank reserves.

The System had purchased $22 billion in government securities, and had used the securities as collateral for issuing $20 billion in Federal Reserve notes. Many of these notes (probably about $6 billion) became a part of the total cash reserves of nonmember banks. The commercial banking system already had excess reserves, so Reserve Bank credit to the banks did not increase by very much. All commercial banks bought about $75 billion in government securities with their excess reserves; and altogether the stock of money increased from $54.2 billion in 1940 to $126 billion five years later, an increase of 133 percent over the five-year period. By way of contrast, the same money stock had increased only 20 percent during the preceding *ten years*.

The monetary pattern of previous wars was largely repeated. The Treasury dominated the scene. Its major consideration was raising money expediently and cheaply in order to pay the government's bills. It insisted, therefore, on

---

[1]Member banks of the Federal Reserve System held at least 85 percent of all reserves by 1940.

"pegging" prices of government securities above levels that the money market would maintain. When the market rejected Treasury issues because the prices were too high (or yields too low), the Treasury turned to the Federal Reserve System for "assistance." The System can never refuse the Treasury, especially under circumstances of "necessity," and the net effect was a substantial expansion of Federal Reserve liabilities, leading to a multiple creation of money. The Treasury could have created the money itself, given congressional sanction for so doing. Other treasuries had done so in the past. However, a central bank between the Treasury and the public had the advantage of obfuscating the money-creating process and of rendering it politically more palatable.

Postwar Performance

The end of the war saw business picking up with a buoyancy it had not shown since the 1920s. The banking system had extended almost all of its credit by buying government securities that now had low yields relative to those possible from private borrowings. Under booming business conditions, therefore, a sizable fraction of bank-held government securities became unattractive as earning assets, and the commercial banks, as well as private investors, turned to other assets for their portfolios as their government securities matured. This action put downward pressure on security prices. Since the Federal Reserve System was committed to the Treasury policy of supporting these prices, the System felt obliged to undertake open market purchases in 1947–1948 in spite of the fact that the stock of money and the price level were both rising. By late 1948 the Reserve Banks' balance sheet was as shown in Table 21.3.

Table 21.3. All Reserve Banks as of December 1948
(billions of dollars)

Assets		Liabilities	
Gold certificates	23.0	Federal Reserve notes	24.2
Government securities	23.3	Member reserves	20.5

Reserve ratio: 49 percent

A comparison of this balance sheet with Table 21.2 shows that the principal changes since 1945 were increases in gold certificates and corresponding increases in member bank reserves. The support of government security prices by Federal Reserve buying in the open market was not reflected in the balance sheet primarily because of *Treasury* monetary policies. In 1945 the Treasury had deposit accounts of $25 billion with the banking system and Federal Reserve Banks. As government securities were turned in for redemption in 1946–1948, the Treasury repurchased them by disinvesting its cash accounts with the banking system. This process did not increase bank reserves; it simply canceled out liabilities of the banks to the Treasury (the Treasury's demand deposit accounts) for liabilities of the Treasury to the banks (government securities held by the banks). The banks were then in a position to make loans to private individuals and businesses in place of the government securities given up.

The Federal Reserve System neither acted to control the postwar inflation by restrictive policies nor tried to neutralize the postwar gold inflows. Gold inflows increased member bank reserves just as if no central bank existed. The System did not aggravate the situation, nor did it buy very many government securities on net balance; but it was prevented from taking remedial action against inflation by its subservience to the Treasury's government security policy.

Late in 1948 and through much of 1949 the economy suffered from its first postwar recession. Government security prices had become stabilized, so the Board felt free to sell government securities throughout 1949 even though the strength in security prices was an index that inflation had abated. By December 1949, the Reserve Banks' balance sheet was as shown in Table 21.4.

Table 21.4. All Reserve Banks as of December 1949
(billions of dollars)

Assets		*Liabilities*	
Gold certificates	23.2	Federal Reserve notes	23.5
Government securities	18.9	Member reserves	16.6

Reserve ratio: 55 percent

E. A. Goldenweiser remarked on this policy: "Sales of securities by the Federal Reserve were diminishing member-bank reserves at a time when bank credit was contracting in a recession."[2] Reserve requirements and discount rates were lowered to offset the recession, but the effects of these policies were too slow to counteract the depressive results of open market sales. Not until the Treasury once again "needed" funds in order to finance government operations during the early stages of the Korean War did the Federal Reserve System increase its holdings of government securities. By this time the economy had largely recovered from the recession of 1949. Booming business under the catalyst of wartime spending called for central bank restraints, but again

---

[2]E. A. Goldenweiser, *American Monetary Policy* (New York: McGraw-Hill Book Co., 1951), p. 211.

the Federal Reserve System was called upon to act as a handmaiden for Treasury financing. Purchases of securities to support Treasury policy added to member bank reserves and were a further stimulus to spending. Fortunately, Treasury fiscal operations were stringent enough to keep the volume of deficit financing minimal. Nevertheless, in the two years between December 1949 and December 1951, the Fed added $5 billion in government securities to its portfolio. (See Table 21.5.)

Table 21.5. All Reserve Banks as of December 1951
(billions of dollars)

Assets		*Liabilities*	
Gold certificates	21.5	Federal Reserve notes	25.1
Government securities	23.8	Member reserves	20.1

Reserve ratio: 48 percent

The Federal Reserve System is not to be blamed for following Treasury "leadership." As Thomas Hobbes, the great political philosopher, once wrote: "When two men ride on a horse, one has to ride in front." When decisions of policy are to be made at the highest executive level, one group must be able to get its will into action. The Treasury was and is politically dominant because of its position in the executive branch of the government. Conflict over policy, however, cannot be resolved by a simple institutional change. The Federal Reserve System is a child of Congress, and Congress has constitutional control over monetary policy. Therefore, executive dominance of monetary policy is also executive usurpation of congressional powers. This problem became acute in the late forties.

Resolution of the Conflict between the Treasury and the Federal Reserve System

Federal Reserve support of government security prices during the 1940s has been aptly described by one economist as follows:

> In short, we are now on what may be called a "low-yield government security standard," for the Federal Reserve stands ready to monetize all the debt that others are unwilling to hold at the selected pattern of yields. And the commercial banks can, of course, expand their credit by a multiple of any new reserves furnished to them by this process, just as they can in response to increases of the monetary gold stock.[3]

---

[3]Lester V. Chandler, "Federal Reserve Policy and the Federal Debt," *American Economic Review*, Vol. 39, No. 1 (March 1949), p. 419.

Economists and others generally condemned the support policy as well as the political subservience of the Federal Reserve System to the Treasury Department. The System had been created on the supposition that it would be independent of just such political connections. The Treasury's motives were clearly expedients; they were also superficial and ineffective. What good to the general welfare was a policy that maintained the money value of just one "commodity" (government securities) when the indirect effects of such a trivial goal at the same time forced all other prices to rise, thus vitiating as well the real value of the price-supported securities?

The general criticisms of Treasury policy were valid, but other factors gave support to Treasury dominance. The Treasury had to integrate its fiscal policy with the general economic policy of the administration, and the administration could not afford to have monetary policy out of step with overall economic policy no matter how reprehensible were the details of the general monetary program. No administration is liable to subject itself to the views of an "independent" authority when it feels strongly that the authority's values and opinions are incompatible with its own.

So great was the furor over the Federal Reserve–Treasury dispute that Congress formed the "Douglas Committee" (Subcommittee on Monetary, Credit, and Fiscal Policies of the Joint Committee on the Economic Report) in 1949 to thresh out the matter.[4] The Committee's *Report,* in effect, threw much congressional support on the side of the Federal Reserve System. "The essential characteristic of a monetary policy that will promote general economic stability," the *Report* stated, "is its timely flexibility." Federal Reserve policy during and after World War II, by way of contrast, had been "to maintain an orderly market for government securities" with a rigid pattern of yield rates on the various issues of these securities.[5] Such rigidity, the *Report* advised, denied the possibility of timely flexibility in the conduct of monetary policy. It concluded that the Federal Reserve System was responsible to Congress, that it was not and should not be an arm of the executive branch, that maintenance of orderly conditions in the government securities market was desirable, but that

the advantages of avoiding inflation are so great that they should be pursued even if the cost is a significant increase in the service charges on the federal debt and a greater inconvenience to the Treasury in its sale of new securities for new financing and refunding purposes.

---

[4]*Monetary, Credit and Fiscal Policies: Report of the Subcommittee, Joint Committee on the Economic Report,* 81st Congress, 2nd sess., 1950, Senate Document No. 129. Reprinted in part in Lawrence S. Ritter, ed., *Money and Economic Activity: Readings in Money and Banking* (Boston: Houghton Mifflin Co., 1961).

[5]The yield pattern had been ⅜ of 1 percent on 90-day Treasury bills, ⅞ of 1 percent on nine- to twelve-month certificates, 2 percent on ten-year bonds, and 2½ percent on the longest bonds.

Finally, the *Report* concluded, Congress by joint resolution should issue general instructions to the Federal Reserve System and the Treasury that would charge both agencies to "be guided primarily by considerations relating to their [policies'] effects on employment, production, purchasing power, and price levels, and that such policies shall be consistent with and shall promote the purpose of the Employment Act of 1946."

The effect of a congressional report is not merely analytical and reportorial, and it not only paves the way for further action by Congress. It also "legislates," in an unofficial manner, the intention and opinion of an influential segment of Congress. The Douglas Subcommittee report, therefore, was supposed to serve both as a reprimand to the Treasury's unbelievably adamant and illogical policy of low interest rates at any price (level), and as reinforcement for Federal Reserve freedom from Treasury subjugation.

The Treasury Department, and the Truman administration generally, were extremely stubborn about retreating on their policies. After the outbreak of the Korean War the financial necessities of the government gave further impetus to the administration's compulsion for intervention and control. The climax came in January 1951 when Secretary of the Treasury John Snyder, after one of the frequent luncheon meetings between Treasury and Federal Reserve officials, made a public statement implying that the Federal Reserve had agreed to continue support of the Treasury's interest rate policy. In fact, no such agreement had been made by the Board of Governors at the meeting. Secretary Snyder's intention clearly was to "present the Reserve System with a fait accompli."[6] In the same month, after an executive meeting that included President Truman and the Board, Secretary Snyder used the same tactic again. The President authorized a press release stating that the Federal Reserve had pledged "cooperation" in maintaining the market for government securities at "present levels." But the minutes of the executive meeting between the President and the Board of Governors showed no such agreement. Once again the administration was attempting to bring the Federal Reserve System into line. When the details of this attempt became known, both public and congressional opinion swung around even further in support of the System.[7]

These events finally led to an "accord" between the two agencies on March 4, 1951, in which debt management was thenceforth to be the responsibility of the Treasury and credit control the responsibility of the Federal Reserve System. From this time on Federal Reserve policy, whatever its other constraints and peculiarities, was not responsible for supporting the government securities market. Interestingly enough, after Federal Reserve support was

---

[6]Marriner S. Eccles, "The Climax of the Treasury–Federal Reserve Dispute," reprinted in Ritter, ed., *Money and Economic Activity.*

[7]The complete and fascinating account of the political maneuvering in this fracas is well reported by Eccles in his article. It reveals that the "independence" of the Federal Reserve was truly mythical and that the Board of Governors, except for Eccles, had no stomach for resisting the demands of the administration.

removed the prices of government securities showed little change until 1954, at which time they *rose* by approximately 8 percent. By 1956, they were again at the same level as in 1951.

Policy during the Recession of 1953

The Consumer Price Index continued to show a slight rise through 1952, but the Wholesale Index turned down early in 1951. By the middle of 1953 a business downswing was clearly in progress. To offset the developing recession, the Federal Reserve reduced member bank reserve requirements for the different classes of banks from 24, 20, and 14 percent to 22, 19, and 13 percent, effective in July 1953. At the same time, open market purchases of about $1 billion were made. Discount rates were reduced from 2 percent to 1½ percent, effective in May 1954, and reserve requirements were again lowered in the summer of 1954 to 20, 18, and 12 percent. All these actions had the effect of increasing free reserves[8] of member banks from $−0.9 billion in late 1952 to $0.8 billion two years later.

The combined balance sheet of all Reserve Banks showed little change for several years after 1951 except for the slight increase in government security holdings in 1953–1954. In spite of the recession, no major problems arose requiring large-scale actions. The reserve requirement changes and discounting operations used in 1953–1954 had no direct effect on the combined balance sheet.

The "Bills Only" Doctrine

Federal Reserve freedom from the Treasury's compulsion to support the prices of government securities was helpful, too; but in 1953 the Federal Reserve substituted a self-imposed constraint in place of the Treasury domination from which it had been so recently freed. This new twist became known as the "bills only" policy. It also has been labeled "the Martin Doctrine," after the Chairman of the Board of Governors, William McChesney Martin. Finally, it evolved into "bills usually" or "bills preferably," and since 1960 has gradually and quietly slipped into limbo.

Its ground rules of operation were simple enough and were stated explicitly by the Federal Reserve Board. The Board (1) recognized that open market operations in government securities are the primary means of carrying out

---

[8]"Free reserves" are total excess reserves of member banks less member bank borrowings at Reserve Banks. When borrowings exceed excess reserves, the item is referred to as "net borrowed reserves."

central bank policies. However, (2) such operations, the Board argued, should be conducted only in *short-term* government securities, that is, in those securities with maturity dates of less than one year. (3) It also held that no support should be given in any way to Treasury financing operations. (4) The technical rationale for this policy was that central bank operations in short-term securities have the least influence ("minimum intervention") on private decisions of savers and investors in securities markets.[9]

For the Federal Reserve to have slipped loose from the shackles of the Treasury only to cut short its newly found freedom with a self-imposed rule seems peculiar to say the least. It seems even more peculiar when the long history of Federal Reserve antipathy to "rules" is recalled. Many times in the past Federal Reserve officials had testified before Congress and declared in professional journals that even general rules pertaining to either ends or means, such as maintenance of a stable price level or fixed percentage increases in the stock of money, would be inappropriate, not to say impossible, for the Federal Reserve to follow. Why, then, a self-imposed rule, and especially one that had such a weak and tenuous rationalization?

The most logical answer to the enigma seems to be chiefly political. Federal Reserve officials, while enjoying their emancipation from the Treasury, were not so naive as to think that it necessarily would be permanent, especially in view of the Treasury's possible fiscal needs for the Korean War and the continuing cold war. By establishing an official "tradition" of dealing in bills only, the System could absolve itself of any responsibility for supporting long-term security prices in the open market. A Treasury "request" to do so could be met with the cool response that "We do not deal in the long market."

The final question might be, "Why pick the short-terms over the longs?" The answer here is that *prices* of short-term issues fluctuate much less than prices of long-term issues, while *yield rates* on shorts fluctuate much more than yield rates on longs.[10] Prices of short-term securities thus would need little support. This "natural" stability together with a "tradition" of dealing only in shorts would maximize the chances for the System to remain independent of the Treasury's political hand.

---

[9]A more exhaustive discussion of the "bills only" policy may be found in Ritter, ed., *Money and Economic Activity*. See also *Federal Reserve System: Purposes and Functions* (Washington, D.C.: Board of Governors of the Federal Reserve System, 1961), Ch. 5. The 1963 edition of the *Purposes and Functions* booklet does not even mention the policy.

[10]The reason for these divergences is clear. Given some real "shock" in the money market, such as an anticipation of continued inflation, current prices of long-term bonds would fall farther than prices of short-term securities because the long-term bonds reflect much more of the anticipated time deterioration in the value of the dollar. A short-term security could not depreciate very far in absolute terms before it was paid off. The pattern for changes in yield rates, on the other hand, is just the contrary. The supply of funds for short-term securities is very inelastic. The sources of this supply are primarily the many kinds of banks and financial institutions, all of whom want a short-term repository for contingency funds. Long-term commitments can be much more discriminatory. (See Chapter 5.)

Table 21.6 shows how maturities of security holdings of the twelve Federal Reserve Banks changed during the period of "bills only." Not only did the System's holdings shift into maturities of one year and less, a sizable fraction also came into the less-than-90-day category.

Table 21.6. Maturity Distribution of Federal Reserve Banks'
Holdings of U.S. Government Securities, 1951–1960
(billions of dollars)

December 31	Total	Less than 90 Days	91 days–1 year	1–5 Years	5–10 Years	Over 10 Years
1951	23.8	0.7	14.4	5.1	1.0	2.6
1952	24.7	5.1	10.5	6.7	1.1	1.4
1953	26.0	7.1	9.9	6.2	1.4	1.4
1954	24.9	6.2	13.2	3.1	1.0	1.4
1955	24.8	5.9	14.9	1.6	1.0	1.4
1956	24.9	7.0	15.1	0.4	1.0	1.4
1957	24.2	7.0	14.4	1.4	0.1	1.4
1958	26.4	7.8	13.2	3.9	0.2	1.3
1959	26.7	7.7	10.9	6.5	0.4	1.1
1960	27.4	6.1	9.2	10.7	1.2	0.3

Source: Board of Governors of the Federal Reserve System, *Federal Reserve Bulletin*, selected issues.

The total quantity of government securities held remained almost constant from 1951 to 1958 except for the purchases that countered the recession of 1953–1954. During this period the Treasury Department maintained a "hands off" policy that was notable. In view of the Treasury's forbearance, Federal Reserve apprehension somewhat lessened. After 1958, Federal Reserve holdings of one- to five-year certificates increased appreciably, and bill holdings were substantially reduced.

The Recession of 1957–1958

The combined balance sheet for the System in September 1957 (Table 21.7) shows little change from its composition in 1951. (See Table 21.5.) The Wholesale Price Index, after increasing from 111 to 114 between 1955 and 1956 and from 114 to 118 between 1956 and mid-1957, showed no further increase in the last six months of the year. The Consumer Price Index behaved comparably. However, unemployment figures showed a significant increase—from about 2.6 million persons in August 1957 to a peak of 5.2 million in March 1958.

The Federal Reserve System began counter-recession maneuvers in October 1957. During the next six months, discount rates were lowered from 3½ percent to 1¾ percent; open market purchases supplied commercial banks with about $2 billion in reserves; and reserve requirement reductions from 20, 18, and 12 percent to 18, 16½, and 11 percent "released" another $1.5 billion in member bank reserves for credit expansion. On net balance the free reserve position of member banks changed from $−0.5 billion in mid-1957 to $0.5 billion in mid-1958.

Table 21.7. All Reserve Banks as of September 1957
(billions of dollars)

Assets		Liabilities	
Gold certificates	21.1	Federal Reserve notes	26.9
Government securities	23.3	Member reserves	19.0

Reserve ratio: 47 percent

As Table 21.8 shows, total monetary obligations of the Reserve Banks (the basis of the economy's money supply) hardly increased at all in spite of System policies. However, reductions in reserve requirements had "stretched" reserves so that the existing amount would go farther, and lower discount rates had made bank borrowing easier. Prices were again buoyant and unemployment figures declined but remained at about 5 percent of the labor force through 1959.[11]

Table 21.8. All Reserve Banks as of June 1958
(billions of dollars)

Assets		Liabilities	
Gold certificates	20.8	Federal Reserve notes	26.7
Government securities	25.4	Member reserves	18.8

Reserve ratio: 47 percent

---

[11]For different reasons, but in a fashion similar to price index biases, unemployment figures also have had an "inflationary" bias since about 1958. They read larger than they "should" due to the influence of the baby boom in the 1940s. The babies of that era just started to enter the labor force in the late 1950s, thus increasing the *rate* of increase in employable people. Minimum wage laws have also generated unemployment among the lower wage groups since 1956, when the current escalation of the minimum began.

Summary of Federal Reserve Policy in the Fifties

Federal Reserve policy between 1951 and 1960 was fairly consistent in some respects. The most notable feature was a constant reduction in member bank reserve requirements with only a little activity in the government securities market. In part, the reliance on changes in reserve requirements was an attempt to get these values closer to the middle of the allowable range. The weighted average of the requirements on demand deposits for all member banks in the System fell from 19.6 percent in June 1951 to 14.9 percent by December 1960 — a quasi-increase in dollar reserves of 31 percent. At the same time actual dollar reserves were reduced from $20.3 billion to $19.3 billion. On net balance these two changes resulted in an increase of demand deposits, from $93 billion to $111 billion, for this period.

Another reason for central bank emphasis on reserve requirement changes, rather than on open market operations, was the desire of the Federal Reserve authorities to avoid dealings in government securities in order to discourage, again, any presumption of the executive that these prices should be kept "orderly" (meaning, supported). But the executive branch interfered little if at all after 1951.

Table 21.9. Yearly Averages and Rates of Change in the Stock of Money and All Time Deposits, and the Consumer Price Index, 1951–1960

Yearly Averages of	1951	1952	1953	1954	1955	1956	1957	1958	1959	1960
Currency and demand deposits (billions of dollars) M_1	115	121	124	125	131	133	134	135	141	138
Time deposits (billions of dollars) Td	60.0	63.7	68.3	73.3	77.1	80.6	85.7	95.5	101	104
Change in M_1 (% per year)	—	5.0	2.5	0.8	4.8	1.5	0.7	0.7	4.4	−2.1
Change in Td (% per year)	—	6.1	7.1	7.2	5.1	4.5	6.4	11.4	5.8	3.0
CPI	90.5	92.5	93.2	93.6	93.3	94.7	98.0	100.7	101.5	103.1

Sources: Department of Commerce, *Historical Statistics of the United States, Colonial Times to 1957* (Washington, D.C., 1960), Section X; and Board of Governors of the Federal Reserve System, *Federal Reserve Bulletin*, selected issues.

Table 21.9 summarizes monetary developments during most of the decade of the fifties. The so-called "narrow" stock of money—currency outside banks and demand deposits adjusted for interbank holdings—grew very nominally, the average annual growth rate for the years shown being 2.0 percent. Time deposits grew more than three times as rapidly, or at an average annual rate of 6.3 percent. This difference reflected the higher interest rates paid by the banks for time deposits, and probably the greater demand of the public to obtain them as contingency reserves. Only in this period did the monetary uncertainties bred by the Depression years begin to dissipate. This fact is reflected in the income velocity of money, which increased by 26 percent, and approached the values it had shown in the twenties.

The Consumer Price Index registered only one year-by-year increase as large as 3 percent (1956–1957). Such a record must be judged as very good, especially because of some upward bias in the index itself (see Chapter 2), and also by comparison with the record of Federal Reserve performance at previous times.

As the 1950s closed, however, a new situation began to appear: the search for an international monetary policy that would provide stability with economic freedom. An evaluation of policy in the sixties must include this matter as well as domestic developments.

Selected Bibliography

Ahearn, Daniel S. *Federal Reserve Policy Reappraised, 1951–1959.* New York: Columbia University Press, 1963.

Beard, Thomas R. "Debt Management: Its Relationship to Monetary Policy, 1951–1962." *The National Banking Review,* Vol. 2 (September 1964), pp. 61–76.

Lutz, Friedrich A., and Lloyd W. Mints, eds. *Readings in Monetary Theory.* Homewood, Ill.: Richard D. Irwin, 1951. Besides the articles on monetary theory, this collection contains several important articles on monetary policy.

Mints, Lloyd W. *Monetary Policy for a Competitive Society.* New York: McGraw-Hill Book Co., 1950. A general discussion of monetary policy.

Ritter, Lawrence S., ed. *Money and Economic Activity: Readings in Money and Banking.* Boston: Houghton Mifflin Co., 1961. A good collection of readings on the interest pegging policy and "bills only."

Warburton, Clark. *Depression, Inflation, and Monetary Policy.* Baltimore: Johns Hopkins Press, 1966.

Federal Reserve Monetary Policies

Senate Committee on Banking and Currency,
Subcommittee on the Federal Reserve

This paper affords the student an opportunity to gain valuable insight into the operating relationship between Congress and the Federal Reserve System. It clearly demonstrates how System officials deliver economic policy information to Congress and in return gain a better understanding of congressional attitudes. Also indicated is the Federal Reserve System's thinking, as represented by the then Chairman of the Board of Governors, William McChesney Martin, on economic tools and policies during the 1950s.

The subcommittee met, pursuant to call, at 10:10 a.m., in room 301, Senate Office Building, Senator J. Allen Frear, Jr. (chairman of the subcommittee) presiding.

Present: Senators Frear, Robertson, Douglas, Proxmire, Bricker, and Bennett.

Also present: Senators Fulbright, Clark, Bush, and Case.

Senator Frear. The subcommittee will come to order.

For several years the Senate Banking and Currency Committee has called upon the staff of the Federal Reserve Board to furnish the committee with an up-to-date economic briefing at the beginning of each new session of Congress. This we have found helpful and necessary because of the vital role played by Congress, and especially this committee, in the formulation of policies which have great impact on the national economy....

During our last briefing session with the Board's staff, which was held on January 24, several members of the committee expressed a desire to discuss the policy aspects of the economic picture as well as the factual data which the staff presented. Obviously, the Board's staff could not discuss policy issues, with sufficient responsibility, as members of this committee desired. Therefore, we have requested the Chairman of the Board of Governors of the Federal Reserve System, the Honorable William McChesney Martin, Jr., to appear before us to discuss these matters, and he has kindly consented.

Chairman Martin, we are very pleased to have you with us this morning. I assume that you have a statement prepared to give us. And then there will certainly be some questions from the members of the committee.

Mr. Martin. That will be fine, Mr. Chairman. May I proceed?

Senator Frear. You may.

Hearing before a subcommittee of the Committee on Banking and Currency, U.S. Senate, 85th Congress, 2nd sess., February 19, 1958.

Mr. Martin. The year 1957 was a difficult one for those of us charged with appraising financial and economic events and formulating appropriate monetary policy. From its opening and on during much of the year, inflationary pressures were dominant in this country and abroad.

In commodity markets, industrial prices were continuing to advance despite generally downward reaction in prices of some internationally traded basic materials following the Suez crisis. In consumer markets, prices of goods and services were advancing at a very rapid pace for a nonwar period....

In spite of Federal Reserve actions taken to resist inflationary trends — including six increases of Federal Reserve bank discount rates in 1955 and 1956 and the pursuance of a restrictive credit policy — money lost its value at a rate that was a matter of great concern to all. Inflationary excesses had clearly gotten ahead of us, and the economy stood in danger of an inflation crisis. The adjustment problems that the economy is confronting today are the aftermath of those excesses.

In response to this change in basic economic conditions, Federal Reserve bank discount rates were reduced from 3½ to 3 percent.

Since that time, the use of open-market and discount policies has been complementary. Open-market operations have provided sufficient reserves to permit member banks not only to repay a substantial portion of their indebtedness to the Reserve banks, but also to accumulate some addition to reserves available for bank credit expansion. Discount rates were lowered again in mid-January, from 3 to 2¾ percent....

We are all, of course, well aware that reasoning by analogy may be misleading and that history does not repeat itself. Nevertheless, it may be noted that the downward movement from the third quarter 1957 peak has been reminiscent in many ways of the declines that occurred in 1948–49 and in 1953–54. In these two postwar recessions, lows in activity were reached in less than a year from the cyclical peak, and recovery to new high levels of output, demands, and employment was rapid and substantial. In both recessions, the industrial production decline was limited to about 10 percent from high to low. With the exception of the catastrophic depression of the early 1930s, the downward phase of every cycle since World War I has been over or virtually over in the course of about a year....

When contractive tendencies in economic activity set in, there is always the hazard that recession may be deeper and more protracted than many anticipate, with a greater degree of underutilization of manpower and industrial resources and with manifest deflationary tendencies. In such an eventuality further monetary action would need to be considered, both to increase the liquidity of the economy and to encourage expansion of spending financed by credit.

Monetary policy by itself, however, cannot assure resumption of high-level employment and sustainable economic growth, although ready availability of credit at reasonable cost is certainly an essential ingredient for recovery.

Those of us charged with responsibility for national economic policies must at all times reckon with the dangers both of inflation and of deflation. The central policy problem, in one sense, is to prevent either inflationary trends or deflationary trends from becoming dominant. Public policies for one objective or another can have effects that go far beyond those that are intended. Both fiscal and monetary policies must be carefully formulated to exert enough pressure or ease but not too much. That is certainly a difficult task. It is one that you and I both must live with every day and do the very best we can to reach the judgments and come to the decisions which in the long run will prove to have been wise.

As I have said on many occasions, anti-inflationary policies and antideflationary policies are inseparably linked. Excesses on the up side must be avoided in order to avoid the heavy costs and personal hardships that unfortunately develop during the ensuing contraction. Now that we are in the contractive phase, we must take whatever actions are needed to minimize the hardships and to foster vigorous recovery. But in so doing we also must recognize that excessive stimulus during recession can sow seeds of inflation that can grow to jeopardize our long-run stability and our economic strength at a time when as a Nation we are confronted with a special urgency to maintain all the productive strength we can muster on a sustainable basis....,

Senator Frear. Mr. Chairman, do you think an economic upturn will occur in March?

Mr. Martin. I have to answer that by saying I do not know.

Senator Frear. There has been a great deal of publicity regarding March as the month of upturn.

Mr. Martin. Well, I have tried to keep out of the prediction business.

Senator Frear. The Federal Reserve Board has been given various tools which it can employ to promote economic stability. Perhaps it would be helpful, Mr. Chairman, if you would briefly outline what your main tools are, along with, if you care to, your opinion as to the relative value of these tools and under what circumstances they can be most helpful.

Mr. Martin. Well, I think the three tools that we have are well known to you.

The discount rate is the rate that we charge the member banks that borrow reserves from us.

Our open market operations by the purchase or sale of Government securities supply or absorb reserves in the market.

With respect to reserve requirements, we are given authority in the Federal Reserve Act to vary reserve requirements by classes of banks....

Concerning the use of these instruments, I think you have to evaluate the position that [the] economy is in at a given time. We have felt that the reserve requirements is probably the bluntest of our instruments. There has been quite a bit of discussion during the restrictive monetary policy of, "Why didn't you raise reserve requirements?"

Reserve requirements, in my judgment, got too high for the type of monetary policy we are now trying to operate, during the period when we had a pegged market. They were being asked to do things that were not contemplated.

Fundamentally, reserve requirements are the fulcrum around which monetary policy becomes effective....

Senator Frear. What is its relative importance to the others, in your opinion?

Mr. Martin. The way I would put it is this: We would probably be better off if we made only major adjustments in reserve requirements. But first, we need to arrive at some better system of reserve requirements than we have at the present time. That has been a most difficult thing for us to achieve because of the disagreements between bankers, which represent, I am sure, honest differences of view.

I think the geographic classification is largely outmoded today. But I do not think it is totally outmoded. What I would like to see is an ultimate reserve requirement that would be based on size of bank, velocity or turnover, and the nature of the business, in preference to mere geographic distinctions....

Now, as a fulcrum, we have tried to have an overall reserve of about 16½ percent. I am pulling all of these ratios together in an average here. I think it would be desirable if we had a little different system of reserve requirements. But, since we do not have a different system of reserve requirements, I think we have to be careful and not favor one class of banks against another competitively just because at that particular point it looks like you would reasonably inject more reserves into the money market. We should not favor one group or another group, but try to look at the national policy as a whole.

The reserve requirement instrument is one that we have labored with about as strenuously as we possibly can, but we still have differences of opinion in our own Board and among our presidents as to the exact way in which it should be used.

Senator Frear. That is stimulating also. The differences of opinion are stimulating.

Mr. Martin. That is indeed. I am very glad to say we have differences in the Federal Reserve.

Senator Frear. Do you think Federal Reserve actions can be as helpful in stimulating investment during a recession as they are in retarding investment during a period of inflation?

Mr. Martin. I do not think they can be quite as helpful because of the human factor.

Let me put it this way: They may be equally as effective in either direction, but it is harder to put people under restraint, even though it may be desirable in an expanding economy, and it is easier to get people to ease money in a declining economy.

If you operated without those human factors, I would think that you would be much more effective in restraining than you are in stimulating. But I think that those human factors have a tendency to even up the effectiveness.

Senator Frear. How do you account for the 1956–57 inflation despite the Federal Reserve's strict credit policies?

Mr. Martin. Well, I account for it by the fact that all of us underestimated the strength of the boom, and I think that we went on a spending spree and an expanding spree. Where I think Federal Reserve policy is vulnerable is that we should have been tighter — not that we were too tight in the policy. And I think that we should have had more support from a larger budget surplus and from other restraining factors in the economy, including the management of the Federal debt.

I think we tended to be slow in our start, and then the momentum gathered up on us, and then, at the tail end of it, it was perfectly obvious to a lot of us that it was being overdone.

When you lose more than $10 billion of your gross national product in a markup in prices without any additional goods and services, you know something has gone wrong.

The cost of living index was going up every month on us. It just got away from us. And, I think as the result, we are now suffering from the inevitable aftermath.... Chairman Fulbright?

Senator Fulbright. Mr. Chairman, I have 1 or 2 questions.

I would like to pursue a bit your last observation that you did not act soon enough or fast enough and your only criticism of your policy was you were not tough enough.

You recall this committee had a hearing in the spring of 1955, did it not, on this subject?

Mr. Martin. You did.

Senator Fulbright. Did the committee not try to urge you and others to take note of the inflationary tendencies in our economy?

Mr. Martin. I think that hearing was very helpful, and we did take some action subsequently. We did not take as —

Senator Fulbright. You took some, but did any other agencies in the Government? Did the Treasury take any note of it or do anything in respect to their policies?

Mr. Martin. Well, they did not do enough. Let's put it that way.

Senator Fulbright. Would you not say that the tax bill of 1954 contributed to the overexpansion of the productive capacity?

Mr. Martin. As things developed; yes.

Senator Fulbright. It was quite clear in 1955 that that would be the effect, was it not? That is what this committee — certain members at least — alleged; was it not?

Mr. Martin. Well, I am inclined to agree with you, but it is a matter of judgment there.

Senator Fulbright. But it is not a matter of judgment now. The facts bore out the views of the committee at that time; did they not?

Mr. Martin. I think subsequent events did.

Senator Fulbright. Is that not the proof that they were correct at the time?

Mr. Martin. Well, for that period; yes.

Senator Fulbright. That hearing did not amount to shouting "Fire" in a crowded theater and did not cause an undermining of the economy of the country; did it?

Mr. Martin. No.

Senator Fulbright. You recall the committee was accused of doing that; do you not? You remember that; do you not?

Mr. Martin. I remember it very well.

Senator Fulbright. Recently Mr. Burns, who was, as you know, formerly Chairman of the President's Council of Economic Advisers, was reported to have said in the New York Times on Sunday, February 16, and I quote for the record:

> Professor Burns believes that the recession which began after the peak in July and August 1957 will continue "at least for some weeks or months." The contraction will not be ended by a revival of business investment, of export demand, or any other economic development but only by "massive" Government intervention.

Do you agree with that statement?

Mr. Martin. No; I do not think I do.

Senator Fulbright. I wish you would comment on it. I would like to see your difference of view about it.

Mr. Martin. Well, I have some question about massive Government intervention. To me, I have no question about the strength and vitality of this American economy. And I think that recovery is assured.

As I have stated recently, I look on it as a patient — to put it in those terms — who has overexerted himself. You want to do all you can to help that patient. You do not want to punish him on account of the fact that he has overexerted himself; you want to give him all the solace and comfort and whatever medication you can give him.

But you have got to be very careful that you do not rush in with a hypodermic that will temporarily create stimulus that will cause him to get up and run a 100-yard dash and then fall back in a worse state than he was before.

Now, I think that that is where you have to watch massive Government intervention. And I think what is required here is that our recovery is assured on a sustainable basis — provided we do not engage in too much foolishness about it and we just go about it in an orderly, sensible, intelligent way....

Senator Fulbright. As of today you do not see the need for a substantial tax cut?

Mr. Martin. I do not as of today.

Senator Fulbright. How about substantial expansion of Government expenditures on public works?

Mr. Martin. I do not see that as of today.

Senator Fulbright. As between those two, would you have any preference if you had to make a choice today? Would you have any preference between one or the other procedure?

Mr. Martin. No; I would not think either one of them would be — I think that public works expenditures would be preferable to a tax cut.

Senator Fulbright. That is what I mean.

Mr. Martin. Yes.

Senator Fulbright. Supposing you had to make a choice.

Mr. Martin. If I had to take one —

Senator Fulbright. You would take public works over taxes?

Mr. Martin. Right....

Senator Fulbright. One last thing. I thought it would be helpful to the committee if in addition to your discussion of reserve requirements you could say a little about your open-market operations. They go hand in hand, do they not, as to their effect?

Mr. Martin. Yes. Well, with our open-market operations, as indicated in the paper, we began to lessen pressure in that way in mid-October. Then after the cut in the discount rate —

Senator Fulbright. You began to buy bonds, did you?

Mr. Martin. That is correct....

Senator Fulbright. What happened? Would you describe it a little?

Mr. Martin. We had a minus reserve, net borrowed reserve, of about $500 million that we were running in late October and early November, and today we have free reserves. This has been done over a gradual period of time by purchases of bonds in the market. We have free reserves of $200 million, approximately. So that is about a $700 million swing in a period of about less than 3 months.

Senator Fulbright. What has been the effect on prices of Governments?

Mr. Martin. It has been a very sharp decline in rates generally.

Senator Fulbright. Putting it in other words, an increase in the price of Governments on the market?

Mr. Martin. That is right....

Senator Fulbright. I will conclude by saying that within your jurisdiction, the Federal Reserve, I think you all have done a very good job, with the exception that you were a little slow in 1955, as you have already stated, in taking hold....

Senator Robertson. You said the pattern of this recession should follow all of our other recessions — except the big one of the thirties when it was worldwide — lasting not over a year.

Then you give us seven encouraging things on the side of a recovery, without saying whether it is going to be March, April, May, June, or July. You say there is going to be recovery, and here are the reasons you think so:

There is an ample supply of credit.
There is a population increase.
Consumer incomes have held up mighty well.
There will be large Federal and local spending.
There will be a big defense budget.
And there is no depression in Western Europe.

Those things are on the favorable side — at least you think — and there will be a recovery.

Then you wind up with a statement leaving us, of course, to make the application, as pointed out by Senator Fulbright. You say that we must take whatever actions are needed to minimize the hardships but avoid excessive stimulation.

I heard a story once about a good old Methodist sister who complained that her preacher smoked a pipe, and she said:

"Now, Doctor, don't you think that is wrong?"

He said, "No, Sister, not unless he smokes to excess."

"Well," said the sister, "what would you call excess?"

He said, "Smoking two pipes at once."

I understand that for the time being the 7 pipes that you have lit on the recovery side are all that you think are needed, and that if we were to light, for example, big deficit spending or a tax cut, which certainly would go first to consumer spending such as a $100 increase in personal exemptions, that would be smoking 2 pipes at once? It would be excessive at the present time?

Mr. Martin. At the moment I think so; yes, sir.

Senator Robertson. Is that the proper application of your philosophy?

Mr. Martin. Yes. I do not have any —

Senator Robertson. You did say recovery would be stimulated by a reduction in prices. The last presentation of the economic picture by your experts was that there had been no cut, no appreciable cut, in wholesale prices although there was considerable unemployment. There had been a reduction in production, yet wholesale prices held up.

How are we going to get any reduction in prices if the manufacturers do not cut, if the wholesale houses do not cut? You cannot expect the retailer to take it all, can you?

Mr. Martin. Well, that is the market process. I think the pressure will force some reductions. And, of course, you are on unpopular ground with anybody when you suggest he cut prices if he has got a stock that he hopes to be bailed out of either by waiting until the recovery gets a little bit further ahead or some other stimulus will come in and save him.

Senator Robertson. Some of my banker friends tell me that a cut in the reserve rate would be more stimulating to them than a cut in the rediscount rate. Have you had many requests from member banks that you cut reserve rates?

Mr. Martin. Yes; we have heard that. We have had the story on both sides. If you took our mail, we have a good many people who think we should not have cut the rediscount rate. There is a smaller number as time goes on, but you have some. There are some who think the way to have handled it would have been to reduce reserve requirements.

Senator Robertson. In other words, do you think that credit at the present time is sufficiently easing to take care of creditworthy risks that are applying for capital?

Mr. Martin. I think that the availability of credit has been steadily improving, Senator.

Now, I do not say that it has been totally adequate. I think that is something you have to measure from day to day and week to week. And that is one of our major concerns right now. If we had a sudden resurgence of activity, a real boom, we would consider reversing monetary policy in the direction of putting the discount rate back up. But if, on the other hand, the decline continues, we have got to look at the situation as it is and be certain that there is availability of credit.

There is no question that the availability of credit has improved. You can see it in the mortgage market. It has been steadily improving there.

Now, it is not running out everyone's ears yet, but I think you have got to be very careful that you do not force credit. This is borrowed money.

Senator Robertson. According to the records of the State unemployment offices, we have over 4 million unemployed at the present time, and for them this is a real depression. They are suffering hardships, but, as you pointed out, we have a better system of unemployment compensation than we had in any previous real depression and that is helping to tide us over. But there are some hardships.

And you say that we should take action to minimize the hardships. But you said an immediate tax cut is not one of them. Pump priming is not one of them. You said reducing prices would be one of them, but that is something we cannot in Congress control.

What would you specifically recommend?

Mr. Martin. Well, I have no recommendation at the moment, Senator. I think we have got to watch the situation. I think that the patient, to get back to that, needs convalescence. I do not know that my medical knowledge is very good, but I think a certain period of convalescence is required, and you have to gauge the patient on the basis of that.

Now, I think that in terms of minimizing hardships through credit and monetary policy —

Senator Robertson. This language that "we must take whatever actions are needed to minimize the hardships" largely indicates a sympathetic attitude on your part, but you do not have anything particularly in mind?

Mr. Martin. The Federal Reserve Board is very distressed at any unemployment. We want to do everything within our power to be helpful.

Senator Robertson. But you say that monetary policy alone will not either put it up or bring it down but that you can do a better job in keeping it from going too high than you can bringing it up again.

The question I raise is this: I pointed out that some bankers think money is not yet easy enough and that if you did not tie up as much of their reserves as you do at the present time they would feel a little easier on making greater loans.

Mr. Martin. That is a matter of judgment that we have to weigh very carefully in the System; and if we come to the conclusion that that is correct, you can be sure that we will act.

Senator Robertson. You would not hold back, if that would be a remedy, until we get forced into a tax bill, would you?

Mr. Martin. I would not hold back 1 minute. The minute the Board is con-vinced—and we are studying this every day—that that would be helpful and would do something for the economy, we are going to do it....

Senator Bennett. I would like to go back, Mr. Martin, to the sentence on page 9 which Senator Robertson mentioned and refer to the comment about the maintenance of prices.

All last summer and fall the Finance Committee, of which three members of this committee are also members, was engaged in a hearing on what was then the current economic situation—a situation of inflation. It was obvious to me as a member of the committee that there is a philosophy in this country which suggests that the way to cure inflation is to raise wages—on the theory that then the wage earner will be able to buy more merchandise and that will prime the pump.

There is some evidence that within the next 2 or 3 weeks we are going to be visited here in Congress as a part of an organized campaign to support that theory that the minimum wage should be raised to $1.25 and current collective-bargaining programs should produce massive wage increases. Do you believe that that is sound policy in a situation where we have unemployment and prices are still rising?

Mr. Martin. Well, as I pointed out in this statement, Senator, wage rates were pressing against productivity and exceeding productivity in some in-stances, and that was one of the reasons for the inflation getting ahead of us. And I think that is one of the factors that has to be considered at the present time.

I do not think that you can justify wage increases beyond productivity and —

Senator Bennett. Can you do that at any time?

Mr. Martin. I do not think you can at any time. And I do not think you can spend yourself prosperous. I just do not agree with that theory.

Senator Bennett. Sitting in on those hearings, it was obvious to me that there is a line of thinking in this country which says that the way to cure inflation is more inflation, that in periods of inflation the policy of the Federal Reserve Board should be to ease money, thus producing more purchasing power, which presumably would fill up the gap produced by the current underuse of productive facilities.

Is it not logical, to follow that same reasoning, to assume that in a period of recession like this the correct policy should be a tight monetary policy? And would you believe that in your position as Governor of the Federal Reserve System you would recommend tight monetary policies in time of recession?

Mr. Martin. I certainly would not.

Senator Bennett. Then you believe you really were following the correct program during the inflationary period, and that by releasing more capital or more reserves now that business has fallen off a little you are also following the correct policy?

Mr. Martin. I do.

Senator Bennett. I think the record would not be injured too much if I asked you if you ever heard the story of the man and the lions? You have not so I will proceed to tell it to you.

The story is that there was a man in an automobile going through the main thoroughfare of a busy town, and about every half block he threw out half a newspaper. Finally the traffic policeman caught up with him and said, "Here, what are you doing? You can't do that. That's against the law."

He said, "I'm protecting this community against wild lions."

The policeman said, "There aren't any wild lions around here."

The man said, "See. My program works."

I wonder if this theory that in periods of inflation we should have more inflation is not based a little bit on that same kind of reasoning?

Mr. Martin. Well, I think it is an incorrect theory. . . .

Senator Douglas. You mentioned at the end of your statement, on page 10, that monetary policy by itself cannot assure resumption of high-level employment and sustainable economic growth. In other words, there is a place for fiscal policy too?

Mr. Martin. Yes, under certain conditions.

Senator Douglas. What would those conditions be? You say now is not the time, but there might be a future time. What criteria do you have for determining when you should add fiscal policy to monetary policy? Fiscal policy could consist either of an increase in expenditures or a reduction in tax receipts.

Mr. Martin. Well, I think it would have to be dependent primarily on whether you think the decline is spiraling and coming in —

Senator Douglas. What indexes would you use to determine whether the decline was spiraling?

Mr. Martin. I would not use any one index. I would —

Senator Douglas. What group, what family of indexes would you use?

Mr. Martin. Well, I think we would have to cover the whole waterfront on that.

Senator Douglas. Let's get to some of the docks on the waterfront. Production?

Mr. Martin. Production index.

Senator Douglas. Employment?

Mr. Martin. Employment.

Senator Douglas. Unemployment?

Mr. Martin. Unemployment.

Senator Douglas. What else?

Mr. Martin. Mr. Young [Director, Division of Research and Statistics, Federal Reserve System], what would you —

Mr. Young. I think you would go across the board — on new orders —

Senator Douglas. What?

Mr. Young. You would go across the board on new orders and inventories —

Senator Douglas. If you go across the board, what would you look at?

Mr. Martin. New orders, inventories —

Mr. Young. What is happening in the securities markets?

Senator Douglas. What is happening to production? It was 145 in August.

Mr. Martin. January, 133.

Senator Douglas. A fall of 12 points. What is that?

Mr. Young. Around 8 percent.

Mr. Martin. Seven to eight percent.

Senator Douglas. If it should go down below 10 percent would you regard that as significant?

Mr. Young. I think you would want to look at the movement against typical patterns in the past also.

Senator Douglas. You say in past recessions the fall in production has not exceeded 10 percent?

Mr. Young. For a moderate recession it is something like 10 percent.

Senator Douglas. All right. Now, then, suppose it exceeds 10 percent. What I am trying to get at is that you are the doctor, one of the doctors, sitting by the bedside of the patient. And that is your own analogy; that is not mine. I did not say the patient was sick; you said the patient was sick.

Now, you feel his pulse. You find out what his temperature is. An M.D. has certain standards. If the temperature rises to, say, 103, something is wrong. He does not worry very much at 99½.

Do you have anything in the back of your mind as to where you might have a critical point? Would you say a fall of 10 percent in production should begin to —

Mr. Martin. I would not want to be pinned to a level. I think that you have got to —

Senator Douglas. Suppose you had a fall of 15 percent. Would you worry?

Mr. Martin. The further the fall —

Senator Douglas. You do not think fiscal policy should come in if production fell 15 percent?

Mr. Martin. I would not — just could not answer that on a specific basis.

Senator Douglas. Suppose it fell 20 percent?

Mr. Martin. I am not —

Senator Douglas. Twenty-five percent? You would not be concerned with 25 percent?

Mr. Martin. Senator, I am sorry but I just cannot say that I —

Senator Douglas. You see, you are the doctor. You say, "Have faith in me."

Mr. Martin. No; I —

Senator Douglas. We want to find out what you are having faith in, what indexes you are watching.

Mr. Martin. I am not saying, "Have faith in me."

Senator Douglas. Let's turn to unemployment. The census says we have 4½ million unemployed. If you add the part-time workers to this you get an equivalent of 1.2 million more or 5.7 million. The total working force is a little less than 67 million. That is 8.5 percent. But this 67 million includes the self-employed, 9 million self-employed plus a million more wives and elder sons or elder daughters, self-employed. So you really have to deduct them in getting an index of unemployment. And when you come to the number of wage and salary workers in the country, a little less than 57 million, then you have 5.7 million equivalent unemployed. That is a 10-percent unemployment ratio. Do you think that is significant?

Mr. Martin. I certainly do. I think that —

Senator Douglas. But you say it is not yet time for fiscal action. By how much would it have to increase before you think it would be time?

Mr. Martin. Well, I cannot answer that categorically, but I want to say that these unemployment figures ought to be studied awfully carefully too. You have questioned the Consumer Price Index. I think all of these indexes have got to be put in the context of what is the truth about it.

Senator Douglas. You see, here is the point. You will say, "I am moving because the Consumer Price Index is this way." Then you will shift. The pea will be under another thimble, and so on. You chase these around. What I am trying to do is assemble these various indexes and try to see when you would believe that fiscal policy should be carried out.

Mr. Martin. Well, I cannot tell you precisely.

Senator Douglas. You are not in control of fiscal policy. We are in control of fiscal policy. Presumably we have to make up our minds. We are coming to you for advice.

Mr. Martin. Well, I am not trying to be presumptuous in what I am saying now, but I am saying that I think you, in studying your problem, just as we in studying our problem, should look at the whole picture and not just at one index or the trend in a few indexes.

Senator Douglas. Oh, that is my whole quarrel with you—that you looked at only one index, the Consumer Price Index, and ignored export figures, ignored the spot price figures, and ignored the employment figures. I think we should look at employment and production as well as the Consumer Price Index.

Mr. Martin. Well, I do not want to belabor it, but I did not look at just one price index.

Senator Douglas. You made up your decision on the basis of the Consumer Price Index.

Mr. Martin. No; I would not say that. I made it on the basis of overall inflation.

Senator Douglas. There was no inflation in primary products.

Mr. Martin. There was a —

Senator Douglas. On the contrary, there was deflation in primary products....

Senator Clark. ... And having therefore established somewhat of a rapport, I wonder whether you would agree that a deficit for the current fiscal year is practically inevitable and is quite probable for the next fiscal year.

Mr. Martin. I think it is probable, yes.

Senator Clark. In view of that, is it not important we increase the debt limit ceiling promptly?

Mr. Martin. Well, I think you have no alternative.

Senator Clark. And, therefore, you would favor it?

Mr. Martin. I would favor it.

Senator Clark. Do you not think in the interest of flexibility the sooner it is done the better?

Mr. Martin. I do.

Senator Clark. Well, now, in order to help cure this recession, could we not afford to put a good many billions of dollars into public improvements in the public sector of the economy without running into a renewed threat of inflation?

Mr. Martin. I think at the moment you can, but the point I am trying to stress there is that I would not be too discouraged on your point, because time does quite a lot in this. This is a process—the sort of movement that does not occur in a 30-day swing or a 90-day swing. It reverses itself over a period of 6 months to a year.

Senator Clark. That I understand.

Mr. Chairman, I will wind it up with just the note that I hope and I am sure that our very good and most able friend is not going to come down here and tell us we should not move very fast indeed with a strong housing program and, if we can get it through the Congress, a strong school construction program, not only because we need them so desperately for our civilization but because it is going to help us get out of this recession.

This is your last chance to say no.

Mr. Martin. I will reserve comment.

Senator Clark. Thank you, Mr. Chairman. Thank you very much.

Senator Frear. Thank you.

Mr. Chairman, we are indebted to you for spending some time with us this morning and answering the questions in very enlightening manner. I think most of the members of this committee—as a matter of fact, I believe all of them—have great confidence in you. Especially the chairman of this subcommittee is always happy when you come down. I think we get a stimulus from your answers, and we like the manner of disagreement at times.

It has been nice to have you with us, sir, and any time this committee, or especially this subcommittee, can be of assistance to the Federal Reserve System—which is probably a suggestion in reverse—we offer our services.

Mr. Martin. Thank you very much.

Senator Frear. The subcommittee is adjourned.

(Whereupon, at 12:25 p.m., the subcommittee was adjourned, subject to the call of the chairman.)

22

Federal Reserve Policy in the 1960s

The Recession of 1960–1961

Economic activity of the late 1950s set the stage for 1960 policy actions. The 1957–1958 recession, shortest of the postwar period until that time, was followed by the shortest postwar expansion—25 months. Although GNP in money terms increased some 15 percent—from a low of $434.7 billion per year in the first quarter of 1958 to a peak of $504.7 billion per year in the second quarter of 1960—unemployment never fell below 5 percent. During this expansion the FOMC moved free reserves from a high of $546 million in July 1958 to a low of −$557 million (i.e., net borrowed reserves of $557 million) one year later. Subsequently, free reserves began to rise again as the FOMC assisted in Treasury financing operations.

The money supply declined for twelve months at an annual rate of 2.7 percent following the July 1959 peak. The National Bureau of Economic Research (NBER) records May 1960 as the peak of economic activity during that period and February 1961 as the trough. Although the FOMC did not recognize the peak in economic activity until two to three months after it occurred, free reserves had been moved up steadily in prior months.

Persistent balance of payments deficits and resulting gold outflows in the late 1950s, in conjunction with a slowing domestic economy during 1960, presented the Federal Reserve System with a traditional problem. If the economy were allowed to cool further, the resulting downward pressure on prices would lessen the international problem by making U.S. export goods and services more competitive in world markets, but domestic unemployment also would increase. Measures to stimulate the economy that would lower interest rates, expand the flow of income, reduce unemployment, and raise prices would reduce exports, increase imports, and cause foreign capital to seek higher returns in other parts of the world. Further gold outflows would be inevitable. The solution attempted was to "twist" or "nudge" the interest rate structure so as to solve both problems simultaneously. A brief review of debt management is necessary before a full explanation of this policy is intelligible.

Debt Management

The debt under consideration is that part of the gross debt outstanding in the hands of the public (see Table 12.3). It excludes government securities held by government agencies and trust funds, such as the Social Security Administration and the Federal Reserve System.[1] Management of the debt has particular reference to changes in its maturity structure, not to changes in its total size. The changing size of the debt and the selection of appropriate marketing techniques pose problems, but attention is directed here only to the debt's composition in terms of its average time to maturity.

Debt management may be performed by either the Federal Reserve System or the Treasury. Proponents of this policy point to two channels through which it might work. During recession, the maturity structure of the debt is to be shortened by the Federal Reserve's (or the Treasury's) simultaneously selling short-term securities and buying long-terms. The sale of short-term securities is supposed to drive down their price and drive up their yield rates. Simultaneously, the purchase of long-term securities is supposed to pull up their prices and lower their yields. The rise in short-term rates generally may be ignored, but the lowering of long-term rates is supposed to stimulate domestic investment in machinery and equipment. Keynesian reasoning then holds that investment thus stimulated works through the multiplier to raise income and output.

The change in the maturity of the debt is also supposed to have a liquidity effect. A debt of shortened maturity is a more liquid debt. Assuming that the public's liquidity is raised beyond the desired level by the government's action, increased consumer spending reestablishes liquidity to the desired amount. Similar to the increase in investment, greater consumption stimulates investment through the accelerator, and increased investment generates increased income and output. This line of reasoning implies that the debt's maturity should be lengthened during inflation and shortened during recession.

One disadvantage of the plan, however, is the difficulty of selling long-term securities during inflation. Also, such sales usually have to be made at interest

---

[1] For a more detailed account of the public debt outstanding, see Chapter 29.

yields conflicting with the Treasury's conventional constraint of minimizing interest payments on the national debt.

During the late 1950s, a proposal was advanced that the Federal Reserve System use debt management to ameliorate the twin problems of a gold outflow and domestic recession. In February 1961, the chairman of the Federal Open Market Committee announced to the press that the committee was resuming operations in long-term government securities. This declaration marked the end of the self-imposed period of "bills only" and the beginning of "Operation Twist."

Operation Twist

To implement Operation Twist, the FOMC sold short-term securities in the open market while simultaneously purchasing longer-terms ones. The action of raising short-term interest rates was supposed to attract the highly liquid, short-term, portfolio-type capital that moves rapidly from country to country in taking advantage of interest yields. In other words, the FOMC attempted to mitigate the gold outflow problem by keeping foreign capital in the country through more attractive short-term security yields. Lowered long-term rates and increased debt liquidity were to stimulate capital equipment expenditures and consumption so as to bolster the desultory domestic economy.

Though Operation Twist was not officially started until February 1961, the minutes of the November 13, 1960, FOMC meeting show that the general consensus of the committee was to keep the Treasury bill rate as high as possible from then on. Between February and August 1961, the FOMC purchased significant quantities of securities with a maturity of more than one year while offsetting them in part by short-term sales. This policy increased the System's net holdings of government securities by $700 million. The System traded in various securities and increased its net holdings by another $1.6 billion during the remainder of the year. Regulation Q, specifying the maximum amount of interest banks could pay on time deposits, also was raised effective January 1, 1962. With the resumption of economic growth, the need for depressing long-term interest rates lessened although the balance of payments problem continued.

The success of Operation Twist has been seriously questioned by academic economists. Some critics doubt the ability of the FOMC to twist the rate structure for any but extremely short periods. Other economists feel that the narrower spread between short-term and long-term rates (at that time short-term rates were below long-terms) was due to a relaxation in the System's Regulation Q and the subsequent rapid growth of CD's rather than effective twisting efforts through open market operations. Still other critics contend that the rise in short-term interest rates adversely affected business inventories, causing a new reduction, not an increase, in business investment. If these contentions are true, debt management policies may have aggravated rather than counteracted the 1960 recession. The small gold flow gain that may have resulted from higher short-term rates was poor compensation. Still other economists question the assumed liquidity impact of changes in the structure of the debt. Recent tests suggest that this effect is small indeed.

The 1960–1961 recession can be traced to two sources. Following a government deficit of $13 billion in fiscal 1959, the federal budget moved to a surplus in fiscal 1960. If it is anything, a surplus is deflationary and has an influence that is not quickly removed. Kennedy's election campaign shibboleth to "get this country moving again" was directed toward those dissatisfied with the business contraction.

Monetarists also find support for their theories during this period. The money supply peaked in July 1959 and then suffered a 12-month decline. The NBER reference cycle peak in economic activity followed the peak in the money supply by eight months, a lag clearly within recognized bounds of probability. Similarly, the June 1960 trough in the money supply was followed eight months later by the business cycle trough.

Institutional Changes in the Early Sixties

As of December 31, 1962, the Federal Reserve Banks' combined balance sheet was as shown in Table 22.1.

Table 22.1. All Reserve Banks as of December 1962
(billions of dollars)

Assets		Liabilities	
Gold certificates	15.7	Federal Reserve notes	30.2
Government securities	30.8	Member reserves	17.5

Reserve ratio: 32 percent

Gold certificates are seen to have declined by more than $6 billion in the four and one-half years between this balance sheet and the balance sheet for June 1958 (Table 21.8). Increased holdings of government securities more than offset the gold losses. Federal Reserve note issues also increased appreciably, while member bank reserves declined. However, the decline in the latter item was offset by further reductions in reserve requirements—from 18, 16½, and 11 percent to 16½ percent for central reserve and reserve city banks, and to 12 percent for country banks.[2]

---

[2]The classifications of "central reserve city" and "reserve city" banks were reduced to just "reserve city" banks as of July 28, 1962. Central reserve cities formerly were Chicago and New York.

Another change instituted in this period was the ruling that allowed vault cash in banks to count as a part of their legal reserves against deposits. Up to December 1959, only member bank reserves (deposits) with the Federal Reserve Banks were used in computing reserve ratios. During 1960, however, by a congressional amendment to the Federal Reserve Act, vault cash in member banks was phased into allowable reserves for meeting member bank reserve requirements. This action substantially increased the demand for currency by member banks.

Prior to this time, any vault cash was held in addition to required reserves in the banks' reserve accounts and thus at the expense of interest-earning assets they might otherwise have held. Vault cash holdings, therefore, had been minimized. After 1960, the Federal Reserve Banks' consolidated balance sheets show a substantial increase in Federal Reserve notes outstanding and only nominal increases in member reserves. (Compare Tables 21.8 and 22.1 above and 22.2 below.)

Balanced Economic Expansion — 1961–1964

Following the February 1961 trough in economic activity, the economy experienced four years of rapid economic expansion with remarkably little inflation. As seen in Figure 22.1, real GNP increased at a 6.5 percent annual

Figure 22.1. Demand and Production
(quarterly totals at annual rates, seasonally adjusted)

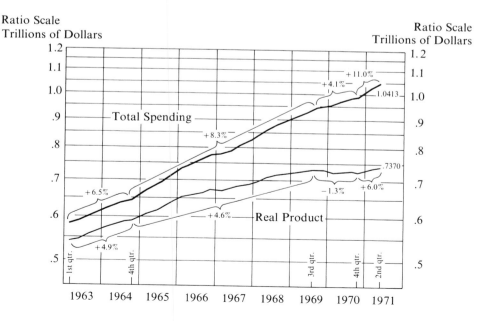

rate between 1963 and 1965, while the Consumer Price Index increased only 1.3 percent (Figure 22.2). These data indicate that real output (GNP adjusted for price index changes) increased at an annual rate of 4.6 percent.[3] Unemployment was reduced from the 1961 level of approximately 7 percent to less than 5 percent toward the end of 1964.

Figure 22.2. Prices

Ratio Scale   Ratio Scale
1967 = 100   1967 = 100

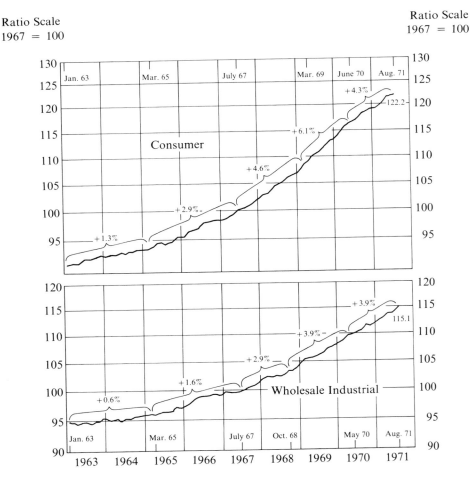

[3]Here again is demonstrated the possible importance of bias in the price index. The bias due to quality changes and other factors increases the computation for the *real* rate of growth by the amount of the bias. A "biased" rate of growth of 5.4 percent becomes 7.4 percent if the price index bias is as much as 2 percent. Thus, a 2 percent annual bias in the price index may lead to a 37 percent error in the computed real rate of growth in the economy.

Through various means the 1960 balance of payments deficit of $3.9 billion was reduced to $2.4 billion in 1961 and to $2.2 billion in 1962. In 1963, however, the deficit worsened. The Federal Reserve System continued efforts to keep short-term interest rates high, while the President called on Congress to pass an interest equalization tax to slow the sale of foreign securities in the United States. The bill was not passed until 1964, but the knowledge that it was retroactive to July 19, 1963, evidently had some effect. In any case, the deficit was held to $2.7 billion for the year.

Figure 22.3. Fiscal Measures (+) Surplus; (−) Deficit
(quarterly totals at annual rates, seasonally adjusted)

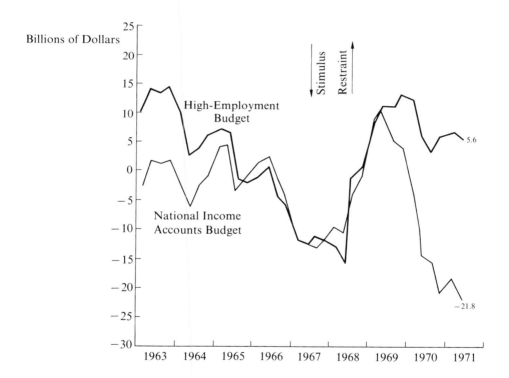

In other congressional action the presidential proposal of a tax cut was finally approved in early 1964. This measure, coupled with increasing military expenditures for Vietnam, shifted the influence of the federal budget from restraint to stimulus by 1965. (See Figure 22.3) The money supply, which had been increasing at less than 3 percent per year, now increased at a much more rapid rate. (See Figure 22.4.)

Figure 22.4. The Money Stock
(monthly averages of daily figures, seasonally adjusted)

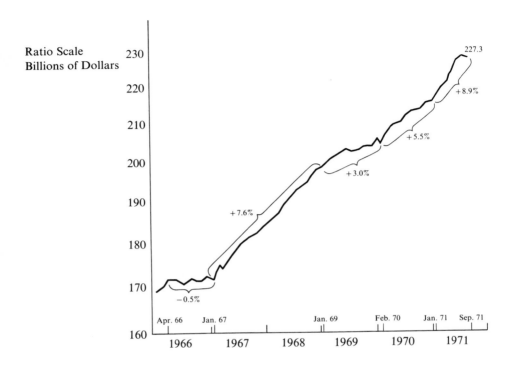

The Inflation of 1965–1966

Table 22.2. All Reserve Banks as of May 1965
(billions of dollars)

Assets		*Liabilities*	
Gold certificates	14.0	Federal Reserve notes	34.4
Government securities	38.7	Member reserves	18.0

Reserve ratio: 27 percent

The shift of the federal budget to a deficit position and the failure of the
Federal Reserve System to keep increases in the money supply nominal led

Figure 22.5. Excess Reserves and Borrowings of Member Banks (weekly averages of daily figures)

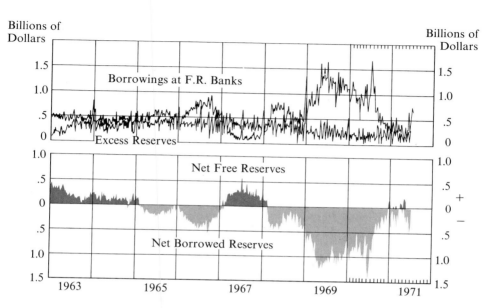

to an increase in total spending in the economy in excess of the increase in output. GNP in dollar terms increased at an annual rate of 10.3 percent between the fourth quarter of 1964 and the first quarter of 1966, and then at an annual rate of 7.6 percent through the end of 1966. While prices had been increasing at an annual rate just slightly above 1 percent from 1961 to 1964, they rose by approximately 2 percent during 1965 and by more than 3 percent during 1966.

Balance of payments difficulties were tackled by several legislative actions, including an extension of the interest equalization tax and a change in the duty-free allowance for U.S. citizens. The administration also established a "voluntary" program that brought pressure on bankers and businessmen to limit loans and investments made abroad. The balance of payments deficit in 1964 was $2.8 billion but was reduced to $1.3 billion in 1965 and held approximately constant during 1966.

In other actions Congress in early 1965 removed the "gold cover" against member bank deposits at Federal Reserve Banks. (Previously, Federal Reserve Banks had been required to hold gold certificates equal to 25 percent of the value of their major demand liabilities—deposits and Federal Reserve notes outstanding.) With only Federal Reserve notes now requiring gold reserves, $5 billion in gold was "freed" to meet international claims on the remaining U.S. gold stock of $13 billion.

Table 22.3. All Reserve Banks as of April 1966
(billions of dollars)

Assets		Liabilities	
Gold certificates	13.2	Federal Reserve notes.	36.5
Government securities	40.7	Member reserves	18.7

Reserve ratio: 36 percent

The Credit Crunch of 1966

The gentle decline in free reserves begun in 1961 continued through late 1965 (Figure 22.5). After a brief reversal, free reserves (then net borrowed reserves) declined sharply through 1966, reaching a trough of −$431 million in October. The money supply stopped growing in April 1966 and actually declined slightly up to January 1967. Bank reserves also declined, interest rates increased, and disintermediation[4] occurred. In an attempt to be restrictive, the Board of Governors approved raising the discount rate in December 1965. They also raised reserve requirements on certain types of time deposits from 4 to 5 percent in July 1966, and then to 6 percent in August. On September 1, 1966, Federal Reserve Banks sent to members what has come to be known as the "September 1 letter." This letter called on members to restrict their expansion of business loans — a formalized example of moral suasion.

Undoubtedly as a result of these measures, business expansion cooled considerably. Industrial production dipped, housing starts dropped sharply, and real GNP increased at an annual rate of less than 1 percent between the fourth quarter of 1966 and the second quarter of 1967. Some economists have dubbed this period a "mini-recession."

Table 22.4. All Reserve Banks as of January 1967
(billions of dollars)

Assets		Liabilities	
Gold certificates	12.7	Federal Reserve notes	38.1
Government securities	43.5	Member reserves	18.8

Reserve ratio: 33 percent

[4]When market interest rates on securities rise above governmental interest rate ceilings imposed on time and savings accounts and on savings and loan shares, many households and business firms disinvest themselves of these assets and buy the more attractive marketable securities. This process is labeled "disintermediation."

Expansion and Renewed Inflation, 1967-1970

The Federal Reserve Board reversed its tight money policy in November 1966. Free reserves moved swiftly into the positive range by March 1967 and peaked at $298 million in August. The money supply shot upward at a 7.3 percent annual rate between January 1967 and January 1969. Its annual rate of growth in some months exceeded 11 percent. Fiscal policy also proved to be excessively stimulative, and the high employment budget deficit reached $16.1 billion (annual rate) in the second quarter of 1968. As could be expected, GNP increased considerably. It achieved an annual rate of increase of 9.1 percent between the second quarter of 1967 and the fourth quarter of 1968. Inflation, as measured by the increase in the Consumer Price Index, accounted for almost half of this increase, with prices rising in some months at an annual rate of 7 percent.

Another institutional change that occurred in 1968 was removal of the final gold cover requirement of 25 percent against outstanding Federal Reserve notes. From this time on, all gold certificates in Federal Reserve Banks could be classified as "free gold reserves." More simply, no reserve ratio was any longer applicable to the Federal Reserve Banks.

This change separated even further the quantity of gold from the money supply. In fact, the divorce would now seem to be complete. Since the creation of money cannot occur in a vacuum, the Federal Reserve System perforce is left with complete responsibility and discretion over the quantity and value of the money supply in the United States.[5]

Table 22.5. All Reserve Banks as of January 1969
(billions of dollars)

Assets		*Liabilities*	
Gold certificates	10.0	Federal Reserve notes	42.8
Government securities	52.1	Member reserves	23.1

Reserve ratio: (None applicable after March 1968.)

Tables 22.4 and 22.5 embrace the two-year period during which most of the inflation took place. They show an $8.6 billion increase in System holdings of government securities, a $4.7 billion increase in Federal Reserve notes, and a $4.3 billion increase in member bank reserves. These increases in the high-powered money base explain the increase in medium-of-exchange money—

---

[5]For further discussion on the political position of the Federal Reserve System, see Chapter 28.

currency and demand deposits — from $170 billion to $194 billion. Furthermore, as the price level responded to these inflationary increases in the stock of money, households and firms economized money holdings more and more. This behavior defines an increase in the rate of spending — the velocity of money. Because of this increase in velocity, somewhat more inflation was generated than the simple increase in the stock of money by itself would have suggested.

After considerable delay Congress passed the Revenue and Expenditure Control Act in June 1968. Its major provisions called for a 10 percent surcharge on income taxes, retroactive to January 1, 1968, for corporations and to April 1, 1968, for individuals. It also extended excise taxes and imposed a ceiling on federal spending. The federal budget quickly moved to a surplus position in late 1968.

Table 22.6. All Reserve Banks as of November 1969
(billions of dollars)

Assets		*Liabilities*	
Gold certificates	10.0	Federal Reserve notes	46.6
Government securities	57.3	Member reserves	23.4

Federal Reserve tightening, as indicated by the level of free reserves, resumed in late 1967 and continued until the passage of the surtax. The FOMC, anticipating quick and effective results from the surtax, relaxed existing monetary restraints in the third quarter of 1968. The results of the tax, however, were not entirely as anticipated. Consumers absorbed much of the increase in taxes, viewed as temporary, by reducing their rate of saving. Consumption, therefore, could continue unabated. With the economy booming and prices continuing to rise, monetary restraint was again applied but this time with more force. Free reserves dropped, and by May 1969 had reached a negative level of $1.1 billion. Bank reserves were sharply reduced; interest rates reached record levels; the rate of growth of the money supply slackened to an annual rate of 3 percent through 1969. Again as in 1966, both bank and nonbank disintermediation occurred and housing starts dropped markedly. Throughout 1969 real GNP slowed its rate of increase, but the momentum of the inflation continued to be reflected in price level increases through 1970 and into 1971. The surtax also was extended into 1970, but continued military spending, expanding domestic programs, and a tax revision saw continuation of a substantial federal budget deficit.

The policy of monetary restraint undertaken in 1969 began to show its effects just about a year after its inception. Unemployment grew slowly but steadily through 1970 until it was around 6 percent by the end of the year. Gross National Product in real terms failed to register an increase — a reflection of the unemployment. However, GNP in dollar terms increased nominally — a reflection of continued price level increases. Market interest rates reached a peak toward the middle of 1970 and fell precipitously at the end of the year. All these factors gave undeniable evidence of a recession from the inflation of the previous three years. In fact, the inflation, if it was to be stopped, made the recession inevitable.

Table 22.7. All Reserve Banks as of November 1970
(billions of dollars)

Assets		*Liabilities*	
Gold certificates	10.8	Federal Reserve notes	49.6
Government securities	61.2	Member reserves	22.7

As soon as the recession showed its early warning symptoms, the Federal Reserve System accelerated the growth of the money supply. Where the growth rate in the narrow money stock had been reduced from about 7½ percent in 1968 to 3 percent in 1969 in order to stop the inflation, it was allowed to increase at a 5½ percent rate in 1970. A comparison of Tables 22.6 and 22.7 shows the changes that made such growth possible. Most of the increase in high-powered money again was in Federal Reserve notes. As the year ended, price level increases were less pronounced, but a moderate amount of unemployment continued.

Selected Bibliography

Beard, Thomas R. "Debt Management: Its Relationship to Monetary Policy, 1951–1962." *The National Banking Review,* Vol. 2 (September 1964), pp. 61–76.

Economic Report of the President Transmitted to Congress February 1968, Together with the Annual Report of the Council of Economic Advisers. Washington, D.C.: U.S. Government Printing Office, 1968.

Keran, Michael W., and Christopher T. Babb. "An Explanation of Federal Reserve Actions (1933–1968)." *Review;* Federal Reserve Bank of St. Louis, Vol. 51, No. 7 (July 1969), pp. 7–20.

Minutes of the Federal Open Market Committee, 1936–1960, and of Its Executive Committee, 1936–1955. Rolls No. 6–16, Microcopy No. 591, Record Group 92. Washington, D.C.: The National Archives, 1965.

Modigliani, Franco, and Richard Sutch. "Innovations in Interest Rate Policy." *American Economic Review,* Vol. 56, No. 2 (May 1966), pp. 178–197.

Ross, Myron H. "'Operation Twist': A Mistaken Policy?" *The Journal of Political Economy,* Vol. 74 (April 1966), pp. 195–199.

Van Horne, James C., and David A. Bowers. "The Liquidity Impact of Debt Management." *The Southern Economic Journal,* Vol. 34, No. 4 (April 1968), pp. 526–537.

The Role of Monetary Policy

Milton Friedman*

Professor Milton Friedman has been introduced so often that any further words about him seem banal and repetitious. Suffice it to say that he is the Paul Snowden Russel Distinguished Service Professor of Economics at the University of Chicago, a profound thinker, and a brilliant and controversial figure on the contemporary economic scene.

One of Professor Friedman's particular gifts is his ability to contribute original analysis to both economic theory and economic measurement. Another of his endowments is his facility for bringing the results of sophisticated original analysis into the ken of the interested and intelligent layman. The selection reprinted here was addressed to professional colleagues, but it is also geared to reach anyone with more than a passing interest in monetary policy. Its apparent simplicity emphasizes its logic and clarity. While it contains many facts on the evolution of monetary policy, its special utility here is to convey the posture monetary policy has taken in the last decade together with some prescriptions for future policy.

There is wide agreement about the major goals of economic policy: high employment, stable prices, and rapid growth. There is less agreement that these goals are mutually compatible or, among those who regard them as incompatible, about the terms at which they can and should be substituted for one another. There is least agreement about the role that various instruments of policy can and should play in achieving the several goals.

Presidential address delivered at the Eightieth Annual Meeting of the American Economic Association, Washington, D.C., December 29, 1967. Reprinted by permission of the American Economic Association and the author.

*I am indebted for helpful criticisms of earlier drafts to Armen Alchian, Gary Becker, Martin Bronfenbrenner, Arthur F. Burns, Phillip Cagan, David D. Friedman, Lawrence Harris, Harry G. Johnson, Homer Jones, Jerry Jordan, David Meiselman, Allan H. Meltzer, Theodore W. Schultz, Anna J. Schwartz, Herbert Stein, George J. Stigler, and James Tobin.

My topic for tonight is the role of one such instrument—monetary policy. What can it contribute? And how should it be conducted to contribute the most? Opinion on these questions has fluctuated widely. In the first flush of enthusiasm about the newly created Federal Reserve System, many observers attributed the relative stability of the 1920s to the System's capacity for fine tuning—to apply an apt modern term. It came to be widely believed that a new era had arrived in which business cycles had been rendered obsolete by advances in monetary technology. This opinion was shared by economist and layman alike, though, of course, there were some dissonant voices. The Great Contraction destroyed this naive attitude. Opinion swung to the other extreme. Monetary policy was a string. You could pull on it to stop inflation but you could not push on it to halt recession. You could lead a horse to water but you could not make him drink. Such theory by aphorism was soon replaced by Keynes' rigorous and sophisticated analysis.

Keynes offered simultaneously an explanation for the presumed impotence of monetary policy to stem the depression, a nonmonetary interpretation of the depression, and an alternative to monetary policy for meeting the depression and his offering was avidly accepted. If liquidity preference is absolute or nearly so—as Keynes believed likely in times of heavy unemployment—interest rates cannot be lowered by monetary measures. If investment and consumption are little affected by interest rates—as Hansen and many of Keynes' other American disciples came to believe—lower interest rates, even if they could be achieved, would do little good. Monetary policy is twice damned. The contraction, set in train, on this view, by a collapse of investment or by a shortage of investment opportunities or by stubborn thriftiness, could not, it was argued, have been stopped by monetary measures. But there was available an alternative—fiscal policy. Government spending could make up for insufficient private investment. Tax reductions could undermine stubborn thriftiness.

The wide acceptance of these views in the economics profession meant that for some two decades monetary policy was believed by all but a few reactionary souls to have been rendered obsolete by new economic knowledge. Money did not matter. Its only role was the minor one of keeping interest rates low, in order to hold down interest payments in the government budget, contribute to the "euthanasia of the rentier," and maybe, stimulate investment a bit to assist government spending in maintaining a high level of aggregate demand.

These views produced a widespread adoption of cheap money policies after the war. And they received a rude shock when these policies failed in country after country, when central bank after central bank was forced to give up the pretense that it could indefinitely keep "the" rate of interest at a low level. In this country, the public denouement came with the Federal Reserve–Treasury Accord in 1951, although the policy of pegging government bond prices was not formally abandoned until 1953. Inflation, stimulated by cheap money policies, not the widely heralded postwar depression, turned out to be the order of the day. The result was the beginning of a revival of belief in the potency of monetary policy.

This revival was strongly fostered among economists by the theoretical developments initiated by Haberler but named for Pigou that pointed out a channel — namely, changes in wealth — whereby changes in the real quantity of money can affect aggregate demand even if they do not alter interest rates. These theoretical developments did not undermine Keynes' argument against the potency of orthodox monetary measures when liquidity preference is absolute since under such circumstances the usual monetary operations involve simply substituting money for other assets without changing total wealth. But they did show how changes in the quantity of money produced in other ways could affect total spending even under such circumstances. And, more fundamentally, they did undermine Keynes' key theoretical proposition, namely, that even in a world of flexible prices, a position of equilibrium at full employment might not exist. Henceforth, unemployment had again to be explained by rigidities or imperfections, not as the natural outcome of a fully operative market process.

The revival of belief in the potency of monetary policy was fostered also by a re-evaluation of the role money played from 1929 to 1933. Keynes and most other economists of the time believed that the Great Contraction in the United States occurred despite aggressive expansionary policies by the monetary authorities — that they did their best but their best was not good enough.[1] Recent studies have demonstrated that the facts are precisely the reverse: the U.S. monetary authorities followed highly deflationary policies. The quantity of money in the United States fell by one-third in the course of the contraction. And it fell not because there were no willing borrowers — not because the horse would not drink. It fell because the Federal Reserve System forced or permitted a sharp reduction in the monetary base, because it failed to exercise the responsibilities assigned to it in the Federal Reserve Act to provide liquidity to the banking system. The Great Contraction is tragic testimony to the power of monetary policy — not, as Keynes and so many of his contemporaries believed, evidence of its impotence.

In the United States the revival of belief in the potency of monetary policy was strengthened also by increasing disillusionment with fiscal policy, not so much with its potential to affect aggregate demand as with the practical and political feasibility of so using it. Expenditures turned out to respond sluggishly and with long lags to attempts to adjust them to the course of economic activity, so emphasis shifted to taxes. But here political factors entered with a vengeance to prevent prompt adjustment to presumed need, as has been so graphically illustrated in the months since I wrote the first draft of this talk. "Fine tuning" is a marvelously evocative phrase in this electronic age, but it

---

[1]In [2], I have argued that Henry Simons shared this view with Keynes, and that it accounts for the policy changes that he recommended.

has little resemblance to what is possible in practice—not, I might add, an unmixed evil.

It is hard to realize how radical has been the change in professional opinion on the role of money. Hardly an economist today accepts views that were the common coin some two decades ago. Let me cite a few examples.

In a talk published in 1945, E. A. Goldenweiser, then Director of the Research Division of the Federal Reserve Board, described the primary objective of monetary policy as being to "maintain the value of Government bonds.... This country" he wrote, "will have to adjust to a 2½ percent interest rate as the return on safe, long-time money, because the time has come when returns on pioneering capital can no longer be unlimited as 'they were in the past" [4, p. 117].

In a book on *Financing American Prosperity,* edited by Paul Homan and Fritz Machlup and published in 1945, Alvin Hansen devotes nine pages of text to the "savings-investment problem" without finding any need to use the words "interest rate" or any close facsimile thereto [5, pp. 218–27]. In his contribution to this volume, Fritz Machlup wrote, "Questions regarding the rate of interest, in particular regarding its variation or its stability, may not be among the most vital problems of the postwar economy, but they are certainly among the perplexing ones" [5, p. 466]. In his contribution, John H. Williams—not only professor at Harvard but also a long-time adviser to the New York Federal Reserve Bank—wrote, "I can see no prospect of revival of a general monetary control in the postwar period" [5, p. 383].

Another of the volumes dealing with postwar policy that appeared at this time, *Planning and Paying for Full Employment,* was edited by Abba P. Lerner and Frank D. Graham [6] and had contributors of all shades of professional opinion—from Henry Simons and Frank Graham to Abba Lerner and Hans Neisser. Yet Albert Halasi, in his excellent summary of the papers, was able to say, "Our contributors do not discuss the question of money supply....The contributors make no special mention of credit policy to remedy actual depressions.... Inflation... might be fought more effectively by raising interest rates.... But...other anti-inflationary measures...are preferable" [6, pp. 23–24]. *A Survey of Contemporary Economics,* edited by Howard Ellis and published in 1948, was an "official" attempt to codify the state of economic thought of the time. In his contribution, Arthur Smithies wrote, "In the field of compensatory action, I believe fiscal policy must shoulder most of the load. Its chief rival, monetary policy, seems to be disqualified on institutional grounds. This country appears to be committed to something like the present low level of interest rates on a long-term basis" [1, p. 208].

These quotations suggest the flavor of professional thought some two decades ago. If you wish to go further in this humbling inquiry, I recommend that you compare the sections on money—when you can find them—in the Principles texts of the early postwar years with the lengthy sections in the current crop even, or especially, when the early and recent Principles are different editions of the same work.

The pendulum has swung far since then, if not all the way to the position of the late 1920s, at least much closer to that position than to the position of 1945. There are of course many differences between then and now, less in the potency attributed to monetary policy than in the roles assigned to it and the criteria by which the profession believes monetary policy should be guided. Then, the chief roles assigned monetary policy were to promote price stability and to preserve the gold standard; the chief criteria of monetary policy were the state of the "money market," the extent of "speculation" and the movement of gold. Today, primacy is assigned to the promotion of full employment, with the prevention of inflation a continuing but definitely secondary objective. And there is major disagreement about criteria of policy, varying from emphasis on money market conditions, interest rates, and the quantity of money to the belief that the state of employment itself should be the proximate criterion of policy.

I stress nonetheless the similarity between the views that prevailed in the late twenties and those that prevail today because I fear that, now as then, the pendulum may well have swung too far, that, now as then, we are in danger of assigning to monetary policy a larger role than it can perform, in danger of asking it to accomplish tasks that it cannot achieve, and, as a result, in danger of preventing it from making the contribution that it is capable of making.

Unaccustomed as I am to denigrating the importance of money, I therefore shall, as my first task, stress what monetary policy cannot do. I shall then try to outline what it can do and how it can best make its contribution, in the present state of our knowledge — or ignorance.

I. *What Monetary Policy Cannot Do*

From the infinite world of negation, I have selected two limitations of monetary policy to discuss: (1) It cannot peg interest rates for more than very limited periods; (2) It cannot peg the rate of unemployment for more than very limited periods. I select these because the contrary has been or is widely believed, because they correspond to the two main unattainable tasks that are at all likely to be assigned to monetary policy, and because essentially the same theoretical analysis covers both.

Pegging of Interest Rates

History has already persuaded many of you about the first limitation. As noted earlier, the failure of cheap money policies was a major source of the reaction against simple-minded Keynesianism. In the United States, this reaction involved widespread recognition that the wartime and postwar pegging of bond prices was a mistake, that the abandonment of this policy was a desirable and inevitable step, and that it had none of the disturbing and disastrous consequences that were so freely predicted at the time.

The limitation derives from a much misunderstood feature of the relation between money and interest rates. Let the Fed set out to keep interest rates down. How will it try to do so? By buying securities. This raises their prices and lowers their yields. In the process, it also increases the quantity of reserves available to banks, hence the amount of bank credit, and, ultimately the total quantity of money. That is why central bankers in particular, and the financial community more broadly, generally believe that an increase in the quantity of money tends to lower interest rates. Academic economists accept the same conclusion, but for different reasons. They see, in their mind's eye, a negatively sloping liquidity preference schedule. How can people be induced to hold a larger quantity of money? Only by bidding down interest rates.

Both are right, up to a point. The *initial* impact of increasing the quantity of money at a faster rate than it has been increasing is to make interest rates lower for a time than they would otherwise have been. But this is only the beginning of the process not the end. The more rapid rate of monetary growth will stimulate spending, both through the impact on investment of lower market interest rates and through the impact on other spending... of higher cash balances than are desired. But one man's spending is another man's income. Rising income will raise the liquidity preference schedule and the demand for loans; it may also raise prices, which would reduce the real quantity of money. These three effects will reverse the initial downward pressure on interest rates fairly promptly, say, in something less than a year. Together they will tend, after a somewhat longer interval, say, a year or two, to return interest rates to the level they would otherwise have had. Indeed, given the tendency for the economy to overreact, they are highly likely to raise interest rates temporarily beyond that level, setting in motion a cyclical adjustment process.

A fourth effect, when and if it becomes operative, will go even farther, and definitely mean that a higher rate of monetary expansion will correspond to a higher, not lower, level of interest rates than would otherwise have prevailed. Let the higher rate of monetary growth produce rising prices, and let the public come to expect that prices will continue to rise. Borrowers will then be willing to pay and lenders will then demand higher interest rates—as Irving Fisher pointed out decades ago. This price expectation effect is slow to develop and also slow to disappear. Fisher estimated that it took several decades for a full adjustment and more recent work is consistent with his estimates.

These subsequent effects explain why every attempt to keep interest rates at a low level has forced the monetary authority to engage in successively larger and larger open market purchases. They explain why, historically, high and rising nominal interest rates have been associated with rapid growth in the quantity of money, as in Brazil or Chile or in the United States in recent years, and why low and falling interest rates have been associated with slow growth in the quantity of money, as in Switzerland now or in the United States from 1929 to 1933. As an empirical matter, low interest rates are a sign that monetary policy *has been* tight—in the sense that the quantity of money has grown slowly; high interest rates are a sign that monetary policy *has been* easy—in the sense that the quantity of money has grown rapidly. The broadest facts of experience run in precisely the opposite direction from that which the financial community and academic economists have all generally taken for granted.

Paradoxically, the monetary authority could assure low nominal rates of interest—but to do so it would have to start out in what seems like the opposite direction, by engaging in a deflationary monetary policy. Similarly, it could assure high nominal interest rates by engaging in an inflationary policy and accepting a temporary movement in interest rates in the opposite direction.

These considerations not only explain why monetary policy cannot peg interest rates; they also explain why interest rates are such a misleading indicator of whether monetary policy is "tight" or "easy." For that, it is far better to look at the rate of change of the quantity of money.[2]

Employment as a Criterion of Policy

The second limitation I wish to discuss goes more against the grain of current thinking. Monetary growth, it is widely held, will tend to stimulate employment; monetary contraction, to retard employment. Why, then, cannot the monetary authority adopt a target for employment or unemployment—say, 3 percent unemployment; be tight when unemployment is less than the target; be easy when unemployment is higher than the target; and in this way peg unemployment at, say, 3 percent? The reason it cannot is precisely the same as for interest rates—the difference between the immediate and the delayed consequences of such a policy.

Thanks to Wicksell, we are all acquainted with the concept of a "natural" rate of interest and the possibility of a discrepancy between the "natural" and the "market" rate. The preceding analysis of interest rates can be translated fairly directly into Wicksellian terms. The monetary authority can make the market rate less than the natural rate only by inflation. It can make the market rate higher than the natural rate only by deflation. We have added only one wrinkle to Wicksell—the Irving Fisher distinction between the nominal and the real rate of interest. Let the monetary authority keep the nominal market rate for a time below the natural rate by inflation. That in turn will raise the nominal natural rate itself, once anticipations of inflation become widespread,

---

[2]This is partly an empirical not theoretical judgment. In principle, "tightness" or "ease" depends on the rate of change of the quantity of money supplied compared to the rate of change of the quantity demanded excluding effects on demand from monetary policy itself. However, empirically demand is highly stable, if we exclude the effect of monetary policy, so it is generally sufficient to look at supply alone.

thus requiring still more rapid inflation to hold down the market rate. Similarly, because of the Fisher effect, it will require not merely deflation but more and more rapid deflation to hold the market rate above the initial "natural" rate.

This analysis has its close counterpart in the employment market. At any moment of time, there is some level of unemployment which has the property that it is consistent with equilibrium in the structure of *real* wage rates. At that level of unemployment, real wage rates are tending on the average to rise at a "normal" secular rate, i.e., at a rate that can be indefinitely maintained so long as capital formation, technological improvements, etc., remain on their long-run trends. A lower level of unemployment is an indication that there is an excess demand for labor that will produce upward pressure on real wage rates. A higher level of unemployment is an indication that there is an excess supply of labor that will produce downward pressure on real wage rates. The "natural rate of unemployment," in other words, is the level that would be ground out by the Walrasian system of general equilibrium equations, provided there is imbedded in them the actual structural characteristics of the labor and commodity markets, including market imperfections, stochastic variability in demands and supplies, the cost of gathering information about job vacancies and labor availabilities, the costs of mobility, and so on.[3]

You will recognize the close similarity between this statement and the celebrated Phillips Curve. The similarity is not coincidental. Phillips' analysis of the relation between unemployment and wage change is deservedly celebrated as an important and original contribution. But, unfortunately, it contains a basic defect — the failure to distinguish between *nominal* wages and *real* wages — just as Wicksell's analysis failed to distinguish between *nominal* interest rates and *real* interest rates. Implicitly, Phillips wrote his article for a world in which everyone anticipated that nominal prices would be stable and in which that anticipation remained unshaken and immutable whatever happened to actual prices and wages. Suppose, by contrast, that everyone anticipates that prices will rise at a rate of more than 75 percent a year — as, for example, Brazilians did a few years ago. Then wages must rise at that rate simply to keep real wages unchanged. An excess supply of labor will be reflected in a less rapid rise in nominal wages than in anticipated prices,[4] not in an absolute decline in wages. When Brazil embarked on a policy to bring down the rate of price rise, and succeeded in bringing the price rise down to about 45 percent a year, there was a sharp initial rise in unemployment because under the influence of earlier anticipations, wages kept rising at a pace that was higher than the new rate of price rise, though lower than earlier. This is the

---

[3]It is perhaps worth noting that this "natural" rate need not correspond to equality between the number unemployed and the number of job vacancies. For any given structure of the labor market, there will be some equilibrium relation between these two magnitudes, but there is no reason why it should be one of equality.

[4]Strictly speaking, the rise in nominal wages will be less rapid than the rise in anticipated nominal wages to make allowance for any secular changes in real wages.

result experienced, and to be expected, of all attempts to reduce the rate of inflation below that widely anticipated.[5]

To avoid misunderstanding, let me emphasize that by using the term "natural" rate of unemployment, I do not mean to suggest that it is immutable and unchangeable. On the contrary, many of the market characteristics that determine its level are man-made and policy-made. In the United States, for example, legal minimum wage rates, the Walsh-Healy and Davis-Bacon Acts, and the strength of labor unions all make the natural rate of unemployment higher than it would otherwise be. Improvements in employment exchanges, in availability of information about job vacancies and labor supply, and so on, would tend to lower the natural rate of unemployment. I use the term "natural" for the same reason Wicksell did—to try to separate the real forces from monetary forces.

Let us assume that the monetary authority tries to peg the "market" rate of unemployment at a level below the "natural" rate. For definiteness, suppose that it takes 3 percent as the target rate and that the "natural" rate is higher than 3 percent. Suppose also that we start out at a time when prices have been stable and when unemployment is higher than 3 percent. Accordingly, the authority increases the rate of monetary growth. This will be expansionary. By making nominal cash balances higher than people desire, it will tend initially to lower interest rates and in this and other ways to stimulate spending. Income and spending will start to rise.

To begin with, much or most of the rise in income will take the form of an increase in output and employment rather than in prices. People have been expecting prices to be stable, and prices and wages have been set for some time in the future on that basis. It takes time for people to adjust to a new state of demand. Producers will tend to react to the initial expansion in aggregate demand by increasing output, employees by working longer hours, and the unemployed, by taking jobs now offered at former nominal wages. This much is pretty standard doctrine.

But it describes only the initial effects. Because selling prices of products typically respond to an unanticipated rise in nominal demand faster than prices of factors of production, real wages received have gone down—though real wages anticipated by employees went up, since employees implicitly evaluated

---

[5]Stated in terms of the rate of change of nominal wages, the Phillips Curve can be expected to be reasonably stable and well defined for any period for which the *average* rate of change of prices, and hence the anticipated rate, has been relatively stable. For such periods, nominal wages and "real" wages move together. Curves computed for different periods or different countries for each of which this condition has been satisfied will differ in level, the level of the curve depending on what the average rate of price change was. The higher the average rate of price change, the higher will tend to be the level of the curve. For periods or countries for which the rate of change of prices varies considerably, the Phillips Curve will not be well defined. My impression is that these statements accord reasonably well with the experience of the economists who have explored empirical Phillips Curves.

Restate Phillips' analysis in terms of the rate of change of real wages—and even more precisely, anticipated real wages—and it all falls into place. That is why students of empirical Phillips Curves have found that it helps to include the rate of change of the price level as an independent variable.

the wages offered at the earlier price level. Indeed, the simultaneous fall *ex post* in real wages to employers and rise *ex ante* in real wages to employees is what enabled employment to increase. But the decline *ex post* in real wages will soon come to affect anticipations. Employees will start to reckon on rising prices of the things they buy and to demand higher nominal wages for the future. "Market" unemployment is below the "natural" level. There is an excess demand for labor so real wages will tend to rise toward their initial level.

Even though the higher rate of monetary growth continues, the rise in real wages will reverse the decline in unemployment, and then lead to a rise, which will tend to return unemployment to its former level. In order to keep unemployment at its target level of 3 percent, the monetary authority would have to raise monetary growth still more. As in the interest rate case, the "market" rate can be kept below the "natural" rate only by inflation. And, as in the interest rate case, too, only by accelerating inflation. Conversely, let the monetary authority choose a target rate of unemployment that is above the natural rate, and they will be led to produce a deflation, and an accelerating deflation at that.

What if the monetary authority chose the "natural" rate—either of interest or unemployment—as its target? One problem is that it cannot know what the "natural" rate is. Unfortunately, we have as yet devised no method to estimate accurately and readily the natural rate of either interest or unemployment. And the "natural" rate will itself change from time to time. But the basic problem is that even if the monetary authority knew the "natural" rate, and attempted to peg the market rate at that level, it would not be led to a determinate policy. The "market" rate will vary from the natural rate for all sorts of reasons other than monetary policy. If the monetary authority responds to these variations, it will set in train longer term effects that will make any monetary growth path it follows ultimately consistent with the rule of policy. The actual course of monetary growth will be analogous to a random walk, buffeted this way and that by the forces that produce temporary departures of the market rate from the natural rate.

To state this conclusion differently, there is always a temporary trade-off between inflation and unemployment; there is no permanent trade-off. The temporary trade-off comes not from inflation per se, but from unanticipated inflation, which generally means, from a rising rate of inflation. The widespread belief that there is a permanent trade-off is a sophisticated version of the confusion between "high" and "rising" that we all recognize in simpler forms. A rising rate of inflation may reduce unemployment, a high rate will not.

But how long, you will say, is "temporary"? For interest rates, we have some systematic evidence on how long each of the several effects takes to work itself out. For unemployment, we do not. I can at most venture a personal judgment, based on some examination of the historical evidence, that the initial effects of a higher and unanticipated rate of inflation last for something like two to five years; that this initial effect then begins to be reversed; and that a full adjustment to the new rate of inflation takes about as long for employment as for interest rates, say, a couple of decades. For both interest rates and employment, let me add a qualification. These estimates are for changes in the rate of inflation of the order of magnitude that has been experienced in the United States. For much more sizable changes, such as those experienced in South American countries, the whole adjustment process is greatly speeded up.

To state the general conclusion still differently, the monetary authority controls nominal quantities—directly, the quantity of its own liabilities. In principle, it can use this control to peg a nominal quantity—an exchange rate, the price level, the nominal level of national income, the quantity of money by one or another definition—or to peg the rate of change in a nominal quantity—the rate of inflation or deflation, the rate of growth or decline in nominal national income, the rate of growth of the quantity of money. It cannot use its control over nominal quantities to peg a real quantity—the real rate of interest, the rate of unemployment, the level of real national income, the real quantity of money, the rate of growth of real national income, or the rate of growth of the real quantity of money.

II. *What Monetary Policy Can Do*

Monetary policy cannot peg these real magnitudes at predetermined levels. But monetary policy can and does have important effects on these real magnitudes. The one is in no way inconsistent with the other.

My own studies of monetary history have made me extremely sympathetic to the oft-quoted, much reviled, and as widely misunderstood, comment by John Stuart Mill. "There cannot...," he wrote, "be intrinsically a more insignificant thing, in the economy of society, than money; except in the character of a contrivance for sparing time and labour. It is a machine for doing quickly and commodiously, what would be done, though less quickly and commodiously, without it: and like many other kinds of machinery, it only exerts a distinct and independent influence of its own when it gets out of order" [7, p. 488].

True, money is only a machine, but it is an extraordinarily efficient machine. Without it, we could not have begun to attain the astounding growth in output and level of living we have experienced in the past two centuries—any more than we could have done so without those other marvelous machines that dot our countryside and enable us, for the most part, simply to do more efficiently what could be done without them at much greater cost in labor.

But money has one feature that these other machines do not share. Because it is so pervasive, when it gets out of order, it throws a monkey wrench into the operation of all the other machines. The Great Contraction is the most dramatic example but not the only one. Every other major contraction in this country has been either produced by monetary disorder or greatly exacerbated by monetary disorder. Every major inflation has been produced by monetary expansion—mostly to meet the overriding demands of war which have forced the creation of money to supplement explicit taxation.

The first and most important lesson that history teaches about what monetary policy can do—and it is a lesson of the most profound importance—is that monetary policy can prevent money itself from being a major source of economic disturbance. This sounds like a negative proposition: avoid major mistakes. In part it is. The Great Contraction might not have occurred at all, and if it had, it would have been far less severe, if the monetary authority had avoided mistakes, or if the monetary arrangements had been those of an earlier time when there was no central authority with the power to make the kinds of mistakes that the Federal Reserve System made. The past few years, to come closer to home, would have been steadier and more productive of economic well-being if the Federal Reserve had avoided drastic and erratic changes of direction, first expanding the money supply at an unduly rapid pace, then, in early 1966, stepping on the brake too hard, then, at the end of 1966, reversing itself and resuming expansion until at least November, 1967, at a more rapid pace than can long be maintained without appreciable inflation.

Even if the proposition that monetary policy can prevent money itself from being a major source of economic disturbance were a wholly negative proposition, it would be none the less important for that. As it happens, however, it is not a wholly negative proposition. The monetary machine has gotten out of order even when there has been no central authority with anything like the power now possessed by the Fed. In the United States, the 1907 episode and earlier banking panics are examples of how the monetary machine can get out of order largely on its own. There is therefore a positive and important task for the monetary authority—to suggest improvements in the machine that will reduce the chances that it will get out of order, and to use its own powers so as to keep the machine in good working order.

A second thing monetary policy can do is provide a stable background for the economy—keep the machine well oiled, to continue Mill's analogy. Accomplishing the first task will contribute to this objective, but there is more to it than that. Our economic system will work best when producers and consumers, employers and employees, can proceed with full confidence that the average level of prices will behave in a known way in the future—preferably that it will be highly stable. Under any conceivable institutional arrangements, and certainly under those that now prevail in the United States, there is only a limited amount of flexibility in prices and wages. We need to conserve this flexibility to achieve changes in relative prices and wages that are required to adjust to dynamic changes in tastes and technology. We should not dissipate it simply to achieve changes in the absolute level of prices that serve no economic function.

In an earlier era, the gold standard was relied on to provide confidence in future monetary stability. In its heyday it served that function reasonably well. It clearly no longer does, since there is scarce a country in the world that is prepared to let the gold standard reign unchecked—and there are persuasive reasons why countries should not do so. The monetary authority could operate as a surrogate for the gold standard, if it pegged exchange rates and did so exclusively by altering the quantity of money in response to balance of payment flows without "sterilizing" surpluses or deficits and without resorting to open or concealed exchange control or to changes in tariffs and quotas. But again, though many central bankers talk this way, few are in fact willing to follow this course—and again there are persuasive reasons why they should not do so. Such a policy would submit each country to the vagaries not of an impersonal and automatic gold standard but of the policies—deliberate or accidental—of other monetary authorities.

In today's world, if monetary policy is to provide a stable background for the economy it must do so by deliberately employing its powers to that end. I shall come later to how it can do so.

Finally, monetary policy can contribute to offsetting major disturbances in the economic system arising from other sources. If there is an independent secular exhilaration—as the postwar expansion was described by the proponents of secular stagnation—monetary policy can in principle help to hold it in check by a slower rate of monetary growth than would otherwise be desirable. If, as now, an explosive federal budget threatens unprecedented deficits, monetary policy can hold any inflationary dangers in check by a slower rate of monetary growth than would otherwise be desirable. This will temporarily mean higher interest rates than would otherwise prevail—to enable the government to borrow the sums needed to finance the deficit—but by preventing the speeding up of inflation, it may well mean both lower prices and lower nominal interest rates for the long pull. If the end of a substantial war offers the country an opportunity to shift resources from wartime to peacetime production, monetary policy can ease the transition by a higher rate of monetary growth than would otherwise be desirable—though experience is not very encouraging that it can do so without going too far.

I have put this point last, and stated it in qualified terms—as referring to major disturbances—because I believe that the potentiality of monetary policy in offsetting other forces making for instability is far more limited than is commonly believed. We simply do not know enough to be able to recognize minor disturbances when they occur or to be able to predict either what their effects will be with any precision or what monetary policy is required to offset their effects. We do not know enough to be able to achieve stated objectives by delicate, or even fairly coarse, changes in the mix of monetary and fiscal policy. In this area particularly the best is likely to be the enemy of the good. Experience suggests that the path of wisdom is to use monetary policy explicitly to offset other disturbances only when they offer a "clear and present danger."

III. *How Should Monetary Policy Be Conducted?*

How should monetary policy be conducted to make the contribution to our goals that it is capable of making? This is clearly not the occasion for presenting a detailed "Program for Monetary Stability"—to use the title of a book in which I tried to do so [3]. I shall restrict myself here to two major requirements for monetary policy that follow fairly directly from the preceding discussion.

The first requirement is that the monetary authority should guide itself by magnitudes that it can control, not by ones that it cannot control. If, as the authority has often done, it takes interest rates or the current unemployment percentage as the immediate criterion of policy, it will be like a space vehicle that has taken a fix on the wrong star. No matter how sensitive and sophisticated its guiding apparatus, the space vehicle will go astray. And so will the monetary authority. Of the various alternative magnitudes that it can control, the most appealing guides for policy are exchange rates, the price level as defined by some index, and the quantity of a monetary total—currency plus adjusted demand deposits, or this total plus commercial bank time deposits, or a still broader total.

For the United States in particular, exchange rates are an undesirable guide. It might be worth requiring the bulk of the economy to adjust to the tiny percentage consisting of foreign trade if that would guarantee freedom from monetary irresponsibility—as it might under a real gold standard. But it is hardly worth doing so simply to adapt to the average of whatever policies monetary authorities in the rest of the world adopt. Far better to let the market, through floating exchange rates, adjust to world conditions the 5 percent or so of our resources devoted to international trade while reserving monetary policy to promote the effective use of the 95 percent.

Of the three guides listed, the price level is clearly the most important in its own right. Other things the same, it would be much the best of the alternatives —as so many distinguished economists have urged in the past. But other things are not the same. The link between the policy actions of the monetary authority and the price level, while unquestionably present, is more indirect than the link between the policy actions of the authority and any of the several monetary totals. Moreover, monetary action takes a longer time to affect the price level than to affect the monetary totals and both the time lag and the magnitude of effect vary with circumstances. As a result, we cannot predict at all accurately just what effect a particular monetary action will have on the price level and, equally important, just when it will have that effect. Attempting to control directly the price level is therefore likely to make monetary policy itself a source of economic disturbance because of false stops and starts. Perhaps, as our understanding of monetary phenomena advances, the situation will change. But at the present stage of our understanding, the long way around seems the surer way to our objective. Accordingly, I believe that a monetary total is the best currently available immediate guide or criterion for monetary policy – and I believe that it matters much less which particular total is chosen than that one be chosen.

A second requirement for monetary policy is that the monetary authority avoid sharp swings in policy. In the past, monetary authorities have on occasion moved in the wrong direction – as in the episode of the Great Contraction that I have stressed. More frequently, they have moved in the right direction, albeit often too late, but have erred by moving too far. Too late and too much has been the general practice. For example, in early 1966, it was the right policy for the Federal Reserve to move in a less expansionary direction – though it should have done so at least a year earlier. But when it moved, it went too far, producing the sharpest change in the rate of monetary growth of the postwar era. Again, having gone too far, it was the right policy for the Fed to reverse course at the end of 1966. But again it went too far, not only restoring but exceeding the earlier excessive rate of monetary growth. And this episode is no exception. Time and again this has been the course followed – as in 1919 and 1920, in 1937 and 1938, in 1953 and 1954, in 1959 and 1960.

The reason for the propensity to overreact seems clear: the failure of monetary authorities to allow for the delay between their actions and the subsequent effects on the economy. They tend to determine their actions by today's conditions – but their actions will affect the economy only six or nine or twelve or fifteen months later. Hence they feel impelled to step on the brake, or the accelerator, as the case may be, too hard.

My own prescription is still that the monetary authority go all the way in avoiding such swings by adopting publicly the policy of achieving a steady rate of growth in a specified monetary total. The precise rate of growth, like the precise monetary total, is less important than the adoption of some stated and known rate. I myself have argued for a rate that would on the average achieve rough stability in the level of prices of final products, which I have estimated would call for something like a 3 to 5 percent per year rate of growth in currency plus all commercial bank deposits or a slightly lower rate of growth in currency plus demand deposits only.[6] But it would be better to have a fixed rate that would on the average produce moderate inflation or moderate deflation, provided it was steady, than to suffer the wide and erratic perturbations we have experienced.

Short of the adoption of such a publicly stated policy of a steady rate of monetary growth, it would constitute a major improvement if the monetary authority followed the self-denying ordinance of avoiding wide swings. It is a matter of record that periods of relative stability in the rate of monetary growth have also been periods of relative stability in economic activity, both in the United States and other countries. Periods of wide swings in the rate of

---

[6]In an as yet unpublished article on "The Optimum Quantity of Money," I conclude that a still lower rate of growth, something like 2 percent for the broader definition, might be better yet in order to eliminate or reduce the difference between private and total costs of adding to real balances.

monetary growth have also been periods of wide swings in economic activity.

By setting itself a steady course and keeping to it, the monetary authority could make a major contribution to promoting economic stability. By making that course one of steady but moderate growth in the quantity of money, it would make a major contribution to avoidance of either inflation or deflation of prices. Other forces would still affect the economy, require change and adjustment, and disturb the even tenor of our ways. But steady monetary growth would provide a monetary climate favorable to the effective operation of those basic forces of enterprise, ingenuity, invention, hard work, and thrift that are the true springs of economic growth. That is the most that we can ask from monetary policy at our present stage of knowledge. But that much — and it is a great deal — is clearly within our reach.

References

1. H. S. Ellis, ed., *A Survey of Contemporary Economics*. Philadelphia 1948.
2. Milton Friedman, "The Monetary Theory and Policy of Henry Simons," *Jour. Law and Econ.*, Oct. 1967, *10*, 1–13.
3. Milton Friedman, *A Program for Monetary Stability*. New York 1959.
4. E. A. Goldenweiser, "Postwar Problems and Policies," *Fed. Res. Bull.*, Feb. 1945, *31*, 112–21.
5. P. T. Homan and Fritz Machlup, ed., *Financing American Prosperity*. New York 1945.
6. A. P. Lerner and F. D. Graham, ed., *Planning and Paying for Full Employment*. Princeton 1946.
7. J. S. Mill, *Principles of Political Economy*, Bk. III, Ashley ed. New York 1929.

Section Four

International Exchange

23

A Schematic Sketch of International Money Flows

The Price-Specie-Flow Mechanism

A simplifying and useful dictum employed by mathematicians in teaching logarithms is the axiom *Logarithms are exponents*. If students understand exponents, the path to understanding logarithms is less difficult.

The same device can be employed in introducing the subject of the exchange of foreign money for domestic money. Throughout the sections on the theory of money, readers have been urged to remember that money is one thing and commodities something else. However, moneys that originate under foreign political systems are a different story. Thus this generalization: *All foreign moneys are commodities*. This statement applies both to foreign moneys that are bank notes and checks issued within a bona fide metallic standard system and to the fiat paper money issues of national governments. Three possible exceptions should be noted: (1) A supranational world money issued by an organization having universal sovereignty would eliminate the distinction; no foreign money would exist. (2) A money universally accepted because of its intrinsic and well-recognized value as a commodity would serve the same purpose as a universal fiat money. Gold and silver in their day approximated this kind of money. (3) A domestic paper money may obtain such universal recognition and prestige due to its stability of value over long periods that other national economies use it as their own. A foreign government may even declare such a money legal tender, in which case the foreign and domestic moneys again become unified.

These qualifications modify the axiom given above only to this extent: *Foreign currencies not generally used as money in a domestic economy should be treated as if they are commodities.* The most important reason for emphasizing this approach is that it makes plausible the slightly incongruous sight of money being bought and sold for other money. Once the *"commodityness"* of foreign moneys is grasped, their purchase and sale can be accepted as a matter of fact.

Gold developed as the most popular monetary base for use in domestic economies. Its monetary utility was even greater for international transactions. Its only important rival was silver. Each of these metals was universally recognized and accepted, and each had the usual characteristics of a good money —portability, divisibility, durability, and relative stability in value.

Due to differences in nomenclature of weights and measures in different countries, units of account came to have different names and sizes. Thus, a gold coin minted in England and called a "sovereign" had no relationship to a gold coin minted in the United States and called a "dollar," except that both contained a defined weight of pure gold. The gold sovereign could be exchanged for goods and services in England, and the U.S. gold dollar could be exchanged for goods and services in the United States. When governments got into the act and declared that defined weights of gold would be legal tender for clearing debts of a specified number of the units of account in both countries, the acceptability of metallic money became absolute and each coin then had a common basis of value with the coin in the other country.

The simplest processes of international exchange and of equilibration in international payments can be demonstrated by assuming that two countries, say, the United States and England, are on fully operational gold standards. Let the unit of account—the conventional expression of monetary value—be the "dollar" in the United States and the "pound" in England. Both dollar and pound are defined as equivalent to a fixed amount of gold by the respective governments, the dollar, say, equal to $1/12$ ounce and the pound to $1/5$ ounce of gold. This definition implies that each government would strike gold coins of the defined weights for those who wanted the metal monetized, and that these coins would serve as legal tender for all debts public and private to the extent of their defined monetary values. The coins would have nothing in common except their substance—gold; but, of course, this similarity would be sufficient for stating the ratio of *gold* values for the two coins. Since $2.40 would be equal in gold value to £1, the exchange rate between the two moneys would be $2.40 = £1.[1] Even if the two governments had acted completely independently in setting up their monetary systems, and even if each was motivated only by nationalistic considerations, the two gold currencies could

---

[1]The official ratio of exchange from 1834 to 1931 was $4.8665 = £1. The ratio of $2.40 = £1 is used here because it is the current exchange rate as well as the most convenient denominational ratio. At this rate, one U.S. penny equals one English pence. There are 240 pence in £1 sterling.

be exchanged for goods and services between the two countries almost as easily as either one could be exchanged for goods within either country.[2]

Since each country has some specialized goods and services that could be produced in the other country only at higher real (or opportunity) costs, international trade normally would take place once communication between the countries had been established and if no legal impediments to exchange were imposed. Every purchase and sale of goods between the two countries, however, would not require a corresponding exchange of gold. Although the cost per unit for transporting gold is nominal, it is a cost and is to be avoided if possible. The sale of English goods to U.S. importers promotes a demand by these importers for English pounds — the money acceptable in England. The sale of U.S. export goods to English importers similarly gives rise to a demand for U.S. dollars. These demands and the corresponding supplies that satisfy them are reciprocal: *The demand for pounds is a supply of dollars, and the demand for dollars is a supply of pounds.* The final requirement is that the demanders and suppliers meet in markets, so that they are able to communicate bids and offers to each other.

A market in which this activity takes place is called a foreign exchange market. "Foreign exchange" in England is non-British money available to British importers who need it. "Foreign exchange" in the United States is non-U.S. money similarly available. Dealers in foreign exchange, who make such a market operational, establish contacts or institutions for handling such exchanges in those financial centers that are loci of export-import activity. These markets ordinarily function very effectively. Competition is prevalent due to the large number of buyers, sellers, and brokers who have reason to deal in foreign exchange, and due also to the impracticality of restricting competition simultaneously on both sides of a political boundary. Furthermore, the products are homogeneous — any one dollar is just like any other dollar — and communications in the market are good.

Figure 23.1 describes the reciprocal nature of demands for and supplies of foreign exchange. In the two markets, hypothetical demand and supply schedules for £ sterling and dollars are constructed. These schedules are graphed conventionally and appear as $D_£$, S , $D_\$$, and $S_\$$. The demand for sterling in the "Dollar Market for £ Sterling" means that dollars are being supplied on specific terms, the terms being described also by the supply of dollars ($S_\$$) in the "£ Sterling Market for Dollars."

Once one of these schedules is known, its reciprocal in the other market is given and can be derived by simple arithmetic. For example, the quantity of £ sterling demanded at a price of $3.50 per £1 is 20 million £ sterling per day. Thus, $70 million would be offered at this price to buy 20 million £ sterling.

---

[2]Governments, including the U.S. government, have frequently specified lists of foreign coins that were allowable as legal tender.

Figure 23.1. Dollar Market for £ Sterling (top) and
£ Sterling Market for Dollars (bottom)

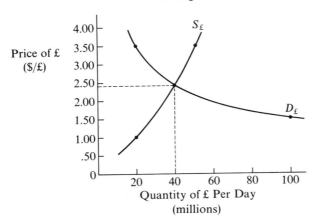

Demand for £	
p of £	q of £
$1.50	100 mil.
2.40	40
3.50	20

Supply of £	
$1.00	20 mil.
2.40	40
3.50	50

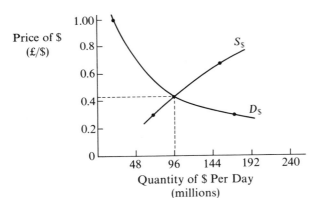

Demand for $	
p of $	q of $
£ 0.286	175 mil.
0.417	96
1.000	20

Supply of $	
£0.286	70 mil.
0.417	96
0.667	150

When the price of a £ sterling is $3.50, the price of $1 in terms of £ sterling is the reciprocal of this expression, that is, £1/$3.50, or approximately £0.286/$1. Therefore, $70 million would be supplied to the British market at a price of £0.286 per dollar, and this point appears accordingly on the $S_\$$ schedule. Every other point on the $D_£$ schedule corresponds similarly to a point on the $S_\$$ schedule, and the same relationship holds for the $S_£$ and $D_\$$ schedules.

The "two" markets, therefore, are really one basic market expressed in terms of the two different currencies. The market equilibrium in terms of dollars is £40 million demanded and supplied per day at a price of $2.40 per £1. The same equilibrium to the British is $96 million demanded and supplied per day at a price of £0.417 per $1.

If under a gold standard system the value of British pounds demanded exactly equals the gold value of U.S. dollars demanded, the moneys exchange with no net flows of gold. The value of the pounds demanded is a value of dollars supplied, and the value of dollars demanded is the value of pounds supplied. In effect, importers and exporters in both countries simply "swap" their currencies in the foreign exchange markets at the £ sterling-dollar exchange rate. But if the *demand* for British pounds exceeds the *demand* for U.S. dollars, and therefore exceeds the *supply* of British pounds, the *price* of British pounds in terms of U.S. dollars tends to rise.[3] This "price" is the exchange rate. The exchange rate might rise above £1 = $2.40. If it did, the operation of a smoothly working gold standard would see U.S. demanders of British pounds shipping gold coin or bullion to England. The gold would exchange at the rate of £1 for ⅕ ounce of gold plus the cost of shipment. Since the cost of shipping the gold is, say, one half of 1 percent of the value depending on the size of the shipment, insurance, and other cost factors, gold would flow from the United States to England when the price of pounds in terms of dollars reached a value of approximately £1 = $2.412. It would flow the other way when the price became £1 = $2.388.

Gold ordinarily flows when events buoy up prices of domestically produced goods and services.[4] Since the price of a foreign money is one such domestic price, prices of foreign moneys (exchange rates) tend to rise with increases in all prices so long as the real value of the foreign money is not deteriorating at the same time in its own domestic environment. Increased prices for domestic goods and services stimulate demand for substitute foreign products and hence for foreign moneys. Under an international gold standard, gold then flows to make up the balance, that is, to pay for the "excess" goods and services purchased from foreigners.

Equilibrium in this process comes about through the corrective monetary effects set in motion by the flow of gold. Since gold is used as reserves by the banking system, the reaction to a loss of gold is a multiple contraction of bank credit. Money prices and money incomes, being functions of the stock of money, then fall in the gold-losing country and rise in the gold-gaining country. Prices that had been attractive in the exporting country become less so, and the lower prices in the gold-losing country encourage buyers, both domestic and foreign. Equilibrium occurs when trade is attended by no appreciable changes in the stock of money in either country.[5]

---

[3] This situation is described by saying that the United States has a deficit in the balance of trade, or that England has a surplus. Sometimes a deficit is referred to as an "unfavorable" balance of trade, and surplus as a "favorable" balance of trade.

[4] Common occurrences that have tended to raise prices of domestic items include domestic gold discoveries, issues of paper money by governments, and expansions of bank credit.

[5] Even if gold mining is a major industry, so that the economy could expect to export gold continuously, the stock of *money* in such a country *may* not increase by any more than the increase in the output of goods and services. It may even decrease if price levels in other countries are falling drastically enough.

Countries that allow a bona fide gold-price-flow mechanism to adjust their international balances must adhere to the following rules:

1. Each country must specify its unit of account in terms of a weight of metal, and this statutory relationship must not be changed capriciously.
2. Money prices and wages must be reasonably flexible, which is to say that a competitive market system must prevail.
3. Restrictions must not be imposed on the flow of gold, and, at worst, only nominal restrictions (tariffs) can be levied against the flow of goods and services.

Adjustments in the system take the form of changes in money prices, wages, and other costs that stem from the alterations in the quantity of money brought about by the flow of gold. Prices, wages, costs, and incomes — all money values not fixed by contract — fall in the gold-losing country and conversely rise in the gold-gaining country, while the exchange rate remains constant (within the limits specified above). For the gold-losing country this process hurts. Prices, wages, and incomes, even if they are very flexible, never fall proportionally. Some depression and unemployment inevitably are experienced. However, an economic system that follows the rules can be assured that the gold flow process will ultimately restore incomes and employment. Furthermore, the process is self-regulatory and takes place automatically, that is, without the agency of policy makers using discretion.

The Use of Nonmoney Debt in International Exchange

The simplest type of gold standard mechanism is the one described above, in which the world's economies produce goods and services, issue national moneys, and base their monetary systems on gold. A more realistic world, of either the present or the past, is one that also contains both public and private debts — fixed claims payable in the money of account.

If, in the example cited above, the demands by U.S. importers for British pounds exceeded the demand by British importers for U.S. dollars by $24,000 (or by £10,000 sterling), 2,000 ounces of gold would need to be shipped from the United States to England to make up the deficit in the balance of trade. In a world that includes debt instruments, U.S. importers may forego the shipment of gold by borrowing the pounds sterling in the British capital or money markets to pay for the deficit. This action would generate an "export" of British capital.[6] They might even obtain the credit they need directly from

---

[6] In a world system of multilateral trading, the lender-investors may be from some other country. Anyone who had British pounds available could lend to the U.S. borrowers. For simplicity's sake the discussion here is confined to markets in these two countries.

the British exporters, but the exporters are not ordinarily credit purveyors. So the U.S. importer-borrowers would try to get the pounds in one of the capital markets in which borrowings and lendings are handled.

No matter how the details of the lending process are performed, some U.S. importers must sign interest-bearing evidences of debt. These notes (short-term) or bonds (long-term) would be purchased ordinarily by private individuals or institutions in England that are interested in obtaining interest-earning assets. The larger the trade deficit, the greater the demand of the U.S. importers for credit and the higher the rate of interest they would need to pay in order to borrow British money. Higher interest rates mean higher costs for those paying them, and consequent discouragement of a limitless continuation of the borrowing process. Higher interest rates on investment goods mean a narrowing of the margin between expected returns from investment and the real costs of investment. If the imports are consumption goods or services, the cost of getting the credit with which to purchase them reduces the margin of advantage the U.S. importer enjoys between buying the goods in England and buying them in the United States.

The additional credit demanded by the U.S. importers may or may not generate new money in England. If English banks have excess reserves and if some unemployment exists (as would be the case during a business recession), the additional credit demands probably would generate new demand deposits as well as reemployment of idle factors of production. The new income can be thought of as equal to the increase in the quantity of money times its velocity; or the net foreign balance can be thought of as an autonomous expenditure, and the new income as equal to this balance times an "export multiplier." (See Chapter 26.) In either case aggregate spending and total incomes would increase in England and decrease in the United States.

If the demand for credit did not increase the stock of money in England because of no excess reserves in the British banking system, the supply of British credit granted to U.S. importers would be at the expense of those people in England who wanted the same accommodation for domestic purposes. The willingness of U.S. importers to bid away the credit by paying higher interest rates would stimulate British export goods industries relative to other industries and have a corresponding effect on *relative* prices in England. Here again the price-wage-income effect would be felt; and while it would be in one sector of the economy relative to another, it would also be a general increase in demand due to an increase in the velocity of the pound inspired by burgeoning U.S. demands resulting from, say, a paper money inflation in the United States. If such an inflation continued, the monetary demands of U.S. importers would find no limit, and the British capital market would come to doubt that the credit it was extending would be repaid in units of similar value. That is, a buyer of U.S. debt might question whether the debt could be repaid in units of constant purchasing power — in terms of either goods and services or gold. He might reason that the U.S. economy could not maintain the convertible (into gold) value of the dollar. In such a case, the credit needed by U.S. importers would become so costly that gold would have to flow. If the United States then ran out of gold, further increases in the volume of paper dollars would simply force the U.S. economy off the gold standard — which is to say that the exchange rate between dollars and pounds could no longer remain constant.[7]

Capital flows — the sale of short- and long-term debt by public or private agencies in foreign money markets to pay for a deficit in the balance of trade — may diminish the volume of the gold outflow either partly or completely. In fact, sufficiently large sales of such debts can *reverse* the gold flow, thus allowing the country with the trade balance deficit to obtain a net increase in gold! This occurrence is rare, but it has happened. Again, if a country is a net creditor in its capital accounts, and returns enough of its capital claims for liquidation to a country currently enjoying an export balance on goods and services, but which is a net debtor in its capital position, gold may flow from the exporting country to the importing country.[8]

Capital flows also include the sale of domestically issued common stock to foreigners. To emphasize the similarity between this kind of sale and a sale of goods or services, note that a foreigner may buy either a Plymouth made in the United States or a share of Chrysler Corporation stock issued in the United States. If he wishes to buy the Plymouth, he uses his currency, say, pounds, to buy dollars, and with the dollars he buys the Plymouth through the usual export-dealer channels. If he wishes to buy the share of stock, he also uses his own money to buy dollars, and with the dollars he buys the stock certificate through investment market channels. In either case, he demands dollars with his own currency, and the monetary effects in the foreign exchange market are identical. Whether the purchase is accounted in "trade" or in "capital flows" is purely a matter of classification. In general, any transaction that causes foreigners to demand dollars for any purpose — to buy commodities, services, bonds or stocks, or to make gifts of money to people in the United States — has a tendency to raise the price of dollars in the foreign exchange market and, under a gold standard system, to generate a flow of gold to the United States. On the other hand, the same kind of transactions by U.S. households and firms generates the opposite effects. In accounting a "balance," therefore, to determine one country's net payment position with respect to another country's, all trade and capital exchanges, plus private and public gifts and grants, plus gold flows and changes in domestic money balances held by foreigners, must be included. Such an accounting statement is called a "balance of payments," and it must balance because it includes all items included in exchanges.

---

[7]Essentially this process took place in the United States from 1862 to 1879. (See Chapter 10.)

[8]This phenomenon was observed in the United States during 1893–1896. The United States had a favorable balance of trade for much of this period, but the return of government securities by foreigners "paid" the export balance and prevented any sizable inflow of gold. (See Chapter 18 again.)

International Exchange in a Multimoney World

General adherence to metallic standards in international exchange, whether accompanied by capital flows or not, calls for changes in domestic money prices, costs, and incomes to pivot around nearly fixed exchange rates in order that equilibrium conditions in the balance of payments be maintained or restored. When stocks of money are issued under the fiat of national governments and without reference to a metallic base, the exchange rates between moneys have no common ground in law. However, they do have commonalty in their respective purchasing powers. Each country's national money may buy a bundle of domestically produced goods and services similar to one obtainable from foreign countries. Exchange rates, being prices of "commodities" (that is, of foreign moneys), are determined in the same fashion as other market prices — by supply of and demand for the foreign moneys in terms of the national money in question. Of course, supply and demand for currencies operates through markets under a metallic system, too. Even though the movement of the price of money in terms of gold is narrowly limited by the statutory equality of gold to the unit of account, *some* change in the exchange rate must occur or gold would not flow. Within a narrow compass, therefore, exchange rates are also "freely fluctuating" under an international gold standard, while domestic money prices, costs, and incomes are freely fluctuating without bounds.

When exchange rates are free to fluctuate without limit because of no legal relationship of gold to the unit of account, domestic money prices, costs, and incomes may remain almost constant, although they do not necessarily do so. Under a nonmetallic monetary system the quantity of national money is determined by deliberate and conscious decision of the money-supplying agency. Once the economy has a given stock of money, all relative values are expressed in monetary terms. Since a foreign money may be used to claim the goods and services produced in a foreign country, it, too, comes to have a monetary value relative to the monetary values of similar goods and services produced in the domestic economy. Foreign goods and services can be evaluated relative to domestic goods and services so long as they fulfill an identifiable function, that is, have similar utility effects for individuals, and so long as they are "close substitutes" for goods and services produced domestically. The ability of the foreign money to exchange for those foreign goods and services that can be so evaluated gives foreign money its "price" in terms of domestic money. A variation of the old axiom of plane geometry can be applied here: Things [almost] equal to the same thing are [almost] equal to each other.

At the same time that domestic evaluation of foreign goods, and hence of foreign money, is operating, the same process is occurring in the foreign country. Chances are that importers in each country recognize "bargains" in the other country due to the international specialization of products and services. Assuming that two countries, say, the United States and England, each start off with a quantity of national money, an equilibrium exchange rate might be established that would again find £1 exchanging for $2.40. (See Figure 23.1 above.) Such an exchange rate would simply mean that the demand by British importers for dollars, the analogous demand by U.S. importers for pounds, the supply of dollars by English exporters, and the supply of pounds by U.S. exporters were all brought into an *equilibrium flow* at a price of £1 = $2.40. An equilibrium flow of dollars for pounds implies that the underlying determinants of supply and demand for the two moneys are such that the price of one money in terms of the other has no tendency to change.

National economies over time usually undergo changes in production and distribution, so the "underlying determinants" do not necessarily remain fixed. To take the simplest case of disequilibrium, suppose that the rate of change of the dollar supply in the United States is greater than the analogous rate of increase of British pounds sterling. To keep the example perfectly simple, assume that the supply of British pounds increases at a constant rate and that this rate keeps a price index of British goods and services constant. Assume also that a general price index in the United States increases at, say, 5 percent per year, due to a constant but inflationary rate of increase in U.S. dollars. The rate of increase in the prices of goods and services does not necessarily imply that the rates of increase of prices in any two sectors of the economy would be identical. Prices of exported goods, especially, would tend to rise more slowly than the general average of prices due to worldwide competition. For simplicity's sake, however, again assume that prices of domestically consumed goods and services and of those exported tend to increase homogeneously.

British importers who bought dollars at the old rate of $2.40 = £1, would find, during the ensuing year, that their dollars tended to buy fewer goods and services in the United States. In fact, since they would undoubtedly have price information on the goods and services potentially importable, they would realize before they bought the dollars that the value of the dollar had depreciated. In the case of an annual 5 percent depreciation, sellers of pounds would have to get $2.52 for £1 to obtain the same dollar purchasing power for the pound as they obtained before the price level increase. Likewise, U.S. importers would have more dollars to offer and therefore would be willing to pay more dollars to get the pounds to buy British goods. This change would be seen in Figure 23.1 as either a shift to the right in the demand for pounds (D£) or a shift to the right in the supply of dollars (S$). In this fashion, increases in the prices of foreign exchange would reflect domestic price level increases.

The general domestic inflation in the United States would also include higher dollar costs of production for all goods and services, whether these items were purchased by households and firms in the United States or by their counterparts in England. In an "ideal" system—one in which all money prices change by the same percentage and without lags or frictions—the increase in the exchange rate for British pounds would match the increase in dollar costs of production for exported goods and services, thus keeping the real costs to British importers what they were before the inflation. In actual inflations, prices and costs do not increase equiproportionally; lags in some prices and in many costs are experienced. Therefore, some distributional effects occur and change the relative allocations of factors of production between export and domestic industries.

Another possibility of international disequilibrium may result from differences in domestic productivity growth even when price levels remain constant. If English growth in real income was, say, 5 percent per year with an identical rate of increase in the supply of pounds (to keep the British price level constant), and if the corresponding rates of growth in real output and the money stock in the United States were, say, 3 percent per year, no *price* effects would be evident.[9] Since the demand for goods and services is a function of both relative prices and real incomes, the relative change in real income between the two countries would induce shifting demands. In general, demands in both countries would shift toward superior goods (sometimes improperly referred to as "luxury" goods) and away from inferior goods. Of course, in England the shift would occur more rapidly. For the determination of international flows and international equilibrium the question would be whether internationally traded goods and services were superior or inferior with respect to domestically consumed goods and services. In the event that they were neither, that is, had an income elasticity of demand equal to one, exchange rates would stay constant. If both countries' importers regarded the other's product specialties as superior, exchange rates might stay constant, but the volume of internationally traded goods and services would increase faster than the increase in domestic purchases.[10]

The chances are that most foreign goods and services, particularly things such as tourist travel in foreign countries, are considered "superior" to domestic alternatives. Assuming this generalization true for both the economies considered here, total international trade would increase, but the British demand for U.S. goods and services would increase more rapidly than the reciprocal demand by U.S. importers. The pressure for change would then be on the exchange rate and "in favor" of the dollar. The British would demand more dollars and they would supply more pounds. The value of dollars in buying pounds would become relatively greater than the value of dollars in buying domestic goods and services, *even though the total value of dollars spent would increase in both areas of purchase.* In such a case, resources would

---

[9]In the previous example real income was kept constant and relative prices of moneys were allowed to change. In the example here, relative prices of moneys are kept constant and real incomes are changed.

[10]*Both* could increase, of course; and in an economy in which real income is increasing, total demands would be for superior goods and services merely by the assumption that real income is increasing. The issue of spending for domestic products or spending for foreign commodities would depend on which bundle was "more" superior, that is, on which bundle had the higher income elásticity of demand.

shift away from industries concentrating on production for domestic needs and into industries specializing in export commodities and services. In an expanding economy, again, both sectors could utilize more resources. However, under the conditions of this example, the export sector would gain in a relative sense.[11]

International prices usually must adjust to changes in domestic price levels (values of moneys), to changes in real incomes in the world's economies, and to changes in relative prices within national economies. For the sake of clarity, these possible causes for change have been separated here. International movements of capital could also modify the adjustment process in the same way that they do under gold standards. In the case of freely fluctuating exchange rates, however, an economy that was a net exporter of goods and services would suffer relative decline in the international value of its unit of account when it imported more capital than the dollar value of its current trade surplus.

Selected Bibliography

Enzig, Paul. *The Foreign Exchange Market*. London: Macmillan Co., 1964.

Walter, Ingo. *International Economics: Theory and Policy*. New York: Ronald Press, 1968.

Yeager, Leland. *International Monetary Relations*. New York: Harper & Row, 1966.

International Payments and Foreign Exchange

Leland Yeager

This selection, written by Professor Leland Yeager of the University of Virginia, presents many real world details of the international payments system and the foreign exchange market not discussed in Chapter 23 itself.

---

[11]Many industries produce for both foreign and domestic consumption, so the cleavage is not necessarily as sharp as implied here.

These data should enlighten the reader considerably by their demonstration of the innate flexibility and simplicity of the foreign exchange market. Indeed, if any single feature stands out here, it is the implication that this market functions at least as efficiently as any other market so long as governments let it alone.

Professor Yeager is an eminent scholar and theorist. He has published many high-quality articles and books in both monetary and international economics. His works are well recommended to those readers who wish to pursue further this branch of economics.

International Payments

The goods and services moving in private international trade are priced and paid for in ordinary national currencies. Loans and investments are also expressed in national money. Private business firms and banks use no special kind of international money....

An American importer buying British goods priced in pounds sterling pays in sterling funds on deposit in a British bank. He transfers the money to his British supplier by a draft, check, or cabled order that he buys for dollars from his own bank in the United States. His bank, or a larger American bank with which his bank has a correspondent relationship, has been holding a sterling deposit in a British bank for just such purposes. The American bank is continually replenishing its sterling deposit by buying checks and similar claims on British bank balances from American exporters and other customers who have been receiving payments in sterling.

If the British exporter in this example has priced his goods and has received payment in dollars rather than sterling, it is he, rather than his American customer, who takes the initiative in exchanging dollars for sterling. The difference is unimportant. When the Briton receives payment in a dollar check, he sells it for sterling to his own bank, which has the amount credited to its dollar deposit in an American bank. The British bank maintains such a deposit as an inventory from which to sell dollars to British importers and other customers needing dollars.

The Foreign-Exchange Market

Only by great coincidence would a bank's sales and purchases· of foreign money in transactions with its own customers exactly match each other. In each country, some banks are developing a shortage and others a surplus of foreign money. The banks can largely even out their positions by buying and

selling foreign bank balances among each other. Every major financial center
has an interbank or "wholesale" market in foreign exchange. (Although it
includes actual foreign coins and banknotes, foreign exchange consists mostly
of claims on foreign currency, such as bank accounts and short-term negotiable
paper.) The banks deal with each other by telephone — usually, for convenience,
through the intermediary of brokers.

It would still be a coincidence if the banks in each country were buying no
more and no less of each foreign money from their customers than they were
selling to their customers. Perhaps American banks are acquiring too many
pounds sterling, while British banks are acquiring too many dollars. Then the
solution is obvious. International telephone and teleprinter facilities link the
individual financial centers together into a single worldwide foreign-exchange
market (except as government controls hamper this unification). Because of
this linkage, it does not much matter whether the British goods imported into
the United States are priced and paid for in dollars or in sterling. In either case,
dollars appear on the market in exchange for sterling. The difference concerns
merely whether the British exporter takes the initiative on the British retail
sector of the worldwide foreign-exchange market or the American importer
takes the initiative on the American sector.

Imbalances in some geographic sectors of the world foreign-exchange
market can cancel out opposite imbalances in others. But what, if anything,
assures the *overall* balance that permits the mutual offsetting of local imbalances? Under a system of freely flexible rates, the foreign-exchange market
clears itself in much the same way as a competitive market for any ordinary
commodity does: each exchange rate, like an ordinary price, moves to the level
at which supply and demand are equal. When a system of fixed exchange rates
prevents this automatic clearing, central banks or other government agencies
buy and sell on the market to absorb surpluses and supply deficiencies of
foreign currencies at the fixed rates. How extensively and how long the government agencies can keep on doing so, and with what consequences, are questions
to be discussed later.

Equilibrium on the Foreign-Exchange Market

For a simple explanation of what keeps the foreign-exchange market
cleared, let us consider American transactions with the rest of the world as
a whole. We shall lump all foreign currencies together under the name "foreign
exchange." This simplification is legitimate; for in the absence of restrictions,
one foreign currency can be sold for any other almost instantly at a competitively determined exchange rate belonging to a consistent pattern of rates.
Multilateral currency arbitrage maintains this consistency. (Arbitrage consists
of dealing to profit from discrepancies between prices prevailing at the same

time in different submarkets.) Suppose, for example, that the "broken cross rates" prevailed of 60 Belgian francs per dollar, 10 Belgian francs per German mark, and 3 German marks per dollar. An arbitrageur (typically a large bank) could profit by buying 60 francs with $1, buying 6 marks with the 60 francs, and buying $2 with the 6 marks. Transactions like this on a large scale would strengthen the franc against the dollar (perhaps toward a rate of 50 francs per dollar), strengthen the mark against the franc (perhaps toward 12½ francs per mark), and strengthen the dollar against the mark (perhaps toward 4 marks per dollar). This or some such consistent pattern of rates would emerge at which no further arbitrage was profitable. Even small discrepancies of the sort exaggerated here would motivate enough arbitrage to wipe them out in a few minutes.

Let us suppose that some disturbance to overall balance in transactions makes American purchases of goods, services, and claims abroad exceed American sales abroad. Desired purchases of foreign exchange with dollars exceed desired sales of foreign exchange for dollars. On a market free from official manipulation, this imbalance would bid up the price of foreign exchange in dollars (reduce the value of dollars in foreign money). As translated at the new exchange rate, the higher dollar prices of foreign goods, services, and claims would cause Americans to buy fewer of them. At the same time, foreigners would buy more American goods, services, and claims because they had become cheaper in foreign money. The totals of desired transactions in the two directions would become equal again (no doubt at a changed level) because the exchange rate would move to just the necessary figure. If the adjustment should overshoot the mark and make the dollar too weak on the foreign-exchange market, the rate would move back toward its new equilibrium level, just as the dollar would strengthen toward a new equilibrium if the initial disturbance had been the opposite of the kind we assumed.

Official Exchange Stabilization

In the real world of constant change in national price levels, tastes, technology, weather, political conditions, and other factors, flexible exchange rates would be responding with continual (though usually mild) fluctuations. For various reasons governments usually hold exchange rates almost rigid, apart from rare deliberate adjustments. When a country's currency shows signs of weakening under the pressure of excess imports of goods, services, and securities, the central bank or other official agency supports it by buying it with foreign exchange (or gold) held in reserve for that purpose. In doing so, the agency fills the gap between the total value of imports of goods, services, and securities and the smaller value of exports. Actually, the agency maintains as well as fills the gap; for if it were not filled, it could not exist. Instead, the value of the country's imports (in the broad sense considered here) would necessarily shrink to the value of its exports in some way or other—by depreciation of the home currency or by controls designed to choke off demands for foreign exchange. The agency can go on filling the gap only as long as it has reserves left or is able to borrow more abroad.

An opposite imbalance would require the central bank to absorb foreign exchange, paying with home money, to keep its currency from strengthening against foreign currencies. In doing so—and thus financing and maintaining the country's excess of sales over purchases in foreign transactions—the central bank faces no limit as definite as the limit to its support of a weak home currency. It can *create* its home currency if necessary to keep it from strengthening and to pay for foreign exchange (or gold) bought; but a central bank in the opposite position cannot, of course, just create foreign money.

Nowadays, instead of holding their exchange rates absolutely rigid, most countries let them fluctuate in a range narrower than 1 percent on either side of parity. When practically everyone is confident that these "support limits" to the range of fluctuation will hold firm, private movements of funds will reduce the necessary scale of official intervention. When the home currency sinks almost to its lower support limit, speculators will realize that it cannot sink much further and that any change in its rate will be upward. In buying the home currency, they will help make their expectations come true. At the opposite extreme of the range, speculative sales of the home currency (purchases of foreign exchange) will reinforce the official intervention and reduce the amount needed to hold the exchange rate within the declared limits.

Speculators act quite differently when they seriously doubt that the exchange-pegging agency will succeed in maintaining these limits. If the home currency is under intense downward pressure and requires heroic support, the chance of its devaluation far outweighs any slight chance of its being revalued upward. (The terms "devaluation" and "upward revaluation" refer to deliberate changes in the level of exchange-rate pegging. When a distinction is intended, "depreciation" and "appreciation" refer to free-market movements in unpegged rates.) Speculators expecting a fall in the home currency and a rise in the price of foreign exchange face practically a "heads-I-win-tails-I-break-even" opportunity, since their possible loss if the official defense of the rate succeeds is slight in comparison with their gain if devaluation occurs. Speculative transactions then reinforce the ordinary transactions that may exhaust the central bank's foreign-exchange reserves and force devaluation. Even shifts in the timing of ordinary commercial payments (so-called "leads and lags") may come into play: merchants ordinarily wanting to sell foreign exchange for home currency will delay doing so, waiting for a possible devaluation, while merchants needing to buy foreign exchange will hasten to do so before a possible rise in its price in home currency.

Conversely, if people suspect that a currency under strong upward pressure will be revalued upward, speculators enjoy their so-called "one-way option" in the direction opposite to the one just described. "Leads and lags," similarly, work in the direction of hastening purchases and delaying sales of the strong currency, increasing the volume of official intervention necessary to stave off the expected upward revaluation.

In short, firm confidence in the declared narrow limits to exchange-rate fluctuation enlists private speculation in helping the central bank maintain those limits, but strong distrust works the other way and magnifies the central bank's task. The currency crises experienced since World War II, notably the crises of the pound sterling, reached the crisis stage precisely because devaluation of the currency under suspicion was considered a real possibility.

The Gold Standard

The international gold standard limited exchange-rate fluctuations before World War I in a way slightly different from the way typical now. Instead of regularly intervening directly on the foreign-exchange market, each government or central bank made its currency and gold freely interconvertible at a fixed price. The United States, for example, would coin gold into money and redeem money in gold at the rate of $20.67 per ounce. The British pound sterling "contained" 4.8665 times as much gold as the dollar. When the dollar price of sterling rose above this "mint par" of $4.8665 by more than roughly two cents, arbitrageurs could make a profit. They would redeem dollars in gold, ship the gold to England, have the gold recoined there into pounds sterling (or sell it to the Bank of England at a corresponding price), thereby obtain sterling for dollars more cheaply than at the exchange rate, and sell the sterling on the foreign-exchange market for more dollars than they started with. In so doing, the gold arbitrageurs would check any further rise in the dollar rate on sterling. At the opposite extreme, when the dollar price of sterling fell more than roughly two cents below mint par, arbitrageurs could profitably redeem sterling in gold, ship the gold to the United States and convert it into dollars, thereby obtain more dollars for their sterling than corresponded to the exchange rate, and have a profit in dollars after buying back their original amount of sterling on the foreign-exchange market. By so doing, they would check any further fall in the dollar rate on sterling.

The spread between the mint par and each of the two so-called "gold points" on either side of it corresponded to the costs of crating and shipping and insuring the gold, the interest lost on wealth tied up in gold in transit, and other costs of carrying out the arbitrage. Since the interest loss and other costs of gold arbitrage changed from time to time and since some of the costs were matters of rough estimate anyway, the spread was not constant and precise. Still, the limits to exchange-rate fluctuation under the gold standard ordinarily stayed close to mint par, as our example suggests.

Before 1914, in short, each government typically left exchange-rate-stabilizing operations to private gold arbitrageurs. With only minor exceptions, it restrained itself to maintaining two-way convertibility between its monetary unit and a fixed amount of gold.

In those days, incidentally, the term "convertibility" meant the unrestricted redeemability of a currency in a fixed amount of gold. At present, with redeemability considered out of the question, at least for private holders of money, "convertibility" has been watered down to mean freedom from government restrictions on making payments with a currency and on selling it for foreign currencies. If only foreign holders but not domestic holders of a currency enjoy this freedom from restrictions on what they can do with it, the currency is said to possess "nonresident convertibility," which is a rather common condition nowadays.

When a gold-standard currency had weakened almost to its so-called gold export point, people would realize that it could not weaken much further and that it would probably rise. Speculative or quasi-speculative capital movements then came to the support of the currency and tended to keep gold exports from actually becoming profitable. At the other extreme, outflows of speculative capital from a country whose currency had almost reached its gold import point would tend to keep inward gold arbitrage from becoming profitable. The process was essentially the same as the one that operates when people are confident that exchange rates will remain officially pegged within declared limits. The danger of distrust and of destabilizing speculation was slighter under the gold standard than it sometimes is now because everyone realized that preserving two-way convertibility between each national money unit and a fixed quantity of gold was then almost an overriding goal of policy.

The permanence of this policy rested, in turn, on a connection between a country's monetary gold stock and its stock of all kinds of money, including banknotes and bank deposits. In a country losing gold because of excess imports of goods, services, and securities, the total money supply tended to shrink; a country gaining gold experienced monetary expansion. Even though countries are no longer on a real gold standard, a similar process tends to operate under the present-day system of fixed exchange rates. Policy may, however, either reinforce or neutralize it.

24

International Financial Institutions

Gold in the Monetary System[1]

In 1834, the monetary or mint price of gold was increased by 6 percent, so that an ounce of pure gold could be used to clear a debt of $20.67. This value stood firm for 100 years in spite of assaults from "cheap" money movements and some cataclysmic world events. Such constancy in the face of travail inspired a well-merited confidence in the gold value of the unit of account, even though the value of the gold dollar in terms of all other wholesale commodities increased secularly by about 100 percent during this same 100-year interval. Nonetheless, a standard of value defined in terms of a commodity stable in supply and recognized and used everywhere as a basic medium of exchange proved to be a monetary yardstick that in practice has yet to be surpassed.

The world's long-time adherence to gold and bimetallic standards accustomed the international trading world to the "principle" of fixed exchange rates. A gold standard operating properly can be thought of as a system in which all money prices except one are free to fluctuate. The lone exception, of course, is the price of gold. The vitality and self-regulating nature of such a system depends on the flexibility of domestic money prices and incomes and on their ability to pivot around the combined ceiling-floor price of gold.

---

[1]A more thorough account of the events and institutions in this chapter can be found in Leland B. Yeager, *International Monetary Relations* (New York: Harper & Row, 1966).

These conditions have long been recognized, but the world has nonetheless swung away from gold standards. Both the reasons and excuses for doing so are legion. A basic reason has been the declining rate of increase in the world's monetary gold stocks. A common excuse has been that economic controls accompany wars, and the extension of these controls into the area of international exchange is both necessary and inevitable. Less excusable is the continuation of such controls long after hostilities end. The development of central banks that actively dominate monetary policy also has undermined the power of the gold standard. But at the same time that the world has eschewed the regimen and discipline of an international metallic standard, it has been equally unwilling to give up the forms that accompany the institution. The statutory ceiling-floor price of gold maintained by a national government can be regarded as "the outward and visible sign," and the operation of a gold standard system that sees the inflow and outflow of gold critically affecting national money stocks can be likened to "an inward and spiritual grace." In truth, the world's governments have clung to the outward and visible sign but have repudiated the inward and spiritual grace.

During the 1930s and 1940s, almost all pretense that the international gold standard regulated international finance was dropped. Many countries allowed exchange rates to fluctuate freely for brief periods. But the generally unstable social conditions between 1929 and 1935 were not conducive to free institutions, and flexible exchange rates shared the fate of many other free market prices. Units of account were then given formal definition in terms of a weight of gold, so that nominal gold standard relationships could be maintained among the various national moneys. Under these circumstances gold lost its operational vitality. It was not allowed to be exported or imported freely, nor was it allowed to determine the quantities of national money stocks even within wide margins.

Pegged Exchange Rates

U.S. gold policy was not radically different from the policies of many other countries. In 1934, the President, under authorization granted by Congress, devalued the dollar in terms of gold from $20.67 = 1$ ounce to $35.00 = 1$ ounce. At that time units of account everywhere were undergoing competitive devaluations in efforts to attract exports and inhibit imports and thereby obtain respectable amounts of monetary gold to serve as a base for the "reflation" of money stocks. Since the existing stock of gold in the world was limited and not readily increased by current output, the gold that one country gained had to be the same gold lost by another. Devaluation of the dollar by the United States was just one part of the general free-for-all that was taking place. Every country tried by this means to force the price-specie-flow mechanism to work in its favor. If the flow of gold was in the "wrong" direction, nationalistic policy called for gold price-fixing until the gold was going in the "right" direction.

Many countries went off gold altogether, but the United States retained a "managed" gold standard. The dollar continued to be defined in terms of a weight of gold even though the private ownership of gold coin in the United States was disallowed. Other U.S. moneys were no longer convertible into gold; traffic in gold was permitted only to fulfill international financial obligations with foreign central banks and foreign governments. The price of $35.00 per ounce paid by the United States was not excessively high in terms of purchasing power relative to gold prices of many other countries, but gold flowed to the United States in large quantities between 1934 and 1940 anyway because of political and social uncertainties in the war-threatened regions of Europe.

The end of an operational international gold standard system in the 1930s, and the general adoption of exchange rates fixed by compacts and political agreements, necessitated a new set of operational practices. That is, two countries might agree that the exchange rate of their currencies was to be in an agreed upon ratio, but their agreement also had to specify the limits within which the rate could move (plus or minus a given percent), and each government had to set up machinery for keeping the rate within this range.

As long as the demand for a foreign currency and the supply of a domestic currency are equal in value to the supply of the foreign currency and the demand for the domestic currency at the pegged exchange rate, no governmental or central bank action is necessary. The foreign exchange market price under such circumstances is equal to the statutory price. When these supplies and demands change, however, so that the foreign exchange market prices would change if left to themselves, some sort of governmental price-fixing machinery must be activated to maintain the pegged rate. Many devices may be used either separately or in conjunction with each other, but the most common practice in the 1930s and later was to use an exchange rate stabilization agency or "fund."

These institutions gained prominence during the 1930s. Their modus operandi is to maintain a fixed price for foreign moneys by means of open market operations in some type of securities, usually those of the central government. To understand this operation, imagine that the agreed upon rate between pounds sterling and dollars is £1 = $2.40, and that the demand for pounds sterling exceeds the supply at this price. (Reciprocally, this assumption would also mean that the supply of dollars in pounds sterling exceeds the demand for dollars at this price.) The price of pounds would tend to rise above $2.40. If the exchange stabilization agency had authority to initiate action at, say, $2.42 = £1, it would have to buy pounds and furnish them to the market at this price. Of course, neither a United States central bank nor a treasury department could manufacture pounds sterling the way that either could fabricate dollars; so the agency would have to get the pounds by selling something in England or in other foreign exchange markets where pounds sterling were supplied. One item it could sell to get the pounds would be gold. Ordinarily, if a quantity of gold were available to the free market, the fund's operations would be unnecessary in the first place. In the tightly controlled economies of the thirties, forties, and after, however, gold was not left within the domain of free markets but was put under the close supervision and control of central banks and treasuries. Another possibility is that the fund would have an earmarked supply of foreign currencies for its own use. Even if pounds sterling were not included in its portfolio, it could sell other currencies for pounds and supply the market with pounds at the fixed price. Here again, a universal market system would accomplish the same end.

But this answer basically begs the question. The fund must be supplied with foreign currencies by some means or other in order to have some to sell. Assuming that the fund had no monetary resources to start with, it could get (or have manufactured) a supply of government securities furnished by the central government. Then when the fund needed pounds, it could sell securities in markets that supply pounds in order to obtain the amount that would keep the exchange rate constant. If continued, this operation would need to be undertaken at higher and higher interest rates, so its ultimate effect would depress the domestic economy or raise the costs of financing fresh imports to a prohibitive level. Essentially, such an action is a capital inflow initiated by a government agency for policy purposes. It is no different than an open market operation by the central bank to carry out a price stabilization objective—be it stabilizing a price level or fixing the money price of some particular commodity. In this case, the price fixed is the price of a foreign money. If the price tended to go below $2.40 = £1, the fund could buy back securities, creating dollars by approved central bank technique.

The foreign fund or central bank, in this case the British Exchange Equilization Account or the Bank of England, would probably be undertaking complementary operations to effect the same ends. The exchange rate would have to be agreed upon in advance by political negotiation; otherwise, the central banks might become involved in a titanic struggle for international financial supremacy, a "war of the gods." Once the exchange rate was agreed upon, exchange stabilization agencies would have little trouble maintaining the fixed rates for the short run. However, to agree upon exchange rates might very well impinge upon the domestic monetary policies then current in either country. So fixing the exchange rate might necessarily imply general agreement that price level policies in both countries be roughly homogeneous.

To illustrate this exception further: Assume that the price level in England was falling and that the Bank of England was *not* undertaking countercyclical action. The lower price level would encourage exports and tend to raise the price of pounds sterling in terms of dollars. To maintain the "peg" on the exchange rate, the stabilization fund or other agency charged with the responsibility for such control in the United States would need to sell securities having the depressing effects noted above. As long as the securities could be sold in foreign markets for pounds, the English deflation would be confined to the capital markets; the internal domestic economy of the United States might not need to suffer. Such a qualification, however, could not hold for long. A persistent long-term pressure on the exchange rate cannot be resisted solely by the selling operations of an exchange stabilization fund in foreign markets. No foreign money market is that isolated from a domestic money market. Hence, the operations of such funds have traditionally been supplemented by the rationing of "scarce" currencies, by imposition of other fiscal and monetary policies of the central bank and treasury, and by import tariffs and other restrictions. Just as popular consumer goods are rationed during a war in order that the volumes demanded and supplied per unit of time be equal at the statutory money prices, so foreign moneys may be rationed under the same supply and demand conditions in order that fixed exchange rates be maintained. Import tariffs are simply taxes levied on imported commodities. Any tax, including a tariff, can be so high that it prohibits people from purchasing the item taxed (or tariffed). Imposing tariffs that prohibit popular imports relieves the pressure on the exchange rates by reducing the quantities of foreign goods demanded and hence the quantities of foreign moneys demanded. If these methods do not suffice, the currency tending to become cheaper may be devalued, an action analogous to increasing the ceiling price of a price-controlled commodity.

National economies had widely varying degrees of deflation and inflation during the 1930s and 1940s, and rigid adherence to pegged exchange rates proved impossible. Devaluation became common. Under a gold standard this process traditionally meant that the value of the unit of account in terms of a weight of gold had to be lowered so that a given amount of gold would buy more units of the national money. In contemporary practice this formality is still followed. What devaluation really amounts to now, however, is reduction of the value of the unit of account *in terms of other national moneys*. Clearly, this kind of adjustment may relieve pressure on exchange rates. A lower price increases the foreign demand for the devalued money and correspondingly increases the supply of that same foreign money. Of course, this kind of a "cure" is in part capitulation to the "disease"; a "pegged" currency that is devalued is not really pegged.

If the costs of pegged exchange rates are high, critics can demand that the benefits also be substantial. Generally, all possible systems have both advantages and disadvantages. The relevant question for any one system is: What advantages and disadvantages does it have over alternative systems? Two answers in favor of pegged exchange rates are usually given to this question. The first is political. Its proponents argue that exchange rate agreements are so important politically to foreigners and foreign governments that their abandonment would cause a major world power, such as the United States, to lose its international prestige and influence. A second argument is the assertion or assumption that changes in exchange rates are inherently destabilizing—that a change in an exchange rate sets up the expectation of further change in the same direction. For these reasons, and also because the transition process to any other system has appeared so formidable and costly, governments have continued the pegged exchange rate policies of the 1930s. The principal attempt to get something else on the books in the period following World War II has centered around international monetary organization and cooperation.

The International Monetary Fund and the International Bank for Reconstruction and Development

The proposals for the IMF and the World Bank, as they are popularly known, were in the blueprint stage even before World War II was over. These organizations were just two of several institutions that were developed to handle postwar international economic problems.

The IMF is an autonomous organization although it is affiliated with the United Nations. Its members include almost every country except Russia. A member country pays in capital according to a quota system. "Capital" consists of gold or U.S. dollars (25 percent), the remainder being the country's own currency (75 percent). Voting power and executive control is proportional to any given country's quota in the Fund.

The functions of the Fund are to obtain general agreement among participants (1) *not* to impose restrictions on payments for current international transactions, (2) *not* to become involved in discriminatory currency policies, and (3) to maintain their currencies at "par," par being a fixed rate stated in terms of gold or U.S. dollars. The gold, dollars, and other currency reserves deposited by signatories to the Fund are to be used to assist the member nations to maintain the par exchange rates agreed upon. Each nation was supposed to have determined and advertised its par rate of exchange in the years following the end of World War II. This rate could then have been appreciated or depreciated according to a fixed administrative procedure by as much as 10 percent per year if the financial condition of the country in question required it.

The various currencies and gold in the Fund are only to take care of short-run maladjustments. A country that "needs" other currency to satisfy what seem to be temporary balance of payments difficulties "purchases" the currency it needs from the Fund with more of its own currency. The limits to which any country can draw are: (1) 25 percent of its own quota in any twelve-month period and (2) a total of 100 percent of its original subscription. The Fund's resources are qualitatively limited, too. They are not supposed to be used for relief, reconstruction, or previously contracted war debts.

The Fund in reality is an attempt to maintain pegged exchange rates within a postwar world in which one major currency, U.S. dollars, is (or has been) the dominant and sometimes "scarce" currency. The Fund also has the power to ration such a scarce money. If its reserves of dollars become low, for example, the Fund could require the United States to sell dollars for gold, or it could ask the United States to lend it dollars. Failing in these ventures, the dollar could be "declared" *a scarce currency,* and member nations could impose restrictions on its use in ways they deem proper. In practice, the use of exchange controls by member nations and the accomplishments of economic reconstruction by many countries took international pressure off the dollar without the use of the "scarce currency" provision of the Fund. Capital movements are both permitted and encouraged by the Fund in order to enable a country to relieve its balance of payments difficulties.

The IMF essentially has been a stopgap institution designed to relieve temporary balance of payments problems and to emphasize formal negotiation and administration over exchange rates. In both areas it has been largely ineffective or simply ignored. The large-scale devaluations of the pound and other currencies in 1949 and after were almost without IMF negotiation, approval, or (perhaps) knowledge. Finally, the use of the Fund's resources by members has been very limited.

The organization of the International Bank was carried out conjunctively with the IMF at Bretton Woods in 1944. The Bank has three sources of lending power: (1) funds paid in by capital subscription of participating countries, (2) borrowings in private capital markets for relending on projects it deems worthy, and (3) guarantees of payment of interest and principal on private investments. In practice, so little of the original subscribed capital has been paid in that the Bank has emphasized the second method of raising funds. Most of its borrowing to lend has been from U.S. investors. However, its activities have been very limited due to political, economic, and other uncertainties in the areas that have applied for loans.

Other programs, some under international agreement and some simply ad hoc negotiation among participating countries, have appeared in the postwar world. The European Recovery Program (Marshall Plan), the British Loan by the United States, the General Agreement on Tariffs and Trade (GATT), and more recently, the Common Market Agreement, have attempted by negotiations, grants, loans, guarantees, and, generally, by conscious determination of economic and financial priorities to obtain international stability. Each of these actions must be evaluated on its specific record.

A World Central Bank

The attempts at international financial cooperation discussed above have been largely palliatives or ad hoc arrangements. A more serious, long-run and basic monetary organization in the form of a world central bank is conceivable and has had some recent support.[2]

---

[2]A discussion of this possibility by Robert Triffin appears in Lawrence S. Ritter, ed., *Money and Economic Activity: Readings in Money and Banking* (Boston: Houghton Mifflin Co., 1961), pp. 435–445. The model presented in this text is similar but not necessarily identical to the one Triffin proposes. See also the section in Chapter 25 on special drawing rights.

The international gold standard was an automatic device for supplying the world with growth in its monetary base as well as a means of providing monetary adjustment among national economies. An international central bank can be outlined that would provide an international money along the same lines. The gold standard was "ideal" when it supplied gold to the world at a rate consistent with the "natural" growth of the world's annual product. A world central bank could provide growth in money or in a monetary base at a much more certain and consistent rate than that seen under the gold standard in its best years.

The requirements for such a system would be economically simple yet politically formidable. Each country would have to accept the international unit of account as full legal tender within its own boundaries. In addition, each country would have to allow free entry and exit of the international currency. If countries still issued their own national currencies, as would inevitably be the case, and allowed the extensive use of fractional reserve demand deposit banking, the analogy with the gold standard would be complete. National moneys in the form of currency and bank deposits would have to be convertible into the international unit of account without impediment. Necessarily, such convertibility, and the assurance that particular national money stocks would not grow too fast, would require each government to specify the international medium as some proportion of its domestic money supply. Otherwise, a domestic monetary inflation, for example, would denude the inflating economy of its international monetary medium and render its currency inconvertible. This possibility is again analogous to what could and did occur under gold standards. Gold could be placed in the vaults of the world central bank as a base for the international unit of account much as gold certificates were used in a limited way as reserves for current demand obligations of the Federal Reserve Banks.

The technical transition to the International Central Bank (ICB) would be simple. Each national treasury and central bank would turn over its *basic monetary assets*, the ones on which rested the domestic money supply of the economy, to the new international agency. The ICB would then grant the depositing national agencies a corresponding amount of ICB credit on which the national money supplies would be based. No necessity would exist any longer for controlled exchange rates. The international unit of account would serve as the international medium. Since this medium would largely be in the form of ICB credit on the books of national central banks, no transportation or shipping charges would impede transfers from country to country, such as was the case with gold. If each national economy specified its unit of account as some multiple of the ICB unit of account, fixed exchange rates with margins for establishing movement would again be in effect. When an economy lost ICB units, its monetary system would have to shrink just as it would have done under a gold standard. Of course, national central banks and governments might not need to specify their domestic units of account in terms of the ICB unit. The requirement that national moneys be a multiple of a limited quantity of ICB units would limit the issue of national money stocks. Under such a system exchange rates could be freely fluctuating, but the degree of fluctuation would probably be confined to a narrow range as long as the international agency carefully rationed its extension of ICB monetary units.

Rules for the expansion of credit by the ICB would undoubtedly be a major stumbling block. Even more to the point, and a commentary on current domestic central banking policy, is that *rules would have to be established* for the creation of any international monetary units. No one would trust an international agency to "play it by ear," to use discretion in its general credit policies. Thus, Robert Triffin, an economist who is opposed to rules for the domestic central bank, in his proposal for a world central bank holds that the "threat of inflationary [and, presumably, other] abuses can be guarded against . . . by limiting the Fund's annual lending authority to the amount necessary to preserve an adequate level of international liquidity." Triffin suggests that the net lending of the agency, plus the increase in the total world stock of monetary gold, be 3 to 5 percent per year.[3] One would think that if a world central bank needed rules to protect various sectors of the world from monetary mischief, any domestic economy should need similar protection from domestic purveyors of the same product.

The expansion techniques of the ICB could be as simple as any central bank methods are currently. It could be empowered to buy or sell government securities in any and all of the world's markets in order to secure the monetary targets prescribed for it. This rule of operation would be sufficient; and in being sufficient and accordingly simple it would be optimal.

In summary, the ICB would require that each participating government hand over its fundamental monetary sovereignty to this institution. The ICB would operate by means of an operational rule (open market operations in various and specified government securities) in furtherance of a target rule (an annual percentage increase in the world's monetary base). The ICB unit of account would be legal tender to the same extent that gold was in the past. In fact, the whole purpose of the ICB would be to provide more regularly and exactly what the gold standard was supposed to have supplied "naturally." It could operate with either fixed or freely fluctuating exchange rates—just as a gold system might have so operated if the rate of increase in the gold stock and the ratio of national money to gold had been specified.

The overwhelming improbability of getting an ICB is manifest. No national governments, particularly strong ones, will ever give up sovereignty over an item as important as the stock of money—particularly to an international agency that might be operated by representatives of countries whose political and economic ideas and ideals were not particularly palatable. The inability to get acceptable rules so that the agency would "run itself" further points up the improbability of such an institution. Even so, attempts might be made.

---

[3]Triffin, p. 442. Triffin's proposal would allow for discretionary action within these limits. The actual amount would be basically 3 percent, with 4 and 5 percent possibilities contingent upon majorities of the voting directorship of the agency.

Almost any system would be an improvement over the contemporary one of pegged exchange rates and the multitudinous interventions and restrictions of world trade and finance that accompany them.

Fluctuating Exchange Rates — The Market Solution

Freely fluctuating (or floating or flexible) exchange rates are yet another alternative arrangement to the international financial systems considered above. This system is nothing more than the extension of the free market principle to the determination of foreign exchange rates. Private dealers in foreign exchange would operate very much as they do now in the stock, bond, and commodity markets, and even as they do now to a limited extent in the foreign exchange markets. Prices of foreign currencies would simply reflect underlying forces of demand and supply.

This kind of system has several distinct advantages over the other systems considered. First, any country can adopt a policy of this sort unilaterally, that is, without negotiation and horse trading with other national governments. Second, it is a policy that requires no further policies and interventions by government agencies. Third, it allows domestic monetary policy to operate independently of foreign considerations. If domestic monetary policy results in, say, a relatively stable price level and "normal" growth of the production complex, variations in exchange rates are usually results of destabilizing activities and policies in other economies. The market-directed exchange rate quarantines the domestic economy from possibly undesirable policies of foreign economic systems. Finally, since flexible exchange rates are the extension of the free market principle to the markets for foreign currencies, and since these markets are very efficient in a technical sense, their unregulated use should maximize welfare to the same extent that it is maximized in other free markets.

The most popular professional argument against flexible exchange rates is that they may show "too much" variation and, further, that such variation increases uncertainty in international dealings. If this argument is carried to an extreme, consistency would require that money prices of all goods and services be fixed similarly by statute. The essence of a vigorous system is that relative prices do change.[4] Prices are symptoms; they change because of underlying disequilibria in economic life. *Disequilibrium* conditions are not at all necessarily *unstable* conditions. Only when adjustment to disequilibria is rendered difficult by artificial restrictions — such as pegged exchange rates — is instability likely to result.

---

[4]A *fixed* price is not necessarily a *stable* price, as is often implied. A stable price is one that tends to regain a new equilibrium value after having been disturbed from its original equilibrium value.

Several questions about exchange rates are still to be answered before a complete brief can be presented on the merits of this system vis-a-vis those of alternative systems: (1) Are variations in exchange rates greater under a free system than variations in other money prices? (2) Are variations in flexible exchange rates unstable? (Do changes in rates lead to expectations of further change?) (3) Can nominal variations in flexible rates be handled by a technical mechanism so that changes in the values of foreign moneys do not impinge on the strictly commercial activities of exporters and importers?

Foreign exchange markets traditionally are among the "best" that can be found. They include many buyers and sellers; competition is active, especially because it works on both sides of political boundary lines; and buyers and sellers can easily have full information on the homogeneous commodities they buy and sell. No evidence has so far been cited that shows greater variation in exchange rates than in other money prices, nor would such variation be any more disequilibrating than variations in other prices. That is, changes in price give no "natural" expectation of further changes in the same direction, except possibly under unusual stress conditions such as occurred occasionally during the 1930s. In short, no facts or logic so far presented support the position that movements of free exchange rates are any less predictable than price movements of other goods and services.[5]

The variation in free exchange rates that does take place can be, and is, borne by "speculators" in this type of commodity. Just as a speculator in wheat takes the risk away from the miller or baker, so a dealer in foreign exchange absorbs the risk of exchange rate variation by carrying out a well-understood hedging operation in a futures market. The buyer of foreign goods for future delivery, for example, can guarantee the value of the foreign money he will need when the sale is consummated in the future by contracting for that money in time present. The speculator, or dealer in foreign exchange, who agrees to furnish the money in the future bears the risk. If the foreign money becomes less expensive in the future, the dealer gains; otherwise, he loses. The importer is ensured in any case against an uncertain gain or loss by agreeing to a small but certain loss (cost) for the service rendered by the dealer.

Sometimes the expositions on this principle give the reader the impression (1) that the costs for this service are "high" and (2) that these costs are obviated by fixed exchange rates. Clearly, the cost of guaranteeing a future value *could* be high. If so, the risks must be correspondingly high. The exchange rates on future deliveries of the money in question *reflect* this risk; they do not *cause* it. Secondly, the risks would be there and would be paid for by someone even if the rates themselves were pegged. Suppose the cost of future delivery, again, is "high" but that the government fixes the rate, thus shouldering itself with the risk. How is the risk "paid for"? It is paid for by whatever means the

---

[5]Since an exchange rate is a monetary link between economies in two countries, predictions of changes in the rate would need to make use of monetary data in both economies.

government uses to keep the exchange rate pegged. A high premium for future delivery, for example, might stem from reasonable and realistic suppositions that the domestic unit of account was soon to be depreciated because of current inflationary monetary policies of the government. The cost of getting "futures" would then be a function of the best guesses on how much the unit of account would depreciate relative to foreign moneys. Since the exchange rate or price of a foreign money could not change legally, the adjustment to the general consensus of change would find everyone stocking up on foreign currency. Adjustment under pegged rates would be in the quantity demanded of the foreign currency. The government would have to supply the currency by selling its own securities to get it or by restricting the demand for it through artificial means. Selling securities to get the foreign money, as noted above, would reverse any inflationary portents of the domestic currency's future value and thus take away the problem. If uncertainty of future value is to remain, only restrictions on the demand for the foreign currency would "solve" the problem and still allow a problem (by hypothesis). But even this "solution" does not solve the problem in the usual sense of the word. Demand for foreign currency can only be suppressed by statutory restrictions, such as higher tariffs or currency rationing, in which case the people involved cannot be satisfied. Fixed exchange rates are seen to have the same results as any other legal price-fixing statutes. They make mandatory the use of other controls, such as rationing; they suppress without solving or satisfying. Such costs, too, are formidable.

Adoption of a flexible exchange rate policy is not in and of itself a guarantee of general economic tranquillity. It is at best permissive. It allows the central bank and treasury to carry out monetary and fiscal policies that ensure a high degree of stability without constraints imposed by political commitments or agreements on exchange rates. In short, market-determined exchange rates permit achievement of economic stability by preventing the exchange rate "tail" from wagging the "economic dog." Under this system, the foreign exchange market joins all other markets in presenting forces of demand and supply for appropriate stabilizing monetary and fiscal policies. If these policies are destabilizing, the exchange rate market reflects this fact just as do other markets.

Under viable gold standards, the single area of price fixing that included foreign exchange rates could be tolerated and supported so long as movements of gold exerted their corrective forces on money prices, costs, and incomes. When these corrective factors are prevented, as they are in contemporary economies, rigid adherence to fixed exchange rates is both anachronistic and dangerous. A world central bank possibly offers a better way out, but requires practically unanimous agreement among the participating major powers. Past experience does not encourage the hope that such agreement could be obtained. Freely fluctuating exchanges could be undertaken unilaterally, and little reason or experience suggests their inefficacy.

Selected Bibliography

Several standard works are available on international trade and finance. See the following.

Friedman, Milton. "The Case for Freely Fluctuating Exchange Rates." *Essays in Positive Economics*. Chicago: University of Chicago Press, 1953, pp. 157–203. The best-known essay on freely fluctuating exchange rates.

Nurkse, Ragnar. *International Currency Experience* (League of Nations study). Princeton, N.J.: Princeton University Press, 1944. This has become the basis of much current thinking on international finance. While it is an important study, its policy espousals are predicated on very dubious and sketchy evidence.

Triffin, Robert. *Gold and the Dollar Crisis: The Future of Convertibility*, rev. ed. New Haven, Conn.: Yale University Press, 1961.

Yeager, Leland. *International Monetary Relations*. New York: Harper & Row, 1966.

A Dollar Is a Dollar

Milton Friedman

One of the most refreshing and responsible innovations undertaken by a popular news weekly in recent times has been the inclusion of three columnists writing on economic affairs for Newsweek *magazine who are also respected professional economists. One of the three is Professor Milton Friedman (introduced in Chapter 22).*

During the years 1967–1968—years marked by monetary turbulence in the economy—Professor Friedman devoted several of his columns to observations on international finance and the value of gold and the dollar. Two of those items are reprinted here. They argue for the sensibility of governmental policies that would allow the prices of gold, the dollar, and all foreign moneys to be determined by the free workings of markets. Not only is such a system the simplest and most efficient in an economic sense, it is also the one that comes closest to granting human aspirations for freedom. Professor Friedman's penchant for taking the ceremonial trappings off international monetary institutions and policies should be extremely helpful to the reader in understanding these principles.

A dollar is a dollar is a dollar. But why should it also be exactly 7 English shillings, 1 penny, and 3 farthings; 4 French francs and 94 centimes, and 4 German marks?

The explanation is very different today than it was in an earlier era. In 1913, for example, anyone could take $20.67 to the U.S. Treasury and exchange it for one fine ounce of gold. He could take the ounce of gold to London, go to the Bank of England, and exchange it for 4 pounds, 4 shillings, 11 pence, and 1 farthing; or he could take it to Paris, go to the Bank of France, and exchange it for 107 francs and 10 centimes. As a result, the price of the pound could not vary much from its then official parity of $4.8665 or the franc from its then official parity of $0.1930.

A Real Gold Standard

If the pound became appreciably more expensive than $4.8665, alert U.S. financiers would get pounds, not by buying them on the market, but by exchanging dollars at the U.S. Treasury for gold, shipping the gold to London, and converting it into pounds at the Bank of England. If the pound became appreciably cheaper than $4.8665 (i.e. the dollar became more expensive) alert British financiers would get dollars by reversing the process. In this way, the cost of shipping gold set narrow limits — termed the "gold points" — on the price of the pound sterling.

That was a real gold standard. Gold circulated in the form of coin and gold certificates. Britain and the U.S. in effect had a common currency differing only in the names attached to an ounce of gold. Individuals were free to buy or sell dollars for pounds or pounds for dollars at any price. The price of the one currency in terms of the other stayed within narrow limits for the same reason and in the same way that the price of sugar in New York never deviates much from the price of sugar in Chicago — because if it did deviate, it would pay private traders to ship sugar.

The situation today is very different. The dollar and the pound are no longer names for different amounts of gold. They are names for separate national currencies. There still are official prices of gold. But these official prices serve primarily as a means to calculate the official price of the pound in terms of dollars ($2.40). Holders of paper money cannot automatically exchange it for gold at the official prices — indeed, since 1934, when the official U.S. price was raised to $35 an ounce, it has been illegal for U.S. residents to hold gold, except for numismatic or industrial purposes. Gold is now a commodity whose price is supported by governmental action — like butter. Gold no longer determines the quantity of money.

Pegged Exchange Rates

The price of the pound sterling is kept at $2.40, not by market forces, but by the British and U.S. governments who peg it at that level by buying and selling dollars and pounds at the official price. They can succeed only by controlling the amount people offer to buy and sell. In Britain, it is illegal for residents to trade pounds for dollars except with the permission of a government official. The U.S. still does not have explicit exchange control, but we have extensive informal controls—ask the businessman who seeks to invest abroad or the banker who seeks to lend abroad.

The pegging of exchange rates is the basic reason for our balance-of-payments problem—just as the pegging of rents is the basic reason for the housing "shortage" in New York City; the pegging of the price of silver for the rapid depletion of our silver reserves; the pegging of the price of butter for the accumulation of stocks of butter.

We should set the dollar free and let its price in terms of other currencies be determined by private dealings. Such a system of floating exchange rates would eliminate the balance-of-payments problem, thereby enabling us to abolish the income-equilization tax and informal exchange controls, and to move unilaterally toward freer trade.

Paradoxically, most leaders of the financial community are against this free-market solution. They confuse the present use of gold as window dressing with a real gold standard. Staunch opponents of government price-fixing in other areas, they support it in this one. They need to examine their clichés.

The Price of the Dollar

Milton Friedman

How low we have fallen! The United States, the land of the free, prohibits its businessmen from investing abroad and requests its citizens not to show their faces or open their pocketbooks in foreign ports. The United States, the wealthiest nation in the world, announces that its foreign policy will no longer be determined by its national interest and its international commitments but by the need to reduce government spending abroad by $500 million.

And for what? Are we so poor that we must forgo profitable opportunities to invest capital abroad? The same President who imposes curbs on foreign investment boasts that our income is at an all-time high. Foreign investment in 1967 was less than 5 percent of total investment and less than 1 percent of total income.

Are we wasting so much of our substance on foreign travel that we must be cajoled by our betters to stay home? Total spending on foreign travel in 1967 was less than 1 percent of total consumer spending.

Are government coffers so empty that reducing expenditures abroad by $500 million justifies shaping our whole foreign policy to that end? The President has not hesitated to recommend total Federal expenditures approaching $200 billion.

An Oft-Told Tale

Why then have we imposed such far-reaching restrictions on our citizenry? To put it bluntly, because a small number of public officials — in the U.S. and abroad — cannot as yet bring themselves to admit their impotence to fix the price of the dollar in terms of other currencies. Like modern King Canutes, they have been commanding the tide not to rise — and apparently are determined to continue until we are engulfed by it.

This is an old story. Let the government seek to peg a price — be it of wheat or housing or silver or gold or pounds sterling — and it will be driven, as if by an invisible hand, to impose restrictions on producers and consumers in order to contain a surplus or to ration a shortage. It can do so for a time, but only for a time. The tide is too strong.

"In the meantime," as I testified to Congress nearly five years ago, "we adopt one expedient after another, borrowing here, making swap arrangements there, changing the form of loans to make the figures look good. Entirely aside from the ineffectiveness of most of these measures, they are politically degrading and demeaning. We are a great and wealthy nation. We should be directing our own course, setting an example to the world, living up to our destiny. Instead, we send our officials hat in hand to make the rounds of foreign governments and central banks; we put foreign central banks in a position...to exert great influence on our policies; we are driven to niggling negotiations with Hong Kong and with Japan and for all I know, Monaco, to get them to limit voluntarily their exports. Is this posture suitable for the leader of the free world?"

Set the Dollar Free

We should instead say to the people of the world: a dollar is a dollar. You may borrow dollars in the U.S. or abroad from anyone who is willing to lend. You may lend dollars in the U.S. or abroad to anyone who is willing to borrow. You may buy dollars from or sell dollars to anyone you wish at any price that is mutually agreeable. The U.S. Government will not interfere in any way. On the contrary, it will dismantle immediately its present restrictions: repeal the interest-equalization tax; dissolve the cartel agreement among banks to restrict foreign lending; remove quotas, "voluntary" or otherwise, on imports; stop resorting to World War I emergency legislation to threaten with prison terms businessmen who invest abroad; refrain from interfering with the right of its citizens to travel when and where they will.

If a foreign country wishes to peg the price of its currency in terms of the dollar, we should not interfere. It can succeed only by voluntarily holding dollars, or adjusting its internal monetary policy to ours or engaging in exchange control. In no case can it force us to impose restrictions on the use of dollars.

If we set the dollar free, and at the same time followed responsible fiscal and monetary policies, many another country would be well advised to link its currency with ours. That would promote not only our domestic objectives but also a healthy development of international trade. That is the right way to make the dollar a truly international currency—not behaving like a banana republic.

25

Contemporary International Financial Issues

Gold and the Balance of Payments

Starting about the time of the Great Depression, the function of control over national money supplies was put under the virtually complete jurisdiction of central banks. Some international exchange in gold was still evident; but emphasis on the dollar by the IMF and the World Bank after World War II gave proof positive that the dollar had become the world's prime currency. Exchange rates of the world's currencies were stipulated in terms of gold *or* dollars. Dollars had high repute both because of their purchasing power, especially after World War II, and because half the world's monetary gold was in the vaults of the U.S. Treasury.

The restrictions and interventions of the world's governments in monetary affairs during the forties and fifties did not leave much chance for fundamental changes in the world's monetary structure. Occasionally a country would devalue, as Great Britain did in 1949, and the IMF would put its stamp of approval on the action *ex post facto*. But by and large, the dollar was the world's prime money, and changes in the values of the world's currencies vis-a-vis the dollar could come about only after many years of reconstruction and growth in the production organizations of the major trading countries.

This phase of the world's economic life ended about 1957. The gold certificate component in the Reserve Banks' balance sheets (Tables 21.1, 21.5, and 21.7) showed almost no change between 1940 and 1957, but it declined almost constantly thereafter, reaching a value in 1968 only 50 percent of its value in

Table 25.1

Components for U.S. Balance of Payments Measures
(annual data, billions of dollars)

| | Goods and Services | | | | | Private Capital | | | |
| | Exports | | Imports | | | Long-Term | | Short-Term | |
Year	(1) Goods	(2) Services	(3) Goods	(4) Services	(5) (Military)	(6) Net	(7) (Bank Liabilities to Foreign Official Agencies)	(8) Net	(9) (Liquid Assets)
1960	19.7	7.8	14.7	8.6	3.1	−2.1	0.0	−1.4	−0.1
1961	20.1	8.7	14.5	8.6	3.0	−2.2	0.0	−1.4	−0.2
1962	20.8	9.7	16.2	9.1	3.1	−2.6	0.0	−0.7	0.0
1963	22.3	10.3	17.0	9.6	3.0	−3.3	0.0	−0.8	0.0
1964	25.5	11.8	18.6	10.0	2.9	−4.3	+0.1	−2.0	−0.3
1965	26.4	13.0	21.5	10.8	3.0	−4.6	0.0	+0.9	+1.1
1966	29.4	14.0	25.5	12.6	3.8	−1.8	+0.8	−0.1	0.0
1967	30.7	15.5	26.8	14.2	4.4	−2.0	+0.9	−0.7	−0.2
1968	33.6	17.0	33.0	15.2	4.5	+1.7	+0.5	−0.3	−0.6
1969	36.5	19.0	35.8	17.7	4.9	−0.9	−0.8	−0.5	+0.1
1970	42.0	20.9	39.9	19.5	4.9	−2.3	−0.8	−0.3	+0.3

Government Grants and Loans

(10) Net	(11) (Special Liabilities)	(12) (Transfers)	(13) Private Transfers	(14) SDR	(15) Liquid Liabilities to Private Foreigners	(16) Errors and Omissions
−2.8	0.0	−1.9	−0.4		+0.3	−1.1
−3.0	0.0	−2.1	−0.4		+1.1	−1.1

−2.9	+0.2		−0.5			−1.2	
−3.5	−0.1		−0.6			−0.5	
−3.4	+0.1		−0.6			−1.1	
−3.6	+0.1		−0.7			−0.5	
−3.7	0.0	−2.3	−0.6	+2.4		−0.4	
−4.2	+0.5	−2.2	−0.8	+1.5		−1.0	
−2.5	+1.8	−2.1	−0.8	+3.8		−0.5	
−4.1	−0.2	−2.1	−0.9	+8.7		−2.6	
−3.7	+0.5	−2.2	−0.9	+0.9	−6.2		−1.1

U.S. Balance of Payments Measures*
(annual data, billions of dollars)

Year	Goods (trade balance)	Goods and Services	Current Account	Current Account and Long-Term Capital	Net Liquidity	Gross Liquidity	Official Settlements	Gold Stock (end of period)
1960	4.9	4.1	+1.8	−1.2	−3.7	−3.7	−3.4	17.80
1961	5.6	5.6	+3.1	0.0	−2.2	−2.4	−1.3	16.95
1962	4.6	5.2	+2.5	−1.0	−2.8	−2.7	−2.7	16.06
1963	5.2	6.0	+3.2	−1.3	−2.6	−2.7	−1.9	15.60
1964	6.8	8.6	+5.8	0.0	−2.7	−2.8	−1.5	15.47
1965	4.9	7.1	+4.3	−1.8	−2.5	−1.3	−1.3	14.07
1966	3.9	5.3	+2.4	−1.6	−2.1	−1.4	+0.2	13.23
1967	3.9	5.2	+2.1	−3.2	−4.7	−3.5	−3.4	12.06
1968	0.6	2.5	−0.4	−1.3	−1.6	+0.2	+1.6	10.89
1969	0.7	2.0	−0.9	−2.9	−6.1	−7.0	+2.7	11.86
1970	2.1	3.6	+0.4	−3.0	−3.9	−3.9	−9.8	11.07

Source: *U.S. Balance of Payments Trends*, first quarter, 1971. Prepared by Federal Reserve Bank of St. Louis July 27, 1971.

Note: Certain accounts have been reorganized to maintain consistency with the Department of Commerce presentation. Figures may not add due to rounding.

* The various balance measures can be derived using the following sequence of additions:

A = Trade balance = (1 − 3)
B = Goods and services = A + (2 − 4)
C = Current Account = B + (12 + 13)
D = Current account and long-term capital = C + (6 − 7) + (10 − 11 − 12)
E = Net liquidity balance = D + (8 − 9) + 14 + 16
  Gross liquidity balance = E + (7 + 9 + 11)
  Official settlements balance = E + (9 + 15)

1957. These losses of gold certificates resulted primarily from the recoveries of European economies and from the successful attempts of several European governments in 1958 to restore convertibility of their currencies with gold. Another factor was the large increase in the U.S. money stock since 1934. The price of gold in dollars was fixed at a much higher value than what the market would have given in 1934, but even this price ultimately was lowered in real terms by monetary inflation. Occasionally since 1960, the price of gold in the London market has gone as high as $44 per ounce. Since the formal mint price of gold in the United States is still $35 per ounce, the tendency toward a higher world price has encouraged apprehension that foreign dollar claims against the United States logically might be called for in gold. Unless prohibited by law or political pressure, no foreign dollar holder would refrain from cashing in dollars for gold at $35 per ounce when he could obtain $40 or more per ounce for the same gold in the London market.

Foreign dollar claims have, in fact, become important because of the international trade and capital movements in which the U.S. economy is involved. Exports from the United States in recent years have ranged from $27–$63 billion, while imports have been $23–$60 billion (see Table 25.1). Thus, the United States has experienced a favorable balance of trade on goods and services averaging about $4 billion per year. However, U.S. government grants and transfers of $3–$5 billion per year and private investments and gifts by U.S. citizens and corporations of another $3–$6 billion per year have changed the surplus in the balance of trade to a deficit in the balance of goods and services, capital, and grants combined.[1] The method of accounting this deficit determines how large it is. (See Table 25.1 and Figure 25.1 for various "balance" concepts.)

No matter how the deficit is accounted, it must be financed by some means because balance of all international payments is a datum. Everything bought and sold — goods, services, and capital — must make use of a payments mechanism. While many of the deficits were financed by the usual means of transferring dollars and other short-term claims to foreigners, about one third of the total deficit was paid for with gold. Decline of the Federal Reserve Banks' gold certificate account at the rate of about $1 billion per year during the ten years 1958–1968 reflected this means of adjustment. During 1968, most of the world's monetary gold was impounded by international agreement, so the U.S. gold stock could no longer be used as a balancing item.

---

[1]When a person in the United States invests in the business of a foreign country, he transfers dollar claims to the foreign corporation and receives, say, common stock in exchange. Thus, his investment adds to the dollar claims enjoyed by foreigners. The U.S. investor may be thought of as having "imported," say, a part of a wine factory in contrast to importing a bottle of wine. The bottle of wine would be consumed, but the share in the wine factory simply gives claim to residual income in the future. Of course, claims against foreign income would improve the *future* balance of trade position of the United States, but investment that occurs in the *present* worsens the current deficit.

Besides their gold certificate reserves, Federal Reserve Banks keep an account of earmarked gold, that is, gold held in a special account for foreign governments and foreign central banks. When foreigners presented a claim for U.S. gold, the claim went through a foreign commercial bank and central bank to a U.S. commercial bank and finally to a Federal Reserve Bank. The Federal Reserve Bank was required by law to release the gold to the foreign central bank, but frequently the foreign central bank left the actual gold where it was. The Federal Reserve Bank then debited its gold certificate account and credited the earmarked gold account of the foreign central bank.

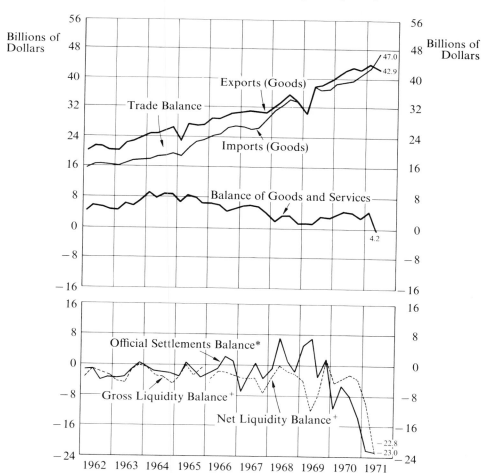

Figure 25.1. U.S. Balance of Payments and Components
(+) Surplus; (−) Deficit
(Seasonally adjusted annual rates, quarterly data)

From 1958 to 1968, the earmarked gold stock increased from $8.54 billion to $13.10 billion, or by $4.56 billion. During the same period the gold certificate account declined from $20.0 billion to $10.0, or by $10.0 billion. In this ten-year period, therefore, the accounted gold outflow was more than twice the actual physical loss. Nonetheless, title to $10 billion in gold was transferred to foreign central banks and governments from the stock held by the Federal Reserve Banks. (See Table 25.2).

Federal grants-in-aid to foreigners must also be financed by some means or other; and while such costs may not be seen directly they are felt in the form of either higher domestic taxes or higher prices on domestic products. If the federal government's budget is balanced before grants to foreigners are authorized by Congress, the amount of the grants would provoke an incipient budget deficit. Taxes then raised to cover this deficit would cause taxpayers to suffer a reduction in real disposable income.

If the resulting deficit is financed by government bond issues instead of higher taxes, the reduction of disposable incomes by new bond buyers is just as onerous as new tax levies. By giving up current income for government bonds, people again have less disposable income. The government then diverts this income to the uses of foreign countries.

Finally, a deficit financed by increases in the stock of money would find holders of money taxed by a decline in the real value of the money units. Since the stock of money must be held by someone, someone must be taxed when the value of each money unit falls. This kind of taxation by inflation is just as real as any other kind. Its final effect is to encourage people to hold less cash, and it thus provokes an increase in the rate at which money is spent.

The persistent gold drain during the early sixties brought the Federal Reserve System up short against its gold certificate reserve requirement. In late 1964, the sum of member bank reserves and Federal Reserve notes outstanding approached $52 billion while gold certificates were falling toward $14 billion. Required gold certificates were approximately $13 billion (25 percent of $52 billion), leaving free reserves of only a little over $1 billion.

Several options were open to the Federal Reserve System and the government at this point. One possible policy was to do nothing—to let the reserve requirement be reached, and then insist that the Federal Reserve maintain the 25 percent requirement by open market sales of its securities when necessary. This policy would have hamstrung the central bank's powers to control the nominal quantity of money in the economy. The Fed would have been forced by the rigor of the law to "run with the wind" instead of "leaning into the wind."

Another option for the Fed lay in the power of the Board of Governors to suspend the gold reserve ratio requirement and to renew this suspension for as long as desired. The only "cost" of this policy was a graduated tax that the Board of Governors was required by the Federal Reserve Act to levy on the deficient reserves of the twelve Federal Reserve Banks. This tax was so

Table 25.2. U.S. Short-Term and Long-Term Debt Due to Foreigners and Due from Foreigners as Reported by Banks in the United States; Gold Reserves of All Federal Reserve Banks and Earmarked Gold, 1941–1968
(billions of dollars)

End of Period	Short-Term Account (demand and time deposits and short-term government securities maturing in less than one year)			Long-Term Account			Gold Reserves of Federal Reserve Banks		Ear-marked Gold with Federal Reserve System	Free Reserves Minus Net Short-Term Balance (+) or (−)
	Due to Foreigners	Due from Foreigners	Net (due to)	Due to Foreigners	Due from Foreigners	Net (due to)	Total	Free		
1941	3.68	0.37	(3.31)	*	0.03	0.03	20.8	15.04	2.22	(+)11.73
1951	9.30	0.97	(8.33)	*	0.40	0.40	21.5	9.91	5.01	(+) 1.58
1958	16.2	2.54	(13.6)	0.02	1.36	1.34	20.0	8.10	8.54	(−) 5.50
1960	21.3	3.61	(17.7)	0.07	1.70	1.63	17.5	5.91	11.8	(−)11.8
1962	25.0	5.11	(19.9)	0.04	2.15	2.11	15.7	3.48	12.7	(−)16.4
1964	28.9	7.96	(20.9)	0.31	3.97	3.66	14.9	2.87	12.7	(−)18.0
1966	31.4	7.78	(23.6)	1.44	4.19	2.75	12.7	2.83	12.9	(−)20.8
1968	31.8	8.71	(23.1)	3.12	3.57	0.45	10.0	10.0	13.1	(−)13.1
1970	41.3	10.80	(30.5)	1.70	3.07	1.37	10.5	10.5	12.9	(−)20.0

Source: Board of Governors of the Federal Reserve System, *Federal Reserve Bulletin*, selected issues.
* Irrelevant amounts.

nominal that it easily could have been paid out of the surplus income the twelve Banks rebate every year to the Treasury. Therefore, it would have had no necessary consequences on policy decisions or direction. The Federal Reserve Board could have gone right on doing what they were doing.[2]

A third option was formal devaluation of the dollar by Congress. If, for example, the price of gold were raised from $35 to $70 per ounce, the existing gold stock would double in dollar value. What was accounted before as $14 billion in gold would have become $28 billion, and the Federal Reserve Banks would have had plenty of free gold reserves once again.

Devaluation of this sort is an ancient device closely related to the practice of debasement. It gets rid of the difficulty in a hurry; and under a true gold standard it encourages exports, discourages imports, increases the domestic stock of gold and money, and stimulates business and incomes. Its disadvantages are the impossibility of knowing how far to devalue, uncertainty over the future course of international trade, and the unsettling international and domestic effects of such a large change in the value of gold to the unit of account. In the nineteenth century, during the heyday of the international gold standard, devaluation was looked upon as a shenanigan indulged in only by governments of less-than-adequate fiscal integrity and responsibility.

A fourth option was to demonetize gold altogether and let exchange rates find their own level in exchange markets. The value of gold then would depend on its utility as a commodity and the supplies made available to the market. The value of the dollar in domestic trade would be what it is anyway—the inversion of the general price level—while in international trade the value of the dollar would be its ability to exchange for foreign currencies. Assuming free markets in foreign exchange and active competition among dealers in those markets, the dollar would exchange for other currencies in proportion to its real purchasing power relative to the corresponding purchasing powers of other currencies. The gold remaining in the Treasury could then be bled off at whatever price was considered "advantageous" by those in authority. (The cost of storing the gold would have to be equated with the possibility of getting better prices for it through limitation of supplies made available.)

Paradoxically enough, formal demonetization of gold and the sale of governmental hoards to private individuals and businesses would probably result in the return of gold contracts and a more general use of gold in international commerce. Gold would have particular utility in foreign trade between countries that had no established national currencies or no well-developed exchange markets.

A final option, and the one actually chosen in March 1965, was abandonment of the legal reserve requirement of gold to member bank reserves. Since mem-

---

[2]For a fuller account of how this provision of law would have applied, see Richard H. Timberlake, Jr., *Money, Banking, and Central Banking,* 1st ed. (New York: Harper & Row, 1965), pp. 313-314.

ber reserves at that time were about $18 billion, this relaxation "freed" approximately $4.5 billion in gold to meet any conversion demands from foreign dollar holders.

The 25 percent gold requirement against Federal Reserve notes was continued. However, the continuing easy money policy of the Fed, heavy open market purchases of government securities, corresponding inflationary rates of increase in the stock of domestic dollars, and the continued outflow of gold soon brought the Fed up short against the remaining reserve requirement. Again, in early 1968, Congress acted. This time the last vestige of the gold requirement, the reserve requirement against Federal Reserve notes, was removed and the Federal Reserve System was left with no gold constraints to hamper its domestic policies.

Another arrangement for stabilizing the price of the world's monetary gold—formation of an international gold "pool"—was begun in 1961. At first the arrangement had eight members, seven western European countries and the United States, with a gold supply of $32.6 billion. Later the membership was extended to include Japan and Canada and labeled the "Group of Ten." Their original actions were more in the nature of a conspiring monopoly to keep as much gold as possible in the pool, but several events put pressure on their supplies. In 1966 the Soviet Union, a large gold supplier, stopped offering gold for sale. The South African industry, the other major supplier, followed suit. In June 1967, the French government withdrew from the arrangement, taking with it its gold share of $5.2 billion. The United States then felt obliged to expand its role in the pool from 50 percent to 59 percent.

British devaluation of the pound sterling in November 1967 again prompted private demands for gold in anticipation of a gold price rise, and reserves in the pool dropped to $26.5 billion in early 1968. A proposal made in Congress called for the United States to withdraw from the pool and to stop automatic gold sales to other governments. This event provoked yet further gold demands in the world's markets. In March, the pool members reaffirmed their determination to support the price of gold by a public communique. Later in March, the U.S. Senate passed the bill that removed the final gold reserve requirement against Federal Reserve notes, releasing the remaining $10.4 billion in gold held by Federal Reserve Banks for international sales. A week later, the seven nations remaining in the pool stated that they would (1) cease supplying gold to the London and other gold markets, (2) no longer feel obliged to "buy" gold in the market, (3) support existing exchange rates between currencies, (4).not sell gold to countries supplying gold to the private market, (5) cooperate more closely than ever to smooth out fluctuations in exchange rates, and (6) provide further aid to the British pound; and they invited other central banks to cooperate in these ventures. Thereafter, the price of gold, which had been above $44 on the Paris market, fell to around $40.

These events marked the beginning of the "two-tier system" of gold prices. The official price of gold in the gold pool remained at $35.00 per ounce, while the price of gold in the free market fluctuated as the forces of supply and demand moved it. Governments that obtained gold at the official price and then sold it on the private market for a profit were to be barred from further official transactions.

By the end of 1969 the private market price of gold had fallen to the official level. The attempt of Russia and South Africa to force up the price of gold seemingly had failed. In fact, world bankers have entertained the possibility of placing a floor under the private price of gold in order to keep it at $35 per ounce in order to prevent South Africa from sustaining losses.

Despite gold or the lack of it, parities between dollars and other currencies were still fixed by political agreement. Occasionally a disequilibrium condition has become so forceful that a change of parity is called for. Usually, such a change is undertaken unilaterally by the affected country. It alters the value of its unit of account with respect to the dollar, and then other currencies fall into line pro rata. The change generally is of a significant magnitude, large enough in the opinion of monetary authorities to cover any further contingencies.

An exception to this procedure occurred in Germany in 1969. Instead of specifying the change, the German government let the deutschmark "float" in the free exchange market for several weeks. When the mark reached what seemed to be an equilibrium value with the dollar, it was re-pegged.[3]

Eurodollars

Eurodollars, a fairly recent phenomenon, have several possible definitions — several because of the quandary over what items to include. The trouble in defining them is similar (perhaps identical) to the problem of defining the stock of domestic money. But it is also complicated by the use of the term as a label for general financial operations in foreign moneys and by the ways in which Eurodollars may be generated. Yeager suggests defining them as "short-term deposits [probably including time deposits] held with British or Continental European banks but expressed in dollars instead of the local currency."[4]

Any bank in the world not proscribed by national law from doing so may hold either foreign currency or deposit claims on foreign banks as part of its reserve assets. Usually, its ordinary depositors would demand the local legal tender for their deposits. But if a foreign money, such as dollars, becomes so current in foreign markets that it has widespread financial usage in that country,

---

[3]The actual revaluation was about 8 percent: from a value of 1 dm = $0.26 to 1 dm = $0.28.

[4]Leland B. Yeager, *International Monetary Relations* (New York: Harper & Row, 1966), p. 467. U.S. currency held by nonbank Europeans and other foreigners should also be included. Most such currency is probably held in banks, so is not additive to their dollar deposits anyway. It is also very hard to estimate the quantity of this currency.

reserves, loans, and deposits all may be accounted in the foreign unit-of-account by banks that traffic in this medium. The dollar claims, in the form of either currency or demand deposits on a U.S. bank, may serve as reserves for the creation of *dollar* liabilities by the foreign bank (or the foreign branch of a U.S. bank). This development could apply to any unit of account regarded as "foreign." Eurodollars are just one such example, and the most significant. Eurosterling, Euroyen, Eurorubles, and similarly Amerimarks, Ameriyen, and Amerirubles are other (academic) possibilities.

In order for this kind of financial development to take place, a national money must be so prestigious that foreigners are willing to use this particular money as a store of value and, to a limited extent, as a medium of exchange. Dollars have come to possess such characteristics. A British financial commentator emphasized this fact in 1966 when he remarked: "The talk at the Paris Club may be about the weak dollar; but the European saver knows different on a longer perspective.... European investors trust dollars more than their own currencies."[5]

The creation of dollars in another country is very similar to their creation in the United States. The first requirement is that the bank in the foreign country have some sort of dollar reserve assets. This reserve could be currency — Federal Reserve notes — but typically it is a deposit claim on a U.S. bank. The foreign bank may attract such deposits because it is allowed to pay interest on demand deposits, a privilege denied U.S. commercial banks. The foreign bank is also free to keep whatever reserve ratio it judges as sufficient to meet deposit claims; that is, foreign banking systems face no minimal reserve requirements. Of course, they keep what are termed "providential" reserves, so reserves are *some* fraction of deposits. But the fraction is much lower than that prevailing in the United States.

Once dollar reserve-deposit claims are the property of a foreign commercial bank, it may make loans and deposits *in dollars*. This process draws down its dollar reserves to some fraction of the original deposit in just the way it would occur in the United States. As long as final recipients are willing to hold the new dollar deposits so created by bank bookkeeping, the world's quantity of dollars grows. The fact that the ratio of prudential reserves to demand and time deposits is lower than in the United States means that the number of dollars created on a given amount of reserves is greater when generated by a European bank than it is when created by a U.S. bank. However, the leakages of reserves from the European banks are more pronounced because the dollars are not used as media of exchange.

As foreign banks create new dollars for borrowers and the borrowers subsequently spend them, the next recipients of the dollars are not likely to use them for ordinary household or business transactions. They are much more

---

[5]Robert V. Roosa and Fred Hirsch, *Reserves, Reserve Currencies, and Vehicle Currencies* (Princeton, N.J.: Princeton University Press, 1966), pp. 30, 34. (Statement was made by Hirsch.)

inclined to exchange them for their own demand deposits and currency, an action that would liquidate the original reserve claim.[6] In the United States, households and business firms would use newly created dollars as media of exchange, and liquidation of reserves would occur only if people wanted to convert new deposits into currency. So, ordinarily, the new demand deposit dollars would stay in existence indefinitely. In sum, therefore, the pyramiding of bank credit in the form of Eurodollars adds some amount of dollars to the world's dollar supply: Eurobank credit is superimposed on U.S. domestic bank credit, which is built on the reserve assets of commercial banks. But the amount of dollars so created is narrowly circumscribed by deposit withdrawals in spite of the lower reserve ratios maintained by European banks.

Special Drawing Rights

Congress passed a bill in 1968 that amended the IMF Agreement in order to create a new monetary device known as Special Drawing Rights (SDRs). The bill also provided for U.S. participation in the plan. The new program is operated by the IMF, which assumes a stature somewhat like a world central bank. The SDRs, similarly, are somewhat like gold certificates, and frequently are referred to as "paper gold."

This plan calls for the IMF to issue SDRs to participating governments in proportion to their existing subscription to the Fund. To the IMF, this item is a deposit liability. To a government that holds an SDR through the agency of the central bank in that country, the SDRs are assets redeemable or convertible into any world currency that is in turn convertible into gold. Thus, the SDRs are indirectly convertible into gold. Their effect is to put another monetary element—another buffer—between gold and national moneys alleged to be convertible into gold. The intent is, of course, to stretch the use of gold in order to maintain the system of fixed parities among national moneys.

The SDRs are issued in denominational units equivalent to the official gold value of the dollar. Participants are required to accept SDRs in an amount equal to three times their allocations, but they are also permitted to accept as many as they wish. A persistent balance of payments surplus in "favor" of a given country would find it piling up SDRs, while a persistent deficit would require the deficit country to purchase foreign currency from the market. Its SDR account at the IMF accordingly would be debited, and the SDR account of the country whence it obtained the currency would be credited.

The original allocation of SDRs is supposed to last for a "basic period" of (normally) five years. Succeeding issues are to be made proportional to IMF

---

[6]Yeager, p. 468.

quotas. No rule was agreed upon or established by which additional issues would be made by the Fund. This void of when and how much to issue, therefore, has by default fallen under the administrative discretion of the Managing Director of the Fund. Before he can proceed to create and allocate additional SDRs, however, he must consult participating members to determine a consensus. To become effective, a proposal must have the approval of a majority of the members, and the majority must have at least 85 percent of the weighted voting power of the Fund. The arithmetic of this requirement means that any country with over 15 percent of the total voting power of the Fund must be included in the majority. (The United States has about 22 percent of the total voting power.)

SDRs have been endowed with limited quasi–legal tender power by the agreement of the participating countries. They virtually must be accepted in payment of international balances. However, the agreement specifies several safeguards and limitations to prevent an inordinate use of SDRs in obtaining other reserve assets, for example, dollars and gold.

The plan was inaugurated in January 1970. The initial issue authorized by agreement of the participating countries was for $9.5 billion SDR units over a three-year period. The first issue of SDRs amounted to $3.5 billion and was made early in 1970. The second issue of $3.0 billion was made January 1, 1971.

Final Notes

The three sections of this chapter have examined three different means of financing international balances: (1) a managed gold exchange standard, (2) a prestigious national money (dollars), and (3) monetary assets — SDRs — issued by an international agency. All of these institutional arrangements involve a certain amount of ad hoc opportunism or political finagling. They also include attempts to avoid the strictures of a true gold standard. The system they constitute is marked by troublesome negotiation, recurring threats of "crisis," and sporadic adjustments of exchange rates made on the basis of highly problematic predictions about the future course of trade. In view of the working infelicities of such a patchwork and the alternative of yet a better system, a good question arises of why such machinery is retained. The alternative to all the administered systems is the "no-system" solution of freely flexible exchange rates. This policy would allow exchange rates to be determined competitively in foreign exchange markets. In this regard, they would be similar to all other prices. Rate changes would occur day by day and would be continuous reflections of underlying economic conditions.

With some exceptions, this policy had been opposed successfully up to mid-1971 by the world's monetary authorities, who profit by the complexity of a system that requires their constant attention. Without "crises," devaluations, international conferences, and the like, the prestige and importance of their jobs would largely disappear. One exception was provided by the Canadian government, however, when it let the Canadian dollar float between 1950 and 1962. After eight years of pegged rates, the Canadian dollar was floated again in June 1970 and has been at a market-determined rate for over a year. The West German mark was also allowed to float for a few weeks in the fall of 1970 in order to determine its "proper" level. Then in June 1971, it, too, was exposed to market forces for the indefinite future. Both of these currencies subsequently appreciated by about 8 percent relative to the U.S. dollar and then settled down to minor fluctuations around their market-determined parities.

The Canadian dollar and the West German mark are two of the three foreign moneys most important in the international dealings of the United States. Still not floating but also undervalued relative to the U.S. dollar was the Japanese yen, the third currency of the group that comprises the major trading partners of the United States.

In a dramatic move to effect equilibrium in the international sphere, the President of the United States announced in mid-August 1971 that the United States would no longer support or be bound by a fixed price of gold of $35 per ounce. The fixed price of gold and fixed prices of dollars for other currencies are not necessarily connected. Even if the price of gold was not supported by government policy, the fixed relative prices of dollars and all other currencies could be maintained by political agreement. However, the implication of the President's announced abandonment of the fixed price of gold was that exchange rates between the dollar and all other currencies would be allowed to seek their market values freely in foreign exchange markets.

Ministers of finance and many foreign central bankers were discomfited by this new policy, but a large majority of economists were in full sympathy. Foreign exchanges were officially closed for a week following the President's announcement because of the alleged "crises" that would appear if market factors were to operate freely. When markets finally were allowed to open in the third week in August, the "crises" were seen to be imaginary. The dollar values of most foreign moneys slowly drifted 1 or 2 percent higher—in effect, the dollar was devalued to this extent. The Japanese yen, however, was kept at a fixed parity by official intervention of the Japanese central bank.

Toward the end of August, the yen was also freed from its official shackles. In the following week, it, too, appreciated relative to the dollar and most other currencies. The market devaluation of the dollar caused more dollars to be bought for yen, less yen to be bought with dollars, some stimulation of U.S. exports to Japan, and some cooling of Japanese exports to the United States.

Most observers doubted that the yen would be allowed to float for long. Incongruously enough, official interventionists are only willing to allow the market to determine a new *level* of exchange rates. Once a new market price relationship for foreign moneys had been established, the official world of financial ministers argued for a re-pegging of rates on the grounds that movements in exchange rates may be destabilizing. Late in 1971, a devaluation of the dollar of 8.7 percent was proposed, with early ratification by Congress anticipated. One would think that the equilibrium the market establishes after a long period of fundamental disequilibrium under pegged exchange rates could only be more thoroughgoing if the market were allowed to function continuously.

Selected Bibliography

Friedman, Milton. *The Euro-Dollar Market: Some First Principles,* Occasional Paper No. 34, Graduate School of Business, University of Chicago, 1969. (Originally published in the *Morgan Guaranty Survey* by the Morgan Trust Company of New York.)

Kindleberger, Charles P. *International Economics.* Homewood, Ill.: Richard D. Irwin, 1968.

Roosa, Robert V., and Fred Hirsch. *Reserves, Reserve Currencies, and Vehicle Currencies.* Princeton, N.J.: Princeton University Press, 1966.

Is Time Money?

C. P. Kindleberger

In what way is the fixed exchange rate system in international finance analogous to the fixed time zone system in the world's temporal structure? Charles P. Kindleberger, Professor of Economics at the Massachusetts Institute of Technology, takes issue in this article with his renowned adversary on exchange rate policy, Professor Milton Friedman of the University of Chicago.

In an earlier article, Professor Friedman argued that society adjusts its clocks (rather than its human habits) by means of daylight saving time in order to coordinate the time unit of account to the "living" day. This occasional adjustment, Friedman stated, is analogous to the adjustments that exchange rates would make if they were determined in free markets.

To Professor Kindleberger, however, fixed time zones are themselves analogous to fixed exchange rates among countries. He notes that flexible exchange rates between one nation and another are not necessarily optimal,

From *Interplay Magazine,* August-September 1969, pp. 40–42. *Interplay Magazine*©. Reprinted by permission of the publisher and the author.

and that rates could be allowed to fluctuate freely within nations, within regions, and even between persons! He points out that such an absurd reduction of the monetary domain demonstrates the necessity for fixed rates at some level. Otherwise, under a completely fractionalized world currency system, the cost of doing business between any two areas would be prohibitively expensive.

The use of the time analogy to support two different points of view should force the reader to think through carefully the arguments for and against both fixed and flexible exchange rates. And even if he maintains his views on proper exchange rate policy, he should learn something about time conventions. He might also be reminded of an old maxim: Analogies do not prove anything.

Every time a new foreign exchange crisis erupts, sending out shockwaves that shake the nerves of bankers, government officials and whole nations, more economists flock to the standard of the flexible exchange rate. What is this ever-more-popular panacea? Under a system of flexible exchange rates, the foreign exchange market would be cleared by simple changes in the exchange rate: if, for example, the Spanish peseta were in difficulties, it would simply be devalued, temporarily, to the level which international traders considered realistic—which reflected, in other words, their evaluation of its true worth. This would, in theory, bring about an adjustment of the balance of payments in the short run—and in the long, as well. It would, moreover, cushion or even eliminate altogether the shocks set up by recurrent international monetary crises.

For purposes of comparison, let us briefly recall how our present fixed-rate system operates. Day in and day out, the government (or central bankers) clears the foreign exchange market at the fixed price for a given currency by buying up surpluses and providing foreign exchange out of reserves—as long as they last—to meet deficits. So much for the short run. In the long run, the balance of payments must be adjusted by increases in wages and prices in countries with a surplus and by painful deflation in countries with deficits.

The disadvantages of the fixed-rate system are obvious—but are flexible rates the answer? Most of the economists who have been and are being converted to the flexible-rates theory do not specialize in international economics. And "practical" men—bankers and government officials—abhor the proposed system instinctively or on principle—though most of them would be hard put to it to define the principles involved.

Some specialists in international trade, on the other hand, have pushed the argument for flexible rates far beyond the real needs of the day. For them, the key criterion is the "optimum currency area"—that is, the right-sized economic unit to enjoy a flexible exchange rate. Why, they ask, should this unit necessarily be a country: why shouldn't it be a region, such as Appalachia or Canada's maritime provinces, which might want to depreciate its local currency in order to curb its unemployment and improve its balance of payments? Why not, for that matter, a state like West Virginia—or a depressed textile town like Manchester, New Hampshire? To carry the argument to its (not very) logical extreme, an "optimum currency area" could even be a man or woman who fails to find work at the local minimum wage rate: the term itself is so flexible that it could designate a single individual — or the entire population (plus land and all other resources) of the globe.

A particularly gifted and articulate advocate of flexible exchange rates is Dr. Milton Friedman of the University of Chicago. In a paper in *Essays in Positive Economics* which received a considerable amount of well-merited attention, Dr. Friedman offers an arresting analogy between flexible exchange rates and, of all things, daylight saving time. He reminds us that instead of changing our daily habits with the waxing and waning of the extent of daylight hours we simply change our clocks. Analogously, he suggests, we should, rather than adjust wages and prices to a fixed exchange rate, simply bring the exchange rate into line with wages and prices.

At least two occurrences during this past year have led me to question the appositeness of this analogy. The first was a personal experience: living in Atlanta, Georgia, in the western part of the Eastern Standard Time zone, and observing how dark it was still at 8 o'clock of a winter morning, I found it necessary — and not very difficult — to adjust my habits, with relation to the sun, rather than my watch. The second was an event in Britain: February 18, 1968 marked the end of Greenwich Mean Time there, and the adoption (on a three-year experimental basis) of year-round summer time — that is, of the same time as Western Europe. In the realm of time, events seem to be running counter to the Friedman thesis: the "optimum time zone," to extend the analogy, appears to be expanding rather than contracting.

In the past, I have explored the analogy between money and language (in "The Politics of International Money and World Language," Princeton *Essays in International Finance,* No. 61, August 1967). In this article I shall look at money and time. The analogies differ. In relation to language, the essence is its role as a medium of exchange; in relation to time, as Friedman intuitively understood, the emphasis is on the unit of account.

Time, to be sure, *is* money. We spend, save, make, budget, lose, waste it. It is thus a store of value. "He has a year to live," or "three weeks off," or "an afternoon free." A number of economists, *e.g.,* Becker and Linder, are investigating how the day may be a more significant budget constraint in an affluent society than income. The cost of a haircut is not $2.25 plus tip but $2.25 plus tip plus 25 minutes of normal working time. This constraint does not apply to youth, which is immortal, or to the old or unemployed, for whom time hangs heavy. Time is rarely a medium of exchange or a standard of deferred payment. Our interest is in time as a unit of account, and in rates of exchange between these units in different locations.

A few years ago, the brilliant Swiss journalist Herbert Luethy wrote a book on France (in the American edition, *France Against Herself*), with the title in French *A l'Heure de son Clocher,* "each clock on its own time." The reference was to France before its postwar economic upsurge. The Italians have a similar expression, *campanilismo,* which emphasizes the separateness of individual villages, each regulated by the *campanile,* or bells of the village church. In primitive economies time stands still or goes its separate ways. In a modern, interdependent economy, by contrast, time not only flies or marches on; it does so in unison.

There is debate over the criteria for the optimum currency area. Robert Mundell of Chicago, who devised the concept, sought a separate currency, with an independent exchange rate, for any political entity whose labor and capital were not joined with those of other communities. The analogy with the uncalibrated clocks of separate villages is exact. The emphasis of a critic, Roland McKinnon, is on closed economies which carry on little trade with the outside world. They require "exchange illusion," or the capacity to ignore the impact of changes in foreign-trade prices on the level of living. (Time illusion is the essence of the Friedman point: we adjust our watches in order to alter our daily routines as against the sun, or God's time.)

A third aspect of the optimum currency area has been put to me by Claudio Segre. It is a supplement to those of Mundell and McKinnon, rather than a substitute for them. An optimum currency area, Segre contends, is one with coordinated macro-economic policies. Communities which are joined by factor movements, and by extensive trade which bulks large in the cost of living of their members, are incapable of sustaining a single currency area unless their monetary, fiscal and commercial policies are mutually adjusted.

What is the optimum *time* zone? The answer, again, is that it is a function of factor movements, commercial intercourse and coordinated policies. For the macro-temporal unit of account, measured by the calendar, it is the world. Since 46 BC, the Julian calendar, slightly modified by Gregory in 1582, has spread its sway, overcoming major rival systems, such as that of the Greek Orthodox church, and winning out over other local methods of reckoning which survive mainly in holy days and holidays, such as the Jewish and Chinese New Years, the Tet lunar New Year, etc. For the most part, the world follows one calendar and adjusts festivals thereto. In Australia and New Zealand, Christmas is celebrated in full summer, despite its pagan origin (as to timing) in the European winter solstice. Christian and pagan legends have been carried below the equator intact: there, evergreens, Yule logs, red-coated Santa Clauses or Father Christmases abound, despite their unseasonable character in mid-summer.

The Difficulties of Reform

One strong similarity exists between the calendar system for measuring time and the world monetary system: the difficulty of effecting rational reform. In the first area, we operate by a standard Rome decreed when she was the pivot of world power. Short of world government, it is impossible to obtain agreement to bring the Roman year up to date and into phase with 20th-century production possibilities and tastes, and the functional residues of tradition. Proposals for reform are easily worked up, as are hybrid world languages and schemes for world monetary reform. But worldwide agreement on any such proposal remains elusive. In the measurement of time on the macro level, as in language and money, the world is stuck with an archaic standard of a single national origin, which is impossible of reform in a world of nation-states.

At the micro-temporal level, the optimum time zone is smaller than the world but bigger than the locality. Greenwich Mean Time dates from 1675, but British cities continued to operate independently of one another chronometrically until about 1800. The clocks of Plymouth, in the west of England, for example, ran 16 minutes later than those of London.

The railroads changed all this. G. M. Young has explained that railroad timetables rendered the English middle-class public conscious of precise time and disposed to carry watches. The 24-hour gate clock on the Royal Observatory building in Greenwich was installed in 1852 to measure time for Great Britain. North American railroads found it desirable to adopt not only the British standard gauge of track width, but also time zones based on Greenwich. Greenwich finally came into its own as the international time standard at a conference held in 1884 at Washington. The need for such a world standard arose from the increased speed of steamers equipped with screw propellers, which crossed the Atlantic in days instead of weeks.

Fixed time zones are analogous to stable exchange rates, and both were increasingly needed, in the last quarter of the 19th century, to accommodate the substantial and rising volume of world trade. The width of the optimal time zone was determined by the earth's diurnal revolution relative to the sun, and the consequent need to divide the circumference of the earth, at every latitude, by 24 hours. At the equator, where the circumference of the globe is approximately 25,000 miles, the optimum time zone is about 1,040 miles wide. There was no need to be precise in fixing the time zones, as a glance at the frequently-erratic northward or southward course of the time boundaries will indicate (except, of course, on a Mercator's projection, in which east-west distances are increasingly magnified moving north and south of the equator). Many hard battles were fought, in the U.S. at least, to prevent communities with substantial intercourse from being placed in different zones.

Daylight saving time was an outgrowth of the flight to the suburbs in the 1920s. Initially, in the U.S., it was left to state and local governments to decide whether or not to adopt daylight time, and on which day in the spring to make the switch. Farmers, whose day is regulated by the sun, were against adjusting the clocks and altering the schedules of milk trains; and thanks to the failure of most state legislatures to reapportion voting districts in line with population shifts, their opposition continued to be effective long after their economic importance had shrunk. As a result a number of states with large urban populations held out against the adoption of daylight saving time up until World War II.

Today, few people over 50 cannot recall the confusion that system of partial daylight saving time engendered with regard to travel and long-distance telephoning. The existence of different time zones makes things difficult enough even now, when fast air transport and long-distance telecommunication are cheap and abundant. "If it is 11:30 in New York, has our California representative come to his office yet?" "If I take off from Los Angeles at 2, can I still make that dinner in Washington?"

Flexible daylight saving complicated matters further still: in the 1920s and 1930s, railroad timetables were adjusted to daylight saving time, but printed in standard time. This confused all but the most organized travelers—all of them male—as they strove to recall which states and cities were on standard and which on daylight time, and whether the hour should be adjusted forward or back.

Lack of uniformity became intolerable in the jet age. In consequence, most, and I think all, states in the United States now move to daylight time on the fourth Sunday in April, and back to standard time again on the fourth Sunday in October. In January 1968, the Georgia legislature considered going its separate way and holding out against the change of clocks on April 28. It is of some interest to note that the conservatives no longer used the hard lot of farmers, the exigencies of milch cows, and God's time as debating points. Instead, opponents cited the problems of children waiting in the dark for buses to take them to school.

That this is a real argument is shown by the death of two five-year-old boys, who were struck down and killed by cars in different parts of Britain as they were walking to school in semi-darkness at 9 o'clock one morning last November, after the government had introduced an experiment in retaining summer throughout the year. This gave rise to an outcry against the time change. But, of course, the attempt in Georgia to get out of lock-step was unsuccessful.

Turning from time to money, economists put little faith in money illusion, which occurs when income-recipients are guided in their behavior by their money incomes and disregard changes in the cost of living. For some reason, however, a good many of them believe that *exchange* illusion is a dependable weapon: that flexible exchange rates can work smoothly and efficiently to restrain spending under devaluation with full employment. Is *time* illusion something to take seriously? I think not.

The man who consistently sets his watch ten minutes fast to get to appointments on time is usually regarded as a simpleton. Stopping the clock at midnight on December 31 to extend the time for debating the budget (as in France under the Fourth Republic), or ripping the clock off the wall on the last day of the legislative session in Georgia, are sometimes regarded as legitimate devices to escape a severe time constraint, although they involve changing the rules rather than fooling anybody. Time illusion is no longer available, however, to the local community locked into the matrix of synchronization over a continental system of timetables, radio and television schedules and business habits. Fixed time rates of exchange are necessary to the maintenance of an intercommunicating society. Daylight saving time has been altogether given up in Western Europe, and adopted year-round in Britain. The British initiative in adopting the same temporal unit of account as the Continent did not, as we have seen, go unchallenged. It nevertheless occurred, and its significance as an earnest of British desires to join the European economic (social? political?) community is profound.

Unifying the Units

Money as a unit of account makes it possible to compare economic values; by the same token, time as a unit of account makes possible the comparison of temporal values. Economic transactions involve comparisons of economic values. Economic, social and political transactions involve the establishment of temporal values. Communicating societies need identical time units or, if distance makes this physically impossible, units of account joined by fixed conversion coefficients.

The hippie movement wants to dispense with both money and time. The economist must take tastes as given. His task is to calculate the economic cost of alternative policies. I have a hard time seeing how to go about estimating the cost to the United States and to the world of abandoning a single unit of account for time, but I think it would be substantial. I question further whether international trade and capital movements can flourish in a world without fixed exchange rates and watches calibrated through fixed time differences. In a world economic system money illusion, exchange illusion and time illusion are probably impossible. If the optimum currency area and the optimum time zones are the whole world, it would seem sensible to abandon the idyllic romance of flexible exchange rates and to move to coordinate economic policies as has long been done in the temporal sphere.

Yeager's excellent textbook on *International Monetary Relations* quotes the Friedman analogy with approval. It also cites another analogy from Roepke: a circus clown makes a big production of moving a grand piano to the stool, when it is obviously easier to move the stool to the piano; by analogy, it is much easier to adjust the exchange rate to economic policies than the reverse.

But suppose the composition is Mozart's concerto for three pianos, and the stools must be placed where the pianists can see each other, the orchestra and the conductor?

Section Five

Some Current Issues in
Monetary Theory and Policy

26

The Velocity of Money and the Investment Multiplier in the U.S.

The Alternative Theories for Testing Purposes

A great deal of controversy has appeared in monetary economics since the years of the Great Depression (1929–1940). Prior to that time, most economists uncritically accepted the quantity theory of money as the theoretical means for expressing monetary behavior. The Great Depression and the reappraisal of monetary influence initiated by J. M. Keynes swung most economists around to a view that belittled the quantity theory and the use of monetary policy for countercyclical purposes. The new approach placed *investment spending decisions*, rather than *the stock of money*, at the heart of spending behavior. Neither acceptance of the quantity theory before 1929, nor its rejection and the corresponding embrace of the income investment theory during the 1930s, resulted from much more than superficial empiricism that seemed to explain the present state of the economy. With few exceptions among economists, either theory was accepted or rejected by hunch, intuition, and reliance on authority.

The lack of emphasis on empirical research and testing procedures is excusable to some extent. First, theories had to be refined and simplified before they were capable of being tested operationally. Second, reliable statistics had to be collected over a period of time sufficiently long to allow significant results. Third, statistical techniques had to be developed so that the testing of theories could be evaluated reliably. Once these three conditions were fulfilled, tests might determine whether one theory was scientifically more valid than another.

Both the investment (or Keynesian) theory of money income determination and the quantity theory are logically valid. The questions posed for empirical testing are (1) which theory is more relevant to monetary behavior (2) which theory is more useful, and (3) under what specific conditions are there differences in the answers to the first two questions?

The brief of the quantity theory is that the quantity of money is a major factor in the determination of the total flow of money expenditures.[1] It also argues that absolute *changes* in the quantity of money lead to or determine absolute *changes* in total money expenditures. These two propositions can be written in equation form as follows:

$$Y = a + V'M \tag{1}$$

and

$$\Delta Y = V' \Delta M \tag{2}$$

where Y is money income (or money spending) of the economy during some time period—usually one year; V' is the income velocity of money; M is the stock of money; and a is a constant to indicate that the series does not start at zero. ΔY and ΔM are annual *changes* in the flow of income and in the stock of money.

Testing for the correlations between M and Y and between ΔM and ΔY should indicate the constancy or inconstancy of V', the income velocity of money. The earlier monetary theorists either implicitly or explicitly considered V' a constant. The Keynesian theory threw open this assumption to question and debate, and in fact concluded, largely on deductive grounds, that V' is not a constant. In place of V' the Keynesian theory substituted an autonomous expenditures multiplier. Such expenditures presumably are independently initiated; they are not derived from other expenditures but lead to other forms of spending. For example, net investment is considered a major autonomous expenditure. The expenditure theory then posits that the flow of money income depends on autonomous expenditures times a "multiplier" analogous to the inverse of the marginal propensity to save (the investment multiplier) discussed in Chapter 6.[2] The equations given by this theory are:

$$Y = g + K'A \tag{3}$$

and

$$\Delta Y = K' \Delta A \tag{4}$$

---

[1]Much of the subsequent text is a rewrite and condensation in more elementary terms of the 1960 study by Milton Friedman and David Meiselman for the Commission on Money and Credit. See "The Relative Stability of Monetary Velocity and the Investment Multiplier in the United States, 1897-1958," *Stabilization Policies* (Englewood Cliffs, N.J.: Prentice-Hall, 1963), pp. 165-268.

[2]For simplicity's sake, investment was the only autonomous form of spending included in the analysis in Chapter 6. In the real model tested here all autonomous expenditures must be included.

where Y again is income, A is autonomous expenditures, K' is the multiplier, and g is a constant. ΔY and ΔA are again the annual *changes* in Y and A. Correlation tests between A and Y and between ΔA and ΔY should show the degree of stability in K'. The problem, then, is to determine which of the two assumed constants, V' or K', is in fact the most constant and under what conditions.

Before correlation tests could be run on the testing equations, they had to be put into forms that would inhibit spurious correlations. A and Y in Equation (3), for example, would show a spurious correlation because $Y = C + A$ (where C equals consumption spending). Thus, Y would be correlated with a part of itself. The real job for A, as an independent variable predicting a determinate variable, is to predict C, consumption spending. Consumption is what is left when A is subtracted from both sides of Equation (3). When this adjustment is made, the testing equation reads:

$$C = h + KA \tag{5}$$

where K is the multiplier of autonomous expenditures in determining C and h is an algebraic constant.[3]

Changing the income equation to the form expressed in (5) necessitates the same sort of change in the money velocity equation, even though no such spurious correlation could exist in the money equation. Nonetheless, one of the two dependent variables, income or consumption, may be easier to predict than the other. In the interests of consistency, therefore, Equation (1) is changed to the following form:

$$C = d + VM \tag{6}$$

where V is the velocity of the money stock used in consumption spending.

This form of the money velocity equation puts a somewhat heavier burden on the stability of the velocity value, V. The quantity of money was always held to be a predictor of *total* income, not of any single component of income. V', therefore, is logically more constant than V. (In actual testing, however, this handicap did not appear.)[4]

Equations (5) and (6) are adequate for determining simple correlations between autonomous expenditures and consumption and between money and consumption. If money and autonomous expenditures are independent, each simple correlation would show how effective each of the two independent

---

[3]Simple algebra shows that $K = (K' - 1)$. For $K' = \dfrac{Y}{A}$ and $K = \dfrac{Y - A}{A}$ or $\dfrac{Y}{A} - 1$. Therefore, $K = (K' - 1)$.

[4]For an explanation of this phenomenon, the interested student should consult Friedman and Meiselman, especially pp. 176–177.

variables is in explaining C. In fact, the two "independent" variables are not independent of each other; and they need not be, no matter which of the two hypotheses is assumed. The general quantity theory predicts that changes in the quantity of money affect all expenditures, alleged "autonomous" expenditures as well as consumption. The expenditure theory predicts that changes in the quantity of money (under most conditions except those of deep depression) influence interest rates in the opposite direction. Changes in interest rates wrought by changes in the quantity of money then may encourage or discourage investment, a principal autonomous expenditure. Therefore, another testing equation to show the potential correlation between M and A is necessary. This equation is simply a combination of (5) and (6) and is expressed as:

$$C = d + VM + KA \tag{7}$$

The advantage of this equation is that it demonstrates how much of the explanations given separately by M and A in the simpler expressions is due to a relation between M and A. The operational concept of a multiple correlation expression is that it obtains correlation values between each independent variable and the dependent variable, with the other independent variable held provisionally constant during the testing process. The simple correlation coefficients, therefore, should be greater than the partial correlation coefficients if the two "independent" variables actually have a degree of dependency. Nonetheless, the simple correlations show the correct direction of relationship. And if, for example, the quantity of money has some influence on autonomous expenditures (as seemed to be the case), the simple correlation between money and consumption would have more significance than the partial value.

Once testing equations are constructed they must be given the substance of empirical data. In the case studied here, the data are in time series of money stocks and income flows. Inevitably, such series need refining, reevaluation, and reconstruction. The question of which stock of money to use is a perpetually knotty problem, and one that economists have debated for centuries. The study summarized here uses the stock that includes currency outside banks, plus demand deposits in all commercial banks adjusted for interbank deposits, plus all time deposits in commercial banks.[5]

The selection of autonomous expenditures requires the heaviest intellectual effort, largely because no one had ever tried to put together an actual set of values for such a series. Finally, included in this series were net private domestic investment, the government deficit on income and product account, and the net foreign balance.[6]

---

[5]The logic of this selection is explored further in Chapter 27 and in the reading selection at the end of that chapter.

[6]The authors were quick to point out the tentative nature of their judgments. They enjoined others who had different opinions on what to include to submit them for further experiment. (See Friedman and Meiselman, p. 185.)

The Results of the Tests

Test results were obtained for the 60-year period from 1897 to 1958 divided into eleven overlapping subperiods and selected so as to include business cycle troughs and peaks, and selected also in a way that would avoid a division during a war period. Results were also obtained for the 1929–1958 period and for quarterly data from 1945–1958. The major results of the tests are summarized in Table 26.1.

Table 26.1. Correlations between Synchronous Variables in Nominal Monetary Terms*

| Period | Income Expenditure Theory | | | Quantity Theory | | |
	r_{CA}	$r_{CA[M]0}$	r_{CM}	$r_{CM[A]0}$	r_{YM}	r_{AM}
(1)	(2)	(3)	(4)	(5)	(6)	(7)
Annually						
1897–1958	0.756	−0.222	0.985	0.967	0.988	0.791
1897–1908	0.587	−0.496	0.996	0.996	0.991	0.622
1903–1913	0.485	−0.127	0.997	0.996	0.987	0.495
1908–1921	0.672	0.400	0.995	0.993	0.975	0.646
1913–1920	0.791	0.423	0.991	0.980	0.975	0.761
1920–1929	0.569	0.288	0.968	0.956	0.933	0.524
1921–1933	0.843	0.884	0.897	0.923	0.810	0.586
1929–1939	0.937	0.688	0.912	0.529	0.915	0.880
1933–1938	0.935	0.414	0.991	0.938	0.985	0.921
1938–1953	0.397	−0.328	0.958	0.955	0.966	0.500
1939–1948	0.173	−0.562	0.963	0.974	0.967	0.327
1948–1957	0.747	0.361	0.990	0.980	0.986	0.719
1929–1958	0.705	−0.424	0.974	0.957	0.983	0.784
Quarterly						
1945_3–1958_4	0.511	0.044	0.985	0.979	0.980	0.512
1946_1–1958_4	0.687	0.286	0.985	0.973	0.978	0.660

* This table is taken almost verbatim from the Friedman-Meiselman study. It does not include the correlation for real values. In general, real values behaved much as did nominal (monetary) values.

The values in Table 26.1 can be interpreted as follows. For example, during the period 1903–1913 autonomous expenditures in monetary terms had a correlation value with monetary consumption expenditures of 0.485 (r_{CA}). For the same period the quantity of money and consumption expenditures had a correlation value of 0.997 (r_{CM}). Since the quantity of money and autonomous expenditures are themselves significantly correlated, as indicated by the value

0.495 (r_{AM}), the correlation values of the first two relationships are reobtained in Columns 3 and 5 by the partial correlation method. The value −0.127 $(r_{CA[M]_0})$ shows the correlation between autonomous expenditures and consumption expenditures when the influence of the money stock is withheld, and the value 0.996 $(r_{CM[A]_0})$ gives the relationship between the stock of money and consumption expenditures when the influence of autonomous expenditures is taken out. Column 6 gives the value of the correlation between the stock of money and monetary income in a separate test. As would be expected, these latter values are very similar to the correlations between money and consumption spending.

The general conclusions are self-evident. The velocity of money — the multiplier of the stock of money — is decidedly more stable than the autonomous expenditures multiplier in every period except 1929–1939. Even in that period the differences between the two values are not great. The authors of the study also experimented with leads and lags in the period for which they had quarterly data (1945–1958). They found that the stock of money on the average is correlated slightly higher with consumption two quarters later than it is with synchronous consumption.

The high correlation values between money and money expenditures, and the still higher correlations of money and consumption expenditures when expenditure values lag money values by two quarters, point to the significant effects the stock of money exerts on spending behavior. The consistency of this pattern also suggests a high degree of stability in the monetary multiplier — the velocity of money. If velocity had shown a pronounced variation, the relationships between the stock of money and money expenditures of different types would be much more random than the actual data of Table 26.1 indicate are the case.

The data give *average* relationships over a secular time period. If an observer knows what is happening to the stock of money, he can predict what would happen to money expenditures at some time in the future with a great deal of certainty. He cannot, however, predict very well what would happen "tomorrow." Spending behavior as influenced by the stock of money takes an average of two quarters to adjust to a new equilibrium. Furthermore, the average of two quarters has a great deal of dispersion. Sometimes the lag is only six weeks; sometimes it is almost a year and a half.[7]

The income-expenditure theory, on the other hand, is seen to be almost completely useless as a *general* theory purporting to describe empirical relationships. It seems to be a useful theory only under the special circumstances of instability in income, severe unemployment, a declining price level, and pervasive uncertainty in the business climate. It was in such a context, in fact, that Keynes developed the main lines of this theory.

---

[7]See Friedman and Meiselman, p. 214. For a contrary view, see John Karaken and Robert Solow, "Lags in Fiscal and Monetary Policy," also published in *Stabilization Policies,* pp. 14–24.

The Friedman-Meiselman study not only tests the two contrasting theories, but it also offers a useful lesson in the laboratory techniques of statistical estimation. In this regard it is a ground-breaking study. But in the mode of most such innovations, it raises as many questions as it answers. The questions subsequently debated have dealt with (1) the methods of testing, (2) the assumptions of the model (or models) tested, (3) the choice of variables to be included in autonomous expenditures, and (4) the choice of variables to be included in the stock of money. Many of these issues were debated in later journal articles. Some of the most prominent are summarized in the next section and in subsequent chapters or readings.

Rebuttal of the Income Theorists

After the Friedman-Meiselman study had been assimilated and digested for a few years, several income theorists offered rebuttals to some sections of the original argument. Three separate counterarguments were prepared by the following economists: Albert Ando and Franco Modigliani, Michael DePrano and Thomas Mayer, and Donald Hester. The first two of these papers, plus Friedman and Meiselman's replies, plus the final rejoinders of the critics, were published as a symposium in the *American Economic Review*.[8] The Hester article appeared in an earlier issue of *The Review of Economics and Statistics*.[9]

Many of the arguments and counterarguments between the principals in this debate go far beyond what would be intelligible and useful in an elementary text. Their analysis must be left for further study at the graduate level. Some of the arguments, however, involve the fundamentals of monetary theory and statistical testing methods as well as the logic and utility of definitions, and these issues can be usefully discussed at any level.

One of the most telling criticisms of the original exposition is that no detailed and operational list of autonomous expenditures was made by those who profess its utility, despite the ubiquitous use of the concept. Friedman and Meiselman proposed a list that included net investment, net exports, and the government deficit. They professed no great confidence, however, that their list included either all the autonomous spending variables or the proper ones. Ando and Modigliani maintained not only that other spending entities should be included in autonomous expenditures but also that the determinants of total

---

[8]Albert Ando and Franco Modigliani, "The Relative Stability of Velocity and the Investment Multiplier" (and "Rejoinder"), Michael DePrano and Thomas Mayer, "Tests of the Relative Importance of Autonomous Expenditures and Money" (and "Rejoinder"), Milton Friedman and David Meiselman, "Reply," *American Economic Review*, Vol. 55, No. 4 (September 1965), pp. 693–792.

[9]Donald Hester, "Keynes and the Quantity Theory: A Comment on the Friedman-Meiselman CMC Paper," "Reply to Donald Hester," and Hester's "Rejoinder," *Review of Economics and Statistics*, Vol. 46 (November 1964), pp. 364–372.

spending act in a manner too complex for valid expression by a simple linear equation. In particular, these critics believed that Friedman and Meiselman's "autonomous" variable, *A*, includes certain induced components. For example, net exports are gross exports minus gross imports. But gross imports are partially a function of income. Therefore, *net* exports are in part induced by present and past income, and they therefore cannot be considered primal in the spending sequence. In Ando and Modigliani's view, gross exports should have been the spending component included in autonomous expenditures.

Another important point of contention is the size of autonomous expenditures. The rationale of the whole spending approach is that some forms of spending are bellwethers for aggregate spending. In order for this theory to be operational and useful, the list of spending leaders cannot be too extensive. Obviously, if a large enough assortment of autonomous spending variables is used, total spending is virtually *defined* rather than *predicted*. Reason suggests as well that the list of expenditures properly regarded as autonomous—the ones having no previous ancestry in income already generated and arising from spontaneous or capricious decisions—should be a relatively small fraction of total expenditures.

Friedman and Meiselman presented a table that specifies the percentages of induced and autonomous expenditures for their own study and for the Ando-Modigliani and DePrano-Mayer models. These values are reproduced in abbreviated form in Table 26.2.

Table 26.2. Division between Induced and Autonomous
Expenditures for Four Spending
Models, 1947–1958

	Friedman-Meiselman	Ando-Modigliani	DePrano-Mayer	
	A	A_1	A_2	A_3
Percentage of autonomous expenditures in determining Y	10.7	45.2	31.6	41.7
Percentage of induced expenditures in determining Y	89.3	54.8	68.4	58.3

This table pointedly demonstrates two of the issues. What is not autonomous is induced; the sum of each vertical column must add up to 100 percent. It also shows that the Friedman-Meiselman model uses 10.7 percent of expenditures to predict the remaining 89.3 percent of total expenditures, while the other models use 30 to 45 percent of the total to predict 70 to 55 percent of the remainder. Predicting a small volume of induced expenditures with a large volume of expenditures *defined* as autonomous is not very useful. If carried to an extreme, it uses all the data to predict nothing! But how large or how small each component should be is a discretionary matter, as is the issue of what expenditures can be regarded as autonomous.

The distinction between autonomous and induced has yet another facet. Since the definition of what is included as "autonomous" determines the size of what is left to be "induced," the independence of the two spending categories is called into question. Statistical testing of the type used in these studies presumes an independent variable with causative properties that is able to predict the movements of some dependent variable. If the "independent" variable is not really independent, the validity of the testing procedures is in serious doubt.

The way that the various factions defined and used money in their tests also reflects major differences in concepts and testing methods. Friedman and Meiselman chose a money stock for testing that includes all privately held commercial bank deposits and currency—those items properly qualified for double counting—and government cash balance holdings. They also maintained in their original study that the choice of *a* money stock within rather wide limits does not matter.[10]

Ando and Modigliani, however, observed that generation of the total money stock may involve both autonomous and induced elements. (In fact, Friedman and Meiselman had allowed for this possibility.) While the "high-powered" monetary nucleus of currency and bank reserves has a determining influence on the value of the total money stock, endogenous factors, such as the reserve ratio maintained by the banking system and the currency-deposit ratio maintained by the nonbank public, also affect the size of the total stock. After recognizing these qualifications, and in order to prevent such elements from polluting the autonomy of their conceptual money stock, Ando and Modigliani proposed a money stock consisting of the "maximum amount of money [currency and demand deposits] that *could* be created by the banking system on the basis of the reserves supplied by the money authority,...account being taken of reserve requirements and currency-holding habits."[11]

Their purpose in proposing this concept was to delete the induced effects of changes in income on the stock of money. But in so doing they created a Frankensteinian concept. As Friedman and Meiselman pointed out, to allow this definition of money—the amount that *could* have been generated—is to allow for an infinite quantity in the case, often occurring in foreign countries, that no legal reserve requirements are imposed on commercial bank deposit expansion. It also biases the actual money stock in the thirties, when commercial banks held double the minimum *legal* reserves for many years because of their jaundiced view of the central bank as a "lender of last resort."

---

[10]See the article at the end of this chapter for further discussion of this issue.

[11]Ando and Modigliani, p. 713. (Italics supplied.)

Ando and Modigliani's criticism of a stock of money induced by income may be well taken; but their cure is much worse than the disease and must be rejected. A better means of examining the data for independent monetary effects is to use annual first differences in the actual money supply, and to test their possible effects on annual first differences of some measure of income. The study by DePrano and Mayer and also the one by Hester made more use of this method than either of the other two.[12]

The conclusions of this three- or four-sided debate are hard to assess. Probably the principal conclusion is that nothing even provisionally agreed upon is conclusive. For example, no one disputes very much the high associations between money and total (private) spending. Yet much disagreement still exists over the channels through which money's influence is felt and over the direction in which the associations run.

Another gritty detail that still remains is the definition of autonomous expenditures. Friedman and Meiselman specified as one component of such expenditures the government *deficit* on income and product account, that is, the difference between what the federal government spends and what it receives in taxes. The other two factions argued that government expenditures are autonomous but that tax receipts are induced by income. They therefore include all government expenditures, not just the deficit. What is the answer here? Clearly, much of total tax receipts is induced by income. But much of what government decides to expend is also a "trend"—a carry-over from previously planned programs and appropriations. These expenditures would probably not be made if total income were to decline. The government deficit, however, is the kind of unforeseen "extra" expenditure that should give rise to the type of multiplier effects described in Keynesian theory. Either this net spending item *or* the annual first differences in gross government expenditures would seem to be the most independent and autonomous spending component to fit into the statistical mechanisms constructed here.

These arguments and remarks demonstrate the character of economic investigation and analysis as well as any single exposition could. The permutations and combinations of variables, both in the minds of economists and in the real world, allow only tentative conclusions. They open up more questions than they contribute in the way of answers to old questions and thus, paradoxically, make necessary an even greater volume of research.

---

[12]See, again, the articles at the end of this chapter and the one following.

Selected Bibliography

Andersen, Leonall C., and Jerry L. Jordan. "Monetary and Fiscal Actions: A Test of Their Relative Importance in Economic Stabilization." *Review.* Federal Reserve Bank of St. Louis (November 1968), pp. 11–24. Comments on the St. Louis position appear in the April and August 1969 issues of the *Review.*

Ando, Albert, and Franco Modigliani. "The Relative Stability of Velocity and the Investment Multiplier." *American Economic Review,* Vol. 55 (September 1965), pp. 693–728.

DePrano, Michael, and Thomas Mayer. "Tests of the Relative Importance of Autonomous Expenditures and Money." *American Economic Review,* Vol. 55 (September 1965), pp. 729–752.

Friedman, Milton, and David Meiselman. "The Relative Stability of Monetary Velocity and the Investment Multiplier in the United States, 1897–1958." Commission on Money and Credit, *Stabilization Policies.* Englewood Cliffs, N.J.: Prentice-Hall, 1963.

Keran, Michael W. "Monetary and Fiscal Influences on Economic Activity — The Historical Evidence," *Review,* Federal Reserve Bank of St. Louis (November 1969), pp. 5–24. Provides historical support of the Andersen-Jordan position.

The Stock of Money and
Investment in the United States, 1897–1966

William P. Gramm and Richard H. Timberlake, Jr.

Keynesian theory regards most of investment spending as an exogenous element in the total spending process and as a major determinant of total spending. The Friedman-Meiselman study found some evidence that autonomous expenditures, which include a large element of investment, are inspired by the stock of money. However, they did not treat this question at length or make a comprehensive analysis.

From *American Economic Review,* December 1969, pp. 991–996. Reprinted by permission.

The authors are, respectively, associate professor of economics, Texas A&M University and professor of finance, University of Georgia. They are indebted to the late David McC. Wright for suggesting this topic for investigation and to James Fortson for helpful comments on earlier drafts of this paper. They are also indebted to two graduate students, J. R. Conner and J. W. McFarland, for technical aid and leg work. From *American Economic Review,* Vol. 59, No. 5 (December 1969), pp. 991–996.

The following article attacks this question explicitly. The hypothesis is that changes in the stock of money determine changes in gross private domestic investment—a major component of all income and of autonomous expenditures. Results of the tests were positive and indicated that the stock of money has about the same effect on investment expenditures as it has on consumption expenditures. Various explanations of these results are offered, and some interest rate relationships are explored.

The last decade has seen an array of empirical studies for testing possible associations between the stock of money and relevant flow variables, such as consumption and income. These studies originated with the comparison by Milton Friedman and David Meiselman between the relative stability of monetary velocity and the autonomous expenditure multiplier; and they include the comments, criticisms, and further investigations the F-M study has provoked [1], [2], [4], [5], [6], [7], [8], [9].

For good reason, the original study by Friedman and Meiselman uses consumption rather than income as the dependent variable in estimating the relative stability of velocity and the multiplier [4, pp. 175–76]. While a persistently high relationship between the stock of money and consumption is found, the Quantity Theory of Money nonetheless hypothesizes more generally that the stock of money is a major factor in the determination of total money expenditures.[1] A brief supplementary test is included in the F-M study using income as the dependent variable. However, no explicit examination of gross private domestic investment as a dependent spending variable is undertaken. Net private domestic investment is included in the F-M definition of autonomous expenditures for testing the stability of the multiplier. Since consumption correlates better with the money stock than does total expenditure-income, Friedman and Meiselman conclude: "The correlation between money and autonomous expenditures is so low that adding autonomous expenditures to consumption in order to correlate their sum (income) with money approximates adding a random variable to a variable systematically related to M [4, p. 211]."[2]

In their criticism of the F-M study, DePrano and Mayer note that the problem involved in defining autonomous elements is complex because "even fixed private domestic investment might be endogenous" due to the acceleration principle [2, p. 732]. The time lags assumed in acceleration theory, however, bring DePrano and Mayer to agree with F-M that fixed private domestic investment must be regarded as autonomous.

---

[1]The Friedman-Meiselman analogy of "... the half miler being required to run the mile race," due to the use of consumption rather than income as the dependent variable in their analysis, is not necessarily valid [4, p. 176]. Since consumption is only a part of the total money expenditures to which the Quantity Theory applies, the miler in the F-M study is being asked to run a race of something less than a mile.

[2]However, in assessing possible routes for money in influencing spending, F-M state: "An initial increase in the stock of money will tend, *via* its impact on the demand for other assets, to produce an increase in money expenditures on all varieties of them and hence on both what is termed investment and what is termed consumption" [4, p. 220].

The purpose of the investigation made here is to test the effect of the money stock (the assumed independent variable) on gross private domestic investment, measured in both nominal and real terms. By analyzing investment as an induced and dependent variable, this study attempts to determine the impact of the stock of money on investment and to assess the realism of the possible acceleration effect of money acting through consumption and income on investment.

Changes in the stock of money, taken as the independent variable, may affect the dollar value of gross private domestic investment in three ways. First, an increase in the stock of money, *ceteris paribus*, tends initially to lower the market rate of interest. A lower interest rate may induce more investment spending because it allows investors to move out farther along their marginal efficiency of investment schedules. This effect may be designated as the interest-rate effect.

Second, a neutral increase in the stock of money tends to produce a real balance effect in the business sector. One of the channels by which businessmen may attempt to disinvest themselves of cash balances is by expenditures on investment goods. This possible reaction may be labeled the business sector real-balance effect.

Third, an increase in the stock of money, through the real-balance effect in the consumer sector, increases consumer spending. A change in consumer spending, given various production capacity constraints, may generate an inducement to further investment spending—the familiar acceleration effect.

At less than full employment, all of the resultant increases in investment almost certainly would include both nominal and real elements. At full employment, any real increase would have to be at the expense of real consumption (forced savings). If only nominal increases in investment were recorded, no utility would be gained in distinguishing the functional causes of investment from any other kind of spending. That is, the economy would simply experience a general price level effect.

To test for these possible effects, the raw data for narrow money (M_1), defined as the sum of currency and demand deposits outside the banks and government, for wide money M_2, defined as M_1 plus time deposits in commercial banks, and for gross private domestic investment I are serialized annually and first differences taken. The data are then correlated for the various time periods shown in Table 1, a categorization similar to the ones used in other studies of this type. Correlation tests are run for first differences on both nominal n and real values r, the latter being nominal values adjusted by a price index.

The results of the tests for first differences are shown in Table ·1 under r_{M_1I} and r_{M_2I}. The most striking feature of the nominal first difference correlation values recorded here is their close similarity to the first difference correlations for the stock of money against income [9]. Correlation coefficients in both cases are approximately .80 for the periods of the 1920s and 1930s. Again, during the 15-year period 1938–53, values obtained both for money against investment and for money against income are not significantly different from zero. This similarity substantiates the credibility gap in recorded spending during the war years. In the late 1950s and early 1960s, first difference coefficients in both cases show recovery toward previous highs with values between .60 and .66. Only in the earlier decades does any significant difference show up.

The reliability of this test is substantiated further by the contrasts of nominal n and real r correlations. When employment is continuously at a high level, real investment can increase at the same rate as money only if the rate of increase in money happens to correspond to the actual rate of investment or produces forced savings. Investment can increase rapidly, with concomitantly rapid increases in money, only when business depression has been pervasive. Under either of these circumstances, correlations for nominal and real values should be close together, and this effect is seen here during the 1930s and 1950s.

When the stock of money increases rapidly at a time of relatively full employment—exemplified in this study by the 1913–20 period[3]—increases in real investment being limited to the secular growth in resources cannot be expected to keep up the pace. However, nominal expenditures should increase due to the price-level effect. Under such conditions, therefore, a disparity between the nominal and real values could be expected. The test results confirm this expectation both for the 1908–21 period and for the 1913–20 period.[4]

The remarkable similarity of money's effects on investment spending and on total spending for so many years may be interpreted in the several ways hypothesized above. First, changes in money could effect changes in investment, which in turn might provoke changes in income through a multiplier. Second, changes in money might change consumption that in turn might effect changes in investment through an accelerator. Third, changes in money might prescribe both types of spending simultaneously. Fourth, measured investment spending and measured consumption spending may be in truth taxonomic identities drawn from the same homogenized population, in which case if money associates well with one it would also correlate well with the other. Certainly, much of what is included in consumer expenditures, such as most consumer durables, is technically investment spending. A similar case may be made for much that is measured as investment expenditure in gross private domestic investment, due to the interdependence between consumption spending and depreciation and inventory changes.

If income is to provoke an accelerator effect, or if investment is to generate a multiplier, consumption spending should correlate positively with investment but with contrasting leads and lags. If classical behavior is hypothesized, an

---

[3]The 1938–53 and 1939–48 periods would provide similar test cases if the data for constructing the tests were reliable. Because these periods very probably contain spurious data, nothing can be gleaned from them. They neither prove nor disprove anything.

[4]In the 1920–29 period real values for M_1 and M_2 are markedly different. This difference is the result of a $-.597$ first difference correlation between changes in real time deposits in commercial banks and changes in real investment.

Table 1. Simple Correlations of First Differences in Two Stocks of Money on First Differences of Investment and on the Interest Rate for Both Nominal and Real Values, Simple Correlations of First Differences of Other Spending and of the Rate of Interest on Investment in Nominal and Real Values, 1897–1966

	r_{M_1I}		r_{M_2I}		r_{M_1R}‡		r_{M_2R}		r_{SI}§		r_{RI}	
	n*	r†	n	r	n	r	n	r	n	r	n	r
1897–66	0.363	0.166	0.388	0.161	0.237	0.006	0.222	0.005	0.170	−0.247	0.327	0.265
1897–66 Excluding War Years	0.536	0.362	0.565	0.350	0.168	0.071	0.180	0.065	0.593	0.349	0.362	0.328
1897–08	0.559	0.398	0.467	0.265	0.665	0.538	0.644	0.510	−0.211	−0.300	0.654	0.629
1903–13	0.590	0.441	0.652	0.485	0.545	0.338	0.521	0.313	0.366	0.234	0.779	0.762
1908–21	0.673	0.097	0.720	0.032	0.429	−0.306	0.409	−0.598	0.434	−0.334	0.409	0.339
1913–20	0.401	0.153	0.686	0.307	0.541	−0.342	0.543	−0.561	−0.066	−0.565	0.216	0.066
1920–29	0.813	0.810	0.596	−0.003	0.273	−0.428	0.243	−0.677	0.332	−0.205	0.047	−0.030
1921–33	0.733	0.512	0.560	0.270	0.238	−0.198	0.197	−0.074	0.547	0.413	215	0.152
1929–39	0.866	0.722	0.731	0.491	0.318	0.274	0.245	0.172	0.809	0.709	0.452	0.374
1933–38	0.873	0.686	0.840	0.483	−0.076	0.010	−0.241	−0.267	0.710	0.385	0.040	0.015
1938–53	−0.021	−0.057	−0.101	−0.113	−0.225	−0.558	−0.207	−0.574	−0.554	−0.728	0.035	−0.120
1939–48	−0.225	−0.146	−0.277	−0.170	−0.617	−0.763	−0.569	−0.747	−0.863	−0.865	0.224	0.030
1948–57	0.445	0.382	0.085	0.063	0.314	−0.096	0.138	−0.377	0.025	−0.078	0.172	0.103
1958–66	0.615	0.593	0.418	0.338	0.682	0.634	0.302	0.217	0.533	0.572	0.823	0.799
1929–66	0.313	0.144	0.336	0.139	0.275	0.029	0.369	0.124	0.108	−0.285	0.443	0.340

Sources: Original data for the money supply M_1 to 1957 were taken from: U.S. BUREAU OF THE CENSUS, *Historical Statistics of the United States, Colonial Times to 1957*, Washington, 1960, Series X, p. 646. Data for the period 1958–66 were taken from current issues of the *Survey of Current Business* and the *Federal Reserve Bulletin*. Data for money stock M_2 to 1958 were taken from the Friedman-Meiselman study [3, pp. 259–60]. Data for the period 1959–66 were taken from current issues of the *Survey of Current Business*. Gross Private Domestic Investment (I) and *Gross National Product* from 1929–50 were taken from: A Supplement to the *Survey of Current Business, National Income, 1951 ed.*, Washington 1951, p. 150. Data for the period 1951–66 were obtained from current issues of the *Survey of Current Business* and the *Federal Reserve Bulletin*. The data for Gross Private Domestic Investment for 1897–1928 were constructed from data found in *A Study of Savings in the United States* by R. W. Goldsmith, Princeton 1955. Other spending S was computed by subtracting Gross Private Domestic Investment from Gross National Product. The interest rate R on 4–6 month prime commercial paper for the period 1897–1957 was taken from the *Historical Statistics of the United States, Colonial Times to 1957*, Washington 1960, p. 654. Data for the 1958–66 period were taken from current issues of the *Federal Reserve Bulletin*. The price deflator was the consumer price index (1954 = 100).

* Represents nominal values.
† Represents real values.
‡ R is the interest rate.
§ S is other spending.

increase in money should be expected to correlate with all nominal spending simultaneously. In real terms at full employment, changes in investment should correlate negatively with other spending (consumption).[5] (See Figure 1.)

In one of the tests conducted here, changes in investment were staged to lag changes in the money stock by one year in order to test for hypothesized accelerator or multiplier effects. In every period this operation made positive correlation values smaller and negative correlation values larger.[6] The same result was experienced in testing for the effect of money on income. These findings suggest a lag of less than a year in money's effect both on what is labeled consumption and on what is labeled investment.

The positive relationship between first differences in nominal money stocks and interest rates that shows up for all time periods except the 1930s and 1940s would seem to deny the generality of a Keynesian liquidity preference thesis. The positive values suggest that any presumed negative effect of changes in the quantity of money on interest rates is ephemeral, i.e., less than a year. As Friedman has pointed out in a recent paper, an increase in the stock of money increases spending and prices and shifts the liquidity preference schedule to the right. When the money stock continues to increase pervasively and at more than a nominal rate, reasonable expectations of further price level increases give additional and positive impetus to interest rates [3, pp. 6–8]. The results of the test here support this contention.

While simple correlations between other spending and investment are consistently high in all periods, the simple correlations of first differences, r_{SI}, are highly variable from period to period (see Table 1). In other tests run, in which investment was lagged one year behind other spending, simple correlations of first differences in most periods were lower than those given in Table 1. One possible explanation for the results in Table 1 is the accounting necessity for other real spending to decline when real investment increases. In real terms the acceleration principle can hold only with unemployed resources. A rise in other spending, given capacity constraints, may produce a stimulus for investment; but at static full employment, resources going to other spending units must decline for real investment to rise. The real, simple correlations of first differences for the periods 1929–39 and 1933–38 seem to exhibit the above mentioned properties though the results are by no means consistent or conclusive.

In general, the tests carried out by this investigation tend to deny the presence of a multiplier or accelerator. At the same time, they seem to substantiate the classical position that a change in the money stock affects all private spending without regard to the categories under which such spending may be defined.

---

[5]To associate investment with income is to introduce spurious correlation. Thus, investment is correlated with other spending S.

[6]The specific results of the lagged tests are not included here.

Figure 1. Possible Monetary Effects

1. Multiplier

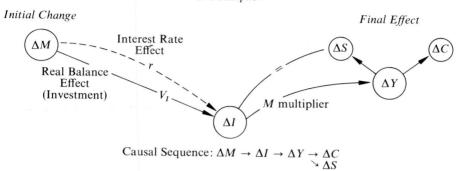

Causal Sequence: $\Delta M \rightarrow \Delta I \rightarrow \Delta Y \rightarrow \Delta C$
$\searrow \Delta S$

2. Accelerator

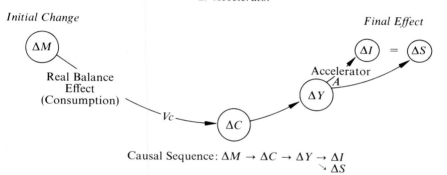

Causal Sequence: $\Delta M \rightarrow \Delta C \rightarrow \Delta Y \rightarrow \Delta I$
$\searrow \Delta S$

3a. Classical Monetary

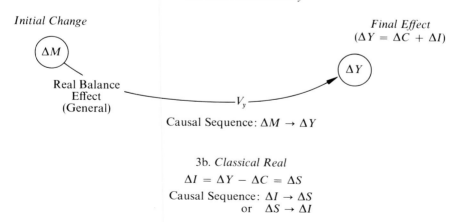

Causal Sequence: $\Delta M \rightarrow \Delta Y$

3b. Classical Real
$$\Delta I = \Delta Y - \Delta C = \Delta S$$
Causal Sequence: $\Delta I \rightarrow \Delta S$
or $\Delta S \rightarrow \Delta I$

References

1. A. Ando and F. Modigliani, "The Relative Stability of Monetary Velocity and the Investment Multiplier," *American Economic Review*, September 1965, *55*, 693–728.

2. M. DePrano and T. Mayer, "Tests of the Relative Importance of Autonomous Expenditures and Money," *American Economic Review*, September 1965, *55*, 729–52.

3. M. Friedman, "The Role of Monetary Policy," *American Economic Review*, March 1968, *58*, 1–17.

4. M. Friedman and D. Meiselman, "The Relative Stability of Monetary Velocity and the Investment Multiplier in The United States, 1897–1958," Commission on Money and Credit, *Stabilization Policies*, Englewood Cliffs, 1963.

5. M. Friedman and D. Meiselman, "Reply to Ando and Modigliani and to DePrano and Mayer," *American Economic Review*, September 1965, *55*, 753–85.

6. M. Friedman and D. Meiselman, "Reply to Donald Hester," *Review of Economics and Statistics*, December 1964, *46*, 369–76.

7. D. Hester, "Keynes and the Quantity Theory: A Comment on the Friedman-Meiselman CMC Paper," *Review of Economics and Statistics*, December 1964, *46*, 364–68.

8. R. H. Timberlake, Jr., "The Stock of Money and Money Substitutes," *Southern Economic Journal*, January 1964, *30*, 253–60.

9. R. H. Timberlake, Jr. and J. Fortson, "Time Deposits in the Definition of Money," *American Economic Review*, March 1967, *57*, 190–94.

27

Nonbank Financial Institutions and "the" Stock of Money

The Possibility of Money Substitutes

Throughout most of the preceding sections, "money" has been treated as if it were a stock of exchange units clearly distinct from the goods and services for which it is exchanged. In a blessedly simple world a sharp distinction between money and other things would be permissible; but in a real world, which includes stocks of nonmonetary financial assets, the line dividing money from other things may not be very well defined. The moneyness of money may merge into the moneyness of nonmoney assets with no benchmark for distinguishing one from the other. "The" stock of money then could not be defined; one person's intuition and judgment on what to include as "money" would be as good as any other person's.

If money had only the function of exchange, this question would not arise. In such a case, the stock of money would be all those things used as media of exchange and nothing else. But in fact money has the additional function of being a store of value. Since other assets can also serve as stores of value, a link is immediately available through which money and other assets may substitute for each other. The "other assets" suggestive of some monetary characteristics are: (1) time and savings deposits in (a) commercial banks and in (b) savings and mutual savings banks; (2) share capital of savings and loan associations; (3) government securities in the hands of the nonbank public, both (a) short-term and (b) long-term; (4) policy reserves of life insurance companies, insofar as these "reserves" correspond to cash surrender values; and (5) shares and deposits in credit unions.

All of these possibilities are fixed dollar, interest-bearing obligations of either nonbank financial institutions or the government and appear on the right side of the balance sheets of these institutions. They differ from currency and demand deposits, which are also fixed dollar liabilities, in that they bear interest and are not legal tender or convertible into legal tender on demand. However, they usually are convertible into legal tender after a very short interval. Their widespread use and their rapid growth during the last 50 or 75 years require that their possible functions as money substitutes be assessed (see Table 27.1). And fundamental to that growth is the growth of the institutions that generate them.

Time and Savings Deposits

The item most likely to bear some monetary characteristics is time (and saving) deposits. These deposits are generated by commercial banks and savings banks. Over time, commercial banks have been responsible for 60 to 75 percent of the total amount of these deposits in the United States. They face a reserve requirement on account of these deposits just as they do for demand deposits, but the percentage required is much lower—usually 3 to 6 percent. Since a time or savings deposit cannot be checked against (except trivially in the United States), they cannot be generated in the fashion of demand deposits, that is, by the loan- and discount-creating process of fractional reserve banking. Largely, they are created by primary deposits of cash for which the banks give a short-term interest-bearing obligation. They are more in the nature of supplies of reserves to banks on the basis of which the banks can create assets bearing higher interest rates. Nevertheless, to their owners (depositors) they may seem to have some monetary properties, especially if they can be readily converted into currency or demand deposits, as is usually the case.

Policy Reserves of Life Insurance Companies

The first life insurance company formed in the United States was the Corporation for Relief of Poor and Distressed Presbyterian Ministers and of the Poor and Distressed Widows and Children of Presbyterian Ministers. It began operations in 1759. Among its early activities was a loan of £5,000 to the Continental Congress in 1777. Still in operation as the Presbyterian Ministers' Fund, it is the oldest continued life insurance company in the world.

In terms of dollar volume of assets, life insurance companies are the largest financial intermediaries (see Table 27.2). By the end of 1967, the more than 1,700 legal reserve companies in the United States had passed the milestone

Table 27.1. Savings Deposits in Selected Financial Institutions, 1925–1970
(billions of dollars)

Year-End	Savings Associa- tions*	Mutual Savings Banks†	Commercial Banks‡	Credit Unions§	Postal Savings‖	Total
1925	3.8	7.2	16.3	¶	0.1	27.4
1926	4.4	7.7	17.2	¶	0.1	29.4
1927	5.0	8.3	18.7	¶	0.1	32.1
1928	5.8	8.8	19.3	¶	0.2	34.1
1929	6.2	8.8	19.2	¶	0.2	34.4
1930	6.3	9.4	18.6	¶	0.2	34.5
1931	5.9	10.0	16.0	¶	0.6	32.5
1932	5.3	9.9	12.1	¶	0.9	28.2
1933	4.8	9.5	11.0	¶	1.2	26.5
1934	4.5	9.7	12.0	¶	1.2	27.4
1935	4.3	9.9	12.9	¶	1.2	28.3
1936	4.2	10.1	13.7	0.1	1.3	29.4
1937	4.1	10.2	14.4	0.1	1.3	31.1
1938	4.1	10.3	14.4	0.1	1.3	30.2
1939	4.1	10.5	14.9	0.2	1.3	31.0
1940	4.3	10.7	15.4	0.2	1.3	31.9
1941	4.7	10.5	15.5	0.3	1.3	32.3
1942	4.9	10.7	16.1	0.3	1.4	33.4
1943	5.5	11.7	19.0	0.3	1.8	38.3
1944	6.3	13.4	23.9	0.3	2.3	46.2
1945	7.4	15.3	29.9	0.4	2.9	55.9
1946	8.5	16.8	33.4	0.4	3.3	62.4
1947	9.8	17.8	34.4	0.5	3.4	65.9
1948	11.0	18.4	34.7	0.6	3.3	68.0
1949	12.5	19.3	34.8	0.7	3.2	70.5
1950	14.0	20.0	34.9	0.9	2.9	72.7
1951	16.1	20.9	36.3	1.1	2.7	77.1
1952	19.2	22.6	39.0	1.4	2.5	84.7
1953	22.8	24.4	41.7	1.7	2.4	93.0
1954	27.3	26.4	44.4	2.0	2.1	102.2
1955	32.1	28.2	46.0	2.4	1.9	110.6
1956	37.1	30.0	48.2	2.9	1.6	119.8
1957	41.9	31.7	53.4	3.4	1.3	131.7
1958	48.0	34.0	59.6	3.9	1.1	146.6
1959	54.6	35.0	62.7	4.4	0.9	157.6
1960	62.1	36.3	66.8	5.0	0.8	171.0
1961	70.9	38.3	76.7	5.6	0.7	192.2
1962	80.2	41.3	91.0	6.3	0.5	219.3
1963	91.3	44.6	102.9	7.2	0.5	246.5
1964	101.9	48.8	116.6	8.2	0.4	275.9
1965	110.4	52.4	134.2	9.4	0.3	306.7
1966	114.0	55.0	146.3	10.1	0.1	325.5
1967	124.5	60.1	167.6	11.2	¶	363.4
1968	131.6	64.5	184.9	12.3	—	393.3
1969	135.7	67.1	181.4	13.6	—	397.8
**1970	146.7	71.5	216.4	15.3	—	449.9

Source: *Savings and Loan Fact Book, 1971* (Chicago: United States Savings and Loan League, 1971), p. 15.
* All types of savings.
† Regular and special savings accounts.
‡ Time and savings deposits of individuals, partnerships, and corporations.
§ Shares and members' deposits.
‖ Outstanding principal and accrued interest on certificates of deposit.
¶ Less than $50 million.
** Preliminary.

of $1 trillion worth of life insurance in force. The premiums paid to these companies exceed the cost of benefit payments during the early years of a policy. The difference is used to build "policy reserves," which may be invested until needed for benefit payments. Thus, all life insurance policies carry some element of saving in them. Endowment policies with pre-death benefits provide the most savings, and term policies include the least (almost none).[1]

Table 27.2. Total Assets of Selected Financial Intermediaries
at Year-End in Selected Years, 1945–1970
(billions of dollars)

Financial Intermediary	1945	1955	1960	1965	1970
Commercial banks	160.3	210.7	257.6	377.3	570.6
Life insurance companies	44.8	90.4	119.6	158.9	206.2
Savings and loan associations	8.7	37.7	71.5	129.6	176.6
Mutual savings banks	17.0	31.3	40.6	58.2	79.0
Finance companies	3.8	17.3	25.0	41.6	60.3
Investment companies	1.3	7.8	17.0	35.2	47.6
Credit unions	0.4	2.7	5.7	10.6	17.4
Noninsured pension funds	1.8	17.6	36.8	70.2	105.9
State and local pension funds	2.5	10.6	19.7	33.5	56.7
Total	240.6	426.1	593.5	915.1	1,320.3

Source: *Savings and Loan Fact Book, 1971* (Chicago: United States Savings and Loan League, 1971), p. 53.

Life insurance company liquidity needs are relatively predictable. While an individual policy holder may not know when he may cause a "withdrawal," mortality tables provide life insurance companies with accurate projections of cash outflows. Stability of income and certainty of return on investments are, however, important to the companies. For this reason mortgages and bonds account for about 40 percent of their assets.

The possible moneyness of life insurance policies to the insured person is in the cash surrender value (CSV) of his policy. When a $10,000 policy is first started, it has almost no "saving" included in its benefits. It promises to pay the beneficiary $10,000 upon the death of the insured. The premiums continuously paid by the insured, however, are more than enough to cover the probability of his death at any given age. These excess payments constitute an increasing cash surrender value on the policy. The insurance company invests this income, usually in "safe" long-term securities, and also pays nominal

---

[1]Term insurance is "pure" insurance. The premiums pay for the actuarial risk of guaranteeing a specified income to the beneficiary in the event of the insured's death.

interest on this amount to the insured. Thus, after ten years, the policy may insure the life (really the *income*) of the insured for $10,000 and also include $1,000 of CSV. The insured may "cash in" his policy and get his $1,000 in the form of cash on very short notice; or he may "borrow" a large fraction of his own cash, say $900, and pay it back over time with interest. This action would also lower the death benefits to $9,100 until the "loan" was repaid.

These features make an insurance company look something like a bank, while the CSV may have the appearance of a time deposit. People are generally loathe, however, "to tamper" with their insurance, and frequently will borrow from an ordinary commercial bank at 12 percent before they borrow against their CSV at 4 to 6 percent! Nonetheless, policy reserves as a proxy for CSV must be examined for their possible monetary effects.

Savings and Loan Association Shares

Savings and loan associations in the United States had a rather inauspicious beginning. On January 3, 1831, a group of citizens gathered at Thomas Sidebotham's inn at Frankfort, Pennsylvania, to form the first cooperative home-financing society in America—the Oxford Provident Building Association of Philadelphia County. Most such early savings and loan associations were formed by individuals wishing to buy houses. By pooling their resources the individuals as a group were able to lend the amount necessary for some one of their members to purchase a house. The associations often continued only until all of the members had purchased houses, and were then dissolved. The present-day savings and loan associations have added nonborrowing members as a source of funds, but the main purpose and many of the attributes of the old associations continue. Today savings and loan associations are the major suppliers of home mortgages.

Savings and loan associations are financed by "shareholders," not by depositors. The shareholders are owners and not creditors. They take part in the associations' meetings, if they wish, and vote for its management. The shares owned by the shareholders are, however, fixed dollar claims similar to time deposits and may be converted into cash. (Demand deposits are neither accepted nor allowed.)

Since conversion of shares into cash is not common, liquidity needs of the associations are minimal, and they can purchase assets of low liquidity. Home mortgages comprise the bulk of their portfolio—accounting for 85 percent of the value of associations' assets. Of course, these assets also satisfy the original home ownership purpose of these institutions.

Presently, there are approximately 6,000 savings and loan associations in the United States. A dual system for their chartering and regulation exists just as it does for commercial banks. About two thirds of the associations in the country are state-chartered; the rest have federal charters. In 1932, the federal government created the Federal Home Loan Bank System. This organization is similar in concept and in administrative functions to the Federal Reserve System. It consists of a Federal Home Loan Bank Board located in Washington, an Advisory Council, twelve regional Banks, and the association members. The Federal Home Loan Bank Board both charters and regulates federal associations. While membership in the Home Loan Bank System is required of federally chartered associations, most states allow their associations the choice of joining the system or not. The Federal Savings and Loan Insurance Corporation (FSLIC), counterpart of the FDIC, is governed by the Home Loan Bank Board and provides insurance for all federally chartered associations and those state-chartered associations that qualify. Almost three fourths of the savings and loan associations in the country are insured. The noninsured associations are usually the smaller, less active ones.

Since World War II, the savings and loan industry has experienced tremendous growth due to the postwar demand for mortgage loans and housing. The strong demand for mortgage loans has resulted in interest returns high enough to allow savings and loan associations to pay competitive dividend rates to shareholders. In return, these attractive rates draw funds from other forms of saving and investment into the savings and loan industry. The rapidly rising interest rates of the late 1960s, however, caused the industry some problems. To remain competitive in attracting funds, savings and loan associations were forced to raise their dividend rate to shareholders more rapidly than the average yields on their loan portfolios could be increased. Their profits suffered correspondingly. Commercial banks, with shorter-term assets, were able to "roll over" their portfolios more quickly to take advantage of rising rates. The spread between the yield to shareholders in savings and loan associations and the rate of return now paid on time accounts in commercial banks has narrowed considerably. At the same time, both associations and banks have been experiencing difficulty in attracting new savings as market rates of interest have climbed above the rates they legally are allowed to pay. Investors and savers have come to deal directly with the capital and money markets. This process of bypassing financial intermediaries in order to save or invest directly is called "disintermediation." It was experienced in 1966 during the period of credit stringency and again in 1969. By way of contrast, a prolonged period of falling interest rates, should one occur, would prove to be lucrative to the savings and loan industry because the average yield on its long-term portfolio then would become high relative to dividend rates being paid.

Mutual Savings Bank Deposits

Mutual savings banks were founded in the early 1800s in order to encourage the wage earner to save in a safe institution. Commercial banks of the period did not cater to small accounts, nor did small savers especially trust commercial banks. As industrialization developed in the United States, two savings banks were opened: The Provident Institution for Savings in Boston was chartered in 1816, and the Philadelphia Savings Fund Society opened its doors that same year—although it did not receive a charter until later.

Savings banks were usually founded by altruistic and wealthy men who wished to see the working class better itself through thrift. Even though the depositors in savings banks were the legal owners, the founders retained control through a self-perpetuating board responsible for selecting the bank's managers. The low liquidity needs of the banks, because of the large number of small deposits all of a time nature (no demand deposits), encouraged mutual savings banks to invest mainly in home mortgages. Although the managerial control of the two institutions differ somewhat, savings and loan associations and mutual savings banks closely resemble each other today in asset and liability structure.

About 900 mutual savings banks are currently in operation in the United States, including the two founded in 1816. These banks are located primarily in the New England area, where industrialization was first felt and where thrift was first hallowed as a heavenly virtue. All are state-chartered institutions; two thirds have obtained deposit insurance, FDIC or other; and a few are members of the Federal Home Loan Bank System. Their assets are in excess of $79 billion.

Finance Companies

Two types of finance companies can be identified. They are distinguishable by their lending methods, though the differences in methods are narrowing. Sales finance companies primarily lend by purchasing consumer installment paper from retailers, while consumer finance companies—better known as small loan companies—primarily lend directly to consumers. These companies finance themselves by issuing debt to other financial institutions and nonfinancial corporations. (The placement of commercial paper by sales finance companies as a means of raising money was discussed in Chapter 12.) Both sales and consumer finance companies also borrow money from commercial banks and issue long-term debt. Sales finance companies account for about 30 percent of the total installment credit in the United States (see Table 27.3). They mainly purchase automobile paper.

Consumer finance companies are active in making small loans to low-income individuals who are often unable to borrow from other sources. Most states have special small loan laws to govern these operations. Loans of this sort are usually exempt from normal state usury laws; interest rates on them may be as high as 48 percent per year. The justification given for such interest rates is the high risk associated with these types of loans and the relatively high bookkeeping costs involved in administering them. Government officials see small

Table 27.3. Installment Credit in Selected Years, 1962–1970
(billions of dollars)

End of Period	Total	Commer-cial Banks	Sales Finance Companies	Credit Unions	Con-sumer Finance	Other	Auto-mobile Dealers	Other Retail Outlets
			Financial Institutions				**Retail Outlets**	
1962	48.7	19.0	11.4	4.9	4.8	1.8	0.3	6.5
1964	62.7	25.1	13.6	6.3	6.5	2.4	0.3	8.5
1966	77.5	31.3	16.7	8.2	7.7	2.8	0.3	10.5
1968	89.9	37.0	18.2	10.2	8.9	3.2	0.3	12.1
1970	101.2	41.9	31.1*	12.5	*	*	0.3	13.8

* Finance companies consist of those institutions formerly classified as sales finance, consumer finance, and other finance companies. Miscellaneous lenders include savings and loan associations and mutual savings banks.

loan companies charging 40 to 50 percent interest rates as preferable to the loan shark (illegal lender), who often operates in states that do not have small loan laws. Interest rates in the thousands of percent are not uncommon in loan sharking operations, and brutal methods of collection are often imposed on the tardy.

Investment Companies

Investment companies provide a means for the investor of small means to obtain a wide diversification in stock market equities. Open-end (mutual fund) investment companies issue unlimited amounts of their common stock to interested purchasers at asset value (the value of total net assets divided by the number of shares outstanding) plus a "load" or sales commission of 8 or 9 percent. Mutual funds use the money so acquired to purchase the common stock of companies in different industries, and the mutual fund shareholder thus has a cross-sectional slice of ownership in these companies. Shares can be redeemed at any time for approximately net asset value. At the end of 1970, open-end investment company assets were about $48 billion, down from $53 billion two years earlier due to the decline in common stock values.

Closed-end investment companies issue a fixed number of shares. Persons wishing to buy or sell them must do so on the open market rather than deal directly with the company. While investment companies have been in existence since the early 1800s, their major growth has come since 1940. Closed-end companies once accounted for the majority of investment company activity, but mutual funds now control most of the industry's assets.

Government Securities

All the institutions so far analyzed have "balanced" balance sheets: They buy fixed dollar assets of longer term and higher yield, and they sell fixed dollar obligations in equal amounts of shorter term and lower yield. Even fractional reserve commercial banks can be thought of in this light. However, they are better regarded as fundamentally different from other financial institutions because they create demand deposits, which are undeniably money by anyone's definition.

The obligations of the federal government are in another category. These obligations are also fixed dollar claims, and they can be long- or short-term. However, the government's balance sheet need not be, and almost never is, balanced: It has outstanding much more in dollar obligations than it has in tangible assets to cover them. It is a net debtor to the private sector of the economy. It makes up for its balance sheet deficit by an intangible asset—the power to tax. This power is exclusive; only governments have it.

The *total* outstanding volume of government debt, however, is not net to the private sector. In the first place, many government agencies, such as the Social Security Administration, hold government securities. Second, many billions of government securities are held by commercial banks as assets and are collateral for the demand deposits the banks have created.[2] This amount of the debt, therefore, has been monetized and is not a net asset to the private economy. The amount owned by financial institutions has likewise been financed by issues of their obligations; so if their liabilities are to be considered a quasi-money, the government securities they hold as assets cannot also be counted. By the process of elimination, only government securities in the hands of individuals and nonfinancial corporations can be said to contribute to money-ness without actually having been monetized or converted into hypothetical money. Currently, the amount so held is on the order of $164 billion—66 percent of the total public debt outstanding.

The Theory of Money Substitutes

One way to approach the question of what to include in the stock of money is to admit as money those things that are used ubiquitously in exchange and that are accepted unequivocally by universal consensus. Other assets can then be included on the basis of some measurable criterion (other than subjective judgment). To begin with, everyone agrees that hand-to-hand currency—legal tender paper money and coin—must be included in any hypothetical stock of

---

[2]See Chapter 29 for a discussion of the federal debt and its management.

money.[3] Everyone also agrees that demand deposits subject to check (excluding interbank deposits) must also be included. At any instant of time, explicit amounts of these two moneys exist, and their sum can be called "the stock of money narrowly defined," or simply "narrow money."

But at this point consensus breaks down. In addition to (1) currency and demand deposits, the list of additional items that have been suggested by the presence of nonbank financial intermediaries discussed above includes the following: (2) time deposits in commercial banks, (3) all time deposits, and, finally, (4) all the items in (3) plus share capital of savings and loan associations, plus policy reserves of life insurance companies, plus the stock of government securities in the hands of the nonbank public. Economists who favor this last and extreme view of "money" deny that any useful line can be drawn separating money from other financial assets. Monetary theory, they argue, must be replaced by a general theory of financial assets. Any group of assets called "money" is hopelessly enmeshed in real life with other near-money assets. Even provisional segregation of anything called money, according to this group, is both useless and impossible.[4] Others of a more "fundamentalist" faith think that the items included in the narrow stock of money are unique and that other forces explain the demand for so-called near moneys. Since both views are logical, only empirical testing can bring forth any objective answers.

The question at issue can be stated in the following manner: Assuming the stock of money narrowly defined remains constant, do changes in the stocks of nonfinancial assets in the hands of the general public influence the spending rate of the narrowly defined stock of money in the same direction? That is, do changes in nonmoney assets positively change the velocity of money narrowly defined? One way to get an empirical answer to this question is to define money stocks that are more and more inclusive of the alleged near moneys and see which of them (if any) best predicts aggregate money spending over time. If this method is pragmatic, it is also objective. It presumes axiomatically that money causes spending. If spending is seen to be determined by nonmonetary forces, then obviously this kind of test is not valid. Since the evidence so far is that money does influence spending markedly, this method must be accepted until further refinements or revisions make it obsolete.

Prior to arranging financial assets and money into test-worthy time series, some preliminary principles must be heeded. First, the stock of any assumed near money must be a relevant fraction of the total stock of money before any significant effect on spending can be experienced. If the candidate for the role of money substitute meets this qualification, its monetary influence must be recorded by its ability to substitute for narrow money as a store of value. (If the candidate were also used as an exchange device, it would be money proper

---

[3]The stock of currency must exclude currency held by banks, since the currency in banks is a reserve base for another kind of money, demand deposits. To include currency in banks *and* demand deposits of banks obviously would be double counting.

[4]The best-known source for this argument is John Gurley and Edward Shaw, *Money in a Theory of Finance* (Washington, D.C.: The Brookings Institution, 1960).

and the whole issue would be nonexistent.) When the stock of the hypothesized money substitute is increased, narrow money is "released" to serve as a medium of exchange. The stock of narrow money itself being numerically unchanged, the average velocity of each unit would have to increase. On the other side of the equation (of exchange) prices would rise, or output of real product would increase, or both would occur. The degree of moneyness — the "monetary specific gravity"—possessed by the financial asset serving as a money substitute would be given by its effect on the velocity of narrowly defined money.

Interest (or yield) rates are another factor that would have an influence on monetary substitution. All of the assets classified as potential money substitutes realize nominal returns. They may be held, then, because they yield income, or because they are good stores of value, or for a combination of these two reasons. If they are held because they yield income, they are, more logically, similar to common stocks and commodities for which money is exchanged. Thus, the higher the yield rates these assets enjoy, the less likely they are to be treated as money, and the fewer the monetary characteristics they are likely to exhibit. By the same token, if they are treated less as money, they are treated more as commodities when their yields are high. Since many of the financial assets show much variation in their yield rates over time, the possibility must be faced that the total degree of moneyness they impart to the economy may vary inversely with their yield rates.

Unfortunately, many conceptual or theoretical difficulties and many empirical problems in measurement must be overcome before the interest rate effects of nonmoney assets on the demand for money can be estimated accurately. In the first place, a method that sees some quantity of money demanded as an inverse function of the "price" (interest rate) on some other asset is neither the most direct nor the most satisfactory way of dealing with hypothesized relationships. It is tricky to set up the function, and it is difficult to evaluate the results.

Another difficulty is the determination of "high" and "low" interest rates. The nominal value of an interest rate is not necessarily its real value any more than a nominal price is a real price. Nominal interest rates must be adjusted for expected rates of change of prices, for example, before they can be considered real. For these reasons, only the nominal *quantities* of alleged money substitutes are used empirically below in testing the money substitute hypothesis. A substantial amount of current professional research is still being applied to this issue. (See the bibliography at the end of this chapter.)

Empirical Tests of the Money Substitute Hypothesis

In order for the stocks of any hypothetical money substitute to have become a significant fraction of the total stock of money, the growth *rate* of the substi-

Table 27.4. Various Stocks of Money and Financial Assets, 1897–1960
(all values in billions of dollars and as near June 30 as possible)

Year	Income Per Year	Currency plus Demand Deposits (M_1)	Currency plus Demand Deposits plus Time Deposits in Commercial Banks (M_2)	All Time Deposits (Td)	Currency plus Demand Deposits plus All Time Deposits ($M_3 = M_1 + Td$)	Share Capital of Savings and Loan (L)	Policy Reserves of Life Insurance Companies (P)	Government Securities Held by Non-bank Investors (B)	($L + P + B$)	($M_4 = M_3 + L + P + B$)
1897	11.6	3.88	4.48	2.31	6.19		1.08	0.380	1.46	7.65
1898	12.9	4.58	5.14	2.40	6.98		1.16	0.383	1.54	8.52
1899	15.4	5.34	6.03	2.62	7.96		1.26	0.544	1.81	9.77
1900	15.5	5.75	6.38	3.02	8.77		1.38	0.499	1.88	10.7
1901	17.1	6.60	7.34	3.32	9.91		1.51	0.455	1.97	11.9
1902	19.4	7.15	8.01	3.57	10.7		1.66	0.420	2.08	12.8
1903	19.4	7.51	8.52	3.80	11.3		1.83	0.383	2.21	13.5
1904	19.2	7.82	8.98	4.05	11.9		2.01	0.334	2.34	14.2
1905	22.7	8.70	10.1	4.46	13.2		2.20	0.328	2.53	15.7
1906	24.7	9.26	10.9	4.77	14.0		2.38	0.283	2.67	16.7
1907	25.1	9.57	11.6	5.35	14.9		2.56	0.215	2.78	17.7
1908	23.7	9.10	11.2	5.49	14.6		2.74	0.164	2.90	17.5
1909	27.3	9.46	12.4	6.27	15.7		2.93	0.130	3.06	18.8
1910	29.4	9.98	13.0	6.94	16.9		3.13	0.138	3.27	20.2
1911	28.8	10.4	13.7	7.34	17.7		3.35	0.386	3.74	21.5
1912	32.7	10.9	14.7	7.89	18.8		3.58	0.382	3.97	22.8
1913	32.6	11.0	15.3	8.36	19.4		3.82	0.362	4.18	23.5
1914	32.7	11.6	15.9	8.35	20.0		4.05	0.139	4.19	24.2
1915	35.4	11.4	17.0	9.23	20.6		4.28	0.151	4.43	25.1
1916	44.6	13.9	20.2	10.3	24.2		4.55	0.150	4.70	28.9
1917	57.0	15.8	23.7	11.5	27.3		4.87	2.59	7.45	34.8

Year										
1918	65.4	18.1	26.0	11.7	29.9		5.22	8.35	13.6	43.4
1919	66.4	21.2	30.3	13.4	34.6		5.62	14.8	20.4	55.0
1920	73.1	23.7	34.2	15.8	39.6		6.08	18.9	25.0	64.5
1921	61.8	20.8	32.3	16.6	37.4		6.62	18.8	25.4	62.8
1922	64.7	21.4	33.2	17.4	38.8		7.18	16.7	23.9	62.7
1923	74.6	22.7	36.0	19.7	42.4		7.79	15.7	23.5	65.9
1924	76.7	23.1	38.0	21.3	44.3		8.54	14.6	23.1	67.4
1925	48.6	25.0	41.4	23.2	48.1		9.43	13.6	23.0	71.1
1926	37.7	25.6	43.0	24.8	50.3		10.5	12.8	23.3	73.7
1927	83.5	25.5	44.1	26.5	52.0		11.7	11.8	23.4	75.4
1928	82.8	25.9	45.8	28.5	54.4		12.9	10.4	23.3	77.7
1929	91.8	26.2	45.9	28.6	54.8	5.99	14.3	10.0	30.3	85.1
1930	77.3	25.1	44.9	29.0	54.1	6.27	15.6	8.87	30.7	84.8
1931	62.7	23.5	41.7	29.0	52.4	6.11	16.8	8.77	31.7	84.1
1932	43.6	20.2	34.7	24.8	45.0	5.62	17.6	9.86	33.1	78.1
1933	40.0	19.2	30.7	21.7	40.8	5.04	18.0	11.3	34.3	75.1
1934	49.5	21.4	33.2	22.9	44.3	4.60	18.6	12.1	35.2	79.4
1935	57.6	25.2	38.2	23.9	49.1	4.36	19.7	13.1	37.1	86.2
1936	65.6	29.0	42.7	24.9	53.9	4.22	21.1	15.7	41.0	94.9
1937	72.7	30.7	45.0	25.9	56.6	4.14	22.5	17.4	44.1	101
1938	68.6	29.7	44.8	26.2	56.0	4.08	23.9	17.3	45.3	101
1939	73.3	33.4	48.5	26.8	60.2	4.10	25.2	18.2	47.5	108
1940	80.3	38.7	54.2	27.5	66.1	4.22	26.5	18.7	49.4	116
1941	94.6	45.5	61.5	27.9	73.4	4.50	28.1	20.6	53.1	127
1942	127	52.8	70.4	27.3	80.1	4.81	29.9	37.0	71.6	152
1943	141	71.9	89.2	30.3	102	5.22	31.9	61.4	98.5	201
1944	154	80.9	106	35.7	117	5.90	34.3	89.9	130	247
1945	160	94.2	126	44.3	138	6.84	37.1	111	155	294
1946	164	106	138	51.8	158	7.96	40.2	115	163	321
1947	182	108	144	55.7	164	9.15	43.3	114	167	331
1948	204	108	145	57.4	166	10.4	46.5	111	168	333
1949	201	107	145	58.5	166	11.7	49.8	112	174	339

Table 27.4 (continued). Income and Various Stocks of Money
and Financial Assets, 1952–1970
(billions of dollars)

Year	Income Per Year	Currency plus Demand Deposits (M_1)	Currency plus Demand Deposits plus Time Deposits in Commercial Banks (M_2)	All Time Deposits (Td)	Currency plus Demand Deposits plus All Time Deposits ($M_3 = M_1 + Td$)	Share Capital of Savings and Loan (L)	Policy Reserves of Life Insurance Companies (P)	Government Securities Held by Non-bank Investors (B)	($L+P+B$)	($M_4 = M_3 + L+P+B$)
1950	220	110	148	59.7	170	13.2	53.2	115	182	352
1951	241	115	153	60.0	174	15.1	56.8	113	185	359
1952	251	121	162	63.7	185	17.7	60.6	111	189	374
1953	262	124	168	68.3	193	21.0	64.6	114	199	392
1954	268	125	173	73.3	199	25.1	68.8	110	204	403
1955	289	131	180	77.1	208	29.7	73.1	113	216	424
1956	298	133	183	80.6	214	34.7	77.6	114	226	440
1957	319	134	188	85.7	219	39.5	81.9	112	233	452
1958	323	135	196	95.5	231	44.9	86.3	106	237	468
1959	352	141	206	101	242	51.3	91.3	117	260	468
1960	366	138	205	104	242	58.4	96.2	124	279	521

Sources: Data for Income and (M_2) were taken from the Friedman-Meiselman study (see Chapter 26). Other data were derived from *Historical Statistics of the United States, Colonial Times to 1957* (Washington, D.C.: Department of Commerce, 1960), Section X, and *Federal Reserve Bulletin*, December 1962, pp. 1662–1667, and May 1963, p. 739. Data for the early years of column 7 may be found in: Raymond W. Goldsmith, *A Study of Saving in the United States*, Vol. I (Princeton, N.J.: Princeton University Press, 1953), p. 441. These values are not included here because they are irrelevantly small. All the values given in columns 7 and 8 are interpolations of year-end data.

Year	Income* (Y)	Currency plus Demand Deposits (M₁)† ADF	Currency plus Demand Deposits plus Time Deposits in Commercial Banks (M₂) ADF	All Time Deposits (Td)† ADF	Currency plus Demand Deposits plus All Time Deposits ($M_3 = M_1 + Td$)† ADF	Share Capital of All Savings and Loan (L) (end of year)	Policy Reserves of Life Insurance Companies (P) (end of year)	Government Securities Held by Non-financial Private Investors in U.S. (B) (end of year)	(L + P + B) (end of year)	($M_4 = M_3 + L + P + B$) (ADF and end of year)
1952	268.1	125.2	164.9	61.32	186.5	19.14	62.58	85.1	166.8	353.3
1953	280.8	128.3	171.1	66.04	194.3	22.78	66.68	86.4	175.9	370.2
1954	285.0	130.3	177.2	71.22	201.5	27.33	70.90	82.9	181.1	382.6
1955	315.0	134.4	183.7	75.28	209.7	32.19	75.36	88.2	195.8	405.5
1956	333.1	136.0	186.8	78.87	214.9	37.15	79.74	84.6	201.5	416.4
1957	351.3	136.7	191.8	85.06	221.8	41.91	84.08	82.6	208.6	430.4
1958	349.8	138.4	201.2	94.09	232.5	47.98	88.60	81.8	218.4	450.9
1959	386.2	142.8	209.6	99.67	242.5	54.58	93.98	90.8	239.4	481.9
1960	400.0	140.9	210.0	103.62	244.5	62.14	98.47	84.9	245.5	490.0
1961	416.9	143.2	221.7	115.77	259.0	70.89	103.29	84.6	258.8	517.8
1962	438.1	146.2	237.3	131.46	277.7	80.24	108.38	84.7	273.3	551.0
1963	460.7	150.6	256.1	148.73	299.3	91.31	114.30	86.9	292.5	591.8
1964	495.2	156.4	275.8	166.93	323.3	101.89	120.70	88.0	310.6	633.9
1965	540.9	162.6	300.2	189.06	351.7	110.39	127.62	87.9	325.9	677.6
1966	587.7	169.8	323.8	208.15	378.0	114.00	134.71	89.6	338.3	716.3
1967	608.3	176.4	349.7	231.72	408.1	124.49	142.42	86.3	353.2	761.3
1968	662.3	187.6	379.7	255.25	442.9	131.62	150.31	89.9	371.8	814.7
1969	717.3	198.3	396.6	263.45	461.8	135.49	158.55	95.2	389.2	851.0
1970	752.4	210.0	418.4	277.88	487.9	NA‡	167.56	92.5	NA	NA

Sources: Board of Governors of the Federal Reserve System, *Federal Reserve Bulletin, 1952–1971*; Department of Commerce, *Survey of Current Business, 1952–1971*, and *Statistical Abstracts, 1952–1971*.

* Income in this column equals personal consumption expenditure plus gross private domestic investment.

† Averages of daily figures.

‡ NA = not available.

tute must have exceeded the growth *rate* of the narrow stock of money for some considerable period of time. This condition is necessary but not sufficient. For even if the asset has become significant in quantity, its character might still be nonmonetary. The tests for moneyness, then, ought to indicate not only how moneyish are the hypothesized money substitutes, but also how inclusive *the* stock of money can be. Any nonmoney assets that possess a high degree of moneyness must be included in *the* stock of money. And if no well-defined stock of money emerges, a more general category of "all financial assets" as a monetary quantum must be given serious consideration.

The four nonmonetary financial assets mentioned above—time deposits, savings and loan shares, policy reserves of life insurance, and government securities in the hands of the nonbank public—are usually considered to be of sufficient monetary importance to warrant investigation. Of these four items, only government securities are unmatched by corresponding offsetting private debt, and only the portion of these securities in the hands of the nonbank public has not been monetized. Possession of the securities might encourage the public to hold less of its other money. At the same time, the government can be thought of as an organization too big and too powerful to worry about its "debt." It may, therefore, hold on average no greater a cash balance than it would in the absence of outstanding debt.[5] The other three groups of assets considered are obligations of banks, savings and loan associations, and insurance companies. These institutions are privately owned and operated, and they face more or less competition in the markets in which they buy and sell. Their outstanding debts currently due must be provided for. Even so, the additional amounts of cash they feel obliged to hold may be trivial.

Assuming for the sake of argument, nonetheless, that the generation of nonmoney assets is not offset by the corresponding generation of liabilities, the first test is to compare the rates of growth in these assets with rates of growth of money and money income. Table 27.4 gives raw values for various stocks of money, financial assets, and annual money income (spending) for the years 1897–1960 and for the recent period 1952–1970. Table 27.5 then summarizes the average growth *rates* of several of these time series for a long period (1897–1960), for two half-periods (1897–1928) and (1929–1960), and for a recent period (1952–1968).

All the growth rates of the hypothesized substitutes are significantly greater than the growth rates of money and money income, but the rates for the substitutes show a marked decline from the first half-period to the second. The very rapid growth rates in the 1897–1928 period may simply indicate a "novelty" effect; the rates of growth in automobile sales and in many household durables undoubtedly showed similar values for this period.

---

[5]In general, this judgment is probably valid. The federal government, in spite of much political handwringing over the "size" and "burden" of the national debt, carries no great amount of cash balances, since it has the power to tax in order to raise revenue for interest payments. State governments are probably more apprehensive about their outstanding obligations.

Table 27.5. Compounded Growth Rates for Income, Money
(Currency Plus Demand Deposits), Time Deposits, Savings and
Loan Share Capital, and Policy Reserves of Life Insurance
Companies for the Periods Indicated*
(percent per year)

Item	Period			
	1897–1960	1897–1928	1929–1960	1952–1968
Money income	5.03	5.50	4.42	5.82
Narrow stock of money	5.83	6.53	5.33	2.59
Time deposits	6.23	8.75	4.11	5.37
Savings and loan share capital	—	—	7.38	9.32
Policy reserves of life insurance companies	7.38	8.62	6.15	5.63
Savings and loan shares plus policy reserves plus government securities†	6.91	9.66	7.18	5.13

* These rates are obtained by the formula $\log (1 + r) = (\log X_t - \log X_0)/n - 1$, where r is the rate of growth compounded (geometric mean), X_t is the terminal value in the series, X_0 is the initial value, and n is the number of years.
† Growth rates of government securities are not shown separately, but holdings by nonbank investors increased only 6 percent in the period 1952–1968.

The growth of financial assets can also be rationalized on other grounds. Policy reserves of life insurance companies increased in every year of the series, even during the depression years of the 1930s. Their growth can be viewed as a function of real income. That is, as people become wealthier over time, they can afford to buy more insurance. Savings and loan shares existed in only irrelevant amounts until after World War II. Their growth rate reflects the growth of the industry with which they are fundamentally associated, that is, residential construction and real estate. Tax laws that discriminate in favor of home ownership also may have had an effect here.

Rates of growth aside, the question still remains of whether alleged money substitutes have significantly altered total money spending. To answer this question, various money stocks are set up to predict changes in total money income. Table 27.4 includes four of the money stock candidates. M_1 is currency and demand deposits—the narrow stock of money; M_2 is M_1 plus time deposits in commercial banks—the stock used by Friedman and Meiselman; M_3 is M_1 plus all time and savings deposits (Td)—sometimes called the "wide" stock of money; M_4 is M_3 plus the sum of the three financial assets $(L + P + B)$.

These various stocks of "money" can be thought of as "good" or "bad" insofar as they are accurate predictors of money income. Their predictiveness, in turn, can be assessed by the degree to which they correlate with money income over the periods indicated. Table 27.6 shows these correlation coefficients for the raw data and for the first differences of the raw data.

The extremely high correlation coefficient values around 0.98 and 0.99 for the raw data of all the hypothetical money stocks against money income suggest that all of them might be good predictors. These values must be read, however, with this well-known adage in mind: Correlation does not imply causation. The coefficients also suggest, in the absence of any nonstatistical logic, that money income is a good predictor of the various money stocks![6]

A second feature of these values gives more concern. All of the correlations, including those for nonmoney assets against income, are so high that there is very little basis for choosing one over the others. Government securities (B) and share capital (L) could probably be rejected, but both time deposits (Td) and policy reserves (P) show reasonably high correlations with money income.

A more difficult and also a more valid test is for the different money stocks to predict *changes* in money income by the *changes* in their own values. Correlation values of annual first differences indicate how well they do this job. Clearly, such correlations may have much lower values than the correlations on the raw data because changes may be completely out of phase while trends of the raw data correlate almost perfectly. At the same time, first differences are much more likely to lead to valid statistical results, for the raw data readings in these time series are certainly not independent of each other from year to year. This contrast is seen in Table 27.6 for the first difference correlation between policy reserves (P) and money income during the period 1897–1928. The raw data return a correlation coefficient of 0.945, but the first difference coefficient is only 0.104. These values suggest that money income and life insurance purchases are related, but that changes in their values are very poorly related—perhaps due to a time lag between the generation of money income and its expenditures on life insurance, and perhaps due to other factors that induce people to buy this service.

In general, the first difference correlations of the various stocks of money against money income show up much better than do the differences of nonmonetary financial assets against money income. Time deposits, the most likely candidate of the nonmoney assets, by themselves do not show high correlation values, but their inclusion in other money stocks improves the performance of some of these stocks for some time periods. Changes in M_4—the stock that includes all the financial assets—seem to be no better at prediction than changes in M_3—the stock that includes only time deposits.

The most consistently good predictors of changes in money income are the M_1 and M_2 stocks. M_1 includes only currency and demand deposits. Its performance as a predictor tends to deny the utility of adding other financial assets to the narrow stock of money. The reasonably good showing of M_2 can be explained, first, by the fact that it is made up largely of M_1 and, second, by the

---

[6]The lag effects of money and money income, discussed in Chapter 26, would tend to deny this hypothesis.

Table 27.6. Correlation Coefficients for Selected Stocks of Money with Various Nonmoney Assets and Money Income and for Their First Differences, for the Time Periods 1897–1960, 1897–1928, 1929–1960, and 1952–1968

Item	1897–1960		1897–1928		1929–1960		1952–1968	
	Raw Data	First Differences	Raw Data	First Differences	Raw Data	First Differences	Raw Data	First Differences
M_1	0.977	0.494	0.933	0.707	0.964	0.399	0.989	0.797
M_2	0.987	0.573	0.990	0.645	0.982	0.501	0.990	0.688
M_3	0.988	0.511	0.986	0.620	0.986	0.421	0.992	0.694
M_4	0.986	0.557	0.982	0.570	0.983	0.473	0.997	0.737
Td	0.984	0.385	0.963	0.220	0.981	0.313	0.992	0.601
P	0.981	0.543	0.945	0.104	0.986	0.498	0.994	0.747
B	0.936	0.332	0.872	0.257	0.892	0.266	0.541	0.547
L	—	—	—	—	0.894	0.408	0.988	0.117
$(P + B + L)$	0.982	0.519	0.945	0.377	0.981	0.437	0.992	0.646

fact that the time deposits contained in M_2 are liabilities of the same banks that generate demand deposits.[7] This category of time deposits might well have some degree of moneyness because many people simultaneously hold time and demand deposits in the same commercial bank. When a depositor's demand deposit account becomes depleted, a telephone call is the only effort required to augment his demand deposit account with balances from his time deposit account.

The time and savings deposits in noncommercial banks cannot share this expediency. Not only are deposits probably made in these latter banks with little intention on the part of the depositors to withdraw them or to change their form, but withdrawal and subsequent redeposit in commercial banks involve much more administrative difficulty and cost than does the single transfer of an account in the same bank.

The last column in Table 27.6 presents results of the money substitute tests for the period after World War II (1952–1968). Not only do the data for this period get away from the highly suspect values for the war years, they allow for the possibility of recent change in the monetary properties alleged money substitutes might contain.

The results for this period indicate a resurgence in the reliability of M_1, the narrow stock of money, for predicting money income. M_1 had shown a higher value for the earlier era but a much lower value in the 1929–1960 period. Correlation tests of all the data for shorter (NBER) cycle periods (not presented here) show that M_1 is invariably a poor predictor when data for the years of World War II (1942–1948) are included, and that test results always improve considerably when data for the war years are excluded.[8]

In order for the traditional influence of money to be contradicted, the correlation values for first differences in M_4—the stock that includes all nonmonetary financial assets—would need to be greater than the values for any other stock. In fact, the values for changes in this stock are somewhat less in most periods than similar values for M_1, M_2, and M_3. This datum generally negates any "financial asset" hypothesis. The presence of exclusively financial assets in the total stock of monetary assets has no significant monetary effects.[9]

The hypothesis presented earlier indicated the means by which money "substitutes" might have influenced the spending properties of money through the displacement of store-of-value money. The other side of the coin is that the alleged substitutes are in fact held as capital assets yielding streams of future income, and that their purchases are made in competition with purchases of consumer goods and services. The "typical" consumer is interested

---

[7]At the end of 1970, all private time and savings deposits totaled $301 billion. Commercial banks were responsible for $229 billion, or about 76 percent of this total.

[8]See the article at the end of this chapter.

[9]The question of whether nonbank financial institutions have come to influence saving, investment, and consumption flows is distinct from the question of their possible monetary influences. Only the monetary question has been investigated here.

in providing for his future and may use up a portion of his current income by buying assets instead of buying everyday "necessities." An increase in the supply of such assets, other things being constant, would then lower security prices, raise interest rates, and lower commodity prices. In essence, the given stock of money would have to perform more overall work by transacting both ordinary commodities and services as well as financial assets.

Future research on such innovations as credit cards may call for a reassessment of money's uniqueness. Until more conclusive results are seen, however, the money used in markets for exchanging goods, services, and capital — currency and demand deposits — must be regarded as fundamentally distinct in function and behavior from other financial assets.

Selected Bibliography

Black, Robert P., and Doris E. Harless. *Nonbank Financial Institutions.* Richmond, Va.: Federal Reserve Bank of Richmond, 1968.

Friend, Irwin. *Study of the Savings and Loan Industry.* Washington, D.C.: U.S. Government Printing Office, 1970.

Goldsmith, Raymond W. *Financial Institutions.* New York: Random House, 1968.

Gurley, John, and Edward Shaw. *Money in a Theory of Finance.* Washington, D.C.: The Brookings Institution, 1960.

Latane, Henry. "Portfolio Balance — The Demands for Money, Bonds, and Stock." *Southern Economic Journal* (October 1962), pp. 71–76.

Laumas, Gurcharan. "The Degree of Moneyness of Savings Deposits." *American Economic Review,* Vol. 58, No. 3 (June 1968), pp. 501–503.

Lee, T. H. "Substitutability of Nonbank Intermediary Liabilities for Money: The Empirical Evidence." *Journal of Finance* (September 1966), pp. 441-457.

Mill, John Stuart. *Principles of Political Economy,* ed. W. J. Ashley. New York: David McKay Co., 1923. See Book III, Chapters 8 and 12 for a discussion of the theory of money substitutes.

Timberlake, Richard H., Jr. "The Stock of Money and Money Substitutes." *Southern Economic Journal* (January 1964), pp. 253–260. The test of substitutability of alleged substitutes.

Timberlake, Richard H., Jr., David Ott, and H. L. McCracken. "Correction and Comment." *Southern Economic Journal* (October 1964), pp. 149–152.

Yeager, Leland B. "Essential Properties of the Medium of Exchange." *Kyklos,* Vol. 21, No. 1 (1968), pp. 45–62.

Time Deposits in the Definition of Money

Richard H. Timberlake, Jr., and James Fortson

This selection is reprinted here for several reasons. First, it has a direct relationship with the subject matter of both this chapter and the previous chapter. Second, it carries some of the monetary testing further than was done by the papers in the symposium summarized in Chapter 26. Third, it focuses directly on time deposits, one of the items most frequently conjectured for inclusion in the stock of money. Finally, it makes use of a simple but useful method for testing monetary relationships.

The original study by Milton Friedman and David Meiselman [3][1] on the competitive abilities of a stock of money and autonomous expenditures to predict money income in the United States has been subjected recently to an intensive reappraisal and review [1] [2] [4]. The essence of the arguments seems to be that the accuracy of autonomous expenditures in predicting money income or consumption depends critically on the definition of autonomous expenditures chosen as a predictor. To a lesser extent this same issue can be raised about the various possible inclusions made in constructing "the" quantity of money used for testing purposes. Essentially, the question boils down to the "moneyish" influence time deposits exert on the "narrow" stock of money (currency and demand deposits).

The analysis presented below purports to develop a pragmatic answer to this question by allowing annual first differences in three diverse stocks of money to compete at predicting annual changes in money income. In order to check the results of the simple correlations, annual first differences in the narrow stock of money and annual first differences in all time deposits are then structured in the form of a multiple correlation to estimate annual changes in money income. The multiple correlation analysis also tests the data for a significant coefficient of moneyness in time deposits.

The raw data for currency, demand deposits, and time deposits may be used to construct an infinite number of money stocks. Each stock would include the

---

The authors are, respectively, professor of finance and director of operations research, University of Georgia. From *American Economic Review,* Vol. 57, No. 1 (March 1967), pp. 190–194.
[1]Hereafter, references to the work of these authors is abbreviated to "F-M".

first two of these items plus some percentage (weight) of all time deposits. F-M chose to include in their money stock the percentage of time deposits in commercial banks. Both expediency and logic recommended this choice. It is expedient because reliable estimates for this definitional stock of money can be obtained for a much longer time period than can be obtained for other money stocks;[2] and it is logical because of the distinct possibility that time deposits and demand deposits may be held as close substitutes for each other when they are claims against the same commercial bank. However, the case can also be made that the narrow stock of money is the only one that can be used for transactions and is, therefore, the only stock that influences spending.[3] Yet another and contrary view sees *all* time deposits generating liquidity in the monetary system, and thus making more efficacious the spendability of the narrow money stock. Each of these concepts is logical, and each has intuitive plausibility. The choice, however, must be made in terms of the empirical relevance shown by the various stocks in predicting money spending.[4]

The groundwork for this study required time series data of the three most relevant stocks of money: the narrow stock, M_1, the F-M stock, M_2, and the narrow stock plus all time deposits in commercial and savings banks, M_3. Data for money income from the spending side, Y, were taken from the original work by F-M and supplemented to 1965 using their definition. Annual first differences in the various money stocks were then correlated with annual first differences in money income for the reference cycle periods defined in the original F-M study.[5] The results of this series of tests are summarized in the first four columns of Table 1.

The correlation values shown here make possible some interesting inferences that are obscured when only the values for longer periods are computed. First, the correlation coefficients for all the money stocks in most of the subperiods covered show extremely high degrees of association between changes in money and changes in income. Second, while the F-M money stock, M_2, has the highest correlation value over the entire period, the narrow money stock, M_1, has higher values in more of the years than either M_2 or M_3. This seeming anomaly results from the inclusion of data from the war years (1942–46) in the tests, and the much poorer performance of M_1 in that period. Third, time deposits improve the correlation values only in the 1933–38 period.

The first inference — that any of the stocks of money influences spending — needs no interpretation beyond that given by F-M. Second, the irregular values

---

[2]Reliable data for *all* deposits in commercial banks are available back to 1875, but accurate breakdowns of these data into time and demand components are available only from 1914.

[3]This argument is tantamount to assigning irrelevant monetary influence to financial assets that are not transactive.

[4]This methodological postulate is the one adopted by F-M and not seriously challenged by anyone so far.

[5]First difference correlations for the whole period are mentioned in the original study and are computed in a later investigation by one of the authors of this paper (Timberlake) [7], but only for the whole period (1897–1960) and the two half-periods (1897–1929) and (1930–1960).

Table 1. Simple Correlations of First Differences in Three Conceptual Stocks of Money on First Differences in Nominal Money Income, the Percent of All Time and Savings Deposits in Commercial Banks, and Coefficients for a Multiple Regression of First Differences in Narrow Money and Time Deposits on First Differences in Nominal Money Income

Period Annually (1)	$r_{Y \cdot M_1}$ (narrow) (2)	$r_{Y \cdot M_2}$* (F-M) (3)	$r_{Y \cdot M_3}$ (all time) (4)	Per Cent All Time Deposits in Commercial Banks (average for period) (5)	b_1 (6)	b_2 (7)	b_2/b_1 (8)	$R_{Y \cdot M_1}$ (9)	$R_{Y \cdot M_1, T}$ (10)
1897–1908	†	0.890	0.820	†	†	†	†	†	†
1903–1913	†	0.788	0.813	†	†	†	†	†	†
1908–1921	†	0.766	0.726	†	†	†	†	†	†
1913–1920	0.796	0.786	0.727	63	3.086	−1.131	−0.3664	0.796	0.803
1920–1929	0.775	0.700	0.702	70	4.939	−1.035	−0.2096	0.775	0.779
1921–1933	0.883	0.801	0.772	68	6.922	−1.128	−0.1630	0.883	0.894
1929–1939	0.891	0.882	0.865	58	3.170	0.4467	0.1409	0.891	0.893
1933–1938	0.785	0.766	0.865	53	1.224	9.791	7.997	0.902‡	0.987
1938–1953	0.028	0.006	−0.145	63	0.3812	−1.620	−4.249	−0.419‡	0.471
1939–1948	−0.019	−0.009	−0.171	63	0.3681	−1.660	−4.510	−0.410‡	0.458
1948–1960	0.495	0.408	0.285	64	1.162	−0.4902	−0.3032	0.496	0.514
1953–1965	0.667	0.609	0.633	68	1.919	0.2903	0.1521	0.667	0.692
1929–1960	0.398	0.501	0.427	62	0.8945	−1.146	−1.281	0.401‡	0.504
1897–1960	†	0.573	0.517	54	1.004	0.7277	0.7251	†	0.518

Sources: Original data for M_4 and T to 1957 were taken from: *Historical Statistics of the United States, Colonial Times to 1957* (Washington, D.C.: U.S. Bureau of the Census, 1960), Series X, p. 646. Data for M_2 and Y to 1957 were taken from [3, pp. 259–60, Table II-B]. Data for the period 1953–1965 were obtained from current issues of the *Survey of Current Business* and the *Federal Reserve Bulletin*. Percentages in Column (5) were computed by the authors.

* Most of these values correspond to ones given by F-M in [5, p. 375, Table I].

† Separate estimates for demand and time deposits in commercial banks before 1913 are not reliable.

‡ These values are for the correlation coefficient of *time* deposits on income. Only the higher of the two values in a multiple correlation (without regard to sign) is registered by computer. To compare the simple coefficient of the narrow stock of money on income, see Column (2).

for the periods embracing the war years obviously result from biases in the raw data and confirm Donald Hester's observation on the original F-M study, viz: "Indeed it is remarkable that the monetary model failed to reflect these conditions [in the 1942–46 period] more vividly" [6, p. 367].[6] The raw data associations for the various money stocks and money income do not reflect wartime discrepancies because of the dominance of trend in the series. First difference correlations do emphasize the warpings of normal spending relationships by abstracting trend. Price controls, rationing, much higher taxes, and exhortations not to spend, dammed up money in peoples' pockets or caused "under the table" spending, the effects of which could not be measured. This alteration continued to some degree through most of the Korean War. The 1953–65 correlation values indicate a gradual return to more normal relationships.

Third, the better performance of M_3 during 1933–38 can be attributed to two "real" factors also not measurable cardinally. First, very low interest rates on time deposits discouraged their attractiveness as investments and encouraged their use as quasi-transaction balances. Probably more important, however, was the influence of the bank debacle in the early 1930s on deposit holdings. Demand deposits lost some of their moneyness due to the additional risk imputed to them by depositors after the monetary blood-letting of 1932–33. Time deposits seemed less risky to both banks and their depositors, so the deduction reasonably can be made that moneyness was lost by demand deposits and gained by time deposits.

To test these conclusions further, and also to test for a significant monetary coefficient of time deposits, a multiple regression analysis was conceived using first differences in the narrow stock of money, M_1, and in all time deposits, T, to predict changes in money income, Y.[7] The form of the testing equation is:

$$\Delta Y = a + b_1 \Delta M_1 + b_2 \Delta T \tag{1}$$

or

$$\Delta Y = a + b_1[\Delta M_1 + b_2/b_1 \Delta T] \tag{2}$$

If time deposits have some degree of moneyness, the ratio (b_2/b_1) should be greater than zero but less than one. A value of one for this fraction would imply that time deposits had moneyness equal in degree to the items in the narrow stock of money. A negative value for (b_2/b_1) implies that time deposits serve more in the nature of investments: that people actively reduce their transactions balances to "buy" time deposits.

---

[6]F-M's effort to include *all* data in their original study is commendable, but surely they leaned too far when they included monetary and income data for 1942–46.

[7]We are indebted to Milton Friedman for suggesting this method.

As can be seen from Table 1, the fraction (b_2/b_1) is between -1 and 0 except for the period 1933–38. In this period the ratio jumps up to 7.997! Furthermore, bringing time deposits into the picture as a multiple correlate to the narrow stock of money does not add significantly to the simple correlation coefficient in any of the periods except 1933–38. [See Columns (9) and (10).] But in this period first differences in time deposits are better predictors of changes in money income than are changes in the narrow money stock, and the multiple correlation coefficient becomes a whopping .987! Such dramatic results confirm the supposition that time deposits gained appreciably in moneyness due to the depreciation in confidence people had in demand deposits.

The value for (b_2/b_1) then becomes large and negative for the periods that include the war years, emphasizing the efforts of people to keep purchasing power they were enjoined from spending in a form that obtained some return. Only in the last 12 years does the ratio of (b_2/b_1) become a positive fraction of a magnitude that would give some credence to the theory of moneyness in time deposits, and even in this case the additional predictability gained from including time deposits in the analysis is insignificant (.667 to .692).

References

1. A. Ando and F. Modigliani, "The Relative Stability of Monetary Velocity and the Investment Multiplier," *American Economic Review*, September 1965, *55*, 693–728.

2. M. DePrano and T. Mayer, "Tests of the Relative Importance of Autonomous Expenditures and Money," *American Economic Review*, September 1965, *55*, 729–52.

3. M. Friedman and D. Meiselman, "The Relative Stability of Monetary Velocity and the Investment Multiplier in The United States, 1897–1958," Commission on Money and Credit, *Stabilization Policies*, Englewood Cliffs, 1963, pp. 165–268.

4. M. Friedman and D. Meiselman, "Reply to Ando and Modigliani and to DePrano and Mayer," *American Economic Review*, September 1965, *55*, 753–85.

5. M. Friedman and D. Meiselman, "Reply to Donald Hester," *Review of Economics and Statistics*, December 1964, *46*, 369–76.

6. D. Hester, "Keynes and the Quantity Theory: A Comment on the Friedman Meiselman CMC Paper," *Review of Economics and Statistics*, *46*, December 1964, 364–68.

7. R. Timberlake, Jr., "The Stock of Money and Money Substitutes," *Southern Economic Journal*, January 1964, *30*, 253–60.

28

Pressure Group Inflation

Individualism and the Group

One variation of the Equation of Exchange discussed in Chapter 3 was Theorem III, "the Political Theorem." According to the argument posited in that case, prices increase because some pressure group, organization, or economic behemoth pushes up the returns of the factors it represents. Groups commonly involved in such practice include labor unions, farm blocs, industrial combines, "small" businessmen, "institutes," "chambers," "associations," and the like, all interested in structuring big and little monopolies to further the cause of the organization that is "represented." Any such combine that is to succeed in raising its return above a competitive level can do so only because of a specialized and sheltered economic position, or because of a political alliance with the government that gives it some special marketing advantage. Basically, both of these alternatives amount to the same thing in that both include monopolistic power factors. To the extent that the thesis of group influence is valid, it vitiates any purely monetary theory of prices. Therefore, while it is a "nonmonetary" phenomenon, it must be examined here for its possible significance.

No one doubts that the intention of a special interest group is to further the cause of the group. The main questions are: (1) Can an interest group muster enough power to give reward to its efforts? (2) Can it realize gains that are not at the expense of other members of the group itself? (3) Can it make such gains permanent? (4) If the interest group is able to raise real returns to its participants, does it then have an inflationary effect on the general price level? If so, monetary theory must be supplemented with some sort of bargaining power theory.

Every individual, Adam Smith observed, "is led by an invisible hand to promote an end which was no part of his intention." His intention may be to establish a monopolistic or specialized position for himself in furtherance of his own self-interest. Since every other man is trying to do the same thing, the actions of others in a free society impede the attainment of a special position for anyone. An organized group forms in order to reduce the check and balance that unorganized individuals exert against one another. It also mobilizes the energies of its members to work in one direction.

Organizing people into a pattern also has its costs and also includes intrinsic checks and balances. As a formal organization develops, the discipline within it becomes progressively weaker; its internal strength deteriorates as the number of signatories increases. Yet the numbers of a restrictive group must include enough of the people concerned to be effective. In short, a combination must include enough people with similar interests to obtain results, but too many members make internal policing difficult. The costs come to outweigh the gains.

Given that a pressure group forms and undertakes collective action for its own benefit, the next question is whether all the individuals in it benefit or whether one part of the group gains at the expense of another. A labor union able to raise real wages of some of its members may find that it can do so only at the expense of unemployment to others. Or one union may raise real wages of all its members but at the expense of lower wages or unemployment in some other sector of the economy. A union member who becomes unemployed would realize that his own self-interest would be furthered by taking a lower wage than by getting no wage at all. And, needless to say, he would not belong to a union that offered him no returns for the cost of membership.

The time period of adjustment is also important for estimating economic gains from monopolistic organization. Demand elasticities, especially, can vary considerably over time. The first effect of, say, higher wage demands by a tightly knit monopolistic union might have to be conceded because of an inelastic demand for this labor in the relatively short run. Given time to adjust, however, firms find all sorts of ways to substitute for factors that are artificially expensive.

The Cost-Push Process

The returns to factors of production, according to traditional analysis, are results of productivity, and returns paid to these factors are costs to the firm.

This analysis assumes a constant price level. The theory of inflation, according to the quantity theory of money, states that when the stock of money is increased, people try to spend the new money on goods and services. Prices rise and business booms. Firms try to get more of the limited factors of production. Since the "pull" of increased demands cannot bring a larger quantity of factors into existence, prices of already existing factors are bid up. This analysis rests primarily on monetary determinants and the responsiveness of prices, wages, and incomes to increases in the money stock.

The cost-push theory of inflation alleges that owners of factors of production can be independently successful in raising their own returns. Costs can be "pushed" up beyond gains in productivity, and prices then must be increased to cover the higher costs. A more sophisticated cost-push theory argues that only some costs, and thus some prices, are pushed up. Cost-pushers may be "right-wing," "left-wing," or eclectic. The right-wingers see labor unions as the dominant pushers; the left-wingers see big corporations in a similar role; the eclectics see both, with assistance from big government. Many times, however, big government is seen as a force that shifts its weight from one side to the other in order to maintain a "balance of power."

Most prices according to the cost-push analysis, are fairly flexible upward but rather inflexible downward. Therefore, other prices in the economy cannot *compensate* downward for prices that are cost-pushed up. Obviously, if some prices hold steady while others rise, the general average (index) of prices must also rise. Since the stock of money does not increase by hypothesis, the rise in prices is not a result of monetary phenomena; and since the velocity of money has no reason to increase, total spending must remain constant. If total spending (MV) remains constant, a higher price level means that total transactions decline; that is, R (Gross National Product) is the dependent variable, and P (the price level) is the independent variable. The Equation of Exchange then takes the form

$$R = \frac{1}{P}[MV]_o$$

This form of the equation says that total product decreases by the same proportion as the increase in prices. A decline in total product necessarily implies that a corresponding decline has occurred in the use of resources, that is, in total employment. The question then arises: In which sector does the unemployment appear—in the cost-pushing area or in other industries where prices might have fallen but did not?

While this question cannot be answered on deductive grounds alone, the best judgment is that unemployment would occur in those areas of factor usage for which substitutes can be found most easily, that is, in the least specialized sectors, which are also the least organized trades. Here, too, the longer the time period of adjustment allowed to the firms in their efforts to substitute factors, the more elastic are the demands of the firms. The group initiating the cost-push would almost necessarily include factors whose services are specialized and inelastic in the short run. The unemployment pressure would then be shifted to other factors. On the other hand, the increase in returns to the cost-pushing organization relative to the (zero) increase received by other groups would provide more incentive for entrepreneurial attempts to substitute factors in the cost-pushed area. In the longer run, therefore, the cost-pushing organization may suffer more unemployment than groups that do not "push" for more than is merited by their productivity.

Most current opinion that leans toward cost-push analysis argues that the issue of unemployment is more or less academic — that unemployment would not get a chance to develop in either the cost-pushed industry or the economy generally because of the social anxiety over unemployment and the corresponding political commitments by both major political parties to the ideal of "full" employment. As a cost-pushed business recession tended to develop, pressure would be brought to bear by any administration on the money-supplying agency (central bank) to "rationalize" the new cost-price structure with an "adequate" volume of bank credit. The quantity of money would then be increased to correspond with the new level of prices so that total real product and employment would remain at some reasonably high level. If this alternative is factual, the Equation of Exchange takes the form

$$M = P\left[\frac{R}{V}\right]_o$$

The quantity of money is the dependent variable and prices are independent, a form of the equation just the reverse of the quantity theory! (See Chapter 3.) Stable prices in conjunction with some unemployment or slightly rising prices with full employment, the proponents of this thesis argue, are the choices contemporary industrial economies face.

The Counterargument

When prices of commodities or services, including wages, are raised someone must raise them; the decision must be arrived at; the operational aspects of the change must be carried out. And certainly the intention of every person who owns a factor of production, including his own knowledge and other capital, is to increase the returns from it. These trite observations apply whether returns are pushed up by cost increases, are inflated by creations of new money, or are realized rewards of productivity increments. The fact that groups organize in order to have a cost effect does not mean that they are successful in this effort. Labor unions, for example, have long enjoyed credit for getting wage increases that may have resulted anyway from the competitive unorganized bargaining process.[1] Unions, in fact, have had so much publicity as wage pushers that one sometimes wonders whether laborers received anything at all before the advent of labor organizations.

Money wages can be thought of as similar to money prices, that is, as functions of the quantity of money. Doubling the quantity of money, other things being equal, should on the average double all prices, including the price (wages) of labor, dividends to the stockholder, and residual income claims to the entrepreneur. Of course, not all these returns would change at the same rate or by the same amount, any more than commodity prices do. Wages fixed by contract would lag other wages, just as contractual prices lag changes in prices of ordinary goods and services.

Increases in productivity must also be paid for by competitive industry to the factors it hires. Over time, productivity of the various factors increases for all sorts of good reasons. A union that obtains better and better wage contracts for its members during a long-run time period again may not be getting anything that would not have been obtained by individual bargaining.

The only part of total returns that can be attributed to an economic pressure group proper is the gain that results from organizational monopolization (or monopsonization). The amount of such a rent, however, would seem to be small. An effective organization, such as a militant labor union, must *gain more and more power* if it is to continue getting year-by-year increases for its members beyond what they would have obtained anyway. Otherwise the formation of a monopolistic labor union would result in a once-and-for-all wage increase, but all subsequent raises would be due to increases in productivity or to some amount of inflation.

While a disciplined union may control its own wages and the number of people working under its auspices, it cannot affect significantly consumer demand for the goods or services its workers cooperate to bring to market.[2] A combine may be successful in monopolizing its market just as technical progress makes its product obsolescent. Union organization in the coal industry is a good example.

A closely related evasion of monopoly is the substitution of other factors over time for the factor monopolized. However, an industry that presses forward with labor-saving devices to become capital intensive in opposition

---

[1]The CIO, for example, organized during the upswing of business in the late 1930s and, except for 1938 and 1949, has operated in a climate of rising prices during its whole existence.

[2]During an auto workers' strike shortly after the end of World War II, Henry Kaiser reportedly granted the wage increase decided upon by an arbitration board because he felt that "his workers were also his best customers." This rather (too) liberal statement may have had a grain of truth to it. In view of the fate of the Kaiser car, his workers may have been his *only* customers.

to a strong union may very well pay higher and higher wage *rates*. The labor that is marginally displaced by machinery is almost always the unspecialized "pick-and-shovel" type. If 50 pick-and-shovel workers are replaced by a power shovel, the pick-and-shovel workers (temporarily) lose their jobs. They swell the supply of pick-and-shovel workers generally available, thus holding down wage rates in that occupation. Meanwhile, the wages of power shovel operators are enhanced because the demand for their services has increased, and the techniques and skills a laborer must learn to operate the power shovel involve real costs on his part. The very fact that this evolution has occurred argues: (1) that unions do not have the power to prevent it; (2) that increased wages are not necessarily a function of union bargaining power; and (3) that if wages have been a function of untoward power in the short run, the process of capital intensification has often vitiated any effects that the union could have regarded as "favorable." In general, when the ratio of capital to labor increases, the effect is to force an increase in the marginal productivity of the labor that remains. Some erstwhile pick-and-shovel worker had to learn to operate the power shovel.

The Steel Industry: A Case Study in Cost-Push Inflation

The steel industry during the period 1952–1968 carried out a large capital intensification program. Table 28.1 shows that the number of workers in blast furnaces, steel mills, and foundries declined by 6 percent during this interval, while the total output of steel increased by 42 percent.

The average weekly wage rose from about $78 to about $150. When these values are adjusted for a 31 percent increase in the Consumer Price Index, the real increase in weekly earnings is about 47 percent. Total real wages paid show an increase of 40 percent due to the decline in the number of workers in the industry; so the real gain in wages amounted to approximately 2 percent per year.

Over this same period, the whole economy's real product increased by 90 percent. The total number of employed persons increased from 61.3 million to 75.9 million, and the real product per employed person improved by slightly more than 54 percent, or 2.3 percent per year.

These data hardly offer any immediate conclusions supporting monopolism of workers in the steel industry. If real wage incomes did not increase as rapidly in the steel industry as they did in the economy generally, any effective monopolism by the steelworkers' unions stimulated enough new capital structure to keep down the number of workers needed. The workers that remain may realize monopoly rents, although the benefits they receive may also call for increased productivity on their part.

Table 28.1. Selected Statistics on Wages, Number of Workers, Output, and Prices in the Steel Industry, and of GNP and Consumer Price Index Values for 1952, 1962, and 1968

Item	1952	1962	1968
Average wage per hour for nonsupervisory employees			
Blast furnaces and steel mills	$1.99	$3.25	$3.76
Iron and steel foundries	$1.77	$2.63	$3.32
Average weekly earnings of nonsupervisory employees			
Blast furnaces and steel mills	$79.60	$127.40	$154.16
Iron and steel foundries	$72.22	$106.52	$139.44
Wholesale Price Index for total steel produced (1957–1959 = 100)	73.7	99.3	106
Total output of steel (millions of tons per year)	93.2	98.2	132
Number of nonsupervisory workers (in thousands)			
Blast furnaces and steel mills	518	480	504
Iron and steel foundries	224	165	189
Totals	742	645	693
Index of industrial production	84	118	165
GNP for United States (billions per year)	$348	$554	$861
Total employed persons in United States, excluding military (millions)	61.3	67.9	75.9
CPI (1957–1959 = 100)	92.5	105	121
WPI (1957–1959 = 100)	94	101	109

Source: *Statistical Abstracts of the United States*, 1952, 1962, and 1968 (Washington, D.C.: Department of Commerce).

The price index for steel products increased by 44 percent, while the CPI increased by 31 percent. Therefore, relative or real prices of steel increased by 10 percent (144 ÷ 131) in sixteen years. In some other sectors of the economy, relative prices increased much more. Real hospital and medical costs, for example, increased 35 percent during this same period.

Steel in fact has become a laggard industry. Plastics, nonferrous metals, and general economizing in the use of steel have cut its market. So even though steel prices have increased, one can hardly argue that such a standstill industry could be exerting price leadership on the whole economy. In fact, the rise in steel prices coupled with substitution of other products for steel suggests that the steel industry may be even less a price "leader" than the laundry industry.[3]

---

[3]This analysis is not meant to be either conclusive or exhaustive. It is presented here to demonstrate that the common inference—wage-price increases in the steel industry cause general price increases—is not necessarily valid, certainly not without a great deal more empirical verification than has so far appeared.

Cost-Push and the General Price Level

The inability of cost-push theorists to verify the effects of pressure groups on either real returns or relative prices in the cost-pushed industry has not stopped most of them from taking the argument one step further. The eclectic cost-push analysts, for example, allow that monetary inflation may be critical at some times, but they also insist that cost-push inflation is more pertinent at other times. They agree that the 1945–1952 period was one in which monetary factors were dominant, but they also maintain that between 1953 and 1963 cost-push inflation prevailed. The increase in prices during 1945–1952 was on the order of 37 percent (6 percent per year), while during 1953–1963 the price rise was about 14 percent (less than 1½ percent per year). Unemployment in the earlier period was only trifling; but it gradually worsened and was generally around 5 to 6 percent of the civilian labor force in the early 1960s. (In 1929, by way of contrast, unemployment was only 3 percent of the civilian labor force.)

These facts suggest that the immediate postwar period was one of inflationary readjustment in response to wartime stresses and to the voluminous increases in the quantity of money held by the public. The later period shows only gradually rising prices but in conjunction with a volume of unemployment that was higher than what should be regarded as "frictional." Therefore, the inflation of 1953–1963 is seen as differing in "quality" from the inflation of the previous period. In particular, the later inflation is regarded as cost-pushed. Only by allowing some unemployment, the argument goes, can price increases be checked. If the central bank "gives in" and rationalizes every push of the various power groups with new issues of money, the economy might experience price increases of perhaps 5 percent per year. The alternative is a 1 to 3 percent per year price rise in conjunction with a constant 5 to 6 percent unemployment.

The possible social "trade-off" that would call for higher levels of unemployment as the "price" to be paid for greater stability in the price level has given rise to what is known as "Phillips curve" analysis (after the originator of the idea, Professor A. W. Phillips). It was originally meant to be simply an empirical description of the alternative combinations of unemployment and inflation as these characteristics had appeared in the British economy over time. It suggests a schedule showing the various possible levels of unemployment associated with alternative possible rates of increase in the price level (see Figure 28.1).

A well-defined unemployment-inflation schedule is demonstrated by H_1. If conditions in the economy give the alternatives described by this schedule, unemployment can be reduced to the 3 percent "frictional" value only when prices increase at the rate of 6 percent per year; and a "stable" price level that shows an increase of only 2 percent per year would be achieved at a "price" of 6.5 percent unemployment in the labor force.

Figure 28.1. The Phillips Curve

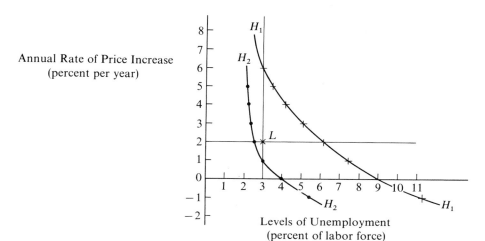

Another possible Phillips curve, by way of illustration, is H_2. If this schedule prevails as descriptive of the economy, relatively stable prices and full employment would be compatible. The only problem for official policy makers would be one of choosing between, say, 3 percent unemployment and 1 percent inflation or 4 percent unemployment and 0.0 percent inflation. Since "frictional" unemployment – laborers between jobs, the semi-indigent, and others – cannot be reduced below about 2 percent under any conditions, or under 3 percent generally, this much of a margin of unemployment must be allowed in classifying the economy as "fully employed." Likewise, a usual bias in the price index of 1 to 2 percent, due to quality improvements and other factors, allows the price *index* to increase by this amount without prejudicing unduly the principle of a "stable" price level.

If a 3 percent level of unemployment and a 2 percent per year increase in the price index are allowed, any achievable combination "southwest" of point L in Figure 28.1 could be considered satisfactory. Some part of curve H_2 enters this area, but none of curve H_1.

A fair amount of empirical work has been done during the past ten years in an attempt to find out just what kind of an inflation-unemployment schedule actually exists for the U.S. economy. The patterns that appear when unemployment is plotted against price or wage data are not well defined. The points making up any such schedule show a large amount of dispersion, suggesting that different amounts of unemployment are associated with any given rate of change of prices. This kind of result implies in turn that institutional conditions in the economy are not homogeneous over time. The most influential determinant of "given conditions" is government policy that specifies the rules of the game under which the market system is supposed to operate. A specific case in point is the minimum wage law. If this law has real teeth in it, its principal result is to generate unemployment in those marginal (low wage) areas where the productivity of workers does not come up to the minimum wage rate stipulated by the law. Thus, if the economy were operating somewhere on the full employment–stable price level schedule H_2 and a minimum wage were imposed, the whole schedule would shift out toward H_1. To restore full employment, the central bank would have to inflate the economy to some degree. Then, if the minimum wage scaled upward in successive future periods, the schedules describing the character of the economy would keep shifting out from the origin. The data for the whole period, however, would plot on the graph as an undefined mass of random points. Nothing in the data itself would tell the observer that several different schedules were involved at different times and under different institutional conditions.

Other factors of measurement and definition would have similar effects. Unemployment statistics, for example, are subject to "errors" of classification. With a given population, more or fewer people may consider themselves in the labor force and more or fewer may be measured as in the labor force. At a time when labor force participation is increasing faster than the total population, "frictional" unemployment may well be greater than the "normal" 2½ or 3 percent. This change, if unrecorded, would also shift the schedule out from the origin.

Price behavior during business fluctuations would have similar effects. When the economy is coming out of a depression the amount of unemployment may be high relative to the rate of increase in prices (see Chapter 20). Similarly, when an inflation-boom is forced to an end by restrictive central bank policy, wage and price level increases carry on upward from the momentum generated during the previous phase of the "cycle," even though some unemployment is developing. (The recessions of 1958 and 1970 are cases in point.) For all these reasons, empirical data used to describe *a* Phillips curve must be qualified considerably before it can be regarded as an analytical device useful for specifying a general relationship.

Selected Bibliography

Phillips, A. W. "The Relation between Unemployment and the Rate of Change of Money Wage Rates in the United Kingdom, 1861–1957." *Economica*, New Series, Vol. 25 (November 1958), pp. 283–299. The classic article on this subject.

Ritter, Lawrence S., ed. *Money and Economic Activity: Readings in Money and Banking.* Boston: Houghton Mifflin Co., 1961. Provides a good basis for study.

Selden, Richard. "Cost-Push versus Demand-Pull Inflation, 1955–1957." *Journal of Political Economy* (February 1959), pp. 1–20. See also R. J. Ball, "Cost Inflation and the Income Velocity of Money: A Comment," *Journal of Political Economy* (June 1960), pp. 288–296; and Richard Selden, "Cost Push versus Demand Pull: A Reply," *Journal of Political Economy* (June 1960), pp. 297–300.

Wright, David McCord, ed. *The Impact of Unions.* New York: Harcourt Brace Jovanovich, 1951. An excellent series of papers on the effects of labor unions. Not only are the papers by outstanding economists, but discussions of each paper by all participants are included.

Is Secular Inflation Likely in the U.S.?

Allan H. Meltzer

Monetarists — that group of economists who regard monetary aggregates as the *determining variables for establishing the quality of the business and economic environment — think of nominal costs and prices as functions of the stock of money. Nonmonetarists, on the other hand, argue that prices are pushed up by costs of production. This view has overwhelming popular support because of the* apparent *linkage between the costs of labor and other resources purchased to the prices of final products sold by the individual businessman.*

In this selection, which originally was delivered in 1967 as a paper to the Third Annual Conference on Economic Affairs at Georgia State University, Professor Allan Meltzer of Carnegie-Mellon University presents simple but convincing arguments and facts that expose the fallacies in the cost-push thesis. Professor Meltzer has published widely in the professional journals and is regarded as one of the brightest stars in the monetary firmament.

A few years ago there was much talk in the financial press, in business periodicals, and in popular magazines about the prospect of long-run secular inflation. Much of this talk died in the United States during the early 1960s. It was replaced by talk of lagging growth rates as the rate of price increase

From the proceedings of the Third Annual Conference on Economic Affairs, *Monetary Problems of the Early 1960's,* ed. Paul K. Gatons and Richard S. Wallace. Reprinted by permission of the publisher and the author.

slowed or stopped, depending upon the index chosen to measure inflation. Now that prices have risen again, a few voices have raised the old secular inflation question. Is the long-run prospect for the United States a gradual steady increase in the broad-based measures of prices? Are we likely to experience secular inflation in the U.S.?

Recent experience in the U.S. and other countries suggests that the answer to these questions is yes, most likely there will be secular inflation in the U.S. My reason for giving this answer, however, is not based on the usual charge that labor unions, profiteers, or other malefactors will push up prices. I do not believe that it is useful to talk about inflation induced by union pressure. Further, I do not know any worthwhile evidence that labor unions or business groups have produced inflation of the kind generally known as cost-push. Since I believe it is misleading to talk about cost-push inflation, I cannot look to cost-push as a likely cause of inflation.

Inflation starts as a result of government policy—not private decisions. Consumers and businessmen, workers and union leaders do not produce inflation out of thin air. Inflation is always and everywhere the consequence of government policies that pump up total expenditure. Indeed, we can simplify and say that inflation is the result of the government's monetary policy since, notwithstanding popular opinion to the contrary, there is very little evidence that government budget deficits are inflationary unless they are financed by large additions to the money supply. Or to put the point in another way, businessmen, and others, believe that budget deficits are inflationary because the deficits are financed by increases in the quantity of money. If the quantity of money increased at the same rate without the deficit, the evidence suggests that we would experience the inflation, though not at the identical rate.

The reason that I expect inflation to occur in the United States—and elsewhere—is that there are a number of popular beliefs that will prevent governments from taking appropriate action in the future, just as they have prevented governments from taking appropriate action to control inflation in the past. Of these, one of the more important is the belief that there is a trade-off between inflation and unemployment. I will comment on that belief in some detail, noting that the argument for a trade-off is undeveloped and that evidence from several countries and from different time periods provides little support for the widely held view. Then I will discuss recent U.S. monetary policy in the light of this argument. Finally, I will conclude that secular inflation is likely because of the belief in the trade-off and because the errors that policymakers will make in the future will differ little from the errors made in the past.

The Trade-Off between Inflation and Unemployment

The belief in a trade-off between inflation and unemployment suggests to some that policymakers can make explicit choices about the tolerable rate of inflation. The notion is that, in principle, some type of cost-benefit analysis could be applied to weigh the costs of inflation against the gain from reduced unemployment. In practice, policymakers must make the choice using less formal procedures, but the notion is conveyed clearly that a choice of this type can and should be made. In the technical literature, the arguments can be found in any one of several articles about the shape and position of the so-called Phillips' curve.

I will argue that there is very little reason to expect a trade-off between unemployment and inflation, and very little evidence to suggest that such a trade-off exists. In fact, there appears to be much more evidence pointing in the opposite direction. If I am correct, policymakers who attempt to reduce unemployment by having just a little bit of inflation will succeed in getting the inflation but will reduce unemployment only temporarily.

Let me state my argument in more detail. Suppose we start by thinking about an economy like the U.S. economy, with real G.N.P. growing at 3 percent per annum and some broad-based index of prices remaining unchanged so that there is no inflation. Suppose that, under these conditions, the unemployment rate remains stable at approximately 4 percent of the labor force. Policymakers now decide that they will trade-off a bit of unemployment for a bit of inflation and try to obtain a 3.5 percent unemployment rate by permitting the broad-based price index to rise by 2 percent a year. To accomplish this, they increase aggregate demand; for example, they raise the growth rate of the money supply by 2 percent. The initial effect of increased demand on employment and output is exactly as expected. Initially, there is very little effect on the price level. Since the increase in aggregate demand is spread over a large number of commodities, individual sellers cannot be certain whether they are faced with a temporary change arising from their own competitive efforts or the more pervasive effect of expansionist government policy. For them, the two are intertwined and mixed up with the random changes that all producers experience. Once it becomes apparent that the increase in demand is systematic, output expands, the demand for labor increases, prices and wages rise in the now familiar pattern.

Once this process gets underway, consumers and businessmen are confronted with announcements of rising prices much more frequently than they were in the past. Where price changes had been less frequent and more or less evenly distributed between revisions upward and downward, announcements of price increases tend to exceed announcements of price reductions. Others are led to examine the prices they charge for the goods or services they sell and to question whether their prices should be adjusted upward.

The process I have described is one part of the familiar process by which an economy adjusts to an increase in the growth rate of money. A more subtle process, however, accompanies the price adjustment: businessmen and consumers learn to expect price increases. Each new announcement of an increase reinforces those expectations. Where the prevailing belief at the margin was that there would be no inflation, there is now an expectation that prices will rise in the future. The expectation of inflation has supplanted the expectation of price stability.

Individuals and businessmen attempt to protect themselves against the consequences of inflation or to profit from those consequences. They sell bonds and spend money balances to reduce their holdings of claims fixed in terms of money. They seek to borrow to increase their liabilities fixed in terms of money. They switch, at the margin, from assets with face values fixed in terms of money to assets whose prices will rise with the general price level under the impact of inflation.

All these responses can be summarized by saying that the market rate of interest rises as a result of the expectation of future inflation. Once the market rate of interest rises by an amount equal to the expected rate of change of prices, there is no longer any stimulus to employment if the expected rate of inflation is maintained. To keep the increase in employment induced by the increase in the growth rate of money posited at the outset of this example, the rate of inflation must increase. Maintaining the expected rate of inflation will not maintain the increased demand for labor.

There are a number of ways in which I can state this conclusion to bring out the main points. I will try several:

First, the argument says that the trade-off between inflation and unemployment is not durable. The reduction in the unemployment rate vanishes as soon as the public, at the margin, anticipates the rate at which prices are expected to rise.

Second, the argument says that if the rate of expansion of money (or, if you prefer, of monetary and fiscal policy variables) is maintained at the higher level, the country gets the inflation as a permanent feature but does not reduce the unemployment rate permanently.

Third, the argument says that unanticipated inflation is a tax on wealth. Unanticipated inflation transfers wealth from creditors to debtors. Once the creditors take protective action, there is no longer a gain to debtors from the inflation.

In short, the rise in employment resulting from government policies that pump up aggregate demand cannot be maintained with a steady rate of inflation. However, the contrary belief seems so widespread that it is a main reason for expecting inflation in the future.

Once the economy has adjusted to a 2 percent inflation, policymakers desirous of maintaining employment must accelerate aggregate demand. In my example, they must increase the growth rate of the money supply. If the higher rate of monetary growth is unanticipated, the unemployment rate is reduced once again. But, again, the rise in employment or reduction in unemployment cannot be maintained without moving to a still higher rate of growth in the money supply and a higher rate of inflation. Each new attempt to force the unemployment rate down by raising the growth rate of money increases the rate of inflation.

Most developed countries can, indeed do, stop inflation before it accelerates. The point of my argument is that if the country is committed to a policy of limiting the rate of inflation, there is no point in choosing a rate of inflation other than a zero rate.

Some Evidence

Let us look at various sources of evidence for this proposition. Consider a country that has experienced a substantial inflation. There are many countries that one might choose for this purpose. If there is a trade-off between inflation and growth of real output, we would expect high rates of inflation to be accompanied by higher rates of growth in the same country at different points of time. In general, growth rates of output and rates of inflation are not closely related. In fact, such countries provide an important additional source of evidence. When the growth rate of money is reduced, and the rate of inflation is slowed, the initial effect is almost always a *rise* in unemployment. Once the economy has adjusted to the new rate of monetary expansion, output and industrial production rise and unemployment is reduced. For example, a reduction in the growth rate of money that lowers the rate of price increases from 75 percent to 50 percent per annum brings a reduction in output and employment even though the growth rate of the money supply remains extremely inflationary. Once the public becomes adjusted to the slower rate of inflation, output and employment rise and unemployment falls to about its former level. Additional attempts to reduce inflation — say from 50 percent to 25 percent per annum — have similar effects on unemployment.

Another example is much closer to home. A few years ago, the Canadian and U.S. unemployment rates were approximately the same, slightly lower in Canada than in the U.S. During the two years from mid-1964 to mid-1966, the Canadian money supply increased about twice as fast as the U.S. money supply, approximately 12 percent per annum in Canada, on the average. The unemployment rate in Canada dropped well below the U.S. unemployment rate and reached a level of 3.4 percent in the fourth quarter of 1965, while the U.S. rate was almost 1 percentage point higher. Canadian unemployment then began to rise despite higher average rate of monetary growth that was maintained in early 1966. On my interpretation, the Canadian unemployment rate rose, in part, because the inflation in Canada was greater than the inflation in the U.S. and, in part, because the public had learned to expect the higher rate of inflation and was adjusting to it.

Evidence of this kind from country after country that has experienced inflation is contrary to the widely accepted view that we have, within our power, the ability to choose a little more inflation as a way of getting a little more employment. The reason policies based on these notions fail is that they presume ignorance on the part of the public. They assume that the public does not learn to anticipate the rate of inflation and does not take action to protect itself. In fact, the protective action is of two kinds, and both forms are used. First, in the financial markets, interest rates rise for the reason I discussed above. Second, in the markets for goods and services and for labor, prices and wages rise.

When we look into the reasons for the rise in interest rates, prices, and wages we find very similar mechanisms at work. In financial markets lenders observe that there are more borrowers—or, as economists say, demand has increased. Though there are more borrowers, there are fewer lenders willing to make loans at the existing prices. Supply has decreased. It really matters very little whether interest rates rise because the lenders recognize that rising prices have wiped out a large part of the return that they expected to earn from loan contracts made in the past, or whether borrowers recognize that it is now more profitable to buy inventories, real capital, land, and other assets that rise in price during inflation. Both effects work in the same direction, so in either case the result is exactly the same. Lenders are willing to lend less at the prevailing market interest rate because rising prices reduce or eliminate their profits; borrowers wish to borrow more because rising prices have made it more profitable to buy assets that rise in price during inflation and to issue debts (bonds, mortgages, etc.) whose prices do not change. Once businessmen and workers recognize that inflation is occurring, it is to their advantage to borrow money now and repay it when prices are higher. Once the rate of inflation is anticipated, once people believe that prices are going to rise, there is no longer a gain to debtors or a loss to creditors. Market interest rates adjust to reflect the rate of price change, that is, the prevailing rate of inflation. The lender now charges the old interest rate plus compensation for the fact that prices will be higher when the borrower repays the loan.

Similar responses take place in the markets for goods and services. As buyers and sellers become more aware of the inflation, prices rise. Some prices are fixed for relatively long periods of time and cannot respond immediately to the inflation. For example, rents on buildings and apartments are usually settled annually or at longer intervals. These prices do not, therefore, rise initially but adjust over longer periods of time.

An Interpretation of "Cost-Push"

A good deal of misinterpretation and error has resulted from the failure to recognize that during an inflation all prices do not rise together. Frequently, this error is propagated under the name "cost-push" inflation. The notion is that prices rise because unions and perhaps other sellers such as landlords suddenly decide to ask for higher wages and prices. These attempts to raise wages undoubtedly raise costs of production and thus force an increase in prices.

Like most examples of its kind, the argument contains a grain of truth and a large amount of misinterpretation. The grain of truth is that wages are a cost of production and that many businessmen, faced with an increase in demand, raise prices and wages. The misinterpretation arises because the rise in wages and prices is both a response to excess demand and a result of the government's policy of inflation. They are not separate events, although they may appear that way to the casual observer or to the businessman.

As an illustration of the process, let us consider the behavior of wages in 1966 and their expected pattern for 1967. Unionized workers in the U.S. received an average wage increase slightly less than 4 percent in 1966. Prices rose by the same percentage, so unionized workers, on the average, were no better off at the end of the year than at the beginning. They had lost, or not gained, the reward for higher productivity. In the sectors such as wholesale and retail trade where about 95 percent of the workers are not unionized, the average wage increase in 1966 was about 1 percent higher. Workers in other nonunion sectors had similar or better experience. On the average, nonunion workers were compensated for the loss in purchasing power due to rising prices and received, in addition, all or part of the return from higher productivity.

What do these facts show? Why did the nonunion workers fare much better than the union workers in the inflation of 1966? On one interpretation, the figures reveal the statesmanship of organized labor and its reluctance to violate the government's wage-price guideposts. The problem with this interpretation is that unionized and nonunionized workers have similar experience in the early stages of other inflations when there were no wage-price guideposts. The wages of union workers almost always rise more slowly than nonunion workers in the early stage of an inflation. We can therefore dismiss increased labor statesmanship as a special factor in 1966. Our previous interpretation fits the facts much better. The unionized workers are under contract; the nonunionized workers generally are not. There is no reason to believe that one or the other of these groups learns about the inflation faster than the other. The effect of increased aggregate demand is spread over much of the economy without regard to degree of unionism and appears as an increase in the demand for labor. In the nonunionized sector, the contract wage is paid to workers with less skill and lower productivity. Unions that have their contracts reopened during the year are able to raise wages. Other unions must wait until contract time comes around.

This pattern became quite clear in U.S. labor negotiations when several unions demanded "cost of living" adjustments and for the first time in many years asked for escalator clauses to protect them against inflation. Although unionized workers as a group lost purchasing power in 1966, unionized workers whose contracts were renewed in 1966 did at least as well as the nonunion workers. The others will try to get compensation when their contracts become negotiable in 1967 or in later years.

If you think about the process I have just described, you will see why the effect of increased aggregate demand on prices is spread through time and will recognize that the effect of increased demand on prices should not be expected to occur all at once. Indeed, it is to be expected that the process will be spread through time because some contracts are fixed, because information does not reach all individuals at the same time, and because rising aggregate demand does not affect all sectors simultaneously.

It is not at all surprising, therefore, that when there are sudden shifts in monetary policy from very expansive to very contractive as in 1966, the response of prices to the inflationary policy may continue long after the expansive policy has stopped. This is our current situation. Output in many sectors declined in the first quarter of this year in response to the overly restrictive policy of the last part of 1966; some prices are responding to the inflationary monetary policy early this year; some are responding to the very expansive monetary and fiscal policies now in effect.

It must be emphasized that there is no inconsistency between rising prices and falling output. There is no need to assign special names such as cost-push inflation to this phenomenon. And there is no reason to introduce special policies — guideposts or other informal price controls — to deal with the problem. Indeed, to the extent such devices are effective, they delay the response in prices, add to the inefficiency, and thus raise the cost of the adjustment to inflationary government policies.

The mechanism I have used to illustrate the way in which the economy adjusts to inflation also explains why there is no reason to believe in a trade-off between inflation and unemployment. Just as individuals, businessmen, and unions learn gradually that prices are rising, they learn to expect them to rise in the future and take action to adjust current and future prices to the expected rate of demand. To maintain a higher level of demand, the government must increase the rate of price change — that is, it must accelerate the inflation. Such action imposes a new burden of adjusting and sets off a new wave of inflation, but it cannot lead to a higher maintained rate of employment.

Recent U.S. Monetary Policy

A third source of evidence suggesting the absence of a trade-off between inflation and employment is provided by the behavior of the U.S. economy in recent years and its response to Federal Reserve monetary policy. I will first consider the monetary policy pursued in the U.S., then I will comment on some of its effects.

Like the long-term record of which it is a part, the experience of the past ten years shows periods in which money increased too much, followed by periods in which it increased too little to maintain the fullest use of resources without inflation. These alternating periods of over- and under-expansion of money are often connected by sudden, sharp changes in the direction of policy, so that excessive increases in the stock of money were followed by excessive contractions of the stock and later by periods of insufficient growth of money. Moreover, the periods of over- and under-expansion are themselves a sequence of large and small increases and decreases that on the average produced the high or low rates of monetary growth.

There is very little indication in any recent (or more distant peace-time) period that a consistent steady monetary policy has been pursued. From 1956 through the middle of 1957, changes in money (currency and demand deposits) rose and fell intermittently. On the average, the growth rate of money declined. At the peak of the expansion in the economy's output, August 1957, money grew at an annual rate of 1 percent, far below the level required to maintain the expansion. During the fall of 1957, the growth rate declined further and the money supply fell, despite clear recognition by the Federal Reserve that a recession had started.

At the beginning of 1958, monetary policy changed direction and, in a series of erratic moves, the annual growth rate of the money supply reached 5 percent by the end of the year. A year later, the growth rate was back to zero and, at the peak of the aborted expansion in May 1960, the money supply was falling at a rate of 2 percent per year.

For the next two years, the annual growth rate of the money supply rose and fell. An indication of the difference in monetary policy between 1959 and 1961 as compared to 1961–63 is given by the fact that in 1961 the monthly money supply figures were often below the levels of two years earlier while 1963 generally showed an increase of $7 to $8 billion (4.5 to 5 percent) over 1961.

The alternating periods of monetary expansion and contraction, and of high and low growth rates of money, leave a clear imprint on the movements of output during the period. Each period of sustained growth in the stock of money is followed by sustained growth in output, and each period of low growth or decline in money is followed by a recession or low growth in output. The very low growth rate of money in the early sixties is reflected in a low growth rate of output that gave rise to widespread fear that the U.S. was unlikely to experience – and unable to achieve – full employment. This is the so-called lagging growth argument of the Kennedy campaign. Once the rate of monetary growth increased, these fears began to dissipate.

From late 1962 to the spring of 1966, the money supply grew at one of the highest average rates of growth in any peacetime period in U.S. history. The $25 billion expansion in currency and demand deposits in the three and one-half years from September 1962 to April 1966 is larger than the increase in money during the preceding ten years. Once again, a sustained expansion in output followed the high average rate of monetary growth. And, contrary to popular belief, the rate of expansion in output began well before the 1964 tax cut was enacted. Indeed, during the early months of the expansion, fiscal policy was most often described as a "drag" on the economy.

After March 1964, a slightly lower rate of monetary growth and a more expansive fiscal policy combined to raise further the rate of expansion of output. Employment continued to rise and it was quite likely that the attempt to maintain the expansive monetary and fiscal policies would produce inflation.

In late 1964 and early 1965, the Federal Reserve decreased the average rate at which it supplied bank reserves and currency. As a result, the rate of monetary growth declined during the winter of 1965. Although monetary policy remained overly expansive and prices began to rise, the Federal Reserve was moving in the appropriate direction.

Unfortunately, the direction of policy reversed again in the fall of 1965, and bank reserves and currency were supplied by the Federal Reserve at a substantially higher rate. Increasingly, the Federal Reserve and other government agencies resorted to exhortation or to mild anti-inflationary actions (such as the rise in the discount rate in December 1965) that were insufficient to counter the excessively expansive rate at which the Federal Reserve supplied base money. A further stimulus to expansion was provided later in 1966 by the government's fiscal policy.

One often repeated and widely accepted view of policy in 1966 is that the Federal Reserve was attempting to restrain inflation but was unable to counter the pressures arising from the government's budget and from the private sector. This interpretation fits the facts badly. From December 1965 to April 1966, the seasonally adjusted money supply grew at a rate 30 percent higher than the rate in the preceding five months.

It was not until the summer of 1966 that the Federal Reserve undertook anti-inflationary action. In early July, it raised the reserve requirements at member banks. Unfortunately, the airplane strike that started in July led to a very large increase in float, temporarily thwarting the Federal Reserve's purposes. When the strike ended, the volume of bank reserves and currency contracted sharply and the money supply started to decline. The second rise in reserve requirements in September, and the effect of open market operations during the fall, contributed to the continued decline in the money supply during the fall.

The Effect of Recent Policy

To understand the effects of these recent policies, we have to separate changes in prices from changes in output and discuss the way in which changes in money affect both prices and output. Inflation and deflation are descriptive of changes in a broad-based index of prices; expansions and recessions refer to changes in the rate at which goods and services are produced. There is nothing contradictory or surprising if various combinations of changes in price and output occur together for a time. Inflation may take place during a recession or during an expansion; prices may fall or rise when output and production are falling or rising. Monetary policy in 1956–1958 produced rising prices during the 1957–58 recession; the monetary policy of 1965–1967 will have a similar effect throughout much of 1967.

There are two main reasons that inflation is likely to continue during at least part of this year. First, the average rate of growth of the money supply was maintained at a high rate for too long in 1965–66. As always, the initial effects of this high monetary growth rate were felt in the credit markets and later on output. It is not until sales and output increase that businessmen and workers begin to believe that they can raise the prices at which they supply goods and services. At this point, past changes in the money supply begin to influence price changes, and prices begin to rise following the pattern previously described. Second, as prices rise, the public becomes convinced that prices will continue to rise and acts on this expectation. Both workers and businessmen attempt to protect themselves against expected future increases in prices by adjusting upward the prices at which they supply goods and services when contracts are due for renewal.

The pattern just described is typical of the behavior in periods of economic expansion when, as is often the case, the growth rate of the money supply remains too high for too long a time. Once formed, the expectations of further price increases are not easily removed. They persist even if monetary and fiscal policies have moved in a contractive or anti-inflationary direction. It is partly for this reason that prices continued to rise while output fell sharply in the recession of 1957–58. The expectations of rising prices and the past rate of monetary expansion continued to influence prices even though the policy in 1957 had produced a fall in output. The sudden reversal of policy in 1958 came before the full effect of the previous low rate of increase or decline in the stock of money had reduced the rate of change of the price level to zero. It was not until the period of "lagging growth" in both money and output during the early 1960s that expectations of inflation were eliminated. Once a high growth rate of money was reintroduced in 1962, the main effect was on output. Expectations of inflation had been eliminated and did not reappear for several years.

One of the more unfortunate consequences of recent policy has been the revival of inflationary expectations. Had the Federal Reserve persisted in the policy that reduced the growth rate of the money supply in early 1965, expectations of inflation would not have been as widespread. By pursuing an inflationary policy in late 1965 and 1966, the Federal Reserve has reduced the chance of maintaining full employment without inflation.

The fact that the change in the growth rate of the money supply last summer was both large and sudden—changing from an expansion of 6 percent to a contraction of 2 percent or 3 percent is a large change—has important consequences for the future. It means that the expansive influence of money on output was replaced by a sharply contractive influence. This caused a sudden decline in the growth rate of output, although prices continued to rise under the influence of widely held expectations of rising prices induced by the previously high rate of monetary expansion.

An anti-inflation policy starts as an anti-expansion policy. This is only another way of saying that to prevent further inflation, the Federal Reserve will first produce a decline in output or in its growth rate. If it does not do the latter, it is unlikely to do the former. Or, to put the same point in still another way, if monetary policy affected prices first and output later, there is little reason to believe that it would have much effect on output at all. Changes in output are a most important step in the process by which changes in money produce rising or falling prices.

Conclusion

Let me return to my main theme, the prospect for secular inflation. I have emphasized one part of the problem: the belief in a trade-off between inflation and unemployment. I do not expect, however, that this belief will lead to an acceleration of price changes. Whenever inflation takes hold, policymakers react to the inflation by reducing the rate of increase in the money supply or, all too frequently, reducing the money supply.

The effect of these actions is that output or the growth rate of output declines. Unemployment starts to rise. The demand to "do something" about unemployment mounts. Once the rate of price increase slows, policymakers begin to combat rising unemployment. They increase or accelerate the rate of monetary expansion.

A main result is that the expectations of inflation are not eliminated, they are reinforced. Instead of periods of rising and falling prices that average out to about zero rate of change, we have periods of rising prices and no periods of falling prices that average out to a positive rate of change of prices. As in past peacetime periods, businessmen and consumers learn to expect prices to rise. Recent history generally supports this expectation. The "stop and go" policy in Britain and the postwar experience in Western Europe are, broadly speaking, examples of this kind. The main counter examples are the experience of the U.S. from 1958 to 1961, and Canada during a similar period, when a very slow average rate of monetary expansion eliminated the expectation of inflation for a time. I do not expect this experience to be repeated. As a consequence, I expect that, on the average, prices will rise and that the U.S. will experience secular inflation.

29

Peripheral Issues
in Banking Theory and Policy

100 Percent Reserve Commercial Banking

Economists and official policy makers have come to regard legal reserve requirements for fractional reserve commercial banking systems as a social necessity—in earlier times to ensure bank liquidity sufficient to meet current demand obligations and in more recent times to control the volume of bank-created credit. In the first quarter of the twentieth century, some theoretical discussions of this issue examined the extreme case of a 100 percent requirement, and a policy favoring 100 percent reserves was developed explicitly by the well-known economist Irving Fisher.[1] The idea itself was first broached in modern times by a professional chemical engineer, Frederick Soddy.[2] Many economists also came to accept various aspects of the concept, although no clear-cut majority ever gave it full sanction.[3]

The philosophical argument for 100 percent reserves and the practical means of attaining it are both fairly simple. The commercial banking system would be required to keep 100 percent reserves in currency, or in central bank credit convertible immediately into currency, against all demand deposits. Bank

---

[1]Irving Fisher, *One Hundred Per Cent Money* (New York: Adelphi, 1935).

[2]Frederick Soddy, *Wealth, Virtual Wealth, and Debt* (New York: E. P. Dutton & Co., 1933).

[3]See Albert G. Hart, "The Chicago Plan for Banking Reform," *Readings in Monetary Theory,* ed. Friedrich A. Lutz and Lloyd W. Mints (Homewood, Ill.: Richard D. Irwin, 1951), pp. 437–456.

creation of derivative demand deposits would not be possible, nor would a bank be able to make loans, discounts, and investments with primary demand deposits. The commercial bank would be only a warehouse for the deposits of the nonbank public and would charge a fee for its service. Since no bank could make loans that bear interest, no bank would be able to offer interest to attract new deposits. Banks would compete with one another in offering their warehousing services at as low a cost as possible. This cost is one that banks must meet in any deposit system, even though it may or may not be fully charged to the depositor. Neither logic nor experience suggests that its real value would be any different under a 100 percent system than it is under present conditions even though its incidence might change if 100 percent reserves were adopted.

The balance sheet of a hypothetical 100 percent reserve bank, after it had taken in, say, 100 units of currency as reserves for checkbook credit, might look as shown in Table 29.1. If the bank wished to make loans and investments it would have to obtain the funds for this purpose from the capital market; that is, it would need to issue stock as a corporation and use the proceeds from the stock sale to make loans and investments. The bank might sell stock for another 100 units of currency. Its balance sheet would then change to that shown in Table 29.2; and after it had made all the loans and investments possible with its resources, its balance sheet would appear as in Table 29.3.

Table 29.1. 100 Percent American Bank

Assets		*Liabilities*	
Currency reserves (government-issued legal tender)	100	Demand deposits	100
	Reserve ratio: 100 percent		

Note: Once again, furniture and fixtures are excluded for the sake of simplicity.

Table 29.2. 100 Percent American Bank

Assets		*Liabilities*	
Currency reserves	200	Demand deposits	100
		Net Worth	
		Capital	100
	Reserve ratio: 100 percent		

Table 29.3. 100 Percent American Bank

Assets		*Liabilities*	
Loans, discounts, and		Demand deposits	100
investments	100		
Currency reserves	100		
		Net Worth	
		Capital	100

Reserve ratio: 100 percent

The net financial effect of the bank on the economy would be as an intermediary between those borrowers who demand short-term fixed dollar claims and the suppliers of such funds who are willing to take residual income claims from the common stock of the bank. The bank would convert one kind of claim into the other. This process is in contrast to the arrangement used currently in which a bank issues demand deposits, 85 percent of which are created by the bank itself, and takes in return fixed dollar claims payable after a time interval (short-term commercial paper). Under 100 percent reserves, the bank would still generate short-term notes, but it would no longer create new money to finance the notes. Its stock flotations would be its only source of loanable funds, and the only claim against the bank's interest-earning assets would be the residual income claims of stockholders. All demand deposit claims would be covered by currency reserves.

A common argument against this scheme is that banking firms would not be able to make short-term commercial loans to businessmen. The process of getting funds through the capital market is alleged to be too cumbersome for banks to undertake, so short-term financing of business operations by banks would supposedly dry up under a 100 percent reserve system. No direct empirical evidence can support or refute this argument because neither 100 percent reserve banking nor anything close to it has ever been tried. However, what is possible for all other private business organizations should also be possible for banks. Traditional methods of business financing—the single proprietor-investor, the closed family corporation, and multi-person ownership through the usual investment channels available to the public—should be as expedient for banks as they are for other businesses. Banks could also reinvest capital earnings, as do other corporations, if they wished to expand their lending activities.

The major advantage of 100 percent reserve banking is that it would take the power of demand deposit creation and destruction out of the hands of private persons. To the extent that initiation or aggravation of inflation and depression are results of changes in the stock of money, business fluctuations would be largely dampened by an arrangement that kept the banking system from magnifying monetary fluctuations. Even in today's monetary world, in which the stock of money is basically controlled by central banks, month-to-month fluctuations and lags in effects of monetary policy might be significantly reduced.

The technical transition to a system of 100 percent reserves could be accomplished easily in an economy that uses paper money and that has in it a large volume of government securities held by commercial banks. The transition problem is primarily an accounting operation. It can be demonstrated by modifying an actual balance sheet of all commercial banks for, say, June 29, 1968.

Table 29.4 includes a significant volume of time deposits. There are differences of opinion over how this item should be handled. For the sake of simplicity if nothing else, they are handled here as if they are demand deposits. In a 100 percent system, which permitted time deposits on the basis of only nominal reserve requirements, the whole principle of requiring a dollar of tangible reserves for a dollar of deposits might well be evaded. Banks could carry out all their operations as before, using "time deposits" in place of demand deposits. For this reason both time deposits and savings deposits in commercial and mutual savings banks would probably have to fall under the same constraint as demand deposits. For purposes of argument, therefore, total deposits of $413 billion are referred to here as "demand deposits."

Table 29.4. Combined Balance Sheet for All U.S. Banks as of June 29, 1968 (billions of dollars)

Assets		*Liabilities*	
Loans (less bank borrowings)	290	Time deposits (less interbank)	251
U.S. government securities	63	Demand deposits (less interbank)	162
Other securities	74		
Cash assets (excluding interbank borrowing)	76	Total deposits	413
		Other liabilities	49
		Net Worth	
		Total capital accounts	41
Total net assets	503	Total net liabilities and capital	503

Reserve ratio: 18.4 percent

Source: Board of Governors of the Federal Reserve System, *Federal Reserve Bulletin*, Vol. 54, Part 2 (October 1968), p. A19.

The reserve ratio in this balance sheet is approximately 18.4 percent (76 ÷ 413). Simple monetization of bank-held government securities would raise this ratio appreciably. Either the central bank or the treasury could print legal tender and buy back these securities while reserve requirements were raised correspondingly so that no "excess" reserves developed. When the securities had all been repurchased, the balance sheet for the system would appear as in Table 29.5.

Table 29.5. Commercial Banking System Combined Balance Sheet
(billions of dollars)

Assets		Liabilities	
Loans	290	Total deposits	413
Other securities	74	Other liabilities	49
		Net Worth	
Cash assets (76 + 63)	139	Total capital accounts	41
		Total net liabilities and	
Total assets	503	capital	503

Reserve ratio: 33.7 percent

The banking system's reserve ratio would almost double by this simple accounting operation. Banks would lose some interest-earning assets, and the government's outstanding debt would be effectively reduced. Further repurchases of securities by the government from nonbank holders with corresponding increases in reserve requirements might be possible. People probably would deposit the new currency received from the sale of government securities. But since this behavior could not be guaranteed, continued purchases and increases in requirements might simply cause transitional hardship for the banks by forcing them to liquidate the rest of their portfolios.

A simpler system for attaining the remaining currency reserves would be by government deposits of currency directly in banks. In Table 29.5 the banking system still had a deficit of $274 billion (deposits of $413 billion minus cash reserves of $139 billion) in reserves to overcome before it could reach the goal of 100 percent reserves. Let the government now issue $274 billion in paper money to the banks, thus enhancing the banks' capital and surplus. At the same time, legal reserve requirements would be raised to the 100 percent limit. The balance sheet for the system would then appear as in Table 29.6. Interest-bearing assets of the banks would equal their capital accounts plus other liabilities ($364 billion), and total cash assets would equal total deposits ($413 billion).

The government could make this capital an outright gift, or many banks might liquidate in order to realize large capital gains. At the same time, government ownership is not desired or desirable. The banks, therefore, might have to issue some kind of nonvoting, nonparticipating, nonincome-earning stock to offset or balance the government's currency issue, which would be a once-and-for-all action. Currency would be retired whenever a bank liquidated. Once the system was embarked on 100 percent reserves, bank credit expansion of

Table 29.6. Commercial Banking System Combined Balance Sheet
(billions of dollars)

Assets		*Liabilities*	
Loans	290	Total deposits	413
Other securities	74	Other liabilities	49
		Net Worth	
Cash assets (139 + 274)	413	Total capital accounts	315
		Total net liabilities, capital,	
Total net assets	777	and "surplus"	777

Reserve ratio: 100 percent

interest-earning assets would have to be matched by expansion of bank capital through orthodox investment channels. Government monetary policy would be the means, and the only means, for getting new money into circulation. It would occur largely through open market purchases of government securities from private investors or dealers. The securities would be paid for by a central bank check which, if deposited in a commercial bank, would go back to the central bank as a deposit in the commercial bank's reserve account. In fact, central bank deposit accounts for commercial banks and currency would be completely interchangeable.

The equality of total deposits and total cash assets would mean that banks would no longer affect, however unconsciously, the quantity of bank deposits. Furthermore, liquidity demands would be no problem to the banks under this system, so the banks would have no liquidity motive for holding idle cash. A commercial loan could be made entirely on the merits of the loan itself.

Another argument against a policy of 100 percent reserves is that it is not absolutely necessary for accomplishing desirable monetary policies: The central bank can operate effectively through a commercial banking system on fractional reserves. This point is valid, even though a great improvement in monetary administration would be probable. At best, the 100 percent system is only desirable, not necessary. Conversion to this system is also inhibited by false fears of any change from the status quo, and uncertainty due to technical ignorance on how such a change could be effected without hurting the banks.

Zero Reserve Requirements

A more recent excursion into the controversy over reserve requirements asks why *any* reserves should be required; that is, why not have zero reserve requirements?[4] Since most of the reserves of commercial banks are no longer

---

[4]See Deane Carson, "Is the Federal Reserve System Really Necessary?" *Money and Economic Activity: Readings on Money and Banking,* ed. Lawrence S. Ritter (Boston: Houghton Mifflin Co., 1961), pp. 238–252.

tangible and no longer serve as a means for paying off demand obligations, this argument goes, reserve requirements serve no bank liquidity function. Furthermore, open market operations are both an optimal and sufficient means of carrying out monetary policy, so reserve requirement changes are unnecessary as a control device. In further support of this position is the fact that many countries with advanced monetary and banking systems do not have legal reserve requirements even though they all maintain some amount of reserves that can be altered by open market operations.

The absence of legal requirements would not mean that banks would keep no reserves. In the nineteenth century under the constraint of converting demand obligations into gold, commercial banks kept ratios of specie to demand liabilities of between 5 and 15 percent. Now they no longer face the obligation of converting notes or deposits into gold, but they must be able to convert demand deposits into legal tender paper currency. Therefore, they must keep "providential" or "contingency" reserves either in the form of Federal Reserve notes or as deposit accounts with a Federal Reserve Bank.

Obviously, if the absence of legal reserve requirements meant that banks would keep no dollar reserves of any sort, bank credit would expand immediately and infinitely. Banks would, however, keep contingency reserves just as nonbank households and business firms keep cash balances against impending obligations, risks, and uncertainties. Thus, bank-generated demand deposits would be no more likely to expand to infinity under such a system than the velocity of money would expand to infinity because of the capricious behavior of households and businesses.

The principal advantage of the no-required-reserves system—and also, paradoxically, of the 100 percent reserve system—is that either system would get rid of unnecessary central bank intervention in the commercial banking industry. Commercial banks would be free to promote their own business as they wished without concern over changes in the rules of the game, while the central bank could carry out monetary policy—control the quantity of money—objectively and dispassionately, using various targets or rules of thumb in the money markets.

The possibilities for reforming the existing system of reserve requirements raised by these extreme points of view really emphasize more fundamental factors: the difference between monetary *policy* and banking *regulation,* and the archaic practice of continuing the practice of reserve requirements as a vehicle for either function. In fact, given the obsolescence of reserve requirements, any stipulated reserve requirement would be as good (or bad) as any other. So the least bad policy would be one of fixing a statutory requirement at some value between zero and 100 for all banks, national and nonnational, member and nonmember, and then letting this value stand permanently. The clear distinction that now emerges between banking regulation and monetary policy raises the more extensive questions of whether any of the many Federal Reserve banking and credit regulations is either desirable or justifiable, and whether the Federal Reserve should not limit itself to control of the money supply through open market operations. The interested reader can explore these issues in more depth by consulting the professional literature.

Monetary-Fiscal Coordination

The most orthodox and unregulated monetary-fiscal policy — the one generally favored during the nineteenth century — included (1) the self-regulating gold (or bimetallic) standard for controlling the quantity of money in the economy and (2) a perennially balanced budget as a proper norm for fiscal practice. Various events already discussed led to gradual abandonment of metallic standards and to their replacement by central banks. Other events, principally wars and depressions, sporadically prevented the achievement of balanced budgets. When budgets were in deficit, the national debt increased, thus "staining" the record of the administration so unfortunate as to have been in office at the time. Frequently, subsequent administrations would curtail spending enough to generate budget surpluses and pay off some of the national debt.

Much myth and nonsense was (and still is) voiced in Congress and in the financial press over the "evils" and ignominy of a national debt. So great has been the propaganda against it that the fiscal austerity of surplus budgets almost or entirely obliterated the debt three different times between 1791 and 1914. It was reduced to a relatively low figure before the War of 1812; it was entirely eliminated by 1835, then held to only a nominal figure up to 1860; and it was reduced again to almost nothing before World War I. Since World War I, it has been a sizable fraction of total debt and of Gross National Product. More importantly, it has also been a significant fraction of the total stock of money.

To discuss the debt critically, its ownership must be spelled out. Not all of the gross debt resides in private hands, so not all of the debt influences private decision making. (See Table 29.7.)

Existence of this size debt, while it would never impoverish our grandchildren, is a financially cumbersome obligation of the federal government. On net balance it has increased by over $100 billion during the past 25 years, even though its size relative to other monetary variables has diminished. Much of this debt falls due every year and must be refinanced along with any additional debt incurred by fiscal deficits. This situation is in contrast to the days of balanced budgets and relatively small national debts.

Table 29.8 presents the outstanding public issues of government debt (not all of which is held by the public) according to their times to maturity. Also given is the weighted time to maturity for the total marketable debt. This value declined from 5 years, 1 month in 1963, to 4 years, 2 months in 1968, and to 3 years, 8 months in 1970. The import of this statistic for, say, 1970 is that the

Table 29.7. Breakdown of Total Outstanding National Debt
and Relationship to GNP and Stock of Money, 1963, 1968, and 1970
(billions of dollars except for percentages)

	1963	1968	1970
As of December 31, the total gross debt was	$309 billion	$358 billion	$389 billion
of which	89	130	159
was held by U.S. government agencies and trust funds and the Federal Reserve System, leaving a net public debt of	220	228	230
Commercial banks and mutual savings banks held	70	69	66
leaving	150	159	164
in the hands of the nonbank public. Of this amount, insurance companies and corporations held.................	30	23	18
state and local governments held ...	21	27	23
private individuals held	68	75	82
foreign and international organizations held	16	14	20
and miscellaneous investors held ...	16	20	21
Gross National Product was	584 per year	866 per year	977 per year
The outstanding net public debt was, therefore, ...	38 percent	26 percent	24 percent
of GNP. The narrow stock of money in December was.......................	153	195	215
and the outstanding net public debt was..	144 percent	117 percent	107 percent
of the stock of money. The net public debt adjusted for price level changes was..	100 percent	90 percent	95 percent
of its 1963 value.			

Source: Board of Governors of the Federal Reserve System, *Federal Reserve Bulletin*, selected issues.

total marketable debt of $307 billion must be completely refinanced or "turned over" at least once in the next 3 years, 8 months, or at the rate of $229 million per day! Even if the national debt is simply something "we owe ourselves," the sheer administration and paperwork required for this amount of refinancing involve substantial costs. If investment dealers, for example, charge and earn a 3 percent commission on gross sales, refinancing this volume of debt costs over $2.5 billion per year. This amount is a net refinancing cost exclusive of the cost of purchases and sales by the Federal Reserve System and private investors.

Table 29.8. Average Times to Maturity of Government Debt (Public Issues), Marketable and Nonmarketable, 1963, 1968, and 1970

| | Total Public Issues | Time to Maturity Marketable Government Debt | | | | | | Nonmarketable | Weighted Average Time to Maturity for Marketable Debt |
| | | 90-Day Treasury Bills | 1-Year Certificates | Bonds | | | | | |
				1–5 Years	5–10 Years	10–20 Years	Over 20 Years		
Billions of dollars outstanding, December 31, 1963	260	52	38	59	36	8.4	15.6	51	5 years, 1 month
December 31, 1968	294	75	34	68	35	8.4	16.4	57	4 years, 2 months
December 31, 1970	307	88	36	82	23	8.6	10.9	59	3 years, 8 months

Sources: *Federal Reserve Bulletin*, selected issues, and *Treasury Bulletin*, April 1971, p. 21.

Such a volume of debt, with its mixed maturities "hanging" over the market, requires the Treasury Department to involve itself in what is known as "debt management." Since the Federal Reserve System acts as a fiscal agent for the Treasury, and operates as well in the securities market in carrying out monetary policy, it too must heed the same problems of managing the debt that are important to the Treasury. Too much of the debt should not enter the market at once; it should dovetail with the Fed's open market operations; it should be floated when market conditions are propitious; international factors must be taken into account; etc., etc. Obviously, consideration and analysis of the many security market factors that lead to efficient debt management require a large use of human and computer resources.

Interestingly enough, virtually all of these costs could be avoided by the use of consols in financing the debt. Consols, having no maturity value, need never be refinanced. The Treasury would sell them at the market price, being careful to choose times when sales could proceed in an orderly manner, and would repurchase them at the market price whenever fiscal surpluses permitted. Once on the market, however, they would be of no further administrative concern. Not only would a general security issue of this type considerably reduce Treasury costs, but it would guarantee almost no conflict of policy interests between the Treasury and the Federal Reserve System. Its only "negative" aspect would be a reduction in the number of government fiscal experts required to perform the ceremonious tasks of debt management. Certainly a trial issue to see how the securities market would accept it is warranted.

Political Structuring of the Central Bank

The interest that both the Treasury and the Federal Reserve System have in the government securities market has frequently gotten them into conflicts. These squabbles have usually followed a pattern: Due to some sort of fiscal "emergency," government expenditures greatly exceed tax receipts. The Treasury then must try to sell large volumes of securities in a short time. The effect on the securities markets is to depress prices and raise effective yield rates, both of which are anathema to the good housekeeping image the Treasury feels it must maintain with Congress.

As government security issues turn "soft," the Treasury, and perhaps the whole majority party in the White House and in Congress, pressure the central bank to support the securities markets by buying some of the securities. The central bank is easily in the best technical position to carry out such an operation, but it can only do so by creating new money, thus generating inflation. In short, the central bank cannot fight inflation and support Treasury selling operations *simultaneously*.

The similarity of functions and technical operations of the two agencies is in contrast to their institutional structures. The Treasury is very much "political." The Secretary of the Treasury is a presidential appointee; he goes in and out with the President; he is largely responsible for the financial policy of the administration; he must deliver the goods or go down to political defeat with his chief. His office, as a part of the Cabinet, is subject to indirect approbation or rejection at the polls.

The Federal Reserve System, in contrast, was designed to be outside politics. Little policy at all was to be made or could be made contrary to the movements of gold. It was to be regulated primarily by the demands and motives of the commercial banks. Its only regulatory device was manipulation of the discount rate. Appointment to the Board of Governors was staggered at two-year intervals so that no President could appoint a dominant majority. Finally, government securities were largely forbidden to Federal Reserve Banks; under the original scheme commercial paper was the principal policy item.

The virtual abandonment of the gold standard after 1934, and the absence of any rules or prescriptions to take its place, left the Federal Reserve System without direction or method. Some of this vacuum was filled by central bank initiative; but no matter what methods have been developed for attaining policy ends, the formal political position of the Federal Reserve System has not changed from what it was 50 years ago.

Members of the Board of Governors are still appointed for fourteen years. The system is still referred to as "independent." Monetary policy is supposed to be above the level of partisan politics. Some observers believe this method of structuring the central bank is dangerously anachronistic because it does not allow democratic processes to operate in the formation of monetary policy. Just as in all other fields of policy that embrace sharp cleavages of opinion, the democratic process must include three political principles: (1) The majority must have the ability to get its will into action. (2) The minority (or minorities) must be allowed full expression and criticism of majority decisions and actions. (3) The machinery for succession between an erstwhile majority and a former minority must operate smoothly and efficiently.

The contemporary Federal Reserve System in conducting monetary policy is subject to none of these conditions. It was meant *not* to be subject. It is always influenced by the strongest power factor; and when the chips are down, the strongest power factor has been not a group of monetary economists, but the Treasury Department specifically and the executive branch generally.

Three possible reforms suggest themselves for preventing unseemly conflicts between these two agencies in the future. One is to give either agency full executive responsibility for combined monetary-fiscal policy. The Treasury is the logical repository for this responsibility because the political machinery for governing it is already set up. The physical structures and technical functions (check clearing and so on) of the central bank could continue as before; but the Secretary of the Treasury would be the executive head. He would be responsible for all monetary-fiscal policies. All his actions would be subject to the full review, inspection, and judgment of Congress, just as his fiscal policies are at present. Congress would, however, prescribe general rules and limits for policies to whatever extent was compatible and necessary with the constitutional provision "to coin money and regulate the value thereof."[5]

A second possibility for reform is to put the executive heads of both agencies (Secretary of the Treasury and Chairman of the Board of Governors) on an equal footing. In practice, this method would bring the Chairman of the Board of Governors into the presidential Cabinet, where he would serve "at the pleasure" of the President.[6] Since both men would be appointed by the President, no deep-seated differences of monetary-fiscal philosophy presumably would exist between them. If such differences arose, the President could reconcile them through the usual procedure of "requesting" a resignation.

The third method suggested is to proscribe discretionary monetary policy for both agencies and to put the essential operations of policy under a system of rules. The Treasury–central bank might be limited, for example, to issuing no debt other than consols. It might be authorized, alternatively, to issue paper money when a deficit occurred and destroy such money when it had a fiscal surplus in order to effect built-in, countercyclical stability. Or it might be ordered to increase the stock of money at a fixed rate of, say, 3 to 5 percent per year. It might be enjoined to maintain stability of a price index within tolerances of, say, 1 or 2 percent per year. Or it might be detailed to keep unemployment at a minimum percentage of the labor force by means of appropriate monetary policy.

The number of possible rules is legion; and while some are good, some are not so good. Certain characteristics of good rules are the following. The rule has to be simple; it also must be easily understood. It must be technically attainable, and its achievement or failure must be apparent. Finally, the rule must be acceptable to a consensus of the political-economic leviathan, or the rule would not stand, and would in fact be no rule. This last point is the major stumbling block of rules. A consensus on rigid rules is almost impossible to obtain — especially among economists and politicians. Monetary policy is too controversial and economic and political opinions on what ought to be done are too diverse for any line of policy action that could not be compromised to be acceptable. Therefore, any good rule, to be accepted and effective, must be specific on what is to be accomplished, but it must also be tolerant and flexible within some limits. A good quantity-of-money rule, for example, might specify that the quantity of money be increased at the rate of 3.65 percent per year (0.01 percent per day), but it might allow the quarterly or monthly rate to vary between 1 and 7 percent per year.

---

[5]Congressmen have often noted that day-to-day policy must be handled by the executive branch, but with veto powers over executive action always within the scope of congressional action.

[6]This plan has been suggested by a number of people. See Michael D. Reagan, "Political Structure of the Federal Reserve System," *American Political Science Review,* Vol. 55 (March 1961), pp. 64–76. No one suggests going the other way and setting up the Treasury under the same loose arrangement now used for the Federal Reserve System.

If the controversial nature of monetary theory and policy prevents the adoption of a rule, this same trait indicts a system that does not allow democratic channeling of these differences. "Nonpolitical" monetary policy is not only a contradiction in terms, it is not possible and it is not desirable. It implies that both policy means and policy ends are "scientific" and subject to no differences of opinion. An institution that operates under such false pretenses becomes authoritarian if controversy over what ought to be done is present but repressed or ignored by the dogmatism of the institution. Students interested in central bank policy must therefore be concerned with what the central bank is as a political institution as well as with what it does in the area of monetary policy.

Selected Bibliography

Carson, Deane. "Is the Federal Reserve System Really Necessary?" *Money and Economic Activity: Readings in Money and Banking,* ed. Lawrence S. Ritter. Boston: Houghton Mifflin Co., 1961, pp. 238–252.

Fisher, Irving. *One Hundred Per Cent Money.* New York: Adelphi, 1935.

Friedman, Milton. *A Program for Monetary Stability.* New York: Fordham University Press, 1959.

Hart, Albert G. "The Chicago Plan for Banking Reform." *Readings in Monetary Theory,* ed. Friedrich A. Lutz and Lloyd W. Mints. Homewood, Ill.: Richard D. Irwin, 1951, pp. 437–456.

Joint Economic Committee. *Standards for Guiding Monetary Action.* Report of the Joint Economic Committee, Congress of the United States. Washington, D.C.: U.S. Government Printing Office, 1968.

Reagan, Michael D. "The Political Structure of the Federal Reserve System." *American Political Science Review,* Vol. 55 (March 1961), pp. 64–76.

Selby, Edward B., Jr. "Nodes of Power within the Federal Open Market Committee." *Mississippi Valley Journal of Business and Economics,* Vol. 5, No. 2 (Winter 1970), pp. 1–9.

Warburton, Clark. "Rules and Implements for Monetary Policy." *The Journal of Finance,* Vol. 8 (March 1953), pp. 1–21.

Nodes of Power within the
Federal Open Market Committee

Edward B. Selby, Jr.

Centers of power form in every organization and not necessarily in coincidence with the "official" chain of command. The Federal Reserve System is no exception. Within the Federal Open Market Committee the power center shifts depending upon whether the operations are defensive or dynamic. This article explores the power relationships.

Renewed interest in monetary policy on the part of a growing number of economists has led to a reexamination of the structural and functional evolution of the Federal Reserve System.[1] That its internal power structure differs from what was originally created by the Federal Reserve Act is generally recognized. Hastings and Robertson have formally specified this awareness by setting forth the following "nodes of power," which they feel apply to the System as a whole:

1. Chairman of the Board of Governors
2. Other Governors
3. The Board's staff, especially senior advisers
4. The Federal Open Market Committee (FOMC)
5. The open market account manager
6. The New York Federal Reserve Bank president
7. Other Federal Reserve Bank presidents
8. Directors of the Federal Reserve Banks
9. System-wide standing and ad hoc committees
10. The Federal Advisory Council[2]

This paper is not concerned with the power structure of the System as a whole but with the nodes of power in the Federal Open Market Committee as revealed by the *Minutes* of that committee between 1951 and 1960.

Two node structures exist within the aggregate framework of the FOMC, one for "defensive" operations and another for "dynamic" decisions.[3] The

---

Adapted from an article of the same title which appeared in the *Mississippi Valley Journal of Business and Economics,* Vol. 5, No. 2 (Winter 1970), pp. 1–9.

[1]For example, some observers feel that the "regional" structure of the System is outmoded and should be abandoned. See Michael D. Reagan, "The Political Structure of the Federal Reserve System," *American Political Science Review,* Vol. 55 (March 1961), pp. 64–76.

[2]Delbert C. Hastings and Ross M. Robertson, "The Mysterious World of the Fed," *Business Horizons* (Spring 1962), pp. 98–99.

[3]As used here, the aggregate framework of the FOMC refers not only to the voting members of the FOMC but also to the nonmember presidents in attendance, the account manager, and the FOMC's staff.

attempt to achieve long-run goals, such as stable prices, a high level of output and income, and a reasonable balance in international payments is usually referred to as a dynamic operation, while the attempt to offset the impact of short-run disruptive forces in the monetary system is called a defensive responsibility.[4]

Defensive nodes include:

1. The open market account manager
2. The FOMC's staff
3. The FOMC

Dynamic nodes include:

1. The FOMC
   a. The Chairman
   b. The president of the New York Bank
   c. Other members
2. The FOMC's staff
3. The open market account manager

Of course, the ordering of these nodes is subjective. It is substantiated, however, by a careful reading of the FOMC *Minutes*. Statements made therein give a feeling for the relative powers of the participants. These feelings are enforced by other sources as well.

Defensive Nodes

Defensive operations are used mainly to offset fluctuations in member bank reserves that occur as a result of changes in float, seasonal currency demands, and gold flows. These operations are required by the open market account manager's attempt to achieve the target (or targets) set for him by the FOMC. Also, it is impossible for the FOMC to anticipate changes in all of these factors in order to give the account manager detailed instructions on how to handle them. Clearly, then, one of the duties of the account manager is to detect and counter market fluctuations that would interfere with the smooth conduct of

---

[4]Robert V. Roosa, *Federal Reserve Operations in the Money and Government Securities Market* (New York: Federal Reserve Bank of New York, 1956), p. 105.

policy. The awareness of the account manager's importance in such operations is evident in the following statement by the Board of Governors:

> The task of taking into account changes in these factors [such as the float] ... is essentially an operating problem rather than a policy problem. It is a part of the Account Manager's job — with the help of the staffs at the Federal Reserve Bank of New York and the Board of Governors — to detect such variations and to make prompt adjustments to them.[5]

The almost total dependence of the FOMC on the judgment of the account manager for defensive activity is perhaps best illuminated by his behavior at a time of crisis. On July 18, 1958, a telephone conference of the FOMC was called at the request of Mr. Robert Rouse, the account manager. Rouse reported a sharp deterioration in the price of government securities and the corresponding concern of the Treasury. "Mr. Rouse then stated that he would recommend that the Committee authorize purchases of bonds for the Account today up to a certain dollar amount in order to steady the market wherever soft spots appeared."[6] Authority was so granted.[7] Later in the day a second telephone conference was held. Rouse stated that the market was disorderly and that the committee should consider the proposal, made by Governors Mills and Robertson earlier, that an announcement be made.

> Mr. Shepardson inquired of Mr. Rouse whether he would contemplate support at a fixed level or on a scale following the market down, and Mr. Rouse replied that for the time being he would have to use the word "pegging." He added that, as Mr. Mills and Mr. Robertson had suggested earlier, the announcement itself might help a great deal and tend to minimize the volume of operations that may be necessary.[8]

Rouse was then given the requested authority to make purchases in the market without limitation, and an announcement was approved for release.[9]

As indicated above, the role of the staff of the Federal Reserve Bank of New York and the Board of Governors' staff (both referred to here as the FOMC's staff), is to assist the account manager in detecting variations in reserves and in adjusting to them. The *Minutes* disclose that reserve projections are made

---

[5]*The Federal Reserve System: Purposes and Functions* (Washington, D.C.: Board of Governors of the Federal Reserve System, 1967), p. 247.

[6]*Minutes of the Federal Open Market Committee, 1936-60, and of Its Executive Committee, 1936-55*, Roll 13, Microcopy No. 591, Record Group 82 (Washington, D.C.: The National Archives, 1965), f. 14. Hereafter referred to as *Minutes*, with the roll and frame number (f.) or frame numbers (ff.) following.

[7]*Minutes*, Roll 13, f. 21.

[8]*Minutes*, ff. 26-27.

[9]*Minutes*, ff. 27-30. The announcement stated: "In view of the conditions in the U.S. Government securities market, the Federal Open Market Committee has instructed the Manager of the Open Market Account to purchase long-term Government securities in addition to short-term Government securities."

by these staffs to anticipate disruptive factors, and that these projections are often presented to the FOMC. For example, during the committee meeting of January 11, 1955, staff economist Thomas reported that in the absence of open market operations, it was projected that free reserves might increase by $250 million during the next statement week ending January 12, $410 million the next week, and $129 million the next. He then suggested that certain bill (short-term securities) sales would have to be made, or maturations would have to be allowed, in order to prevent free reserves from rising above desired levels.[10] During the following executive committee meeting, it was decided that free reserves should be pushed downward from their existing $300–$440 million level.[11] Thus, the account manager, in carrying out the policy objective of lowering free reserves, was also to counteract at his discretion the imminent reserve increase that had been projected by the staff.

The role of the FOMC in daily defensive operations is passive. At 11 o'clock on each trading day there is a telephone conference in which the account manager in New York and several members of the FOMC participate. This procedure, initiated in 1954, allows the account manager to give the committee up-to-the minute reports on events in the market and on actions he contemplates for the day in fulfilling instructions from the last regular meeting.[12] According to Governor Brimmer,

> In the discussion, other participants may contribute information they have obtained independently or may comment on the planned operations. I might note, however, that there is a strong tradition—shared by individual Committee members participating as well as the staff—against attempting to impose personal judgments on the Manager; all recognize that the Manager bears the final responsibility for executing the policies laid down by the full Committee and that he must be prepared to defend the actions he takes at the next meeting.[13]

However, even at the regular committee meetings and especially at those called in times of crisis, the committee must rely on the account manager's judgment for defensive tasks. The account manager is thus the most important node of power in defensive operations, followed successively by the FOMC's staff and the FOMC members themselves.

---

[10]*Minutes,* Roll 9, ff. 6–10.

[11]*Minutes,* ff. 33–34.

[12]Andrew F. Brimmer, "Tradition and Innovation in Monetary Management," *Monetary Economics: Readings,* ed. Alan D. Entine (Belmont, Calif.: Wadsworth Publishing Co., 1968), pp. 282–284.

[13]Brimmer, p. 283.

Dynamic Nodes

Today the Federal Reserve System recognizes that its general purpose "is to foster growth at high levels of employment, with a stable dollar in the domestic economy and with over-all balance in our international payments."[14] The System attempts to fulfill its purpose by influencing money and credit conditions in the economy, primarily through open market operations. In performing such operations, the System is said to be meeting its dynamic responsibilities.

The power structure for the achievement of these long-run goals is substantially the reverse of that used in the realization of defensive responsibilities. That is, the FOMC makes policy decisions, with the advice of the various staffs, and the decisions are then carried out by the manager of the open market account. A simple test of this decision-making process is to examine the dates of shifts in FOMC policy and compare them with changes in the target variables used by the FOMC but controlled by the account manager. If a target variable changes prior to a decision by the FOMC, then the account manager is making policy that is only confirmed by the FOMC.[15] If the target variable changes after a decision by the FOMC, then the account manager is subordinate to the committee and is carrying out its policy. Table 1 illustrates such a test. In every case free reserve changes follow committee decisions, confirming that policy decisions are made by the committee and then carried out by the account manager.

The staff of the FOMC, primarily the Board's staff, may influence open market decisions in several ways. First, the staff prepares written economic reports prior to each meeting and then makes oral reports preceding the discussion by committee members. These reports are undoubtedly the major source of current economic information received by the committee. Second, in December 1964 the staff began submitting analyses of major economic and financial questions. According to Governor Brimmer, these papers were found "to be of great value."[16] Third, the staff, at the pleasure of the FOMC and/or

---

[14]*The Federal Reserve System*, p. 2.

[15]Not all economists would agree that the account manager follows committee instructions. Brunner and Meltzer have contended that "The Manager permits or encourages changes in the level of free reserves, and the Committee often ratifies his prior decision." Karl Brunner and Allan H. Meltzer, *The Federal Reserve's Attachment to the Free Reserve Concept*, Subcommittee on Domestic Finance, House Committee on Banking and Currency, 88th Congress, 2nd sess., May 1964, p. 47. This author has argued elsewhere that Brunner and Meltzer improperly dated the response of the committee to economic changes (due to the unavailability of the *Minutes*), which resulted in the erroneous conclusion that the account manager initiates changes. See "The Inside Lag of Monetary Policy, 1953–58," *The Quarterly Review of Economics and Business*, Vol. 8 (Spring 1968), p. 45.

[16]Brimmer, "Tradition and Innovation in Monetary Management," p. 286.

the Board of Governors, undertakes research on the operation of the monetary mechanism. Such investigations may include criticism of the various tools of monetary control in addition to the proper targets and indicators for the committee to follow.[17] Finally, the staff may offer direct suggestions on the appropriateness of current policy. For example, these comments were made by staff economist Thomas during the May 6, 1958, FOMC meeting: "Perhaps the time has come when consideration should be given to whether further credit expansion at the rate and of the type which has taken place in the recent past should continue to be encouraged.... Perhaps easy money has done all it can in mitigating recession and promoting recovery until other essential adjustments are made."[18] Yet in spite of all these services, the FOMC itself still holds the policy reins and may accept or reject any or all suggestions from either inside or outside the System.

Table 1. Dates of FOMC Policy Changes and Changes in Free Reserves, 1953–1958

Committee's Policy Change	Free Reserve Change	Lag
May 6, 1953	May 27, 1953	21 days
November 9, 1954	December 1, 1954	22 days
October 22, 1957	October 23, 1957	1 day
July 29, 1958	August 13, 1958	15 days

Source: The dates of the committee's response were discerned from an analysis of the *Minutes of the Federal Open Market Committee, 1936–60, and of Its Executive Committee, 1936–55*, Rolls 6–16, Microcopy No. 591, Record Group 82 (Washington, D.C.: The National Archives, 1965). Free reserve changes are from Karl Brunner and Allan H. Meltzer, *The Federal Reserve's Attachment to the Free Reserve Concept*, Subcommittee on Domestic Finance, House Committee on Banking and Currency, 88th Congress, 2nd sess., May 1964, p. 42.

Nodes of power are also seen within the FOMC itself. Even a cursory examination of the *Minutes* reveals that the chairman wields much the greatest influence. His standing in the committee is perhaps the result of both position and personality. According to Hastings and Robertson, "The tradition of

---

[17]For example, Frank de Leeuw and Edward Gramlich, members of the Board's staff, have this to say about the econometric model completed for the System: "The major purpose is to be able to say more than existing models about the effects of monetary policy instruments—both in themselves and in comparison with other instruments. No existing model has as its major purpose the quantification of monetary policy and its effects on the economy." "The Federal Reserve–MIT Econometric Model," *Federal Reserve Bulletin*, Vol. 54 (January 1968), p. 11.

[18]*Minutes*, Roll 12, f. 335.

Chairman domination was, of course, started during the reign of Marriner S. Eccles, but it has reached a new high under Chairman William McChesney Martin, Jr."[19]

The influence of the chairman in the FOMC meetings may take several forms. Though he is usually the last to speak during the "go-around" (the expression of policy views by Governors and presidents), the chairman will quite often indicate his opinion before the "go-around" by suggesting that a change in policy should be considered by members. For example, in the November 12, 1957, meeting, Chairman Martin made the following comments:

> Last Friday the members of the Board had an economic go-around which made it clear that there was no longer a question of forecasting a change in the economy; it was a question of recognizing what was on us. In the Chairman's opinion, the Committee would be blind if it ignored these developments.[20]

At the November 9, 1954, meeting of the executive committee of the FOMC, the chairman wanted a full discussion of current policy because he felt that the FOMC directive might be out of date. "Chairman Martin felt that the Committee should consider the problem even though it was a very difficult position to make a change in its operations in view of the Treasury financing coming up."[21] He went on to suggest that the committee should consider lowering its free reserve target. The committee decided on such a policy change during the meeting.[22]

At the end of the discussion during FOMC meetings, the chairman normally makes a consensus statement that is an attempt to summarize the views of the members of the committee. Hastings and Robertson imply that the chairman often colors this statement to make it more closely fit his own views.[23] It is interesting to note that William P. Yohe, in studying the 1955–1964 voting patterns of the FOMC on policy directives, found that Chairman Martin had never been on the losing side.[24]

A second prominent source of power within the FOMC is the president of the Federal Reserve Bank of New York. During the FOMC meetings the New York president is almost without exception fully prepared for discussion and in fact usually makes a lengthy economic statement that is often quoted

---

[19]Hastings and Robertson, p. 99.

[20]*Minutes,* Roll 11, f. 673.

[21]*Minutes,* Roll 8, f. 336.

[22]*Minutes,* ff. 340–348.

[23]Hastings and Robertson, p. 101.

[24]William P. Yohe, "A Study of Federal Open Market Committee Voting, 1955–1964," *The Southern Economic Journal,* Vol. 32 (April 1966), p. 399.

verbatim in the *Minutes*—a courtesy not afforded to all members.[25] He is the vice-chairman of the committee, he is president of the bank where open market operations are conducted, and he is the account manager's immediate superior. It is entirely conceivable that a strong New York Bank president may rival a weak chairman in influence.[26]

Table 2. Average Number of Times per Meeting
FOMC Participants' Names were Recorded in the *Minutes*, 1956

Board of Governors		Bank Presidents		Staff	
Martin	22.6	Sproul	16.3	Rouse	9.7
Robertson	8.2	Hayes	11.5	Thomas	5.8
Mills	6.6	Johns	5.9	Young	3.0
Vardaman	4.4	Mangels	5.2		
Balderston	4.3	Leach	4.9		
Shepardson	3.3	Williams	4.9		
Szymczak	2.8	Allan	4.8		
		Bryan	4.5		
		Erickson	4.2		
		Leedy	4.2		
		Irons	4.2		
		Powell	3.8		
		Fulton	3.5		
		Earhart	3.0		
		Young	1.5		

Source: *Minutes of the Federal Open Market Committee, 1936–60, and Its Executive Committee, 1936–55*, Roll 10, Microcopy No. 591, Record Group 82 (Washington, D.C.: The National Archives, 1965).

During FOMC meetings, the chairman, the president of the New York Bank, and perhaps one or two others carry on the bulk of the discussion concerning economic policy. Table 2 records the average number of times those in attendance at the 1956 FOMC meetings had their names recorded in the *Minutes*. The other FOMC members, with notable exceptions, agree with the chairman,

---

[25]For example, see *Minutes*, Roll 9, ff. 11–16, and Roll 12, ff. 176–180.

[26]The System has probably not forgotten the power that Benjamin Strong once commanded. Of course, that was prior to the Banking Act of 1935, which essentially established the present FOMC structure and placed more power in the hands of the Governors. See Milton Friedman and Anna J. Schwartz, *A Monetary History of the United States, 1867–1960* (Princeton, N.J.: Princeton University Press, 1966), pp. 411–416; and Hastings and Robertson, p. 99.

the New York Bank president, and the staff once a strong case for changing policy has been made. The strength of each of the other members must derive from his personality and intellectual ability—not his position. Thus, within the FOMC proper, the chairman has been and apparently continues to be the strongest node of power, followed by the president of the New York Bank and then the remaining members of the committee.

Conclusions

The decision-making structure of the Federal Open Market Committee in its task of purchasing and selling government securities on the open market cannot be considered unidirectional. One must separate the responsibilities of the committee in order to discern the decision-making process. In the case of defensive operations, the open market account manager is the chief decision maker. He is held accountable for maintaining FOMC policy in spite of the destabilizing forces of the float, currency drains, and other such factors. In the case of dynamic operations, the FOMC itself holds the reins. Within the FOMC proper, the greatest influence, by virtue of position and personality, is exercised by the chairman, who is followed by the president of the Federal Reserve Bank of New York and then the other members.

Index